SOCIOLOGY

DIVERSITY AND CHANGE IN THE TWENTY- FIRST CENTURY

DAVITA SILFEN GLASBERG • KENNETH J. NEUBECK

Kendall Hunt
publishing company

Cover image © Shutterstock, Inc.

Kendall Hunt
publishing company

www.kendallhunt.com
Send all inquiries to:
4050 Westmark Drive
Dubuque, IA 52004-1840

Copyright © 2013 by Kendall Hunt Publishing Company

ISBN 978-1-4652-2376-0

Printed in the United States of America
10 9 8 7 6 5 4 3 2 1

CONTENTS

CHAPTER 1 THE SOCIOLOGICAL IMAGINATION.. 1

Personal Troubles and Public Issues: Dana's Story.............................. 2

The Sociological Imagination in Action 5

Sociology: Intellectual Traditions And Core Concepts 8

    Sociology's European Roots 8

    The Functionalist Perspective 9

    Émile Durkheim: Influential Functionalist Thinker 10

    The Conflict Perspective 11

        Karl Marx: Proponent of Radical Change 12

        Max Weber: Student of Social Stratification and Bureaucracy 13

    Reflecting Back on Dana's Story 14

    Symbolic Interactionism: People Constructing Social Reality 15

Different Perspectives, Different Voices: the Benefits...................... 16

Chapter Summary... 17

Thinking Critically 17

Key Terms... 18

CHAPTER 2 RESEARCH METHODS 19

The Research Process 20

    Use of Hypotheses and Open-Ended Research Questions 20

    Steps in the Research Process.. 21

Types of Research Methods 22

    Experimental Research 22

        Establishing Experimental and Control Groups........................ 22

Research Example: Teacher
Expectations and Student Performance..23
Advantages and Disadvantages of Experimental Research 23

Field Research 24
Making Field Observations 24
Research Example: Manufacturing Classroom Failure..........................25
Advantages and Disadvantages of Field Research 26

Survey Research 26
Survey Procedures..26
Research Example: Gatekeeping in High Schools 27
Advantages and Disadvantages of Surveys 27

Historical Research 28
Uses and Sources of Historical Data 28
Research Example: The Origins Of School Tracking Practices.................28
Advantages and Disadvantages of Historical Research 29

Analyses of Existing Data...30
Secondary Data Analysis 30
Advantages and Disadvantages of Using Existing Data 30

Research Ethics and Politics 31
The Ethics of Research...31
The Politics of Research 33

Chapter Summary.. 34

Thinking Critically 35

Key Terms.. 36

CHAPTER 3   **MACRO SOCIAL STRUCTURES**.. 37

Social Structure.. 38

The World-System 39
Global Patterns and Their Consequences
for Individuals' Life Chances 42
The Role of Raw Materials in the World-System..45

Societies 47
Two Views of Social Structure..48

Institutions... 49
The Family...53

Religion 54

The Economy 56

Education 58

The State 60

Institutions as Dynamic Structures 63

Social Movements: Challenges and Change **64**

Chapter Summary **65**

Thinking Critically **67**

Key Terms **67**

CHAPTER 4 **SOCIAL STRUCTURE: MICRO- AND MID-LEVELS** **69**

Status **70**

Achieved And Ascribed Status 71

Master Status 71

Roles **72**

Role Strain 73

Role Conflict 73

Role Sets 74

Groups and The Individual **74**

Primary Groups 75

Secondary Groups 77

Group Structure: Bureaucratic Versus Democratic Organization **79**

Bureaucratic Organization 79

Features of Bureaucracy 79

Bureaucracy and Control in the Workplace 80

Bureaucracy and the Declining Power of Workers 81

The Bureaucratized Society 83

Democratic Organization 84

Democratic Workplace Cooperatives 84

Features of the Democratic Workplace 85

How Bureaucratic and Democratic
Organizations Affect People's Lives 86

Informal Organization **87**

Some Functions of Informal Organization 88

Workers' Resistance to Management 89

Social Networks **91**

Strong and Weak Network Ties 91

Networks and Social Advantage 92

Chapter Summary **93**

Thinking Critically **94**

Key Terms **95**

CHAPTER 5 **CULTURE** **97**

Norms **98**

Folkways 100

Mores...100

Laws...101

Values **102**

The Relationship Between Values and Norms *103*

Culture and Language **104**

Language: Describing the World 105

Language: Constructing Reality...105

Language: Vehicle for Change 107

Corporate Culture **108**

Agents of Cultural Transmission **110**

Mass Media 111

Schools 113

Subcultures **115**

Countercultures... **119**

Chapter Summary **121**

Thinking Critically **122**

Key Terms **123**

CHAPTER 6 **SOCIALIZATION** **125**

Socialization as a Learning Process **126**

Symbolic Interactionist Perspective... **127**

Charles Horton Cooley: The Looking Glass Self 128
George Herbert Mead: Significant and Generalized Others 128
Symbolic Interaction as a Dynamic Process................................129

Conflict Perspective.. **129**
Conflict in Social Psychological Explanations 129
Conflict in Structural Explanations 131

Socialization, Conflict, and Social Structure **132**

Agents of Socialization **133**
Families 134
Peer Groups 134
Schools 134
Religious Organizations..135
The Workplace 136
The Media 136
Toys, Games, and Recreation 137
The State...138

Class Socialization **139**
Family 139
Schools 140

Gender Socialization... **140**
Family..140
Schools 141
Work...142
Media..143
Toys, Games, and Recreational Activities 144
Effectiveness of Gender Socialization 145

Racialized Socialization **147**
Family..147
Schools 149
Media..151
Toys, Games, and Recreational Activities 152

Political Socialization.. **153**
Schools 153

Toys and Games 154

Media 155

Chapter Summary 157

Thinking Critically 158

Key Terms 159

CHAPTER 7   **SYSTEMS OF INEQUALITY** 161

Economic Inequality 163

Wealth, Income, and Poverty 163

Different Perspectives on Economic Inequality 166

The Functionalist Perspective on Economic Inequality 166

Critiques of Functionalism 167

A Conflict Perspective on Economic Inequality 169

Racialized Inequality 172

The Concept of "Race" 172

Personal Racism 174

Institutional Racism 175

Racism and the Economy 175

Racism and the State 176

Gendered Inequality 179

The "Biology Is Destiny" Ideology 180

Male Chauvinism And Institutional Sexism 181

Women and the Labor Force 182

Are Males Harmed by Gender Inequality? 183

Sexual Orientation and Inequality 184

The Ideology of Heterosexism 184

Mistaken Notions about Homosexuality 185

Discriminatory Practices Against Gay Males and Lesbians 186

Some Signs of Change 187

Able-Bodiedness and Inequality 189

The Ideology of Ableism 190

Problems Experienced by People with Disabilities 191

Chapter Summary 191

Thinking Critically 193

Key Terms 193

CHAPTER 8   **INTERSECTIONS OF RACE, CLASS, AND GENDER** 195

Patriarchy in the Lives of Wealthy White Women 197

Gendered Inequality in the Upper Class 197

Upper Class Women's Subordinate Gender Roles 197

White Women Employers and Domestic Workers of Color 199

Racial and Class Inequalities in Household Settings 199

Women Oppressing Women 201

African American Men in the Lower Class 202

When Race and Class Trump Male Privilege 202

Effects of Ghettoization on African American Men 204

Racism and Middle-Class African Americans 205

Economic Success in the Face of Racism 205

Racial Segregation of the Black Middle Class 206

Diverse Experiences Among Women of Color 208

The Importance of Recognizing Women's Diversity 208

Challenges Facing African American Women 209

Experiences of Chicanas in U.S. Society 209

Special Challenges Facing Women with Disabilities 211

When Gender and Disability Meet 211

The Oppression of Women with Disabilities 212

Unraveling The Matrix of Systems of Inequality 214

Chapter Summary 215

Thinking Critically 216

Key Terms 216

CHAPTER 9   **DEVIANCE, CRIME, AND SOCIAL CONTROL** 217

The Social Construction of Deviance 218

The Role of Power in Defining Deviance 221

Norms that Restrict Women 221

Appearance Norms 222

Motherhood Norms 222

Challenges to the Label "Deviant" 224

Deviance and Resistance 225

Deviance as Behavior Versus Deviance as Being................................ 225

Resistance to Being Labeled Deviant for One's Behavior 226

Resistance to Being Labeled Deviant for One's Being........................ 227

Crime as Deviance 229

Bias in the Treatment of Different Types of Crimes 229

The Case of White Collar and Corporate Crime.............................. 230

Explanations for Deviant Behavior 233

Physiological Explanations 234

Psychological Explanations.. 235

Social-Psychological Explanations 235

Differential Association Theory... 236

Control Theory 236

Containment Theory.. 236

Social Reinforcement 237

Labeling Theory.. 237

Shortcomings of Social-Psychological Explanations 237

Sociological Explanations 238

Opportunity Structure Theory 238

Deviance and Capitalism 239

Crime and Punishment: Differential Application of Sanctions......... 241

Do Societies "Need" Deviant Behavior?...................................... 244

Deviance and Social Change 246

Chapter Summary.. 248

Thinking Critically 249

Key Terms.. 250

CHAPTER 10 **SOCIAL CHANGE AND SOCIAL MOVEMENTS**...................... 251

The Meaning of Social Change... 251

Explaining Social Change.. 252

Cyclical Theory 253

Evolutionary Theory 254

Equilibrium Theory *254*

Marxist Theory *255*

Modernization, Development, and Underdevelopment **256**

The Meaning of Development 256

Dependency and Development 258

Trade Dependency *258*

Dependent Development *260*

Debt Dependency *261*

Technological and Social Changes **264**

Energy Production 265

Technological Change and the Labor Process 266

Technology and Reproductive Issues 267

Technological Innovation, Power, and Inequality 269

Social Movements **269**

Types of Social Movements 271

Explaining Social Movements 273

Absolute versus Relative Deprivation *273*

Resource Mobilization *274*

External Forces 279

Chapter Summary **280**

Thinking Critically **281**

Key Terms **282**

CHAPTER 11 THE STATE, CAPITAL AND POWER **283**

The Relationship of State and Economy **284**

Pluralism **286**

Group Pluralism 286

Elite Pluralism 288

Power Elite Theory **289**

The Military-Industrial Complex 293

A Power Elite Analysis of the State and Economy Relationship 296

Voting: Who Participates? **297**

The State in Capitalist Society **303**

Business Dominance Theory 303

Capitalist State Structuralist Theory 304

Class Dialectics and the State 305

**The State and Political Economy: New Federalism
and Welfare "Reform"** **306**

New Federalism 306

Welfare Reform 309

Dismantling the Welfare State? 310

Chapter Summary **312**

Thinking Critically **312**

Key Terms **313**

CHAPTER 12   WORK AND ECONOMY **315**

The Meaning of Work **316**

The Structure of the Formal Labor Market **318**

The Changing Structure of Paid Work **318**

Causes of the Structural Transformation of the Economy **320**

Technology 320

The Global Economy 321

Capital Mobility 321

Investment Abroad *321*

Runaway Shops *323*

Mergers *323*

Deindustrialization 324

Changing Corporate Organizational Structure 326

The Great Twenty-First-Century Economic Recession **327**

Economic Structural Transformation and Inequality **328**

Unemployment 328

Underemployment and Declining Income from Existing Jobs 330

Gendered and Racialized Inequality and the Labor Market 331

The Declining Middle Class 335

Prospects for Change **336**

Chapter Summary **340**

Thinking Critically 340

Key Terms 341

CHAPTER 13 FAMILIES 343

Defining Family 344

Diversity of Family Forms 347

Family Forms: Cultural Choice or Institutional Response? 348

Reasons for the Rise in Single-Parent Families 349

Divorce *349*

Unwed Motherhood *350*

Reasons for the Rise in Other Nontraditional Family Forms 351

Poverty and Families 352

The Effect of State Policies 352

The Effect of Marital Dissolution 353

Poverty in Nontraditional Families 356

Family Dynamics and Family Issues 356

Family Violence 357

Power Differentials in the Family 358

Sources of Stress in Families 359

Prospects for Change: Reducing Family Violence 362

Reproductive and Parenting Rights and Issues 363

Contradictions between Work and Family 365

Future Trends 368

Chapter Summary 369

Thinking Critically 371

Key Terms 371

CHAPTER 14 EMERGING ISSUES 373

**Global Population: The Youth Explosion
of the Periphery and the Graying of the Core** 375

The Youth Boom of the Periphery 379

The Graying of the Core 380

Environment: Toxic Imperialism and Environmental Racism **383**

    Toxic Imperialism 384

    Environmental Racism 386

Technology and Globalization: The Digital Divide **388**

    Cyberspace and the Promise for Social Change 396

Globalization, Militarism, Terrorism, and Social Change **397**

    Export of Arms 398

    Terrorism 400

Chapter Summary **403**

Thinking Critically **405**

Key Terms **406**

REFERENCES **407**

GLOSSARY **469**

THE SOCIOLOGICAL IMAGINATION

A glance at newspaper headlines or television nightly news reveals political turmoil and civil strife, military violence, serious economic breakdowns, famines, and natural disasters in societies around the world. In comparison to many other societies, the United States seems relatively calm and tranquil, even as it has had to contend with terrorist acts and their aftermath and economic crises. Beneath this relative tranquility, however, millions of people in the United States face problems that leave them yearning for relief and anxious for change in their circumstances.

Many, for example, have difficulty finding or keeping decent-paying jobs. Others find themselves living in tension-filled and abusive partner or family situations. Still others face prejudicial attitudes and discriminatory treatment. Individuals sometimes view such experiences as their own personal burdens to bear and fail to appreciate just how widely their problems may be shared. The discipline of sociology can contribute to our understanding of the sources of such commonly experienced problems and help offer solutions.

Sociology is the scientific study of society, of the ways in which society is organized and operates, and of the factors contributing to both societal stability and social change. Sociologists are interested in analyzing how people create, maintain, and go about altering the society in which they live. They are also interested in analyzing the effects that various features of society have upon its members. Sociology provides research-based knowledge about the organization and operation of society that can often help individuals to put the problems they encounter in their personal lives in perspective and perhaps deal with them more effectively. It does this by encouraging people to view the sources of their problems in a larger context.

In chapters that follow we will underscore the fact that people's lives are very much influenced by not only who they are, but by <u>what</u> they are, where they fit in the larger society, and the opportunities available or inaccessible to them. In U.S. society, individuals' opportunities and **life chances** (one's ability to experience life and all its beneficial offerings) are unequally distributed. They vary by whether people are affluent or poor, male or female, white or of color. People's lives are likewise affected by virtue of their being either young or old, able-bodied or experiencing a disability, heterosexual, homosexual, bisexual, or transgendered. Race, class, gender, ability, and sexuality are significant organizing principles in society, affecting the available opportunities for individuals, and therefore their life chances.

As you will see in subsequent chapters, sociological research has generated a great deal of knowledge about class, gendered, and racialized inequalities, as well as many other factors that shape people's experiences in society. Such knowledge not only contributes to a better understanding of the sources of harmful societal conditions that can and should be changed. Sociological knowledge may also point to ways to go about making the changes. Sociologists' research findings and advice thus have often proven useful to politicians, planners, policymakers, journalists, intellectuals, social workers and reformers concerned with contemporary social problems.

Sociology differs in significant ways from other social sciences. The discipline of psychology, for example, focuses primarily on the internal mental functioning of individuals and its effects on their behavior. In contrast, sociologists are principally concerned with the impact of social groups and societal conditions on people's thinking and behavior. Sociologists seek to understand how and why people are influenced by their group memberships, their everyday social interactions with others, and the broader social, economic, and political conditions under which they function. We examine the effects of how we are organized as a society on the lives of individuals.

Psychologists and sociologists do at times overlap in the interests of their academic disciplines and share insights. For example, some sociologists and psychologists share common interests in the specialized area of social psychology, which includes such research arenas as attitude formation and change, the behavior of people in small groups, and the socialization process through which people learn to participate in social life and develop social identities. But in general it is fair to say that sociologists are more prone than psychologists to be interested in the "big picture," which means looking at how the organization and operation of society affects its members, as well as how its members' thinking and behavior affect society.

Sociologists also trade ideas with their social science colleagues in economics and political science. Sociologists, however, view economic and political systems as only two of many types of social institutions central to the functioning of society. Finally, there is a good deal of common ground between sociology and anthropology in their concepts and research concerns. While there are many exceptions, anthropologists have historically emphasized the study of non-Western, preliterate societies, particularly their cultural characteristics, while sociologists have tended to emphasize analysis of the organization and operation of industrialized and post-industrialized societies, particularly those in the West.

Earlier we defined sociology as the scientific study of society, of the ways in which society is organized and operates, and of the factors contributing to both societal stability and social change. This chapter will address the following questions:

- What is the "sociological imagination" and how does sociology contribute to it?
- What major theoretical perspectives have historically shaped sociology?
- What are some of the highly useful concepts that have come out of these perspectives?

As we address these questions, we hope readers of this textbook will begin to share our own sense of excitement and enthusiasm about the discipline of sociology.

PERSONAL TROUBLES AND PUBLIC ISSUES: DANA'S STORY

Before moving to a discussion of the "sociological imagination," we will begin with a story about Dana, a sincere and pleasant young woman of 19. Dana grew up in a racially and ethnically diverse middle-class neighborhood with her parents and two younger brothers. She was a relatively good student in high school, although she was the first to admit she coasted whenever she could. To provide the family with basic necessities, Dana's parents were both employed. They gave up vacations in order to put a small amount of money aside each month to help pay for their children's college costs. Dana and her brothers found part-time jobs to pay for their personal expenses, just as her older sister did when she was a teenager before she enlisted in the Marines. There were few luxuries. Dana's family was proud last year when she went off to a public college that had a good reputation. She was one of the first children of color in the neighborhood to go to this college. It was barely affordable with Dana's summer earnings and a modest loan from the financial aid office. She was on track. But now her world is falling apart.

Dana's father was laid off over six months ago, one of thousands of workers thrown out of work by the severe economic recession of the twenty-first century. His employer, a large manufacturing firm where he had worked his way up to a middle-management position, "downsized" its number of employees to reduce labor costs. To his dismay, the best job he was able to find was that of evening shift supervisor at a telemarketing firm. As a typical service-sector job, it paid far less and did not provide the healthcare benefits he used to receive from his manufacturing firm position. He was suffering downward mobility. Dana's father wondered how much being in his early fifties had to do with his limited job prospects or if his physical disability, the result of a car accident, counted against him. He took it for granted that his dark skin could be a liability.

Dana's mother had been employed ever since her youngest child was old enough to care for himself after school. But her salary as a data-input worker in an insurance company was not sufficient to offset the family's drop in income from her husband's job change. When Dana inquired about more financial aid, the college aid office told her that the federal government had tightened the eligibility rules in response to the weak economy and reduced tax revenues. The school couldn't give her anything more. Even with the part-time jobs she was holding down, Dana could not afford to stay at college.

Clearly, asking her parents for more financial help was out of the question: In addition to supporting Dana and her two younger brothers on her father's underemployment and her mother's limited income, her parents are also raising young twin grandchildren while their mother, Dana's older sister, is deployed with the Marines in Afghanistan. And to make matters worse, the family's home is now "under water": It is now worth less than the amount the family still owes on the mortgage, thanks to the collapse of the mortgage industry and the tsunami of foreclosures blighting neighborhoods all over the nation. If they don't somehow find the money to continue to pay their mortgage, Dana's parents may lose their home. Needless to say, the economic and emotional stress in the family is quite strong.

When Dana arrives home, she finds her family in turmoil. Stress seems to be ripping apart her parents' marriage. Mutual hostility and periodic outbursts of physical abuse mar their relationship. Dana's father was always strict but fair with his children. Now he behaves unpredictably and at times drinks to excess. Her brothers seek refuge with their friends and try to avoid their father. They are also beginning to get into trouble at school; her mother is receiving a stream of calls and notes from school authorities. Even Dana's niece and nephew, her sister's two young children, are acting out, getting into trouble at the daycare where they spend their days. The director of the daycare has already told Dana's mother that if the twins continue to be disruptive they cannot return, leaving Dana's mother little choice but to quit her much-needed job to care for them at home. Dana spends a lot of time in her room, anxiety-stricken and chronically depressed by the overwhelming facts of her difficult situation. Away from her friends and the refuge of school, Dana suffers alone.

If Dana and her family were part of a small handful of people in our society facing crises associated with employment difficulties, pressures of military deployment, the prospect of foreclosure and possible homelessness, and family discord, we might simply suggest that they all get counseling and wish them well. It would be logical to conclude they were just suffering from what sociologist C. Wright Mills called **personal troubles.** These are matters involving a person's character and his or her relations with others over which the individual has some control, and commonly affect relatively few people. As such, personal troubles typically can be resolved in local environments by those directly involved (Mills, 1959). But a substantial body of social science research suggests that the kinds of crises and challenges confronting Dana and her family are extremely widespread and have far more to do with crises in the economy, international politics, and education than with individuals' personalities (Newman, 1999; Sklar, Mykyta, and Wefald, 2002).

Mills, a renowned scholar whose writings were often very critical of the workings of U.S. society, made a distinction between personal troubles and **public issues**. Public issues "have to do with matters that transcend local environments of the individual" (Mills, 1959: 8). When millions of men and women in our society are unable to achieve economic success and job security, as is so often the case today, this is a public issue. The individuals involved cannot all correct their plight simply by an act of personal will. Rather, it is necessary to look at what is wrong with the economy as an institution in order to determine what steps can be taken to improve employment opportunities and incomes. This may require the active intervention of other major social institutions, such as the state.

Dana's father is caught up in a situation that he may be experiencing as his personal trouble, but it is really a reflection of a larger public issue. Widespread national and global economic crises and "deindustrialization" of the U.S. economy, involving the decline of secure, well-paying jobs in the goods-producing manufacturing sector, and their replacement with often lower-paying jobs that involve providing services, has become a fact of life in the United States (Newman, 1999). The severe contraction of the economy that began in 2008, and that quickly spread abroad, left the greatest number of workers unemployed and underemployed we've seen since the Great Depression of the 1930s (Ferguson, 2012). Dana's father and mother are among many blue-collar and white-collar workers who have found their work and family lives and economic situations transformed and disrupted by the economic crisis, the foreclosure crisis, wars in places like Afghanistan and Iraq, and the deindustrialization process. Notice, too, that Dana's own situation is not at all of her making: She is caught in the swirl of the institutional crises hampering her parents' ability to help invest in her education and therefore help her move up the economic ladder. She has done everything expected of her: She has earned good grades and maintains a part-time job to contribute to the costs of her education.

The plight of Dana's family reflects other public issues that go beyond personal troubles and resist individual-level solutions. Despite anti-discrimination laws, millions of adults face discrimination in the labor market on the basis of their skin color or age. Approximately 40 million Americans have disabilities and many confront hiring prejudices on the part of employers.

Women across U.S. society continue to face pressures to bear the bulk of childcare and domestic responsibilities in their households, often simultaneously caring for aging parents and their own offspring, and sometimes their grandchildren when their adult child is deployed in the military. This situation, combined with sex discrimination in the work force, makes it difficult for women to perform successfully as sole providers of the family income (Albelda and Tilly, 1997). Unemployment and other job-related problems may have a damaging impact on personal and family life, fostering tensions and even contributing to family violence (Neubeck, Neubeck, and Glasberg, 2006).

Studying sociology can help us become sensitive not only to the difference between personal troubles and public issues but also to the connections that often exist between the two. It is common for people like Dana's parents to view job loss, downward mobility, and economic stress as their own personal trouble and to accept the full burden of responsibility for it. They blame themselves, and may be blamed by others, for their plight. The solution to personal troubles rests with the individuals involved. But when many people experience these same troubles, and the causes lie with forces and decisions that are largely beyond their control, it is more appropriate to treat such personal troubles as a public issue. In that case both the causes and solutions lie with how the society is organized and run.

THE SOCIOLOGICAL IMAGINATION IN ACTION

C. Wright Mills coined the term **sociological imagination** to refer to a way of thinking that enables individuals to understand how they are affected by broad features of the society in which they live. In *The Sociological Imagination* (1959), Mills noted that many people tend to get so caught up in their own "personal orbits" of everyday life that they often ignore what is happening in the larger society. Family, school, work, and personal relationships absorb much of people's attention, time, and energies. Yet their personal orbits are very much open to influence by broad societal trends and key events.

In order for us to place ourselves in that broader societal and historical context, we need information and facts, and an ability to use that information, often collected from multiple sources, to develop a logical, well-reasoned, critical analysis. Sounds pretty straightforward. But do consider this: Where do we get our facts and information? Many of us rely on newspapers, magazines, books, television, radio, and the Internet for information of the world around us. Unfortunately, we cannot simply accept without question the information we get from these sources. First, information on the Internet is not necessarily vetted for accuracy before it is posted, which is why many teachers will not accept Wikipedia as a valid, sole source. We must corroborate what we learn on the Internet with information gleaned from other sources before accepting it as fact.

We might turn, then, to newspapers, magazines, books, television, and radio as sources to verify what we can glean from the Internet; but these are all elements of the media industry, which is structured much like any other industry. Major corporations own and control the output and the productive facilities of these seemingly varied media outlets, and there is a strong process of increasing concentration in the industry, such that fewer and fewer corporate entities own and control more and more of the informational output. There are, for example, over 2,300 newspapers, 11,000 magazines, 9,000 radio stations, 1,500 television stations, and 2,400 book publishers (www.census.gov/compendia/statab/cats/information_communications.html), which together are owned by just three corporations. Why does this matter? Such concentration of ownership produces a private ministry of information and culture (Bagdikian, 2000) that has the power to shape and frame how we understand the world around us and to determine which facts and information we can access.

In addition, relying on facts and information we can get from media sources may produce the **homogenization of news** (Chomsky, 2002), a process that produces a single perspective and a single analysis of highly complex stories regardless of the variety of media sources we consult. This is because they are commonly owned and controlled by the same media conglomerates who determine their output. And if they are owned and controlled by a small handful of corporate media giants, they will disseminate a common viewpoint. How likely is it, then, for these media outlets to report on stories damaging to their interests? How likely is it that they will report stories and information from viewpoints other than their own?

This caution about the validity of information available to us does not mean we can never really get adequate information. Scholars typically do research by gathering their own data as a strategy to verify information found in the media or to generate information unavailable through the media. In the next chapter we will discuss the different methods scholars may use to do this. But for now, it is important to realize that when we gather facts and information as one of the necessary ingredients to exercising a sociological imagination, it is important to look not only at mass media sources, but to consult scholarly journals and books for unimpeded research. Once we have information that broadens our perspective about individuals' social and historical contexts, we are in a better position to exercise a sociological imagination.

The exercise of the sociological imagination, then, involves striving to understand (1) how society is presently structured or organized, (2) how and why it seems to be changing, and (3) how people's personal "biographies" or individual life experiences fit within and are affected by the society's structure and the flow of social change. Mills believed the sociological imagination gives power to anyone possessing it. It allows individuals to identify problematic circumstances they share with others, circumstances over which they may seek to capture some control. Let's look briefly at Dana's parents' situation. How might exercising the sociological imagination be useful to Dana, her parents, and other members of her family?

Many people like Dana's father are losing their jobs because of shifts in the capitalist world economic system. The widespread housing and mortgage crisis and the sudden and deep economic recession that began in 2008 and that continues to plague much of the world was ignited by shifts in the way financial institutions operate: They began to engage in high-risk and predatory mortgage and investment practices that were not allowed after the Great Depression of the 1930s, but were made possible in the 1990s and beyond with the repeal of federal banking regulations that controlled such behavior (Ferguson, 2012). The result: Millions of people are losing their homes to foreclosure and losing their jobs entirely as companies go bankrupt or reduce their workforce.

In addition, the dominant economic position occupied by the United States since World War II has been undergoing challenge by Japan, members of the European Union, and a host of other capitalist nations that are successfully competing to provide manufactured goods for the world market. To deal with the competition and meet their profit goals, corporations in the United States have been taking steps to reduce production costs and increase efficiency. Often this means downsizing or trimming the ranks of management and other supervisory and white-collar staff, substituting automated machinery for blue-collar workers, and moving some production activities to low-wage plants elsewhere in the United States or abroad. The pursuit of profit maximization has led some corporate executives to engage in "corporate deviance," in this case unethical and illegal financial practices which at times (as in the case of Enron) have led to criminal charges, corporate bankruptcies, and extensive employee job loss.

Many of the manufacturing jobs that have disappeared in the United States due to deindustrialization have been replaced by jobs in the service sector (e.g., finance, communications, real estate, retail sales, healthcare, food services). But high-level service jobs often require skills that former manufacturing workers do not possess, and the skill-level requirements and pay levels of many of the new service-sector jobs are often less than those for the blue-collar and white-collar jobs that are disappearing. Some argue that the pace at which U.S. manufacturing sector jobs have been lost has increased since the mid-1990s when the U.S. government established new economic relations with Mexico and Canada (under the North American Free Trade Agreement, or NAFTA). Both the world and domestic economies are undergoing a major reordering, reflecting decisions being made by top-level corporate and political elites. Members of the U.S. labor force are experiencing effects of these decisions, over which they exercise no say.

Using a sociological imagination, Dana's parents might view their predicament more constructively. They could see how deindustrialization, downsizing, and economic difficulties are troubling millions of workers and homeowners in the United States, and that they are by no means alone or to blame for their plight. They might see value in joining collectively with others to actively press for needed political and economic solutions on the local, state, and national levels. Finally, were Dana and other family members to view problems families like theirs are having with employment and income, housing, and family care as public issues, they would see how important it was to give Dana's parents needed support and encouragement. Each family member could do more to help the others cope, and family members together might opt to join with people caught up in a similar predicament in mobilizing politically to demand solutions.

Our goal in writing this textbook is to help readers develop a sociological imagination. The sociological imagination can help individuals understand the importance of acting with others to affect history and thereby influence the series of life experiences that constitute individual biographies. The sociological imagination can help people who are struggling under harmful societal conditions to avoid placing blame on themselves or innocent others for situations that they did not create (for a classic critique of "blaming the victim," see Ryan, 1976). The sociological imagination can redirect attention toward more productive and appropriate analyses and strategies for social change from which many can benefit (Johnson, 1997).

The exercise of a sociological imagination, then, involves not only gathering facts and information to broaden our perspectives; it also involves taking that information and framing it in a reasoned analysis by using theoretical and conceptual lenses that help us find order in a jumble of seemingly disparate facts. In order to help readers develop a sociological imagination, we will draw upon a number of core concepts used by sociologists, in particular the concepts that are discussed in Part 1 of this book. **Core concepts** are fundamental ideas that are helpful in analyzing features of U.S. society as well as those of other societies. They provide a language to use in formulating research questions that lead us to take a deeper look at society's workings. Armed with facts from such research, people are in a better position to determine what, if anything, they might hope to change.

The core concepts used by contemporary sociologists in the United States derive from or reflect the influence of major intellectual traditions that have historically shaped the discipline. In the next section we will address these intellectual traditions and some of the core concepts that flow out of them.

SOCIOLOGY: INTELLECTUAL TRADITIONS AND CORE CONCEPTS

Sociology's European Roots

The actual origins of sociology lie in antiquity. For hundreds of years, social thinkers and philosophers in the East and West have expressed views on the workings of the organized social life of their own and other societies. Contemporary sociological thinking in the United States, however, has been most directly influenced by intellectual developments arising in the late eighteenth and nineteenth centuries, particularly in France and Germany. This was a time when rapid and radical social changes were occurring in European societies (Ritzer, 2009). Social movements, like the one that led to the French Revolution in 1789, challenged and undermined hierarchical social relationships between the rich, aristocratic classes and the poor, common people. These relationships had long been taken for granted by elites and common people alike as part of the natural order of things. In addition, advances in science opened up alternative ways of thinking about the natural and physical worlds, prompted by exciting new ideas and discoveries. The increasing stature of science threatened the traditional monopoly over truth and knowledge claimed by church authorities.

Research and technological innovations fostered new means of producing goods as well as advances in transportation and communication. These provided the basis for the Industrial Revolution, which dramatically changed many people's lives. The expansion of trade with the colonies and with non-European nations, along with changes in domestic production, meant that fewer European workers were needed in traditional agricultural pursuits and more were needed to labor in newly built factories. Increasing numbers of families were forced to leave rural farms, estates, and villages and seek out a livelihood in these factories, which were often located in growing urban centers. In these centers an emerging class of business owners and merchants was busy accumulating political and economic power and aggressively using this power to further its interests in profits and wealth accumulation.

The late eighteenth and nineteenth centuries were disruptive and unsettling, as more and more people across Europe experienced the loss and transformation of their traditional ways of life. It was also an era in which many people—including the intellectuals of the day—worried about high rates of crime, widespread squalor, street rioting, and threats of rebellion by impoverished workers and unemployed people in the burgeoning cities. This, then, is the social, economic, and political context within which early European sociological thinkers developed their ideas.

European scholars approached the study of society out of deep concern over the harmful social conditions they observed (Zeitlin, 2009). Impressed by breakthroughs in the physical and natural sciences made possible by the systematic use of scientific methods, these scholars believed it was possible to study society scientifically as well. The knowledge generated, early sociologists believed, could be employed to help solve social problems. Sociologists were not to study society simply to accumulate information about it, but were to generate knowledge that could be used to guide social progress.

Almost from the very beginning, however, sociologists found it difficult to agree on how to approach the study of society and its problems (Zeitlin, 2009). What concepts should be used to analyze the workings of society? What were the societal problems that needed to be solved? Disagreements among scholars over such issues gave rise to two European intellectual traditions whose impact on sociological thinking lingers even to this day. We will refer to these two traditions as the "functionalist perspective" and the "conflict perspective."

The Functionalist Perspective

The **functionalist perspective** is often associated with French thinker Auguste Comte (1798–1857), who helped to popularize the term "sociology," and even more so with his fellow countryman Émile Durkheim (1858–1917). This perspective posits that human society is a naturally stable, harmonious social system. This stability of the social system is maintained by a culture that includes values, rules, and practices that are widely shared. People become participants in a society by learning its culture. This occurs through a process known as socialization.

The socialization process includes learning how to fill existing social positions and to perform necessary social roles in major social institutions, such as the family, the economy, religion, and the political system. Each of these institutions is said to be interdependent and interrelated with other institutions, and to serve critical functions for society as a whole. The various features of society—from social institutions to systems of inequality—are said to be there for a reason and should be changed using great caution, if at all.

From the functionalist perspective, the appropriate relationship of the individual to society is one of accommodation and adaptation. Individuals are constantly being born, participating in social life, and then dying. Yet, society and its institutions go on regardless of the changes in societal membership. The ongoing operation and continuity of society requires that everyone cooperate with the socialization process, carried out by social institutions such as the family, religion, and education. Through the process of socialization, individuals are groomed for their appropriate places in society's division of labor. Along with a commonly shared culture, the cooperation among people called for by the division of labor is itself important to societal stability. In the big scheme of things, the needs of society are far more important than the needs of those individuals who participate in it.

It is assumed, from the functionalist perspective, that human nature contains a tendency toward irrational behavior that must be kept in check by proper socialization. When individuals are not adequately socialized, their behavior is likely to depart from shared values, rules, and practices. Deviant behavior can be highly disruptive to stability and harmony within the social system. Important positions and social roles may not be adequately performed, and this can interfere with societal functioning.

Thus, from the functionalist perspective it is important for society to evolve means to exercise social control over deviant behavior and to discourage society's members from engaging in it.

While minor expressions of deviant behavior can usually be dealt with informally by those who find them offensive (e.g., teachers, neighbors, family members, or friends), formal agencies of social control such as police, courts, and prisons exist to handle the most serious cases of deviance.

Punishment of society's deviants is said to serve as a reminder and reaffirmation of the cultural values and rules that its members share in common. Most individuals are either responsive to the socialization process or coerced to conform by the ever-present weight of cultural values, rules, and negative sanctions for deviant behavior. Individuals' conformity with society's demands contributes to order, without which, from the functionalist perspective, there can be no social progress (see Figure 1.1).

Émile Durkheim: Influential Functionalist Thinker

Frenchman Émile Durkheim, a nineteenth-century thinker whose sociological writings are still widely read and cited, has been perhaps the most influential proponent of the functionalist perspective. Durkheim's writings range across a wide variety of topics (Ritzer, 2009). He addressed the importance of culture and the functions played by commonly shared moral values, beliefs, ceremonies, and rituals in encouraging societal harmony and stability. In more contemporary societies, where population diversity may outweigh commonalities among people, Durkheim saw stabilizing functions also played by the complex division of labor, arguing that it renders people and their activities highly interdependent. Likewise, Durkheim saw social order being helped along by the appearance and consequent condemnation of deviant behavior such as criminal acts. Condemnation of deviance functioned to remind even members of diverse societies that they shared certain fundamental values in common.

Durkheim also stressed the important function of **social facts**. These are social and cultural features of a society, existing independently of the individuals who make it up, which

Figure 1.1: Functionalist and Conflict Perspectives

Measure	Functionalist Perspective	Conflict Perspective
Notable features of society	Common culture, stability, harmony	Societal diversity, power differences, systematic inequalities
View of human nature	Irrational, in need of control	Rational or "good"
Individual's relation to society	Individuals should adapt to society's needs	Society should be organized to meet its members' needs
Sources of deviant behavior	Failure of people to be adequately socialized	Alienation of people from harmful features of society
View of deviance	Disruptive, dangerous	Inevitable
Basis for social progress	Order in society	Conflict leading to transformation of society
Means to social progress	Conformity to social roles and the demands of social institutions	Social movements for fundamental societal change
Influential European thinkers	Comte, Durkheim	Rousseau, Marx, Weber

influence people's behavior. The size and makeup of the general population, dominant ideas and ways of thinking, the division of labor, groups to which people can belong—all are examples of social facts. Durkheim believed that analyses using social facts would lead to highly valuable sociological explanations of human behavior, reducing reliance on often-problematic biological or psychological explanations. He showed, for example, that the members of different religious denominations have different rates of suicide, suggesting that the groups in which one holds membership (a social fact) can help explain even highly personal acts. In other words, suicide rates can be explained sociologically and without recourse to biological or psychological explanations.

Finally, Durkheim also brought a functionalist perspective to bear in his thinking about inequality in society (Kerbo, 2011). In Durkheim's view, if contemporary society and its division of labor were to function properly, and social progress was to occur, individuals with the appropriate talents had to be encouraged and permitted to move into those positions to which they were best suited. The rewards (money, power, prestige) attached to different positions were often highly unequal. However, this was less important to Durkheim than the undermining of social order that could occur if people grew disruptive because they could not move into positions where they could exercise their talents. In his stress on the importance of meeting society's needs for order, Durkheim failed to see inequality as a matter for concern.

Functionalist thinkers like Comte and Durkheim articulated ideas that very much expressed the views and supported the interests of the privileged classes in European society. But, while in retrospect functionalist thinkers may have acted as apologists for the status quo in their theorizing about how society works, they also embraced and emphasized core concepts that still serve as important tools for analyses of the organization and operation of society. We will see aspects of this intellectual tradition reflected later in this textbook when, for example, we discuss the functions of different social institutions, culture, views on socialization, and explanations for class inequality and deviant behavior.

If the functionalist perspective emphasizes the importance of order as a prerequisite for social progress, a second intellectual tradition emphasizes the role of conflict in bringing about change. Proponents of the "conflict perspective" argue that struggles between groups with different degrees of wealth, prestige, and power are to be expected and are necessary if social progress is to occur (see Figure 1.1).

The Conflict Perspective

Like the functionalist perspective, the **conflict perspective** represents an intellectual tradition within sociology whose roots go back to late-eighteenth and nineteenth-century Europe and the changes underway at that time. Thinkers within this second tradition emphasize social splits and divisions that often characterize human society. While proponents of the functionalist perspective tend to emphasize what societal members share in common (e.g., common cultural values), conflict perspective proponents stress heterogeneity and diversity within society. In the rapidly industrializing capitalist societies of the late eighteenth and nineteenth centuries, wealth and income, prestige, and power were very visibly unequally distributed.

Unlike functionalist thinkers like Comte and Durkheim, social thinkers adopting a conflict perspective tended to side with the common people regarding the widespread injustices being inflicted by the privileged and powerful, and in seeing a need for radical social change. Needless to say, their views were dismissed and condemned by members of Europe's privileged classes. Jean Jacques Rousseau (1712–1778) found class inequality in pre-Revolutionary France to be unnatural and in violation of human nature. It had to be fought. In Germany Karl Marx (1818–1883) concluded that industrial **capitalism**—an economic system in which the means of production were owned by relatively few—would produce class inequalities so severe as to call forth worker-led social movements leading to the system's downfall. Both were disturbed by the unequal distribution of life chances and opportunities among society's members that systematic political and economic inequalities promote and maintain.

The conflict perspective accepts the notion that human society is naturally harmonious and stable, but it sees the creation of systems of inequality (such as class inequality under capitalism) as producing outcomes that are contrary to social order. Social movements can be expected to arise as people refuse to submit to unjust and harmful conditions within systems of inequality from which they see no escape. Conflict is to be expected, as groups or classes holding little power or privilege struggle to improve their lot, while the advantaged strive to protect what they have. A society with haves and have-nots is inherently unstable. From this perspective, social progress often requires social conflict.

Proponents of the conflict perspective tend to adopt a more positive view of human nature than proponents of functionalism. Human beings are seen as being fundamentally rational or "good." The conflict perspective holds that individuals are capable of acting effectively on behalf of their own best interests. Karl Marx, for example, was generally respectful of workers' ability to make the right choices when it came to bringing about needed social change, encouraging them to do so in political pamphlets like *The Communist Manifesto*.

Persons who question the societal status quo, who refuse to adapt to the demands of authority and the rules of the existing order, are viewed from the functionalist perspective as poorly socialized deviants. From the conflict perspective, however, such persons instead may be seen as expressing their alienation from an oppressive and exploitative social system that fails to meet their needs. Order cannot depend upon socializing deviants into the existing social system, for the system is harming them. Such a situation regularly arises whenever a social system is organized and operated to systematically benefit only a few.

Hence, unlike the functionalist perspective, the conflict perspective places priority on the well-being of society's members. Their physical and psychological needs are of primary concern, and proponents of the conflict perspective argue that society and its institutions should be organized in ways that meet these needs. The failure of the social system to meet many of its members' needs makes their lives intolerable, and this situation gives rise to social movements to bring about change. Social progress occurs out of the conflict such movements produce, and conflict thus is as necessary as it is inevitable.

Karl Marx: Proponent of Radical Change

To nineteenth-century German thinker Karl Marx, perhaps the most important feature of any society was the nature of its economic system. In his view, the economy significantly affects a society's culture and value system, its class structure and class relations, and the functioning of the state.

Marx was particularly critical of the European industrial capitalist economy of his day. It was an economy based on the private ownership of the means of production (e.g., factories, mines, transportation systems) by a relatively small number of affluent individuals who comprised a **bourgeoisie** or capitalist class. The overwhelming majority of society's members—who constituted a **proletariat** or working class—could only survive by selling their labor power to the capitalists. The latter took advantage of the workers' desperation, profiting mightily by paying workers very low wages and requiring that they labor under the worst of conditions. Workers who did not like the situation could leave or were fired. The state sided with the capitalists by passing laws that prohibited workers from organizing and unionizing and provided police to forcibly suppress protests and protect capitalists' property.

Marx believed that a society organized around capitalism was highly unstable, conflict-prone, and contained the seeds of its own destruction. Conflict between the bourgeoisie and the proletariat was inevitable, given the contradictions in their self-interests. Yet, he noted, workers often blamed their suffering on fate, higher powers, or their own poor decisions. Workers possessed what Marx called **false consciousness**, in that they did not understand that capitalism itself created their poverty and misery. Marx believed this false consciousness would eventually give way to **class consciousness**, wherein workers would understand that capitalism itself was the problem and that their poverty and poor working conditions could only be ended with **socialism**, or worker ownership of and control over the society's means of production.

As a proponent of the conflict perspective, Marx believed that social progress required conflict. He assumed that economic exploitation of the proletariat by the bourgeoisie would eventually spark widespread worker rebellion and radical change that would benefit the majority of society's members. Marx's analyses have been highly influential and have provided inspiration and a rationale for participation in social movements for exploited and impoverished people in many nations. Marx's writings have also been important to sociologists interested in developing a conflict perspective on the present-day dynamics of capitalism, the class structure, and capitalism's impact on society's members.

Max Weber: Student of Social Stratification and Bureaucracy

While Karl Marx is often considered the central figure in the development of the conflict perspective, it is just as important to mention contributions that his fellow German sociologist Max Weber (1864–1920) made to this intellectual tradition. Weber was nowhere near as critical of capitalism as was Marx. Moreover, Weber placed more emphasis than did Marx on the importance of analyzing other features of a society than its economic system, such as its political and cultural characteristics. Weber is best understood as developing many of his ideas in reaction to Marx, providing his own approaches to some of the issues with which Marx was concerned (Zeitlin, 2009).

Like Marx, Weber was interested in inequality. But he did not limit his analyses to capitalism and to classes defined in terms of those who either owned or did not own society's means of production. His interest in inequality encompassed differences in individuals' political power and prestige. Weber noted that power and prestige did not always derive from property ownership. In some instances important social positions, such as religious or military positions, carried power and prestige but not wealth. Moreover, power and prestige was at times rooted in an individual's charisma, personality characteristics to which others responded by granting that person respect or authority. Weber thus emphasized the importance of analyzing **social stratification** in society, or the bases on which different positions and the people in them are ranked or "stratified" from high to low in terms of wealth and income, prestige, or power.

Weber viewed the unequal distribution of power and conflict as central features of society. But, unlike Marx, Weber associated these phenomena with trends that went beyond capitalism. Weber observed that traditional ways of organizing social life in Western societies, which relied heavily on past practices and the authority of elders, were rapidly being displaced by more scientific and rational approaches. This shift was reflected in the growing use of bureaucratic forms of organization to carry out business activities and governmental affairs. A **bureaucracy** is an organization in which people perform specialized roles under a system of explicit rules and within a hierarchy of authority.

Weber viewed bureaucracy as a highly efficient tool for getting various societal tasks accomplished. He was, however, very concerned over the implications of society becoming more and more bureaucratized and run by bureaucratic elites, those in top organizational positions. Just as capitalism was a problem to Marx, bureaucracy was a problem to Weber. Weber was pessimistic that the trend toward bureaucratic domination could be overcome, suggesting instead that the hierarchical social relations characterizing bureaucratic organization (in business, government, religious institutions) would give rise to constant conflicts and struggles between bureaucratic elites and the rank and file over elites' exercise of power and authority.

Reflecting Back on Dana's Story

Social thinkers like Rousseau, Marx, and Weber helped launch an intellectual tradition that encouraged contemporary sociologists to utilize core concepts such as capitalism, bureaucracy, class, power, and social movements in their efforts to understand the workings of society. Core concepts important to the conflict perspective will play a prominent role in the chapters that follow. Indeed, we already drew upon such concepts in discussing how a sociological imagination might help one see Dana's family problems as connected to public issues.

For example, Dana's father's loss of his manufacturing sector position and the prospect of losing their home to foreclosure stemmed from his firm and his mortgage bank putting profit maximization before the jobs and homes of workers, a decision being made by many firms within the U.S. economic system of *capitalism*. Needing more financial aid, Dana found that she would now have to drop out of college due to the limits on aid established by the federal government *bureaucracy*. Her father's downward mobility, coupled with her mother's limited earning ability, had made the *class* position of Dana's family less secure. This was compounded by the necessity of her parents to financially and emotionally care for her niece and nephew while her sister was deployed in Afghanistan. Helpless to solve their problems simply on their own as individuals, we suggested that members of Dana's family could gain *power* by joining with others in *social movement* activities to demand change.

Consideration of the functionalist and conflict perspectives raises some interesting questions. Can people successfully avoid adaptation to the demands being made upon them by the social system in which they are embedded? Can people ignore, resist, or even alter the system? To what degree can Dana's family, and people facing similar problems, realistically hope to alter the trajectory of their biographies? In thinking about such questions, it is helpful to consider a third intellectual tradition that has helped to shape contemporary sociology in the United States.

Symbolic Interactionism: People Constructing Social Reality

The functionalist and conflict perspectives approach society and its key features from very different standpoints, and each also has a different conception of the relationship of the individual to society. The functionalist perspective views people's lives as by necessity being "determined" by society and its institutions, to which people had best adapt. The conflict perspective likewise views society as placing constraints on people, but in ways that foster alienation, not adaptation, and that may prompt people into movements for social change (Figure 1.1).

Among contemporary sociologists there is disagreement over the degree to which people are pushed to behave in certain ways by prevailing features of society, whether it be the demands of shared cultural values (the functionalist perspective) or social conditions that do harm (the conflict perspective). Are human beings really little more than robots who march in response to abstract "laws of society" or other social forces? Or are people active agents? Do people's minds count? To what degree and in what ways do people exercise their own "free will" to act autonomously within and upon society?

The term **human agency** is often used to refer to the ability of humans to react to and change the social conditions surrounding them. It stands in contrast to the term **social determinism,** which is used to stress the importance of society's features as determinants of what happens to individuals. How much emphasis sociologists should place upon the role of human agency in understanding the operation and course of society is a key issue within contemporary sociology. This question is addressed by a third sociological perspective, one which focuses on people's thinking and behavior on the level of their everyday social interactions.

Symbolic interactionism is an intellectual tradition that evolved in the United States out of the scholarship of such sociologists as George Herbert Mead (1863–1931) and W. I. Thomas (1863–1947). Proponents of symbolic interactionism have often been highly critical of functionalist and conflict perspectives, arguing that they overemphasize the significance of external social forces, such as cultural values or systems of inequality, in determining individuals' behaviors. Indeed, symbolic interactionism arose in the United States partly in response to the failure of the functionalist perspective to treat individuals as intelligent, thinking social actors.

Symbolic interactionists acknowledge that individuals are influenced by the social environments in which they find themselves. However, they stress that individuals are also active, autonomous agents who, unlike robots, initiate thought and behavior. Proponents point to the important fact that human beings are capable of self-reflection, self-criticism, as well as efforts at self-development and change. People also can think imaginatively, and they actively interpret and bestow meaning on situations and events. All these activities are possible due to humans' use of language and other symbols in combination with social interaction.

Symbolic interactionism focuses upon such topics as the ways in which shared meanings among individuals develop or change through social interaction. It addresses the role that social interaction plays in the individual's development of a sense of "self." And, of particular importance to scholars of social movements and social change, symbolic interactionism explores how people, interacting through the medium of language and other symbols, construct understandings of external reality on which they then may act.

From a sociological perspective, the reality that is objectively "out there" is not nearly as important as the reality that subjectively exists in people's minds. Symbolic interactionism will, for example, inform aspects of our discussion of the importance of language in constructing social reality, our treatment of how individuals develop social identities, including gender identity, and our discussion of the processes by which people come to be labeled by others and to see themselves as deviants.

DIFFERENT PERSPECTIVES, DIFFERENT VOICES: THE BENEFITS

We have presented the functionalist, conflict, and symbolic interactionist perspectives as distinct intellectual traditions. In the United States, sociologists have tended to lean toward one or the other of these traditions in their attempts to understand the workings of society. Others have moved back and forth between traditions over the course of their careers. Today it is common for sociologists to borrow core concepts from different intellectual traditions, although they may find some concepts more useful than others in their analyses. Our own interest in "personal troubles" and "public issues" has led us to draw heavily upon concepts central to the conflict perspective in writing this textbook. However, we also freely rely upon many concepts that are central to alternative ways of viewing society and its participants, such as the functionalist and symbolic interactionist perspectives.

In recent decades the influence of voices that were often muted or largely ignored by mainstream sociology has grown much more prominent. In part, this has occurred as the sociological community in the United States—long dominated by white, male academics—has become much more diverse and inclusive. Today, for example, this community is coming to appreciate the intellectual power and unique contributions of important sociologists of color such as W.E.B. Dubois (1868–1963) and Oliver Cromwell Cox (1901–1974), pioneers in analyzing racial inequalities. The sociological community is likewise very much aware of the path-breaking contributions to understanding gender inequalities by women in sociology, particularly since the 1960s (Lengermann and Niebrugge, 2007; Rogers, 2001). In recent years, the voices of scholars of color and feminist sociologists have encouraged new ways of thinking about how the intersections of race, class, and gender simultaneously affect people.

Much of the diversity and scholarly creativity within sociology has come from the discovery of new questions and new ways to use the discipline's core concepts as stepping stones to knowledge about society, whatever the intellectual traditions with which they are historically associated. In chapters that follow, we will define and flesh out sociology's core concepts and show how contemporary sociologists have used them in their scholarly work. Such concepts are central to the exercise of the sociological imagination.

Reflecting the contributions of different perspectives and different voices, sociology seeks to provide a systematic, evidence-based understanding of the world humans have constructed. At its best, sociology does more than simply identify obstacles to change. It points to contradictions within society that are potential change levers, suggests public issues around which people can organize, and stimulates continual assessments of the status quo. In short, sociology is meant to be done, studied, and used for the betterment of humanity.

CHAPTER SUMMARY

- Sociology is the scientific study of society, of the ways in which society is organized and operates, and of the factors contributing to both societal stability and social change.

- Sociology is useful in that it can help people distinguish between their own "personal troubles" or problems that individuals might hope to solve, and "public issues" entailing socially harmful societal conditions whose solution requires collective political action.

- In order to understand the difference between personal troubles and public issues, it is helpful to develop a way of thinking called the "sociological imagination." That imagination is fueled by knowledge about how society is presently structured; how and why it seems to be changing, and how features of society affect people's biographies.

- A sociological imagination allows people to play an active role in influencing the directions their biographies are likely to take. Human beings need not simply be passive objects to whom life happens. Working alongside like-minded others, people have the capacity to exercise influence and capture some control over their series of life experiences.

- Contemporary sociology is influenced by important intellectual traditions that we have termed the functionalist, conflict, and symbolic interactionist perspectives. While quite different in their ways of perceiving society and its members, each has contributed to the core concepts that sociologists use in asking research questions and generating new knowledge about the workings of society.

- The functionalist perspective stresses the importance of order and stability within society as a prerequisite for social progress. It examines functions served by different features of society and the contributions they make to the organization and operation of society as a whole. Core concepts associated with the functionalist perspective include culture, socialization, deviant behavior, and social control.

- The conflict perspective emphasizes features of society that can be harmful to people's life chances. This perspective suggests that social progress may require conflict in order to end harmful conditions. Core concepts associated with the conflict perspective include capitalism, class, systems of inequality, power, bureaucracy, and social movements.

- The symbolic interactionist perspective focuses on people as active and autonomous agents. Symbolic interactionists explore how individuals come to view and define themselves, and the ways in which people use language and other symbols to interpret and bestow meaning on situations and events. Core concepts associated with this perspective include "self," social identity, and the construction of social reality.

THINKING CRITICALLY

1. When a couple's marriage ends in divorce, it is usually dismissed as their own personal trouble and a matter of their individual failings. Yet the divorce rate is very high; some 50 percent of all marriages end in divorce. How might our understanding of the causes of divorce be enriched were we to view it as a public issue?

2. Since 2008, many students graduating from college have had a difficult time finding jobs. Some have experienced unemployment. Others could find only part-time or temporary positions, or were forced to take lower-paying full-time jobs that often didn't really require a college education. Many graduated and returned home to live with their parents. Who or what is to blame for this situation? How does the way one answers that question suggest different solutions?

3. Do you believe that members of society can change harmful social conditions under which they or others are living? To what degree and in what ways do people have "free will" to make such changes? If there are obstacles, who or what are they? What might it take for these obstacles to be overcome? Give examples.

4. C. Wright Mills believed that the sociological imagination would be empowering to anyone possessing it. A counterargument might hold that the accumulation of knowledge about how the surrounding social world affects us could prove to be overwhelming, even paralyzing. Where do you stand in this argument?

 KEY TERMS

sociology **1**

life chances **1**

personal troubles **4**

public issues **4**

sociological imagination **5**

homogenization of news **6**

core concepts **7**

functionalist perspective **9**

social facts **10**

conflict perspective **11**

capitalism **12**

bourgeoisie **13**

proletariat **13**

false consciousness **13**

class consciousness **13**

socialism **13**

social stratification **14**

bureaucracy **14**

human agency **15**

social determinism **15**

symbolic interactionism **15**

RESEARCH METHODS

In order to exercise the sociological imagination, as discussed in Chapter 1, it is important to become skilled in distinguishing between opinion and fact when it comes to discussing the workings of society. Many people base their knowledge of the social world upon "facts" handed down from others in the past or traditional thinking, without questioning whether the facts still hold true (or ever did). Other people make hasty generalizations about social groups or various features of society largely based on their personal experiences. While one's own personal experiences may themselves be valid, this does not mean that they are necessarily at all typical, correctly understood or interpreted, or that they can be broadly generalized.

Sociologists make special efforts not to fall into the trap of confusing opinion with fact. They tend to be cautious or even skeptical about ideas concerning the workings of society, even ideas that many people take for granted as being true. As we noted in Chapter 1, scholars commonly gather their own data or rely on verifiable data rather than data from the mass media as one strategy to avoid the homogenization of news. Sociologists seek to base their observations about society on facts that have been scientifically established through objective investigation and systematic data gathering. When sociologists report their research findings, they describe the methods and data that produced them. If they receive funding for their research projects, they reveal its sources. This information helps other researchers assess the probable validity of the research findings being reported.

Sociologists use a variety of research methods to conduct their investigations. These methods are important tools, for they are the means by which sociologists seek to generate new knowledge. No one research method is intrinsically "better" than another, just as a hammer is no "better" a tool than a screwdriver or pliers. As a unique tool, each research method has its appropriate uses, as well as its relative advantages and disadvantages. The toolbox of different research methods is invaluable for furthering our understanding of the ways in which society is organized and how it operates, and the factors contributing to social stability and change. It is no exaggeration to say that the effective use of research methods makes the sociological imagination possible.

Whatever the research methods sociologists choose to use, opportunities for unethical behavior may arise in the course of carrying out investigations. In addition, sociological research could in some instances conceivably be conducted for purposes that contribute to social injustice. Like other professionals, sociologists have a responsibility to pursue their activities ethically and to avoid bringing harm to others.

This chapter will focus attention on several questions:

- What are the main research methods that sociologists use in their investigations?
- What are the relative advantages and disadvantages of the different methods?
- What kinds of ethical issues may at times arise for sociological researchers?
- What is the importance of the political context in which research is conducted?

THE RESEARCH PROCESS

Use of Hypotheses and Open-Ended Research Questions

Social scientists are trained to use a variety of different **research methods**. Research methods are procedures designed to establish facts about the social world. These methods include experimental research, field research, historical research, and survey research (Babbie, 2010; Schutt, 2008). Usually such research methods are used to gather information relevant to hypotheses. A **hypothesis** is a carefully formulated statement that may be either verified or discarded on the basis of the examination of relevant data. At times, the hypotheses being tested have important implications for social policy.

For example, a sociologist may formulate a hypothesis that states, "Mother-headed families receiving welfare, whose heads enter the labor force under federal and state welfare reform requirements, are likely to rise out of poverty." The sociologist would then gather data on the work behavior and poverty circumstances of such mothers to see whether the hypothesis receives support. In testing a hypothesis, researchers look for systematic relationships between the variables contained in their statements. **Variables** are attitudes, behaviors, or conditions that can vary.

There are two main types of variables, *independent* and *dependent*. An **independent variable** is one that affects another variable. A change in the independent variable causes the other variable to change. A **dependent variable** is the one in which change is caused. In short, when an independent variable changes, a change in the dependent value should follow. Sociologists use statistical techniques to manipulate (change) independent variables in order to see whether and to what extent dependent variables then undergo change, and to identify the circumstances under which that change is likely to happen. In the example above, the sociologist is interested in whether welfare-reliant mothers' entry into the labor force (the independent variable) results in their families rising out of poverty (the dependent variable).

Sometimes researchers believe that they do not know enough about a given social phenomenon to develop and test specific hypotheses about it. In such instances researchers may pursue **open-ended research questions**. They are "open-ended" in the sense that no particular answers are necessarily assumed or anticipated to be tested. Rather, questions are posed in ways that may generate new and at times detailed and often unexpected information. Open-ended questions can be very exploratory and leave the sociologist a good deal of flexibility in deciding what he or she will consider relevant and useful data sources.

For example, a sociologist may ask, "Why is there a high rate of hunger within the U.S. population?" Sources of data bearing on this question might include people patronizing soup kitchens and food banks; caseworkers in social service agencies and homeless shelters; staff of public health clinics, hospitals, and schools; leaders of anti-hunger groups, and government officials.

Steps in the Research Process

The sociological research process proceeds through a series of steps (see Figure 2.1). Once having become interested in a particular social phenomenon, and having reviewed existing scholarly literature to learn more about it, the researcher determines the hypothesis to be tested or the research question to be pursued. Next, the researcher chooses a research method. The method selected depends, in part, on the hypothesis or research question. Some methods will be more appropriate than others to answer the questions posed by the researcher's investigation. He or she then gathers data relevant to the hypothesis or research question (or draws upon data already gathered by others). The researcher analyzes these data, records the findings, and reaches conclusions.

Finally, sociological researchers disseminate information about their inquiries. This often involves preparation of a report that describes the purpose of the research, the method(s) used, an explanation of how the data produced were analyzed, the findings, and the conclusions reached. Often, the report will include recommendations for further research. If the research was commissioned by a sponsor (for example, a government agency, foundation, or private firm) the sociologist will give the report to the sponsor. Sociologists also disseminate information about their research in professional or scholarly peer-reviewed journals and books, in the mass media, and through public presentations.

To illustrate the principal methods used in sociological research, we will examine some well-known and classic studies that examine the relationship between schooling and class inequality, a topic to be taken up in more detail in Chapter 12 ("Education"). As we will see, different questions about this relationship, explored with various research methods, have led to valuable insights. The studies to be discussed have been widely cited by sociological researchers and have contributed to debates that continue to this day over how to eliminate the unequal educational opportunities confronting students from low-income backgrounds. The studies chosen employ experimental research, field research, survey research, and historical research. Finally, to round out our discussion of research methods we will discuss analyses of data that have previously been collected by others.

Figure 2.1:   The Research Process in Brief

1. Observing, hearing about, or reading about a social phenomenon of interest.
2. Reviewing existing scholarly literature to learn more about the phenomenon.
3. Framing hypotheses or research question that, if addressed, will generate valuable new knowledge and understandings.
4. Selecting an appropriate research method (or methods).
5. Gathering data that will address the hypotheses or research questions.
6. Analyzing the data gathered, reaching conclusions based on the findings.
7. Disseminating information about the research project, its findings and its conclusions through reports, articles, books, or public.

TYPES OF RESEARCH METHODS

Experimental Research

Most of us are familiar with experimental research from high school physical and life science courses. In the physical and life sciences, **experimental research** is conducted to find out how a particular organism or object is affected by different types of treatment selected by the researcher. While by no means the most common research method used by sociologists, some do find it useful even though experimentation with human beings imposes practical and ethical considerations. Like other scientists, some sociologists even conduct studies in laboratories where they are able to maximize control over experimental procedures and conditions. The basic principles guiding the experimental research method are much the same in both laboratory and natural (non-laboratory) settings.

Establishing Experimental and Control Groups

Researchers begin by establishing at least two groups to be studied. The first is called the **experimental group**. The experimental group is the one to which the researcher will give special treatment in order to determine its effect. The second group, the **control group**, differs only in that it is not subjected to the same special treatment. The control group serves as a baseline of comparison to the experimental group. If the experiment is well designed, differences in thinking and behavior between the two groups should reflect the differences in their treatment. The cause of the differences, if any, is assumed to stem from researcher-designed conditions. Experimental research is typically used to test very specific hypotheses. Unusual experimental outcomes may lead to new ideas to explore, and thus to further hypothesizing and experimentation.

All researchers, regardless of the methods that they use, try to design their research in ways that avoid bias. **Bias** refers to unwanted influences that can produce research results that are invalid or without foundation. In the case of the experimental method, avoidance of bias begins with the way in which subjects are assigned to the experimental and control groups. Typically, researchers will select a sample of subjects. A **sample** consists of a set of subjects that is representative of the total population of subjects. The sample is chosen at **random**, meaning that every individual in the total population has an equal chance of being selected. Then, those selected for the sample are assigned to the experimental and control groups at random. In this way possible sources of bias in assignment will be extremely small.

Avoiding bias also requires the researchers to take care that only members of the experimental group receive the special treatment whose effect is being investigated. Moreover, researchers must be prepared to assess the effects of unexpected factors that may influence what occurs in the experimental or control group. Such cautions are necessary if other social scientists, repeating the same experiment, are to be able to replicate or come up with the same findings.

Laboratories provide researchers with maximum control over an experiment because they impose artificial conditions on the two groups. But while the artificiality of the control may not be a significant issue in biology or chemistry research, it is a substantial issue for sociological research. That's because people do not live in laboratories, nor are the conditions to which they are normally subjected as neatly timed and delineated as they are during laboratory experiments. Laboratory research may thus produce findings that may be reproducible by other laboratory researchers but that do not necessarily apply to people's thinking and behavior in the "real" world. Hence it is desirable to conduct experimental research in natural settings when possible.

Obviously, there are many natural settings that are not easily replicated or that cannot even be imitated in a laboratory. A public school is such a setting. Yet, oddly enough, schools actually resemble research laboratories in some ways. For example, school staff members provide students with an "experimental treatment" in the form of teaching, and they expect this treatment to have a certain outcome in the form of learning. In the example of experimental research we will describe, researchers manipulated the treatment of students by teaching staff.

Research Example: Teacher Expectations and Student Performance

It has long been observed that students from poor and working class backgrounds, on average, get lower scores on intelligence quotient (IQ) tests and other standardized tests of achievement than do students from the more affluent middle and upper classes. Researchers Robert Rosenthal and Lenore Jacobson wondered whether the lower achievement could at least in part be due to low expectations on the part of teachers toward children of the less affluent. The researchers thus set out to test the following hypothesis: "Within a given classroom those children from whom the teacher expected greater intellectual growth would show such greater growth" (Rosenthal and Jacobson, 1968a: 61).

The researchers conducted their experiment in a West Coast elementary school whose students came for the most part from low-income families. Rosenthal and Jacobson began by giving the children in all six school grades a test. The teachers were deceived into thinking that the test results would predict which students would bloom intellectually over the school year. The researchers then gave the teachers a list consisting of 20 percent of the school's students who should be expected to do well. The researchers had compiled this list by randomly selecting students, such that the "difference between the special children and the ordinary children . . . was only in the mind of the teacher" (Rosenthal and Jacobson, 1968a: 175). The so-called special children comprised the experimental group, and the other 80 percent of the school's children comprised the control group. Members of the experimental group would, presumably, be subject to different treatment by their teachers under the expectation that they would intellectually spurt ahead.

At the end of the school year, each student was given the same test again, and the gains made by the experimental and control groups were compared. The experimental-group students not only experienced intellectual growth (at least as measured by the test) but were perceived by their teachers as displaying more positive learning and other behavioral characteristics than control-group students.

Some controversy surrounds this classic study because of mixed results in subsequent efforts by other researchers to replicate it. Still, Rosenthal and Jacobson's innovative experiment made a major contribution in suggesting that the nature of teachers' interactions can play an important role in the intellectual growth of children from less affluent backgrounds. School experiences that discourage intellectual growth can contribute to poorer children's social and economic marginalization as adults and help to perpetuate class inequalities.

Advantages and Disadvantages of Experimental Research

To summarize, then, experimental research methods are modeled after methods used in the physical and life sciences. When experimental and control groups are carefully chosen and all safeguards against bias and invalid results are put in place, experiments can provide important insights into people's thinking and behavior. Experiments have several advantages: They can demonstrate causal links between experimental treatments and predicted outcomes; they provide researchers with a high degree of control over independent and dependent variables in order to exclude sources of error; and they can be used to study changes in people's thinking and behavior over time. Disadvantages include the sometimes artificial character of experimental settings; the possibility that people aware of their involvement in an experiment may adjust their behavior with this knowledge in mind; and practical limits to the size of samples for many experiments. The latter may limit the generalizability of findings.

Relatively few sociologists use laboratory-based experimental methods, and these are mostly scholars whose research lies within the specialized area of social psychology. Other sociologists look for ways to employ the principles of experimental research in non-laboratory settings. For example, it has become commonplace for sociologists to participate in the evaluation of experimental government "pilot programs" to help policymakers determine if they should be implemented on a wider scale. This type of experimentation has taken place in such areas as education, health-care delivery, job training, and welfare reform.

Field Research

When researchers leave their offices and go out among people to observe or speak with them firsthand, they are conducting **field research**. Direct observation can be useful either when little is known about a group or particular type of social setting, or when enough is known to warrant hypotheses about the group. In the first case, the social scientist may enter the research site with few preconceptions and observe the entire situation just long enough to draw some conclusions about group members' thinking and behavior. When the social scientist already knows enough to have formulated a testable hypothesis before entering the field, direct observation will be much more limited in its focus; only observations pertaining to the hypothesis will be of interest to the researcher.

Making Field Observations

Depending upon the purpose of the study, the types of data needed, and the situation at hand, the researcher may engage in **passive observation**, simply watching, listening, and recording events for later analysis and interpretation. Or, the researcher may engage in **participant observation**, playing an active role even to the point of becoming an actual participant in the activities of those being observed. Participant observation may prove especially helpful if the social scientist is attempting to better understand matters from the position and viewpoint of others.

Whichever observation technique is used, researchers must decide how to handle the issue of revealing their identity and purpose (see Goode, 1996). Should the observations be done covertly or overtly? Should subjects know they are being studied? Would the known presence or participation of the researcher in a group's activities influence behavior and events in ways contrary to the researcher's objectives? There is also the issue of privacy. What rights to privacy do those being studied have? Are there times when people deserve the opportunity to give their informed consent to be research subjects? Thinking back, you will no doubt see ways in which such questions could be readily discussed in regard to the experimental research of Rosenthal and Jacobson.

Field research tends to take place in one particular site, within a given time period, and with a specific sample of people. How do we know whether the findings based on observations of one group at one site will be applicable or generalizable to other people and other settings? One may be more confident in the findings if other researchers come up with similar findings elsewhere. Unfortunately, sometimes a research situation is so unique that the research may not be repeated easily. Because those reading field researchers' findings have not been observers, they must place a great deal of trust in the researchers' honesty, observational skills, and interpretive judgments. Finally, field research—while often rewarding—is also highly labor-intensive. Investigators may have to devote a great deal of time, often over long periods, to gathering observations. This was certainly the case in the well-known study we have chosen to illustrate the use of this research method.

Research Example: Manufacturing Classroom Failure

Aware of Rosenthal and Jacobson's experimental research, sociologist Ray C. Rist conducted a highly-acclaimed study that further explored ways in which schools may actually nurture class inequalities (Rist, 1973). In contrast to Rosenthal and Jacobson's experimental method, Rist chose to pursue his investigation through direct observation of teacher–student interaction in the classroom. He conducted field research in an urban elementary school in the Midwest, observing a group of children from the time they entered kindergarten until they entered the second grade.

Rist began by looking at pre-enrollment information about each child, all of which was available to the kindergarten teacher. For example, the school social worker reported on which children who were about to enroll in kindergarten came from families receiving welfare. Rist noted that none of the pre-enrollment information directly related to the children's academic capabilities or potential. Yet, armed with this information and firsthand observation of the appearance and demeanor of each child, by the eighth day of kindergarten the teacher in the classroom where Rist was observing had established permanent seating assignments.

Seated at Table 1, closest to the teacher, were the better-dressed children in the classroom. None came from families reliant on welfare. Table 1 children seemed most at ease in the school setting, interacted confidently with the teacher and their peers, and tended to speak standard American English. At Tables 2 and 3 were less well-attired children. They were more likely to be from families receiving public assistance, appeared restrained in their interactions, and were likely to speak in street dialect, if they spoke at all.

The teacher told Rist that the students she placed at Table 1 were her "fast learners," while those at the other two tables "had no idea of what was going on in the classroom" (Rist, 1970: 422). Thereafter, she focused most of her time, attention, teaching, and affection on Table 1 children and effectively wrote off the children at Tables 2 and 3 as "unteachable." As he watched the process of differential treatment of the children unfold, Rist concluded that those the teacher had earmarked for school success were the children who were most similar—in their background, appearance, and behavior—to offspring of the educated middle class, the same class of which the teacher was a member.

Children who are not taught usually do not test well either. Hence, it was not surprising to Rist that formal tests of IQ and reading skills that were later used to sort the students into "ability groups" in the first and second grades produced groupings that closely replicated the kindergarten teacher's initial table placements. Tables 2 and 3 students lagged academically behind their more fortunate peers from the first grade on. Rist asked the rhetorical question, "Given the treatment of low-income children from the beginning of their kindergarten experience, for what class strata are they being prepared other than that of the lower class?" (Rist, 1970: 448–449). Using a different research method than did Rosenthal and Jacobson, Rist shed light on some actual classroom practices that provide differential and more negative treatment to low-income children.

Advantages and Disadvantages of Field Research

Field research has a number of advantages. These include the ability of researchers to observe behavior as it occurs, to be flexible in determining what to consider as data, and to obtain information about people in natural settings. Field research also sometimes allows sociologists to study groups engaged in "deviant behavior" who would be unlikely to cooperate with other research methods, such as questionnaire surveys.

Disadvantages lie in the difficulties the researcher may face in gaining entry to and cooperation from a group, the possibility that personal limitations or prejudices may affect the researcher's observations, practical difficulties in recording and analyzing what can be substantial amounts of data, time commitments involved in doing the research, and problems in establishing the reliability of observations when two or more researchers must alternate in field research of long duration.

Sociologists have used field research to gather data in a wide range of settings, including poverty-stricken neighborhoods, college dormitories, tattoo studios, race track stables, factory assembly lines, communities in suburbia, nude beaches, private schools, hospital emergency rooms, working class bars, the headquarters of religious cults, and homes of the wealthy. Field research has vastly increased our knowledge of the social forces and conditions affecting human behavior and has challenged many stereotypes and false assumptions about different populations.

Survey Research

Perhaps you have been asked to fill out a written questionnaire or answer a series of questions over the telephone or in person. Or, maybe you have participated in a course evaluation in college. If so, you have participated in a survey. A **survey** is a set of questions administered to a sample of people.

Survey Procedures

When social scientists use surveys to investigate a topic, they must follow strict procedures. The most important is choosing the sample. It is usually impractical for researchers to survey every single person in the population under study. Care, then, must be taken to use proper techniques to choose a sample that is representative of the population about whom the researcher is seeking to generalize. To avoid bias, the researcher selects randomly from this population. For example, researchers wishing to study views on people of color moving into a close-knit white suburban neighborhood may decide to seek interviews at every third home on each block.

The wording used for survey questions must be as neutral as possible. Frequently, researchers will pretest their questions and rephrase any that seem biased or confusing to subjects. Both sample selection and survey-question development are carried out in accordance with rules designed to minimize sources of bias and error that might cast doubt on the research results.

Surveys may be undertaken simply to gain descriptive information or to gather data relevant to previously formulated hypotheses. In the example we present here, the researcher was interested in gathering descriptive information on students' experiences with their course curricula.

Research Example: Gatekeeping in High Schools

In her classic study *Keeping Track: How Schools Structure Inequality* (1985), Jeannie Oakes explored the connection between high school education and class inequality. Most high schools in the United States have formal or informal schoolwide policies of **tracking** (Lucas, 1999). In many instances, tracking involves dividing course offerings into academic (college-bound) and one or more vocational (employment-bound) curricular programs or "tracks." The different tracks are supposed to prepare students for what teachers, counselors, and school administrators believe they should be doing after graduation. Some schools may subdivide various academic subjects into separate classes designed for different ability levels. Students are assigned, often after standardized achievement tests and teacher recommendations, to a given classroom ability level as determined by school guidance counselors and teachers.

Oakes examined the tracking experiences of students surveyed in 25 high schools located in 13 different communities. Each school was carefully selected to represent the population of students in U.S. secondary schools. Her findings pointed to distinct patterns of placement in tracks. Students from low-income backgrounds and students of color were found to be disproportionately present in the non-college bound tracks. Once students were placed, they were exposed to very different course content. Those in college preparatory classes were presented with knowledge similar to what they would later encounter in college and university courses, including critical thinking skills. In the non-college bound classes, students were exposed to extremely basic materials often requiring little more than rote learning.

Oakes's research results led her to criticize tracking policies. Students from economically disadvantaged backgrounds, particularly students of color, were likely to be channeled away from courses, knowledge, and high school credentials that could facilitate future upward mobility. Oakes concluded that high schools act as **gatekeepers**: They function to open up different doors of opportunity for different populations (see also Page, 1991). It is noteworthy that high school dropout rates are highest for students in non-college bound tracks, suggesting that track placement by itself can lower students' educational aspirations and commitment to schooling.

Advantages and Disadvantages of Surveys

Surveys are advantageous when one wishes to learn about the thinking and behavior of large populations. Since the ability to sample means that everyone in the population does not need to participate in the survey, costs can be kept down. People who are widely dispersed geographically can easily be reached by mail or phone if necessary. Respondents to phone or mail surveys often accept assurances of anonymity, which may make it easier to gain information about sensitive topics. Sampling and data analysis may often be done quickly and efficiently with the aid of computer technology.

There can also be disadvantages to survey research. A survey usually provides information about people's behavior and thinking only at a given point in time. Arranging and conducting surveys using face-to-face interviews can be time-consuming and require special interpersonal skills. The quality and dependability of survey results depend upon the representativeness of the sample chosen to be surveyed, the care with which questions are constructed, and the degree to which respondents are cooperative and truthful. But even with these disadvantages, surveys have become an important source of data for sociologists and other social scientists, as well as for decision makers in business and government. We may have escaped being part of someone's experiment or field research, but few of us have escaped being surveyed.

Historical Research

We have seen how research using experimental, field, and survey methods has in each case made a different kind of contribution to our understanding of the relationship between schooling and class inequality. Our next example of a research method shows that social scientists may also look at the historical record in order to understand the workings of society.

Uses and Sources of Historical Data

Much of the research in the social sciences deals with contemporary phenomena. But many researchers are concerned with establishing facts about the past. This approach is known as **historical research**. Sociologists using this method may want to gain more understanding of people's behavior in contemporary society by comparing it with that of an earlier era. Or they may want to determine origins of present-day practices. The motivation for historical research may be to understand patterns of continuity as well as change in society over time. Frequently, two or more of these motivations operate at the same time. Historical research may help test a strictly defined hypothesis, but it may also be used to answer questions that are open-ended. Usually, the questions pursued go beyond "Who?" "What?" "When?" and "Where?" Social scientists go one step further and want to know *why* history looks like it does.

Historical research involves using available data to re-create the past. Data may be found in **primary sources**, such as original records and diaries, official documents, and eyewitness accounts. In recent years a great deal of attention has been given to the use of oral history as a primary source: People are interviewed and asked to recount perceptions and make observations about earlier life experiences. This source of data may be particularly useful when written sources are inadequate or lacking. Data may also be found in **secondary sources**, such as historical data described in the publications of scholars.

Research Example: The Origins of School Tracking Practices

The desire to better understand the present-day relationship between schooling and class inequality informs the well-known study *Schooling in Capitalist America* by Samuel Bowles and Herbert Gintis (1976). These researchers wanted to determine why tracking systems were originally established in order to more fully understand their contemporary significance. Bowles and Gintis, using secondary sources for the most part, traced the origins of these policies back to the beginnings of mass public education in the United States well over 100 years ago.

The world of work back then, as is even more so the case today, was a hierarchy of varying occupational levels. Each level required different degrees of skill and allowed for different amounts of autonomy, responsibility, and privilege. Bowles and Gintis found that public schooling was, from the very beginning, designed to guide individuals toward these different levels. In order to carry out this process, the economic and political elites who organized mass public education deemed it necessary to sort children into various curricular tracks. Tracking systems were rationalized as the most efficient way to make sure each child received a school experience appropriate to his or her potential. However, biases in track assignments destined many poor and working class children for the lower rungs of the occupational ladder, while children of the more privileged middle and upper classes usually received quite a different education and hence had quite different occupational trajectories.

Bowles and Gintis asked if the objectives of those economic and political elites who maintained control over mass public education in the nineteenth century are still being played out today. In their view this is indeed the case: Schooling is organized in such a way as to serve the labor needs of hierarchical workplaces. However, schooling does not seem to be performing this function satisfactorily in the eyes of many of today's employers. Indeed, much of the recent corporate interest in improving the quality and effectiveness of U.S. public schools stems from employers' desire to increase worker productivity at different levels of the occupational structure.

In short, historical research can help shed light on a variety of social phenomena. This research method has been used to better understand the evolution of relations between developed and underdeveloped nations, the factors producing revolutions and other movements for social change, the effects of technology on the workplace, the origins of the modern welfare state, the changing nature of the health-care system and the medical profession, and approaches to the definition and handling of crime, mental illness, and other forms of "deviant behavior."

Advantages and Disadvantages of Historical Research

Perhaps the key disadvantage of historical research is the possibility of inaccuracy and bias in the sources. Primary sources such as eyewitness accounts may exaggerate or fabricate reality, contain errors of fact, or be intentionally self-serving. Documents are often not intended for research purposes, and their content may be built around a depiction of reality that departs from actual events. Secondary sources are written from a scholar's point of view. The selection of source material and the meaning the scholar derives from his or her selection must be assessed critically. Anyone conducting historical research thus must be satisfied with the closest approximation of reality possible, based on review of all available information. Social scientists are obligated to be meticulous in documenting the sources of their historical data, for others must be able to judge the credibility of their research.

The principal advantage of historical research is its helpfulness in understanding not only the past but also the present: Knowledge of history provides a unique context within which we can better assess present-day issues. Indeed, Jeannie Oakes's path-breaking work on the significance and implications of tracking as a gatekeeping process was clearly assisted by the historical research on the origins of tracking published several years earlier by Bowles and Gintis.

While we face many public issues today that are new and unprecedented, most of the issues we grapple with are not. Contemporary phenomena such as school failure, unemployment, poverty, substance abuse, different forms of criminal behavior, discrimination, and family-related problems—to mention just a few—may be rendered less mystifying and more open to change when viewed within a historical context. Moreover, we may find out that certain strategies being proposed for addressing these phenomena have never worked and thus be more open to thinking about new approaches.

Analyses of Existing Data

Secondary Data Analysis

Not all research requires that social scientists go out and gather their own data. Sociological researchers often rely on data that have already been gathered by others, data that often had originally been collected for totally different purposes. When such data are analyzed by sociologists engaging in their own research, they are performing **secondary data analysis**.

An enormous volume of data is readily available for secondary data analysis. Most of these data are in the form of statistics and often are generated by government agencies. For example, federal census data on the characteristics of the U.S. population are available for the nation as a whole as well as by region, state, city or town, and on down to the neighborhood level. The federal government also generates statistics on such topics as education, healthcare, employment, and immigration. Both government agencies and many business groups collect data to track government spending, assess the effects of government programs, and determine the need for new legislation. Nonprofit organizations and advocacy groups frequently develop data concerning social problems and policy issues with which they are concerned. Much of this data, particularly that generated by government, is in the "public domain." This simply means that anyone interested can access and use it.

Advantages and Disadvantages of Using Existing Data

Being able to analyze data already gathered by others is invaluable in saving sociological researchers a great deal of time and money. In some instances, sociologists are even able to serve in roles that influence the kinds of data being gathered, particularly by government agencies. For example, when George W. Bush was president of the United States, he tried to reduce and in some cases eliminate the data collected on the status of women by the Census Bureau. Social scientists protested vigorously against this attempt to limit the collection of important data; ultimately, the Bush Administration backed down and rescinded its effort. On the other hand, not all secondary data are in the public domain, especially data collected by corporations and business groups. In addition, data that are generally available are not always as up-to-date as a researcher may wish, and researchers needing data extending over a period of years may find gaps or inconsistencies in what has been collected. Finally, data originally intended to be used for quite different purposes do not always provide the best fit with the kinds of research questions that sociologists are seeking to answer. Nonetheless, secondary data analysis is an important research method on which many sociological researchers rely.

RESEARCH ETHICS AND POLITICS

The different types of research methods illustrated above generate facts that can help us exercise the sociological imagination. Yet the conduct of sociological research and the reporting of findings do not take place in a vacuum. Under certain circumstances, unless care is taken, research may cause harm to people. Researchers have an obligation before they even begin an investigation to consider the ethical and political implications of what they are about to do (Babbie, 2010: Chapter 3). Failure to do so not only may be harmful to others but is likely to make it more difficult for future researchers to obtain the cooperation and legitimacy they need to pursue their own inquiries. This is not to say that researchers must avoid controversy. Newly discovered facts are often controversial, if only because they may be differently interpreted depending upon one's personal or group values. Rather, social scientists must be reflective and ready to take responsibility for the impact of their research undertakings.

The Ethics of Research

Perhaps the most well-known case of research generating widespread debate over ethics is Laud Humphreys' work, published under the title *Tearoom Trade* (1975). Humphreys was interested in male-to-male sexual behavior. He decided to investigate the sexual behavior and social backgrounds of men who visited public restrooms of a Midwestern city park for mutually consenting, but anonymous and highly impersonal, sexual encounters. Humphreys' research findings exploded the popular stereotype that such men lead very deviant lifestyles in general. Most of the men were married, had families, and were respected members of their communities. They came from all walks of life, occupations, and professions. Few were exclusively homosexual in their sexual orientation. Yet, when Humphreys reported his findings, the facts were forced to compete with a torrent of debate about the ethics of his research procedures. Let us briefly describe what he did that raised debate.

Humphreys gathered his data using the field research technique of participant observation. His research took place in a park located in a major Midwestern city. To observe the sexual behaviors of the men in question, he offered to play the role of lookout at the park's public restrooms, warning of the arrival of possible intruders (including the police). Besides systematically keeping track of the patterns of sexual behavior he observed, Humphreys also managed to take down the automobile license numbers of the men. Using friendly contacts in the local police department, but telling them only that he was performing some kind of "market research," Humphreys located the home addresses of his subjects. Using a disguise to avoid being recognized as the restroom lookout, Humphreys interviewed the men as part of a survey he said he was conducting on the health of males in the community. In this way he was able to gather a wide variety of information on their lifestyles and backgrounds.

One of the ethical issues Humphreys' procedures raised was that of individuals' rights to privacy. Some researchers argued that the subjects' privacy rights were invaded by Humphreys, both in his participant observation and through the interviews. Others argued that Humphreys had rights as a scientist to pursue and to disseminate new knowledge. Another issue was that of deceit; he had pretended to be a lookout at the restrooms, a market researcher at the police station, and a survey interviewer at the subjects' residences. Some researchers argued that deceit was often the only way to gain access to groups who are likely to reject being studied. Others argued that this type of activity spawned distrust among citizens and violated fundamental values about what kinds of behavior were just and fair.

But Humphreys' critics went beyond the issues of privacy invasion and deceit. They pointed out that he risked doing harm to the subjects by seeking out their identities and places of residence. If, despite safeguards that Humphreys had established, their identities had somehow leaked out, the lives of these men could have been ruined. As it was, once the research findings and sociologists' debate over his methods entered the public arena and were picked up by the mass media, some of the men—clearly panicked—privately sought reassurance from Humphreys that their anonymity was not in jeopardy. Perhaps others, who chose not to contact him, lived in a state of fear. Psychologically, one could argue, harm was done.

The debate among sociologists over the ethics of Humphreys' research methods was useful because it helped make members of the discipline more aware of their responsibilities to their research subjects. The American Sociological Association, a scholarly organization to which most professional sociologists belong, has a Code of Ethics. This code requires that people being studied give the researcher their informed consent. Such consent may be waived under certain conditions, according to the code:

> Despite the paramount importance of consent, sociologists
> may seek waivers of this standard when (1) the research
> involves no more than minimal risk for research participants,
> and (2) the research could not practicably be carried out
> were informed consent to be required (American Sociological
> Association, 1997: Section 12.01).

The Code of Ethics addresses the principle of keeping information provided by research subjects confidential. For example, the code states:

> Sociologists have an obligation to ensure that confidential
> information is protected. They do so to ensure the integrity
> of research and the open communication with research
> participants and to protect sensitive information obtained
> in research . . . Confidential information provided by research
> participants . . . is treated as such by sociologists even if there
> is no legal protection or privilege to do. Sociologists have an
> obligation to . . . not allow information gained in confidence
> from being used in ways that would unfairly compromise
> research participants . . . (American Sociological Association,
> 1997: Sections 11 and 11.01).

Although unusual, adherence to the code's principles of confidentiality may place a sociologist in conflict with legal authorities. Rik Scarce, who has done research on animal rights and environmental activists, was jailed for almost six months in 1993. Scarce had refused to answer a federal grand jury's questions about research interviews he conducted with members of a group called the Animal Liberation Front (ALF). In 1991 ALF members allegedly broke into a research laboratory at Washington State University, released mink, coyotes, and mice that were being used for experiments, and did $150,000 worth of damage. Police were unable to locate the suspects. Scarce, jailed under a charge of civil contempt, took the position that he would not breach any guarantees of confidentiality he might have made to the subjects of his research. As he put it:

> *I am concerned that activists in the environmental movement*
> *may refuse to speak to me if I testify. . . . Other social scientists*
> *might find themselves less able to gain the trust of sources . . .*
> *[Social scientists] also would be less willing to go out and do*
> *research which in some instances does require of us that we*
> *grant promises of confidentiality (Monaghan, 1993).*

Researchers put themselves at great risk if they break the law themselves in order to be able to gain access to and maintain rapport with a group they are studying. Sociologist Patricia Adler, who studied upper-level drug smugglers and dealers, acknowledges witnessing criminal behavior, including drug transactions that occurred in her own home. In addition, she admits to possessing and consuming marijuana and cocaine along with her research subjects. Adler states that it would have been impossible for a non-drug user to gain admittance and acceptance into the drug underworld that she studied. In the course of her research, Adler risked the serious dangers of arrest in a drug "bust" and police seizure of her research materials as "evidence" of her own and others' criminal behavior (Adler, 1985).

Although the question of the risk to the researchers themselves is certainly not irrelevant, most universities and other institutions where researchers conduct investigations using human subjects have Institutional Review Boards. The purpose of these review boards is to ensure that any human subjects are protected from harm, both physical and mental, that vulnerable populations (such as prisoners, children, and people with mental disabilities) are particularly protected, and that subjects' rights to confidentiality, anonymity, and self-determination are strictly adhered to. Human subjects must have a clear, honest understanding of the true nature of the research and be able to provide informed consent to participate in the project. Even after they sign a letter indicating that they have given their informed consent to participate, they must have the right to discontinue that participation at any time in the project, even if that means compromising the research project's goals and objectives. The mission of Institutional Review Boards, then, is to ensure that the interests of science do NOT trump the interests of potential subjects to the right to privacy, confidentiality, anonymity, and self-determination.

The Politics of Research

Researchers not only must be sensitive to ethical issues in the conduct of their research. The fact that all research is conducted within a larger political context can raise issues for researchers as well (Neuman, 2009). While ethical concerns usually involve sociological research methods and the handling of data, political issues can arise from the purposes or substance of the research and the uses to which findings may be put. A well-known case in point involved "Project Camelot," a research project that became the object of international condemnation.

In the early 1960s the U.S. Department of the Army asked researchers at American University to engage in a research project that would enable it to "predict and influence politically significant aspects of social change in the developing world" (Horowitz, 1967: 47). At that time, Latin American nations—in which a number of U.S. corporations had important investments— were the Army's principal focus. In many such nations, impoverished people were rebelling against strong, often brutal dictatorships. The Army wanted research conducted that would help it predict where rebellions were most likely to occur so it could help these Latin American governments head them off. It was, in short, a research project aimed at helping the powerful remain powerful. Those social scientists who agreed to participate in Project Camelot accepted, whether consciously or not, that political bias.

Project Camelot was to cost millions of dollars over a three-year period and was to draw upon social science expertise across the United States and in Latin America as well. Yet, less than a year after Project Camelot began, the Army dropped the whole idea. The U.S. government was highly embarrassed when news of the research leaked to the mass media. Governments and scholars around the world strongly condemned the United States for this planned intrusion into other nations' internal affairs and the political uses it was making of social scientists.

The widespread controversy surrounding Project Camelot alerted sociologists to the importance of understanding the interests of their sponsors, the implications of the research questions they were being asked to pursue, and the sponsors' intended uses of the research findings. The controversy made many sociologists sensitive to the potentially harmful political uses to which their skills and knowledge can be put. In our view sociologists have an obligation—much like that of medical researchers—to pursue knowledge that will aid in reducing human suffering and enhancing human potential. By that criterion, research like Project Camelot should simply not take place.

 CHAPTER SUMMARY

- Sociologists study society in order to generate knowledge helpful in exercising the sociological imagination.

- In studying society, sociologists seek to base their conclusions on facts that have been scientifically established through objective investigation and systematic data gathering.

- The research methods used by sociologists are usually intended to gather data relevant to a hypothesis, a statement that may be verified or discarded on the basis of the data collected. Sociologists also may ask open-ended research questions when not enough is known about a social phenomenon to state a hypothesis.

- In pursuing their research questions, sociologists may engage in experimental research, field research, surveys, or historical research in order to establish facts about the social world. Sociologists also often engage in secondary data analysis.

- Experimental research involves studying the effects of treating members of an experimental group and a control group differently under carefully controlled conditions.

- Field research entails direct personal contact with those whose attitudes or behaviors are being studied, using such techniques as passive or participant observation.

- Surveys involve the gathering of data from individuals through questionnaires or interviews, making possible the study of large populations.

- Historical research involves the study of both continuity and changes in various aspects of society over time, utilizing primary or secondary data sources.

- Secondary data analysis entails analyzing already existing data gathered by others, often for quite different purposes.

- In carrying out their research, sociologists have a special obligation to conduct themselves in ways that avoid bringing harm to people. This means being fully aware of the ethical and political implications of their research, including the unintended uses to which their research findings could be put.

THINKING CRITICALLY

1. Assuming that you had the education, training, skills, and resources, which aspect of society would you most like to study and why? What, specifically, would you want to find out? How would you go about doing so? What research methods do you think you would use? What kinds of problems do you think you would run into in doing your research?

2. In order to gain access to groups that are likely to resist being the objects of sociological research, sociologists sometimes conceal their professional identities and intentions. What issues does this raise in your mind, and where do you stand on them? Are there situations where people's rights to privacy must come before the sociologist's right to freedom of scientific inquiry? What would be an example?

3. In this chapter we discussed research which suggests that U.S. public education operates in ways that deny equal educational opportunities to children from less affluent backgrounds. We also mentioned research that suggests that men who have sex with other men come from all walks of life and that many are married men with families. Sociological research findings like these may make some people uncomfortable. In your view, is this good or bad? Why?

4. Discuss the differences between fact and opinion. What opinions concerning poor people and recipients of welfare are contrary to actual facts? Where do you think these opinions come from? Do you think they easily change when those who hold them are presented with factual information? Why or why not? What are the risks of basing policies regarding the poor on opinions and not facts?

5. Is it possible for social science research to be entirely unbiased? Why or why not?

KEY TERMS

research methods **20**
hypothesis **20**
variables **20**
independent variable **20**
dependent variable **20**
experimental group **22**
control group **22**
bias **22**
sample **22**
random **22**
open-ended research questions **20**

experimental research **22**
field research **24**
passive observation **24**
participant observation **24**
survey **26**
tracking **27**
gatekeepers **27**
historical research **28**
primary sources **28**
secondary sources **28**
secondary data analysis **30**

MACRO SOCIAL STRUCTURES

Most people interact regularly with a relatively small handful of other individuals on a face-to-face basis. Yet each person's daily existence is likely to be affected by many other unseen, unknown people throughout the world. This observation raises several questions:

How are the world and the societies in which people live organized to link individuals in meaningful ways?

How might your life be affected by people halfway around the world and from all walks of life, and how might you affect them?

Is the way societies are organized unchangeable, or do people have an ability to resist and affect the patterns of social organization?

To begin to explore these questions, look at the labels inside the clothes you are wearing. Where were the garments made? If you drive a car or own a cell phone, where was it manufactured? And have you or has someone you know been sent as a member of the U.S. military to another country to participate in an armed conflict (perhaps to Iraq or Afghanistan), to deliver medical and food supplies to an embattled nation (maybe in Somalia in the 1990s or South Sudan in the 2000s), or to participate in a peacekeeping mission (say, in Bosnia or Kosovo in the 1990s), or simply to be part of an ongoing presence (in Europe or Asia)?

Your answers to these questions should illustrate to you that no one is isolated from the rest of the world. On the contrary, everyone is part of a world-system, linked to other countries and the people who live there through the economic and political relationships forged between nations. Moreover, each individual is linked to society through participation in its central institutions, including the family, education, religion, economy, and the state. The shaping of individuals' lives can be understood in terms of how each person is positioned within these three levels of social structure: the world-system, society, and its institutions. These are the three levels of what sociologists refer to as macro-level social structures, and they will be the focus of this chapter. Although these macrostructures are powerful forces affecting people's life chances, they are not absolute in that power: People can affect these macrostructures through collective actions, thereby introducing flexibility and change into such structures. This notion will be explored in more depth at the end of the chapter and throughout the book.

SOCIAL STRUCTURE

Social systems are the ongoing ways that groups of people organize themselves and relate to one another in order to survive. Individuals are born into and die out of social systems, or may immigrate into or migrate out of social systems. But the ways in which these systems are organized, or the social structures, of the world's individuals enter and leave remain in place. What are these social structures, and how do they affect individuals as members of these social systems? Sociologists refer to **social structure** as the means of organizing recurring patterns of relationships within a social system. **Macro-level social structures** are large-scale mechanisms that organize and distribute individuals in an entire society, as opposed to small-scale, or interpersonal, structures (on the mid- or micro-level—see Chapter 4). Social structures can be arranged along a continuum, from the most macro to the most micro (see Figure 3.1).

In addition to falling along a continuum, you will notice in Figure 3.2 that social structures are arranged in a nesting pattern: The more macrostructures contain the elements of the more microstructures below them.

Figure 3.1: Social Structures

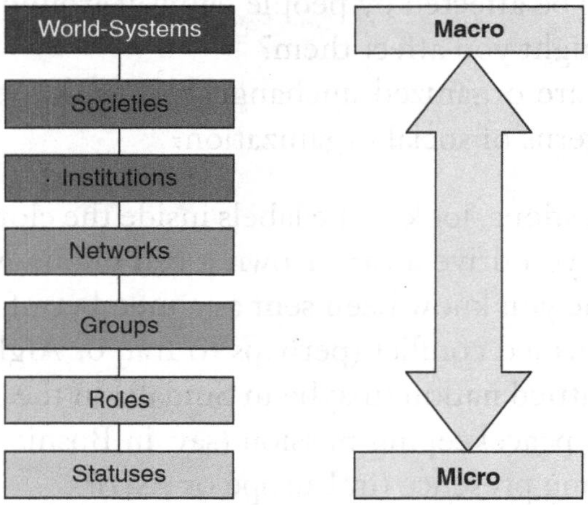

World-Systems
Societies
Institutions
Networks
Groups
Roles
Statuses

Macro

Micro

Figure 3.2: Nesting Nature of Social Structures

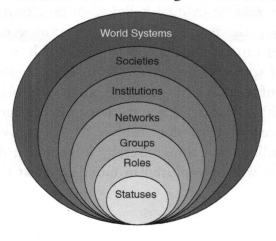

World Systems
Societies
Institutions
Networks
Groups
Roles
Statuses

Note that the focus here is not on individuals and their personalities; rather, what is important is how the positions that individuals occupy in society are organized and how they are related to the positions occupied by other individuals. Social structure is analogous to an apartment building in which tenants may come and go but the building itself remains intact. Some members of the social system die or leave, new ones are born or migrate into it, but the social structures remain to organize the positions that these individuals fill. For example, national and international labor markets are large-scale structures that organize tasks of production and distribution of goods and services in our society and around the world; they also operate as a sorting mechanism, distributing individuals into jobs to carry out these tasks. Individual workers and managers may retire, quit, or die, and others may be hired to replace them. But the way the jobs are organized to produce and distribute goods and services remains unaltered by the changes in individuals performing the work: Managers typically decide what to produce, how much to produce, how to produce it, and how much to pay workers to get the job done. Workers, in turn, follow the orders dictated from management and are paid a negotiated wage in exchange for their labor. That structure of work does not change even though personnel may come and go. So it is with social structures: Individuals may come and go, but the way society is organized largely remains stable.

The patterns produced by the organization and distribution of individuals in society are beyond any single individual's day-to-day control, but they remain powerful and significant forces in contouring people's existence. They shape people's experiences, possible alternatives for action, their world view, and their feelings about themselves. What, then, are these macro-level social structures, and how do they contour individuals' lives?

Let us begin by considering how individuals may be affected by events and relationships in other countries.

- How is it possible for issues and problems in one place to affect individuals across oceans and continents?
- How do people influence what happens in their nation and around the world?
- In what ways are all people members of an organized world-system?
- How is this relevant to individual experience?

THE WORLD-SYSTEM

All nations are connected to each other in a **world-system**. This is the most complete macro-level structure, as it encompasses all the other levels of social structure below it on the continuum of social structures. A world-system is an international social system of "cultural, normative, economic, political, and military relations"; these are organized around the exchange of goods and services (Chase-Dunn, 1998: 348). In a world-system, nations may trade goods and services, share common goals in international treaties, allow foreign productive facilities and military bases to locate within their borders, share a common history or heritage, or exchange labor. Such relationships are not necessarily between equal partners, nor need they produce equal or mutually beneficial outcomes. Indeed, they often do not (Peet, 1999).

Let's consider, for example, the role different countries play in producing the world's goods and services. There is a **global division of labor** in which the work required to produce these goods and services is broken into separate tasks, each performed largely by different groups of countries or groups within countries. Some countries may be classified as industrial and postindustrial or **core nations,** in which production is based on technology that relies more on the most modern machinery than on human labor and in which human labor is relatively skilled and highly paid. In these nations most employment is increasingly in the service industries rather than in basic manufacturing. While such countries tend to be wealthy overall, most of the people who live in them are not. Examples of core nations include the United States, Great Britain, Japan, Canada, and Germany.

In **peripheral nations,** production is based on technology that relies more on cheap human labor than on expensive machinery and state-of-the art technology, except in cases where such technology is imported from the core nations. Employment is primarily in manufacturing, mining and agriculture. Such countries are typically quite poor overall; however, not everyone who lives in the periphery is poor. Elites in peripheral nations tend to be wealthy compared with the poverty of the masses. Examples of peripheral nations include Bangladesh, Vietnam, Sri Lanka, Nicaragua, Zaire, and Lesotho.

Finally, still other countries may be classified as **semiperipheral nations.** These are countries in which production is based on a mixture of intermediate levels of machinery, modern technology, and human labor and in which human labor is semiskilled and paid intermediate levels of wages. Employment in these nations is commonly in manufacturing, mining, agriculture and some service industries. Such countries are neither as poor as peripheral countries nor as wealthy as core countries. And as with core and peripheral nations, wealth and poverty coexist within their populations. Examples of semiperipheral nations include India, Mexico, Egypt,

Figure 3.3: The World-System of Global Inequality

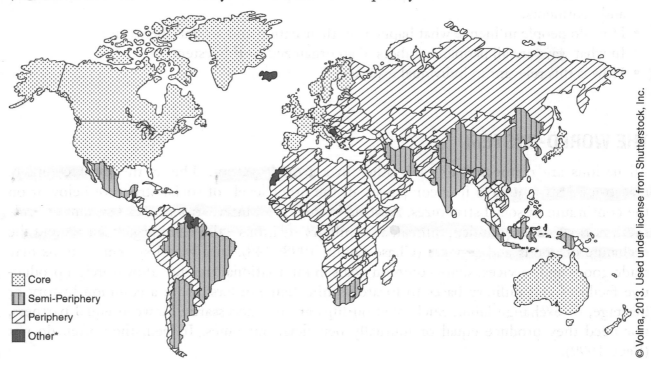

Core

Semi-Periphery

Periphery

Other*

Figure 3.4:   Global Division of Labor

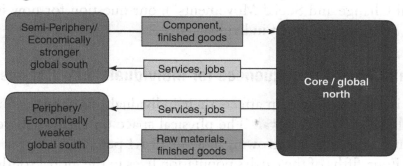

Kuwait, and South Africa (Wallerstein, 1974; Chase-Dunn, 1997) (see Figure 3.3 for a map of the global distribution of these classifications).

Each type of country plays a different role in producing and consuming the world's goods and services. Together, these different roles are part of what sociologists call a **division of labor, an arrangement of work in which tasks are broken into steps or jobs performed by different individuals or nations**. In the international division of labor, peripheral and semiperipheral countries provide the raw materials needed for production and manufacture more and more consumer goods, which the core nations consume. Meanwhile, the economies of core nations increasingly revolve around service sector operations, such as finance, management, sales, and information processing (see Figure 3.4). But do notice that the distribution of these nations' roles in the global division of labor is hardly random.

If you look at the map in Figure 3.3, you will notice a pattern for where each group of nations is located: Core nations are generally Western (North America, Western Europe), with the notable exceptions of Japan and Australia. Peripheral nations are largely located in Africa (especially sub-Sahara), Southeast Asia, Central America, and the Caribbean. Semiperipheral nations fall largely in South America, Eastern Europe, the Middle East, and West Asia. This distribution is hardly accidental or random: centuries of colonialism, imperialism, and unequal economic exploitation have plunged peripheral nations into severely disadvantageous situations relative to the core and left semiperipheral nations to struggle to remain above subsistence. Increasingly, then, some sociologists have begun to take issue with the terms *core*, *peripheral*, and *semiperipheral*, because these imply that industrialized and postindustrialized nations are somehow more advanced or more important than the others. But each plays an important role in the global division of labor, and the respective positions in that division of labor arise not from each nation's choice but from centuries of unequal power in politics, military, trade, and production relations. The terms most recently used to categorize nations in the world-system to reflect historical power and economic inequalities are *global north* and *global south nation*.

Global north nations are industrialized and post-industrialized nations that are and have historically been relatively powerful economically, politically, and militarily, and thus able to assert their interests over and above those of less advantaged and powerful nations. **Global south** nations are semi-industrialized or largely agrarian nations that are relatively less powerful economically, politically, and militarily than the global north nations. They are often impoverished after centuries of exploitation and oppression, and many of these nations have histories of colonialism and imperialism at the hands of global north nations.

While we'll return to an analysis of the dynamics of producing this division of labor in Chapter 10 ("Social Change and Social Movements"), our question for now is: How do these global patterns and relationships affect individuals' lives?

Global Patterns and Their Consequences for Individuals' Life Chances

Where people live in the world system affects their individual **life chances**, or their quality of life and their very likelihood of survival. The physical space on earth is shared by 6.9 billion people, a population that is currently growing at a rate of 1.1 percent each year. But that space is not shared equally: Four-fifths of the earth's population lives in the global south, where extreme poverty and hunger run rampant. Population growth rates are higher in these nations than in the global north nations: In global south nations the **death rates** (the number of deaths in a given year per 1,000 people in the population) are lower than **birth rates** (the number of births in a given year per 1,000 people in the population) (www.census.gov). These rates are greatly affected by age distributions in the world population: Nearly 90 percent of those under age 25 (prime child-bearing years) live in global south countries. Contrast this to more affluent global north countries where the number of people aged 65 and older is growing faster than those under 25 (www.census.gov).

Some observers argue that poverty and hunger in the global south are caused by the strong population growth rates in such nations, an analysis that implies poverty and hunger to be personal problems that can be solved by individuals choosing to have fewer children. However, a conflict perspective (see Chapter 1) would emphasize how extremely widespread poverty and hunger are in global south nations. That observation suggests that hunger and poverty are public issues rather than personal problems and that their cause may lie in how the structure of the world-system affects the distribution of power and resources between and within nations (Lappe and Collins, 1986). For example, by 1998 it was already clear that the wealthiest fifth of the world's population consumes 86 percent of all global resources, compared to the poorest fifth who consume 1.3 percent (UN Human Development Programme, 1998). That disparity has not improved. How does the structure of the world-system contribute to this pattern of global inequality?

The position of global south countries in the world-system's division of labor affects population dynamics and the life chances of everyone living in these nations, from birth on. Both the land and the resources are controlled by a small privileged class, an elite group interested primarily in generating private profits by trading with large corporations in the global north. Much of the land is thus used to produce cash crops (those grown for profitable sale rather than immediate consumption or barter by the grower) and luxury commodities (such as sugar, coffee, and cocoa), rather than the food needed for survival by most of the people in the global south country itself. As a result, chronic malnutrition or undernutrition and poor health severely limit the life chances of the vast majority of people living in these countries.

Additionally, the cultivation of a limited number of cash crops for many years requires the use of chemical fertilizers to replenish lost minerals and pesticides to protect the crops. After years of exposure to these chemicals, many workers suffer from debilitating and life-threatening diseases. Moreover, when countries emphasize cash crops grown for profit, they must increasingly rely on technology to make production more efficient and raise profits. This displaces human labor and provokes widespread unemployment. Unemployment, malnutrition, and lack of control of fertile land combine to undermine the life chances of working people in the global south. In particular, women and children suffer most.

Statistics show a stark gap between life chances in wealthy global north nations and those in impoverished global south ones. As Table 3.1 indicates, adults can expect to live decades longer and infants have a far greater chance of survival in the global north nations. In many global north countries the number of children who die in the first year of life per 1,000 live births per year (i.e., the **infant mortality rate**) is seven or fewer. In contrast, in some global south countries in Africa and Asia, anywhere from 50 to more than 119 infants per 1,000 live births die before the first birthday. Moreover, it is relatively rare for children in the global north to die before age 5 (1 per 1,000 people in the total population). Those who do die are usually victims of accidents. In contrast, *half of all deaths in global south countries are children under 5 years old*, and the typical cause of their deaths is not accidents but disease (www.worldbank.org; www.census.gov). In global south nations, malnutrition severely increases children's susceptibility to diseases; when water supplies are contaminated, intestinal irritations like diarrhea become deadly. Indeed, diarrhea is one of the major causes of death among these children. The poor distribution of food and unequal control over arable land often impose a death sentence on children in global south countries.

Table 3.1:   Global Contrasts: Wealth And Survival, 2011

Nation	GDP Per Capita	Infant Mortality (Per 1000 Live births)	Life Expectancy
Sweden	$57,091	2	81
Japan	45,903	2	83
United States	48,112	6	78
Germany	44,060	3	80
France	42,377	3	81
Nigeria	1,502	78	52
Pakistan	1,189	59	65
Haiti	726	53	62
Bangladesh	743	37	69
Ethiopia	357	52	59
Sierra Leone	374	119	48
Afghanistan	543	73	48

Source: World Development Indicators database, World Bank, 2012 (www.worldbank.org/indicator)

In many global south countries multinational corporations based in global north nations conduct manufacturing for export. But the people they employ do not derive many benefits. For example, in electronics factories in the Philippines, young women who work for eight to 12 hours per day peering into microscopes strain their eye muscles and endanger their eyesight. Workers in garment industries (who are primarily women) commonly work in sweatshops where severe overcrowding, and inordinately long days with few if any breaks threaten their well-being (Soyer, 1999). And slave labor remains a common and rapidly increasing feature of production in the global economy (Bales, 1999). Wages are extremely low, even by local standards of living, endangering workers' general health because their low wages are hardly enough to subsist on, much less support families. According to the Institute for Global Labour and Human Rights, while the average hourly wage for garment workers in the United States in 2009 ranged between $8.25 to $14, it was 93 cents in China (the world's largest apparel manufacturer); in Vietnam (the second largest exporter of garments to the United States) garment workers earn 52 cents in urban areas and 36 cents in rural areas (www.globallabourrights.org/alerts?id=0297). In India (a major trading partner with the United States) unskilled garment workers earn 55 cents, and skilled sewing operators earn 68 cents. And in Mexico (a partner of the North American Free Trade Agreement with the United States and Canada), the minimum wage for garment workers was 50 to 53 cents. While some might argue that these wages are related to significantly lower costs of living in these countries, it is notable that these wages are in fact well below a living wage: Workers paid these wages are extremely poor even by their national standards of living.

Beyond the severely low wages, in some of these nations' factories exposure to toxic chemicals and fumes causes lung and respiratory diseases, miscarriages, cancer, and other life-threatening diseases. Some corporations respond to workers' complaints of less-than-living wages and unsafe work conditions by automating, replacing people with technology. This only increases unemployment, poverty, and hunger among workers in the global south.

Since these workers do not own or control the corporations they work for, and since they are typically not unionized, changing production arrangements to improve their life chances becomes extremely difficult. Recent developments, however, suggest that such resistance is not impossible: Fair trade coffee networks have developed, for example, linking small producers in Latin America with consumers in the Northern Hemisphere "around the values of solidarity and fairness" and rejecting the corporate values of capital accumulation at the expense of human rights (Renard, 1999). Environmental nongovernmental organizations (NGOs) like Greenpeace, the Sierra Club, and Friends of the Earth have also had some success in pressuring individual transnational corporations in global south countries to assume greater responsibility toward the environment in their production processes (Fabig and Boele, 1999).

In this world-system, global north countries aren't immune from hardship either. When global south countries' economies are in crisis, these nations may sharply increase their exports to core countries like the United States and flood global north markets with cheaper goods. These cheaper goods then compete with more expensive products, undermining sales of domestic goods. Declines in sales of domestic products may produce widespread layoffs and unemployment in affected U.S. industries, such as textiles, garments, computers, and electronics. In addition, poverty in global south countries produces a cheap labor pool that can be exploited by multinational corporations based in the global north. When U.S. corporations move their plants to the global south to take advantage of the cheap labor, workers in the United States lose jobs. U.S. workers' wages and job opportunities are also affected by mass migration of unemployed and impoverished workers into the United States: Corporations can pay migrants substantially lower wages, thereby creating competitive pressures between workers. That competition enables employers to pay U.S. workers lower wages as well. All of this works to the benefit of corporations. The social structure of global relationships thus affects people in both global south and global north countries.

The Role of Raw Materials in the World-System

Dependency on imported raw materials affects the U.S. economy, its military relations, and its population. For example, heavy dependence on foreign sources of oil leaves the United States vulnerable to political and economic upheavals over which it has little control. In 1973, when the Organization of Petroleum Exporting Countries (OPEC) restricted its production and export of oil, the United States suffered a serious recession. Industries that relied on oil and petroleum products for production had to pay four times as much for these raw materials. Production became much more costly, raising the price of consumer goods. The resulting decline in consumption, together with the increased costs of production, caused thousands of U.S. workers to lose their jobs and left everyone suffering from dramatic inflation in prices. High inflation rates reduced the amount of goods and services that wages were able to purchase, thereby lowering their standard of living. In the year 2000, when oil producers restricted production in an effort to enhance prices, the cost of home heating fuel and gasoline soared in the global north nations, leaving many poor families, as well as elders on low-level fixed incomes, to choose between food and fuel; many in the middle class felt the economic pinch as well.

Reliance on imported oil also affects international political relations. When Iraq's invasion of Kuwait in 1991 threatened U.S. access to Mideast oil, President George H.W. Bush mobilized the most massive military force since the Vietnam War. As a result, thousands of people found their employment and education disrupted and their lives at risk when their reserve units were sent to the Middle East. In many families, income dropped sharply while wage earners were away at war. And, of course, some Americans lost their lives, many others suffered injuries, and still others endured the emotional turmoil of being captured as a prisoner of war. It is unlikely that U.S. decision-making leaders would have cared so deeply about Iraq's invasion of Kuwait had oil not been involved. Note, for example, that the United States did not mobilize military forces when the Soviet Union invaded Afghanistan in the 1980s, when the Taliban in Afghanistan began its campaign against the rights of women in that country in the 1990s, or when the Bosnian Serbs slaughtered Muslims in their "ethnic cleansing" campaign in that same decade. Note, too, that while gross human rights violations in the Balkans or in Sudan did not persuade the United States to exercise its military strength, the geographic significance of Yugoslavia did: Its position on the global map allows access to oil-rich areas in the Black Sea and Caspian Sea, and thus is important to the United States in its quest for global resources (Chossudovsky, 1997). It was not difficult, then, to understand the willingness of the United States and its global north allies to send troops to the former Yugoslavia in 1999 (Gervasi, 1996; Chomsky, 1999).

Moreover, while it is clear what effect such military ventures have on the indigenous populations in the global south, people in the global north nations are not immune. The 1991 U.S.

attack on Iraq caused outbreaks of political conflict in the United States. Many people questioned whether U.S. troops should be sent to war to protect access to Mideast oil. But those who protested against the war often found themselves labeled unpatriotic by powerful political elites and by members of the public who supported the war. Similar charges were lodged against people who protested the buildup toward war against Iraq in 2003, which was politically framed more as a war against terrorism than a war to secure oil resources for the United States.

Economic and trade relations between countries thus can seriously affect the social and political relations within them. This is in part why so many people felt compelled to protest the World Trade Organization (WTO) in Seattle in 1999 and 2000. The WTO is an international bureaucracy, dominated by countries in the global north, whose mission is to reduce economic conflicts or differences in order to smooth the way to the international production and trade of goods and services. Essentially, the WTO is supposed to mediate the global economy of primarily private corporate producers by moving countries toward common policies about such things as labor laws, environmental regulations, economic restrictions such as trade tariffs, and immigration laws and restrictions.

Some people consider the WTO to be the international agent reinforcing and maintaining the impoverished status of poorer nations (Brecher, Costello, and Smith, 2000). They point to the effects of the North American Free Trade Agreement (NAFTA) of 1994 between Canada, the United States, and Mexico, in which trade and investment barriers between the three countries were relaxed to encourage trade. Supporters of NAFTA argued that the policy would equalize wages between the three countries, increasing Mexican wages to U.S. levels and thus discouraging illegal immigration and encouraging consumerism to benefit the economies of all. After just five years, NAFTA had served to depress wages by 29 percent in Mexico, thrusting 60 percent of the Mexican labor force below the poverty line (Wallach and Sforza, 1999; see also www.globallabourrights.org/alerts?id=0297).

Furthermore, the push for mediating the differences in environmental laws between the countries has meant relaxation of the tougher laws in Canada and the United States, resulting in an increase in toxic waste dumping and an increase in public health problems. One 12-year border study found a connection between the boom in border-area production in the *maquiladoras* (foreign-owned factories where low-paid workers assemble imported parts in the production of goods for export) in Mexico and severe birth defects in both Mexico and the United States (Wallach and Sforza, 1999). Critics saw NAFTA as a smaller scale of WTO, which they argued would produce the same intensification of inequality on a global scale, and consequently they launch protest demonstrations against the WTO every time it meets. These protests are frequently met with the full force of military and police power to subdue the demonstrators and protect the meetings and their attendees, and thus the economic agenda of the global north nations represented at WTO meetings.

In addition to protecting U.S. trade interests, the military often facilitates international production. A strong U.S. military presence in or around countries in which multinational corporations have a stake helps secure the political environment. This military presence often requires treaties and leases to forge political interrelationships between countries. Such arrangements involve an unspoken understanding that issues like human rights violations may be overlooked in the interest of preserving the agreements. For example, for many years the United States did little to acknowledge the beating, torture, and killing of dissenters in the Philippines, in part because the Philippine dictatorship had been avowedly anti-Communist, a position consistent with U.S. economic and political interests. International relations in the world-system, then, affect the structure and experiences of whole nations and the people in them.

To sum up, where individuals are located in the global division of labor strongly influences their lives. Factory workers all over the world live less well than corporate executives, but factory workers in Mexico, the Philippines, and Vietnam are far more poverty-stricken than their counterparts in the United States.

It is important, too, where people are located within the society that links them to the world-system. Just as there is differentiation between nations, there is differentiation within them. What is the relationship between the individual and the larger society of which he or she is a member?

SOCIETIES

The world-system is a network of many nations and societies. A **society** is an organization of people who share a common territory, govern themselves, and cooperate to secure the survival of the group. Not all societies are nations; there may be several societies within a single nation. For example, in the United States many surviving populations of Native Americans constitute societies within the national boundaries of the country. Similarly, before its breakup, Yugoslavia contained within its boundaries several societies, including Serbs, Muslims, and Croatians; Spain contains a society of Basques as well as the more dominant Spaniards; and Iraq, Iran, and Turkey share the society of Kurds. In Israel, societies of Jews and Palestinians live a tense coexistence. Sometimes the presence of many societies in a single nation can produce diversity, richness of history, and gradual change. Other times, the presence of many societies within a single nation can become a source of serious conflict and sometimes war. In Iraq, Iran, and Turkey, for example, Kurds are persecuted and Shiite and Sunni Muslims engage in deadly clashes for dominance and control. In Yugoslavia in 1991, Serbs, Muslims, and Croatians resumed old conflicts in a struggle for control of land, a struggle that continues even now. And in Israel, despite ongoing efforts to forge a treaty for coexistence, tensions between Jews and Palestinians often erupt in violence.

Nations are political entities with clearly defined geographic boundaries usually recognized by neighboring nations. Nations are generally characterized by the viewpoint and interests of their dominant societies. Thus, although nations may contain several societies, not all these societies are necessarily equal in power or benefit equally from social, political, and economic arrangements. For example, the Kurds in Iraq were oppressed by a more powerful prevailing society under Saddam Hussein. And although blacks in South Africa are now in the political majority, for many years they were exploited and oppressed economically, socially, and politically by the dominant white society in that country. In the United States, Native Americans do not share the political or economic power of the nation's white-dominated society. Indeed, the dominant legal system may render aspects of Native American culture illegitimate. For example, federal laws prohibit Native Americans from using substances that the federal government defines as illicit drugs in their traditional rituals, despite the fact that such substances may have been an integral aspect of their societies' rituals for centuries.

Two Views of Social Structure

Some sociologists adopt a **functionalist perspective,** in which they view societies as adaptive social structures that help human beings adjust to their physical, political, economic, and social environment (Parsons, 1951) (see Chapter 1). When changes or challenges occur in that environment, the structure of a given society becomes the mechanism for organizing responses, adjustments, or preemptive strategies. For example, our use of fossil fuels has contributed to the **greenhouse effect,** a phenomenon that occurs when carbon dioxide released and trapped in the atmosphere by the burning of fossil fuels raises the earth's temperature and prompts significant global climate change. Functionalists would argue that U.S. society has made structural adaptations so that it can continue to survive. Our political structures have enacted and enforced clean-air and recycling laws, and our economic structure has made fossil fuels more expensive to discourage unnecessary use. Thus, society functions to adapt to the greenhouse effect. In this sense, society's structure is functional or beneficial in meeting its members' needs.

In contrast, other sociologists offer a **conflict perspective** on social structure (Chapter 1). They challenge the assumption in the functionalist analysis that all of society benefits from the way it is structured and from the ways it adapts to challenges. Moreover, they argue that such policies are often driven by power struggles. These critics point out that some groups enjoy advantages and privileges that allow them to impose their views on others and to influence the adaptive strategies society may adopt. In this analysis, the way society is organized significantly affects not only how (and if) people might alter their lifestyle in response to environmental challenges but also who benefits and who is hurt by the strategies chosen (Lowe, 1994; Foster, 1999).

What forces might influence decisions concerning energy policy? In the United States, the power of large-scale corporations, particularly energy and utility corporations, greatly influences that policy. The nation's energy policy today struggles to encourage use of renewable sources of energy, but continues to emphasize heavy reliance on nonrenewable, potentially hazardous sources of energy such as nuclear power plants and burning fossil fuels. After the United States had gone to war to protect its access to cheap foreign oil in 1991, President George H.W. Bush put forth a national energy policy that reflected a corporate agenda. The proposal called for a renewed investment in nuclear power generation as an alternative to reliance on oil and other fossil fuels; it made no provision for the development of less hazardous renewable sources of energy (such as solar, wind, or geothermal energy) or for conservation measures. And while President Barack Obama's energy policy does attempt to encourage wider use of solar and wind energy and the increasing development of electric cars, it also championed the development of a pipeline for gas and oil from Canada and enabled "fracking" (the process of fracturing rock layers by drilling and injecting highly pressurized fluid) to access rich veins of natural gas below the ground. Such a policy largely benefits the energy corporations, and their wealthy stockholders, that own the nuclear power plants, at the expense of the rest of society. Similarly, current policies relaxing environmental restrictions against cutting mature trees in national forests in the United States favor the logging industry's interests, and proposals to allow oil drilling in Alaskan national forests favor energy corporations' interests, at the expense of the environment.

In many global south countries, global inequalities in the world-system encourage policies that favor the wealthy elites, reinforce oppression of workers, and may intensify environmental challenges. Large landowners in countries like Brazil cut down millions of acres of rainforest a year to export wood or to create more land for cattle grazing in order to export beef to industrialized nations. Since trees are the natural consumers of the carbon dioxide released by burning fossil fuels, massive deforestation in rainforest-rich global south countries contributes to the greenhouse effect and global climate change (Durning, 1994). Thus, the structural position of countries in the world-system affects policies that in turn can affect the earth's environment. Indeed, protestors against the World Trade Organization in Seattle in 2000 raised precisely these issues.

Ironically, even political and economic power cannot protect corporate executives from the personal effects of global warming. At some point, it would seem, health issues would be expected to outweigh the profit motive in steering energy policy. For example, certain rare medicinal plants used to treat life-threatening illnesses may be found only in the rainforests now undergoing destruction. Thus far, however, personal and public health issues have not been connected to energy policy changes. People tend to address the greenhouse effect and change in terms of personal lifestyle issues (such as whether to buy large, fuel-inefficient cars like sports utility vehicles or energy-efficient hybrids like the Prius, whether to carpool to save gas usage, and whether to invest in solar energy for one's own home). Framed this way, the hazards are analyzed as personal problems of lifestyle rather than as public issues of energy policy driven by profit motives.

Societies respond to the need to adapt to their environment in many ways, *always influenced by their social structures.* Thus, there is no single, universal response to a given problem. For example, some societies may respond to the threat of the greenhouse effect and climate change by outlawing the burning of fossil fuels altogether. Others may attempt to reduce the use of fossil fuels for some purposes but not for all. Still others may ignore the threat, seeing it as minimal in the near future and therefore not a pressing concern.

The strategies societies develop to respond to environmental challenges affect not only their own survival but that of the entire world-system. For example, if societies choose to rely on nuclear power as an alternative to burning fossil fuels, they run the risk of nuclear accidents that may poison the air, land, and water of other societies in the world-system. In 1986, the accident at the Chernobyl nuclear power plant in the then- Soviet Union contaminated a large area of land and water in that nation and the radiation drifted into several neighboring countries. On the other hand, societies that insist on burning fossil fuels may be contributing to the growing threat of the greenhouse effect and climate change, and that will affect everyone.

How, then, do societies resolve the problem of survival, and how are individuals linked in the process of social survival? How do factors such as one's class, gender, and race affect each person's relationship to the larger society? How does society control and distribute access to important resources? These questions point to social structures called institutions.

INSTITUTIONS

To survive, every society must successfully address the same fundamental social needs. Sociologists using the functionalist perspective call these needs **functional imperatives** (Parsons, 1951). Talcott Parsons identified six basic functional imperatives, each of which is discussed below.

1. All societies must *organize the activities of their members* to obtain and distribute the basic goods and services necessary for survival (such as food, clothing, shelter, fuel, potable water), without irreparably upsetting a balance with the environment. Societies can obtain food, for example, by relying on what they find growing around them, or they can cultivate products that may or may not deplete the fertility of the soil. Alternatively, societies can trade with other societies for food, or they can invade another country or society to seize its food, perhaps at a cost to their own national security.

2. Societies must *protect their members* from both external and internal threats. External threats include invasion by other societies and destructive natural disasters like hurricanes, tornadoes, and earthquakes. Internal threats include crimes like robbery, murder, rape, and embezzlement and health epidemics like AIDS, measles, polio, and the flu.

3. All societies must *replace members* lost by death or emigration. One strategy may be to encourage increased reproduction, as many Orthodox Jewish leaders have done to replace members lost in the Holocaust. Alternatively, societies may provide incentives to draw immigrants from other societies, as the United States did in the 1800s to mid-1900s to attract the large labor force needed for industrial expansion. Another way to replenish labor is to seize people from other societies, as slave traders did during the 1700s to 1800s. While slaves certainly did not officially count as full citizens of U.S. society, they did count as greatly needed labor. As such, they filled a particular position in the social structure of plantation life, and slavery represented one strategy for replenishing diminished labor power in society.

4. Whenever societies gain new members, they must *transmit knowledge* of the rights, obligations, responsibilities, and expectations of appropriate behavior to the newcomers (whether they are native-born children or adult migrants). New members must also be taught the skills they will need to participate as productive members of the society.

5. All societies must *motivate both new and continuing members* to fulfill their responsibilities and conform to expected behaviors, even if these may be personally dangerous or onerous. This may be accomplished by a variety of approaches, among them providing significant rewards or meaning and purpose to activities and behaviors or by using force and punishment.

6. Finally, societies must *develop mechanisms for resolving conflicts*. Otherwise, conflicts may disrupt a society's ability to satisfy other needs and may even destroy that society altogether.

The social structures that all known societies possess to fulfill these fundamental social needs are called **institutions.** These structures develop the standardized methods that societies use to cope with problems of survival. While most members of society accept these conventional coping mechanisms as legitimate, there may be some debate about them within a society. The dominant groups in society are generally able to prevail over the interests and viewpoints of the nonelite or subordinate groups in society. For example, although there is evidence this is increasingly challenged, dominants in the United States strongly insist on defining the institution of the family as a heterosexual married couple and their offspring, a viewpoint reinforced by a wide range of laws. However, organized challenges by gay couples have pressed for such changes as the repeal of the Defense of Marriage Act (which explicitly defines marriage as a legal union between one man and one woman), extension of health benefits for life partners and the right of gays to adopt children. By 2013 10 states passed legislation recognizing same-sex marriages as legitimate; nine more legally recognize same-sex civil unions or domestic partnerships (and both California and Rhode Island recognize out-of-state same-sex marriages), and the number of states that join them are rising each year. Thus, resistance and organized challenges to the powerful groups' view may affect the content and operation of institutions.

Despite debates or changes in their form, institutions as social structures survive over time. Because they strongly influence our lives, they often become the focus of attempts at change. How can the problems experienced by individuals be viewed within the context of societal institutions? In order to answer this question, it is important to first establish what it is that institutions do.

Five basic institutions can be found in all known societies: *the family, religion, economy, education,* and *the state.* Each institution is intended to address one or more of the functional imperatives determining society's survival, and often more than one institution addresses the same imperative. Sociologists who adopt a functionalist perspective call such goals the **manifest functions** of the institution. However, in carrying out these manifest functions, institutions also produce unintended and often unrecognized outcomes or consequences, or **latent functions** (Merton, 1968). In addition, when institutions carry out their manifest functions, they also sometimes inadvertently produce consequences that reduce the adaptability and flexibility of societies and hence may threaten the very survival of the society the institutions are presumably there to secure. It is important to note that not all latent functions are necessarily negative; some positive outcomes may occur as well that were not intended or even noticed. For example, the global climate change resulting from the greenhouse effect poses a serious threat to the environment as an unintended consequence of the operation of powerful interests in economic institutions. This unintended threat to the environment produced by economic institutions fulfilling their manifest functions has also produced the unintended outcome of greater awareness of how people live, and growing creativity in balancing lifestyles with the health of the ecosystem. As such, the manifest function of economic institutions, dominated by powerful private interests, to obtain and distribute vital goods resulted in both negative and positive latent functions.

Functionalists argue that, in general, the purpose of institutions is to provide for the collective or common good by attending to the survival needs of society. However, a conflict perspective points out that institutions often serve some portions of the societal population better than they serve others. Institutions may even provoke or exacerbate systemic inequalities between groups within society. For example, when the United States went to war against Iraq in early 1991, the state was fulfilling its function of protecting U.S. society from external threats. Indeed, President George H.W. Bush argued that it was necessary to go to war to "protect our way of life," because Iraq's invasion of Kuwait threatened U.S. access to Mideast oil. And when the U.S. waged war against Iraq again in 2003, the state insisted it was fulfilling its manifest function of protecting the nation from the external threat of terrorism. However, an examination of who was actually deployed to Iraq among the U.S. troops indicates that the "way of life" of certain groups was exposed to disproportionate risk. The troops (particularly the ground troops) in 1991 were overwhelmingly from the working class. None of the chief executive officers of the nation's top 20 corporations, or anyone in the president's Cabinet had children involved in the war (Lacayo, 1990; Siegel, 1991). Moreover, people of color were disproportionately represented among the troops in the Gulf. The percentage of African Americans and Latinos/as in the ground troops was much larger than their proportion in the U.S. population. Of the troops who went to the

Gulf, 30 percent were African American; more than half of the women on active duty in the Army were of color. And on one Native American reservation, 70 members of a total population of 3,600 went to the Gulf (Women's International League for Peace and Freedom, 1991). This pattern repeated itself as the United States went to war against Iraq in 2003: Fully one-third of the active duty troops were people of color (Thomas, 2003). Why are persons of color and working class whites so predominant in the U.S. troops mobilized to serve in war?

When the United States discontinued the military draft system in 1973, the country began to rely on an all-volunteer Army. With unemployment and poverty among African Americans and Latinos/as running double and triple the rate among white Americans, many people of color turned to the military as one of the few sources of employment and social mobility available. Others joined the military reserves as a way to afford college tuition. An Army survey concerning recruits' reasons for joining the military found that 39 percent needed the money for college, and 26 percent needed job skills and training or income from service (DeParle, 1990). Although such motivations are not quite as strong for women as for men (Segal et al, 1998), many of the women in the military still cite similar reasons for volunteering: "for college money, technical training, a way out of a pink-collar ghetto filled with dead ends" (Quindlen, 1991). In many ways, poverty had led the chronically disadvantaged to become the ones who jeopardized their lives in order to preserve "our" way of life.

Note that there is a hierarchy within the military as well, such that people of color are more commonly found in the nonelite branch of the Army but are far less present in the more elite branches of the Navy, Marines, and Air Force. For example, African Americans constitute over 20 percent of the personnel in the Army, but only 18 percent in the Navy, 10 percent in the Marines, and 14.5 percent in the Air Force (U.S. Department of Defense, 2010 at www.militaryhomefront.dod.mil/.../MilitaryHOMEFRONT/.../2010_ Demographics_Report.pdf). This suggests that one latent function of the war mobilization was to reinforce racialized inequality, while the manifest function was to protect our society from external threats to its survival.

Sociologists using a conflict perspective often point out that when institutions reinforce inequalities, they are unintentionally introducing elements that may actually *erode* a society's ability to operate. For example, inequality limits the possibility that all of society's members will have an equal opportunity to develop their creative talents and skills. Inequality also may provoke hostility and distrust of society's ability to be fair or to reward hard work and accomplishment regardless of gender, race, class, age, religion, sexual orientation, or a host of other characteristics. Such distrust and hostility may weaken loyalty to the society among those who feel they have been unfairly denied rewards, and they may resist fulfilling responsibilities, obligations, and expected behaviors (Tumin, 1966). Hence, inequality as a latent consequence of institutions' manifest operations may actually threaten the institutions' ability to ensure a society's survival. At the very least, inequality may lead certain members of society to disregard socially prescribed responsibilities and obligations.

While a functionalist perspective emphasizes the needs institutions are there to meet, a conflict perspective asks who benefits and who is hurt by the way institutions operate to meet these fundamental societal needs. Who benefits and who is hurt by the unintended consequences or latent functions of our institutions? Keep these questions in mind as you read about institutions on the following pages, which compare the functionalist and the conflict approaches in an analysis of key institutions.

The Family

Functionalist sociologists view the **family** as the institution whose manifest function is to contribute new members to society. Families also teach the new members what is expected of them, and they try to motivate members to fulfill those expectations. The family may help contain and resolve conflicts within it, including disputes over inheritance. Finally, it ideally resolves the issue of the support of members of society whose capacity to produce may be limited (such as the very young, the very elderly, and the infirm). However, while the family attends to these important manifest functions, it may also produce several unintended consequences.

A conflict perspective, in contrast, would note that families may reinforce racialized, gendered, and class inequalities in the way they transmit expectations regarding appropriate behaviors and goals. Girls and boys may be assigned chores that reinforce traditional gender distinctions: Girls may be expected to babysit and wash dishes, while boys may be expected to take out the garbage or help with household or car repairs (Antill et al., 1996). Children of the working class may be taught behaviors and skills that are consistent with jobs requiring little or no autonomy and creativity, while children of the middle class may be instilled with expectations of autonomy, creativity, initiative, and responsibility (Holstrom, Karp, and Gray, 2002). Gender, however, can affect families' class influences on children's socialization: Women in relatively prestigious positions often place significantly more value on autonomy than men in similar positions (Xiao, 2000).

Similarly, families may reinforce prejudice and discrimination on the basis of race, religion, and sexual orientation. Parents, guardians, older relatives, and siblings are important sources of such values, stereotypes, and preconceptions of superiority and inferiority of different groups (Dennis, 1981). As families fulfill their manifest functions, they may unknowingly perpetuate inequalities, hostilities, and unnecessarily low aspirations and goals. Over time these prejudices can undermine society's ability to develop human resources and form a consensus, both of which may strengthen a society's ability to survive.

Families can also perpetuate economic inequalities by consolidating their wealth through marriages between wealthy families or through inheritance. Kanfer (1993), for example, offers a detailed historical analysis showing how three generations of the Oppenheimer family achieved highly concentrated wealth in South Africa through their monopolistic hold over the DeBeers diamond mines, and ultimately over the world's diamond market. By the early 1990s, the Oppenheimer family controlled 90 percent of the global supply of diamonds.

Instead of facilitating conflict resolution, families may actually produce the unintended consequence of increased conflict and violence. For example, some families in southern states were instrumental in instigating lynchings to avenge perceived injustices or insults against family members (Cutler, 1969). Their actions tended to inflame the existing conflicts rather than resolve them.

In addition, in a context of diminishing resources and increasing external pressures, family conflict in the form of domestic violence and child abuse may increase (we will discuss this in detail in Chapter 13). Domestic violence in the United States does not occur in the vacuum of family structures. Society itself provides the context for using violence to resolve conflict. This can be seen in both popular culture and political relations. For example, television and film graphically show the use of violence as a method of resolving differences. Furthermore, the United States has a long history of participation in international wars to resolve global conflicts. Film footage on the U.S. labor movement (1900s–1980s), the civil rights movement (1950s–1970s), the antiwar movement (1960s–1970s), and protests against the World Trade Organization in 2000 and Occupy Wall Street in 2012 chronicles the use of force and violence by military and police organizations to quell challenges to government policies and private corporate practices. And private videos have documented police violence directed against people of color, as in the 1991 beating of Rodney King in Los Angeles. So prevalent is the use of violence in society that it is not surprising if it comes to be accepted as a legitimate form of conflict resolution within families at home.

On the other hand, some families may transmit expectations of behaviors that challenge the predominant ones. Some parents, for example, argue against violence and in favor of nonviolent ways of resolving conflict, shielding their children from viewing violent films and television and banishing violent video games and toys such as guns from their homes. And some children are repelled by the state-sponsored violence and war they see in news clips and by the violence they see in their own or friends' families; it may offend their sense of justice to see people being clubbed or beaten, for example, or even killed. Indeed, nightly news footage of the horrors of the Vietnam War did more to raise a public outcry against the war than any debate ever could. In such instances, individual reactions to the social setting can affect the latent functions of the institution.

When families teach their children to challenge or question institutional arrangements and their limitations, they may open the door to changing social institutions, such as the family itself. The tension between alternative and dominant expectations and behaviors in families does not necessarily indicate a breakdown of the institution. It may become a front edge of change in the structure of the family as an institution. Different conceptions of family and different needs will give rise to a variety of forms of that institution, including child-free couples, gay and lesbian couples (perhaps with children), "blended" families of partners and their children from previous relationships, and so on. These variations can potentially challenge inequalities of race, class, and gender. For example, new divisions of labor may necessarily arise that do not conform to traditional gender-based divisions. Whoever is available for childcare must do the babysitting; whoever is available may have to cook dinner if the family is to eat; and so on. Then, too, the gendered construction of the household may not be conducive to a traditional division of labor: There may not be any women, or there may be only women. These issues will be explored in greater detail in Chapter 13 ("Family").

Religion

Functionalist sociologists emphasize that the institution of **religion** manifestly motivates members to comply with their responsibilities and obligations by assigning meaning and purpose to such activities. It attempts to reinforce the family's transmission of appropriate behaviors and goals to new as well as continuing members of society, and it parallels the family's role as a mechanism of conflict resolution. And religious institutions reinforce the family's legitimacy by sanctifying and protecting the family as an important institution.

However, a conflict perspective suggests that religious institutions often reinforce gendered inequalities by promoting notions of appropriate and inappropriate gendered behaviors and reproductive roles within the family. This typically means that sexual intercourse (and therefore parenthood) is forbidden until a couple has been formally married. The father is considered the breadwinner and authority figure ("head of the family"); the mother is the caregiver, house-keeper, and child rearer, and is subordinate to the father. Such interpretations of appropriate family roles imply that departures from this model are in many ways sacrilegious. Indeed, one young single mother in Nigeria became the focus of an international outcry in 2001 because she was sentenced to death by stoning for bearing a child out of wedlock. Religious institutions thus often sanctify a particular family form, such as the nuclear heterosexual family, and denigrate or punish others (especially homosexual family forms and heterosexual cohabitation without mar-riage). This reduces society's ability to adapt to changes.

Religious institutions may also underscore gendered inequalities within their own power structure. For example, the Roman Catholic Church does not recognize the legitimacy of women as priests. The Orthodox branch of Judaism similarly does not recognize the legitimacy of women as rabbis, nor does it allow women to be included in minions reading the Torah or leading services. Orthodox men and women cannot sit together in synagogues to pray; men who pray each morning include a passage in which they thank God they were not born a woman. Some interpretations of Islamic doctrine do not recognize women as equal to men: Men are dominant and superior to women. In some fundamentalist Islamic countries women must cover themselves completely when outside the home by wearing the traditional chador. Islamic women in Saudi Arabia are not permitted to drive. Whenever they wish to go anywhere, they must have a male as both a chauffeur and an escort. Women in Afghanistan were forced by the Taliban to leave their jobs, and they were forbidden to attend school. Similar Taliban restrictions against education for girls in Pakistan prompted a 14-year-old girl, Malala Yousafzai, to protest and demand an education in 2012; she was shot (but survived) in an attempted assassination by the Taliban.

Finally, religious institutions may unintentionally reinforce existing inequalities and social problems by emphasizing belief in an afterlife, when sufferers will be rewarded. This attitude may impede attempts to improve social conditions and increase society's survivability.

But despite their general tendency toward conservatism, some religious institutions chal-lenge existing inequalities (Smith, 1996). Several denominations of Judaism, including Conser-vative, Reform, and Reconstructionist Judaism, recognize women as equal to men; they allow men and women to sit together in temple, encourage women to participate in prayer services, and permit women to function as rabbis. Some more liberal Muslims note that nothing in the Koran specifically indicates that women are less valuable than men or that women must neces-sarily live circumscribed roles. Some Christian and Jewish religious groups have begun to accept homosexuals as legitimate members as well as leaders. Black churches in the United States were instrumental in challenging racialized inequalities as part of the civil rights movement (Morris, 1984; McAdam, 1999). And many religious groups have actively opposed inequality and have participated in antipoverty activities for decades. Indeed, many faith communities have become vocal partners with labor organizations in the United States in their push for a living wage in the new century, in their protests against welfare "reform" in the 1990s, and, more recently, in their protests against the wars in Iraq and Afghanistan. And in Latin America, many churches preach Liberation Theology emphasizing protest against poverty and oppression.

Another unintended consequence of religion as an institution can be an increase in conflicts rather than the decrease of hostilities and the development of peaceful consensus. Some religions have for centuries nurtured hostilities toward one another as competitors for souls. Wars such as the Crusades have been waged in the name of God, church, and religion. People who have not conformed to the prevailing religious dogmas have been killed, as in the Salem witch trials in colonial America, the Spanish Inquisition of the thirteenth century, and in Islamic Iran and Afghanistan. Indeed, Iran's religious political leaders issued an international death warrant against novelist Salman Rushdie in 1989 when they decided that his book, *The Satanic Verses*, was a blasphemous attack against Islam and God.

The Economy

In the United States, the institution of the **economy** includes corporations, organized markets, the banking community, international trade associations, labor unions, and consumer organizations. In noncapitalist societies, the economy might include the state-controlled production collectives, worker cooperatives, bartering and trading systems, and so on. For functionalists, the purpose of economic institutions is primarily to produce and distribute goods and services throughout society. They also discipline and motivate members of society to perform their role in the production, distribution, and consumption of goods and services. In a capitalist economy, workers (including managers) are motivated to do their jobs through the rewards of salaries, wages, and bonuses or the punishments of unemployment and poverty.

A conflict perspective, in contrast, would emphasize that the economy is often imperfect in achieving its manifest purposes and in reality produces unintended consequences depending on how people design that institution. For example, the economy in some socialist countries (such as the former Soviet Union), where the profit motive is not the principal guide to economic activity, may not produce the consumer goods people need to survive; instead, the economy may focus on state-defined needs, such as military production. A capitalist economy does not always produce the goods and services that people need to survive, either, but in this case the situation occurs because the economy focuses on profits. Grain and cheese may be warehoused and milk dumped into the ocean (despite great hunger here and abroad) because marketing too much of these products can reduce their profitability. Drugs needed to treat rare diseases, or products designed to help physically challenged individuals participate more fully in society's mainstream, may be difficult to find or very expensive because the market is considered too small to be profitable.

On the other hand, corporations may produce many goods and services that are profitable but not needed. In spite of mounting evidence of the dangers to both smokers and nonsmokers alike, cigarettes continue to be manufactured because of their profitability. Manufacturers are targeting younger consumers through advertisements and sponsorship of sports events and concerts. These marketing strategies are declining in effectiveness, but apparently still working: While the percentage of smokers in all age groups has declined in the last 20 years, and teenage use of tobacco is at an all-time low, the decline in tobacco usage has been slowest among 12- to 17-year-olds, and nearly 20 percent of all teenagers are smoking cigarettes by the time they leave high school (National Institute on Drug Abuse, at www.samhsa.gov/data/NSDUH/2k11Results/NSDUHresults2011.htm#4.1). Young consumers are replacing the losses among older, more educated, and health-conscious consumers. Thus, the economy as an institution provides incentives to produce harmful or useless goods and disincentives to produce important, needed goods. People often pressure the state to step in to control harmful consequences, demanding more ordinances regulating smoking in public places such as elevators, airplanes, restaurants, stores, and offices.

The economy can also reinforce class, racialized, and gendered inequalities. When workers' wages are kept low to increase corporate profitability, the workers are less able to purchase the goods they produce. Low wages thus reduce the consumption of goods and services produced, thereby periodically provoking recessions and unemployment and aggravating class inequalities.

Seniority systems within both corporations and labor unions institutionalize racialized and gendered inequalities. This is because a "neutral" principle of "last hired, first fired" ensures that women and people of color—historically more likely than white males to be the last hired in many job categories—will be the most vulnerable to recessions and corporate downsizing (although the recession of 2008–2013 has hit men harder than women—a notable difference from previous patterns that we will discuss in Chapter 12 ["Work and the Economy"]).

Inadequate access to jobs, coupled with racial discrimination in the labor market, perpetuates class and racialized inequalities by assigning different economic roles to different races and classes. In the face of dwindling opportunities, the poor, both whites and persons of color, are more likely to volunteer for military service as a job. Thus, the people who are least likely to benefit from the existing economic structure become the ones most likely to endanger their lives to protect it and the superior advantages it provides others.

In the United States the economy is supposedly based on a system of free enterprise and open competition, suggesting equal opportunity for all members of society. However, the economy actually protects the advantages of the already privileged. Large corporations that dominate most industries prevent small businesses from entering an industry and competing successfully. For example, small mom-and-pop clothing stores, grocery stores, and restaurants find it difficult to compete with the price advantages of large national department stores like Walmart and fast-food chains like McDonalds; many go bankrupt as the national chains continue to grow and expand. And relatively small auto producers like the American Motors Corporation have found it impossible to remain competitive with General Motors, Ford, and Chrysler (indeed, Chrysler eventually bought American Motors; by 1998 Chrysler itself was bought by Daimler-Benz, making it an even larger firm in an industry with fewer and fewer separate, competitive auto producers).

When the economy fails to equitably and adequately produce and distribute the basic goods and services needed for survival, those members of society who are denied them may turn to other, sometimes illegal ways to survive. For example, when the Soviet Union existed, a thriving underground economy of black-market trading developed there to give consumers access to commodities (commonly at a very high price) that were unavailable to them through state-run stores. In the United States, some women consider prostitution an opportunity for employment in an economy that offers few jobs (although, to be sure, not all prostitutes make a lucrative living in a safe environment; many are exploited by pimps and work under very dangerous conditions). Drug trafficking provides a lucrative (although extremely risky) source of income. Thus, although not all crimes are the result of economic need, and not everyone with desperate economic needs commits crimes, one unintended consequence of the way the economy is organized may be increased by crime.

More advantaged members of society may also receive unintended incentives for criminal behavior. Executives are more likely than assembly-line workers to embezzle corporate funds because the structure of the corporation places them in a position to do so. In the United States, for example, lack of regulatory oversight of the savings and loan institutions in the 1980s facilitated executive abuse, embezzlement, and fraud, costing taxpayers billions of dollars (Calavita and Pontell, 1991). In the same decade, illegal insider trading of stocks became a common practice among stockbrokers (Zey, 1993). And by 2008, it was clear that repeal of federal banking regulations had unleashed the common practice of predatory lending that resulted in massive foreclosures of delinquent mortgages, costing millions of homeowners their share of the American Dream and igniting the worst economic recession since the Great Depression of the 1930s (Ferguson, (2012). One consequence of our economy, then, may be that people place a greater emphasis on the value of money and personal gain than on the value of integrity and societal or collective gain.

The priority of profit making in the U.S. economy also provides incentives for corporate crimes. For example, it was profitable for Pacific Gas & Electric Company (PG&E) to discharge massive amounts of chromium 6, a cancer-causing chemical that is potentially highly toxic to anyone exposed to it, and allowed it to seep into the groundwater of Barstow, California (a case made famous by the film *Erin Brockovich)*. Although PG&E knew about the extreme toxicity of the chemical as early as 1965, it continued its practice but did not notify the community or the local fire department as required by law. Instead, the company watched as the entire community drank, bathed, swam, and cooked with the contaminated water, and supplied contaminated water to the all-volunteer fire department (Ascenzi, 2000). By 1996, after severe clusters of cancer, birth defects, and miscarriages began surfacing in the small town and Erin Brockovich doggedly pursued the case against PG&E's resistance, the firm was forced to pay a settlement of $333 million to residents of Barstow. PG&E had maintained its profitability at the cost of human lives and at the expense of the taxpayers, who ultimately will have to pay to clean up such sites.

These latent consequences of the economy combine to weaken its ability to ensure adequate production and distribution of basic goods and services to all, and to protect its members from internal threats. It then becomes increasingly necessary for other institutions, such as the state, the family, and religion, to redirect societal priorities so as to discourage the profit motive from overwhelming society's basic needs. Some of these issues will be taken up in greater detail in Chapter 11 ("The State and Power") and Chapter 12 ("Work and the Economy").

Education

When functionalist sociologists study the institution of **education,** they see a system whose manifest function is to transmit the basic skills that all young members of society need to become productive members of society as adults. Thus, the purpose of schools is to teach basic skills such as reading, writing, and math. In the United States, free public education is available to all children up to the age of 18. The Supreme Court's 1954 decision *(Brown v. Topeka Board of Education)* that separated educational institutions based on race are inherently unequal underscored the government's commitment to equal education for all.

A critical conflict perspective reveals, however, that in the United States, schools in fact reinforce the status quo because they *reproduce* inequality as an unintended consequence through a variety of mechanisms. For example, most school systems fund their budgets through local property-tax revenues. This method of funding creates unequal school budgets, since school systems located in wealthy areas with high property values have access to greater tax revenues than do those in poor locales with low property values. For example, in 2009–2010 the city of Bridgeport, Connecticut, spent $13,101 per student on a student population that was 91.4 percent children of color; in contrast, the nearby affluent community of Westport spent $16,959 per pupil on a student population that was 91 percent white. Greater per-student expenditures appear to have contributed to a more advantageous environment for success in Westport: Nearly 96 percent of Westport students go on to attend college, compared with 75 percent in Bridgeport. Compare the proportions of students in these school districts who pursue higher education to those who enter the military instead: In Westport, only 2.4 percent of the high school graduates went into the military, but nearly 12 percent of Bridgeport's graduates did so (Connecticut Department of Education, 2011). Why do per-student expenditures affect such high school outcomes as college attendance versus military service? Students in wealthy school systems tend to study an enriched curriculum in well-appointed facilities with low student/teacher ratios; students who attend school in poor systems commonly study a spare curriculum in deficient facilities (including lack of adequate books) with high student/teacher ratios. The method of providing local school budgets thus re-creates past patterns of class and racial inequalities.

Another latent function of education is mate selection. This is because our educational institutions are structured so as to place large numbers of similar-aged people in the same school or classroom. While this may be the most cost-efficient manner of imparting basic knowledge, it has the unintended consequence of serving as a marriage and mate-selection mechanism at the high school and college levels. By matching privileged students with one another and economically disadvantaged students with one another, schools and colleges seriously reduce the possibility that an upwardly mobile, college-educated individual will mate with someone less advantaged or less educated, whose chances of mobility are limited. Thus, the educational institution reproduces economic inequalities and unequal access to mobility.

Schools also perform the latent function of mitigating pressures on the economy during recessions by delaying the entry of young adults into a tight labor market. Indeed, many college graduates in the early 1990s and again during the 2008–2013 recession, faced with the worst job market for college graduates in more than a decade, opted for graduate school as a haven from unemployment (McFadden, 1991; Luzer, 2010 at www.washingtonmonthly.com/college_guide/blog/economic_meltdown_causes_surge.php). Schools therefore reinforce the legitimacy of the economy by reducing the pressures that could be created on a restricted labor market if all high school and college graduates demanded jobs simultaneously.

On the other hand, educational institutions can also be powerful mechanisms for social change. When skills taught by schools include independent, critical, and creative thinking, they produce the potential for challenges to society to alter inequalities and discrimination (Ayers, Hunt, and Quinn, 1998; Finn, 1999). It was to prevent such challenges that the antebellum South prohibited teaching African American slaves to read. More recently, critical thinking in colleges and universities and the consequent challenges to institutions promoted pressures to pass and implement civil rights laws, to question U.S. involvement in Vietnam, and to demand an end to the reliance on sweatshop labor to produce the licensed merchandize bearing the schools' name and logo. When people can read and think critically, they are less likely to accept without question practices and policies they see as problematic or unfair. That latent function of the manifest mission of educational institutions often becomes the vanguard of social change.

The State

The **state** is the structure of the political system that includes all governmental branches and agencies, which together exercise power and authority over a particular nation. This is different from the notion of **government**, the people who govern within that structure who determine overall policy direction and make laws. Government, then is but one of several elements of the state. While people in governing bodies make laws, these laws are enacted or implemented by other administrative agencies; the military and police enforce the laws; and the judiciary interprets the laws, resolves the disputes in their application, and applies sanctions for transgressions. The state, then, is composed of the people in governing bodies together with people in administrative and enforcement agencies.

In the United States, for instance, the government is Congress and the President, state legislators and governors, municipal and town councils and mayors, and other policymaking bodies (such as Boards of Education). The administrators of the laws and policies passed by these decision makers include bureaucracies such as the Department of Labor, the Environmental Protection Agency, and the Department of Health and Human Services. The military and police forces (including the various branches of the armed services) help enforce the policies passed by Congress and signed into law by the president, both within the United States and abroad. The judiciary, including the Supreme Court, criminal courts, civil courts, and courts of appeal, interpret the laws and policies Congress passes and may impose sanctions against those who do not comply. Together these various agencies and branches (whose personnel are both elected and nonelected) are the state in the United States.

Functionalist sociologists conventionally view the state as an institution designed to protect society's members from internal and external threats. To meet this obligation, the state frequently becomes the only institution that can legitimately use force and violence, doing so through its police force and militia (Weber, 1947). Except in police states, there are controls on state power as well: When the state exceeds legitimate use of its power, even its agents can be brought to trial, as in the case of police officers who brutally beat up suspects and military interrogators who abuse prisoners of war.

The state also establishes penal and civil codes to formally define standards of acceptable and unacceptable behaviors, responsibilities, and obligations, and it specifies sanctions for violations of these standards. These codes help transmit prevailing standards and expectations and motivate society's members to comply with them. Ideally, the laws also serve to resolve conflicts through clearly defined legal processes, to be conducted in courts before impartial judges and a jury of one's peers.

Finally, the state is designed to aid the economy by developing social welfare programs that distribute goods and services to individuals the economy cannot support. By enhancing the ability of the poor to consume goods and services, such programs indirectly support the private producers and the economy.

On the other hand, a conflict perspective of the state reveals activities that may reproduce racialized and class inequalities. When the state is controlled by interests that are already advantaged (for example, white, wealthy, corporate interests) its legitimate use of force and violence may be directed against challengers to the system. As noted earlier, this has historically been the case in the U.S. labor and civil rights movements.

At other times, the state may become the agent of change. In the United States the state is not a single entity controlled by an absolutely powerful elite. Instead, the state is composed of several levels of government in a hierarchy that allows the federal government, within limits, to act to force local governments to change. For example, the federal government used individual states' National Guard to enforce court-ordered school desegregation in southern states in the 1950s.

The state may reinforce advantages of corporations over labor and advantages of the affluent over the poor through its tax structure. A study by Citizens for Tax Justice reported that in 2011, as a group, the wealthiest members of U.S. society paid a lower effective tax rate (of 15.3 percent) than the rate paid by the poorest members as a group (who paid a rate of 21.3 percent). This occurred because of hidden entitlements and tax breaks for the affluent and an emphasis on regressive sales and excise taxes, as opposed to progressive ability-to-pay income taxes (Citizens for Tax Justice, 2012 at http://ctj.org/ctjreports/2012/04/buffett_rule_bill_before_the_senate_is_a_small_step_towards_tax_fairness.php). Sales taxes are regressive in that everyone, regardless of income, must pay the same tax on purchases; this means that the poor pay a higher proportion of their income than do the wealthy on food, clothing, transportation, fuel, and so on.

Moreover, the tax structure provides the affluent with tax breaks that are not accessible to the poor, thereby reducing the affluents' share of the total tax burden. For example, mortgage interest is tax-deductible. Since far more people in the middle and upper classes than in the poor and working classes are likely to own their homes, such a deduction mainly benefits the wealthier taxpayers. Indeed, while only 25.5 percent of U.S. taxpayers earn more than $75,000 per year in 2010, they are the recipients of more than 75 percent of mortgage deductions. And while an income of $75,000 per year is not considered wealthy by current standards, three-fourths of U.S. workers earn less than that amount (www.irs,gov/taxstats); thus, mortgage tax breaks are inaccessible to the vast majority of the population. A mortgage tax deduction, then, not only reduces the tax burden of the relatively privileged few; it also becomes a form of welfare for them.

This same tax policy, manifestly designed to encourage home purchases, may have the indirect latent consequence of stimulating job creation in the construction and supply industries (lumber, concrete, brick, plumbing, electrical supplies, durable goods, shipping and moving, and so forth). The state as an institution thus may serve the latent function of reproducing inequality while simultaneously stimulating upward mobility through the creation of jobs in high-paying industries.

The state may reinforce other inequalities as well. The Medicaid program, for example, is manifestly designed to extend healthcare to the poor, thereby reducing economic inequalities and promoting a healthy work force as well as promoting public health. However, since the program focuses largely on acute-care needs, it neglects the needs of the chronically ill and people with physical and mental disabilities, thus underscoring and aggravating such persons' problems.

Furthermore, the state may reinforce dominant ideologies in its development and implementation of laws. For example, while civil rights legislation legally ensures equal rights regardless of race, sex, ethnicity, religion, or physical ability, in fact people of color, women, individuals with disabilities, and religious minorities may find their protections limited by the various ways the laws are interpreted. Moreover, some minority interests remain unprotected, even in the written policy. Homosexual equal rights, frequently under attack, are often defined as outside the realm of the state. Thus, one consequence of the structure and process of the American state is continued domination by privileged wealthy, white, largely male, heterosexual and often corporate interests.

The state does not always provide equal protection under the laws. People of color frequently charge that they are harassed or unfairly treated by police, courts, prisons, and laws that remain insensitive to issues of discrimination (Free, 1996; K. Russell, 1998; Mauer, 1999). Studies in several cities have noted that prosecuting lawyers often challenge African Americans during jury-selection processes and effectively keep them off juries that are likely to hear cases involving African American defendants (*Harvard Law Review*, 1988: 1472 Kennedy, 1997). This raises the questions of whether these defendants are being tried by a jury of their peers and whether the judicial system is neutral. Moreover, people of color are frequently the target of police brutality and excessive use of force on the streets, as evidenced by the Stolen Lives Project (1999), which has documented more than 2,000 such cases nationally, and are also the victims of denigration and excessive force and violence at the hands of their guards in prisons (see also Johnson, 1990; McQuiston, 1990).

Unequal protection is also manifested as a class issue. During the 1980s, the U.S. government increasingly initiated policies that favored the wealthy. The ability of the affluent to drastically reduce their share of the federal tax burden (and thus indirectly of the state tax burden) through deductions, write-offs, and loopholes has effectively meant that they have decreased their financial support of public services at all levels. Faced with reduced funding, the local levels of the state are finding it difficult to maintain adequate police forces, and the protection provided to the public is often insufficient. At the same time, however, the affluent do not suffer. Instead, they purchase their own protection by hiring private security guards. Thus, the state's decision to shift the responsibility of protection to the local level, coupled with its policy of tax structures that overwhelmingly favor the wealthy, means that the state provides unequal protection to society's members on the basis of class (Cole, 1999).

Similarly, gender is an issue in the state's unequal approach to crime. Women who have been raped still complain of being psychologically raped a second time by insensitive police, lawyers, judges, and other members of the judicial system who inquire about their previous relationships and their manner of dress when these women attempt to bring their attackers to justice. Debates still continue over whether a victim's past relationships are admissible evidence during a rape trial. And many communities still treat spouse or partner abuse as a private matter of domestic dispute to be dealt with by the parties involved, rather than as a violation of the law. Fortunately, more and more communities are beginning to treat such abuse as a crime of assault and battery, thereby opening the possibility for greater state protection of women. However, protection of women is still quite imperfect: Once an attacker has served the specified term, the state does not typically follow up with restrictions for the attacker.

There is some evidence to suggest that a pattern defines who receives less-than-perfect protection. Those groups in society who have relatively little power, particularly women, people of color, homosexuals, and the poor, have found themselves to be the victims of state neglect, at best, and of violence at the hands of agents of the state, at worst. The state appears to provide the best protection to those who already benefit most from the way the state is organized and who have the power to ensure that this organization continues. In particular, the affluent in the United States, who are largely white, have historically had the power to protect the state from serious challenges and in turn have benefited from its protection of their safety, their affluence, and their position.

Institutions as Dynamic Structures

Institutions are not inexorable and unchangeable. The form and content of institutions such as the family and the state may vary from one society to another or from one time period to another within a single society. There may also be several simultaneous alternative forms of a given institution within a single society. But the institution itself, in some form or another, remains identifiable as an institution everywhere. For example, there are many contrasting structural forms that may still be classified as family: nuclear families (two parents of opposite sex who are married and their offspring), extended families (nuclear families plus other related individuals, such as grandparents, aunts, uncles, cousins), single-parent families, child-free couples, gay and lesbian couples, live-in couples (two people of opposite sex who are not married), blended stepfamilies, and so on. All are families, grouping individuals into a common living arrangement to obtain the necessary goods and services for survival. They all transmit to their members the knowledge and skills needed to function in society. And they often replenish the population.

Institutions, then, are not set in concrete. They are dynamic structures that respond to changes and challenges. But what remain, regardless of alterations in form, are structures of organized social life that are designed to satisfy fundamental social needs and that often produce both positive and negative unintended consequences.

The basic institutions do not operate in isolation either. They interact and affect one another. For example, the institutions of the economy and the state affect the family and education. When the state determines that education systems must be funded by property-tax revenues, it affects schools' curricula and facilities and thus how effective these will be. In this way, decisions made by the state reinforce the schools' latent consequence of perpetuating class (and often racialized) inequality.

When the economy is in a recession, it affects the family by altering the employment status of family members. This may in turn affect gendered roles as well as reinforce class inequalities, since low-wage production and service workers are typically the first and hardest hit in a recession. When the state awards child custody primarily to the mother (except in extreme cases) during a divorce, but does not enforce child-support payment responsibilities, it is reinforcing gendered inequalities (see Weitzman and Maclean, 1992; Allen, Nunley, and Seals, 2011). So great are the inequalities in earnings between males and females and the gendered division of paid and unpaid (that is, housework) labor that in the first year after a divorce the mother's income typically declines substantially while the father's *improves* (Morgan, 1991). More recent research indicates that men's incomes are most likely to increase after divorce if they were the sole or primary breadwinner; men whose partners contributed substantially to the total household income actually lost income after divorce (McManus and DiPrete, 2001). This suggests that one latent consequence of traditional roles in marriage is the reproduction of gendered inequalities after divorce, since the state does not typically evaluate women's unpaid labor as equal to the monetary income paid to men who work outside the home. Moreover, the state's approach to child-custody arrangements also has the latent consequence of supporting some family forms and undermining others. Single parenthood becomes an economic liability, particularly for single mothers, whereas the nuclear family becomes an asset. These issues will be elaborated in Chapter 13 ("Families").

SOCIAL MOVEMENTS: CHALLENGES AND CHANGE

Although institutions may produce inequalities, people are not powerless to affect how they fulfill their functions. **Social movements,** for example, are organizational structures within which individuals working together may alter how institutions, whole societies, and even world-systems operate. In Poland in the 1980s, workers organized in the outlawed union Solidarity were able collectively to strike, ultimately shifting the Polish communist government by 1989 to one that permitted free elections of noncommunist leaders. Prior to this elections were not part of the country's political structure, nor was participation by any party other than the Communist party.

The feminist movement in the United States (which has been, in fact, several movements, depending upon the kinds of changes sought) has had variable success in obtaining legislation and Supreme Court decisions designed to promote social and political rights, greater control over reproduction, and greater protection from sexual harassment. There is still a gulf between legislation and implementation, and legislation still does not guarantee equal economic rights, but the feminist movement has succeeded in weakening many traditional gendered barriers to participation in U.S. society.

Black South Africans, organized in the outlawed African National Congress (ANC), collectively defied the white minority government, holding mass funerals and demonstrations and enlisting world support for their struggle. Together, they succeeded in forcing the white government to dismantle the discriminatory institution of apartheid in 1994. Under that system, blacks were not allowed to vote; were segregated in public as well as private facilities, housing, education, and transportation; were forced to relocate into tribal "homelands" designated by the government; and were denied the right to freedoms of assembly, speech, and movement. Such restrictive institutional practices would have been daunting for an individual to alter, but the collective pressure applied by the ANC and its international allies facilitated a change in South African social and political structures that many had thought impossible. Today the ANC holds the reins of government in South Africa after the first election in which South Africans of all racial and ethnic groups were allowed to vote.

The civil rights movement in the United States linked individuals and groups (such as churches, civic groups, student groups, and local black organizations) in a coalition to pressure and change institutions that reinforced racial inequality. Their efforts led to the Supreme Court ruling that separate educational institutions on the basis of race are inherently unequal. This fundamentally altered the structure of schools' populations, if not the manner in which schools are funded. Pressure from the movement also ultimately elicited civil rights legislation mandating voting rights and equal opportunity and affirmative action programs. These laws made it illegal to deny access to political, educational, or occupational opportunities on the basis of race. And while the civil rights movement's efforts have certainly not eradicated racism or eliminated the inequalities that white-dominated institutions may reproduce, they have altered in some ways how such institutions operate.

The disability rights movement has been somewhat less visible, but it has been fairly successful in redressing grievances and inequalities generated against people with disabilities by social institutions. Part of its success may be traced to the public perception that unlike more stigmatized groups (such as gays and the poor), people with disabilities are a "worthy" minority. Moreover, disabilities affect all races, classes, and genders, making it likely that individuals each know someone personally who has a disability; and given the longer life span of people in the United States, it is likely that individuals today may very well confront a disability in their own lives at some point. Thus, the disability rights movement may face a less hostile public than other groups. Whatever the reason for its success, however, the movement has been able to produce important institutional changes. In many cases legislation has given people with disabilities greater access to public transportation. The movement's efforts have also resulted in making buildings more accessible, with ramps to accommodate wheelchairs, elevators with floor indicators in Braille, and bathrooms with wider stalls, low handles, and raised seat levels. Many cities also construct sidewalks that slope at street corners so wheelchairs can negotiate the streets. And in some cities "walk–don't walk" lights emit loud signals so that visually impaired pedestrians can know when it is safe to cross the street. Most recently, efforts of the disability rights movement helped gain passage of the Americans with Disabilities Act in 1990.

And the burgeoning Students Against Sweatshops movement in the United States is quickly building a potential ability to affect trade and production processes in the world-system. It is pressuring well-endowed universities to refuse to enter into licensing contracts with manufacturers who produce goods with exploited child labor and workers who are paid less than living wages in underdeveloped countries. For example, in 2000 the University of Michigan, among several other major universities, refused to renew its licensing agreement with Nike because that firm would not agree to the general principles and guidelines against the use of sweatshops (Featherstone, 2000).

This discussion of social movements suggests that changing institutions may be a very long, slow process but that change is not impossible. It also suggests how individuals may affect macrostructures. Individuals acting alone are not likely to be successful; but when people join together in a common effort, they can, in fact, collectively act as agents to alter these structures (We will explore this more fully in Chapter 10 ["Social Change and Social Movements"]).

 ## CHAPTER SUMMARY

How do events and relationships around the world affect individuals' everyday lives?

- Social systems link individuals to one another as organized mechanisms for survival. When these linkages are organized and recurring, they form social structures, some of which are quite large and complex.

- Everyone is situated within a world-system; the society where an individual may live is only one part. Changes in the relationships among the world-system's components—for example, the invasion or domination of one nation by another—can have ramifications that reach right down into the lives of individuals in societies around the world. Individuals' personal lives are not explicable without reference to where their own society stands within this world-system. The powerful position of the U.S. economy in the world-system has begun to erode in recent years as, for example, other nations successfully compete against the United States in international markets. This has affected everything in the United States, from the ability of individuals to find decent-paying jobs to the quality and cost of public services upon which people depend.

- Just as all persons are linked to the world-system through their societal membership, so are they linked to their own society through participation in its institutions. In one way or another, everyone has some kind of relationship to the central institutions of family, religion, the economy, education, and the state. The functioning of these institutions influences individuals' biographies directly, often affecting them differently depending upon their race, class, and/or gender. These factors come to be organizing principles around which institutions frequently operate. For example, until the recession of 2008–2013, in times of economic stagnation the persons who have often experienced the highest rates of unemployment have tended to be those working in the lowest-paying jobs and thus most likely to be individuals of color and females. In comparative terms, then, those who are white, affluent, and male were less likely to lose their jobs, and if they did, they were likely to find work sooner. That did change in the Great Recession of 2008–2013, owing to the structure of the labor market, when men's unemployment was higher than that of women (we will take this up later in Chapter 11 ["Work and the Economy"]). Suffice it to say for now, the structure of the institution of the economy affects individuals in profound ways, and commonly those who are already disadvantaged feel these effects in the most pronounced ways.

- To sum up, as relationships among components of the world-system change, the operations of entire societies may be affected, and within societies the functioning of central institutions may exact costs from some people and not others. Sometimes, however, concerted collective actions undertaken by individuals may alter institutional and societal operations; even the world-system itself may consequently undergo change.

- While it is true that each person is part of a much larger set of structures through participation in institutions, society, and the world-system, people are not entirely powerless to affect how these macrostructures operate or are organized. Change occurs at all levels of this set of structures, whether out of consensus on the need for change or out of conflict over the status quo. Each individual can be involved with others in making change; people need not be only acted upon by society.

The discussion of social movements raises the question of how individuals are linked to these more abstract levels of structure. Just as there are macro-level structures, there are micro-level and middle-range structures that distribute and organize individuals locally, defining positions and behaviors of individuals and linking them to the macro-structures. These more local structures will be examined in the next chapter.

THINKING CRITICALLY

1. Global trade and production relationships form macro-structures that influence our daily existence. Discuss how these relationships affect your own life.

2. Select an important and current problem facing nations all over the world (such as population growth, nuclear danger, AIDS, food shortage, homelessness). Analyze how different social structures in at least two different nations may contribute to how these nations approach the problem.

3. Examine your own family (or your religious organization or the educational system you attend) and identify the manifest and latent functions it performs. Describe how the institutions may produce the latent functions you identify.

4. At the start of the chapter you were asked where your clothing was made and where your car or cell phone was manufactured. What social structures contributed to bringing these items into your possession? What are the manifest and latent functions of these structures in the manufacture of consumer goods?

5. You may know someone (perhaps yourself) who has been deployed and stationed with a military unit somewhere in the world. Identify the location of the military assignment and discuss the social structures that may have contributed to the assignment. Discuss the manifest and latent functions of the assignment. How did the social structures affect the daily life of the individual stationed abroad? How did they affect his or her family?

KEY TERMS

social structure   38

macro-level social structures   38

death rate   42

birth rate   42

world-system   39

global division of labor   40

core nations   40

peripheral nations   40

semiperipheral nations   40

global north nations   41

global south nations   41

infant mortality rates   43

society   47

nations   47

functionalist perspective   48

greenhouse effect   48

critical analysis   00

functional imperatives   49

institutions   50

manifest functions   51

latent functions   51

family   53

religion   54

economy   56

education   58

state   60

government   60

social movements   64

SOCIAL STRUCTURE: MICRO- AND MID-LEVELS

4

One of the most fascinating features of society–one often taken for granted—is the degree to which people's daily lives are patterned and organized. For the most part, individuals' daily interactions with others are not random. Rather, they reflect the wide variety of social positions that each individual occupies and the interpersonal relationships and group memberships that these positions require or make possible. In this chapter, we will explore questions such as the following:

- What are social statuses and roles, and how are people's lives tied to and shaped by them?
- What are the distinguishing characteristics of social groups, and why are group and organizational memberships important for individuals?
- How do bureaucratic and democratic forms of organization differ in their features and in their effect on people?
- What functions do social networks play in people's lives and how does individuals' access to social networks vary along the lines of class, race, and gender?

Like Chapter 3 ("Macro Social Structures"), this chapter introduces sociological concepts useful for thinking about how society is organized and the types of demands that people face by virtue of being participants in society. Knowledge about the ways in which society is organized can help in the development of a sociological imagination, in that such knowledge increases our understanding of both sources of social order and sources of social conflict and change.

Most human beings spend very little time alone or in isolation from others. From birth, people are engaged in ongoing social relationships. At first relationships are with members of the family, neighbors, and playmates. Later, additional social relationships develop with other people in school, in clubs, on sports teams, at places of worship, and at work. Any setting in which people regularly interact—from a street in a low-income neighborhood to a corporation boardroom—provides opportunities to enter into and maintain social relationships.

As we saw in Chapter 3, the term **social structure** refers to the organization of recurrent and patterned social relationships. Chapter 3 focused on macro-level forms of social structure, including world-systems, societies, and institutions. Macro-level social structures entail large-scale mechanisms that organize social relationships within and between entire societies. In the present chapter we examine micro- and mid-level forms of social structure.

Micro-level social structure refers to social relationships based on interaction between small numbers of individuals, e.g., between family members or between occupants of a dormitory floor. Such relationships often take place within the context of "primary groups," which are discussed in a later section. Social structure at this level is small-scale or "micro" in the sense that the interpersonal social relationships involved, while important, involve relatively few people.

In contrast, we use the term **mid-level social structure** to refer to larger webs of social relationships. "Secondary groups" and social networks, also to be discussed later, are examples of mid-level social structures. At this mid-level, participants are involved in varied forms and degrees of interaction with others. Consider, for example, a restaurant as a mid-level form of social structure. Restaurant waitstaff interact with a changing cast of customers at their tables, while maintaining ongoing relationships with the floor manager, the bartender, cooks, and table-clearing staff. Mid-level social structure differs from micro-level in the greater number, formality, and complexity of the social relationships in which individuals are enmeshed.

As we will see, at both micro- and mid-levels the nature, frequency, and content of the interaction that takes place between individuals are often guided by role expectations. Different role expectations accompany the various social statuses or positions that individuals occupy. In the examples above, there are certain widely held role expectations as to how people will behave who hold positions as family members, dorm floor residents, waitstaff, or cooks. But because people are typically participants in many micro- and mid-level social structures at the same time, they frequently find themselves caught up in role expectations that are contradictory or conflicting and at times impossible to meet. We will take this topic up as well.

Finally, this chapter will address ways in which particular mid-level forms of social structure where people are involved affect and help to shape their lives. For example, secondary groups in which people participate may be democratically organized or fashioned along the lines of a bureaucracy. As will be discussed, these two ways of organizing activities call for very different types of social relationships among group participants and may have very different effects on their behavior and thinking. Likewise, most people are involved in social networks, another form of mid-level social structure. The nature of the social networks in which people participate— in effect, the ties people develop within and outside their own social circles—can likewise have important life consequences, as we will see.

Overall, then, this chapter seeks to encourage sociological thinking in response to the following question: What is the importance of participation in social structures at the micro-levels and mid-levels for the biographies and lived experiences of individuals?

STATUS

People participate in a variety of micro- and mid-level social structures. People's social positions in these structures are referred to by sociologists as their **status**. The term *status* is often used interchangeably with the term *prestige*. But here we are using *status* to refer to the social *position* a person occupies regardless of the prestige of that position. For example, a young person may occupy the status of daughter and granddaughter, as well as sister, at home; student, girlfriend, and basketball player at school; and sales clerk at work. People typically occupy multiple statuses or social positions, some of which change over time. A person is likely to be a daughter and sister far longer than a point guard or girlfriend. One's biography can be mapped by tracing the many statuses an individual has occupied.

Achieved and Ascribed Status

The ability to assume some statuses depends upon whether or not individuals possess the right combination of resources, talent, motivation, and—most important of all—opportunity. An **achieved status** is a social position that is largely contingent upon the structure of opportunities open to an individual. One thus achieves the status of wife, truck driver, business executive, or amateur skydiver. In contrast, **ascribed status** refers to a social position over which one has no real control. In some cases ascribed status is linked to characteristics determined at birth. Sex, race, class, and nation of origin are particularly powerful forms of ascribed status present at birth. And, throughout life, sexual orientation, the presence or absence of disability, and age provide additional sources of ascribed status.

It is important to note that ascribed status can easily function as an impediment to upward mobility in society. One cannot readily change one's ascribed race or gender, and discrimination against women and people of color continues to be a serious problem experienced by millions of people in U.S. society. While it is true that many individuals do achieve mobility upward within the class structure, most members of U.S. society remain at or near the class position of the parents to whom they were born or by whom they are adopted. This is particularly the case for those who suffer discrimination in the world of work (Kerbo, 2011).

Master Status

The meaning people attach to a given status may change over time and place. Thus, being female or male, a person of color or white, gay or heterosexual, experiencing a disability or being able-bodied may mean different things in different contexts. Not all status positions are equally important or salient, either to the individual occupying them or to other members of society. But at times one status occupied by an individual tends to override all others, dictating how a person is likely to be treated. For such cases sociologists use the term **master status**. A female college professor or attorney may find that her sex is more salient than her professional credentials in determining how she is treated by many others, even colleagues.

One's master status may enhance or limit opportunities and thereby affect one's life chances. One of the clearest examples of this involves people experiencing disabilities. Disabilities may interfere with many life activities, such as being able to hold down employment, attend school, or care for members of a household. While there are some 35 to 43 million people with disabilities in the United States (estimates vary by source and definition of disability), only a small proportion were born with the disabilities with which they are challenged. Many adults with disabilities have not completed high school, and the overwhelming majority are not engaged in paid employment, even though most want to work. Poverty among those experiencing disability is much higher than it is among those who are able-bodied. Discrimination, based on the stereotype that to have a disability is to be "defective" and less than human, is widespread (Shapiro, 1993; M. Russell, 1998).

In 1989 a committee of the U.S. Senate conducted hearings on the proposed Americans with Disabilities Act, a significant civil rights bill that became federal law in 1990. The hearings documented the miserable treatment that people with disabilities faced, treatment contributing to their isolation and segregation from those privileged to be able-bodied (U.S. Congress: Senate, 1989). The hearings also uncovered discrimination against caregivers, as well as persons thought to have a disability even if this was no longer or had never been the case.

The senate committee heard testimony from a young woman with cerebral palsy who was denied admission to a movie theater by its owner. It also learned about a zookeeper who would not admit children with Down syndrome because he feared they would upset the chimpanzees; a child with a disability whose teacher claimed he should be excluded from school because his appearance "produced a nauseating effect on his classmates"; a woman who was fired because she was caring for her son, who was suffering from the effects of AIDS; people with arthritis, cancer survivors, and others who were fired or denied jobs not because they could not do them but because of discrimination; and people with disabilities who were denied access to public transportation and accommodations, medical treatment, and housing. The Americans with Disabilities Act of 1990 is intended to provide people with disabilities the same civil rights protections available to people of color and women, persons also often accorded a devalued master status.

Master status has a great deal to do with the distribution of power and the ability of dominant groups in society to decide what is "normal." In a society in which political power is concentrated in the hands of the able-bodied majority, to be otherwise is to be vulnerable to stigmatization and stereotyping, common prerequisites for discriminatory treatment. This is true even though people with disabilities are members of a "minority group" that any person can involuntarily join at any point in life. Likewise, in a society in which political power largely rests in the hands of persons who are heterosexual, gay males and lesbians, along with persons who are bisexual or transgender, are vulnerable to mistreatment. The imposition of unwanted master statuses is possible as long as men have more power than women, whites more power than people of color, the young more power than the elderly, and the affluent more power than the poor.

ROLES

We have said that people typically occupy multiple social positions or statuses. The behaviors expected of those in these positions are referred to as **social roles**. Social roles are not necessarily rigid proscriptions or scripts, although they are often linked to prevailing social norms. Some roles are more flexible than others, permitting the role player more room for innovation and experimentation. For example, the social role of college instructor probably allows more flexibility in ways to go about fulfilling the role than airline pilots are permitted. Failure to fulfill some roles properly can result in more severe sanctions than others. A bank clerk who is short money from his or her cash drawer may be summarily fired; a doctor whose work is suffering due to addiction to prescription narcotics is likely to be referred by a panel of peers for counseling.

Roles do not occur in a vacuum, isolated from all others: Each role implies a reciprocal role played by someone else. So, the role of teacher implies that someone else is playing the role of student; the role of parent suggests that someone must be in the role of child; the role of coach indicates that someone else is playing the role of athlete. The reciprocal nature of roles creates a complicated swirl of social relationships. Let's examine the complications that arise from roles and their reciprocal dimensions.

Role Strain

While roles provide blueprints defining expectations of behaviors of individuals in their various statuses, it is not always easy or even possible to comply with these expectations. Sometimes the expectations are vague or contradictory; other times the expectations of one status conflict with those of another; and at times even if the expectations are clear it may not be possible to comply with them. When people cannot conform to these expectations they may experience distress.

For example, **role strain** refers to the distress experienced by an individual when a particular role contains contradictory demands. Role strain involves the contradictory demands embedded in a *single* role. Consider the role of mother, when this position is occupied by an impoverished woman. Out of economic desperation, poor mothers at times must look to the state to help meet their need for family income support. Yet, a mother receiving welfare is often faced with role strain. She needs a minimum income to support her children. If she enters the welfare rolls, she is liable to be publicly stigmatized and condemned for so-called "welfare dependence." Under current "welfare reform" policies she will be pressured by welfare officials to leave the rolls—voluntarily or involuntarily—as soon as possible and be a "self-sufficient" provider for her children. On the other hand, if she leaves her children in order to be employed and to try to provide for her children in that way, she may be criticized as a "bad mother" by those who feel that the daily care of children—not working outside the home—should be a mother's first and foremost priority (see Edin and Lein, 1997).

The role strain faced by such mothers is made even worse because quality, affordable daycare, afterschool care, and overnight care are in woefully short supply in the United States. Consequently, most working mothers rely on family, friends, and neighbors to care for their children. But not all mothers have social networks adequate to the task. Mothers who are forced by welfare officials to take on day, evening, or night shift employment may at times have little choice but to leave their children home alone (as "latchkey kids") or in less-than-reliable childcare situations. These mothers not only may put their children at risk; they also put themselves at risk of getting into trouble with government child protection agencies. In many instances mothers struggling to rise to the employment demands of welfare policy have been accused of neglect and have had their children taken away by the state (Roberts, 2001). Which way should an impoverished woman go about meeting the role expectations of "mother" (in this instance, mother as caretaker and mother as provider) when faced with such contradictory expectations and demands?

Role Conflict

Along with role strain, **role conflict** can exact costs from people. Role conflict occurs when the demands on a person from *two or more* of the roles he or she must fulfill are at odds; to comply with the demands of one role automatically means failure to comply with the demands of the other. Consider, for example, the case of a college student talented enough to be awarded a scholarship to play basketball. Playing college-level ball is a dream for many young people—including low-income youths who see few other routes to upward mobility and financial success. With rare exceptions, play at this level is a prerequisite to selection by a professional team. Even though there is an extremely small statistical probability that a college player will make it into the pros, many young persons nonetheless harbor this fantasy.

Yet the role of student and the role of athlete do not necessarily coexist easily. Some of the young people recruited to play college basketball lack skills as students. More commonly, the demands made on athletes by their school's coaching staff conflict with those being made by professors. College athletes may find themselves caught in an impossible dilemma: Cut back on time devoted to developing as an athlete and draw the wrath of coaches, or cut back on time invested in being a student and risk losing the grades necessary to maintain athletic eligibility.

Colleges vary greatly in how they react to the student athlete's role conflict. Some schools work hard to support the student role, an important consideration given how few players will actually turn pro. College players will need a track record of academic success to compete for jobs when their athletic careers are over, which is right after college for just about all. Other schools exploit the athlete role, using whatever tricks are necessary to maintain student athletes' eligibility to play and losing interest in players when their eligibility is lost or runs out. In such settings, the graduation rate for athletes is very low and non-graduates are faced with very limited employment opportunities when they leave school.

Role Sets

In thinking about role conflict, it is also useful to consider the fact that individuals occupy reciprocal **role sets**. Any given role exists in relationship to a set of many other roles being played by others, and the individual is therefore simultaneously subject to various expectations and demands from people fulfilling all these other roles. For example, a person fulfilling the social role of student may have to simultaneously satisfy the expectations of individuals with such roles as teacher, academic adviser, roommate, fellow student, friend who is not a student, partner, parent, coach, or employer. A student must find ways to deal with the situation whenever it becomes impossible to adequately fulfill the expectations of all those who are part of his or her role set.

The kinds of role strains and role conflict that people face, and the ways in which strains and conflicts are handled, constitute yet another element of people's individual biographies. Efforts to solve role strain and conflict may become the front edge of change, as when people break out of roles or defy others' role expectations.

The complex interactions between many individuals performing complementary or reciprocal social roles in role sets lead us to take up the topic of *groups*. Sociologically speaking, what is a group and why is group membership significant to individuals?

GROUPS AND THE INDIVIDUAL

Just about everyone in U.S. society has at some time attended a concert or sporting event. People arrive along with hundreds of others, find a seat, hopefully enjoy themselves, and participate by clapping and cheering. Such an audience is not, in sociological terms, a "group." Rather, it is a **social aggregate**, a collection of individuals with no real interpersonal ties or regular, patterned social relationships.

Classrooms of college students on the other hand, are an example of what sociologists mean by the term *group*. The first day of class most people don't know one another and may have little basis for interaction. As time goes on, students begin to recognize one another in and out of class, share gripes and lecture notes, study together for exams, form ties, and develop social relationships. As the professor comes down the hall to enter class, she is likely to hear a lively chorus of conversations that is quite different from the relative silence that may have greeted her entry on the first day. The class meets on regularly scheduled days and times for a specified length of time for a specified number of weeks (either a semester or a quarter). There is a shared understanding of the expected content of the course and a shared understanding of the authority and role of the instructor and the role of the students. And there is an expectation that at the end of the semester or quarter students will earn a grade and hopefully credits toward graduation.

In a sociological sense, then, a **group** occurs only when there is regular interaction among an aggregate or collection of individuals. The interaction provides a basis for a sense of group membership and can facilitate the emergence of leadership and status differences within a group. Through interaction people enter into orderly and predictable relationships with one another. Social order is assisted by the formation and acceptance of rules of group behavior, or **norms**. For example, a group norm may be "You must raise your hand in class to speak," "Never snitch on a friend," or "Men don't work at the office without a coat and tie." If new members join the group, they must learn and adhere to its norms. Failure to adopt these norms will make it difficult for a new member to form or retain the social ties and relationships integral to group participation.

Human beings are social animals. They rely on group memberships for everything from friendship to economic survival. Because of this, the groups in which people are involved form an important part of their personal biographies. Individual members can shape the character of their group, but the group's character also helps shape the thinking and behavior of its individual members. For example, inspirational or charismatic leaders (Weber, 1947) may give specific direction to a religious group, but participation in collective rituals and ceremonies helps members arouse one another's sense of group belonging and the desire to remain involved. Given the influence of groups, sociologists feel it is important to examine the types of groups in which people typically find themselves. The level of influence on our daily lives will be affected by the types of groups and their organizational forms.

Primary Groups

Sociologists generally distinguish between two different types of groups, primary and secondary. The term **primary group** was introduced many years ago by sociologist Charles Horton Cooley (1929). Primary groups tend to be made up of a relatively small number of people who interact frequently face-to-face. Group members share important connections that bring them together, such as common kinship ties, school attendance, residential location, or employment at a workplace. Their frequent interaction gives rise to a sense of group identity and to the emergence of norms, which both guide members' behavior and contribute to group solidarity. Primary groups commonly evoke strong ties of emotion for their members, involve multifaceted relationships, and are enduring over time. The prototypical example of a primary group is the family. Primary groups can be a source of friendship, companionship, and support, yet they may also give rise to serious conflict. Because relationships within primary groups are often both binding and intense, these groups play a central role in people's everyday lives.

A classic study by sociologist Herbert Gans (1982) revealed the importance of primary groups to people's biographies. Gans was interested in looking at the everyday lives of white working-class families. He chose a run-down, low-income neighborhood in Boston's West End, considered a "slum" by city officials and planners (the West End neighborhood would later be torn down and its residents dispersed as part of "urban renewal"). Gans found that the lives of working-class people in the neighborhood revolved around what he termed a "peer group society." In Gans's words,

> *The primary group is a peer group society because most of the*
> *West Enders' relationships are with peers, that is, among people*
> *of the same sex, age, and life-cycle status (Gans, 1982: 37).*

Males and females each had their own primary-group peer affiliations, and these in turn were roughly divided by different ages and generations. Adult peer groups were largely based on family and kinship. Members shared common interests and ethnic backgrounds (most were Italian Americans) and came together regularly. The adult peer group not only provided companionship and a sense of belonging; it was also a source of news and entertainment. It was a setting in which individuals could express their unique personalities and feel they were making a well-received contribution.

The opportunities for personal expression provided by the peer group society were in marked contrast to what the adult men experienced in their low-wage factory and service jobs. For them, the peer group was a place to escape to from the "outside world" of poorly paid, insecure employment. Given the nature of the jobs they could find, the men viewed work in highly utilitarian terms: It was necessary, but not enjoyable, and it provided them with means to participate in the peer group society. For example, it enabled men to play the role of hosts at group get-togethers and to lay claim to the prestige associated with being successful providers and breadwinners.

According to Gans, the peer group society performed other functions for adult women. The women spent most of their free time and communicated most often with relatives and friends of the same sex; Gans felt that their emotional involvement with the peer group surpassed that with their husbands. He believed this was the case because of their families' very marginal and insecure economic position and the heavy stresses of working-class life. Faced with the ever-present possibility of losing a husband through illness or a workplace accident, or through separation or divorce, the women looked to their same-sex peer group members for support that would be available at all times.

The peer group society Gans described also played a negative role. In some ways it encompassed and trapped its members, channeling their thinking and behavior along certain lines. For example, one norm of the peer group was that members focus on being liked and noticed within the group (*person-orientation*). This orientation came at the expense of focusing on particular objectives such as pursuing a career or improving one's material circumstances (*object-orientation*). Object-oriented behavior violated group norms because it involved detaching oneself from a group-life to focus time and attention outward in directions that did not support the peer group society.

Object-oriented individuals were made to feel like traitors pursuing selfish aims. So, if a person wished to enjoy the benefits of the peer group society, he or she often had to suppress aspirations for involvement and success in the "outside world" that conflicted with the norm of person-orientation.

The peer group, therefore, was alternately a comfort and a source of oppressive confinement. Given its benefits, along with the fact that it was linked heavily to family and kinship, the peer group society—as a primary group—could not be rejected by its members lightly.

The example provided by the working-class peer group society may lead to thinking about one's own primary group memberships. As a primary group, the peer group society revolved around intimate, face-to-face relationships. Each individual developed strong bonds with the others and could depend upon the group for support. In return, each member was expected to adhere to the norms of the group. Expressing ideas not shared by others in the group could result in criticism and even rejection by the group's members. How do the features of primary groups of which you have been a member—at home, in high school or college, or at work—compare with those of the peer group society? What benefits or rewards have you gained from being a member of such primary groups? What disadvantages or costs have been associated with your involvement? The answers to such questions can help you assess the importance of primary groups in shaping your own life experiences and thus the ongoing composition of your biography.

Secondary Groups

Secondary groups are very different social phenomena from primary groups, although certainly they are as much a part of people's daily lives. In contrast to primary groups, secondary groups are usually larger, more formally structured, and formed for a purpose, such as accomplishing a certain task (providing fire protection) or achieving a particular goal (making a profit manufacturing and selling cars). Examples of secondary groups include schools, colleges, government agencies, military services, corporations, unions, and voluntary associations. (The latter are secondary groups in which members' involvement is really a matter of choice, participation usually takes only a small portion of members' time, and commitment to the group and its purpose may be highly variable. The Girl Scouts and the National Rifle Association are examples.) Secondary groups vary in composition from relatively few members to thousands of members. The degree and intensity of interaction and personal involvement are ordinarily less than that found in a primary group. Secondary groups typically involve only limited aspects of an individual's existence, in contrast to the multifaceted relationships forged in primary groups.

Note, however, that it is common for primary groups to form as people become acquainted through participation in secondary groups, as is the case when a group of people become close friends at school or in the workplace. Indeed, the large size and impersonal nature of many secondary groups often prompts participants to form primary-group relationships with others for the personal rewards and benefits these relationships can provide. Moreover, as we will see later in our discussion of informal organization within bureaucracies, the formation of primary groups can affect the functioning of secondary groups.

In contrast to a primary group, secondary group members may come and go; their emotional ties to the group are ordinarily not strong enough to make leaving a serious problem.

A secondary group typically continues to accomplish its tasks or pursue its goals even as its membership changes. Individuals become members for a limited purpose and may use their membership in the secondary group to accomplish a personal objective. Even if people are not members of particular secondary groups that exist around them, they usually have some contact with such organizations and feel the impact of these groups' presence.

While employees of a large firm, members of the military, or students at a public university tend to be a heterogeneous collection of people, members of some secondary groups often have more in common than simply the fact of their group affiliation. In the example we describe below, that of a voluntary association, the members happen to share a great deal in common: class position, gender, and race.

In comparison to the amount of knowledge that sociologists have generated about the thinking and behavior of "ordinary people," such as those in the peer group society studied by Herbert Gans, much less is known about the everyday lives of U.S. society's elites. Affluence and power enable elites to have a great deal of privacy, and such persons have little incentive to admit researchers into their personal domains. Nevertheless, the research of sociologist G. William Domhoff (2009) has provided some data on elites (see also Kerbo, 2011). According to Domhoff, social and economic elites constitute an upper class in the United States whose members regularly interact and often intermarry. Their great wealth, high annual incomes, and privileged lifestyles distinguish them from members of other classes. Domhoff estimates that the upper class makes up no more than 0.5 percent of the U.S. population. It is also overwhelmingly white. Upper-class activities often include membership in private clubs (for example, country clubs, hunt clubs, men's clubs, and women's clubs).

Exclusive private clubs that cater to the upper class are examples of secondary groups. It is extremely difficult for sociologists (or non-members generally) to gain access to them. However, G. William Domhoff has carried out extensive research on such clubs, and we draw upon his work here. The example we will use is the Bohemian Club of San Francisco, founded in 1872. For over a hundred years the club has provided a summer camp outside the city, one primarily attended by wealthy men, top corporate elites, and important political figures and government officials (Domhoff, 2002: 51–54). Located on a 2,700-acre forest site called Bohemian Grove, the camp attracts as many as 2,500 men to its annual two-week summer session each July. The membership and guest lists have included most of those who have been president of the United States in past and recent decades, top military officials, as well as numerous chief executives and directors of the nation's largest corporate firms. Besides political and economic elites, some well-known celebrities and university intellectuals are usually in attendance.

Bohemian Grove provides a setting in which some of the most powerful and influential men in the United States can come together privately once a year to engage in informal and off-the-record talk about business and politics, establish or reaffirm social relationships, engage in recreation, and be entertained. Participants reside and attend one another's dinners and parties in over 120 camp sites or lodges with names like Cave Man, Owl's Nest, and Hill Billies. Over the course of the two weeks they swim, canoe, hike, play cards and dominoes, attend talks, and involve themselves in events that have become fraternity-like traditions at Bohemian Grove. Camp attendees act out light-hearted roles in amateur talent shows, participate in camper rituals, and dress up for large-scale, annual ceremonial spectacles with names like "Cremation of Care." The latter, a camp-opening ceremony, "involves the burning of an effigy named Dull

Care, who symbolizes the burdens and responsibilities that these busy Bohemians now wish to shed temporarily. More than 250 Bohemians take part in the ceremony as priests, elders, boatmen, and woodland voices" (Domhoff, 2002: 52).

In Domhoff's view, such clubs contribute to the national cohesiveness of the upper class and tie its members together across geographic and institutional boundaries. In the case of Bohemian Grove, cohesiveness is facilitated by participants' retreat from their everyday activities, where they are sometimes at odds in their political and business dealings. In the camp, they relax into a setting that functions to promote a sense of collective upper-class brotherhood that clearly resembles a fraternity. Membership in the Bohemian Club is highly restrictive and both the club and the camp are off-limits to the public. This exclusivity adds to participants' feelings of being part of a very special in-group, as members of the upper class and their guests bond with one another through club activities.

The Bohemian Club is a voluntary organization and an example of a secondary group, in this case one that caters largely to white male members of the upper class (on private clubs catering to women of the upper class, see Kendall, 2002). The workings of different secondary groups influence people's biographies in a variety of ways. Apart from the makeup of their membership, the organizational form that secondary groups take is of importance to sociologists. In the next section we will discuss how experiences that people have participating in secondary groups can be affected by the group's bureaucratic or democratic structure.

GROUP STRUCTURE: BUREAUCRATIC VERSUS DEMOCRATIC ORGANIZATION

Secondary groups can be structured in different ways. In this section we focus on two particular organizational forms in which people may at times participate: bureaucratic and democratic organizations. People's lives are shaped in important respects by the structure of the organizations in which they are involved. Thus it matters whether a society is characterized more heavily by bureaucratic or by democratic organizations. Most societies contain a range of types of organizations, but some societies tend to be more bureaucratic or more democratic than others in their organizational makeup.

Bureaucratic Organization

The term **bureaucracy** is often used by people complaining about an experience they may have had with a large, impersonal organization, often a business or a government office. People frequently refer to organizational "red tape" that interferes with getting things done or of inflexible "bureaucrats" who say things like "I just work here; I don't make the rules." Sociologists, however, use the term *bureaucracy* to refer to the way in which certain secondary groups are organized. Such groups may or may not be responsive to people's needs, but that is not their defining feature.

Features of Bureaucracy

As was mentioned in Chapter 1, the rise of bureaucratic forms of organization was central to the thinking of German sociologist Max Weber, one of the European social thinkers of the late nineteenth and twentieth centuries whose ideas contributed to the development of contemporary sociology. Weber saw the spread of bureaucracy as a dominant or master trend in the Western world. In his writings, he identified five features of the ideal-type, or model, bureaucratic organization that continue to prove useful to sociologists as they analyze features of present-day society (Weber in Gerth and Mills, 1968):

1. The organization contains a clear-cut division of labor: every member is responsible for particular tasks.
2. Authority is organized in a hierarchy: Everyone (except of course the individual at the top) reports to someone whose directives are considered legitimate and to be obeyed.
3. The activities of all members of the organization are governed by a set of formally established, written rules and regulations.
4. Members are to carry out their organizational responsibilities impartially and without the exercise of favoritism or bias toward others.
5. Recognition, rewards, and status in the organization are based upon meritorious performance.

Bureaucracy and Control in the Workplace

To some extent, most work settings are organized in accordance with the above features. One might ask why this is the case. What functions does bureaucracy perform? In his widely acclaimed historical analysis addressing this question, Richard Edwards (1979) examined the evolution of work organizations in the United States. In his view, while significant changes in ways of organizing work have occurred over the last several centuries, the central issue facing employers has remained the same: how to get as much work as possible out of workers for the least amount of money. In Edwards's view, resolving this problem has required that employers deal with the issue of how workers are to be controlled.

Before the Industrial Revolution, work organizations were relatively small operations in which the "boss" ran the enterprise. Whether the owner or hired supervisors oversaw the work, power over workers was exercised personally and directly. Edwards termed this type of structure **simple control**, a form of organization that still persists today in small firms. In the late nineteenth and early twentieth centuries, as firm owners relied more on technologically advanced machinery and the assembly line became common, power over workers came to be exercised by the impersonal demands of technology. The machinery and other apparatus in the workplace limited the activities of each worker and dictated the pace of work. On an assembly line, for example, working too slowly quickly becomes apparent and laggards can then be disciplined. Edwards called this form of structure **technical control**. Technical control of workers still exists in many of today's factories, although automation and computerization have greatly reduced the proportion of the U.S. labor force employed in assembly-line settings.

During the twentieth century, as work organizations increased in size and the white-collar office sector grew, **bureaucratic control** became dominant in the workplace. Bureaucratic control operates by surrounding people with rules. Employers require that their workers conform to standardized job descriptions, and they evaluate employee job performance on checklists and rating forms. Of course, it is possible to create new job descriptions, alter old ones, and make judgments about job performance, but the power to do so is in the hands of those who occupy the top positions in the organizational hierarchy. The individuals who have the ability to make and change the organization's rules tend to be far removed from the average worker. This is particularly the case in large organizations. Under bureaucratic control, the power over workers wielded by top organization officials is masked. This is because it is the rules—not distant bosses—that workers experience as coercive and controlling. For many workers, one consequence of bureaucratic control is dissatisfaction and alienation (Garson, 1994; Ehrenreich, 2001; Fraser, 2001).

Even persons occupying managerial positions in bureaucratic work organizations are confined and controlled by the nature of the activities and relationships bureaucracy promotes. Sociologist Robert Jackall (1988) demonstrated this in his research on corporate managers. While corporate managers hold positions of substantial responsibility and receive generous financial remuneration, bureaucracy has important effects upon their everyday lives. Here, Jackall sums up the impact of bureaucracy:

> *Bureaucratic work shapes people's consciousness in decisive*
> *ways. . . . [It] regularizes people's experiences of time and*
> *indeed routinizes their lives by engaging them on a daily basis*
> *in rational, socially approved purposive action; it brings them*
> *into daily proximity with and subordination to authority,*
> *creating in the process upward-looking stances that have*
> *decisive social and psychological consequences; . . . and it*
> *creates subtle measures of prestige and an elaborate status*
> *hierarchy that, in addition to fostering an intense competition*
> *for status, also makes the rules, procedures, social contexts,*
> *and protocols of an organization paramount psychological*
> *and behavioral guides (Jackall, 1988: 5–6).*

Jackall's interviews with corporate managers revealed that they were under pressure to conform to an organizational code of morality that often differed from their own. As one former corporate vice president put it, "What is right in the corporation is not what is right in a man's home or in his church. What is right in the corporation is what the guy above you wants from you. That's what morality is in the corporation" (Jackall, 1988: 6). Jackall's research suggests that conformity to an organization's code of morality (its workplace norms) is a key prerequisite for personal success in the world of corporate managers. Research on other categories of white-collar personnel in bureaucratic work organizations, such as persons in sales positions (Oakes, 1990), has revealed similar demands for conformity. On occasion, the corporate code of morality may be loose enough to allow shocking acts of large-scale corporate corruption and malfeasance, as illustrated by the revelations of illegal financial activities involving top officials at Enron and other large corporations in the early 2000s.

Bureaucracy and the Declining Power of Workers

In the past century a large percentage of the U.S. labor force has come to be employed by large, bureaucratic organizations—in both the public and the private sectors. For example, 16.7 percent of the labor force—22.2 million people—work for agencies of government at all levels (including federal, state, and local governments). Nearly 4.5 million work for the federal government alone (U.S. Office of Personnel Management, available at www.opm.gov/policy-data-oversight/data-analysis-documentation/federal-employment-reports/historical-tables/total-government-employment-since-1962/). Figure 4.1 illustrates the vast range of federal offices. Moreover, it

Figure 4.1: Branches, Departments, and Agencies of the Federal Bureaucracy

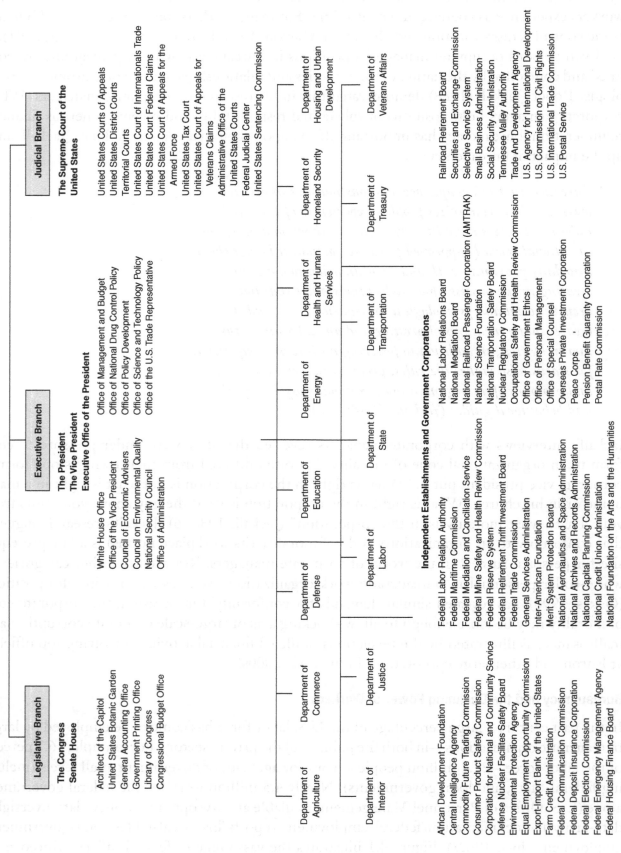

Legislative Branch

The Congress
Senate House

Architect of the Capitol
United States Botanic Garden
General Accounting Office
Government Printing Office
Library of Congress
Congressional Budget Office

Executive Branch

The President
The Vice President
Executive Office of the President

White House Office
Office of the Vice President
Council of Economic Advisers
Council on Environmental Quality
National Security Council
Office of Administration

Office of Management and Budget
Office of National Drug Control Policy
Office of Policy Development
Office of Science and Technology Policy
Office of the U.S. Trade Representative

Judicial Branch

The Supreme Court of the United States

United States Courts of Appeals
United States District Courts
Territorial Courts
United States Court of Internationals Trade
United States Court Federal Claims
United States Court of Appeals for the Armed Force
United States Tax Court
United States Court of Appeals for Veterans Claims
Administrative Office of the United States Courts
Federal Judicial Center
United States Sentencing Commission

Department of Agriculture

Department of Commerce

Department of Defense

Department of Education

Department of Energy

Department of Health and Human Services

Department of Homeland Security

Department of Housing and Urban Development

Department of Interior

Department of Justice

Department of Labor

Department of State

Department of Transportation

Department of Treasury

Department of Veterans Affairs

Independent Establishments and Government Corporations

African Development Foundation
Central Intelligence Agency
Commodity Future Trading Commission
Consumer Product Safety Commission
Corporation for National and Community Service
Defense Nuclear Facilites Safety Board
Environmental Protection Agency
Equal Employment Opportunity Commission
Export-Import Bank of the United States
Farm Credit Administration
Federal Communication Commission
Federal Deposit Insurance Corporation
Federal Election Commission
Federal Emergency Management Agency
Federal Housing Finance Board

Federal Labor Relation Authority
Federal Maritime Commission
Federal Mediation and Conciliation Service
Federal Mine Safety and Health Review Commission
Federal Reserve System
Federal Retirement Thrift Investment Board
Federal Trade Commission
General Services Administration
Inter-American Foundation
Merit System Protection Board
National Aeronautics and Space Administration
National Archives and Records Administration
National Capital Planning Commission
National Credit Union Administration
National Foundation on the Arts and the Humanities

National Labor Relations Board
National Mediation Board
National Railroad Passenger Corporation (AMTRAK)
National Science Foundation
National Trasportation Safety Board
Nuclear Regulatory Commission
Occupational Safety and Health Review Commission
Office of Government Ethics
Office of Personal Management
Office of Special Counsel
Overseas Private Investment Corporation
Peace Corps
Pension Benefit Guaranty Corporation
Postal Rate Comission

Railroad Retirement Board
Securities and Exchange Commission
Selective Service System
Small Business Administration
Social Security Administration
Tennessee Valley Authority
Trade And Development Agency
U.S. Agency for International Development
U.S. Commission on Civil Rights
U.S. International Trade Commission
U.S. Postal Service

Source: Office of Federal Registrar, *United States Government Manual, 2011/2012.* Washington, DC: U.S. Government Printing Office, 2012.

has been estimated that 20 percent of our industrial labor force is employed by a mere 16 of the very largest U.S. corporations (Neubeck, Neubeck, and Glasberg, 2006).

Relatively few employees have very much collective power within their own workplace. The organized labor movement, which traditionally worked to increase the power of workers vis-à-vis employers, has weakened in recent decades. Unions have been adversely affected by the elimination of many unionized industrial jobs and by a climate of employer hostility toward their concerns and activities. Unionized workers on average have higher pay and benefits, better working conditions, and more on-the-job protections of their rights than do non-union workers. Today, however, unions represent less than 12 percent of the U.S. labor force, down from a peak of 35 percent in the mid-1950s (www.census.gov/compendia/statab/2012/tables/12s0664. pdf; see also Mishel et al., 2012, on this trend). Moreover, the unionization rate is much higher among government workers today (36.2 percent) than among workers in the private sector (6.9 percent) where the vast majority of people are employed (U.S. Bureau of Labor Statistics, 2012, available at www.census.gov/compendia/statab/2012/tables/12s0664.pdf).

The typical large, bureaucratic work organization discourages collective activity by workers through its complex reward structure: the substantial numbers of job titles, occupational levels, pay scales, and symbols of prestige that differentiate workers from one another. One feature of bureaucratic control, then, is the way in which it differentiates and divides people, making it very difficult for workers across an organization to be aware of the things they all have in common. White-collar and blue-collar workers, or professional and nonprofessional staff, often fail to realize that they share many of the same workplace problems, such as declining job security and difficulty getting the resources they need to do their work well.

The Bureaucratized Society

Bureaucracy is so common in U.S. society that many people can hardly imagine another way to organize human activity. Large bureaucratic organizations have come to pervade people's everyday lives (Jaffee, 2002). Their subtle influence extends outside the immediate workplace through the promotion of "corporate culture." The latter has encouraged the "McDonaldization" of our eating practices around corporate-designed foods and fast-food eating places, values emphasizing material consumption, and the routinization and rationalization of human activities in a wide range of other settings (Ritzer, 2012).

Sociologist Gary Fine's provocative study of Little League baseball (1987), for example, suggests that even this popular youth sport has fallen to bureaucratization. Little League's bureaucratic organization no doubt helped to facilitate and has been reinforced by the expansion in size and league activities since Fine completed his study (see www.littleleague.org). Little League, Inc., an organization with millions of dollars in assets, operates under a charter awarded by the federal government. Under this charter, Little League is considered to be a quasi-governmental agency whose revenues are exempt from taxes. The charter calls for Little League to file an annual report on its finances and philosophy with the U.S. House of Representatives. Little League is also required to "shape its mission to the needs of the United States government (particularly in dealing with foreign leagues)" (Fine, 1987: 6). Presumably, this means accepting the responsibility of "promoting America" as part of its involvement in international competitions (Fine, 1987: 261).

As of 2012, there were more than 7,000 local Little Leagues with almost 2.4 million baseball players, along with an additional 360,000 softball players (www.littleleague.org). Fine characterizes local leagues as "branches of a large bureaucratic organization" (1987: 7). Each league has a board of directors to oversee its operations, coaches to supervise the children and teach them how to play, umpires to interpret and enforce the official rules, and players who are expected to occupy their assigned positions and perform well. The entire operation of the game—from the length of the base paths to the number of innings to be played—is governed by decisions made by Little League, Inc. With its division of labor, hierarchy of authority, rules and regulations, and recognition based on merit, Little League baseball is an expression of the master trend toward bureaucratization. In the realm of sports, this master trend is especially evident at the professional level—e.g., baseball, basketball, hockey, and football—which are essentially activities run by corporations in which players are employees. Many of those who play such professional sports (as well as those who umpire games) have unionized and on occasion even gone out on strike to assert their collective interests as workers.

Writing in the mid-twentieth century, German social thinker Robert Michels (1962) argued that bureaucratization of human activities was inevitable. He thought that the inevitability of bureaucracy was virtually a social law (much like a law of physics). In Michels' view, organization life is subject to an **iron law of oligarchy**: There is always a tendency for organizations to be ruled by a few, even those that purport to be organized in accordance with democratic ideals. According to Michels, persons who come to occupy an elite organizational status—whether by appointment or election—come to enjoy the special benefits and privileges associated with it. They find they have access to knowledge, resources, prestige, and power that rank-and-file organizational members do not have. Consequently, such elites are likely to manipulate and control others in ways calculated to allow them to retain their positions. Even democratically elected elites are said to act in such ways, doing whatever it takes to gain re-election. In Michels' view, organizational elites seek to protect their own interests over and above the interests of other organizational members and those of the organization as a whole. But, as the next section outlines, there is reason to doubt bureaucracy's inevitability and the existence of such an "iron law."

Democratic Organization

If bureaucracy involves control *of* people, **democracy** involves control *by* people. In organizations structured in accordance with bureaucratic principles, most members have little or no power to shape the policies that affect them; in those structured along democratic lines, group members are empowered to participate in shaping these policies precisely because they will be affected. Democratizing decision-making processes in already existing organizations may be considered a radical idea in a society whose organizational life tends to be highly bureaucratized. When people demand a say in decisions that affect their lives, they are demanding power. In the United States, just as in virtually every other nation in the world, such demands can be occasions for sharp conflict when made in an organization where power has traditionally been monopolized by a few top members who are "in charge."

Democratic Workplace Cooperatives

Despite Robert Michels' view that people are subject to an iron law of oligarchy that makes bureaucracy inevitable, there are work organizations in the United States and in many other societies that incorporate principles of democratic organization. They are intriguing not only because they are less common, but because they contradict the notion that the only way to successfully organize work is to institute a bureaucratic system or some other form of top-down control of workers (Melman, 2001)

Sociologists Joyce Rothschild and J. Allen Whitt studied democratically controlled workplace cooperatives in the United States. Such cooperatives have a history going back to the late eighteenth century. Rothschild and Whitt suggest that since the late 1960s there has been a new wave of creation of such organizations as "alternative newspapers, arts and handicraft shops, food co-ops, publishing houses, restaurants, health clinics, legal collectives, natural foods bakeries, auto repair cooperatives, and retail stores" (1986: 11; see also http://nobawc.org/; http://usworker.coop/front). Such cooperatives are organized at the local, grassroots level, are small in size (often 10 to 20 members), and frequently arise from members' commitment to progressive social change. Their non-bureaucratic organization typically reflects political values that view personal empowerment and involvement in the democratic process as fundamental goals.

Cooperatives are usually organized as a **direct democracy**, in which all members participate in decision making on issues of concern. Their size makes this possible. Direct democracy is quite in contrast to the system of political governance in the United States, which is often called a **representative democracy.** Ideally, the tens of millions of U.S. voters elect others (the members of the Electoral College who vote for the president, representatives, senators) to make decisions for them that serve their interests. Those elected are said to be put in office to represent the "will of the people." But the U.S. representative democracy chronically falls short of this ideal, and many of "the people" often feel that their interests are going unmet. In contrast, organizations set up to allow direct democracy, in theory at least, provide opportunities for all group members to express their needs and work with others in getting these needs met.

Features of the Democratic Workplace

Just as the ideal-type, or model, bureaucracy described by Max Weber has certain key features, the workplace cooperatives studied by Rothschild and Whitt had a set of common characteristics as well:

1. Power is shared within the membership as a whole, and decision making involves discussion, negotiation, and consensus.
2. Rules are minimal; members are assumed to be capable of using discretion and common sense in conducting their activities.
3. There is a sense of community. People do not limit their interactions to the work tasks at hand but feel free to develop close relationships with one another.
4. The division of labor is minimal. Members share their knowledge and take turns rotating jobs when possible.
5. Material rewards are secondary to those otherwise derived from involvement in the group. Just as there is no hierarchy of authority, rewards are shared equally or nearly so.

From this list one might think that cooperatives are utopian forms of organization. But Rothschild and Whitt's research indicates that their members must be ready to confront challenges. For example, democratic decision making can be time-consuming. Differences among group members can at times be very intense and disturbing. Personality characteristics that may mesh well in bureaucratically controlled areas of life, such as a need for authority figures or an inability to make decisions in the face of ambiguity, may create problems when they unexpectedly emerge in a democratic setting. Majority rule under democratic decision making is not a protection against poor decisions. And cooperatives may face external challenges—legal, economic, political, and cultural. Some fail because of internal and/or external challenges or conflicts that cannot be overcome. But many do not fail, and they may often provide enormously rich experiences for their members.

Democratically run work organizations at times find ways to cooperate with and help to sustain one another. For example, in the San Francisco Bay Area, over 55 worker cooperatives ranging from clinics to cafes participate in the Network of Bay Area Worker Collectives (http://nobawc.org). In some instances, cooperatives' activities cross national borders. A U.S.-based cooperative, Equal Exchange, functions as part of an international cooperative network. This organization purchases coffee from small democratic work cooperatives in Latin America and Africa, and sells it through retail establishments—including other cooperatives—in the United States (see www.equalexchange.com).

Some of the most noteworthy examples of workplace cooperatives are outside the United States. In Japan, older workers who have been laid off and are unable to find work using their experience and skills have formed cooperatives, as have retired Japanese workers. Income is shared among the workers, and they are able to have health insurance and other benefits important to elders (Evanoff, 2001).

While most cooperatives are small in terms of the number of workers involved, some are quite large. In such instances, combinations of direct and representative democracy may be necessary in order to maintain workers' participation in democratic decision making. In the Basque region of Spain, workers own and control large-scale manufacturing cooperatives in the industrial city of Mondragon; they produce stoves, refrigerators, steel, and other goods for an international market (Cheney, 2002). In the state of Kerala, in southern India, an industrial cooperative operates with over 30,000 workers, who produce packaged food and tobacco products (Isaac, Franke, and Raghavan, 1998).

These examples suggest that work organizations and other secondary groups do not have to be structured in accordance with bureaucratic principles in order to operate effectively. The issue of how organizations are to be structured is really an issue of the distribution of power—who will have it, and how it will be exercised.

How Bureaucratic and Democratic Organizations Affect People's Lives

Those whose lives are heavily encompassed by highly bureaucratized organizations will behave and feel very differently than those who conduct their lives primarily in democratically organized settings. Bureaucratic organizations expect people to accommodate to their will, to become objects to whom things happen. Highly bureaucratized structures are likely to discourage spontaneity, innovative ideas, or creative group efforts that may call the status quo into question. The more a society is pervaded by bureaucracy, the more its organizational structures exert pressure on and control over the thinking and behavior of its members.

Within democratic organizations people can more easily become subjects who make events happen. Democratic forms of organization can empower participants, providing them with degrees of freedom to decide how to conduct their own affairs. Persons who feel alienated and disgruntled when denied a say in what is going on around them may find that democratic structures open up new opportunities for the expression of their personalities and the achievement of personal goals. This is not to say that in democratic organizations "anything goes" and there are no restraints on members. Participants in democratic structures usually arrive at, if they do not start out with, rules of operation and social norms as to the range of behavior and thinking they are willing to tolerate. These rules and norms, however, may periodically be discussed, criticized, and changed by rank-and-file organization members, something that is unlikely to occur in bureaucratic work organizations that are run from the top down.

Today, people's lives often involve a mixture of daily experiences with bureaucratic and democratic organizations. A person may work in an office, follow the office rules, fulfill the narrow set of duties outlined in a job description, and jump whenever the boss calls. But outside of work that same person may attend an evening meeting of the local parent–teacher organization, functioning as a democratically elected officer; participate with peers in a lunch-hour gathering of a free-wheeling book discussion group that was spontaneously organized; accept an invitation to hear (and decide whether to work on behalf of) a political party candidate; and spend a weekend hunting with fellow members of the collectively owned and operated Fish, Fur, and Feather Club. While people's biographies are affected by participation in bureaucratic organizations, democratic structures shape their biographies in important ways as well.

In societies whose overall mode of governance is dictatorial or authoritarian, political elites may use military and civilian bureaucracies to monitor and control many aspects of people's lives. In such societies, people at times rebel and seek to create democratic organizational structures. Most nations in Latin America, a region long characterized by oppressive military dictatorships, have made a transition to greater democratic rule in recent years in response to popular social movements and political upheavals. Nations in Eastern Europe and the former Soviet Union were shaken apart by social movements that were at least in part a reaction to the concentrated bureaucratic power of their respective states. The democracy movement in the People's Republic of China, brutally crushed in 1989 by tanks in Beijing's Tiananmen Square, will very likely reappear. Resisting bureaucratic control is one way in which many people have sought to gain more say over the directions in which their own biographies will go.

INFORMAL ORGANIZATION

Max Weber's classic model focused on bureaucracy's formal characteristics (its hierarchy of authority, rules and regulations, and so on). Yet anyone who has worked in a bureaucratic setting knows that informal relationships spring up among groups of employees. Often these relationships have little or nothing to do with the bureaucratically prescribed division of labor or people's official job descriptions. Sociologists use the term **informal organization** to refer to social structures that emerge spontaneously as people interact and develop interpersonal ties within bureaucratic settings. Informal organizations provide the evidence for the existence of primary groups within a bureaucratically organized workplace.

Some Functions of Informal Organization

The importance of informal organization was first noted in path-breaking organizational research conducted way back in the 1930s (Roethlisberger and Dickson, 1939). Researchers at Western Electric Company's Hawthorne Works in Chicago, where electrical components were assembled, were interested in helping the firm's management increase levels of production. The researchers assumed that one way to do this was to alter working conditions. They selected a group of workers and observed their reactions to changes in conditions, such as the amount of light in the workroom and the timing of rest breaks. But no matter what the researchers changed, there did not seem to be any consistent relationship between workplace conditions and worker productivity.

The researchers continued their experiment. Finally, they realized that the workers themselves created mutually accepted norms that guided their rates of production. According to management, these norms resulted in less being produced than was possible. The researchers tried to understand this restriction of output. It turned out that the workers were holding back their productivity out of fear. They believed that if management knew they could produce more, it would increase their production quotas without increasing their pay or would decide fewer workers were needed and lay some off. This research was taking place during the Depression of the 1930s, a time of extremely widespread unemployment and scarcity of jobs.

Within their group, the workers denounced and ridiculed those who broke ranks and produced above the norm, calling them "rate-busters" and "speed kings." At the same time, a worker who lagged too far below the norm was criticized as a "chiseler" who could possibly draw unwanted attention from management. Since most workers were concerned with earning and maintaining the respect and regard of their peers, few chose to deviate from the pressures to conform. The researchers concluded that informal relationships are important in influencing productivity levels and that the output of any individual worker should be considered a function of the informal organization in which that person participates.

Sociologists have conducted numerous studies in a variety of work settings and found informal organization to be operating and demanding conformity to its norms (Jaffee, 2002, Chapters 4 and 5). At times, informal relationships actually facilitate work accomplishment, particularly when bureaucratic rules get in the way of handling problems or when established channels stifle communications that are important to organizational functioning. Workers may informally pass along knowledge to one another that enable work to be done more safely and efficiently than official bureaucratic procedures would allow. In some settings informal organization results in activities that distract workers from the mind-numbing nature of their labor and thus actually contributes to their productivity.

Managers and workers obviously occupy very different positions in bureaucratic work organizations. As such, they often have very different perspectives on the work to be done and on the respective roles each should play in the process. Based on in-depth interviews, sociologist Randy Hodson found that workers are often motivated in the workplace by their own agendas rather than those of management. While informal organization may facilitate organizational operations, workers may also choose not to comply with managerial directives. Their behaviors can include resistance to being managed, as well as autonomous, often creative efforts to control and structure the work they must do (Hodson, 2001).

Workers' Resistance to Management

Worker resistance to being managed can take the form of disrupting and sabotaging bureaucratic routine (see Sprouse, 1992; Hodson, 1991, 1995). Let us look at two dramatic examples drawn from the auto industry in the latter part of the twentieth century. In the first example, workers actively resisted management's efforts to plan their role in production. In the second example, workers rebelled in similar ways against a new supervisor's efforts to "shape things up" and enforce previously neglected bureaucratic rules. Auto company managements have sought to overcome the types of disruptive worker behavior contained in these examples and increase control over workers by replacing more and more of them with automated and computerized production machinery, including mechanical robots, and increasing bureaucratization of the production process. Nonetheless, these studies demonstrate that resistance to bureaucracy is possible through informal organization in the workplace.

When Bill Watson (1971) took a temporary summer job in a Detroit auto factory, he was overwhelmed by the frenetic human activity demanded by the constantly moving assembly line. Workers resembled robots, tied to their specialized function and place along the line. The assembly line ran inexorably at a pace that always seemed just slightly too fast. It seemed to dominate all human social interaction or what little was possible given the incredible noise. Yet Watson quickly became aware, on the basis of participant observation in this work setting that not all was what it seemed on the surface.

Watson found that the workers were engaged in daily and often overt struggles with management over everything from working conditions to the quality of the autos being produced. The struggles were made possible and carried out through an informal organization consisting of networks of "fictive kin": chains of friends and acquaintances across the auto plant who kept up channels of communication, did favors for one another, and looked for ways to cooperate in subverting management. The fictive kin network extended outside the plant, through the taverns and bars surrounding it, and into local working-class neighborhoods where many of the auto workers resided.

Workers used the fictive-kin network to establish their own rest break system. Workers in different parts of the plant would find ways to sabotage and break down the assembly line at a specified hour on a given day, allowing everyone time to talk, read, or move about the plant to visit friends. When workers were asked to assemble engines out of parts known to be defective, the fictive-kin network rolled into action. Assembly workers either broke parts or deliberately assembled the engines incorrectly, and workers responsible for inspection cooperated by rejecting the engines and pulling them off the line.

The fictive-kin network made possible a great deal of organized theft. Workers would distract security guards at plant gates while peers smuggled out tools and auto parts. Similar organized distraction allowed workers to smuggle items into the plant. Chaise lounges were brought in, hoisted through ceiling traps in the bathrooms, and placed on the roof. Workers who could manage to "disappear," protected by false excuses given to supervisors by peers, were often able to escape the racket, heat, and oil-filled air by hiding on the roof for brief periods.

The heat in the plant in the summer was debilitating. Workers in one area responded by holding sporadic fire-hose fights; participants were protected by a network of lookouts who warned them whenever supervisors were coming. For a while those involved wore their wives' shower caps to work, a symbol that management could not fathom but that brought glee to coworkers across the plant.

One of management's bureaucratic rules stipulated that workers had to cease work 10 minutes before their shift was over in order to wash their hands. Workers felt that this was a waste of time, since they could wash their hands in less than 10 minutes. Using the fictive-kin network, they agreed to wash for only a few minutes, line up at the exit door, howl the sound of the shift whistle, and proceed to charge out early. For a time the supervisors were unable to mobilize enough counter-force to stop them.

Efforts to enforce conformity to bureaucratic rules among workers who have devised their own ways of accomplishing mind-numbing work may likewise foster rebellion. Ben Hamper, a riveter on a General Motors assembly line, describes workers' feisty reaction to a new supervisor's efforts in this regard:

> *Enter the new boss, a self-proclaimed "troubleshooter."*
> *He had been enlisted to groom the rivet line into a more*
> *docile outpost. . . .With a tight grip on the whip, the new*
> *bossman started riding the crew. No music. No Rivet*
> *Hockey. No horseplay. No drinking. No card playing.*
> *No working up the line. No leaving the department.*
> *No doubling up. No this, no that. No questions asked.*
> *No way. After three nights of this imported bullyism,*
> *the boys had had their fill. Frames began sliding down*
> *the line minus parts. Rivets became crosseyed. Guns*
> *mysteriously broke down. The repairmen began*
> *shipping the majority of the defects, unable to keep*
> *up with the repair load. Sabotage was rather drastic;*
> *however it was an effective way of getting the point*
> *across. We simply had no other recourse. Sometimes*
> *these power-gods had to be reminded that it was we,*
> *the workers, who kept the place runnin'. . . . This new*
> *guy was nobody's dummy. He could see it all slippin'*
> *away, his goon tactics workin' against him. He pulled*
> *us all aside and suggested that we return to our old*
> *methods (Hamper, 1991: 206).*

Do these workers appear irrational? And, whatever happened to the old-fashioned work ethic? Yet, consider the context in which they are made to labor: Assembly-line systems of production are designed by management to leave workers with very little or no say over what they will produce, how it will be produced, the pace of production, and the quality of the end product. Job dissatisfaction and alienation among assembly line workers tends to be high. Yet, while assembly lines minimize workplace freedom, U.S. society simultaneously values democracy and individual rights. The behavior of the auto workers described by Watson and Hamper might be said to represent one expression of the fundamental contradiction between bureaucratic control and democratic values, in this case through the medium of informal organization.

Organizational memberships help to shape people's biographies, but so do the social networks in which people participate. These networks often involve relationships and ties that link the primary and secondary groups with which people are affiliated to other such groups.

SOCIAL NETWORKS

Some 40 years ago, social psychologist Stanley Milgram published an article in which he asked the question, "Starting with any two people in the world, what is the probability that they will know one another?" Taking the U.S. population as a case in point, his answer was that there was a chance of 1 in 200,000. Milgram presented a model showing it was highly probable statistically that any two people in the United States could be linked up through a range of two to 10 intermediary acquaintances (Milgram, 1967: 60–67). Milgram's article stimulated research into his claims and may have prompted some sociologists to take a greater interest in the subject of **social networks**. Networks can be described as the complex patterns of social relationships and ties to others in which individuals are caught up.

Strong and Weak Network Ties

Sociologist Mark Granovetter (1973) was among the first to stress the importance of distinguishing between "strong" and "weak" ties. Some ties are interpersonally strong, as in the case of primary groups. Strong ties develop, for example, among family members and friends. Other ties are weak, as with casual acquaintances and people to whom we might have indirect ties through relatives or friends. Ties that are weak are often typical of our relationships with many others who are in the secondary groups of which we are members. Weak ties may also link us to people in primary and secondary groups other than those to which we belong. They can connect us to people who move in more distant social circles. With computerized communication linkages available through the Internet (including social media like Facebook and Twitter), we can even develop weak ties with people living on other continents and amass huge numbers of "friends."

The importance of social networks, and strong versus weak ties, has been underscored in research into how people find jobs. Newspaper job listings turn out to be far less important in successfully locating employment than the networks in which people are enmeshed (Montgomery, 1992). Figure 4.2 illustrates the relative importance of personal ties in obtaining employment.

Networks function, in effect, as a form of **social capital**, i.e., a crucial social resource that all people possess to a greater or lesser degree. Success in finding jobs has been found to depend not only upon having access to social networks and on their size, but on the relative proportion of weak and strong ties which one's networks contain. In general, if people have to rely most heavily or entirely on strong ties (family, friends), they run out of job-locating assistance very quickly. Those with extensive weak ties (acquaintances, indirect links to friends of friends or to members of other groups) are much more advantaged in this regard. Weak ties, then, have been found to be indispensable in exposing people to a wider range of job information and opportunities (Montgomery, 1992).

Figure 4.2: The Social Network to Employment

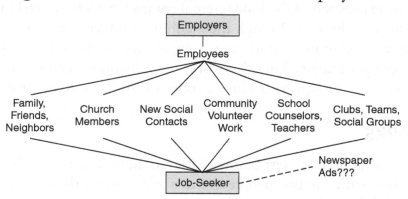

Networks and Social Advantage

People differ in the degree to which they possess social capital—in this case, access to networks and to weak or strong interpersonal ties. But they differ as well as to the relative advantages they possess in terms of what they can achieve through activating such ties and networks. Indeed, variation in social network possession, use, and payoff occurs rather systematically along the lines of race, class, and gender. The affluent, men, and whites have more extensive, richer, and varied networks than do the less affluent or poor, women, and people of color. The latter populations also have fewer weak ties and tend to rely more on strong ties for help with job searches, job advancement, and attainment of higher earnings and bonuses (Ling, 2000).

Using women as an example, researchers have found that those who must take on the primary responsibility for childrearing (especially of very young children) have smaller social networks and fewer ties than men or women without such responsibilities (Munch, McPherson, and Smith-Lovin, 1997). Women engaged in caregiving are drawn more heavily into relationships with family and friends, while their male partners are sustaining and develop their ties outside these circles. Likewise, sex segregation in the labor force means that women who do work outside the home tend to develop ties on the job with those in lower-paying occupations like their own, while men are more likely to develop ties with other men who hold similarly higher-paying positions. Differential access to social networks and the nature of the ties in these networks contribute to the difficulty that women face in competing for jobs on an equal basis with men in the labor force (Ling, 2000: 787–788).

In short, the networks available to those who are already privileged help them to sustain that privilege. As sociologist Nan Ling put it:

> *Resource-rich networks are characterized by relative richness*
> *not only in quantity but in kind—resource heterogeneity. . . . Members*
> *of such networks enjoy access to information from and influence*
> *in diverse socioeconomic strata and positions. In contrast, members*
> *in resource-poor networks share a relatively restricted variety of*
> *information and influence (Ling, 2000: 787).*

Insofar as the social networks in which people of color, nonaffluent people, and women participate are resource-poor, this lack of social capital poses invisible but very concrete barriers to achievement, upward mobility, and social equality.

The statuses and roles, groups, organizations, and social networks into which people's lives are woven are in actuality somewhat fragile, requiring individual and collective acquiescence and collusion in order to persist. People can and do choose to challenge or change social structures within and through which they relate to one another, thus contributing to the dynamic quality of what would otherwise be extremely stagnant social arrangements.

 # CHAPTER SUMMARY

- Social structure, the organization of recurrent and patterned social relationships, provides the framework within and through which human beings relate to one another. Micro-level social structure involves social relationships based on interaction between small numbers of individuals. Mid-level social structure refers to larger webs of social relationships.

- Individuals occupy many different social positions and are involved in a variety of micro- and mid-level social structures. The social positions or statuses that people occupy, and the roles they are expected to perform, organize and define their participation in groups, organizations, and social networks. Statuses and roles may restrict individuals' activities as well as provide opportunities for people to explore their talents and capabilities.

- A status is a social position occupied by an individual. An achieved status is entered into based on an individual's opportunities and decisions. In contrast, an ascribed status is beyond an individual's real control and is often determined at birth. A master status is so socially important to some that it overrides other statuses in terms of how that person may be treated. Some master statuses are unwanted by those who occupy them, but are imposed by dominant groups in positions of power.

- Statuses are accompanied by roles, or sets of expectations as to how those occupying a particular social position are to behave. Individuals may find that a role they are expected to play has contradictory demands, leading them to experience role strain. People may also experience role conflicts, as when different roles or sets of roles carry competing expectations. Such strains and conflicts can prove stressful to the individuals involved.

- Unlike social aggregates or collections of individuals with no real interpersonal ties, social groups are based on recurrent interaction and established social relationships. Individuals participate in many social groups during the course of their lives and are often participants in a variety of groups simultaneously. All groups have rules or norms of behavior to which members are expected to conform.

- There are two different types of groups: primary and secondary. Primary groups are smaller in size and may entail more frequent and informal face-to-face interaction with other group members than secondary groups. The secondary groups in which people participate are likely to be organized around one of two basic principles: bureaucracy or democracy. To the degree that organizations are bureaucratic, individuals are likely to feel that they are objects to whom things happen. This is in contrast to feeling like actors empowered to shape the social scene, as is more often the case for members of democratic organizations.

- Most workplaces in U.S. society are organized in accordance with the features of bureaucracy, one of which is a formal hierarchy of authority. Bureaucracy calls for top-down control of workplace activities and its spread has contributed to the declining power of workers. Bureaucracy in the workplace is not inevitable. Democratic workplace cooperatives exist, proving that workplaces need not be subject to oligarchy or rule by a few. Nonetheless, many arenas of social life in U.S. society reflect the strong influence of bureaucratization.

- Members of bureaucratic organizations frequently form or enter into primary group relationships within the organizational setting. Referred to as expressions of informal organization, such relationships within bureaucratic workplaces may serve to offset bureaucracy's oppressive tendencies and even empower workers to actively resist top-down control.

- People's access to and participation in social networks is a crucial social resource or form of social capital. Network ties may be weak or strong. Those who have the most numerous, diverse, and rich network connections are typically people who are privileged by virtue of class, race, or gender. The social networks in which people are involved help determine their life chances, including opportunities for employment and upward mobility.

 THINKING CRITICALLY

1. Sociologists believe that the thinking and behavior of youths are strongly influenced both by their families and by the peer groups to which they belong. Use examples to characterize the influence these two primary groups have on a teenager. Does their relative influence change over time? How so?

2. Consider the features of the ideal-type, or model, of bureaucratic and democratic organizations. Apply these features in an analysis of the family. How does the family resemble the ideal type of bureaucracies, and how does it differ? How does the family resemble the ideal type of democratic organizations, and how does it differ? Is the family a bureaucratic or a democratic organization? What does this suggest to you about these organizational types?

3. We have said that bureaucracy is extremely common in U.S. society. What arguments could be made for and against organizing many more of our secondary groups, such as schools and workplaces, along democratic principles? What do you see as the obstacles to doing so?

4. Think about the various social roles you occupy and the behavioral expectations associated with these roles. In what situations do you experience role strain or role conflict? How successful are you, usually, in resolving it? Why?

5. Do people single out a particular ascribed status of yours (e.g., race, ethnicity, gender, sexual orientation) and consider it more definitive of "who and what you are" than any of your other personal characteristics? When do you notice this occurring? How does this affect you?

KEY TERMS

social structure **69**

micro-level social structure **70**

mid-level social structure **70**

status **70**

achieved status **71**

ascribed status **71**

master status **71**

social role **72**

role strain **73**

role conflict **73**

role set **74**

social aggregate **74**

group **75**

norms **75**

primary group **75**

secondary group **77**

bureaucracy **79**

simple control **80**

technical control **80**

bureaucratic control **80**

iron law of oligarchy **84**

democracy **84**

direct democracy **85**

representative democracy **85**

informal organization **87**

social networks **91**

social capital **92**

CULTURE

5

In Western societies people marry one spouse at a time, whereas in some African and Asian societies it is common to be married to several spouses simultaneously. Western families commonly contain two or more children; but in China, there have been state-enforced policies mandating one-child families. Women in Western societies take their freedom of movement for granted; women in Saudi Arabia are not even permitted to drive; and women in Taliban-controlled Afghanistan were not permitted to hold jobs, attend school, or leave home unescorted by a male family member. Dogs and cats are pets in Western societies, not meals; cows may be food but are not regarded as sacred objects, as they are among Hindus in India. These varied social practices are part of what is called *culture*.

- Where do these patterns of social practices come from, and why are they different in different societies?

When sociologists conventionally use the term **culture,** they are generally referring to a shared way of life among the members of a society. Culture is an agreement among a society's members about appropriate behavior, values, beliefs, history and heritage, rituals that should be respected and observed, and so on. The members of a society share a way of life described by a set of blueprints that show "what must be done, ought to be done, should be done, may be done, and must not be done" (Williams, 1965: 23). These blueprints, handed down from one generation to another, are learned understandings of acceptable and expected patterns of behaviors.

- But who decides what these patterns are?

Karl Marx and Friedrich Engels once noted that "the ideas of the ruling class are in every epoch the ruling ideas" (1970: 64). In their view, those who control the production of material wealth in a society also control the production of knowledge, and systems of ideas (or **ideology**) and insight, and in this way control the production of an entire way of life. Thus, a society is highly likely to create a culture that justifies reinforces, and reproduces the privileges, advantages, and power of its ruling class.

   Antonio Gramsci (1971) later expanded this insight with his notion of **cultural hegemony:** The ideas and values of the dominant class are diffused throughout society's institutions and imposed on society's less powerful members. Since the members of the dominant class enjoy privileged access to its institutions, as well as to the media, they are in a position to promote the values that support and legitimize their privileged or dominant position. That position also enables them to tolerate only those dissenting viewpoints that do not fundamentally challenge the existing order and to squelch any views that do. The dominant members of society are thus able to define the boundaries of debate and discussion, thereby encouraging the incorporation of their ideologies into the thinking of subordinate members. Culture, then, can be a powerful influence on people's behaviors by restricting their actions and thoughts within "safe" ranges that do not seriously undermine the existing order.

The provocative observations of Marx, Engels, and Gramsci challenge the common assumption that cultures are little more than a blend of the shared contributions of many different groups. Their analysis, therefore, raises several questions:

- Is it true that those who control wealth and production also control the culture?

- If so, how is diversity possible? What do all or most members of society share in common?

- Are people powerless to alter the dominant culture, or do individual and collective efforts make a difference?

- How successful are different groups in gaining widespread acceptance for their ideas?

- To what degree and in what ways can individuals and minorities resist the ideas of dominant groups within society?

Conventionally, sociologists treat culture as a relatively static entity handed down from one generation to another with little or no significant resistance and only superficial modifications. But another way to view culture is as a contested terrain characterized by an ongoing dynamic process of resistance and change: People may challenge prevailing definitions of acceptable and appropriate behaviors as well as existing social arrangements.

- Who has the power to determine the elements of culture?

- How do the dominant groups in society convey their cultural perspectives and how do others convey challenges to those perspectives?

In this chapter we will explore these questions by examining the components of culture, including norms, values, sanctions, language, subcultures, and countercultures.

NORMS

When you come into a classroom, you generally know how to behave. You must sit down, open a notebook, and have a pen or pencil ready to take notes. You know that you should not listen to an iPod or chat on a cell phone during class, you should raise your hand to speak, and you should not swear at the teacher or stand up and shout at friends across the room during a lecture. If you use a laptop or notepad to take notes in class, you know you're not supposed to surf the Web, check your email or Facebook. You know you're not supposed to cheat on exams or turn in plagiarized papers as your own. And you're aware that you should wear clothing to class. How do you know all this without receiving a written list of rules from each individual teacher?

Norms are standards that define the obligatory and expected behaviors of people in various situations. They reflect a society's beliefs about correct and incorrect behaviors. Once these behaviors become second nature, members of society do not have to consciously analyze every situation and decide what their appropriate actions ought to be. Norms also can inhibit the type of thinking that might result in challenges to the dominant members of society. For example, the norms defining appropriate classroom behavior reduce the chances that a student will challenge the teacher's authority in class. Similarly, norms served for generations to inhibit the idea that women and African Americans in the United States could challenge their disadvantaged position in society (we will discuss how this situation changed later in the chapter).

On the other hand, norms also help society control inappropriate or harmful behaviors. For example, until very recently, sexual harassment of women was widely perceived as normative, something women had to learn to live with and endure. Norms are now beginning to define such behavior as inappropriate and unacceptable. Similarly, driving under the influence of alcohol and drugs is now normatively defined as unacceptable, as are other harmful behaviors such as assault, rape, murder, and drug trafficking. And smoking in public places is increasingly frowned upon, if not defined as illegal, in many settings.

Normative indoctrination, or the teaching of norms to individuals, is so successful that people often are taken by surprise when they encounter behaviors that do not conform to prevailing norms. That is, when people's unconscious expectations for behavior are suddenly violated, they experience **culture shock.** For example, on one early episode of the popular television show *Survivor*, contestants ate live beetle larvae and roasted rats. The revulsion viewers expressed illustrated the collective culture shock at having to confront eating norms that contradict those that are more commonly unexamined and taken for granted. People often remain equally unaware of the norms about physical beauty until they see someone whose face is disfigured. Such a person is considered "ugly" and less than valuable, and frequently isolated (Hughes, 1999; Hawkesworth, 2001). In some cases, people may audibly gasp, look away with revulsion, or even scream when confronted with severe facial disfigurement. In other cases, individuals with facial disfigurements are likely to be stared at, pitied, scorned, discriminated against, or made the object of derision.

Culture shock can also be seen in the way some people react to homosexuality. People are largely unconscious of the social assumption that heterosexuality is the only legitimate basis of sexual relationships. Yet, when confronted with members of the same sex kissing or openly expressing physical attraction, people may express shock, revulsion, anger, derision, ridicule, discrimination, or violence. For example, more than half of the public television stations in the United States refused to air the PBS program *Tongues Untied*, about African American homosexuals. In its listing of the broadcast, *TV Guide* warned that the subject matter was not suitable for all audiences. *TV Guide* does not always post such warnings for sexually explicit programs involving heterosexuals. Indeed, fairly explicit heterosexual interactions occur daily on network afternoon dramas, but the program listings appear without warnings.

Culture shock may be a reflection of **ethnocentrism,** in which one's own culture is held to be the standard against which all other cultures are evaluated. Here, the individual not only notices the differences between cultures but ranks them as superior and inferior, with his or her own culture as the superior one. For example, many people in the United States are unable to appreciate the fact that for Hindus in India cows are sacred; no matter how hungry people might be, they may not eat cows there. To many Americans, such a status accorded to the cow even in the face of extreme hunger may indicate an inferior culture. Evaluating India as having an inferior culture on this basis is an expression of ethnocentrism.

There are three types of norms, based on their level of importance to the dominant members of society: *folkways*, *mores*, and *laws*. The negative **sanctions,** or punishments, meted out to violators of norms vary in severity depending upon the type of norm being transgressed.

Folkways

Folkways, the least formal or important norms, involve everyday conventional routines. They belong to the category of behaviors that *should* and *should not* occur, as specified by society or a social group. Folkways may include such things as how many meals members eat per day, when meals are eaten, and what should be eaten at each one. They also include rituals of deference and public deportment, such as where to stand and whom to look at during conversations or public outings.

For example, in the United States, one is expected to maintain an invisible bubble of personal space even when involved in conversations with others. Violation of personal space is tolerated only in unavoidable circumstances such as crowded trains and elevators; even then, one is expected to avoid eye contact as a means of respecting a minimum of personal space. One only makes direct, sustained eye contact and physical touch with another when both are engaged in a mutually intimate relationship; to do so otherwise is considered an act of aggression or inappropriate social behavior. In contrast, people in Latin America consider it rude to hoard personal space and fail to look directly at the individual with whom one is speaking; they will attempt to get physically close to their fellow conversant and will sometimes even touch the other's arm while speaking. Imagine the social dance likely to develop as a person from the United States and someone from Brazil attempt to have a conversation, with the first person backing away and the Brazilian advancing closer, both attempting to conform to their own folkways, and each experiencing confusion and discomfort at the other's failure to conform to their expectations.

Sanctions imposed on violators of folkways are often relatively mild expressions of reprimand, such as stares, frowns, laughter, throat clearing, or tongue clucking. In the hypothetical conversation described above, the person from the United States may frown or stare at the Brazilian or may even laugh nervously, and the Brazilian is likely to do the same. Both are undergoing the culture shock of having a conversational partner violate the expected social behaviors defining roles and physical positions, and each may interpret the violation differently. Each may alternatively interpret the other's behavior as rude, curious, eccentric, deranged, aggressive, or hostile.

Mores

Mores are more formal and important norms than folkways. They generally include behaviors defined as those that *absolutely must* or *must not* occur. Members of society view these norms as absolutes because violation of them is believed to threaten the group's ability to function or its very existence. Given the increased level of importance accorded to mores, violations of mores typically meet with more severe sanctions than do violations of folkways. These include imposition of shame and ostracism upon transgressors, and sometimes exile.

Mores may include rules governing marriage-partner selection. For example, many societies require that mates be selected from the same ethnic, racial, religious, economic, political, or social group. Marriages between people from different groups are seen to threaten a group's existence by diluting its practices and its heritage or by dispersing the group's accumulated material wealth. Intermarriages may be subject to a range of sanctions, including excommunication from a church, abdication of royalty, beating of the "intruding" partner, refusal to acknowledge the marriage as legitimate, and so on. Among certain groups of Orthodox Jews, the family of an individual who has married a non-Jewish partner will sit *shiva*, a ritual of mourning. From that moment on the family will act as if the transgressor had died; many will not even permit the name of the transgressor to be mentioned, and all evidence of the person's existence, past and present, will be destroyed.

Most societies maintain mores defining heterosexuality as the only legitimate sexual orientation. Sexual relationships between individuals of the same sex are at best unacknowledged and at worst punished. In the United States, for example, gay males and lesbians are often ridiculed, chastised, denied housing and employment, subjected to violence, ignored by family members, and erroneously blamed for social problems such as AIDS or child pornography.

Laws

Laws constitute the most formal and important norms. Laws are the folkways and mores deemed so vital to dominant interests that they become translated into written, legal formalizations that even nonmembers of the society (such as visitors) are required to obey. For example, in many communities in the United States no one may purchase alcohol before noon on Sundays; in some communities, alcohol sales are completely forbidden on Sundays, despite the fact that many people do not regard Sunday as the Sabbath. In most states, no one under the age of 21 is permitted to purchase alcoholic beverages, and that includes international visitors who may be allowed to purchase and consume alcohol at a younger age in their own country.

Similarly, same-sex partnerships are not legally recognized as valid marriages in most states in the United States, although the partners may be mutually devoted for many years, even if the partners may come from places where such partnerships are legal. While this is clearly changing (twelve states now legally recognize the rights of gay and lesbian couples to marry), the sanction largely still remains: Few employers allow homosexuals to extend health insurance coverage to their partners, as married heterosexuals are allowed to do. And many states still carry laws that make homosexual acts illegal. When laws are not firmly based on norms shared by the majority, they are difficult to enforce. The constitutional amendment prohibiting the sale of alcohol was repealed in 1933 because so many people regularly violated it. The amendment was championed primarily by the Protestant middle class, with the support of labor and socialist organizations, in an attempt to impose its norms and values on the rest of society. More recently, while many states maintained laws forbidding private, consensual practices by homosexuals, these laws were routinely ignored by homosexuals and heterosexuals alike. These laws were difficult to enforce, both because of the private nature of the act and because the laws were so commonly violated. The Supreme Court in 2003 finally found such laws unconstitutional. Today there remain breaches in the social cohesion underlying laws such as those forbidding the possession and use of marijuana, as well as conflicts between states allowing possession and the federal government that still criminalizes it, an example of laws that continue to be challenged and may change in the future.

Laws concern issues that are so important to dominant interests that sanctions against violations are formalized in the written legal codes and are likely to be quite severe. But one latent consequence of these sanctions is the reproduction of class and racial inequality (Reiman, 1996). For example, monetary fines typically penalize the poor more than the wealthy. The poor are also at a disadvantage in raising bail in order to remain out of jail while awaiting trial, and thus are deprived of the right enjoyed by the affluent of the presumption of innocence until proven guilty. In addition, people of color pay considerably more, sometimes twice the bail, than whites to secure their freedom before trial.

Regardless of whether one believes that sanctions are fair or uniformly applied, the fact that they occur regularly suggests that norms are not necessarily shared and embraced by all members of society. Where, then, do norms come from?

VALUES

Folkways, mores, and laws are shaped by the value system defined by the dominant members of society. **Values** are assumptions and judgments made about the goods, goals, or states of existence that are deemed important, desirable, and worth striving (or dying) for. For example, in the United States respect for private property is a fundamentally important value, as are individual rights to privacy and freedom of expression. Values shape the normative system by defining the criteria for judging which behaviors will and will not be tolerated. However, values do not necessarily *determine* people's behaviors. Norms define the dominant perception of the ideal behaviors in specific situations; they are not necessarily a reflection of real or actual behaviors. Thus, although an important value in the United States is the right of individuals to privacy, it is still fairly common for children to have their personal belongings examined by their teachers and school administrators, for workers to have their private lives investigated by employers and to be subject to random urine tests for drug use, and for individuals' credit histories to be sold to any buyer (Manning, 2000).

Because of the gap between ideal norms and actual behavior, societies generally feel the need to impose negative sanctions (or punishments of violations of norms). For example, jails and courts are overcrowded with hundreds of thousands of violators of society's most important norms—laws (especially drug laws). And parents routinely talk about the need to find effective punishments for children who do not comply with family rules: Is a removal of privileges ("grounding") enough? Is a spanking too much? Many people violate norms, and such widespread violation indicates that norms are not necessarily shared by all. Similarly, not everyone accepts the prevailing value system advocated by dominant groups. Both the norms and values of dominant groups meet with resistance and challenge.

Furthermore, the prevailing value system may contain contradictory values that give rise to debate, challenge, and varying interpretations. For example, one of the ostensible values in the United States is the right to life. As such, laws strictly prohibit the taking of human life. Killing another person is considered the most heinous of offenses. Yet the prohibition against taking a life is suspended during war (and actually redefined in such cases as part of one's patriotic duty) and under circumstances defined as "self-defense"; and some states reserve the right to take a human life in capital punishment. And some people view abortion as a violation of the fetus's right to life. Ironically, to protest the operations of abortion clinics, some abortion opponents have used violence (and, in several cases, the murder of physicians performing abortions in Florida, New York, and Massachusetts, such as the 1998 sniper killing of Dr. Barnett Slepian in his Amherst, New York, home). Contradictory values may serve to help shape a normative system by generating debate and conflict. The process of developing various perspectives through debate, and of resolving conflict, may help identify the priorities of values and the norms to which those values point us.

The Relationship Between Values and Norms

Conventional wisdom holds that norms and values in the culture are the glue that binds society together as a positive, coherent unit, enabling its members to function smoothly and peaceably. However, sometimes the value system gives rise to norms that actually serve to oppress some people. We shall examine the value system inherent in a patriarchy to show this relationship between values and norms.

A patriarchal society values male dominance as a natural, inalienable right, thereby enforcing the inferiority and subordination of women. Normative behaviors derived from this value include institutional discrimination against women in education and in the labor force, resulting in restricted opportunities, lower wages for work, and relative economic, social, and political deprivation (Cubbins, 2001).

Patriarchal values also encourage the treatment of women as property. This is evident in Christian marriage rituals in which the bride is "given away" by a male (usually her father or uncle) to the male she is about to marry. Similarly, in some Jewish marriage rituals the bride's father walks her halfway down the aisle; then he turns her over to the groom, who walks her the remaining way to the rabbi performing the ceremony. At the conclusion of many wedding ceremonies the presider announces, "I now pronounce you man and wife," suggesting that the woman now belongs to the man. Many couples today prefer "husband and wife," which represents their relationship as partners rather than as a man and his possession.

While marriage rituals seem relatively innocuous, the fact that they frequently go unquestioned suggests the power of patriarchy to define values. More extreme cases of patriarchal definitions of female inferiority involve violence against women (Dobash et al., 2000, Kurz, 2001). Even though U.S. culture assumes that women's male partners are to be their protectors, it is also a culture that links masculinity with anger and violence (Kindlon, Thompson, and Barker, 2000). It is not surprising, then, to find these norms coalesce so that women are more likely to become homicide victims in the United States than in 25 other global north countries, and account for 70 percent of all female murder victims in these countries (Hemenway, Shinoda-Tagawa, and Miller, 2002). Furthermore, while men in the United States are more likely to be murdered away from home and by a stranger, women are more likely to suffer violence at the hands of their intimate male partners at home (Hemenway et al., 2002). Indeed, one study found that in nearly 65 percent of the cases of female homicide, the perpetrator was either the victims' current or former partner (Fox and Zawitz, 2010).

In extreme cases the intersection of patriarchy as power and privilege and cultural conceptualizations of women as objects and possessions can often become institutionalized into a "rape culture" in which rape and other forms of violence against women are accepted as a common feature of society (Cuklanz, 2000; Feltey, 2001). Indeed, the widespread use of rape as a weapon of war led the UN Security Council to formally denounce it as a human rights violation in a 2008 resolution as "a tactic of war to humiliate, dominate, instill fear in, disperse and/or forcibly relocate civilian members of a community or ethnic group" (www.ohchr.org/en/newsevents/pages/rapeweaponwar.aspx). Evidence suggests, however, that such a rape culture can be resisted and challenged: The Silent Witness Initiative in the United States notes that homicide rates of women often decline in locales with a greater presence and availability of women's shelters and rape crisis centers and in states that had legislation addressing domestic violence (www.silentwitness.net/old_site/html/results.html).

Patriarchy also implies that women are objects for the sexual pleasure of males. That means women must make themselves attractive partners for sexual pleasure (as well as for reproduction). For many women, being attractive means being thin, and this value leads them to engage in various health-threatening behaviors, such as smoking, and eating disorders, particularly anorexia (voluntary starvation) and bulimia (binge purging). At least 90 percent of the diagnosed cases of these life-threatening disorders are females (www.nationalalcoholscreeningday.org/eat/eat-athlete.htm). Both anorexia and bulimia have tended to be treated as personal troubles, that is, as psychological and medical problems of individuals. Recently, however, more and more researchers have suggested that patriarchal values combined with corporations eager to cash in on the cult of thinness have promoted eating disorders based on the notion that "one can never be too rich or too thin" (Hesse-Biber, 1996; Poulton, 1997; Brand, 2000). Similarly, the tobacco industry aggressively promoted smoking to women as a weight-control tool, despite mounting evidence of its dangers, especially to women (Stauber and Rampton, 1995).

Thus, far from simply organizing society into a positive, unified structure that is beneficial to all members, norms and values may create an oppressive culture for some members. Such oppression may have dire consequences for those who are victimized by the culture. But the normative system is not all-powerful; there is often resistance to the oppression that some members of society may feel. (We will also discuss resistance to the dominant culture in this chapter's sections on subcultures and countercultures.) The question we now ask is: How do societies communicate and disseminate the prevailing normative system, and how do people challenge that system?

CULTURE AND LANGUAGE

Culture contains prevailing knowledge, or "facts" as a particular society construes them; beliefs and assumptions about the way the world works or ought to work; values defining what is important; customs and rituals; and symbols. Together, these elements are a society's **nonmaterial culture,** the body of abstractions defining the way its members think and live. A society's **material culture** consists of the physical artifacts that define the society, such as a style of dress, means of transportation and housing, popular music and food, currency, and so on. Material culture artifacts are items people select to bury in time capsules because they represent the current society for future generations to discover and learn about who we were and how we lived.

But even more powerful than the tangible items of material culture is nonmaterial culture, the abstractions that define who we are, what we value, what we believe, and so forth. The key to the abstractions of nonmaterial culture is **language.** Language consists of patterns of written symbols, audible sounds, and gestures that convey meanings. These meanings are usually shared by the members of a society, so when some members use them, others understand the gist of what is being communicated. Through the exchange of language members of society have access to experience and history beyond their own immediate time and place. It is not necessary to have lived in concentration camps in 1940s Germany to know about the Holocaust and its horrors or in Hiroshima in 1944 to appreciate the devastating effects of nuclear weapons. Nor is it necessary to put one's hands in a fire to learn that it burns. This is because language can categorize objects and events that share perceived or assumed common elements.

There are three main cultural functions of language: It can describe the world; it can create or construct individuals' vision of social reality; and it can be a vehicle to challenge and change social reality. Let's examine each of these functions.

Language: Describing the World

Language may simply describe the world around us. For example, people may categorize as wars all conflicts that attempt to resolve differences by means of violence, weapons, and bloodshed. Thus, even though people today were born after the American Revolution, the Civil War, and World War II, these are widely agreed to all be wars. It is not necessary to analyze why these wars occurred or who was right and who was wrong to understand that these were all wars, because they shared the common elements of violence, weapons, death, and conflicting interests. And this understanding may be extended to the present day, defining as wars such events as armed disputes between urban gangs, the invasion of Kuwait by Iraq, the extended conflicts in the Balkans and the Middle East, and the 2003 use of U.S. military forces against Iraq. Similarly, the word *war* is often used to describe policies and practices aimed at eradicating serious, objectionable situations, such as the war on drugs and the war on poverty. These share with the more common use the word *war* the underlying reality of the use of force and often violence to resolve the problem.

Language: Constructing Reality

Beyond simply reflecting reality, language can also *construct*, or define, reality (Berger and Luckmann, 1966; Sinke, 1999). This is in part because the structure of language contains hidden assumptions about the world around us. For example, the English language contains many implicit assumptions about gender abilities, worth and value, and appropriate behaviors and roles (Sorrels, 1983). When people use words like *fireman* and *congressman,* they are conjuring a mental image of a male, thereby constructing a reality that assumes that only men fight fires and serve in Congress. Such assumptions are similarly reinforced when people use gendered pronouns, such as "the doctor . . . he" and "the nurse . . . she" or "the teacher . . . she" and "the principal . . . he." Even the use of the generic *man* to refer to all of humanity constructs perceptions of a male as the normal embodiment of humanness. This may have the consequence of **symbolic annihilation**, or rendering females invisible and inconsequential (Tuchman, Daniels, and Benet, 1978). In contrast, words like *firefighter* and *congressperson* draw attention to the notion that females as well as males hold these positions.

In fact, anthropologists Edward Sapir (1949) and Benjamin Whorf (1956) suggested that people's understanding of the world around them can be limited by their language: They only know the world by the very words they learn and use, a view referred to as the **Sapir-Whorf hypothesis.** Thus, if an individual's language has only one word to describe economic deprivation, the wide range and degrees of the experience of insufficient money may become difficult to appreciate: Is the cash flow problem temporary or chronic, conscious and deliberate (as in a vow of poverty), or beyond one's control, crushingly fundamental so as to deprive one of the necessities of life or simply a limitation to one's ability to obtain luxuries? This power of language to restrict people's perceptions can be seen in the difficulty of translating ideas from one language to another because not all words or phrases have exact counterparts in all languages. Many a frustrated speaker can often be heard to say after a failed attempt to communicate between two languages, "It loses something in the translation!"

The power of language to construct social reality is captured in the **Thomas theorem,** or the **definition of the situation** (Thomas, 1928): If people define a situation as real, they will behave according to that belief, and the consequences of that definition will be quite real regardless of whether that definition is accurate. For example, if society accepts a definition of women as inferior to men, the consequences may be behavior that reinforces the definition as correct. Members of society, including school administrators, prospective employers, and those holding political power, may believe that women are incapable of tasks requiring intellect, independent initiative, authority, responsibility, and physical strength and stamina. The all-too-real consequences set in motion by this definition of the situation may be women's economic, social, and political disadvantage and deprivation (we will discuss sexism and gendered inequality in greater detail in Chapter 7). Because the very language suggests that men are superior to women, men are considered more qualified for leadership positions, jobs requiring skill and responsibility (which are frequently higher-paying jobs), and decision making in politics and the home. It doesn't matter if that viewpoint is inaccurate; what matters is that those in decision-making positions as well as many others in society believe it to be true and act on that belief; the consequences of their decisions, in unequal wages, unequal educational opportunities, and so forth, will be very real indeed (see Kleinman, 2002; Kleinman Ezzell, and Frost, 2009; Deutscher, 2010).

The idea that women are inferior in the culture is also expressed in the terminology many men traditionally apply to women—descriptive words such as *girls, dolls, broads, babes,* etc. When one executive says to another, "I'll have my girl call your girl," the statement renders both their administrative assistants inferior. Through one small sentence, each administrative assistant becomes a child, her boss's possession, and his servant. Thus, the Thomas theorem describes how language and ideas reinforce each other in the social construction of reality.

Language usage similarly reinforces stereotypes defining racially-linked perceptions. The use in the English language of *black* as a metaphor for "evil" and *white* as a descriptor of "good" and "pure" contributes to cultural images linking racially defined categories of people with such characteristics. For example, villains in film are commonly dressed in black and described as having a "black heart," while the heroes wear white and are described as "pure of heart." African Americans and other dark-skinned people become culturally defined as somehow inherently aggressive, violent, criminal, untrustworthy, and mean-spirited, while light-skinned people become culturally defined as inherently honest, fair, well-mannered, law-abiding, and well-intentioned.

Take, for example, the notable racialized captions on two news photographs in New Orleans after the devastating floods from Hurricane Katrina in 2005: Both showed hurricane victims in chest-deep water dragging plastic trash bags full of bread, milk, and other food they had retrieved from flood-ravaged local stores. The caption under the photograph of the white survivors referred to them as "residents" and said they had "found" food in the store to survive; the caption under the photograph of the black survivor did not refer to him as a resident and said that he had "looted" the store (www.huffingtonpost.com/van-jones/black-people-loot-food-wh_b_6614.html). These comparative captions are powerful in shaping perceptions: The white man and woman are survivors deserving of our sympathy while the black man is a criminal deserving of arrest and punishment.

Similarly, the words used to describe physical and mental impairment also construct individuals' perceptions of various human conditions and the people who have them. The term *handicapped person* implies that an individual who has a physical or mental disability is a "limited person" (Stroman, 1982: 47). The use of such wording defines the person in terms of her or his physical or mental disability and precludes the understanding that the disability is merely one aspect of an entire human being. This social construction affects how people without disabilities respond to those with a disability. People with disabilities are frequently seen as unattractive, unintelligent, immature, incapable of competently performing jobs requiring responsibility, unable to adequately parent children, and incapable of living independently. Replacing the term *handicapped person* with the phrase *person with a disability* reorients the social construction to one in which a specific impairment is seen as only a part of a person. Stroman (1982) suggests that "handicap" be reserved to describe the limitations that culture imposes on those with disabilities through stereotyping and labels. In doing so, Stroman acknowledges the power of language to socially construct reality, and he suggests using that power to *resist* the prevailing social constructions. By using noticeably different words, it is possible to call attention to the inadequacy of the words more commonly used and raise society's consciousness about the realities these words create. Thus, language can also be used to challenge or change culture.

Language: Vehicle for Change

The important role of language in the social construction of reality indicates that individuals who control language have the power to control culture. Those who determine the "appropriate" words for denoting various experiences and objects can strongly influence the way everyone else views the world around them, as well as their own place and the places of others in that world. Language is the means by which culture is passed on (including social constructions of advantage and disadvantage) from generation to generation and to new members of society. But language also allows people who are less powerful to introduce change into culture. As noted above, people can alter established social constructions by deliberately using common words in new ways or by generating new concepts that heighten society's awareness of the power of existing words (Hall and Bucholtz, 1995).

This is also what "politically correct" speech often does. Consider, for example, the effect of changes in the words used to refer to people of color in the United States. Until this century, men of color were commonly called "boy," a derisive pejorative term that dismissed their value as adult human beings. This socially constructed cultural consciousness helped shape the real consequence of denial of the rights and privileges normally accorded to eligible (i.e., white) adult men: voting rights, meaningful jobs (beyond slavery), education, and decent housing. By the 1960s, activists rejected the term "boy" (and its later much-abhorred pejoratives "colored" and "nigger") and instead worked to reframe the social construction of race in the use of "black" as a self-identifier infusing greater dignity and empowerment in a racially charged culture. More recently, many people have noted that "black" still focuses on skin color as a biological marker. Instead, they use the term *African American* to highlight the cultural history of kidnaping and enslavement that is distinct from all other, more voluntary immigrant groups. Notice that the change in words draws attention to different cultural issues and ideas, which in turn shape individuals' consciousness. The controversy over "politically correct" speech, then, may be a reflection of the power of language: Such use of language is a forceful expression of challenge and resistance to cultural assumptions favoring dominant groups (whites in this example).

CORPORATE CULTURE

The discussion of language indicates the ongoing struggle between dominant and subordinate members of society to socially construct reality or to challenge and change these. But what shapes the definition of what is important in society? That is, where do norms and values come from? At the beginning of the chapter, we introduced the idea that powerful groups in society are in a position to define society's norms and values. In the United States, values derive in part from the production and consumption of goods and services for profit. Cultural ideologies create relationships and structures that promote and enhance the production of private profit. Sociologists refer to this fundamental aspect of U.S. culture as the **corporate culture**. Corporate culture includes values based on the cult of **competitive individualism** (Cummings and del Taebel, 1978; Lipset, 1990), in which members of society are taught to believe that individuals are completely responsible for their own personal economic conditions. As such, economic success (wealth) or failure (poverty) is held to be the result of individual effort and competitive capabilities. Individuals who are wealthy are presumed to have earned their privileged economic position; if they did not deserve it, they would not have it. Similarly, many people believe that poor people deserve their poverty because of sloth, laziness, lack of motivation or initiative, or lack of competitive capabilities. If not for these personal failures, the poor would not be poor.

The notion that some people are poverty-stricken because of a lack of motivation to work hard, earn a living, or gain an education is called the **culture of poverty** (Lewis, 1959; Billings and Blee, 2000). This viewpoint assumes that the poor share a value system, or normative culture, that differs from mainstream norms and values because of the effect of poverty on their lives. According to this argument, the circumstances of being poor shapes people's adaptive strategies so that they come to value instant gratification, shun formal education, disrespect law and order, and adopt cynical attitudes about the value of hard work and effort (Banfield, 1974). And they are likely to pass these values along to their children, dooming several generations to be poor. The analysis implies that poverty permanently deprives the poor of any competing cultural input beyond their immediate environment, an implication often interpreted to suggest that the poor consciously embrace the value system of the culture of poverty and thus hinder their own ability to break out of the cycle of poverty.

Such was the ideological underpinning of welfare reforms of the 1990s in the United States. Since work was assumed to be the antidote to poverty, the poor would be coerced out of poverty by being cut off from welfare benefits and forced to adopt the presumably absent work ethic to work outside the home. Not only do such policies ignore the work ethic possessed by most poor people, the culture of poverty thesis does not consider the larger structural constraints that are important factors in producing poverty. For example, can valuing hard work and education ensure upward mobility for individuals if there are not enough jobs paying living wages for all the people who want and need these? Many adults who are poor work full-time, year-round, but the jobs pay so poorly that they are still unable to afford the bare essentials of survival.

In spite of this reality, the mainstream cultural appeal and the power of the ideology of "pulling oneself up by one's own bootstraps" and individual competitiveness remain quite strong. The success of transmitting mainstream values can be seen in public opinion polls regarding economic success issues. In a 2012 survey by Pew Research Center, although 65 percent of respondents recognized that most people who are poor work but can't earn enough money to avoid poverty, suggesting that poverty is beyond the control of individuals, a full 38 percent of these respondents still believed that people are poor because of a lack of effort (www.people-press. org/2012/06/04/section-3-values-about-economic-inequality-and-individual-opportunity). Apparently, even when a majority of people recognize the role that the economy and society play in generating poverty, most still believe that the poor are themselves to blame because of deficient personal characteristics. This contradiction indicates that the twin ideologies of culture of poverty and competitive individualism are powerful, pervasive, and tenacious, even in the face of contradictory information.

These ideologies, transmitted through schools and the workplace, support an acceptance of corporate culture and inhibit any independent thinking that might challenge these notions. For example, is it appropriate or accurate to consider economic achievement in terms of a competition that has winners and losers? Does each generation of contestants begin the competition on a level playing field regardless of their parents' or previous generations' economic positions? Might such a competition, in fact, be rigged at the outset, with some beginning with greater advantages to support success and others carrying heavy institutional hindrances throughout? Is individual effort the most important factor in determining economic success? Are there institutional arrangements and practices in the economy and the state that might shape opportunity structures, making individual effort less important?

The assumption that the affluent have worked hard and earned their wealth ignores that reality that many have likely inherited the wealth they currently enjoy from previous generations. Similarly, the level and quality of education many of the affluent have received, and the consequent good-paying jobs they currently hold, are frequently the result of the economic advantages their parents and grandparents were able to provide. As such, wealth is not necessarily earned by each generation anew, without benefit of the wealth of the previous generations; rather, each generation stands on the shoulders of the advantages of the generations that came before. In that way, individual effort is not the sole determinant of wealth or poverty; rather, the cumulative advantages or disadvantages of one's parents and grandparents structurally set the parameters of opportunities available. It is not that individuals' hard work and great value of education are irrelevant; but structured access to opportunities plays a significant role in affecting whether one will more easily remain poor or continue to be affluent.

The power of U.S. corporate culture is not necessarily restricted to the United States; it is disseminated to other cultures when firms go abroad in search of profits in new markets and when the relatively better-off in many countries seek to enjoy the lifestyle that seems to be accessible to so many in the United States. That is why McDonalds' golden arches can be found in Russia, Mexico, Japan, India, Israel, and many European countries. Coca-Cola and Pepsi ads can be seen all around the world in dozens of languages, as can the logos of many, if not most, of the Fortune 500 corporations.

Most of these firms not only sell products in an international marketplace; they also maintain manufacturing plants abroad, particularly in global south nations where labor can be exploited cheaply. Such inroads make possible a sharing of foods, music, and material goods, but they also spread corporate culture, in which generating profits takes precedence over other cultural norms and ideologies (Held et al., 1999). Sociologist George Ritzer refers to this exportation of U.S. corporate culture around the world and the consequent homogenization of global culture as the **"McDonaldization" of society** (Ritzer, 2012). This term does not mean simply that one corporation—McDonalds—is taking over the world. Rather, it suggests a more widespread issue of **cultural leveling,** in which the diverse and distinctive differences between cultures become blurred as they increasingly come to resemble each other because of the common, dominating presence of corporate culture.

Many countries encourage the presence of U.S. corporations as part of a conscious economic development strategy, but such strategies can also have an enormous cultural impact (Held et al., 1999). For example, corporate producers can disrupt agrarian cultures as land usage and labor activities shift from farming to manufacturing. Sunrises and sunsets, growing seasons, and weather patterns no longer mark the daily clock and annual calendar. Instead, the day and year are organized around the assembly line, production shifts, and workweeks, all dictated by the market for material goods. Rituals and norms associated with agriculture become less meaningful in the face of corporate culture. Less visible, but no less important, is the impact on family and community structures and cultural heritages. Rural farming and fishing communities can no longer compete with the economy of scale posed by large corporate agribusinesses and fisheries, so the community members leave in search of employment in overcrowded cities.

Notably, despite the powerful influence of corporate culture, it is not absolute or immune to change. As more individuals articulate criticisms and organize into action-oriented groups, the likelihood increases that there will be challenges to policies such as tax structures that favor the wealthy (we will discuss social change in Chapter 10).

AGENTS OF CULTURAL TRANSMISSION

How is it possible for members of a large society to learn the subtle and not-so-subtle values, norms, and rituals of the dominant culture? Which members have the power to transmit and impose their cultural assumptions on others? What mechanisms and processes enhance this transmission? Do these processes produce an all-powerful, dominant culture, or is there some degree of resistance, challenge, and diversity?

Several agents combine to facilitate transmission of the dominant group's culture, most notably, schools, the media, the workplace, and the toy, game, and recreation industries. Other agents may variably reinforce this process, including the family, religion, and peers. We shall deal with the processes and agents of cultural transmission, or socialization, in great detail in the next chapter and in Chapter 13 ("Education"). Here, we focus broadly on the special role that schools and the media play in reinforcing the dominant culture.

Mass Media

The mass media are major transmitters of culture. Television broadcasts entertainment that reflects stereotypes of acceptable and unacceptable behaviors and values across a wide range of dimensions, including race, class, gender, age, physical and mental ability, and sexual orientation. The format of the programs often invites viewers to laugh at, despise, or belittle cultures other than the dominant one in the United States. For example, *The Simpsons* has a running joke that depicts Pakistani immigrants as ignorant convenience-store owners and confused taxicab drivers. While broadcasters may be showing some sensitivity to how they present diversity, they have a very long way to go. By 2000, the National Association for the Advancement of Colored People and Latino groups began to publicly criticize the television and film industries for their inadequate representation of people of color in front of the cameras as well as behind them. Consequently, too few faces of color turn up in popular culture, and thus pejorative stereotypes are less likely to be challenged.

News programmers reflect the interests of society's major power groups—corporations and the wealthy, for example, in capitalist nations like the United States—in the stories they select as important, the subjects they choose for interviews, and the way they treat the stories they present. This is not surprising: The media are themselves controlled by major corporate entities and the primary sponsors of programming are corporate advertisers (McChesney, 1999, 2008; www.fair.org/extra/9711/gmg.html). Notably, in a survey of journalists 40 percent admitted that they deliberately refrained from reporting on important stories or "softened the tone" of reports "to avoid harming the financial interests of their own news organization or embarrassing an advertiser" (Pew Research Center for the People and the Press, 2000).

Television commercials encourage a materialistic consumer mentality, regardless of the necessity, safety, or effectiveness of products. Consider, for example, the controversies over the advertisements for highly sugared cereals and junk food that children watch along with their Saturday morning cartoons. (The cartoons, themselves, are often little more than half-hour commercials for toys, movies, and other merchandise related to the main characters of the shows.)

Researchers have long noted the power of commercials and the media to entice consumers to feel the need for products that may be unnecessary, ineffective, frivolous, beyond people's means, or even harmful. The modern world is dominated, both in print and electronic media, by corporate logos, advertisement jingles and catchphrases, and visual images that create a reality that contradicts and often undermines the everyday reality of the individual (Parenti, 1993, 2010; Turow and McAllister, 2009). Indeed, it is remarkable how many millions of viewers eagerly await the commercials aired during the Super Bowl broadcasts as forms of entertainment, often ignoring the powerful ability of these to shape our preferences and perceptions. In his examination of U.S. culture, *Culture Against Man*, Jules Henry describes advertising as "an expression of an irrational economy that has depended for survival on a fantastically high standard of living incorporated into the American mind as a moral imperative" (1963: 45). That is, people are encouraged to believe that it is their duty to maintain a very high level of consumption in order to support the economy. Limited personal budgets are not an obstacle: Credit cards help even those with relatively meager incomes to consume well beyond their means in order to make their contribution to this civic cause (Manning, 2000). Age apparently is no obstacle, either: The advertising industry now uses child psychologists to make advertising more effective by stimulating consumerism and demand among children (Solomon, www.fair.org/media_beat991007/html). Advertising creates a consumer culture in that it defines individuals' needs and then entices them to fulfill these by purchasing goods and services, an activity that is the lifeblood of capitalism. Indeed, referring to consumerism as a moral imperative is not so far-fetched: Experts proclaim that the U.S. economy was slow to rebound from the recession of the early 1990s and again in 2012 because consumers were not spending enough to fuel the recovery.

In *Who Rules America* (2009), G. William Domhoff examines what he calls the *ideology process*, the use of commercials, direct mailing, television-programming productions, and full-page newspaper ads to contour public opinion and the normative system (see also Dines, 1992b). Domhoff identifies as a major force the Advertising Council, an organization dominated by corporate interests. It sponsors conferences "where academics, journalists, and other cultural experts can brainstorm with corporate leaders about problems of ideology and public opinion," thereby helping to solidify the dominant ideology (Domhoff, 2009: 109).

The Advertising Council transmits an ideology favoring dominant interests to the rest of the population in its campaigns of advertising in the public interest. These commercial spots tend to promote the sanctity of free enterprise; to encourage voluntarism in groups like the Red Cross and United Fund (as opposed to pressing for corporate responsibility or state-funded social welfare programs), ignoring the fact that volunteerism and charity are often too haphazard and unpredictable methods to deal with serious need; to present pollution and conservation as problems of individual behavior rather than public issues of corporate misconduct, abuse, and responsibility; and to stress the importance of religion in American life. These issues and viewpoints are ones that the "corporate-dominated boards and advisory committees [of the Advertising Council] believe to be in the public interest" (Domhoff, 2002:108). Since the Advertising Council uses more than 80 percent of the public service airtime that television networks are required by law to provide, its ads, even if unsuccessful, still deprive viewers of exposure to opposing points of view.

On the other hand, when television producers are less dependent on corporate advertisers, they are freer to promote and reinforce values and norms that challenge corporate culture. For example, much of the funding for public television comes from membership dues and federal support. Therefore, it is easier for children's programs like *Sesame Street*, *Barney and Friends*, and *Dora the Explorer* to promote values of cooperation, sharing, acceptance of others, and racial and gender equality. It is not surprising to hear, then, that some advocate eliminating federal funding of public television, and instead making it more reliant on corporate sponsorship to survive. Imagine what could happen to its content were that to occur.

The media, as corporate entities, also tend to choose stories and present them in such a way as to manipulate public opinion about foreign policies that support corporate interests. This filtering process serves to stifle or at least marginalize dissent and to mobilize acceptance and support of corporate interests (Parenti, 1993, 2010; Chomsky, 1997). For example, the media may define victims of violence who challenge U.S. corporate dominance as "unworthy" of coverage and victims who are supportive of that dominance as "worthy" (Elias, 1986; Herman and Chomsky, 1988). Thus, the U.S. media loudly protested the injustice of the murder of a Polish priest ("worthy" victim) by the police in then-Communist Poland, but gave scant coverage to the murders of the archbishop of El Salvador and numerous clergy ("unworthy" victims) protesting treatment of the poor by landowners in El Salvador, killed by paramilitary troops who had been trained by Green Berets at Fort Bragg, North Carolina. Similarly, mainstream media coverage of the Tea Party in the United States sympathetically framed the group as a "grassroots" movement with clearly articulated legitimate issues, despite the evidence that it was bankrolled by the Koch Brothers (among the most affluent in the country); in contrast, the Occupy Wall Street movement was portrayed as unfocused, diffuse, and disruptive, deserving of the violence unleashed by police attempting to clear them from public space. The amount and kind of coverage accorded stories, then, influence perceptions of what U.S. interests are and, in turn, help "manufacture" citizens' consent to foreign as well as domestic policies consistent with corporate interests.

Schools

In addition to the media, schools are cultural-transmission agents. While there is a growing and powerful movement toward a multicultural perspective in curricula, teachers and boards of education often aid the transmission of dominant culture. They determine the subject matter and perspectives to be taught and then select the appropriate textbooks to support that curriculum. In the United States, this policy has often meant that both the curricula and the textbooks—for political and social history, literature, and science—emphasize the dominant white, male, Western perspective, ignoring or downplaying the contributions, and, at times, the very existence, of females, members of the working-class, people of color, or non-Western peoples (Loewen, 1995).

The movement in the United States to broaden and enrich curricula by making them more inclusive encourages teachers and textbook writers to adopt a perspective of **cultural relativity.** This perspective considers other cultures and their points of view as worthy of respect and understanding. It treats others' cultural practices as valid within their own context. More recently, however, there has been a shift to a perspective of **multiculturalism.** Whereas cultural relativity focuses on the perspective of another culture, multiculturalism acknowledges the heterogeneity within societies, examines the contributions and the intersection of many different groups at crucial moments in history, and explores the factors that differentially affect the experiences of each group. For example, cultural relativism might ask people to view slavery as supporting the economy of the southern United States in the 1800s and the profit "needs" of plantation owners. In contrast, a multicultural perspective invites individuals to explore the roles that each group played in the larger political economy and to examine the power differences between slaves and slaveholders. Thus, multiculturalism has brought about a shift in the New York State public school curriculum. The new approach no longer treats Christopher Columbus and the Spanish explorers as benign heroes and native populations as violent and uncivilized. Students are now exposed to primary and secondary sources describing the brutal and exploitative treatment of native populations by the explorers.

Schools in most, if not all, societies, regardless of their political or economic structure, reinforce the dominant culture of their society in addition to providing basic knowledge and skills. In their book *Schooling in Capitalist America* (1976), Bowles and Gintis describe how schools in U.S. society have historically sought to foster common ideological values and perspectives under the guise of mass public education. More often than not, they argued, what is taught are the *ideals* of democracy rather than the realities. Some schools today do encourage critical thinking and discussion about the difference between political ideals and reality. However, many of them still teach that the U.S. is a government of the people, by the people, and for the people, an oversimplified point of view that ignores existing power structures.

Schools can also transmit culture more subtly. In the very way they are structured, schools urge students to acquiesce to bureaucratic rules, regulations, and authorities. This encourages the students to accept authority outside of school as normal and legitimate. While one can debate how much authority children should have in schools, as well as whether all institutions can or should be run on strict democratic principles, it is noteworthy how schools themselves violate the virtues of democracy they extol in their curricula. They frequently violate students' right to privacy by searching their lockers for contraband, instituting random drug testing, and restricting students' freedom of expression in student publications (http://archive.aclu.org/issues/student/hmes.html). Student activism, however, sometimes succeeds in challenging such contradictions of democracy. In schools where they have learned the lessons of the Bill of Rights, students protest intrusions on their rights, and sometimes they win in the courts. Thus, they see the conflicts that are inherent in democratic societies and act to confront them.

Schools and the media often combine as cultural transmitters. Whittle Communications, for example, in 1989 introduced Channel One television, a news service, into public school systems in every state (except Nevada, Alaska, and Hawaii) and the District of Columbia (U.S. Congress: Senate, 1991; DeVaney, 1994). The schools received free media equipment from Whittle Communications in exchange for allowing 12 minutes of news each day plus 2 minutes of commercials to be aired in the classroom. Critics vehemently objected to using students as a captive audience for a barrage of messages promoting consumption (Apple, 1992; Greenberg and Brand, 1993). Many state boards of education—including those in New York, California, and North Carolina (Johnson, 1989; Mater, 1989; Walsh, 1990)—became convinced that Channel One was inappropriate and banned the broadcast from their public schools. Many other school systems, however, drawn by the attraction of free media equipment and a new medium for instruction, have invited the powerful cultural transmitter into their classrooms. By 2003, Channel One, then owned by K-III Communications., was being broadcast to over 8 million students in 12,000 middle- and high schools around the country (www.fair.org).

Channel One is hardly the first mechanism corporations have used to transmit corporate culture to schoolchildren. More than 3,000 large corporations regularly produce and distribute videos, films, posters, comic books, and coloring books to children in public schools (*Business Week*, 1980; Manning, 1999). Teachers faced with severely tight budgets are more than happy to have the free materials. These materials, however, often carry a hidden agenda, defending the legitimacy of various industries, extolling the virtues of their products, and narrowing the critical vision of students. Consider the math exercise book for third graders that uses Tootsie Rolls or M&M candies to teach counting; a business course for elementary and middle school students that demonstrates the value of work by exploring "how McDonald's restaurants are run" (Manning, 1999:11); a scoreboard at a football stadium or basketball gym supported by corporate sponsors whose logos and advertisements dominate the vision of all who wish to see the score; computers donated by corporate sponsors that ensure no student will log on without having to see a barrage of corporate ads; or a school bus whose sides are covered with corporate ads, as are the walls in the halls and cafeteria of the school, bombarding students with corporate culture throughout their day.

Corporate culture has made similar inroads into higher education, as corporations increasingly become major providers of research funding, endowments, and faculty chairs, underwriters of campus athletics and social events as well as financiers of campus buildings and laboratories. That crucial economic role increasingly positions corporations to wield tremendous power to affect curriculum and knowledge production decisions that are more traditionally covered by the norms of academic freedom of individual professors and scholars (Aronowitz, 1998; 2000; Croissant, 2001; Washburn, 2006). For example, a major corporation may use its role as provider of research grants to influence the kind of scholarship researchers pursue, the development of courses that are consistent with its needs (often to the detriment of more critical courses which do not), exerting editorial control over the production and publication of scholarship, and so forth (Press and Washburn, 2000; Washburn, 2006). Thus, the central role economic institutions play in society enables them to influence other institutions like education and to shape them so as to promote and disseminate cultural norms and values that are consistent with business interests. Corporate culture, then, becomes the product of that power.

SUBCULTURES

We have so far discussed culture as a single, powerful national phenomenon that everyone experiences. However, there is cultural variation *within* society. While there may very well be a prevailing dominant culture, people are not necessarily bound to it or forced to conform like powerless robots. Rather, they can experience a great deal of diversity within society and its dominant culture. A wide variety of groups exist whose members participate in the larger society and its institutions while they simultaneously share values, norms, heritages, and rituals that differ from those of the dominant culture. Sociologists call these groups **subcultures.** Members of subcultures do not necessarily reject the dominant culture, but they embrace their own subculture as valid and important even as they participate in the dominant culture.

Subcultures can be based on a variety of factors, including religion, race, ethnicity, age, economic circumstances, and sexual orientation. Gay male and lesbian subcultures have flourished in large urban areas and in smaller towns (often university towns) where there are meeting places and organizations to support their social and political activities. A loose national network provides information about supportive, thriving gay and lesbian communities. Thus, while gay males and lesbians are active participants in the dominant culture—in jobs, educational and religious institutions, and politics at all levels—they often also participate in a subculture containing shared norms and values that support the legitimacy of their sexual orientation.

Age subcultures also thrive in the United States. Communities of middle-class and wealthy retirees, particularly in the warmer climates of Florida and Arizona and in 55+ communities all around the United States, continue to multiply. Residents' lifestyles are arranged around leisure activities and healthcare issues and information. Restaurants in such communities typically provide health-conscious menus and less costly early evening meals ("early bird specials"). Support groups abound for widows and widowers, for people with critically ill partners, and for those who are critically ill themselves. So do clubs and organizations that offer opportunities to meet other retirees, information regarding retirement benefits and entitlements, and chances to get involved in political issues affecting senior citizens. Some planned retirement communities and condominiums maintain social activities and classes and develop "blue books" establishing norms to govern residents' behaviors, including restrictions on the minimum age of residents and on the maximum length of visits by younger people (especially if they bring young children with them).

Similarly, college campuses often become age subcultures. Large segments of the population roughly between ages 17 and 23 (and often older, if there are large numbers of returning military veterans and graduate students) are concentrated in dorms, going to classes together, joining campus clubs and academic and Greek societies, participating in athletic teams and attending games, and engaging in campus activities. While they may embrace the subculture of college students, they still participate in the dominant cultural institutions: They often vote, work part-time jobs, and retain family ties.

Economic circumstances can also impose a subcultural existence on people. Elliot Liebow's study, *Tally's Corner* (1967), and that of Elijah Anderson, *A Place on the Corner* (2003), used research methods of participant observation to examine how poverty and unemployment structured the lives of the men in two different city neighborhoods. The loss of self-esteem caused by inadequate job opportunities created the subculture of the street corner, where men gathered whose lives were characterized by shaky and failed marriages, sometimes by illegal activities, and often by shallow and fluid relationships (because of evictions from homes, prison terms, migrations in search of jobs, and so on). The men did not willingly embrace a culture of poverty. Rather, they were thrust into the street-corner subculture by poverty and by limited or nonexistent opportunities that marginalized them from mainstream society and made them appear unmotivated to settle down.

The economic circumstances of the men in Mitchell Duneier's participant observation study, *Slim's Table* (1992), were clearly better than those of the men in Liebow's and Anderson's studies: These working-class African American men in Chicago had jobs. Every day at about the same time "the regulars" stopped into the Valois cafeteria to break up the monotony of the workday for cheap home-cooked food and, more importantly, to hang out together with the other regulars, sharing stories, offering mutual support, and providing meaning about life's challenges. Like the men on Tally's Corner and Anderson's street corner, the subculture that the men at Valois created by hanging out together was carved out of the intersecting experiences of their work, class, race, gender, and families. Thus, while they may have had a greater sense of choice because of their more comfortable economic status than the men in the other two studies, their subculture was just as structured by economic and social circumstances.

In addition to economic and social factors, subcultures are often also structured by norms and **rituals** (regularly practiced formal ceremonies, usually marking important personal or social events). Many ethnic and religious groups observe rituals and holidays and share folkways of foods, dances, music, and other everyday habits that are part of their ethnic heritage. For example, Jews who participate fully in American political, economic, and social life often still observe Passover and Hanukkah (Festival of Lights), as well as other Jewish holidays. Orthodox

Jews observe their Sabbath even as they participate in the secular world: They leave work early on Friday to get home before sundown, and they avoid the use of electricity until sundown on Saturday. Many Jewish children become bar mitzvahs (boys) and bat mitzvahs (girls) at age 13 as a rite of passage to adulthood. Participants at such events typically dance the *hora*, a spirited dance of joy and celebration. Each Jewish holiday and ritual is marked by a remembrance of history and custom, a reaffirmation of heritage and roots, and a recommitment to maintaining that connection. At the same time, Jews live and fully participate in the larger, non-Jewish society and culture.

It is not always easy for subcultures to maintain such clear and solid connections to their heritage. Jews in the former Soviet Union had to practice their religion in secrecy or not at all. There is a long history of persecution and attempted genocide of Jews, from Jewish enslavement under Pharaoh to banishment and oppression during the Spanish Inquisition to extermination during the Holocaust. And in the United States and in many places around the world today, Jews continue to be the object of serious anti-Semitism. The results of a 2011 survey by the Anti-Defamation League indicate that 15 percent of the people in the United States harbor negative attitudes toward and stereotypes about Jews (an increase from 12 percent in 1998). Respondents' belief that Jews have too much power has also increased, growing from only 13 percent in 1998 to nearly 18 percent by 2011. While these figures indicate that anti-Semitic attitudes are relatively low they are showing a resurgent animosity toward Jews. (Anti-Defamation League, 2011, www.adl.org/PresRele/ASUS_12/6154_12.htm). It is clearly a difficult challenge for the subculture of Jews in the United States to maintain their heritage in such an improving but still hostile atmosphere.

Many ethnic groups have similar histories of oppression; two examples are Native Americans and African Americans. African Americans' ancestors were kidnapped from their tribes in Africa and sold as slaves in colonial America. Torn from their cultures, and unable to communicate with slaves from other tribes who spoke different languages, many lost their cultural connections. Only through concerted, conscious efforts by many African Americans have some threads of African culture been retrieved and nurtured by embracing folkways that emphasize the subcultures' validity. Many African Americans, for example, celebrate Kwanzaa, a festival held to reinforce and honor African heritage according to the principles of unity, self-determination, collective work and responsibility, cooperative economics, purpose, creativity, and faith. During this holiday, celebrants may wear traditional African dress; decorate their homes in the African colors of red, black, and green; arrange a table centerpiece containing the symbols of the harvest and of children; and share a feast with traditional African music and dancing in tribute to their ancestors. Some African Americans have changed their Anglo-American names to Muslim or African ones; prominent examples are writer and civil rights activist Kwame Toure (formerly Stokely Carmichael), boxing legend Muhammad Ali (born Cassius Clay), and basketball great Kareem Abdul-Jabbar (born Lew Alcindor). African crafts (such as batik), music, and dance are increasingly introduced in concert halls, community centers, and schools in African American neighborhoods as vivid reminders of the importance of the African American culture. And an increasing number of students have begun attending graduation ceremonies with a thin, multicolored shawl draped over the traditional cap and gown indicating African unity and pride.

Native Americans have also had to work militantly to preserve their heritage, all but obliterated by the genocidal westward expansion of the dominant white population in the United

States (see LaDuke, 1999). The remaining members of the various Native American nations are recapturing the rituals, spiritual practices, folk medicine, language, dance, norms, dress, and material aspects of their culture (such as pottery, jewelry making, textiles, and architecture).

The ability of ethnic and religious subcultures to piece together and preserve their often-threatened or lost cultural heritages is a testament to their strength and resilience. Indeed, many such subcultures are now so well preserved and maintained that their members often bring parts of their subcultures with them as they participate in the larger society. Such sharing by a wide variety of subcultures diversifies and enriches the larger society. In this way, even dominant cultures can change over time as they adapt to the new cultural elements. Sociologists refer to the gradual sharing and incorporation of a diversity of cultures into the dominant culture as **cultural diffusion.**

Many aspects of this diffusion can be seen in the mainstream culture of the United States. For example, rock music popular in youth subculture is now often used in product commercials. And fashions frequently borrow and incorporate styles from other cultures. In their 1993 line of men's clothing, designers in New York City featured the "Hassidic look": simple black suits, plain-brimmed hats, and long, white, fringed scarves, which constitute the conventional dress of many Orthodox Jewish men. Indian saris and bindhis were popularized in the United States by pop culture figures like Madonna and Gwen Stefani in the late 1990s. Foods of many ethnic subcultures have become standard American fare: pizza from Italy, frankfurters from Germany, tacos from Mexico, sushi from Japan, falafel from the Middle East, and so on. American music and dance incorporates salsa from Latin America; reggae and ska from the Caribbean; jazz, rap, hip-hop, and blues from African American culture; and zydeco from black Creoles. The noted pop and rock star Paul Simon deliberately uses the music forms and instruments of black South African groups and Latin American and Caribbean cultures in his mainstream music. And many schools in the United States have changed their Christmas parties to "winter holiday celebrations," in which children often learn Hanukkah, winter solstice, and, on occasion, Kwanzaa songs in addition to the more traditional Christmas carols. Note, however, that the cultural forms absorbed from subcultures are relatively innocuous. The norms that still prevail tend to be those established by the dominant groups in society. In order to thrive, then, a subculture must maintain its identity apart from and in addition to the mainstream culture.

Sometimes dominant groups adopt aspects of subcultures as a safety valve mechanism. Doing so reduces the probability of open hostility and challenge to the dominant culture. For example, Arizona initially refused to recognize Dr. Martin Luther King Jr.'s birthday as a state holiday. That decision evoked protest marches and boycotts, all of which stopped when the state finally reversed its position and adopted the holiday in 1992. A similar struggle erupted in 2000 in Wallingford, Connecticut. Including King's birthday in the dominant culture of Arizona and Connecticut calmed race relations and reduced the probability that hostile challenges to the state would escalate.

Changes in cultures are not necessarily swift or immediate, however. There is often a lapse between the time a new subculture, technology, or idea is introduced and the time it is accepted and incorporated into the existing dominant culture. Sociologists refer to this time gap as **cultural lag.** For example, the civil rights movement has succeeded in getting legislation passed that legally protects people of color from discrimination. However, the notion that they are equal to whites is still not fully accepted by all. This is not to say that racism in the United States is impossible to eradicate, but the concept of cultural lag points to how the more innocuous aspects of African American culture can become incorporated into the dominant culture while African Americans themselves still struggle against racism in the mainstream.

COUNTERCULTURES

Dominant corporate and wealthy interests shape U.S. culture, particularly its norms and values. However, in spite of this pervasive influence, the persistence of subcultures suggests that the power of such interests is not absolute. Even more telling is the persistence of **countercultures.** A counterculture is a specific type of subculture whose members embrace values, norms, rituals, and lifestyles that directly challenge the dominant culture. Whereas members of other subcultures participate in both the dominant culture and their particular subculture, members of countercultures reject the mainstream and challenge its pressures to conform.

The best-known, relatively recent example of a counterculture is the "hippie" movement of the late 1960s and early 1970s. Members of this loose counterculture denounced the legitimacy of the corporate culture and rejected its values of a button-down 9-to-5 work ethic and competitive individualism, its emphasis on private property and the amassing of material goods ("conspicuous consumption"), its norms of state violence and aggression as means of resolving conflicts and threats (both domestically and internationally), and its reliance on modern technologies that threaten the environment. Moreover, the counterculture rejected mainstream norms of exclusivity in sexual relationships and the right of the state to legislate individual behaviors such as drug use. In essence, the counterculture challenged what it referred to as "the Establishment." Many in the movement were young people who joined urban collectives and rural communes to jointly produce or buy their own food, communally raise their children, eschew the "rat race" of traditional jobs, foster cooperation instead of competition, and drastically reduce or eliminate their reliance on technology. Many communes also endorsed illicit drug use and nonnormative sexual practices. Ironically, many communes reverted to sexist divisions of labor, relegating household chores and childcare largely to women. Many also developed mainstream patriarchal power structures, with men dominating the decision-making process. While not all communes replicated mainstream sexism, its presence in some countercultural settings suggests the powerful influence mainstream norms and values can have.

Gangs can also be seen as countercultures. They tend to emerge from poverty and disenfranchisement from the mainstream's economic, social, and political opportunity structures. In the United States, where the Census Bureau indicates that 22.7 percent of African American families and 22.7 percent of Latino families live below the poverty line, it is not surprising to find that 49 percent of gang members are Latino and 35 percent are African American (www.nationalgangcenter.gov/About/FAQ#q11; www.census.gov). There are also several very active Asian American gangs in New York, Los Angeles, and other major cities (Huff, 1996; Vigil, 1997).

Gangs come in a variety of forms, including social gangs, neighborhood street gangs, and organized-crime gangs. Our discussion here will focus mostly on the neighborhood street gangs. Many of these have spread from specific urban neighborhoods to other neighborhoods, entire cities, or more suburban areas. These gangs often use illegal weapons and violence to commit crimes and control neighborhoods.

Gangs are typically organizations of alienated youths whose experiences remind them that the mainstream culture disdains and disrespects them. Gang members are frequently poorly educated and many live in substandard housing. They are chronically unemployed because urban education systems often do not provide adequate skills training and because there are fewer and fewer jobs for those without such training. Youth gangs can be seen as a countercultural response to blocked opportunities (Long and Ricard, 1996; Sheldon, Tracy, and Brown, 1997). But gangs are not necessarily only typical among poor, urban minorities; increasingly, gangs are emerging in more affluent white suburbs where youth alienation and stagnated opportunities combine with the romanticized portrayal of gangs in movies and videos as icons of rebellion and empowerment to appeal to and attract a wider audience (Monti, 1994; Wooden, 1995). Gangs reject many of the values and norms of the mainstream and form their own often violent and predatory countercultures. For example, dominant cultural norms stipulate that only the state can use force and violence to resolve disputes and that individuals must settle conflicts through negotiations or legal processes. Gangs challenge this notion by brazenly investing powers of violence with individual members. Gang violence also repudiates mainstream norms that call for deference to institutional authorities, such as those in schools and in the criminal justice system; it becomes a means of eliciting a semblance of respect, based on fear, from other gang members as well as the larger community. Gangs often respond to the unavailability of jobs in the mainstream economy by participating in drug trafficking, which can be lucrative although highly dangerous. Larceny and robbery may also be part of gang activity (Hagedorn, 1998; Anderson, 1999).

Gangs reject mainstream culture in more symbolic ways as well. For example, their members' dress (such as the widespread use of bandanas as "colors" identifying gang affiliation), hairstyles, tattoos, and language defy the dominant folkways. Gangs also represent an alternative to mainstream definitions of family as one's unit of procreation and parentage. The gang itself becomes an extended family providing protection as well as approval and support for delinquent and violent acts not accepted by the larger society (Kaplan, Johnson, and Bailey, 1987; Clark, 1991), or acts as a surrogate family when even the opportunity for developing the more traditional form itself becomes more difficult to achieve (Moore and Hagedorn, 1996). (We will discuss family structures in greater detail in Chapter 13.)

In a unique participant observation study of several female gangs in New York City, Campbell (1991) showed how such gangs reject the dominant culture's restrictive gender roles and establish their independence through the use of violence. While she disagreed with the notion that female gangs represent a counterculture, her descriptions of three of them suggest otherwise. For example, her findings indicate that female gangs will not accept members who are not able to "take care of themselves." Prospective members must demonstrate that they are willing and able to engage in a fight. In some instances, once the gangs have established this ability, members are initiated into the gang in a violent ritual called "jumping in." In this initiation they must endure (and perhaps defend themselves against) severe beatings by other gang members for a period of 10 seconds.

Members in the gangs also form strong ties with other members; they do not allow men to come between the "sisters." Members frequently demand extreme loyalty to the gang, over and above boyfriends and even family. Female gangs thus repudiate the mainstream gender prescriptions of females as docile and dependent and as antagonistic rivals.

In some ways, gangs provide an interesting demonstration of how a counterculture can, in fact, embrace dominant cultural values while establishing very different and challenging norms. For example, gangs often accept the mainstream value of economic success and all the material comforts such success affords. But when faced with blocked opportunities, the gangs resort to their own norms for acquiring wealth, such as drug trafficking, robbery, larceny, and extortion of "protection" money from local small businesses (Clark, 1991). Some gangs have spread beyond the local "turf" battles and have organized "franchises" in many cities. These intercity franchises facilitate the movement of stolen goods and drugs. The national network this creates frustrates law enforcement agencies, which have tried in vain to control such gang activities. Gangs' countercultures thus become a parody of mainstream values, even as the gangs adopt normative behaviors that defy the legitimacy of the dominant culture.

CHAPTER SUMMARY

Do people who control wealth and production also control culture? If so, how is diversity possible? Is the dominant value system fixed and inflexible, or can people's efforts, individually and collectively, make a difference?

- Culture is a social construction created by members of society. But not all members' viewpoints concerning values and norms are equally powerful in influencing the contours of mainstream culture. Since culture is transmitted from one generation to another, those members who have enjoyed prior privilege, advantage, and power are in a stronger position than others to impose their values and norms on everyone else. Similarly, since culture is diffused from one society to another, those societies with greater power and advantage are better able to influence the cultures of others.

- Mainstream culture shapes individuals' biographies by defining what is acceptable and unacceptable and what is normal and abnormal in regard to behavior and life circumstances. People's vision of legitimate alternatives becomes narrowed by these culturally defined restrictions. In addition, punishments for violations of these norms may reduce the likelihood that people will challenge existing rules and guidelines and may sometimes prevent them from even considering alternatives. Individuals who depart from the dominant culture may be marginalized and condemned by members of mainstream society.

- Language, as the key to cultural transmission, is a powerful vehicle for constructing reality. Individuals who control what constitutes legitimate language usage can significantly influence the definitions of appropriate and inappropriate behaviors, viewpoints, and values. They can also shape what people consider to be real and viable and what never even occurs to them as possible.

Does this mean, then, that the less powerful members of society are unable to resist the imposition of dominant groups' culture? Does this mean that the forces of cultural domination and cultural hegemony are absolute and all-powerful? Hardly.

- Although the ideas, values, and norms of dominant groups tend to define the dominant culture, cultural diversity and resistance can still exist. The persistence of subcultures, for example, testifies to the fact that diverse values and normative systems can thrive even as the members of the subcultures participate in the mainstream culture. And the presence of countercultures illustrates the power of human effort to challenge and reject mainstream, dominant norms, and values and to push at their boundaries. Moreover, while language may be the key to the social construction of reality by society's dominant members, it may also be used by the less powerful to sharpen people's consciousness about that social construction and to introduce new ways of seeing the world and ultimately helping to change the dominant culture.

- Culture, then, is not simply a static body of ideas and practices handed down unchanged from one generation to the next. It is a dynamic process of power struggles and contested constructions of social reality involving various members of society. While all members of society may know what the dominant definitions of reality might be, subordinate members of society do not necessarily accept these without question; they are likely to engage in struggles to challenge dominant conceptions. These struggles are part of an ongoing historical process in which groups possessing variable resources and abilities strive to articulate and preserve the legitimacy of their social worlds. We will examine this process of organized struggle over the social construction of reality and cultural content in Chapter 10 ("Social Change and Social Movements").

 ## THINKING CRITICALLY

1. Many immigrants and descendents of immigrants express an internal struggle to balance their ethnic identity with their status as an American citizen. Consider your own ethnic heritage. Do you have similar conflicts? What does it mean to be an "American"? Is it necessary to give up your ethnic identity in order to be fully "American"?

2. Many variables may contribute to the development of a subculture. Consider the variety of statuses you have. Which of these might shape a subcultural existence for you? Why? Describe the elements of your subculture that depart from mainstream culture. Do these differences draw sanctions from the larger normative system? Why?

3. Think about situations you have encountered in which the norms differed significantly from those with which you are familiar. How did you react? Why? What norms did these differences define for you?

4. Consider the textbooks, ideas, and materials to which you were exposed in elementary school and high school. Make a list of the images, ideas, norms, and values focused upon in your schools. How closely did they conform to mainstream culture, and how much did they challenge it? Were you invited to debate the ideas presented in the classrooms and in the texts? How? How were uninvited challenges received?

5. Much debate has centered on the notion of "politically correct" language. What is politically correct language? What values does such language invoke? Why might there be considerable resistance to the use of politically correct language? What role does such language play in society? Select a "politically correct" term and explore how it might challenge dominant conceptions.

KEY TERMS

culture   **97**

ideology   **97**

cultural hegemony   **97**

norms   **98**

normative indoctrination   **99**

culture shock   **99**

ethnocentrism   **99**

sanctions   **100**

folkways   **100**

mores   **100**

laws   **101**

values   **102**

patriarchy   **00**

nonmaterial culture   **104**

material culture   **104**

language   **105**

symbolic annihilation   **105**

Sapir-Whorf hypothesis   **106**

Thomas theorem (definition of the situation)   **106**

corporate culture   **108**

competitive individualism   **108**

culture of poverty   **108**

"McDonaldization" of society   **110**

cultural leveling   **110**

cultural relativity   **113**

multiculturalism   **113**

subculture   **115**

rituals   **116**

cultural diffusion   **118**

cultural lag   **118**

counterculture   **119**

SOCIALIZATION

6

When you entered your first college class, you probably knew that you had to take a seat in the classroom rather than sit at the desk in front of the room, take out a notebook and a pen or a laptop computer to take notes, raise your hand to speak rather than simply call out, don't talk on your cellphone during class, and come to class dressed in clothing like jeans and a shirt rather than a bathing suit or pajamas. You also are likely to hold certain attitudes about what you expect of others in your environment: You expect that if you're the first to arrive in the lecture hall you may select any seat you wish; the next person to enter the room may also select any seat, but not the one right next to yours, and not the one you have selected. You may also have some ideas about what your classmates should look like and about whom you would consider a good candidate for a date. And you are likely to have some ideas about what you might like to do when you graduate, and what are your realistic options. How do you know all of this, and where did you get these ideas from?

Sociologists have long recognized that social attitudes and behaviors such as these are learned because of the great variability in cultural patterns throughout the world. As members of a society, individuals learn and adopt social attitudes. Such attitudes are not genetically programmed; people learn them. Are your attitudes similar to or different from those of your friends, your family, or your teachers?

Answer the following questions as honestly as you can: If one person of a two-earner couple has to quit work and remain home because of a family situation, how should the couple decide which person will quit? Do you believe the United States is full of opportunity for anyone willing to work hard? Would you hesitate to marry someone who has a physical disability? Would you be willing to go to war if the president asked you to, even if you didn't understand the reasons for U.S. involvement? What if you didn't agree with the reasons? Suppose you wanted to lease your home to tenants and you receive two similar offers, one from a female-headed family and one from a two-parent family. Which one would you rent your house to, and why? Should the school board of your child's elementary school be permitted to hire a kindergarten teacher who happens to be gay? Suppose you are on the admissions board of a prestigious medical school, and you have one opening left. Two applicants come before you with similar grades and board exam scores. One is the daughter of an unemployed coal miner, and the other is the son of a congressperson. Which applicant will you admit? Would you buy a home in a neighborhood in which most people were not of your race? Should legal marriage be possible for gay males or lesbians? Should capital punishment be abolished? Should retirement be mandatory for everyone at age 65? Your responses reflect your attitudes on a number of social issues. People are not born genetically programmed with such attitudes; these are learned. This raises several questions about their origins:

- How does this learning occur?
- Who does the teaching?
- To what degree is the individual a passive recipient in this process?
- Can an individual transform the persons doing the teaching?
- What sorts of social roles and identities do people learn?
- What are the possible limitations to the process?

This chapter will examine how sociologists have studied the learning process sociologists call socialization.

SOCIALIZATION AS A LEARNING PROCESS

Human beings are social animals by nature and are among the most dependent of animals at birth: When humans are born, the muscles, nervous system, skeletal, and digestive system are not fully developed, and individuals cannot care for themselves. People rely on other humans to nurture and protect them. But the need for other human beings does not end when individuals learn to walk and feed themselves; it is a lifelong, cradle-to-grave process.

Moreover, along the way to addressing their needs over the course of a lifetime, individuals become members of society, finding their place in the world around them and discovering what is and is not expected of them. The ongoing process of learning the ways of one's culture is called **socialization.** During this lifelong process, individuals acquire and modify their social identities. People learn, accept, reject, and modify the norms, values, assumptions, and expectations of the societies in which they live. Finally, members of society develop the political lenses through which they view and analyze their surroundings.

Social scientists often debate the relationship between what people inherit and what they learn. Sociologists call this the **nature versus nurture debate.** Some sociologists argue that many social behaviors appear to be inherited genetically (for example, intelligence and the capacity to learn, aggression or passivity, and sexual orientation) (Kagan, Resnick, and Snidman, 1988). The study of the biological basis of social behavior is known as **sociobiology.** Other sociologists view social characteristics as primarily socially constructed, influenced by such environmental factors as power in relationships and learning. If social traits were biologically determined, they say, such immense variation within families and societies and between cultures in social behaviors and attitudes would be unlikely, and it would be unnecessary to teach and reinforce these (Wilson, 2000).

Yet studies of twins separated at birth and raised apart suggest that some social traits may develop independently of individuals' social environment: Such twins often exhibit surprisingly similar traits, such as shyness, in spite of very different upbringings and surroundings (Bouchard and McGue, 1990). How can the contradictions of evidence in the nature versus nurture debate be reconciled? Many sociologists take a middle ground. They argue that while the *potential* for expressing some social traits may indeed be inherited, striking evidence shows that social characteristics are unlikely to develop without social interaction between individuals as well as between individuals and a variety of social agents.

For example, children deprived of social contacts do not thrive physically and tend to be socially and emotionally immature. Such is often the case with institutionalized children (Cermak and Groza, 1998). In fact, even when infants in institutions are given the best basic care in terms of food, clothing, hygiene, and shelter, their social development is slow at best without regular play and human interaction (Cummins and Dunt, 1988). Such was the case of Anna, an illegitimate child whose mother, fearful of her grandfather's fury, kept the child in an attic where she was fed but otherwise largely ignored. When she was found, she was a 6-year-old child who could not even sit up, much less walk, and she could not talk; she was unable to express any emotion, other than to bite the social workers who worked with her (Davis, 1940). In another case, Genie's father locked her away before she was 2 years old in an isolated room with no human contact beyond the brief visits by family to bring her food. She remained locked away for 11 years, until her mother, herself abused by Genie's father, escaped and took Genie with her. Like Anna, Genie could not speak or stand up straight, and could only walk in the clumsy fashion of a toddler; she was not toilet-trained, and her emotional expression was confined largely to animal-like noises. Doctors described her as primitive and barely human (Curtiss, 1977).

Adults who are similarly deprived as Anna and Genie, such as prisoners in solitary confinement for long periods of time, tend to regress to infantile behaviors (for example, assuming a fetal position and thumb sucking). These cases suggest that the provision of the basic physical needs for survival such as food and water is not sufficient to ensure social or even physical development of the human being in the absence of human contact.

Notably, evidence suggests that children who were deprived of social interaction early in their lives improve in language, social skills, and muscle control when stimulated by increased human contact (Scarr, 1982). In the case of Anna described above, social workers intensively provided interaction and care, and within four years she was able to talk and attempt conversations, and could perform basic functions of daily life, such as brushing her teeth and washing her hands, keeping her clothing clean, walking, and even running. Her emotional range increased regularly (Davis, 1948). Genie showed similar progress once under the intensive care of social workers and physicians. Although both children's eventual development was well behind that of most children of their ages, their astonishing progress highlights the essential importance of human interaction for developing and reinforcing social characteristics. However, they do not tell us exactly *how* individuals learn to adopt certain attitudes and behaviors. In short, how do individuals become members of society? What is the *process* of socialization? Who participates in this process, and what role do they play?

SYMBOLIC INTERACTIONIST PERSPECTIVE

Several theorists maintain that individuals develop social identities through **symbolic interaction,** an interpersonal process using language, symbols, reinforcement and sanctions. It is through that interaction process that individuals come to learn the values and norms of their society: They learn how to behave, what to think, and what to expect of others. Let's look, for example, at what this might entail for some sociologists.

Charles Horton Cooley: The Looking Glass Self

The sociologist Charles Horton Cooley (1902) argued that people acquire a sense of who they are by evaluating themselves through the eyes of others, imagining how these others might react to a particular behavior. He calls this identity the **looking-glass self.** People see themselves as they believe others see them, perhaps altering behaviors they believe others disapprove of. Cooley argued that these others need not be present during this process; people's assumptions and ideas of how they are likely to react are sufficient. For example, when you wish to speak in class, you know you should raise your hand and wait to be called upon, and then avoid using slang and profane words. You do not need a specific teacher in front of you to tell you this every semester and for every class; you become aware over the years as a student that this is what is expected of you, and you are likely to act accordingly.

Cooley's analysis of the looking-glass self did not distinguish among the various others whose perceptions individuals anticipate. Are the opinions of all others equally important to people when they see themselves through others' eyes? Some sociologists, like George Herbert Mead did not think so.

George Herbert Mead: Significant and Generalized Others

Sociologist George Herbert Mead (1934) believed that the child's primary-group relationships (e.g., family, peers) were crucial, as **significant others,** to the development of the self. Harry Stack Sullivan (1953) later argued that the most important primary group member is the mother, who becomes the child's significant other. Since an infant is so dependent on its mother for nurturance and survival, he argued, the mother becomes uniquely important to the child; her judgment and approval are critical in developing the child's sense of self and identity. Later, researchers found that fathers are also significant (Lamb, 1997). In fact, anyone who functions as a child's primary caregiver may be viewed as the significant other. Such persons could be grandparents and other family members, foster or adoptive parents, daycare workers, and so on (Pooley et al., 2000).

As the child matures, the process of acquiring social identity and self-awareness extends to play. For example, children try on a variety of roles through dress-up and playacting. As they mature further, children develop a generalized understanding of how people around them expect them to behave and of what their place is among those people through role-playing. They no longer need the actual presence of known individuals in order to understand their own roles and identities. They now evaluate their behavior through a **generalized other.** Here, play and pretend are highlighted as critical elements in social development (Barnett, 1977).

Mead's analysis speaks of the process of shaping a sense of self as if it occurs only in children. In fact, many different significant others, people who are vitally important to individuals in their daily existence, may appear throughout the life cycle. Anyone who is centrally important to individuals at a particular point in their lives—on-the-job mentors, for example, or coaches, advisers, or partners—may take on the role of significant other. Indeed, many couples in the United States refer to each other one as "my significant other." Some researchers argue that a significant other does not even have to be someone with whom the individual is intimate; nor does it have to be another person at all. For example, television may act as significant other for some people (Newton and Buck, 1985). For others, some notion of a spiritual higher being is sufficient.

Mead's analysis of how individuals acquire social identities suggests that the process of self-development is reflexive, involving the individual as an active agent rather than as a passive recipient. That is, developing a self-identity involves an interaction "between identification by others and self-identification, between objectively assigned and subjectively appropriated identity" (Berger and Luckmann, 1966: 132). Thus, socialization subjects may resist or reject others' definitions of "appropriate" behaviors. However, the focus in Mead's analysis remains the socialization subject. This focus implies that the socialization process moves in one direction only: The agent socializes the subject.

Symbolic Interaction as a Dynamic Process

More recent analyses using a symbolic interaction perspective suggest that the interaction process is a dynamic one: *Both* parties get socialized rather than just one; adults get socialized as well as children. For example, although parents and other primary caregivers may indeed teach the child about appropriate behaviors, the child may also socialize the caregivers, altering their behaviors, values, or attitudes (Peterson and Rollins, 1987). When labor and management engage in negotiations, management is certainly attempting to indoctrinate the workers about appropriate attitudes and behaviors, but the workers are also teaching management about appropriate interaction and bargaining styles, acceptable demand levels, and so forth. Both parties are in fact altering their behavior patterns. Even when one party is clearly more powerful than the other, that power is not absolute. There is usually some room for each side to modify its position in response to the socialization it has undergone.

CONFLICT PERSPECTIVE

Sociologists using a **conflict perspective** argue that socialization processes are, in fact, typified by struggles. Conflict theorists examine the internal as well as external struggles experienced in the process of socialization. They also tend to view socialization as ongoing throughout the life cycle. As individuals encounter new situations and challenges in their lives, they are always shaping and reshaping their social identities. As they move from school to the work world or from single life to marriage, for example, people learn new sets of expectations, some of which may challenge previous social constructions of themselves. Even though some statuses (for example, race and, usually, sex) do not change, people's sense of what they mean may change over time. Other statuses may actually change (such as age, family status, working status, sexual orientation, and physical and mental capacities and capabilities), prompting a personal reconceptualization of self and a reevaluation of expectations. Conflict theorists argue that as people confront and resolve these changes and challenges, they form and redefine their social identity.

Conflict in Social Psychological Explanations

Learning a social identity and how to interact in society is not a smooth or easy process. Many observers have noted how rife with conflict such learning can be. For example, the noted psychologist Sigmund Freud (1946) described a conflict between a primitive, almost feral self that he called the **id** in unsocialized infants, a driving, self-centered force that compels individuals to focus on their own personal pleasure. While the need to satisfy personal demands for pleasure is biologically natural, he argued, it is quite at odds with the requirements of the larger society: Social norms largely do not accept public displays of sexual gratification or defecation on public streets, even if these are widely acknowledged as satisfying actions. People learn to control the urge for instant gratification, primarily by parents setting limits and punishing children's failure to remain within those limits identifying appropriate times and places for satisfaction of personal pleasures. That learning process helps establish the development of the **ego,** or what Freud defined as the rational self that controls the urges of the id. Freud argued that the individual also develops a **superego,** or conscience, as a result of this learning process. Even in the absence of a punishing other to help remind the ego to control the id, the superego functions as that restraining force. Here, the superego is the internalized parental voice, reinforcing the limiting rules of social behavior. The individual's personality and social behavior is thus the site of constant conflict between the id, the ego, and the superego.

Where Freud's analysis emphasized how children become socialized into social beings, in his *Eight Stages of Psychological Development*, psychologist Erik Erikson (1963) argued that individuals develop their identities and attitudes about the world throughout the entire life cycle as they resolve various developmental conflicts and crises. Although he specified the life stages during which each crisis typically occurs, he argued that individuals may always return to earlier crises and rework them or complete unresolved ones. How people resolve these crises shapes their social identities (see Figure 6.1).

The basic conflict during infancy concerns reliance on others to provide food, shelter, protection, and comfort. Infants resolve this problem by developing either *basic trust* or *basic mistrust* that the world around them can be counted on to provide consistently for their needs. Toddlers encountering challenges of personal control (for example, during toilet training) resolve their crisis with either a *sense of autonomy*, if control is mastered, or a *sense of shame and doubt*, if control proves difficult to achieve. Preschool children, whose main challenge is to learn to perform basic tasks independently, develop either a *sense of initiative* born of successful attempts at mastery or a *sense of guilt* from repeated failures. Older children confront increasingly challenging academic

Figure 6.1: Erickson's Stages of Psychosocial Development: Erik Erikson underscored the role of culture in personality development throughout the life cycle. Consider your own personality development: Which development stages are you currently struggling with?

Old Age	Integrity versus Despair
Maturity	Generativity versus Stagnation
Young Adulthood	Intimacy versus Isolation
Adolescence	Identity versus Role Confusion
School Age	Industry versus Inferiority
Preschool	Initiative versus Guilt
Early Childhood	Autonomy versus Shame, Doubt
Infancy	Trust versus Mistrust

(*Source:* Adapted from Erik Erikson, *Childhood and Society*, 2nd ed, New York: W.W.Norton & Company Inc., 1950.)

and physical skills. If they learn that mastery of these skills involves the often frustrating process of trying, failing, and trying again, they are more likely to develop a *sense of industry* and a willingness to work through failures. If they learn that not mastering a task immediately is a personal failing and a character flaw, they are more likely to develop a *sense of inferiority*. Adolescents face the challenge of establishing a clear definition of self. Success in defining "who I am" resolves the crisis with a *sense of identity;* failure to resolve the identity crisis may result in *role confusion.*

Beyond adolescence, Erikson saw three more crises. Young adults face the tension of establishing close personal relationships, many of which may not last for very long. Such crises resolve either in a *sense of intimacy* and a willingness to make one's self vulnerable to another or in a *sense of isolation* and a refusal or reluctance to risk getting close to others. Adults must resolve the crisis of maintaining a *sense of generativity*, involving productiveness and growth, or they may develop a *sense of stagnation*, of being in a rut or not being challenged or excited about their work or lifestyles. Elderly adults, particularly at retirement, resolve the crisis of identity shift either with a *sense of integrity*, feeling they have performed well and lived a good life, or a *sense of despair*, feeling they have wasted their lives or lost sight of their goals. For Erikson, then, identity development is a lifelong process, never fully completed, and often dialectical in nature: Previous crises may be revisited and reworked even as one moves into the next developmental crisis.

Conflict in Structural Explanations

Freud's and Erikson's analyses certainly emphasized conflicts in socialization of individuals as social members of society, but they focused on individuals' psychological processes. In contrast, W.E.B. Du Bois (1989/1903) examined the conflicts resulting from the intersection between identity processes and larger social structures and relationships. He argued that African Americans commonly formed dual, sometimes "warring" identities separated by what he referred to as a *veil.* As strategy for survival in a racist world, the veil allows African American individuals to see themselves as black persons with an individual consciousness, but also to see themselves through white eyes. This does not mean the individual forgets that he or she is African American; but racialized power inequalities require African American people to be conscious of how whites are likely to see them and expect them to behave and to conform to racist expectations, such as deference to whites, as a matter of survival. This is because whites control so much that can affect African Americans' life chances, including jobs, housing, education, healthcare, legal justice, and so forth. The veil functions to preserve and protect the African American identity for expression in safe and supportive circumstances and to send that identity underground in more threatening situations. This dual identity, he argued, produces "this peculiar sensation, this double-consciousness, this sense of always looking at one's self through the eyes of another" (1989/1903:5). A similar analysis of this double consciousness can also be seen among Asian Americans (Min, 1996; Spickard, 1997).

While Cooley spoke of the looking-glass self affecting all individuals in their identity formation, Du Bois referred to the conflict that specifically affects the identity of persons of color in a white-dominated society. In Du Bois' analysis, perceptions of the (white) "other" are likely to devalue the worth of the individual's identity because of racist stereotypes and assumptions rather than the actual behavior of the individual and to have the power to make those assumptions matter. The concept of the veil, then, highlights both the internal conflicts individuals struggle within the development of a general social identity and the external conflicts between the person of color and the white-dominated world in which they must live in particular.

Further complicating the conflict surrounding the development of identity is the rise in multiracial identities. Increasingly, sociologists are recognizing that previous social constructions of racial identity as matters of black vs. white (which later broadened to include categories of Latino/a, Asian American and Pacific Island, and Native American) are no longer valid. Individuals' identities are often defined more by overlaps of a wide range of ethnic and racial backgrounds and heritages as a result of immigration and intermarriage (Root, 1996). This means that identity formation is frequently marked by conflicts in the negotiations between sharply different cultures and loyalties (Hall and duGay, 1996). Du Bois' veil is likely to produce not just a double consciousness, but a more complicated multiple consciousness. The logistics of maintaining several such identities is surely characterized by heightened tension and conflicts as individuals seek to develop positive multiracial identities in a white-dominated society. At least one study, on the other hand, has found that many individuals find multiracial identity actually liberates them rather than isolates and marginalizes them, because their membership in several racial and ethnic groups broadens their social consciousness and makes them wiser and more socially astute. In such cases, race is no longer a matter of imposed social constructions; rather, race is *chosen* by individuals (Korgen, 1998).

SOCIALIZATION, CONFLICT, AND SOCIAL STRUCTURE

Erikson's and Du Bois' analyses introduce conflict rather than consensus as the central characteristic of the socialization process. However, Erikson's model is based on the assumption that specific roles and tasks belong to particular life stages, and it defines success and failure narrowly. And because of Erikson's psychoanalytical perspective, his analysis assumes psychosocial development to be more a personal problem of individual struggles and conflicts than the result of structural restrictions. For example, if an adolescent girl is told she cannot participate in football because she is not strong enough, the feeling of inferiority she might develop would be seen as the result of a personal failure to resolve a developmental crisis. Yet it seems more likely that her feeling of inferiority would be the result of systematic discrimination and differential treatment in the social structure, a point emphasized by Du Bois. Sometimes both personal and social elements are at work. Consider an elderly woman who feels a sense of despair. She may have failed to resolve some personal crises, but she also may feel the burden of a social structure that limits her opportunities, perhaps sharply reduces her income, restricts her access to outlets for usefulness, narrowly defines her roles, and accords senior citizens little respect.

Looking at the role of both internal and institutional conflicts suggests that the process of identity development does not necessarily produce a uniform outcome for all. Some people may, in fact, resist and reject the dominant group's definition of appropriate and inappropriate behaviors. What happens in such cases? In some instances, sanctions may be imposed to punish or correct the "inappropriate" behavior. For example, homosexuals, whose very existence violates the prevailing more of heterosexuality, often suffer the intense sanctions of being ostracized or harassed, denied employment, or fired. Children who display "gender-inappropriate" behaviors may be called names, ostracized by their peers, and "redirected" by guidance counselors who try to steer them to more "appropriate" behaviors and aspirations. Those who violate the mores against intimate interracial relationships may also experience similar sanctions.

When informal sanctions are insufficient to alter an individual's resistance, dominant groups may sometimes attempt to reeducate, or resocialize, the transgressor. **Resocialization** is a process in which the individual's previous self is dismantled and replaced with a new, more acceptable social identity (Fein, 1990; Ichilov, 2002). Sometimes individuals undergoing resocialization may be relocated to entirely new and unfamiliar locations called **total institutions,** in which they are completely isolated from the rest of society as well as from their ordinary surroundings and social networks for an extended period of time. In such environments the individual's life is carefully controlled and the process of resocialization more easily accomplished (Goffman, 1961).

New military recruits experience this situation in boot camp, where they undergo a fairly intense process of resocialization designed to break down civilian values of individuality, freedom of expression, and freedom of choice and replace them with new values. The recruits learn to accept orders unquestioningly, to subordinate individuality to country or troop, and to respect rank, the flag, and the uniform. They learn to accept narrowly defined conceptions of appropriate dress and hairstyles and to suspend personal opinions concerning a broad variety of issues, both personal and global. In some cases, the process may involve a **degradation ceremony,** in which socialization agents assail and devalue the subject's existing identity in an effort to break it down and build an entirely new one (Garfinkel, 1956). For example, drill instructors in military boot camp may publicly call resistant or struggling recruits pejorative names or challenge the manhood of male recruits by referring to them by women's names and attributing feminine characteristics to them. Officers may penalize the recruits by assigning them to publicly demeaning chores such as cleaning bathrooms with a toothbrush, or denying them privileges such as leave time. Goffman (1961) found that similar processes occur among prisoners and patients at state mental hospitals.

Resocialization may also occur in more subtle ways. Changes in life circumstances can bring about transformations of one's social identity. For example, no total-institution setting is required for the changes that accompany the shifts from student to worker, from child-free person to parent, from worker to retiree, and so on.

At the same time that individuals develop a social identity, they also undergo a constant process of **political socialization.** In this process they may internalize a political identity of who they are and how they should behave in the political and economic institutions of society. Moreover, individuals may learn to accept the dominant social structure and its inequalities as just, fair, and legitimate. Socialization, then, can be a means of political control, in which the dominant group may influence and shape individuals' perceptions of acceptable or appropriate political attitudes and behaviors (for example, voting is an acceptable way to express dissatisfaction, but rioting is not), limit their conception of valid options for action, and legitimize its rule and ideology.

AGENTS OF SOCIALIZATION

How do people come to be socially and politically socialized? Who or what are the agents of socialization? **Socialization agents** can be grouped into primary groups such as family members and peers; secondary groups such as schools, religious and work organizations; mass media and language usage; toys, games, and recreational activities; and institutions such as the state. As we pointed out in Chapter 3, institutions operate to address the functional imperatives of societal survival as their manifest function. One of these is to teach the knowledge and skills necessary to be contributing members of society, and to motivate members to perform their roles. Those institutions that perform this function are clearly agents of socialization. But socialization can also produce latent consequences as the institutions address the basic imperatives; the development of social identities is not the manifest function of institutions as socialization agents, but it is a latent function. Let's look at how some socialization agents may prompt this latent consequence.

Families

Just as *families* reinforce "appropriate" social and gender roles, some observers also believe that birth order acts as a passive socialization agent (Steelman and Powell, 1985): One's birth-order position in the family may greatly affect siblings' interactions as well as parent–child interactions. These interactions become part of one's socialization experiences.

For example, firstborn children (if they are not twins) tend to be more strictly disciplined, to receive more attention, to remain in school longer, and to be higher achievers than later-born siblings. With second-born children, parents are more relaxed and tend to be less authoritative; such children may therefore have more relaxed relationships with others and be more playful than firstborns. Second-born children may also be more diplomatic negotiators than firstborns, because they are smaller than older siblings (at least when they are very young) and must therefore rely more on reason and rationality than on brute strength. It is important to note, however, that these social characteristics are based on a middle-class model of the family. Birth-order characteristics may be complicated by such factors as the age and spacing of siblings and parents' differential expectations based on gender, class, ethnicity, and family structure (Kilbride, Johnson, and Streissguth, 1977).

Peer Groups

Peer groups constitute an alternative **reference group** to family members. A reference groups is a group to whom individuals look for approval, guidance, and role models. Peer groups may be an important factor influencing study habits, work aspirations, and lifestyle goals (Allen, McManus, and Russell, 1999). Children and adolescents often develop a greater sense of autonomy from adults by forming coalitions with peers (see McClellan and Pugh, 1999). In extreme cases, gangs and other countercultural groups may develop to challenge authority. Adults who work together often form informal groups of peers that may counteract and contradict rules of managers or corporate culture (see Chapter 5).

People who are subject to systematic prejudice or disapproval may look to peers to help resist being stigmatized and reinforce the validity of their autonomy. For example, the many formal and informal gay and lesbian peer groups found in high schools, colleges, and urban areas serve this dual purpose. Students of color on predominantly white campuses frequently look to peer groups to affirm their validity in the dominant group's culture. And women often form peer groups as a way to countervail patriarchal treatment and share information and strategies that challenge the prevailing attitudes toward women's appropriate roles, rights, and abilities.

Schools

Schools reproduce the dominant culture of society by socializing students about what is valued and appropriate in the culture and what is not (Spyrou, 2000; Rodden, 2001). For example, curricula and texts that stress white, male, privileged European contributions to U.S. society and ignore the legitimacy of contributions of people of color, women, and the working-class reproduce a limited set of cultural values (Deegan, 1998; Parker, 2001). In-school celebration of Christian holidays (such as Christmas) but not of other ethnic or religious groups' holidays (such as Hanukkah, Kwanzaa, or winter solstice) makes Christianity seem more valuable and legitimate than other credos. Likewise, if schools honor Washington's and Lincoln's birthdays, but not Dr. Martin Luther King's birthday, they teach children that King's contributions to U.S. society are less important. The celebration of the dominant groups' culture and the failure to acknowledge the importance of others may socialize whites and Christians to an identity of superiority and privilege while socializing people of color and non-Christians to an identity of marginality and inferiority, and contribute to their symbolic annihilation as "the other."

Similarly, the dramatic rise of daycare as a common feature of many preschoolers' day increases the role of these facilities as socialization agents. Daycare teachers have the potential, as surrogate parents for at least part of the day, to teach very young children core values. While taking turns, sharing, resolving conflicts without violence, and developing good manners are among the common themes many daycare centers foster, attitudes related to gender, race, and class position may also be transmitted by teachers.

Religious Organizations

Religious organizations socialize us to adopt particular attitudes and behaviors, which may or may not be consistent with the dominant culture. For example, an ideology that stresses sacrifice and asceticism, obedience to a higher authority, acceptance of one's lot in life as part of a plan of that higher authority, heterosexual love and marriage, tradition, and hard work is consistent with the values of the dominant culture in the United States. These principles contribute to a social identity based on conformity, which makes it less likely that oppressed or exploited groups subject to this ideology will challenge the authority and privilege of the dominant groups.

On the other hand, some religious teachings stress a refusal to accept poverty, challenge higher authorities if they are oppressive or punitive, civil disobedience, and the legitimacy of nontraditional lifestyles. This religious position has occurred as a social movement in Latin American Catholic churches, where it is referred to as **liberation theology.** This theology may pose a countervailing influence to dominant socialization forces. Indeed, in parts of Mexico, and in Central and South America, the poor are encouraged by local clergy to believe that it is entirely appropriate to challenge landowners and political authorities who oppress and starve them, deprive them of dignity and civil and human rights, and otherwise abuse them.

In the United States, African American churches played a pivotal role in the civil rights movement from the 1950s to 1970s. Unitarian and mainline Protestant denominational churches have come to recognize the legitimacy of women as clergy, and many Conservative, Reform, and Reconstructionist Jewish synagogues have come to accept female rabbis. The Episcopal Church now accepts priests who are homosexual and has generally played an active role in the gay, lesbian, bisexual and transgender movement. Religious organizations throughout the world were often visible and vocal opponents to the Vietnam War, giving legitimacy to such opposition. More recently, churches in the United States have provided asylum for Central American refugees escaping oppression by their governments. Not only have these churches provided refugees with food, clothing, and shelter, but they have also protected them from deportation by U.S. immigration authorities. The participation of religious institutions in the antiwar and asylum movements lends institutional support to people who challenge their governments, both here and abroad. Religious doctrine, then, can contribute to a social identity that includes the entitlement to protest and challenge oppression. It can also contribute to a social identity based on a notion of social justice and altruism.

The Workplace

The *workplace* acts as both a formal and an informal socialization agent, reinforcing capitalist social relations of production. For example, on-the-job training is a formal mechanism of workplace socialization, in which one is taught rules, regulations, expectations of behavior, and recognition of authority figures and status symbols. Individuals who train closely with a mentor tend to become dependent on the mentor, and therefore more susceptible to influence (Shire, 1999).

Training in groups can produce a team spirit that reinforces dominant workplace values. For example, military training in boot camp emphasizes the importance of duty to country, a strong sense of "us" against "them," and the necessity of a buddy system for survival against a common enemy. Corporate softball and bowling teams similarly reinforce many similar principles and create a sense of family and loyalty among the workers for that firm.

Group training can, however, also produce camaraderie among trainees *against* corporate and military authority figures and become a source of resistance to the workplace organization. For example, during the Vietnam War, there were frequent instances of apparent violent retaliation by recruits against abusive or overzealous officers. Assembly-line workers may develop group loyalty to one another in the face of exploitative or overly harsh management, devising ways to set more comfortable rates of productivity and, in extreme cases, sabotaging output. Computer hacking is now emerging as a new form of corporate sabotage, sometimes involving the dissemination of sensitive information about executives and managers whom workers view as dictatorial or arbitrary. While these examples describe conflicts between workers and management, group training can sometimes also produce intragroup forces to conform. The classic Hawthorne studies discussed in Chapter 4 revealed how an informal group of workers punished those whose productivity exceeded the group's informally set rate. The group also covered for colleagues whose productivity fell short for various reasons (Roethlisberger and Dickson, 1939).

Some have noted gender biases in on-the-job training and interaction patterns, such as mentor relationships. Employers place men in advantageous interaction systems more frequently than they do women; the men thus become part of a network tapped for promotion opportunities. Such gender differentiation in training and work opportunities serves to reproduce stereotypical gender differences.

The Media

Media are very powerful, pervasive agents of socialization. Television can play a positive role in the development of language and reading readiness skills, as well as the assimilation of basic arithmetic facts. Programs like *Sesame Street*, in particular, have been highly successful in this area. In addition, *Sesame Street*, *Barney*, and *Dora the Explorer* promote prosocial values like cooperation, helping others, sharing, and self-control.

On the other hand, much debate centers on the effects of media violence on anti-social behaviors (Barker and Petley, 1997; Dudley, 1999; Gunter and Daly, 2012; Martins and Wilson, 2012). Some studies have found that early and frequent television viewing is associated with increased aggression in children and teenagers (Barry, 1993; Cannon, 1993; Boxer et al., 2009;). Many observers agree that the increasing level of violence in both television programs and films teaches viewers of all ages that brute force and violence are acceptable and appropriate avenues for redressing grievances and solving problems and desensitizes the viewer to the horrors of violence (Grossman and DeGaetano, 1999). Some evidence suggests that programming containing violence particularly targeted against women tends to heighten women's feelings of vulnerability and lack of power (Reid and Finchilescu, 1995). Such perspectives can alter women's freedom of movement as they seek to protect themselves from perceived threats to which they may be subjected because they are female.

The power of media may also come from what they do *not* show. By limiting the kinds of people viewers see, especially in positive roles, largely to white, middle class, heterosexual, able-bodied men, the media contribute to **symbolic annihilation** (Tuchman et al., 1978), or "the absence of experience of a group of people in the media" (Lont, 2001:119). When individuals see few people of color, women, gays and lesbians, people with disabilities, or the poor, or hear few of their voices talking about their experiences as valid, it suggests that these people do not exist or are unimportant. While this can happen in other settings besides media, it is especially important in media, since this is such a significant source of information for many people and is so widely accessible.

Evidence suggests that the proportion of females and people of color in media is improving, but still has a long way to go. For example, in the Writers Guild of America, West analyzed the diversity of writers working at 190 broadcast and cable television programs in 2011–2012. They found that writers of color (primarily Asian and Latino/a) "nearly doubled" over the past decade from 7.5 percent to 15.6 percent, and women writers increased from 25 percent to 30.5 percent. As encouraging as that increasing diversity is, however, the study noted that "minorities remained disproportionately underrepresented by a factor of more than 2 to 1 in television staff employment" (Verrier, 2013:D3). Moreover, white males still held three-fourths of the executive producer positions. These figures suggest that the likelihood of diversity in scripts and roles would remain relatively minimal, contributing to the symbolic annihilation of women and people of color.

As influential as media can be, however, there are limits to their power in shaping individuals' identities. For example, while adolescents may not necessarily be able to choose to avoid exposure to the socialization information provided by their parents, schools, and religious organizations, they do have much greater power to select which media messages and information they consume. And the easy availability of social media may act as a potential source of resistance and challenge. As a result, individuals may be more able to "self-socialize" with challenging or contradictory information, values, norms, etc., thereby minimizing the power of other socialization agents (Arnett, 1995).

Toys, Games, and Recreation

In addition to the usual components of media (such as films, television, newspapers, magazines, and the Internet), *toys, games, and recreational activities* serve as socialization agents (Fromberg and Bergen, 1998). Individuals learn much about cultural values from the rules and concepts of various board games. For example, Monopoly rewards greed and cutthroat competition: The winner is the player who bankrupts all the other players. The game of Risk, with its goal of world domination, rewards aggression. Other games also reinforce prevailing social values. Trivial Pursuit rewards the ability to spit back odd bits and pieces of memorized information rather than the ability to present a coherent, critical analysis of a problem.

While most board games and sports tend to emphasize the concepts of competition and winning and losing, some do stress cooperation. For example, Bertel Ollman's game Class Struggle and the more recent Co-opoly sought to deliberately counter Monopoly by rewarding cooperation and an organized struggle against capitalism (interestingly, no major toy company would market the game). Group games of jump rope, particularly Double Dutch, succeed only when everyone cooperates to keep the game going by ensuring that the rope turns with a constant rhythm and accommodates the jumper. And while team sports emphasize competition between teams, they also reinforce the notion of cooperation for the common good among the team members.

Children remain fairly creative in how they approach games, however, and that creativity may pose limits to the power toys and games may have in forcing them to acquire their intended values and norms. Children often alter the rules provided by the makers of manufactured games, sometimes changing the rules mid-game, and sometimes creating entirely new games using the basic pieces out of the box. Further, the interaction process of play provides opportunities for children to actively explore and question the rules, the apparent use of toys (such as doctor kits, kitchen sets, and black dolls by white children), and the meanings of these (Best, 1998).

The State

Finally, *the state* itself is an important socialization agent in its efforts to eliminate "deviance." Laws formally codify the norms of dominant groups, such that noncompliance is likely to be sanctioned with the loss of rights and freedoms, resources, and rewards. For example, welfare reform laws, passed by the affluent and predicated on the false assumption that poverty is caused by individual laziness and a lack of a work ethic, ultimately require recipients of welfare to accept whatever work is available regardless of pay, hours, or lack of benefits. Should a mother whose family receives welfare object (often because there are preschool children or ill family members needing care at home), the state reserves the right to deny her and her children aid.

Similarly, the state normatively defines legitimate political action as voting. Those who violate that norm by participating in protests and demonstrations are often subject to intense state sanctions by police: pepper spray, tear gas, rubber bullets, arrests, beatings, and sometimes death. Witness, for example, the treatment of civil rights demonstrators during the 1960s who were attacked by police using powerful fire hoses. Antiwar demonstrators at Jackson State and Kent State Universities in 1970 were shot at and killed by the National Guard. More recently, demonstrators against the World Trade Organization in Seattle in 1999 and Occupy Wall Street demonstrators in 2012 received the full force of the state's power and violence in an effort to punish and disperse protestors and discourage future demonstrations.

Interestingly, sometimes gendered norms prohibit the social control agents from resorting to force and violence: No use of tear gas or pepper spray, or arrests, marked the Million

Mom March against guns and violence on Washington, DC, in 2000. Motherhood norms hinder the state from viewing women with babies as threatening and from using the level of violence against them more commonly used against primarily male demonstrators. On the other hand, older women without young children in tow do not necessarily receive such restrained response: Witness the octogenarian woman who was pepper-sprayed directly in her face when police sought to evict Occupy Wall Street demonstrators in Oakland.

Taken together, these socialization agents tend to encourage the adoption of dominant values and norms. But beyond a general assimilation of cultural norms and values, what specific roles do these agents socialize us to internalize? There is evidence that they work to reinforce and reproduce roles and identities relating to class, gender, and race, as well as roles and attitudes concerning political values and norms.

CLASS SOCIALIZATION

Families, workplaces, and schools play an important part in class socialization, reproducing and perpetuating class positions and roles. Consider the different socialization processes undergone by professional, technical, and managerial workers, on the one hand, and blue-collar, clerical, and service workers, on the other. The latter operate in a work environment that requires little autonomy or creative initiative. They are rewarded for accepting orders and following directions. Professional, managerial, and technical workers are more likely to get rewards for exercising autonomy, independence, creativity, and initiative in decision making and problem solving (Kohn, 1977). These differential work experiences and reward structures reproduce class differences: they affect how these workers view themselves as well as how their children perceive them as role models (Grant and Sleeter, 1988).

Family

Class differences may persist because parents strive to prepare their children for the work world they are likely to join when they become adults (Majoribanks, 1987). This preparation for future roles is what sociologists call **anticipatory socialization** (Mortimer and Simmons, 1978). Research shows, for example, that the higher parents' socioeconomic status, the more likely they are to emphasize independence in socializing their children, a reflection in part of the presumed qualities needed for the occupations of managers and professionals such children are anticipated to fill. In comparison, parents with lower socioeconomic status are more likely to emphasize obedience in socializing their children, a quality characteristic of rank and file or non-managerial jobs requiring workers to follow the orders of managers and supervisors (Flanagan, 1999). Research also suggests that this pattern is often affected by gender. One study found that middle-class African American women's parents held higher expectations for them than the parents of working-class African American women held for their daughters (Hill, 1997). These different levels of expectations are likely to affect how parents prepare their daughters for their future roles, be they in the workforce or in the home.

Some researchers have noted, however, that class-based differences are declining as middle-class and working-class child-rearing practices become more similar (Alwin, 1984; Amato and Fowler, 2002). Why is this convergence taking place now? It may well be that shrinking working-class opportunities in manufacturing and increasing middle-class opportunities in lower-paying service sector jobs may be making the work experiences of both more similar: Both contend with work that is likely to offer low pay, few benefits, and little job stability. This is escalating in the aftermath of the Great Recession of 2008–2012. In addition, increasing reliance by firms on contingency or temporary work for skilled and managerial workers makes the work world of the middle and upper-middle classes more like that of the part-time and seasonal workers in the service sector. As such, parents' perceptions of the probable work world their children will face may very well be increasingly similar, and this in turn may affect how they socialize their children.

Schools

Schools also participate in socializing children for their future roles in the labor market. Teachers and guidance counselors make assumptions concerning appropriate future education or work roles for students and therefore appropriate curriculum tracks. Affluent students sent to private prep schools are prepared to assume power positions, while students in public schools are more likely to be prepared for following such leaders (Brint, 1998; see also Burke and Attridge, 2011). The class membership, race, and gender of a student may influence school staff more than his or her actual skills and talents (Grant and Sleeter, 1988). Teachers and counselors also tend to emphasize varying degrees of obedience, the necessity to follow rules and take direction, and independent thinking (Franklin, 1986). School officials tend to reward behaviors that they see as consistent with perceptions of future roles; inconsistent behaviors are punished. Taken together, these forces operate to perpetuate differential class positions.

Differential treatment of students on the basis of class becomes a **self-fulfilling prophecy**, a phenomenon in which people achieve to the level expected of them rather than to the level of which they may actually be capable. As such, when teachers assume that poor and working-class children are not capable of achieving high academic performances expected of middle-class and affluent children, it is likely to produce poor performance and feelings of inferiority among lower-class and working-class children (Rosenthal and Jacobson, 1992; Rhem, 1999). Indeed, even when working class and poverty-stricken students succeed later in life as educators and researchers holding advanced degrees, they frequently express feelings of the **imposter syndrome**, of somehow having fooled those around them into thinking that they are deserving of recognition, respect, and acceptance (Ryan and Sackrey, 1984; Morris and Grimes, 1996), and harbor an often debilitating fear of being uncovered as a fraud.

GENDER SOCIALIZATION

Many socialization agents are important forces in the shaping of gender identities. They therefore contribute significantly to reproducing conventional gender roles.

Family

Families may reproduce gender roles by overtly assigning different household chores along traditional gendered lines: Girls babysit, cook, and wash dishes; boys take out garbage and do yard work (Burns and Homel, 1989). Different parental expectations for academic performance may also reinforce gendered differences. Parents often send their children messages about male and female abilities and appropriate future work roles (Howard and Hollander, 1997). Similar gendered information frequently crosses cultural divides around the world (Harkness and Super, 1996). Noted one observer, "girls are raised to 'keep the home fires burning.' Boys are raised to do battle" (Abbott, 1998:1).

The division of household chores between parents also sends a powerful message to children about gendered domestic work roles (Cunningham, 2001). Studies indicate that women do the majority of domestic labor, thereby defining it as women's responsibility (Demo and Acock, 1993). Even when women work full-time outside the home, they still perform most of the household chores, a situation some observers have referred to as the, **second shift** (Hochschild with Machung, 1997; Stohs, 2000). Such role models teach children that the appropriate behavior for women includes cooking, cleaning, and caring for children, regardless of the time spent working outside the home. Similarly, they imply that a man's appropriate role is that of paid worker who is not expected to assume household or childcare responsibilities.

Notably, this may be changing because of the extreme pressures and realities imposed by the Great Recession of 2008–2013: Women are more likely to be employed than men, who suffered stronger losses of jobs than women, and who faced daunting challenges to finding new jobs. That has meant more men at home full time while their partners work full time outside the home, necessitating a shift in who cooks, shops, cleans, takes care of and chauffeurs children (Folbre, 2012). While women still do the majority of the work at home, we are seeing more men take on a larger share of that responsibility. It will be interesting to see if this prompts a shift in gendered socialization in future years.

Schools

Schools also reinforce gendered social roles. For example, researchers have documented the differential treatment accorded males and females in the classroom that reinforces a sense of inferiority and lack of initiative among female students (Sadker and Sadker, 1994; Spade, 2001). Boys are far more likely than girls to be given specific information that guides improvement of their performance (Boggiano and Barrett, 1991). Boys also receive greater encouragement to reach for higher standards for themselves. Girls are thus denied an important part of the education process that encourages students to strive for excellence. Instead, the vague praise girls may receive often implies that whatever they accomplish, however flawed, is "good enough," that it is not necessary for them to try for better achievement.

Researchers have found that school tracking often occurs along gendered lines (Kubitschek and Hallinan, 1996). Girls tend to be tracked away from the STEM (Physical and Life Science, Technology, Engineering, and Math) disciplines and toward the humanities, social sciences, and secretarial studies. They are often encouraged to enter nurturing or helping professions, such as teaching (especially at the preschool and elementary school levels), nursing, social work, and clerical work. Boys tend to be pushed toward more autonomous professions, such as medicine, science and technology, law, business, engineering, and finance, or physical vocations in fields like auto mechanics and electromechanical technology (Peltz, 1990; Riegle-Crumb et al., 2012; see also Shaffer, Marx, and Radmila, 2013).

Textbooks used in schools explicitly and implicitly reinforce gendered roles through both their content and their form. For example, literature texts are often dominated by the works of white males, with a few notable exceptions (such as Emily Dickinson). History texts give scant attention to the serious contributions of women in American and world history. Even in college-level sociology texts, discussions of women tend to be restricted to a single chapter on gender or sprinkled in chapters on topics such as the family and socialization, which have traditionally included women (Ferree and Hall, 1996).

One study of photographs that accompany sociology texts found that only one-third of the pictures contained women of any race. Race and gender were treated as mutually exclusive categories: White women were depicted as women, while women of color were depicted for their race. Moreover, the study found that, overall, white male images dominated the textbook photographs, most particularly in the chapters on politics and economics (Ferree and Hall, 1996). The message here, in sociology textbooks of all places, is that white males are the important actors in the most crucial institutions, while women play a role primarily in the family.

Although Title IX law requires equality in education, and there have been notable improvements since its inception in 1972, there remain serious gendered inequities. Funding for high school and college athletics, including facilities, equipment, travel, and scholarships, tends to reward females less than males (with the notable exception of cheerleading). This inequality is reinforced by the lack of opportunities for women's professional sports. Even in cases where women's sports do receive some institutional support, it lags significantly behind that of men's sports. The lack of positive rewards or adequate funding to support women's sports discourages females from pursuing such activities. This reinforces cultural assumptions that women are genetically predisposed to dislike sports, are not strong, and do not have physical endurance.

Work

Work roles in the paid labor market are also sharply divided along gendered lines, sending a strong message to people about appropriate and inappropriate work aspirations for boys and girls. Most occupations in industrialized societies are characterized as predominantly male or predominantly female. In the United States in 1998, almost 60 percent of the women in the paid labor force can be found in fewer than 50 job categories (out of a total of 219 defined by the Census Bureau) that are predominantly female, which means that at least 80 percent of the employees doing those jobs are women (www.census.gov). Such an arrangement identifies specific work activities based on one's sex and can contribute to the gendered development of aspirations and training for future work roles. Indeed, when individuals pursue gender "inappropriate" jobs, they frequently report pressures from family, peers, teachers, and employers to reconsider. Such is often the case with men who choose to work as daycare providers, kindergarten teachers, and nurses, an experience illustrated in popular culture. Take, for example, the man in the movie, *Meet the Parents*, who suffered the disrespect and severe disapproval of his future father-in-law when he announced that he was a nurse. Similarly, when Ross and Rachel hired a man as a nanny (or "manny," as they called him) for their new baby on the television show *Friends*, an entire episode of jokes revolved around questions concerning his masculinity. Eventually they fired him, the ultimate sanction for being the "wrong" sex for the job and for "poor" socialization.

There is some indication that this may be changing somewhat. More men are beginning to take female-dominated jobs because of shrinking job opportunities in their previous male-dominated jobs (Dewan, 2012). As more men do so, the gender-typing of jobs may be likely to play a reduced role in gender socialization.

Media

The media also contribute to stereotypes and the reproduction of conventional gendered roles. In some media, for example, stark images depict men as aggressive and dominating actors and women as docile, submissive objects (Rollins and Rollins, 1994; Berberick, 2010; Pozner, 2010). Television and films tend to offer very limited roles for women, and those they do offer perpetuate female stereotypes and caricatures. Women in the profession frequently lament the scarcity of roles for strong leading women; they tend to be cast in secondary roles as insecure, punishing, spoiled, prudish, emotionally manipulative or unstable, or childish females (Hanania, 1999; Lont, 2001). And while it is true that many situation comedies depict men in buffoonish stereotypes (Pehlke et al., 2009), there remains a wide and diverse array of images of men to counter these. In comparison, the images of women tend to be more restricted to sharp and demeaning caricatures; in the absence of a wide, diverse array or countervailing images of women, the stereotypes become more significant. Moreover, when men are poorly depicted, they tend primarily to be working-class men, suggesting that there is something about their class, not their gender that causes them to behave so poorly (Butsch, 1995).

The gender bias in media is not surprising, given the industry's power structure. One study of Fortune 500 media and telecom corporations found that while 44 percent of network and national cable news anchors were women, they remained severely underrepresented in the boardroom: Only 15 percent of executives and 12 percent of corporate board members were women (Falk, 2003). Regardless of who reads the news to viewers, those who make the decisions about what to broadcast, whether it is news or entertainment programming, will get to determine what images people see. And when the decision makers are predominantly male, it is likely that male interests, perspectives, and experiences will dominate the programming.

Why does the pattern of gendered media images matter? Research shows that children as young as toddlers imitate behaviors they see on television and that this copying intensifies through adolescence (Comstock and Paik, 1991). Therefore, media images of gender can be powerful socializers. In children's television, very few roles are given to females.

Notably, there are encouraging signs of change: Children's shows like *Kim Possible* and *Dora the Explorer* are beginning to showcase strong, intelligent female characters. In adult programming, the popular television series *Murphy Brown*, *Roseanne*, and *Grace Under Fire* in the 1980s and *Ally McBeal*, *Felicity*, and *The Profiler* in the 1990s all featured independent, powerful central female characters. By 2003, these few shows were gone from prime time, but others have continued the trend: *Alias* and *Buffy the Vampire Slayer* depict strong females as the main characters. Witness as well several formidable women who are lawyers and district attorneys on the *Law and Order* franchise series and the women on the *CSI* franchise series who are top-notch forensic scientists.

That such roles are increasing is a real sign of progress. But there is much work to be done: that such characters stand out reaffirms the persistence of gendered stereotypes as more the norm in television. Moreover, a study of prime time television in 2000–2001 done by Children

Now, a child policy and advocacy organization, found a continuation of gendered images. Men dominated prime time: 65 percent of the characters portrayed in that time slot were male. The marital and parental statuses of females were twice as likely to be identified than males. And while women are seen crossing over into traditionally male jobs, no such crossover of men to traditionally female jobs occurred at all (www.childrennow.org "Fall Colors 2000–01").

Gendered roles for both males and females are generally depicted as appropriate when they are heterosexual. The media, particularly television, still are more likely to treat gay males and lesbians as oddities in overdrawn caricatures, when they portray them at all. Indeed, a very sensitive portrayal on *thirtysomething* in the late 1980s of two homosexual men sitting in bed discussing the horror of losing friends to AIDS was never rerun because of intense objections to the scene by ABC's standards and practices censors. More recently, while the show *Will and Grace* is often credited with bringing homosexuality into the mainstream of television culture, some critics point out that it continues to rely on stereotypes of male homosexuals as feminine and infantile in their behavior (Battles and Hilton-Morrow, 2002). Even shows like *The New Normal* and *Modern Family*, often cited for offering a refreshing portrayal of healthy, committed marriages between gay characters, frequently resort to overdrawn caricatures of gay and lesbian characters in the interest of a comedic bit.

However, there are encouraging signs that television is becoming more comfortable with more positive, accepting images of gays. Since the coming out of Ellen DeGeneres' lesbian character on *Ellen* in April 1997, television has portrayed gays who are comfortable in their identity and productive members of society. Examples include *Will and Grace* (even if the show still reverted to stereotypes of gays), an affirmative depiction of a gay wedding on *Felicity*, an intimate kiss between two women on *Ally McBeal*, and a feature-length positive treatment of lesbian relationships on HBO's *L* and *If These Walls Could Talk, II*, in which a woman struggles for dignity, inclusion, and recognition as the grieving widow by the family of her deceased long-term lesbian partner.

There are also encouraging signs of the ability of media to challenge dominant values and norms. For example, one study found that subjects tended to have a more sympathetic, positive attitude toward homosexuals after viewing the documentary, *The Times of Harvey Milk*, about a gay legislator murdered in California in 1978 (Riggle, Ellis, and Crawford, 1996). The film had premiered in 1984 and was aired on PBS in 1985, a time when affirmative portrayals of gays and lesbians were still uncommon.

Toys, Games, and Recreational Activities

Toys and games teach children a great deal about "appropriate" and "inappropriate" gendered roles and identities (Johnson, Christie, and Yawkey, 1999). Even the packaging plays a part. For example, boxes showing girls playing with dolls and tea sets and boys playing with erector sets, or doctor kits showing a boy as the doctor and a girl as either patient or nurse, send children a message of who is "supposed" to play with these toys or who is "supposed" to assume a particular role when they play. Indeed, girls are encouraged to view the distorted body form of the Barbie and Bratz dolls as the ideal, while boys learn to idolize the aggression of such "action figures" as G.I. Joe, Transformers, and He-Man.

Games are subtle, but powerful, gender socialization agents. For example, Chutes and Ladders is a very popular game among preschoolers and very young elementary school children.

The game very explicitly defines "good" behaviors (rewarded with advancement to the finish) and "bad" behaviors (punished with slides back toward the start). Notably, the behaviors identified in the pictures on the game board are gender-specific: good behaviors depict girls planting flowers, baking a cake, nursing an injured dog, and sweeping the floor, and boys mowing the lawn, rescuing a distressed cat in a tree, and locating Mom's misplaced purse. Bad behaviors show girls eating too many chocolates (girls must be careful not to jeopardize their figures so as to remain attractive) and breaking dishes by attempting to carry too many (girls are not strong enough to carry more than a few), and boys reading comic books instead of the history textbook, breaking a window with a baseball, and pulling a cat's tail. Games such as Sweet Valley High, Girl Talk, and The Barbie Game teach adolescent and preadolescent girls to fit the stereotype of catty, back-biting females as they compete for boyfriends and prom dates.

Video games tend to reinforce conventional gendering as well (Cassell and Jenkins, 1998; Dill and Thill, 2007). One study found that females were absent in more than 40 percent of the games containing characters, rendering females unimportant or invisible. In almost one-third of the remaining games containing female characters, they were depicted as sex objects (for example, Lara in "Lara's Tomb") and targeted by violence in more than one-fifth of the games (Dietz, 1998). It is little surprise, then, to discover that video games are frequently considered boys' toys ("Game Boy") or to find that video arcades are largely populated by boys. The research suggests that the messages contained in these games, coupled with the themes of violence against women in the media, may be desensitizing users to women as human or as deserving of respect and socializing them to accept as normal the treatment of women as objects and as targets of aggression (Gilmore and Crissman, 1997; Burgess, Stermer, and Burgess, 2007). The perception of video games as a male preserve may also encourage the more general notion that the world of computers itself belongs more to males than females.

On the other hand, although female athletics receive less funding than male athletics, sports have in fact become an increasingly important source of activity for girls, largely as the result of protests against sex discrimination in school athletics. The state has been pressured to adopt legislation mandating equal access to and funding for educational activities for both boys and girls through Title IX. This has resulted in a dramatic increase in funding and participation opportunities for girls in athletics (although still not equal to the funding and participation opportunities for boys). By 2000, there was not only a rise in national participation and interest in women's basketball, but in women's soccer and ice hockey, in both schools and the Olympics as well as in professional sports. Of considerable concern, however, is the backlash to Affirmative Action. While the Supreme Court in 2003 reaffirmed the principle of Affirmative Action, legal disputes, including those challenging its Title IX provision that has been crucial in the increase of funding for girls' and women's athletics, continue to work their way through the courts. If successful, these cases may roll back the progress made by women in sports. This is likely to be an area of struggle and contention for some time.

Effectiveness of Gender Socialization

How successful are all these agents of gender socialization in reinforcing conventionally gendered social constructions of appropriate and inappropriate behavior? Gilligan, Lyons, and Hanmer (1990) studied socialization and development of adolescent girls in a girls' school in the

United States, and they found striking evidence that these agents are indeed quite formidable. According to the researchers, girls tend to go through a "moment of resistance" around age 11, in which they experience a clear confidence in their abilities, insights, integrity, and potential roles in the world around them. However, as they get older, girls begin to understand and heed the restrictive messages that socialization agents in their culture send to them: They begin to realize that women are invisible and unimportant in their culture. By age 15 or 16, the girls in the study show signs of succumbing to their symbolic annihilation: They were less outspoken, less sure of their abilities and intelligence, and more docile than the preadolescents. The resistance was gone, or had at least gone "underground"; the girls were more likely to preface their statements and observations with comments such as "This may be silly," and they repeatedly said, "I don't know." The researchers' findings suggest that socialization agents are quite powerful in shaping girls' social identities to conform to gender stereotypes (Gallas, 1998).

The difficulty of generalizing the findings of Gilligan, Lyons, and Hanmer stems from the fact that their study was based on an elite, gender-segregated school. Are their findings gender-specific? Or might they be age-specific to both boys and girls? A 1992 survey found that although both boys and girls do indeed suffer a decline in self-esteem as adolescents, the decline is more pronounced for girls (American Association of University Women, 1992). Another study found that while girls begin kindergarten well ahead of boys in all areas except science, they finish high school *behind* boys in almost all areas because systematic gender bias in the classroom boosts boys' and undermines girls' confidence (Sadker and Sadker, 1994; see also Chalabaev et al., 2013).

The effectiveness of gender socialization of both boys and girls is also evident in their respective recreational activities, peer interactions, and language usage. Sex segregation in peer and play groups begins very early among preschoolers (Schofield, 1981), and it continues in school friendships as children select same-sex tablemates in the lunchroom and in the playground at recess. These groups begin to reinforce gendered roles for both boys and girls. Later, schools, families, and communities support team sports as common, validating experiences for boys, a reflection of the persistent cultural social constructions that define competitive and aggressive behavior as masculine, not feminine (Messner, 2001). This view is reinforced by disproportionate media coverage of men's professional sports and use of male star athletes in advertisements. One result of all this support is that large areas of playground space are controlled by boys playing baseball, football, basketball, street hockey, and so on. Girls often play games such as jump rope and hopscotch, which involve turn taking and cooperation and take up relatively little playground space (Thorne, 1989, 1993). While there have been important advances in organized competitive sports for girls in many schools throughout the United States, owing largely to federal legislation mandating equal opportunity for both boys and girls to participate in school sports, these still lag behind school and media support for boys' athletics.

Boys, then, dominate the "gendered turf" of the playground, where they learn that competition, aggression, and sometimes violence are "normal" aspects of being male. Such lessons extend beyond team sports, as boys' interactions frequently involve contests, challenges and dares, insults, and dictated commands (Goodwin, 1980; Fine, 1986). Girls, in contrast, learn to express disagreement more indirectly, through secrets and shifting alliances (Maltz and Borker, 1983). Instead of using commands and orders, girls learn to use inclusive suggestions, such as "let's" do something (Goodwin, 1980). The gendered messages are obvious: Boys are leaders who dictate orders to others, control greater resources, and confront conflicts and challenges; girls are subordinate to boys in that they control fewer resources, follow rather than lead, and avoid or ignore conflicts. Indeed, research has found that girls tend to more positively respond to female peers who use an inclusive, communal style of interaction, in contrast to boys, who tend to respond more positively to male peers who adopt a more individually goal-oriented style (Hibbard and Buhrmester, 1998).

Thus, family, schools, work, media, toys and games, the state, and language usage operate together in the process of gender socialization, reproducing and reinforcing conventional social constructions of appropriate and inappropriate gendered roles and behaviors. Moreover, the domination in all these agents of heterosexual images and assumptions strongly discourages consideration of homosexuality as a viable and acceptable alternative and together effectively promote a sense of **compulsory heterosexuality**, the adoption of a heterosexual public persona as a prerequisite for acceptance in mainstream society (Neilson, Walden, and Kunkel, 2000; Renold, 2000). For such reasons, young people who know they are, or believe they might be, gay or lesbian are made to feel very negative about themselves.

On the other hand, gender socialization appears to be imperfect: Many women and men transcend its powerful messages and successfully challenge them. For example, in the workplace and in educational institutions, an increasing number of women are breaking barriers considered impenetrable by previous generations. Look at the proportion of female students in your classroom. Perhaps the professor standing before you is a woman. Look, too, at the increases in women in school and professional and Olympic sports, including basketball, soccer, and ice hockey. And notice the increasing number of female executives in corporations and female politicians in Congress, the White House, and governor's mansions all over the United States. Consider, as well, the Houston Oilers football player who in 1993 refused to play in a football game because his wife was giving birth to their first child. He risked a heavy monetary fine and suspension from the team, but after a major public outcry supporting his denial of traditional gendered roles and condemning his punitive coach, the team's management rescinded the sanction. More recently, after the birth of his fourth child in 2000, Tony Blair, Prime Minister of Great Britain, took a brief parental leave of absence to help care for the child. Such cases remain departures from the norm, but the fact that they happen at all suggests that gender socialization, while powerful, is far from absolute in shaping gendered identity.

RACIALIZED SOCIALIZATION

Just as the various agents play a critical role in class and gender socialization, they are vital transmitters of racialized socialization. Racialized socialization reinforces racist stereotypes and race-based roles that legitimize racialized inequality. The agents that are particularly influential here are family, schools, the state, media, and toys.

Family

The family is an important source of values and norms of interaction for children, and it is within families that stereotypes about groups may take on added significance (O'Connor, Brooks-Gunn, and Graber, 2000). Children may go through racialized rites of passage that emphasize white superiority and black inferiority. For example, Sarah Putton Boyle experienced a racialized rite of passage as a white child in the South in the 1950s when she rebuffed an African American child's invitation to play. Here is her poignant description of the event:

> *Crushing back my desire both for his company and for fun, I answered stiffly, "No, I can't." Then I added with proper Southern-lady courtesy, "How are you?" My mother had watched the exchange . . . [and] she said, "Mother saw and heard everything. That was a good girl" (Boyle, 1962: 22).*

When families reward "appropriate" behavior regarding rules and boundaries of interracial interaction, they send a clear message to white children and children of color about the children's "proper" places in society.

On the other hand, some families' socialization processes may encourage resistance to prevailing racist attitudes. For example, African American parents must often teach their children ways to interact with a white-dominated law enforcement system in order to safeguard themselves when they have not violated any laws. Thus, although most families of all ethnic and racialized groups want to impart to their children a sense of the children's places in the social structure and an understanding of social norms, African American families must do so in the context of racism. Unfortunately, that context may not allow their children to develop a positive self-image or pride of group membership. The challenge for people of color, then, is to stand between their children and a hostile environment to reinterpret the significance of the prejudicial attitudes and discrimination likely to confront them (Thornton, 1998; Hill, 1999). Yet not all African American families actively pursue this socialization route.

What factors, then, influence whether and how a family will offer racialized socialization information? Age of the child may be one factor: A study of African American families suggests that in general racialized socialization most frequently emphasizes an appreciation for culture rather than a preparation for bias or a promotion of mistrust. However, parents are more likely to shift toward a focus on preparing their children for bias and discrimination or to more overtly promote wariness of others as their children grow older (Hughes and Chen, 1997). Research also shows that the gender of the child may affect the process: African American adolescent males appear more likely than females to receive cautionary messages about the racist roadblocks they will commonly confront; African American adolescent females are more likely to receive socialization information stressing racialized pride (Bowman and Howard, 1985; Stevenson, 1995). Fathers rather than mothers, especially fathers in the Northeast as opposed to those in the South, were more likely to offer survival strategies for existing in a racially hostile environment; widows and never-married women were less likely to offer such information (Thornton et al., 1990). Apparently, gender helps determine who will deliver the messages that challenge negative stereotypes and racist barriers to achievement as well as who is likely to receive them. Resistance and militant challenge are more characteristic of behaviors considered appropriate for males.

This is not to say that women never receive and send racialized socialization messages that encourage resistance to prejudice and discrimination. Just consider such women as civil rights activist Rosa Parks who challenged racism in the early 1960s by refusing to give up her seat on a bus to a white passenger; attorneys Anita Hill, who testified about sexual harassment by Clarence Thomas in the Senate hearings to confirm his Supreme Court nomination in the 1980s, and Lani Guinier, a highly active and vocal federal civil rights advocate; and award-winning writers

Maya Angelou, Alice Walker, and Toni Morrison. Research does suggest, however, that men are far more likely to be socialized in this way. That such challenges occur at all underscores the role family can play as a proactive socialization agent contradicting racialized messages stressed by other agents.

Schools

Schools reinforce racial inequality and racial socialization through a variety of mechanisms. One of these is funding. Because school budgets depend on property-tax revenues and state matching funds, much better funding is available for schools in middle-class districts than for schools in poor and working-class districts (Walters, 2001). Housing discrimination patterns, coupled with widening economic gaps between whites and people of color suggest that these funding practices are likely to contribute to widening racial inequality as well. Differential funding often occurs *within* districts, where school boards may allocate money unequally from school to school. One study in New York found that teachers' pay in predominantly white suburban Scarsdale averaged $81,410 annually, compared with teachers' annual salaries of $47,345 in heavily Latino/a and African American New York City, a pay gap of 73 percent (Stern, 1998). Funding and allocation decisions can produce differential educational experiences on the basis of race and class (see Swan, 1995).

Texts and curricula also often contain a racialized and ethnic bias. As noted earlier, textbooks tend to exclude racial minorities from analyses of U.S. history. In one early study, only eight out of 45 social science textbooks mentioned Latino/as, and only two talked of Chicano/as (Kane, 1970; Cruz, 2002). Another early study found a similar sparseness of references to Native Americans in texts (Bowker, 1972). When racial minorities were mentioned at all, they tended to be depicted in pejorative terms, as violent, lazy, and resistant to assimilation (Wills, 1994; Shaw-Taylor and Benokraitis, 1995; Cruz, 2002). Although textbook publishers have grown more sensitive to this issue, progress is still needed. Photographs of people of color are most likely to appear in textbook chapters on race-related issues rather than being integrated throughout the book. Some disciplines' textbooks still tend to ignore race-related issues altogether. For example, studies found that introductory economics and American government textbooks tend to "race code" contemporary poverty as an African American problem, but exclude African Americans in more sympathetic portrayals of Depression-Era poverty (Clawson and Kegler, 2000; Clawson, 2002). Anthropology and criminal justice textbooks tend to ignore problems of racism in their presentations (Farrell and Koch, 1995; Shanklin, 2000; Nicholas, 2001). Yet another study noted that introductory sociology textbooks fail to present race-related information outside of specific chapters (such as those on race and ethnicity, family, and stratification) (Ferree and Hall, 1996).

Schools reinforce racialized inequality through interactions between students and teachers. One study found that while African American female students are more likely than white female students to seek contact with and help from their teachers, the African American students are more likely to be ignored or turned away (American Association of University Women, 1992). When teachers do respond to students of color with positive feedback, the praise offered is likely to be more qualified ("that report wasn't bad;" "your project was pretty good, but it could have been neater") than that offered to white students (Freiberg, 1991; American Association of

University Women, 1992). Evidence also suggests that teachers' expectations of students' performances are influenced by race and class (Dei et al., 1997). For example, teachers often have higher prior expectations of white and middle-class students' abilities than of economically poor students and those of color (Allen-Meares, 1990; Majors, Gillborn, and Sewell, 2001; Gillborn et al., 2012).

Such prior expectations get frozen early on in the process of tracking, with the result that students of color are often placed in slower or non-college-bound programs of study. Such students find it difficult to access opportunities to earn college preparatory credits, and they enjoy fewer opportunities for educational and occupational advancement. Evidence suggests that an early placement in a slower track on the basis of race tends to become permanent and impedes academic advancement, regardless of early abilities (Oakes, 1995; Jencks and Phillips, 1998).

Language also plays a part in tracking decisions. Schools tend to devalue languages other than standard English, a position that reinforces white superiority (Baron, 2000; Hartman, 2003). For example, many educators have decried the use of Black English or Ebonics, saying it limits the socioeconomic futures of students (Barnes, 2003) and lacks the rules and syntactical organization of standard English. However, studies have shown that, while certainly different, Black English is just as regulated by rules as standard English (Baratz and Baratz, 1970). Unfortunately, teachers have more power than students to make their interpretations of language usage stick. As a result, African American students who use Black English get labeled as less intelligent than white students or as slow and requiring a less advanced track of study (Woodford et al., 1997). It is important to note that standard English is the language of high-paying occupations in the United States, so preparing students of color to compete for these jobs must include teaching them standard English. The point here is that, while doing so, teachers may not convey that different languages and linguistic styles are appropriate for specific circumstances, but rather denigrate students' common usage.

On the other hand, dialects such as Ebonics can in fact be an important vehicle for resistance and identity formation. Ebonics has been found to provide a framework for the development of greater group cohesion and identity and to provide a vocabulary of resistance to dominant group conceptions of African American inferiority and an empowering celebration of self for those who are often excluded from the mainstream (Green and Smart, 1997; Smitherman and Cunningham, 1997).

Schools may also reinforce racialized socialization through their very structure, in the lack of role models within their personnel. In 2008, only 7 percent of elementary and secondary public school teachers were African American, 7 percent were Latino/a (www.census.gov). By the time students enter college (if they do, in fact, go to college), the proportion of faculty of color dips to 6.6 percent African American, 4 percent Latino/a, 6 percent Asian/Pacific Islander, and less than one-half of one percent Native American (http://nces.ed.gov/fastfacts/display.asp?id=61). While this does not necessarily mean that schools intentionally restrict the number of minority faculty, the decline in role models among teachers does send a visual message to all students that people of color are not as intelligent or capable of holding positions of authority as whites. And it reinforces the effect of **stereotype threat** (Purdie-Vaughns et al., 2008), the anxiety experienced by individuals in marginalized groups when placed in situations there is a potential to perform in such a way as to conform to negative expectations of stereotypes. This can occur when the paucity of role models signals to students of color that they must not be capable, and that in turn compounds the self-fulfilling prophesy of lower performance than their white classmates.

Media

In addition to schools, the media are powerful transmitters of racialized socialization (B. Williams, 1999). For example, many African American and Latino/a actors complain that they are typically cast as drug dealers or users, pimps, prostitutes, rapists, murderers, or muggers but are rarely given positive leading roles (Dennis and Pease, 1996; Rodriguez, 1997; Entman and Rojecki, 2000). The NAACP and Latino/a and Asian American critics in the entertainment industry have forcefully condemned this persistent pattern (Jackson, 2000; Lichter and Amundson, 1997). A similar bias occurs in radio broadcasting. For example, one study of national public radio found that in seven major U.S. urban markets the voices that dominated the airwaves were overwhelmingly white: 88 percent of the daytime hosts and news anchors were non-Latino/a white (Rendall and Creeley, 2002). Although the situation has improved somewhat and the roles have become more varied, positive roles are still more remarkable than typical. Indeed, a study of prime time television in 2003–2004 done by Children Now found that people of color remained marginal and that the greatest racial diversity occurred not in central, continuing roles but in non-recurring characters. Whites were more likely than people of color to be portrayed in professional occupations, in contrast to African Americans who were more likely to be portrayed in law enforcement related positions. And only people of color played the roles of domestic workers, nurse/physicians' assistants, and unskilled laborers, with most of these concentrated among Latino/as (www.childrennow.org "Fall Colors 2003").

Moreover, television has not remained consistently vigilant about increasing the affirmative presence of actors of color in a diversity of roles. Both television and films continue to rely heavily on racialized and ethnic stereotypes. And where there has been an increase in the number of television shows dominated by African Amercian characters, these have been largely restricted to the cable channels like Warner Brothers (WB) and Universal Paramount Network (UPN), and on premium channels like HBO (in shows like *Treme*), rather than on the major networks. Notable exceptions that do not rely on negative stereotypes include the 1980s *Cosby Show*'s positive portrayal of a successful African American family, which was important for the perceptions of both white and African American viewers of families of color as respectable, well-educated, and stable (Rhym, 1998; Havens, 2000). Later, *Bernie Mac* and *My Wife and Kids* depicted middle-class couples struggling successfully with issues confronting many African American and middle-class families. But the more standard fare on television perpetuates racialized stereotypes, reinforcing negative racialized images and making people of color objects of derision.

Television and print news media are often swift to seize on racist stereotypes in their reporting. For example, when Susan Smith claimed an African American carjacker kidnapped and killed her two young sons in South Carolina in 1994, both the police and the press readily and uncritically accepted her story. Later it became clear that she herself had sent her sons, strapped in their carseats, to their death when she deliberately submerged her car in a lake. The repeated emphasis in the press on the racial overtones of the case served to reinforce racist stereotypes of the violence of African American males and the danger they pose for whites.

Toys, Games, and Recreational Activities

The toys children play with may also reinforce racist stereotypes. In 1949 Crayola, the leading manufacturer of crayons, had introduced a peach-colored crayon that it labeled "flesh," implying that normal skin color is peach, not black, brown, yellow, or red. "Flesh" crayons remained on the market for over a decade, but were discontinued in 1962 when Crayola bowed to pressures from the civil rights movement. Crayola was less sensitive to the implications of labeling another color "Indian Red." This color label remained on the market until 1999 when it was changed to "chestnut" (http://kids.inforplease.lycos.com).

Dolls are also persuasive toys. In a classic study (Clark and Clark, 1947), when children were confronted with two dolls, one white and one black, one-third of the African American children selected the white doll as the one resembling themselves. Both white and African American children in the study tended to identify the white doll as good and the black doll as bad. Research suggests that the preponderance of white dolls available in toy stores continues to affect racial socialization and perceptions of beauty and goodness. For example, 65 percent of the African American preschoolers in one study selected a white Cabbage Patch doll over a black version of the doll (Powell-Hopson and Hopson, 1988). Another study done in the West Indies produced similar results, which the author attributed to the continued cultural impact of white colonialism (Gopaul-McNicol, 1995). On the other hand, toys and books do have the power to alter racist stereotypes. In one study, two-thirds of both white and African American preschoolers chose the black doll after exposure to a half hour of stories containing positive images of the black doll (Gopaul-McNicol, 1988).

The use of racist stereotypes as team mascots and logos, both in school and in professional sports, reinforces the image of some groups as less-than-human or as uncivilized. In particular, Native American references are often used as team names (Red Skins, Braves, Indians, etc.) in part because of the cultural image of these as aggressive, violent, savage, and fear-inspiring. The team names are typically combined with demeaning logos, as the savage image of the Atlanta Brave, or the unflattering caricature of the Cleveland Indian. Other groups (and certainly white European Americans as the dominant group) escape such treatment, at least in part because of power differentials: Whites own and control teams and the designation of names, logos, and mascots. African Americans and Latino/as have historically been more politically successful than Native Americans in resisting and challenging these depictions. This is beginning to change: Native Americans are becoming more vocal in their protests and their demands that use of these images end. There is evidence that this is already having some effect, at least in academia: St. John's University now refers to its teams as the Red Storm, and Stanford University's teams the Cardinals; Syracuse University's teams are now simply called the Syracuse Orange.

Taken together, families, schools, media, and toys play critical roles in racialized socialization and the reproduction of racialized inequality. They also contain strong possibilities for interrupting the cycle of the self-fulfilling prophecies that these agents have more commonly perpetuated. While many agents may offer powerful messages that together reinforce racism, they are not absolute: People are not powerless to resist them. And therein lays room for change.

POLITICAL SOCIALIZATION

The same socialization agents that teach members of society about "appropriate" and "inappropriate" behaviors and expectations with regard to gender, race, sexual orientation, and class also socialize members *politically*. **Political socialization** is the process through which individuals come to internalize a political identity that defines who they are and how they should behave in the political and economic institutions of society. Individuals develop a lens that shapes their views on how they expect the world to work and what they consider acceptable or even viable politically and economically. The agents that are particularly important in this process are schools, toys and games, and media.

Schools

Schools have historically helped transfer cultural values, and that function continues today (Zajda, 2000; Gerstle and Mollenkopf, 2001; Norberg, 2001). In U.S. schools students learn the principles of the U.S. Constitution and Bill of Rights, concepts that facilitate individuals' internalization of values such as the preeminence of private property, individual rights and personal responsibility for one's own fate, and civic obligations and duty to country. Students often begin each day with the Pledge of Allegiance and sporting events with the National Anthem, constant reminders of those basic nationalistic values. While in and of themselves these values may not be problematic, the implications of uncritically accepting them may be. These values lead us to believe that ours is a free and open society in which the key to upward mobility and accomplishment is simply individuals' hard work and that each individual earns or deserves his or her position based solely on his or her own efforts. Thus, many people assume that persons who are poor, homeless, illiterate, or powerless have only themselves to blame. The strong implication is that those who may be better off do not have the responsibility to help the less fortunate. If people have successfully internalized these values, they may never question the adequacy of this blaming-the-victim analysis or analyze the role of political and economic institutions in producing such victims (see Euben, 1997). Nor will they likely consider the *structure* of wealth and poverty as institutionalized over generations, or entertain that wealth and poverty may be the accrued product of oppression, exploitation, or unfair advantage or disadvantage several generations ago.

Similarly, textbooks typically portray a sanitized view of American history, which de-emphasizes or ignores altogether the most violent aspects of slavery, the carnage of the Vietnam War, the violence by employers and the state against the labor movement, and the genocide of Native Americans in the westward expansion. This cleaner, crisper view of American history urges students to accept as legitimate the continued power and privilege of the few at the expense of the many, because countervailing or challenging information that invites critical analysis of that view is not readily available.

Schools also teach individuals to revere the electoral process. Through elections for class officers, for example, students learn about their rights and responsibilities as voters, and they learn to value the democratic process as free and open. Along the way, however, they may also learn to accept as normal the highly competitive nature of such a process, as well as notions like

"The winner takes all" and "All is fair in love, war, and politics." The process of elections in the context of principles like "one person, one vote" teaches people to validate the rule of politically and economically dominant groups. This is because all members of society appear to have had an equal chance to participate in selecting that rule, despite the fact that the candidates they choose from are overwhelmingly drawn from the ranks of dominant groups to begin with.

Schools may additionally impart important information regarding capitalist values of consumerism, through the constant bombardment of students with commercial messages. As we noted in Chapter 5, schools have become infused with corporate ideals, including the role of citizens as consumers. Students quickly learn to accept without question the political economy of capitalism and their need to consume mass-produced products and labels (Brint, 1998).

Beyond the political process itself, schools socialize students to accept political structures and values unquestioningly. For example, while competitive school sports prepare us for later physical fitness training, an important aspect of people's lives, they can also prepare people to accept political decisions involving the nation in wars. Warfare is often seen as just another sporting event characterized by team spirit and "us" against "them." People often accept physical injuries and casualties as normal and justified, and to view as legitimate the notion that "to the winners go the spoils." Wars and competitive school sports even share a common terminology. Teams typically select warlike or aggressive figures or symbols for their names, mascots, and logos. And competitive team sports may politically socialize us by channeling violence and aggression into an organized setting governed by rules (Wilson, 1992; Dunning, 1993). Thus, competitive team sports become part of a "civilizing" process that teaches us it is acceptable to inflict bodily harm on players of the opposing team but not acceptable to do so to neighbors, coworkers, or authority figures. Such a civilizing process becomes easily transferable to situations of war, particularly when both settings share terminology and analytical frameworks.

Toys and Games

The toys and games commonly available reinforce the internalization of dominant ideologies and the acceptance of warfare as a game. Video games are dominated by militaristic themes (including one called Contra, in which a Rambo-like figure single-handedly tries to search for and destroy guerrilla rebels). Real lives, violence, and pain become trivialized into blips on a screen, removing the horrors of war from the players' consciousness and developing the eye-hand coordination necessary for actual participation in high-tech warfare. Even the more realistic graphics on video games maintain a cartoon-like edge that implies a divorce of violence from reality. Although video games may improve eye-hand coordination, that physical development is accomplished in the context of militaristic themes that glorify war as normal and acceptable (Cerulo, 2000). Indeed, the military itself began to use video games to train its personnel, using settings in places like Iraq and Afghanistan, in situations like search-and-destroy house-to-house missions (Voakes, 2012). Moreover, as we noted earlier, the gendering of video games as a male activity implies that aggression, war, and violence are "natural" male attributes.

Other toys also tie a political message to play. Almost immediately following the outbreak of the Gulf war in the Middle East in 1991, G.I. Joe "action figures" in desert-beige camouflage uniforms began to turn up in toy stores and remain a dominant fixture in the era of the wars in Iraq and Afghanistan. And just as quickly, Topps, the maker of baseball cards, began selling packets of Operation Desert Storm cards, with pictures of generals and weaponry replacing pictures of star ballplayers. Statistics on individual officers' careers, relative troop strengths, and the capabilities of various weapon systems replaced earned-run averages and runs-batted-in statistics. During the war against Iraq in 2003, department and convenience stores began selling decks of playing cards with the faces of "Iraqi Most Wanted" (identifying Saddam Hussein as the ace of spades). While these cards were originally distributed to American and British troops in Iraq to familiarize them with the faces of "persons of interest," the cards quickly became available as playthings for the general public and implied that all Iraqis are violent criminals.

Media

The media are important sources of information for individuals as they seek to make sense of the world around them. Television is probably the most widely used media source of information in the United States. What effect does television have on the development of political identity? How effective is its influence in shaping this identity? Studies show that television can affect viewers' perceptions of what constitutes important issues and who is responsible for these issues (Iyengar, 1990; Barnhurst and Wartella, 1998; Goidel et al., 2010; Callanan and Rosenberger, 2011). Together, these findings illustrate that television can influence how people see the world and their places in it.

While media provide crucial information to viewers and readers, they also tend to present that information from a mainstream point of view and thus promote acceptance of dominant political values (including the defense of these with individuals' lives in war) (Parenti, 1998; McChesney, 1999; 2004). Reporters cover wars like sporting events, using all the terminology and metaphors of competitive sports, including pep rallies, "up-close and personal" vignettes of "our" various warriors, and nightly score reports of casualties and destruction, as reporters embedded in deployed U.S. troops did in the 2003 war against Iraq.

People tend to more readily accept various wars as necessary and legitimate when the media portray other countries' leaders and citizens as evil or subhuman, deserving of destruction. In 1991 President George H. W. Bush repeatedly described the war against Iraq as a war of good against evil. The media frequently noted that the Iraqis "don't value human life the way 'we' do." In 2003, President George W. Bush referred to an "axis of evil" supposedly created by Iraq, Iran, and North Korea. Exposure to such ideological statements, especially on a recurring basis from multiple media sources, enables people to transcend the usual norms against the taking of human lives. The selectivity of media coverage may foster the impression that "we're all in this together," "we'll all benefit equally from our team effort," and "we all agree that this is right and should occur" (see MacArthur, 1992).

In addition to socializing us to accept war as legitimate, the media may promote the legitimacy of inequality, domination, and capitalism through the stories they select and the perspective they bring to them. This bias on the part of the media is not surprising, given that many mass-media outlets are owned and controlled by large capitalist interests (Hackett and Adam, 1999; McChesney, 2004). For example, the dominant commercial television networks (ABC, CBS, and NBC) are owned and controlled by major corporate investors (McChesney, 1997, 2004). General Electric owns NBC, while Disney owns ABC, and Viacom owns CBS; Fox is part of Rupert Murdoch's News Corporation, an international media empire. In radio, by 1996

Clear Channel owned more than 1,200 radio stations (McChesney, 2004, 2008). The significance of the investors' and interlockers' influence over the networks is that people in the United States are far more likely to use television as their source of news than anything else: Only 67.2 percent in the U.S. read newspapers, but 92.9 percent watch television (www.census.gov). In spite of the growth of cable networks offering some competition, and an increasing use of the Internet for information, the four major commercial networks still dominate in their share of the audience.

Newspapers and magazines are less concentrated than television broadcast media, but many of the top print media are owned and controlled by industry conglomerates. Just 10 newspaper conglomerates account for half of the total newspaper circulation in the United States (Knee, 2003). The conglomerates typically own several major newspapers, magazines, and local television affiliates, thereby promoting **homogenization of news.** This means that people are likely to be exposed to a single perspective and a single analysis of very complex stories no matter how many different media individuals select as their sources of news, particularly if these are all owned or controlled by the same conglomerate.

Concentrated control of both broadcast and print media by large corporate interests contributes to political socialization by empowering these interests to determine what constitutes news and how it is interpreted. Herman and Chomsky's (1988) comparative analysis of which major news stories were covered and which were ignored showed how media elites censor news to reflect and reinforce corporate and wealthy elites' interests.

In spite of how powerful media can be in reinforcing the existing power structures, they can also be an important agent in challenging the status quo (Black and Allen, 2001). For example, film footage documenting the excesses of police against civil rights and antiwar protesters in the 1950s, 1960s, and 1970s contributed to growing public intolerance of abuses of power and the problems of racism and militarism in the United States. More recently, journalistic pursuit of charges of sexual harassment lodged against Supreme Court Justice nominee Clarence Thomas in 1992 and Senator Robert Packwood in 1993 contributed to increased public rejection of abuses of power related to gender. And growing reports in 2003 of decades of sexual abuse by the Catholic clergy have similarly prompted public outcries for the need to punish such abuses of power even when the perpetrator is an otherwise revered and trusted religious leader.

Clearly, as the sole legitimate user of force and violence, the state maintains the power to assert and enforce its own interests and to discourage or suppress challenges to its authority and decision making and to the structure of key institutions. Historically, the state in the United States has resorted to use of violence to squash labor unrest and to silence anti-war protests. At other times local police have jailed civil rights, antinuclear, and antiabortion demonstrators, as well as protestors against the World Trade Organization and those in the Occupy Wall Street movement protesting pronounced and growing gaps between the wealth of a few and the poverty of the many, to name just a few examples. In China, the state called out the army and used tanks to quell the Student Democracy Movement in 1991. In Israel, the military often fires upon demonstrating Palestinians seeking political self-determination. Media coverage of such events can serve as an influential vehicle for socializing the public, including potential future critics, to conform to the dominant group's rule. But it can also backfire and galvanize large numbers of people to challenge and resist that dominant rule and the violence that reinforces it.

Together, schools, the media, the state, and the toys and games many people enjoy contribute to political socialization. People often learn to accept and support unquestioningly the existing political and economic structures and to regard the inequalities of privilege and power produced by these structures as right, inevitable, and legitimate. This is not to say that these institutions necessarily conspire to fool people or that individuals are helpless robots with no ability to resist or change what may seem like "thought control." (We will discuss how people can become agents for change and resistance in Chapter 10 "Social Change and Social Movements.") The point here is that one of the identities learned through the socialization process consists of who individuals are, where they fit in the world around them, and how they should behave in the political and economic institutions of society.

 CHAPTER SUMMARY

How do individuals become members of society? What kinds of things must be learned to become a member, and how are they learned? To what degree is the individual a passive recipient in the process, and to what degree does the individual resist and reshape the social identities created?

- It is important to note that while the various agents of socialization are powerful forces in shaping social identities and political consciousness, individuals are not automatically transformed into mindless clones of one another. There is a considerable degree of individual interpretation of "appropriate" behaviors and expectations, as well as resistance to total conformity. Individuals' input into the socialization process contributes greatly to a broad diversity of outcomes.

- One can easily see personal variations in the "appropriate" behaviors suited to one's gender and age group, the challenges people make against class and racialized inequalities that they perceive as intolerable, and the resistance many people mount (against great odds) to prevailing political doctrines that serve elite interests. This can be seen in the women's movement, the gay rights movement, and the civil rights movement. It can be seen as well in the labor movement, in antiwar protests, and recently in the students against sweatshops movement and the Occupy Wall Street movement. It is also evident in the growing militance of senior citizens in the Gray Panthers and the American Association of Retired Persons. And individuals see it every day in their own personal styles.

- People also often change as they learn new things, collect new experiences, and meet new people with different ideas.

- This highlights the notion that the process of socialization is not absolute and does not flow in one direction only. It is, in fact, an interactive process (somewhat lopsided, to be sure, because of power differences, but interactive nonetheless) between the individual and the various socialization agents, a process typified by conflict and struggle, alterations, and learning.

THINKING CRITICALLY

1. Select one of the attitude questions at the beginning of this chapter. How did you answer this question? Now consider these questions: What values does your answer reflect? How did you acquire your attitudes and values? What agents have had a part in teaching you and reinforcing these attitudes, and how specifically did they do this? Are your attitudes the same as or different from those of your friends, your family, your teachers, your religious leaders, or the media? If they are different, how have you managed to ignore the pressures of such institutions?

2. Select a board game other than those discussed in this chapter (some good ones might be Careers, Careers for Girls, Life, Go to the Head of the Class, Couch Potato, and Stratego, but you may think of others). What are the rules and objectives of this game? What racialized, class, gendered, or political socialization messages are contained in those rules and objectives?

3. Examine your gender, race, class, or political identity, and think about some of the agents of socialization that have played an influential role in shaping it. For example, how did your family, your school experiences, your religious training, your peer groups, or the media affect how you see yourself? What factors influenced the socialization experiences you have had? If you are shaping an identity that challenges institutional messages, what factors influenced your ability to resist them?

4. Select a television show or movie and examine the racialized, class, gendered, and political identity messages it contains. Does the show or movie rely on stereotypes, or does it challenge them? Be specific. How would a symbolic interaction theorist, a functionalist, and a conflict theorist analyze this show or movie? What insights might each perspective offer in analyzing the images you see? What limitations does each perspective contain?

5. Consider your experiences in elementary and high school. What characteristics or factors from your school experience shaped your political perceptions? What shaped your perspectives of the economy, of consumerism, or of capitalism? What shaped your perspectives of the possibility of social change? What shaped your perceptions of your rights and your responsibilities as a citizen? Did you resist your socialization in school? If you did, how? Was your resistance successful?

KEY TERMS

socialization   **126**

nature versus nurture debate   **126**

sociobiology   **126**

symbolic interaction   **127**

looking-glass self   **128**

significant other   **128**

generalized other   **128**

conflict perspective   **129**

id   **129**

ego   **130**

superego   **130**

resocialization   **132**

total institutions   **133**

degradation ceremony   **133**

political socialization   **133**

socialization agents   **133**

reference group   **134**

liberation theology   **135**

symbolic annihilation   **137**

anticipatory socialization   **139**

self-fulfilling prophecy   **140**

imposter syndrome   **140**

second shift   **141**

compulsory heterosexuality   **147**

stereotype threat   **150**

homogenization of news   **156**

50
39.75
5
3.25
7.50
5
6
5
5.50
5
3
7
5.50

$$\frac{174.5}{210} = 83.0$$

SYSTEMS OF INEQUALITY

In U.S. society, many people are treated as subordinates or inferiors on the basis of their class, race, or gender and are often subject to various forms of discriminatory treatment by others. From a sociological perspective, such inequalities are not accidental or distributed randomly, but are an integral feature of how society is organized. In U.S. society, **systems of inequality** are constructed around particular attributes—such as one's income and wealth, gender, skin color (or other characteristics used to socially construct "race"), sexual orientation, and state of ablebodiedness. These systems organize people's access to important resources and opportunities in patterned ways that advantage some and disadvantage others, depending upon their status characteristics. Such systems of inequality have far-reaching consequences for the biographies and life-chances of every member of society.

Sociologists have long been interested in studying and understanding systems of inequality. Karl Marx (1813–1883) drew attention to the processes that produce and maintain economic inequality and poverty in capitalist societies, a concern that is still relevant today. German sociologist Max Weber (1864–1920) was also highly influential in the study of inequality. He encouraged sociologists to analyze societies in terms of their systems of **social stratification**, the ways in which people occupying different social positions are stratified in a hierarchy from high to low.

Weber suggested that in any given society social stratification is likely to be multidimensional. The three dimensions of stratification that Weber considered most important are class (possession of property and marketability of skills to generate income), status (social honor or prestige), and power (the ability to dominate or influence others). In Weber's view, the nature and relative importance of these three dimensions may differ from society to society as well as within any given society over time. Weber's notion that social stratification is multidimensional has influenced our approach to analyzing systems of inequality.

In this chapter we examine five systems of inequality, focusing on the United States: economic inequality, racialized inequality, gendered inequality, inequality based on sexual orientation, and inequality based on ablebodiedness. These systems of inequality are human creations or **social constructions** that tend to differ from society to society and in different historical periods. For example, researchers have found that people in many non-Western societies have very different ways of viewing gender and gender relations than is typically the case in the United States and that in other societies a wide range of sexual practices—including those one might associate with homosexuality—are accepted as normal (Nanda, 1999; Murray, 2000).

Before looking at the five systems of inequality, we wish to set them in a larger context. Not only are they human creations, but these systems also are organized around differences in power. And they commonly confer **invisible privileges** upon those who belong to the dominant group within each status, that is *unearned* advantages that can be counted on without conscious effort simply because one is a member of the dominant group. It is not uncommon for one segment of society to have the ability to set the standards of who or what will be considered "good" or "normal" within a system of inequality, as well as the power to marginalize or impose disadvantages on people who do not conform to that standard and are consequently deemed "bad" or "abnormal."

For example, in male-dominated societies men may reserve certain central social roles for themselves and seek to limit women to other, more marginal roles. In doing so, men decide what role behavior is "normal" for each sex, usually in ways that benefit men. This exercise of male power and its "gendered" outcome are usually justified by an **ideology**. As used here, ideology refers to an organized system of ideas and ways of thinking that may be either critical or supportive of the status quo. In this case we are concerned with ideologies that justify existing systems of inequality.

Ideologies that justify systems of inequality help to keep them going. The ideas they contain typically include the notion that the systems of inequality are necessary and inevitable and therefore unchangeable. When such ideologies are well-integrated into the fabric of a society's culture, the inequalities they foster may be accepted by societal members as little more than the "natural order of things." The term **ideological hegemony** has been used to refer to the dominance of a set of ideas governing ways of doing things, to the point where existing social arrangements—including systems of inequality—are treated by societal members as just a matter of "common sense" (Gramsci, 1971; Seybold, 1987).

For example, not very long ago, peoples of European ancestry waged war with indigenous (native) peoples residing in what are now North American nations: the United States, Mexico, and Canada. European colonists and their military forces took away native residents' lands and forced many to live in destitution. The conquerors justified their actions by an ideology that held that European colonists were racially and culturally superior to native North Americans. The latter were viewed and treated as uncivilized "savages" (Smedley, 1999). To this day many native peoples in North America remain socially marginalized and subject to negative stereotypes that can be traced back to ideologies accompanying European colonization (Brown, 2001).

Systems of inequality commonly generate advantages for those with characteristics of the dominant status and disadvantages for those with the characteristics of the subordinate status. What is crucial about these is that they are invisible and generally *unearned*: Those among the dominant status in a given system of inequality enjoy a set of invisible, unearned privileges based on that advantaged status; those among the subordinate or devalued statuses in a given system of inequality are hindered by *undeserved* disadvantages (McIntosh, 1992; Feagin, 2010). It is important to recognize that this inequality is not about blame: Those who enjoy privileges are not necessarily guilty of denying these to others, and those who are denied privileges are not necessarily deserving of disadvantage because of some personal failure. What is at issue here is how societies are organized so as to advantage some and disadvantage others based not on what they have earned but rather on what status they happen to inhabit through no personal effort or personal fault of their own.

Systems of inequality often give rise to conflict. Some groups seek to bring about social change that will put an end to their mistreatment, while other groups that are privileged within the system fight to maintain the status quo. People's biographies and life chances are strongly influenced not only by their positions in different systems of inequality but also by the presence and outcome of movements for social change. Obviously, if a person is unfavorably situated in a given system of inequality—as is the case for so many people—one way to alter the system is to join or otherwise lend support to such movements.

In the following sections we examine different systems of inequality that directly affect everyone in U.S. society. We address such questions as:

- How unequally are income and wealth distributed within U.S. society?
- Is the system of economic inequality in U.S. society necessary or functional? For whom?
- What ideas or ideologies help to justify and rationalize the existence of economic and other systems of inequality—such as those that are based on race, gender, sexual orientation, and disability status,?
- What invisible, unearned privileges can the dominants in a given system of inequality take for granted?
- What are some of the effects of these various systems of inequality on those occupying subordinate positions within them?
- Are these systems of inequality changing? For the better or for the worse?

ECONOMIC INEQUALITY

One of the enduring features of many societies is **economic inequality**, differences in the wealth and income that families and individuals possess. A great deal of meaning and significance is attached to the possession of such resources, principally because they play a major role in determining how long and how well one will live. For example, people's access to educational opportunities, food and housing, and healthcare is affected by their location within a system of economic inequality. The position people occupy in a system of economic inequality places them in a particular **class**, a term referring to a segment of the population whose members are similar in their economic resources. Let us look briefly at the unequal distribution of wealth and income in the United States and the poverty to which this unequal distribution contributes.

Wealth, Income, and Poverty

Wealth is the value of the assets or property that one owns. A small percentage of families own most of the nation's personally held wealth in the form of corporate stocks and bonds, savings accounts, real estate, cars and boats, and other types of property (Wolff and Leone, 2002). In 2010 the richest 1 percent of the population possessed over a third of all personally owned wealth and almost half of all wealth, if one excluded the asset of owner-occupied housing, while the bottom 90 percent possessed less than one-fourth of the nation's wealth (Mishel et al., 2012). Notably, wealth and all of its advantages can be transferred from one generation to the next, even after the original wealth holder dies.

Wealth is different from **income**, which for most people is money received in the form of hourly wages or annual salaries, or government benefits such as Social Security, unemployment compensation, or public assistance. In contrast to the transferability of wealth, income streams are discontinued when the recipient dies, quits or is fired from a job, or runs out of benefits. Moreover, wealth may itself generate income, as when stockholders receive dividends and capital gains from corporate stock or real estate owners profit from rental payments. Wealth, not earnings from employment, generates the majority of annual household income in the most affluent households. In U.S. society, most adults have incomes of some sort, but few own much wealth, particularly income-generating wealth (Phillips, 2002: Chapter 3; Mishel et al., 2012).

The value of one's assets (wealth), minus the value of one's outstanding debts, is commonly used as a measure of a person's **net worth**. Members of certain groups in U.S. society that have been systematically deprived of equal opportunities for education, jobs, bank loans, credit, and home ownership, such as African Americans and Native Americans, have average net worths that are extremely low in comparison to that of the white population (Oliver and Shapiro, 1995; Mishel et al., 2012; see also http://www.stanford.edu/group/scspi/slides.html).

In the United States, there is substantial inequality in the distribution of income, although it is not as extreme as the inequality in wealth holdings. For example, in 2010 the most affluent quintile, or 20 percent of households, received 51.7 percent of the nation's household income; the least affluent received a mere 3.4 percent. Indeed, the bottom 60 percent of households collectively received only 27.2 percent, while the most affluent 5 percent received 17.2 percent (Mishel et al., 2012:61). People of color, on average, had much lower household incomes than whites and were significantly more likely than whites to fall in the bottom quintiles.

Wealth and income are related in the sense that those with the greatest wealth tend to also receive the highest incomes. Indeed, the top 1 percent of wealth holders received more than 17 percent of all household income in 2010 (Mishel et al., 2012:379). Both the distributions of wealth and of income have become increasingly unequal in recent decades. The gap between rich and poor has increased, and the rich have literally become even richer (Mishel et al., 2012). Often, one hears terms being used like "two-tiered society" to characterize the large and growing gap between the most affluent members of U.S. society and everyone else.

Another dimension of economic inequality is the extent of poverty (see Figure 7.1). In 2010, the U.S. Bureau of the Census defined poverty for a family of four (including two children) as an annual income below $22,314 (the amount changes annually and differs depending upon family size). That year, more than 46 million people in the United States—most of whom were women and children—lived in poverty. Millions more were living in "near poverty," just above the poverty line (www.census.gov; Mishel et al., 2012). While most poor people in the United States are white, people of color are disproportionately found among the poor (Table 7.2). Many people manage to climb out of poverty, but they often don't rise very far. For some the climb out is temporary; meanwhile, others keep plunging in. Job losses in recent years, as well as a rise in the number of female-headed households because of marital breakups, have introduced poverty to many middle-class families who had assumed that their economic status was secure (Albelda and Tilly, 1997; Newman, 1999; Mishel et al., 2012).

Figure 7.1:   Number of Poor and Poverty Rates in the United States, 1959–2011

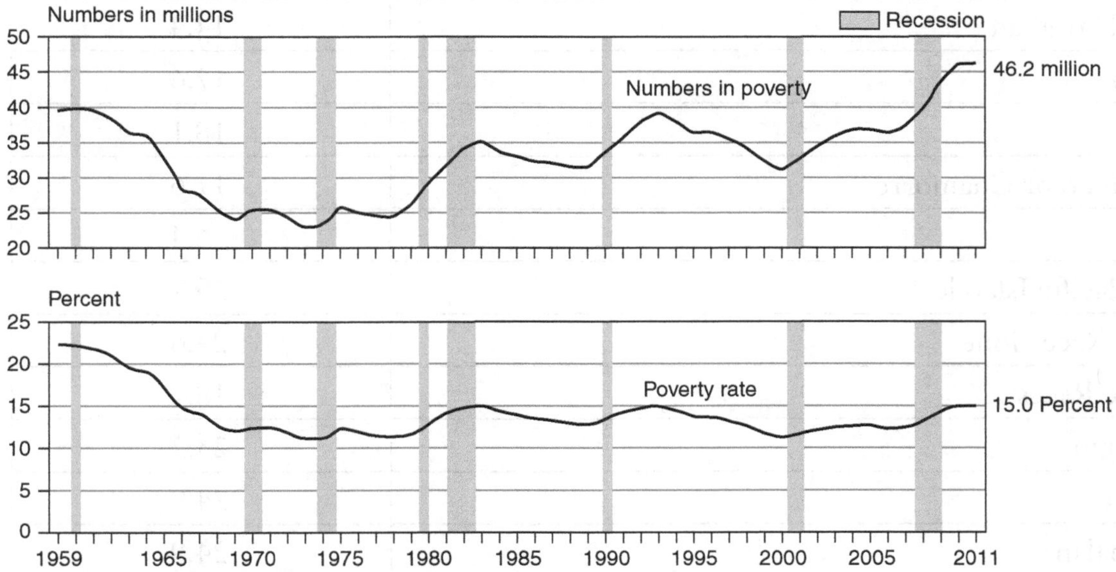

Note: The data points are placed at the midpoints of the respective years. For information on recessions, see Appendix A.
Source: U.S. Census Bureau, Current Population Survey, 1960 to 2012 Annual Social and Economic Supplements

Table 7.1:   Poverty Rates in the U.S. by Race and Latino/a Origin, 2007–2011

Race and Hispanic or Latino/a Origin	Percent below Poverty
Total	14.3
White alone	11.6
White alone, non-Hispanic	9.9
Black or African American alone	25.8
American Indian and Alaska Native alone or in combination	23.9
American Indian and Alaska Native alone	27.0
Asian alone or in combination	11.6
Asian alone	11.7
Asian Indian	8.2
Chinese	13.4
Filipino	5.8
Japanese	8.2
Korean	15.0
Vietnamese	14.7
Native Hawaiian and Other Pacific Islander alone or in combination	15.8
Native Hawaiian and Other Pacific Islander alone	17.6

(Continued)

Race and Hispanic or Latino/a Origin	Percent below Poverty
Native Hawaiian	14.4
Samoan	17.6
Tongan	18.1
Guamanian or Chamorro	11.6
Fijians	6.4
Other Pacific Islander[4]	29.7
Some Other Race alone	24.6
Two or More Races	18.7
Hispanic origin	23.2
Mexican	24.9
Guatemalan	24.9
Salvadoran	18.9
Cuban	16.2
Dominican	26.3
Puerto Rican	25.6

[1] Poverty status is determined for individuals in housing units and noninstitutional group quarters. The poverty universe excludes children under age 15 who are not related to the house holder, people living in institutional group quarters, and people living in college dormitories or military barracks.

[2] The Census Bureau does not advocate the use of the alone population over the alone-or-in-combination population or vice versa. The use of the alone population in sections of this brief does not imply that is the preferred method of presenting or analyzing data. Data on race from the American Community survey can be presented and discussed in a variety of ways. Hispanics and Latinos/a may be of any race. For more information see the 2010 Census Brief, Overview of Race and Hispanic Origin, at <www.census.gov/prod/cen2010/briefs/c2010br-02.pdf>.

[3] Data are based on a sample and are subject to sampling variability. A margin of error is a measure of an estimate's variability. The larger margin of error in relation to the size of the estimate, the less reliable the estimate. This number when added to or subtracted from the estimate forms the 90 percent confidence interval.

[4] Induces other Micronesian (25,000), Other practice islander not specified (17,000), Marshallese (17,000), Other native Hawaiian (8,000), Other practice Islander (7,000), Palauan (6,000), Other polynesian (5,000), Chuukese (2,000), Pohnpeian (1,000), Tahilan (1,000), and other detailed groups.

Source: U. S. Census Bureau, 2007–2011 American Community Survey.
Source: http://www.census.gov/hhes/www/poverty/publications/acsbr11-17.html

The facts about economic inequality and poverty are open to different interpretations. Let us look first at how a functionalist perspective would interpret economic inequality.

Different Perspectives on Economic Inequality

The Functionalist Perspective on Economic Inequality

As was discussed in Chapter 1, the foundations of the functionalist perspective were established by early European sociologists such as Émile Durkheim (1858–1917). He and more contemporary sociologists sharing the **functionalist perspective on economic inequality** have held that economic inequality is the result of beneficial forces and that the different positions that people occupy in society receive quite different rewards because this is in the interests of society as a whole (Durkheim, 1964). Thus, a functionalist viewpoint might hold that it is not a bad thing that the average chief executive officer (CEO) of a large corporation in the United States receives an annual salary that is 231 times that of a typical hourly production worker, or more in a single day than the average worker earns in a year (Mishel et al., 2012:289). Similar, if less dramatic, pay disparities exist throughout the occupational structure.

From a functionalist perspective, attaching different rewards to different positions is "functional," or beneficial to society. It provides incentives for individuals to strive for the most highly rewarded positions. Proponents of this view also argue that the most highly rewarded positions are the most important for the operation of society. It is crucial, therefore, that people who have appropriate talents, and/or who are willing to undergo the necessary training, strive to fill the important positions. Otherwise, the positions could end up being filled by persons who are less competent and society would suffer. Moreover, poverty is seen by functionalists as important to motivate people to strive harder to avoid poverty, and as a social control mechanism penalizing those who refuse to do so. Rewarding different positions unequally—in effect, maintaining an ongoing system of economic inequality—is thus seen as necessary and inevitable.

Those sympathetic to the functionalist perspective might argue that the formerly socialist nations in Eastern Europe abandoned socialism and moved toward the construction of capitalist economies because their previous economic reward systems were not unequal enough. That is, under socialism, the relatively modest gap in rewards between the best-paid and worst-paid positions failed to provide sufficient motivation for people to work hard, be productive, and strive to move up, thus setting the scene for economic collapse. Such an analysis would suggest that capitalism is preferable to socialism because capitalism contains vastly greater economic inequalities. However, the picture is more complex than the functionalist thinkers would have it.

Critiques of Functionalism

The functionalist perspective certainly sounds very logical. Yet it has long been attacked as an ideology that does more to justify economic inequality than to adequately explain it. In the United States this perspective first formally appeared in sociology journals in 1945, by which time World War II had pulled the nation out of the throes of the Great Depression (Davis and Moore, 1945). During the Depression a quarter of the U.S. labor force was unemployed, poverty was extremely widespread, and sharp economic inequalities prevailed. The functionalist perspective on economic inequality, had it appeared in the Depression years, would have counseled calm acceptance and greater individual striving, as opposed to questioning the system of economic inequality itself.

Shortly after the functionalist perspective on economic inequality appeared in the journals, critics assailed it on a number of grounds (Tumin, 1953; Wrong, 1959). The questions the critics asked are still being asked today (Kerbo, 2011):

- Are the most highly rewarded positions indeed the "most important" to society? How could this be proven?
- Do the extremes of enormous wealth and income, juxtaposed to abject impoverishment, have to exist?

- Since the talented at the bottom of the economic ladder necessarily start from a disadvantage, does U.S. society really have an open system of equal opportunity in which all people compete on an equal footing and talent "rises to the top"?
- Is it necessary that some occupations pay millions of dollars per year, while others pay even below the government-set minimum wage or pay so poorly that people in these occupations remain below the poverty line?

Critics of the functionalist perspective on economic inequality have also asked what role access to contacts helpful in obtaining jobs plays in determining a given individual's job opportunities (see the discussion of "social networks" in Chapter 4). For it seems that equal opportunity to compete for good jobs cannot safely be assumed. The already economically successful are privy to resources and connections that may then be used to help others get similar jobs, such as their own friends and family members. In unionized skilled trades and licensed professions members are often able to limit entry or extend it selectively to those of their choosing. Moreover, some trades and professions are able to use their members' collective power to maintain scarcity of their particular skills, and they thus command higher rewards than those in other types of positions.

Physicians, for example, have long been able to use their collective power to restrict the number of accredited medical schools and the number of doctors. They also have been able to make choices as to the geographic areas in which they will practice and whether to serve as general practitioners or specialists. Physicians have thus generated scarcity in relation to demand for their services that has helped to keep their average salaries high. In addition, discrimination on the basis of race and sex in medical student admissions has until fairly recently meant that medical students were overwhelmingly white males. Admissions committees often gave special preference to the sons of physicians who were alumni. By putting obstacles to admissions in front of women and people of color, such practices undermined any open system of competition among the talented to enter medicine.

Critics of the functionalist perspective on economic inequality also often point out that many jobs that one would think are very important to the operation of society, particularly jobs with significant "caretaking" responsibilities, remain poorly rewarded. These are jobs that often involve tasks that families are increasingly unable to perform, especially since most adults today are by necessity full-time participants in the labor force. One need only think of the low pay typically extended to daycare workers, those providing services to patients in nursing homes and hospices, and employees in institutional settings serving the mentally ill, recovering substance abusers, and people with serious disabilities. Many caretaking occupations are disproportionately held by women and are stereotypically defined as "women's work" (Albelda and Tilly, 1997). In a society in which the power of males over females continues to be an issue, the tendency to treat women's work as less important than men's may help to account for the gap between such jobs' pay rates and their arguable importance to society.

Finally, critics have suggested that rather than being functional, or beneficial to society, economic inequality leads to a dysfunctional situation. It harms people in innumerable ways: Economic inequality results in a lack of commitment to the larger society by the economically disadvantaged; fosters antisocial behavior such as crime and substance abuse; generates resentments, jealousies, and intergroup conflicts; and can be a very destabilizing force. Economic inequality may especially serve as source of conflict when it systematically overlaps with skin color, as is the case in the United States (see Table 7.2a and Table 7.2b).

Table 7.2a: Median Income of Families by Race and Latino/a Origin, 1990–2009 (in CURRENT dollars)

Year	All Races(a)	White	Black	Asian, Pacific Islander	Latino/a(b)
1990	35,353	39,915	21,423	42,246	23,431
1995	43,611	42,646	25,970	46,356	24,570
2000	50,732	53,029	33,676	62,617	34,442
2005	56,194	59,317	35,464	68,957	37,867
2009	60,088	62,545	38,409	75,027	39,730

Table 7.2b: Median Income of Families by Race and Latino/a Origin, 1990–2009 (in CONSTANT [2009] dollars)

Year	All Races(a)	White	Black	Asian, Pacific Islander	Latino/a(b)
1990	56,243	58,728	34,082	67,210	37,277
1995	56,755	59,598	36,293	64,783	34,337
2000	63,189	66,050	41,945	77,993	43,899
2005	61,741	65,172	38,965	75,764	41,605
2009	60,088	62,545	38,409	75,027	39,730

a Includes other races not shown separately

b People of Latino/a origin may be any race

Source: www.census.gov

A Conflict Perspective on Economic Inequality

A **conflict perspective on economic inequality** would not view it as natural and inevitable. Rather, this perspective would stress that to understand the unequal distribution of income and wealth, one must look at where power in a society resides. In his classic work *Power and Privilege* (1966), sociologist Gerhard Lenski argued that in societies that produce a surplus—more than the minimum needed for basic group survival—the people with power will determine its distribution. In his view, "power determines privilege." In the United States, for example, the distribution of economic rewards is broadly influenced by government policies toward taxation of income and wealth.

In looking at the United States, one might ask:

- To what extent do the wealthy enjoy special tax breaks not available to others?
- Does the system of taxation reduce or simply maintain economic inequalities?
- How much income assistance (if any) is provided to the poor?

When the affluent or their representatives control government, they can use their power to serve the interests of those who are already economically privileged (see Domhoff, 2009).

Understanding the relationship between power and privilege can be helpful in understanding movements for change in the formerly socialist nations of Eastern Europe. Proponents of a conflict perspective are unlikely to accept the argument that these nations were on the verge of collapse simply because they had too little economic inequality. For example, before its breakup the Soviet Union possessed a highly centralized state-controlled economy. Communist party leaders put priority on strengthening the Soviet military-industrial complex to compete in the Cold War against the United States and its allies, rather than on producing consumer goods and services needed by Soviet citizens. At the same time, the Soviet state was undemocratic and politically repressive, making it extremely difficult for citizens to express their views or have any impact on state and party decisions directly affecting them.

Top Soviet officials had exclusive authority to shop in special stores offering imported goods to foreigners, rode around in expensive government vehicles, relaxed in luxurious state-owned vacation properties, and used their political connections and social networks to get preferential treatment for their family members in regard to educational opportunities, healthcare, and jobs. The visibility of such privilege caused much resentment among Soviet citizens for many years, because it contradicted the egalitarian ideas accompanying socialist ideology (Parkin, 1971). From a conflict perspective, people living in the Soviet Union sought its transformation because they could no longer tolerate political and economic injustices that they believed were undermining their ability to live and the quality of their lives. That transformation did not come simply because the relatively modest gap between the best- and worst-paid Soviet workers stifled worker motivation.

What about economic inequality in U.S. society? Those who interpret economic inequality in the United States from a conflict perspective, as opposed to a functionalist perspective, view this inequality as the outcome of the workings of **capitalism**. In capitalist economies, ownership of a society's means of production is typically in the private hands of a small proportion of the population. In the case of the United States, the enormous income and wealth that is generated by the collective labor of the majority flows disproportionately into the hands of corporate owners. Under the principle of "power determines privilege," who and how many people will be hired (or laid off), where work will be located (or relocated) and how much (or little) workers' pay and benefits will be, are decided by top corporate officials with an eye toward maximizing profits.

Keeping workers' wages low helps to keep corporate owners' profits up and the incomes of corporate executives high. In the United States, unemployment, underemployment, economic insecurity, and poverty—or just the threat of these things occurring in one's life—act to push workers into constant competition with one another for jobs or for better-paying ones. This competition, in turn, helps to keep wages down. Employers can offer lower wages when the competition for work is intense. From the conflict perspective, economic inequality is fostered by the routine workings of capitalism and, insofar as the state intervenes in this process, it is largely on behalf of those who disproportionately receive its economic benefits and not the average worker.

Indeed, in the years since the formerly socialist Soviet Union dissolved, and Russia has been making the transition to a capitalist economic system, economic inequality has sharply increased in that nation. With most economic activity no longer centrally state-controlled and economic activity allowed to go loosely regulated, some Russian citizens have grown extremely wealthy, while others suffer unemployment and poverty at rates never seen under Soviet socialism. Many

Russian entrepreneurs have taken advantage of the state's relaxation of control over the economy to operate outside the law, and their quest for ever greater wealth has unleashed a tidal wave of corruption, organized crime, and white-collar offenses. Meanwhile, among those left poor and unemployed in Russia's new capitalist economy alcoholism, drug abuse, prostitution, suicide, and other social problems have sharply risen.

Similarly, in the United States gross economic inequality means that some members of U.S. society enjoy enormous economic privilege at the same time that millions of impoverished individuals and families experience great suffering. This suffering could be avoided, advocates of the conflict perspective point out, if the state was not far more concerned with tax breaks and other forms of "corporate welfare" from which large corporations and the affluent reap great benefits (Glasberg and Skidmore, 1997). As we have noted, more than 46 million men, women, and children live below the official federal poverty line. Millions more are "near-poor," living just above the poverty line. Many poor and near-poor adults are experiencing unemployment. But there are also many millions of adults who work full-time jobs at wages that keep them and their families below or hovering just above the poverty line. The numbers of such workers have gone up markedly in recent years.

As a consequence of the workings of U.S. capitalism, tens of millions of U.S. society's members regularly confront hunger (Schwartz-Nobel, 2002). Millions must deal with a lack of affordable housing and homelessness (Mittal and Rosset, 1999). Poverty is a major contributor to serious health problems for millions of people in the United States. Compared with the rates in other industrialized nations, U.S. infant mortality and child death rates are extremely high.

Meanwhile, the very affluent may enjoy a range of unearned invisible privileges based on that affluence. For example, affluent people can assume that all their basic needs will be met: They don't need to worry about where they will be sleeping tonight, or where their next meal is coming from. For that matter, the affluent can waste food without concern that they have squandered meager funds. Similarly, they can travel or run errands without having to worry about the cost of gas. They do not need to worry that the burden of debt will ruin them financially. They can purchase whatever they want or need and not worry that it might be too costly. They can conceal family failures and abuse within the privacy of their homes. They do not have to worry about their health or access to adequate care should they encounter physical or mental health issues. They do not have to worry that they will not be able to afford to retire. They enjoy the social perception that they are trustworthy and confront the criminal justice system perceived to be innocent until proven guilty (with the confidence that they will have adequate legal assistance) (see www.everydayfeminism.com/2012/11/30-examples-of-class-privilege). The ability to take these unearned advantages and privileges for granted frees the affluent from the day-to-day worries that plague the less fortunate.

From the conflict perspective, such obvious as well as invisible disparities of wealth and poverty characteristic of economic inequality are not "functional" to society. Such inequality exacts enormous costs from persons who experience it, whether a society's economy is capitalist or socialist. Society as a whole loses as well. A vast pool of potential talent is suppressed, as individuals who might make substantial contributions to the well-being of others are caught up in poverty and economic insecurity. They may never have the opportunity to develop or to utilize their natural gifts. Insofar as a system of economic inequality stifles human potential and shortens life spans for some, everyone suffers. The costs of economic inequality to society can be very high, especially when they include increased crime, illness and disease, and social unrest.

RACIALIZED INEQUALITY

Relationships between peoples having different physical or cultural attributes are often characterized by misunderstanding, tensions, and conflict. Conflict is particularly likely to occur when populations with different physical or cultural attributes occupy unequal positions of advantage in the existing system of economic inequality (Steinberg, 2001). In systems of **racialized inequality**, some groups are subjected to discrimination and exploitation based on their racial "minority-group" status, while others are accorded (or accord themselves) privileges denied to minority group members. A **minority group** is comprised of people who share common characteristics (e.g., skin color or geographic origin), on the basis of which they are singled out and subjected to prejudice and discriminatory treatment by others.

The term *minority group* does not mean the group is relatively small in number; rather, it indicates lack of status and power within one's society. In South Africa, for instance, blacks far outnumber whites, yet for many years black South Africans were a minority group because the dominant white population structured social institutions to ensure that blacks occupied an inferior status. This system of racialized segregation and racialized oppression, known as "apartheid," was finally abolished in 1990 after decades of social movement and protest activity and, in the 1980s, international economic and political pressures. In 1994 the first elections open to South Africans regardless of race resulted in the election of a black president, Nelson Mandela, an anti-apartheid leader who the white political regime had imprisoned for twenty-seven years.

The Concept of "Race"

In South Africa, the United States, and elsewhere, the physical trait of skin color has been used by many whites as a criterion of social worth and as an indicator of racial differences. **Race** is a category into which people are assigned based on the social meaning and significance given to certain physical (and sometimes cultural) characteristics of members of a society's population. Although frequently employed as a means of categorizing people, "race" is actually a meaningless concept in biological terms (Gould, 1996). Regardless of superficial physical characteristics such as skin color, people all belong to one human species. Variations in physical traits exist among members of the human species as a consequence of extremely slow evolutionary changes. These changes have evolved in response to differing demands of the various physical environments to which humans have long been exposed. They are also, in part, the outcome of generations of genetic selection as different groups have come into contact with one another.

Thus, such features as skin color, hair texture, and shape of the eyes, nose, or lips vary among people whose ancestries lie in diverse geographic locations. Biologically speaking, these varying features do not really depict people of different races. Race is a social concept, not a biological one. Hereditarily "pure" races simply do not exist, and existing systems of racial categorization of people are imprecise and arbitrary (Smedley, 1999).

Further, the concept of "race" is not defined by a single, consistent element along which different groups may vary; rather, the defining element changes depending upon what the group dominants in society are identifying. At times members of a dominant group will define others as racially different based on distinctive cultural characteristics (including language and religion) or their geographic origin. When the criteria for defining a group as being of another "race" is at times biological, and at others times cultural or geographic, the fact that races are socially constructed becomes painfully evident. It is not unusual for people use the term "race" to refer to a particular ethnic group. An **ethnic group** consists of persons who share a common culture, which may include a shared heritage, language or dialect, religion, norms, and customs.

Evidence abounds indicating that "race" is a changeable social construction rather than an immutable biological fact. For example, a long history exists in the United States in which the Supreme Court redefined the racial categories of various groups: Jews, Irish, and Italians who were once considered "non-white" were simply redefined as "white by law" (Lopez Haney, 2006. Others, such as East Indians, who were once defined by U.S. Citizenship and Immigration Services and the Supreme Court as white suddenly found themselves redefined as "non-white." And the biological markers defining who is white varies state by state, with some states adopting a "one drop of blood" definition of who is "non-white" and others adopting a definition anywhere from one-sixteenth to one-fourth drop. That means that one may simply travel across the borders from one state to another and suddenly "become" a different race. If race were simply a matter of biology, that would not be possible, nor could the state simply legislate the meaning of race. That such processes occur indicates quite clearly that "race" and racial formation are the result of a process in which dominants socially construct its meaning and reinforce that with an ideology of supposed innate white superiority.

Cultural or geographic origin differences may or may not coincide with skin color. But some people have long argued that people in the United States who are of African ancestry are members of a distinct "race" that is biologically and psychologically inferior to that of whites (Gossett, 1997). Until the mid-twentieth century this was widely taken to be a scientific truth. A number of scientists argued that persons of African descent had smaller brains than whites and therefore, by nature, were less intelligent. Even the famous scientist of evolution, Charles Darwin, stated:

> *With civilized nations, the reduced size of the jaws from lessened*
> *use, the habitual play of different muscles serving to express different*
> *emotions, and the increased size of the brain from greater intellectual*
> *activity, have together produced a considerable effect on [whites']*
> *general appearance in comparison with savages (quoted in*
> *Gossett, 1997: 78).*

Since they were less intelligent, the reasoning went, African Americans were fit only for the low-level work whites set aside for them. This argument for racial inferiority served as part of a larger ideology justifying the enslavement of African Americans and the constitutional declaration that slaves were not fully human, but rather counted only as three-fifths of a human being. Later, the same argument was used by racist politicians to justify segregated public education: Mixing the allegedly less intelligent African Americans with whites in the same classroom would harm the progress of the whites.

Michael Omi and Howard Winant favor the term **racial formation** to underscore the social construction of "race" as a concept (1994). Racial formation is "the socio-historical process by which racial categories are created, inhabited, transformed, and destroyed" (Omi and Winant, 1994:55). Designating a particular population a "race" may be a first step toward singling it out for discrimination. The alleged negative characteristics of a group that is racially categorized are often claimed to be rooted in genetics and therefore impossible to change. This type of thinking can lead to **genocide**, the systematic extermination of a group of people by those who consider themselves racially superior.

A society in which the "race" of people is thought to be significant is likely to be racist; there is no other reason for genetic variations in appearance or cultural differences such as language or geographic origin to be of any particular concern. Systems of racial inequality are socially constructed around the false assumption that a link exists between these features and the ways in which people are likely to think or behave. Just as humans cannot change their skin color or their geographic origins, this view suggests that neither can they escape what these imply about their social worth.

Personal Racism

Sociologists interested in the ways in which racism is expressed have identified two types of racism, personal and institutional (Feagin and Feagin, 1999). The first type, called **personal racism**, is racism expressed by individuals or small groups of people. It is an indication of bigotry or prejudice against those deemed "racially" inferior, and it may take such forms as espousing stereotypes based on alleged racial differences, using racial slurs, and engaging in discriminatory treatment, harassment, and even threats or acts of violence.

Here it is important to distinguish between **prejudice** and **discrimination**. Prejudice involves bigoted *attitudes*, and discrimination involves racist *actions* informed by prejudice. Anyone—including people of color—may harbor racially prejudicial attitudes. But whites are generally much freer to express personal racism by acting upon their prejudices, often with abandon and without concern for consequences, a privilege associated with their dominant power position in this society's system of racial inequality. In that regard, while just about everyone may harbor prejudicial attitudes about people different from themselves, the advantaged status of whites in the United States places them in a position to act on those attitudes in ways that have far-reaching consequences for others, a position not available to racialized minorities.

The view that some people are both racially different and less valuable and more objectionable as a population still exists among many members of the white majority in the United States. This view is reflected in sociologist Joe Feagin's analysis of survey data gathered in the 1990s. Data from one survey, conducted by the University of Chicago's National Opinion Research Center, indicated the following (www.norc.org/GSS):

- More than 33 percent of whites opposed a close relative or family member marrying an African American.
- More than 27 percent of whites said they would oppose living in a neighborhood where half of their neighbors were African American.
- When asked how many African Americans they trusted, more than 44 percent of white respondents indicated "zero."
- Nearly 46 percent of white respondents thought that African Americans received more government attention than they deserved.
- When asked if they ever felt admiration about African Americans and their families, more than 36 percent said "not too often," and an additional 6.5 percent said "never."

One must be cautious in looking at such survey outcomes, for it is possible that some survey respondents are uncomfortable revealing racist ideas to strangers—in this case, survey researchers—as opposed to friends or neighbors. Thus the survey results may underestimate racial bigotry. In any event, surveys routinely indicate that personal racism is alive and well in the United States.

Racist thinking on the part of individuals is both stimulated and reinforced by pseudo-scientific claims that there are biologically based differences in the capabilities of different "races" (e.g., see Rushton, 1997). This notion, of course, requires acceptance of the assumption that biologically distinct races actually exist, which is not the case. In 1994, psychologist Richard J. Herrnstein and political scientist Charles Murray published *The Bell Curve*, in which they argued that there are innate differences in mental abilities along the lines of race. African Americans, for example, were said to be less intelligent on average than whites. Herrnstein and Murray's book was widely reported on in the mass media. Their ideas and the adequacy of their data were overwhelmingly rejected by social scientists as well as biologists, geneticists, and other scholars in the physical and life sciences (see Gould, 1996). Even so, the seriousness with which such ideas are treated by the mass media work to keep alive stereotypes about racial inferiority, and these media stereotypes in turn feed personal racism.

Institutional Racism

As an example of personal racism, one cannot help but recall the horrific 1998 murder in Texas of 49-year-old James Byrd Jr. He was an African American man who was kidnapped by three white men, chained to the back of a pickup truck, and dragged for three miles until he was dismembered ("Life Sentence in Dragging Death," 1999). As outrageous and damaging as expressions of personal racism may be, this form of racism in general has a less far-reaching effect upon the life chances of people of color than does the racism that is built into societal institutions, known as **institutional racism**.

An *institution* is a social structure created by people in order to accomplish certain tasks or perform certain needed functions in society. The economy and the state are examples of institutions. People of color have historically been excluded from key policy-making and decision-making roles in such institutions. This has contributed to institutional racism, whereby the routine everyday operation of societal institutions fosters white privilege and advantage. Institutional racism often operates silently and subtly, through processes that are not immediately obvious and that are difficult to detect and observe (Smith, 1995).

Racism and the Economy

Within the economy, for example, racial discrimination in employment continues to be a major problem. This discrimination helps to keep the income of white households higher on average than those of people of color. A study involving interviews with Chicago-area employers revealed the blatant racist stereotypes and hiring policies of many toward workers of color:

> *When they talked about the work ethic, tensions in the workplace,*
> *or attitudes toward work, employers emphasized the color of a*
> *person's skin. Many believed that white workers were superior*
> *to minorities in their work ethic (Kirschenman and Neckerman,*
> *1991: 209–210).*

As one employer told the researchers,

> *(According to) the energy that they put into their job and trying*
> *to be as productive as possible, I would have to put the white*
> *native-born at the high end and the Hispanic in the middle and*
> *the blacks at the bottom (Kirschenman and Neckerman, 1991: 210).*

Employers, acting on these stereotypes, tried to avoid hiring minority workers as a matter of routine (see also Wilson, 1996 Chapter Five). The study found that as a matter of policy they relied on their white employees to refer friends and relatives for job openings, and regularly placed job advertisements in papers serving particular white communities and white ethnic groups. African Americans or Latino/a Americans who somehow made it as far as an interview would often be screened out at that point.

Racial discrimination also affects career opportunities in higher level positions. For example, the federal government's Glass Ceiling Commission investigated the reasons why so few people of color are hired by top management to be executives in large U.S. corporations. According to the commission's findings,

> *Color-based differences are inescapable but nobody likes to talk about*
> *Them . . . . The unstated but ever-present question is, "Do they look like us?" . . .*
> *Though it is mostly covert, our society has developed an extremely*
> *sophisticated, and often denied, acceptability index based on gradations*
> *in skin color. It is not legally permissible, but it persists just beneath the*
> *surface, and it can be and is used as a basis for decisionmaking, sometimes*
> *consciously and sometimes unconsciously (quoted in Zweigenhaft and*
> *Domhoff, 1998: 110–111).*

Institutional racism need not be as direct as in the examples above. Indeed, some institutional practices have differential and discriminatory effects on people of color that do not appear to be intentional. Take, for example, seniority rules, often seen by unions as important worker pro-tections. The most familiar such rule is "last hired, first fired." Employers abiding by seniority rules dismiss their most recently hired employees first whenever cutbacks or layoffs occur. Since African Americans, Latino/a Americans, Asian Americans, Native Americans, and others who have fought against racial discrimination are often over-represented among the most recent arrivals in traditionally white-dominated work settings, seniority rules are unlikely to protect them from unemployment.

Racism and the State

Another societal institution, the state, often seems less than aggressive in addressing racism and its consequences, or in enforcing laws against discrimination. At the federal level, for example, there are typically vast backlogs of complaints regarding incidents of racial discrimination, and many victims believe it is useless to file a complaint. Institutional racism by the state often takes the form of neglect or indifference. At times, however, state officials have actively tried to water down or retract existing state policies designed to assist victims of racism (Edsall and Edsall, 1992).

For example, the civil rights movement of the 1960s successfully pressured the state to adopt regulations requiring that employers take **affirmative action** to stop discrimination against people of color, as well as women (Reskin, 1998). Affirmative action not only meant that discrimination in hiring was to cease, but also that employers were to take positive ("affirmative") steps to increase the presence of people of color and women in their applicant pools, thus improving the opportunity for such persons to be considered and hired if qualified. Ordinarily, this required little more of employers than that they widen their advertising of openings and drop discriminatory pre-employment screening practices. Only in some instances, when employers clearly resisted taking such positive steps, were they temporarily forced to abide by court-ordered hiring "quotas" aimed at breaking down systemic discrimination. Affirmative action policies have had their greatest effect in government employment and, to a lesser extent, in the corporate sector. When implemented effectively, such policies have allowed individuals who had previously been excluded from particular workplaces to learn of opportunities, become part of applicant pools, and often to successfully compete for employment (Reskin, 1998).

Political opponents of affirmative action claim that discrimination in hiring has disappeared and that affirmative action is a form of "reverse discrimination" against whites and males. Its opponents further claim that unqualified workers have been hired simply to meet race and gender "quotas." Even though research by social scientists has shown such claims to be invalid (Reskin, 1998), they continue to be cited by politicians seeking to court white votes by playing on the white majority's frequent misunderstanding of and hostility to affirmative action (Edsall and Edsall, 1992).

Affirmative action policies were a direct outgrowth of the political pressure applied against the state by the civil rights movement of the 1960s and its supporters. But by the mid-1970s that movement had gone into decline, ironically in part due to its successes. When federal legislation outlawed the most blatant forms of racial discrimination, many movement supporters assumed the struggle for racial equality was over. Soon, the state began to do little more than pay lip service to affirmative action, and public support for it eroded as many politicians called the need for it into question. In turn, state pressure on employers to conform to affirmative action requirements waned, and their enforcement has since remained a low priority. In recent years government agencies have shown little interest in even studying the problems of racial (or gender) discrimination in employment.

In the 1980s top politicians routinely distanced themselves from the issue of affirmative action in political campaigns, and some ran openly on platforms decrying "reverse discrimination." The Reagan administration (1980–1988) and the George H. W. Bush administration (1988–1992) were openly hostile to affirmative action, and strict attention to state enforcement of regulations generally declined. In the 1990s, while never pushing affirmative action as an important government priority, the Clinton administration (1992–2000) did fend off calls for its abolition by its harshest critics. The latter included many strong supporters of the George W. Bush administration that followed.

The increasingly uncertain future of affirmative action was, however, dramatically altered in 2003. Despite the public opposition of the Bush administration, in a case involving the University of Michigan (*Grutter v. Bollinger*) the U.S. Supreme Court narrowly ruled in support of the use of affirmative action to achieve student diversity in higher education admissions

(Greenhouse, 2003a). This ruling was expected to have a broad effect, for it also indirectly supported the legitimacy of efforts that have been undertaken by a number of major corporations to diversify their workplaces. Growing numbers of firms are coming to realize the economic benefits of having a diverse workforce as they seek to sell goods and services to multicultural domestic and global markets.

In large part, institutional racism by the state is a reflection of the state's racial composition. The fact that whites are in the numerical majority in most parts of the country has meant they can—when they wish—block people of color from high elected office (the notable exception is the election of Barack Obama as president of the United States in 2008; that it is a notable exception underscores its rarity). Moreover, at the top levels of state bureaucracy, where crucial public policy decisions are made, positions are typically filled through political appointment. This has made it very difficult for people of color to rise as high as their talents and accomplishments may merit. Those who do may have to sacrifice being assertive about minority interests in return for the employment opportunity they have been afforded by representatives of the white majority.

Recent research on the composition of the nation's "power elite"—those who occupy top positions in government, military, and the corporate world—shows that skin color clearly matters. Prior to the 1960s civil rights movement, hardly any people of color were ever found in such positions. While there is evidence that diversity among members of the power elite has increased since then, African Americans and darker-skinned Latino/as seem to be having the most difficulty gaining admittance into these higher circles of power (Zweigenhaft and Domhoff, 2006).

The state's criminal justice system is also white-dominated. The subject of law enforcement has always been a particularly sensitive one for people of color, due to their mistreatment by the criminal justice system (Mann and Zatz, 2002; Reiman, 2012). The use of racial profiling in routine stop-and-frisk police policies and practices, for example, often results in charges that amount to "driving while black" or in the unfair arrest of people of color even when they have not violated any laws. Until fairly recently, employment discrimination in police departments was rampant as well. Moreover, even today police departments frequently either ignore charges of police officer misconduct and acts of brutality against people of color or perform internal "investigations" of such charges by police officials with little result. Police have a monopoly over the legitimate use of force, but its misuse has led to mistrust, hostility, and occasionally civil disorder. Acts of police brutality have at times generated violent rebellions in ghettos, in barrios, and on reservations. Police brutality was, for example, an issue in the massive disorders in Los Angeles in 1992 that followed the acquittal of white police officers who had been videotaped beating Rodney King, an African American.

The dominant white majority is also over-represented among judges, prosecutors, jurors, prison officials, probation officers, and parole board members. People of color are more likely than whites to be arrested and charged with crimes, to be unable to afford bail, and to lack the funds needed to hire an attorney to defend them. People of color are more likely to be found guilty, to receive heavy sentences, and to be denied requests for parole from prison. Once released, they are likely to face very restricted employment opportunities, a situation that sets the stage for possible further involvement with the legal system. Those convicted of felonies are very likely to face permanent loss of their basic political right to vote. For too many persons, going through the criminal justice process is like being trapped in a revolving door (Reiman, 2012).

There are many unearned, invisible privileges of white skin in the United States. Peggy McIntosh (1992) identified a long list of these, including, for example, white people can shop alone with the assurance that shopkeepers will not follow or harass them. When taught about our national heritage or about "civilization," they will learn that people who look like them are responsible for making it that way. They can assume that they can find foods consistent with their cultural traditions in the supermarket, and a hairstylist who knows how to cut and style their hair. They can buy bandaids labeled "flesh" knowing these will generally match their skin tone. They can speak in public without being asked to speak for all white people. They can assume that when they accomplish something, they are not viewed as "a credit to their race." They can pay for purchases using cash, credit, or checks, without their whiteness affecting assumptions about their financial ability to pay. They can criticize the government and its leaders without being marginalized as a racial malcontent. They can assume that when they are pulled over by the police while driving on the highway that they are not being targeted because they are white. And they can accept a job or enroll in a university without others assuming they got it not because they are qualified but because of affirmative action.

In documenting the effects of racism, most social scientists have (understandably) looked at its effects on people of color. Yet it is clear that all of society's members—including whites—lose as a consequence of racism, if only because the system of racial inequality stifles the potential accomplishments of millions of people from which everyone could benefit. But in addition, whites are not really "free" in a society in which social significance is accorded to physical traits like skin color or cultural traits like geographic origin or language. All whites, not just the visible bigots, are limited in the quality of their social relationships with people of color. Whites can find themselves imprisoned by the minority group anger and resentment to which racial inequalities give rise, spending great amounts of money for private security forces and security systems to protect them from perceived threats and dangers posed by "those people." Even freedom of movement may be affected, insofar as racism-based stereotypes about "dangerous" people guide whites' decisions about where it is safe to go and what events it is safe to attend. It is worth taking time to imagine how everyone's biography might be greatly altered, and certainly improved, by living in a nonracist society.

GENDERED INEQUALITY

Just as systems of economic inequality and racialized inequality have ideologies justifying their existence, so too do systems of **gendered inequality**. Gendered inequality stems from the notion that "biology is destiny," that biological differences between the sexes dictate that the sexes must necessarily play very different societal roles.

Males and females obviously do differ biologically. Their genetic makeups are not the same, anatomical differences are apparent, and their hormones perform different functions. But how much social importance should one attach to such differences? To answer this question, we must make a distinction between two concepts: sex and gender.

Sex refers to the fundamental biological characteristics that people generally use to categorize persons as either female or male. These characteristics are genetically determined and are largely related to different potential roles each may play in reproduction. Rarely is there ambiguity as to the sex of any given newborn once the baby's physical traits are established.

Moreover, sex differences remain the same from society to society across historical time and across borders, a clear indicator that sex is indeed a biological distinction.

Gender, on the other hand, is a social construction, much like "race." Gender refers to the ways of behaving and relating to others that members of society expect of the two sexes; it refers to the different roles males and females are expected to play. Gender is learned, whereas sex is inherited and established in one's DNA. As such, the behaviors associated with gender differ in various respects from society to society, and over time within single societies. For example, in some societies women are expected to be active and aggressive individuals, while in others they are expected to be passive and retiring. Indeed, even within societies the role expectations for women may differ—for example, by age, ethnicity, or class (Lindsey and Christy, 1996; Nanda, 1999). And, role expectations within societies may change over time. The difference between sex and gender, then, is that we ARE a sex by our DNA when we're born, but we DO gender as a practice of social constructions.

Nonetheless, males have used the ideology expressed in "biology is destiny" to create and maintain systems of gender inequality in which they dominate. The concept of **patriarchy** is used to refer to such systems. Not only domination but oppression and exploitation are common themes in societies characterized by patriarchy. While undergoing important changes in the last few decades, U.S. society is still very patriarchal. Men and women are not equal sharers of power—whether it is economic, political, or social. This is the case, to greater or lesser degrees, in most societies around the world. The biology-is-destiny ideology hovers over women, justifying male dominance and advantage, influencing male-female relationships, and affecting the trajectory of both sexes' biographies and life chances.

The "Biology is Destiny" Ideology

According to this ideology, biological differences between the sexes require that there be a **sexual division of labor**, in which men and women take on responsibility for the tasks that each sex is naturally most capable of performing. Hence, because women bear children female biology dictates that they are most fit for child-rearing and caretaking roles in the home. The home is said to be the best place for those whom nature has decreed the "weaker sex." It is a haven from the rough, competitive world of work and politics in which only men, portrayed as biologically the "stronger sex," are able to excel. It is the men's role to protect and provide for their "dependents": women and children.

The ideology suggests that the need for the species to reproduce promulgates yet another important role for women: being sexually attractive. Women thus play an important function when they strive to be, and allow themselves to be, treated as sex objects. This is all in line with nature's grand design.

The biology-is-destiny ideology spills over into the workplace and other institutional arenas outside the home (Lindsey and Christy, 1996). The rigidity of the ideology has eroded somewhat, but most people still accept that there are "men's jobs" and "women's jobs." Few chief executive officers or other top officials of the nation's largest corporations are women (Zweigenhaft and Domhoff, 2006). But most clerks, secretaries, nurses, elementary school teachers, childcare workers, social workers, and domestic helpers are women. Why? According to the ideology, this division of labor simply reflects the basic biological differences between the sexes:

Men are presumed to be naturally equipped to exercise power and authority and to function under demanding circumstances. Women are presumed biologically best suited for supportive, caretaking occupations and professions—those that call upon the particular strengths nature has given women.

Critics of the ideology and the restrictions it imposes on women's life chances include **feminists** and their supporters. Feminism refers to the belief that men and women should have equal political, social, and economic rights. Feminists underscore the difference between sex and gender, pointing out that the gendered roles accorded women are largely of men's making. Women alone are capable of bearing children, but men are as capable as women in playing a nurturing role. They simply choose to allocate most such tasks to women. Nor is there reason to restrict women to the home out of concern that they are the weaker sex. Given the opportunity, women can fulfill virtually any position in work and politics that is presently male-dominated (recall, for example that during World War II women filled innumerable civilian roles for men who left for the military, including riveting, plane and shipbuilding, munitions manufacturing, and other physically demanding and exhausting jobs). Similarly, men are eminently capable of doing so-called "women's work" in the labor force, as is becoming evident as more men, left unemployed and bereft of opportunities in many male-dominated jobs by the Great Recession of 2008–2013 are increasingly entering female-dominated jobs like nursing and elementary education.

Finally, current social conditions make it clear that women can and must be able to support themselves, instead of functioning as males' "dependents." The millions of women who are unmarried, separated, divorced, or widowed—many with children or others to support—are independent by necessity or choice. The demands faced by these women, for their own survival and that of their families, often cannot be met by the earnings accorded to "women's work" (Albelda and Tilly, 1997). Feminists also question the notion that women must put priority upon making themselves attractive to men in order to ensure reproduction of the species. Standards of beauty and attractiveness tend to be set by members of the dominant gender. Most women are unable to meet these standards, but there are always some who can—or can at least meet them better than others. Thus, many women are raised to live in fear of rejection by men and to see other women as threats. Feminists do not see women's role as sex object as natural and inevitable, but as yet another instrument of male domination.

Male Chauvinism and Institutional Sexism

Patriarchy, as a system of gendered inequality, finds expression through practices of **sexism**. This term refers to the systematic subordination of persons on the basis of their sex. Similar to racism, sexism exists both at the level of personal relationships and at the institutional level.

At the personal level, sexism typically takes the form of **male chauvinism**. Men who are chauvinistic express attitudes or behave in ways that suggest that males are superior to females and have a right to insist on females' subordination. Chauvinistic attitudes can range from sexist points of view ("Women are too emotional to be president of the United States") to extreme sexist behaviors ("I wouldn't call it rape—the way she was acting, she was asking for it").

Overt expressions of male chauvinism can be confronted, but such confrontation may sometimes be dangerous in a society in which men hold an unequal share of power. Women who challenge the sexist views and behaviors of a professor or employer, for example, may end up receiving a poorer grade than deserved, being overlooked for a promotion, or being dismissed from work. While feminists and their supporters have pressed the state to provide legal protections for women who are the victims of this type of harassment, it remains widespread.

Institutional sexism fosters male advantage through the routine operations of societal institutions. In the spheres of the economy and the state institutional sexism is pervasive, yet often less visible and less open to direct confrontation than male chauvinism. Given its far-reaching impact, institutional sexism is more of a problem than chauvinism—not only for women but for men as well.

Women and the Labor Force

Despite the biology-as-destiny ideology that stresses women's alleged biological proclivity for homemaking and childcare, by 2010 nearly 59 percent of all women over 16 were in the paid labor force (www.dol.gov). Most were working out of economic necessity, either because they had sole responsibility to provide for themselves (and, in many cases, others) or because their partners were incapable of being the sole providers. This is particularly true in the aftermath of the Great Recession of 2008–2012, when more men than women found their jobs eliminated, particularly in manufacturing and mining, and women's employment opportunities more plentiful in the service sector. Yet by all statistical indicators, women get much smaller rewards on average for their participation in the labor force than do men. And the pay they receive for the work they do is on average significantly lower than that for men. This state of affairs is understandable only in light of institutional sexism.

The U.S. labor market is sex-segregated to the point where it is common for social scientists to use the term **dual labor market** to describe it (Tomaskovic-Devey, 1993). Most women hold jobs in which the majority of their coworkers are female. Women are overly represented in jobs that are the least well paying, offer the least security, and have relatively low prestige—clerical work and service occupations (such as wait staff). Conversely, women are under-represented in the jobs highest in pay, security, and status.

In 2010, the United States Department of Labor reported that working women were paid on average 81 cents for every dollar in wages that men were paid, and women of color earn lower average wages than white women (www.bls.gov). Over 1 million women work in jobs that pay less than the federal minimum wage (www.now.org). This dual labor market is not a reflection of educational differences between men and women; women, on average, have the edge over men in years of formal education completed and average lower pay than men for the same level of educational attainment (www.census.gov). Rather, the dual labor market is held intact by discrimination in employment, promotion, and pay. By paying less for "women's jobs" than for "men's jobs," and by channeling women into the former, employers use the biology-is-destiny ideology to their own economic advantage.

Just as there are unearned invisible privileges of being among the dominant status in other systems of inequality, there are things that can be taken for granted simply because one is male in a male-dominated society: When men speak in a group, they can assume that they will be respected as intelligent; they can remain unmarried for a very long time (or forever) and not be pitied as an unwanted loser or disparaged as an "old maid" (but rather viewed with some envy as a "confirmed bachelor"); they can be reasonably sure that if they do not get the job or the promotion, it is not because they are a man; they can argue with their partner or their colleagues and not have their passion interpreted as linked to their hormones or described as irrational or too emotional; men can take their car into a repair shop or go to a new car dealer and not be talked down to or presumed to be ignorant because of their sex; and they can assume that when they are described to others, their sex will not be used as a qualifier (as in, "Arthur, the male teacher" or "Mark, the male Senator"). These invisible, unearned privileges of maleness, then, affect not only social interactions but also men's and women's experiences in the labor market.

The struggle of women to improve their standing in the labor market is relatively recent and follows upon similar struggles by people of color to end racialized discrimination. But institutional sexism in the economy, like institutional racism, is a routine matter largely because the state does so little about it. Indeed, the state itself is a locus of institutional sexism in employment. Women are poorly represented in the elected and appointed offices that make important policy decisions. They thus have limited power in resolving major issues affecting women's lives. These issues include the level of income maintenance provided to poor female-headed families, government support for affordable daycare for working mothers, the need for programs providing universal healthcare, and the protection of women's reproductive rights (Albelda and Tilly, 1997; Mink 2002).

Are Males Harmed by Gender Inequality?

Does the system of gendered inequality enhance or promote the life chances of men? Do men benefit from patriarchy? Why should society do without the full range of contributions that women can make? The answer is that narrow benefits for some are outweighed by much broader losses for all. Any society in which the opportunities for women—typically half the population— are channeled and restricted is a society that is limited in its development.

Working to change patriarchy would make available a much wider range of biographies for people of both sexes. For example, married men and women with jobs outside the home could each escape the irrational constrictions posed by gendered norms when it comes to household work. As it now stands, even when women work outside the home, they still perform most of the household chores as well. Employers could reduce the rigidity of bureaucratic work organizations, thereby allowing much more flexibility in both women's and men's job assignments and work schedules. This could better accommodate meeting needs at home. Marital partners would be able to more equitably share the burdens and the joys of childcare and other household responsibilities that are now largely considered "women's work."

Were men to significantly increase their contributions to household labor, married women would no longer half-jokingly complain that their daily lives could be improved immensely if only they too had "a wife." As men's roles at home expanded into new arenas of household competence and accomplishment, their female partners would no longer be forced to chafe under a sexual division of labor that so clearly limits their horizons and the uses to which they can put their talents and time. Moreover, were women equitably treated in the labor market, the economic pressure on male "bread-winners" would be less. Their male partners would also be freer to leave unsatisfying jobs or seek additional education in lieu of paid work, options that are currently inaccessible to many men. Clearly, many men would see tangible benefits from the elimination of patriarchy.

SEXUAL ORIENTATION AND INEQUALITY

Sexual orientation is one of the most important aspects of people's biographies. Matters ranging from whom people are likely to choose as a mate to what kinds of protections they are afforded under the law will be influenced by whether people are homosexual, heterosexual, **bisexual**, or **transgendered**. People who are bisexual lean more toward one orientation or the other, engaging in physical and emotional relationships with members of both the same and opposite sex. People who are transgendered may be **transvestites** (dressing in the culturally accepted clothing of the opposite sex) or **transsexuals** (surgically altering or correcting their physical sex to align with their emotional or core sex).

Social science research on human sexual behavior indicates that both men and women occupy places on a broad spectrum in terms of their sexual interests and practices and that there is a great deal of diversity across cultures (Nanda, 1999). Not only is there diversity within U.S. society, but many people move around on this spectrum over the course of their lives. Because of these variations, the terms "homosexual" and "heterosexual" are rather arbitrary categories (Fausto-Sterling, 2000). Only at the far ends of the continuum are individuals who are exclusively lifelong homosexuals or heterosexuals in terms of both their identity and behavior.

Interestingly, it was not until the late eighteenth and early nineteenth centuries that the concept of "homosexual" emerged in Europe and the United States (Greenberg, 1988). Individuals who engaged in sexual activities with persons of the same sex were not seen as unique in any way apart from this behavior. This is not to say homosexual practices were widely accepted. Such behavior was condemned by Judeo-Christian religions and prohibited by law.

The concept of homosexuality emerged largely as a result of the medical profession's claim to have "scientifically" established that such behavior was abnormal and pathological, only engaged in by persons who were a separate and different human type (Fausto-Sterling, 2000; Greenberg, 1988). Despite such allegations, which continue today, no one has yet been able to definitively establish any biological or psychological traits (apart from sexual orientation) that differentiate homosexuals from anyone else. The findings from studies attempting to explore the biological foundations of homosexuality remain inconclusive. Whatever the ultimate findings of such studies, there is no reason that they should be used as a basis for defining homosexuality in negative terms.

The Ideology of Heterosexism

The sexual practices many associate with homosexuality have been found in many cultures and historical periods. It is not unusual for practices associated with both heterosexuality and homosexuality to be part of a cultural repertoire (Nanda, 1999). The dominant culture within the United States, however, is supportive of a system of **inequality based on sexual orientation**. As we will discuss, many people condemn those perceived as fitting into the category of "homosexual," a category that is socially constructed to include gay men, lesbians, bisexuals, and those who are transgendered.

Today, prejudicial attitudes and institutionalized discrimination are widespread against individuals labeled as homosexual. Gay men, lesbians, bisexuals, and transgenders are the daily victims of emotions ranging from disgust to fear to hatred on the part of persons who demand that everyone adhere to the dominant norm of heterosexuality. An ideology called **heterosexism**, which holds that homosexuality is unnatural and immoral, strongly prevails in U.S. society.

Heterosexism affects a large number of people in the United States. Pioneering studies by Alfred Kinsey and others concluded that 10 percent of the U.S. population is predominantly homosexual (Kinsey, Pomeroy, and Martin, 1948; Kinsey et al., 1953). While some would argue that this figure is too high, others believe it is an underestimate (see Marcus, 1999). Many persons who have had or continue to have sexual experiences with members of their own sex do not see themselves as homosexual. Many call themselves bisexual, indicating that their lifestyles also allow for heterosexual practices. All these people, as well as their parents, family members, and friends, are affected by heterosexism. Clearly, the system of inequality based on sexual orientation plays a role in the biographies of a substantial proportion of people in the United States.

In a national CNN public opinion poll, 60 percent said they know someone who is gay (http://politicalticker.blogs.cnn.com/2012/06/06/cnn-poll-americans-attitudes-toward-gay-community-changing). Yet many people continue to accept the myths accompanying the ideology of heterosexism. Many do not want to know about issues of particular importance to homosexuals. Neither the media nor educational institutions have done much to encourage interest, let alone understanding.

Mistaken Notions about Homosexuality

There are many mistaken notions about homosexuality (see Marcus, 1999):

1. *"There aren't many gay people in the United States."* Since so many gay men and lesbians, bisexuals, and transgenders are forced to hide their sexual orientation, there seem to be far fewer than is actually the case.

2. *"Homosexuals are easy to identify."* Many people believe that homosexuals can be identified simply by appearance or gestures. But, in fact, one cannot discern a person's sexual orientation merely by observing him or her.

3. *"Homosexuality is caused by mental illness, willful perversity, or recruitment by other homosexuals."* This view ignores the fact that homosexuality is a natural inclination found in virtually every society. Homosexuals generally are mentally healthy, do not choose their sexual orientation, and come to realize their orientation without contact with other homosexuals.

4. *"Gay men and lesbians lead unproductive, dissolute lives."* In reality, homosexuals are in all occupations, professions, and callings. As accomplished homosexuals in medicine, the clergy, the arts, education, the military, sports, politics, and business increasingly refuse to hide their sexual orientation, the productivity and contributions of gay men and lesbians are becoming more apparent.

5. *"Homosexuals are terribly unhappy people because of their affliction."* Rates of substance abuse and suicidal behavior are thought to be higher among homosexuals than within the "straight" population, but this difference very likely reflects the negative treatment homosexuals often experience, not something innate.

6. *"Homosexuals are likely to give you AIDS."* Not only is this an erroneous stereotype, but it is dangerous. It ignores the high likelihood of contracting AIDS from those who are not gay. There is no reason to avoid homosexuals (assuming one knows who they are to begin

with). It is not possible to contract AIDS through casual contact with homosexuals or, for that matter, heterosexuals.

7. *"With proper treatment, people can change from homosexual to heterosexual."* Consider how improbable the reverse assertion seems: "With proper treatment, people can be changed from heterosexual to homosexual." Homosexuality is not an illness. There are no "treatments" that can change people's basic sexual orientation in either direction.

National public opinion polls reveal very mixed attitudes toward homosexuals, although there is evidence that this is changing. In 2000, 51 percent of adults polled said that gays and lesbians should not be allowed to legally marry, although fewer (46 percent) objected to their entering into domestic partnerships that give same-sex couples the same rights and benefits as opposite-sex married couples (Associated Press, 2000). Less than half of those polled supported providing Social Security, employer health insurance coverage, and inheritance rights to gay partners (Associated Press, 2000). At least a third of registered voters believed that gays should not be allowed to serve openly in the military (Fox News/Opinion Dynamics, 2000). While only 11 to 13 percent of adults thought that racial minorities, religious and ethnic minorities, and women, should not be covered by state hate crime laws, 20 percent would reject applying such laws to homosexuals (Gallup Organization, 1999). By 2012, there was evidence that these attitudes were changing: For example, 54 percent of respondents said that same-sex marriage should be recognized by law as valid (http://politicalticker.blogs.cnn.com/2012/06/06/cnn-poll-americans-attitudes-toward-gay-community-changing). And in 2013 President Obama signed a repeal of the military's "Don't Ask, Don't Tell" policy against gays and lesbians.

Although public opinion does indeed appear to be shifting in favor of the rights of gays and lesbians, they continue to not only suffer harassment and discrimination but have few rights to protection under the law. Indeed, many people believe that there are already too many laws that give "special rights" to homosexuals. In a national poll commissioned by NBC News and the Wall Street Journal in 1999, 42 percent of adults felt this way (NBC News/Wall Street Journal, 1999). Yet, gay males and lesbians, bisexuals, and transgenders deny they want any "special rights" at all. What they do want is the legal rights, protections, and recourse to legal action against discrimination that most other citizens are able to take for granted.

Discriminatory Practices against Gay Males and Lesbians

Many employers discriminate against homosexuals in hiring. Landlords refuse them housing. Insurance companies refuse to provide coverage. Six states have laws and 31 states have constitutional amendments banning same-sex marriage. Child-custody rights or visitation privileges are often at issue for a homosexual parent. And "gay-bashing" has become a common term, denoting violent attacks on both gay males and lesbians, bisexuals, and transgenders by those seeking to uphold the heterosexual norm. In many settings, such attacks are not recognized as hate crimes; sometimes they are not even investigated.

The fear of hate violence among homosexuals is not overstated (Sloan and Gustavson, 2000). After the horrendous 1998 murder of Matthew Shepherd, a gay student at the University of Wyoming who was beaten viciously, tied to a rural country fence, and left to die, 68 percent of adults polled stated that an attack such as this could happen in their own communities (CNN/

Time, 1998). According to the National Coalition of Anti-Violence Programs, a network of 26 organizations that monitor and respond to hate incidents in locales across the United States, rates of violence against people based on their sexual orientation (or their *perceived* orientation) are high, taking forms ranging from harassment and intimidation to assault and even murder (National Coalition of Anti-Violence Programs, 2002).

In the early 1990s the Clinton administration changed Defense Department policy to allow homosexuals to serve discreetly in all ranks and in all military services, a policy reflecting the controversy surrounding the dismissal of many highly talented people found to be gay. Under this policy of "don't ask, don't tell," members of the armed forces were not required to reveal their sexual orientation, but homosexual conduct remained grounds for dismissal. Under this policy, gay service members continued to be dismissed at a high rate, including thousands who were fluent in languages such as Farsi, Arabic, and Sanskrit, leaving the military with a severe shortage of translators in Iraq and Afghanistan. President Obama eventually eliminated that policy, but not before significant damage had been done to both the individuals and the military itself. Notably, even in the absence of overt homosexual conduct, and even after the elimination of "don't ask, don't tell," harassment and violence against those known or thought to be gay remains a serious problem in many military settings. There are numerous unearned invisible privileges associated with being heterosexual in such societies. For example, heterosexual people can hold hands or kiss their partner in public without getting stared at or disparaged with disgust. They can bring their partner to an office party without their sexuality becoming a potential threat to their employment. They can count on their partner being allowed to make decisions about their care should they become too ill to make such decisions. They can count on their partner receiving coverage under their healthcare or pension benefits. They can take advantage of any and all tax deductions and benefits allowed to married couples. They can attend their children's school functions with their partner without jeopardizing their children's social reputations among their peers. They can assume that when they speak in a group they are not asked to speak for all heterosexuals or have their point of view presumed to be biased by their sexuality. And they can assume that when they are described to others, their sexuality will not be used as a qualifier (as in, "Jane, the lesbian teacher" or "Joe, the gay Senator") (see www.everydayfeminism .com/2012/10/30-examples-of-heterosexual-privilege-in-the-US).

Some Signs of Change

In a milestone action, President George H. W. Bush signed the National Hate Crimes Statistics Act of 1990, which requires the Department of Justice to gather nationwide statistics on crimes motivated by prejudice on the basis of race, religion, ethnic background, or sexual orientation. This was the first time a U.S. president ever signed a bill including sexual orientation as a civil rights concern—and the first time gay rights representatives had ever been invited to the White House for a public ceremony in which a bill was signed into law.

Yet, while the Hate Crimes Statistics Act was indeed a milestone, since its passage in 1990 the National Gay and Lesbian Task force and other gay rights advocacy groups have complained that inadequate reporting and data-gathering procedures have produced serious undercounting of the numbers of hate crimes based on sexual orientation that actually occur. Moreover, even with the new data produced, the U.S. Congress has resisted adding sexual orientation to the existing law that allows the government to prosecute hate crimes as a federal offense.

Gay men and lesbians are becoming more visible as holders of responsible positions in key institutions. For example, in 1980 fewer than five elected state or local officials in the nation were openly gay. Today, scores of elected officials are known to be gay and the numbers continue to slowly increase. Shortly after assuming office, President Bill Clinton selected a woman who had publicly acknowledged her lesbianism for a key post in the Department of Housing and Urban Development and appointed a gay male with AIDS to his White House staff. President George W. Bush appointed a gay male to head up his administration's initiative to combat AIDS. In 2012, Tammy Baldwin was elected as the first openly lesbian in Congress. That said, however, it is still the case that openly gay male and lesbian politicians and top government officials remain unusual enough to invite comment.

There have been some improvements in the extension and protection of civil rights for gay males and lesbians. Nine states now recognize the legal right of same-sex marriage, and several others are close to joining them. A number of individual states have passed laws prohibiting discrimination in such areas as employment and housing. Some states have passed so-called hate-crime laws that specifically outlaw and spell out penalties for violent crimes motivated by the sexual orientation of the victim. Yet, most states have not passed such laws.

In many large urban centers in states that do not recognize the right to same-sex marriages, gay male and lesbian couples now may file at city hall for legal recognition of "domestic partnerships." Some states do not go so far as to recognize same-sex marriages as legal, but do grant homosexuals the right to enter into civil unions that carry most of the legal rights accompanying heterosexual marriages. Some of the nation's newspapers have abandoned their wedding and engagement pages in favor of "celebration" pages, to allow public announcement of such partnerships. Many state and local governments, colleges and universities, and well-known corporations provide insurance coverage and health benefits to same-sex domestic partners of their employees.

The civil rights of gay people may be further transformed in the wake of a 2003 landmark U.S. Supreme Court decision, *Lawrence and Garner v. Texas*. Before the court ruled, consensual homosexual activity in private was a criminal offense in four states, including Texas, under laws prohibiting sodomy. (In nine other states, laws criminalized such consensual sexual acts between heterosexuals as well.) In 2003, the Supreme Court decisively ruled that such laws demean the lives of people who are gay. Speaking for the court, one justice noted that "Gays are 'entitled to respect for their private lives . . . The state cannot demean their existence or control their destiny by making their private sexual conduct a crime'" (Greenhouse, 2003b). The unprecedented Supreme Court recognition of the civil rights of homosexuals in this court case is expected to affect cases involving gay males and lesbians in other areas, from employment to family matters.

Nonetheless, gay males and lesbians, bisexuals and transgenders still face an enormous amount of oppression informed by individual ignorance and bigotry as well as systemic discrimination. The system of inequality based on sexual orientation has really only begun to come under attack. That means gay people in the United States will continue to be involved with their supporters in courageous struggles to secure recognition and protection of their civil rights (Clendinen and Nagourney, 2001).

ABLE-BODIEDNESS AND INEQUALITY

In 1990 President George H. W. Bush signed a bill into law that was widely hailed as the most important step taken by the federal government since the 1960s to protect people's civil rights: The Americans with Disabilities Act. This Act was intended to end discrimination against people with disabilities and to foster their participation in the mainstream of economic and social life. The specific areas of discrimination addressed in the Act include employment in the private sector, public accommodations, public services, transportation, and telecommunications (Public Law 101–335, 1990).

The term *disability* is open to different definitions and interpretations. The Disabilities Act uses the term to refer to any physical or mental condition that substantially limits one or more life activities of an individual. Such life activities include walking, hearing, speaking, seeing, learning, or working. Under this definition, it has been estimated that more than 54 million people with disabilities live in the United States (www.census.gov). Figure 7.2 provides some basic information about this population.

Impairments arise from a variety of causes: illness, disease, accidents, environmental hazards, criminal victimization, involvement in war, and problems associated with prenatal development or birth. Persons with disabilities differ in the degree to which they are limited: Some have only one life activity impaired, while others are multiply impaired. And people differ in the degree to which their disability is readily visible to others.

Figure 7.2:   Facts about People with Disabilities in the United States, 2010

- More than 54 million people age 5 and over, or 19 percent of the U.S. population has a disability.
- More than 5.5 million of those with disabilities are between the ages of 5 and 15;
  more than 29.5 million are between the ages of 21 and 64.
- Some 19.2 million of those with disabilities are 65 and over.
- The average annual earnings in 2010 for year-round, full-time employees aged 21–64 who had a disability was $27,000;
  the average income for those no disabilities was $30,468.
- Of those age 15 and older with disabilities:
  - 23.9 million had difficulty walking a quarter of a mile
  - 22.3 million had difficulty climbing a flight of stairs
  - 15.2 million used an ambulatory aid such as a wheelchair, cane, crutches, or walker
  - 17.2 million had difficulty lifting and carrying a 10-pound bag of groceries or carrying small objects
  - 15.2 million had a mental disability
  - 7.6 million had difficulty hearing what was said in a normal conversation with another person
  - 8.1 million had difficulty seeing the words or letter in ordinary newspaper print

Source: Matthew W. Brault, 2012. "Americans With Disabilities: 2010." Current Population Reports P70–131. Available at www.census.gov

People with disabilities face many challenges just living with their conditions, but we are interested here in the system of **inequality based on ablebodiedness**, created and sustained by those without disabilities (Shapiro, 1993; M. Russell, 1998). Again, this system involves persons being victimized by others who are more powerful and who justify their behavior by an ideology based on the alleged inferior attributes of the victimized. In this case the system of inequality is characterized by **ableism**, a system that treats people with disabilities as if they are defective, unwhole, or less than full human beings.

The Ideology of Ableism

The ideology of ableism suggests that the disabling condition is all-encompassing. From this point of view, the objects of attention are not "people with disabilities." The language of the ideology subtly shifts over to talking about "disabled people," a label implying that the disability is the only thing that matters in how they should be viewed and treated (see Linton, 1998). The disability becomes a *master status* (see Chapter 4), one that carries a **stigma**, or a negative mark, signifying doubt as to a person's social worth (Goffman, 1963). Those with physical and mental impairments are viewed as if they are members of some other species, one lacking the "normal" interests and concerns that occupy others of their social class, race, sex, age, and sexual orientation. In short, they are seen and treated as disabled first and as people second.

Often the ideology paternalistically suggests that this "separate species" is childlike in nature. Helplessness, dependency, inability to take on responsibility, and need for guidance are assumed to be innate characteristics of people with disabilities. In communicating with such people, the ablebodied often adopt an obviously conjured air of concern and kindness. Their approach is much like the one many people take when they are first introduced to a friend's dog.

On the other side of the coin, many persons are afraid of people with disabilities, so they avoid eye contact and minimize interaction. Some behave as if the disability was catching, but others are simply fearful of what they do not know. Those who are ablebodied may question their own role: If these are "disabled people" (instead of people who happen to have disabilities), how am I supposed to know how to interact with them? What do I do? What do I say? What might the disabled person want from me? Avoidance can be a way of protecting oneself from the unknown and from the fear of embarrassing or stressful social errors that might arise during interactions with members of this "separate species."

In her testimony before the U.S. Senate on behalf of the Americans with Disabilities Act of 1990, Arlene B. Mayerson of the Disability Rights Education Defense Fund described the situation faced by people with disabilities in these terms:

> *The discriminatory nature of policies and practices that exclude and segregate disabled people has been obscured by the unchallenged equation of disability with incapacity. . . . The innate biological and physical "inferiority" of disabled people is considered self-evident. This "self-evident" proposition has served to justify the exclusion and segregation of disabled people from all aspects of life. The social consequences that attach to being disabled often bear no relationship to the physical or mental limitations imposed by the disability (U.S. Congress: Senate, 1989: 303–304).*

Problems Experienced by People with Disabilities

More than three decades after the passage of the Americans with Disabilities Act, people with disabilities continue to face many serious problems and barriers (www.census.gov):

- Among people with disabilities ages 18–64, only 46 percent were employed full- or part-time, in comparison to 84 percent of those without disabilities. Over two-thirds of those without jobs said they would prefer to be working.
- Those with non-severe disabilities had median earnings of $27,000 per year.
- The poverty rate of people with non-severe disabilities was 12 percent.
- Only 28 percent of people with disabilities had a bachelor's degree or higher, compared with 31 percent of ablebodied individuals.

Those who do not have disabilities can enjoy a range of unearned invisible privileges based on their ablebodied status. For example, ablebodied people can assume that they can enter any building they wish without worrying that they might have problems accessing it. They can take a job or rent an apartment on any floor in a building without worrying about how they will be able to get up there if there's no elevator or if the building suffers a power outage. For that matter, they can assume that if the elevator is not working in an emergency, they can simply escape the building using the stairs. They can assume that when they need to go to the bathroom they will be able to get through the doors and fit in the stalls. They can talk to others and not be shouted at or talked down to as if their ablebodiedness somehow affects their hearing or intelligence. And they can assume that when they are described to others, their ablebodiedness will not be used as a qualifier (as in, "Susan, the blind teacher" or "Michael, the Senator in the wheelchair").

Those who are presently ablebodied can, at any time, join the ranks of those who have a disability. Were this to occur, their biographies would radically change as a consequence of this particular system of inequality. Many obstacles to full incorporation of people with disabilities into mainstream society remain. The Disabilities Act has drawn criticism from advocates for people with disabilities for doing too little to enable full participation in mainstream societal institutions. The Act has also been criticized by some politicians and employers for demanding too much in the way of accommodation to people's disabilities. From the point of view of those whose lives are at stake, as with any system of inequality, what inequalities people have taken the initiative to build, they can equally well take the initiative to pull down (Fleischer and Zames, 2001).

 ## CHAPTER SUMMARY

- Systems of inequality differ from society to society and change over time. One's life chances will not only depend upon the society of which one is a member, but also one's position in the particular systems of inequality contained within that society.

- This chapter addresses five systems of inequality in U.S. society: economic inequality, racial inequality, gendered inequality, and inequality based on sexual orientation and on state of ablebodiedness.

- In U.S. society, each individual is situated within a multidimensional matrix composed of multiple systems of inequality. Most people are disadvantaged within one or more of these systems or will be at some point in their lives. People's biographies are shaped and tempered by where they are situated in this matrix.

- Those among the dominant status in a given system of inequality enjoy a set of invisible, unearned privileges based on that advantaged status; those among the subordinate or devalued statuses in a given system of inequality are hindered by undeserved disadvantages.

- People participate in such systems of inequality involuntarily. Individuals cannot exercise control at will over their economic class, ancestry, sex, sexual orientation, or state of ablebodiedness.

- Individuals who are oppressed and victimized within the different systems of inequality often struggle against such treatment, and changes that occur in systems of inequality affect everyone's biographies.

- Systems of inequality are accompanied by ideologies, or ways of thinking that rationalize and justify them. The ideology justifying a system of inequality is likely to be promoted by those with the power to benefit from it.

- Wealth and income are unequally distributed in the United States, and poverty is a serious problem. While a functionalist perspective views the existence of a system of economic inequality as beneficial to U.S. society, from a conflict perspective this society's high degree of economic inequality is dysfunctional and harmful.

- People may act as if "race" and meaningful racial differences actually exist, but race is a social construction rather than a biological reality. U.S. society's system of racialized inequality is expressed through both personal and institutional racism. Institutional racism has a more far-reaching impact on people of color than personal racism.

- In the United States, a system of gendered inequality exists that is justified by the idea that the sexes should play different social roles because "biology is destiny." Male domination or patriarchy is supported by male chauvinism and institutional sexism. While patriarchy benefits males in some ways, its elimination would benefit both males and females.

- The ideology of heterosexism condemns homosexuality as abnormal, and lends support to a system of inequality based on sexual orientation in the United States. Mistaken notions about homosexuality contribute to widespread prejudicial attitudes and discriminatory practices against gay males and lesbians.

- In U.S. society a system of inequality based on ablebodiedness turns millions of people with disabilities into victims. The ideology of ableism depicts such persons as defective and less-than-whole. Ableism justifies prejudice and discrimination directed toward those who have physical or mental impairments.

- The five systems of inequality do not all show signs of weakening. Economic inequality is worsening. Gendered inequality has been breaking down much faster than inequality built around sexual orientation. Progress toward eliminating racialized inequality may be starting to erode.

THINKING CRITICALLY

1. Of the five systems of inequality discussed in this chapter, which do you feel has had the most important impact on your own life? How so?

2. While important gains in the dismantling of systems of gendered inequality and racial inequality have occurred in the United States, some people would argue that a backlash against further progress for women and people of color is underway. Do you agree? Why or why not?

3. Attitudes toward the rights of people who have disabilities are more sympathetic and tolerant than attitudes toward the rights of people who are homosexuals. How can one explain the differences in these attitudes?

4. Economic inequality in the United States is worsening, not getting better. Why is economic inequality not a lively public issue, compared with other systems of inequality we have described in this chapter?

5. Talented and highly educated women may be pressured to avoid assertiveness and outspokenness in their professional or business lives, lest they be seen as unfeminine. Discuss the effects of such pressures on those who give in to them.

6. Systems of inequality give rise to unearned and invisible privileges based on dominance. What might be some invisible privileges based on holding the dominant status in systems of inequality based on religion, age, or body weight?

 KEY TERMS

systems of inequality   **161**

social stratification   **161**

social constructions   **161**

ideology   **162**

ideological hegemony   **162**

economic inequality   **163**

class   **163**

wealth   **163**

income   **164**

net worth   **164**

functionalist perspective on economic inequality   **166**

conflict perspective on economic inequality   **169**

capitalism   **170**

invisible privileges   **162**

racialized inequality   **172**

minority group   **172**

race   **172**

ethnic group   **172**

racial formation   **173**

genocide   **173**

personal racism   **174**

prejudice   **174**

discrimination   **174**

institutional racism   **175**

affirmative action   **177**

gendered inequality   **179**

sex   **179**

gender   **180**

patriarchy   **180**

sexual division of labor   **180**

feminists   **181**

sexism   **181**

male chauvinism   **181**

institutional sexism   **182**

dual labor market   **182**

bisexual   **184**

transgender **184**

transvestite **184**

transsexual **184**

inequality based on sexual orientation **184**

heterosexism **185**

disability **189**

inequality based on ablebodiedness **190**

ableism **190**

stigma **190**

INTERSECTIONS OF RACE, CLASS, AND GENDER

8

Racism and sexism are among the social forces that shape people's biographies and place limits on the contributions that individuals are capable of making to society. Writing at a time when she was serving as president of Spelman College, a historically black institution, Johnnetta B. Cole commented on her own awareness of racism and sexism:

> *My first awareness of race was when I was about three years old,*
> *and a little white kid called me "nigger." I lived a good deal of my*
> *life more conscious of racism than sexism; for many African-American*
> *women of my generation that would be the response. But the women's*
> *movement helped raise my consciousness about sexism. Once it was*
> *there, the interconnections became clear. ("Race: Can We Talk?" 1991: 36).*

President Cole's words were directed at two of the five systems of inequality we examined in Chapter 7. In that chapter we discussed the fact that individuals occupy different positions in systems of inequality that are based on class, race, gender, sexual orientation, and state of ablebodiedness.

While we examined each of the five systems of inequality separately in Chapter 7, it makes sense to think of these systems as combining to form a multidimensional matrix or grid (Collins, 2000). Every individual occupies positions in every single one of these different systems of inequality and occupies them all simultaneously. These systems, operating together, shape people's personal biographies. In some systems individuals may be members of the more advantaged or dominating groups; at the same time, in other systems they may be among those who are disadvantaged or dominated. One cannot treat society as if it were simply divisible into just two groups, such as oppressors and oppressed. That ignores the ways in which individuals may occupy different positions in the systems of inequality that comprise the matrix (Johnson, 2001).

For example, the phrase "white male privilege" is often used to refer to the benefits that European American males receive within systems of gendered and racial inequality. But this does not mean that all white males are in a superior position to all other people. Their class membership is of great importance. In the United States, only a small proportion of white males occupy favorable and dominant positions in the system of economic inequality. The economic resources that are available to the vast majority of white males are highly limited in comparison to those available to upper-class males, and also upper-class females. Many white males can and frequently do experience economic insecurities and exploitation. Indeed, the more unfavorable

195

their position in the system of economic inequality, the more white males objectively have in common with many women and people of color in this regard. Thus, males may be dominant within certain dimensions of the matrix but not in others. Figure 8.1 illustrates some of the possible variations in an individual's matrix positions.

The term *intersectionality* is sometimes used to emphasize the fact that different systems of inequality are interconnected (Anderson and Collins, 2004). This interconnection affects how individuals experience these systems. One does not, for example, experience life only as an Asian American, or only as a member of the middle class, or only as a female. While at any given moment or situation individuals may find a particular dimension of the matrix to be more salient to their lives than other dimensions, all persons bear effects of the cumulative lifetime experiences of all the dimensions they occupy in the matrix. Thus, an Asian American, middle-class female's everyday or lifetime experiences may vary substantially from those of a person who is the same gender and class, but of a different color and ancestry.

It is also important to underscore the fact that systems of inequality are not static and unchanging. Indeed, these systems often give rise to intergroup tensions and conflicts. At different historical moments, one or another system of inequality may undergo collective protest and resistance by those who experience disadvantage within it. The challenged system may consequently change, thereby altering also the nature of the overall matrix. For example, in the last several decades the civil rights, feminist, and gay rights movements have produced changes in systems of inequality that have in many ways transformed the matrix, changing social relationships, and thus reshaping individuals' biographies across U.S. society.

Viewing systems of inequality as combining to comprise a matrix not only raises the interesting question of how different systems are interconnected, but also the question of why, at times, those who are subordinated within a given system of inequality are divided against one another. As sociologist Allan G. Johnson has put it, ". . . subordinate groups are often pitted against one another in ways that draw attention away from the system of privilege that hurts them both" (Johnson, 2001: 55).

For example, some white politicians use rhetoric that pits poor and working-class whites against other low-income people who have a different skin color. Politicians may intentionally do so as they take public stands against affirmative action in employment or subtly stereotype welfare as predominantly serving African Americans. Seeking to attract whites' votes, their rhetoric subtly plays the "race card," dividing people and encouraging those of different skin color to see one another as problems. Consequently, both whites and persons of color may be blinded to the very important difficulties they have in common in terms of class disadvantages. Politicians may use the race card to divert attention away from government's failure to help provide decent-paying jobs, affordable housing, access to healthcare and educational opportunities for poor and working-class people, needs that all people have regardless of their racialized identity.

In the last decade or so, more and more sociologists have begun exploring the complex and multidimensional matrix of inequality. In this chapter we do so by focusing on several questions:

- What does occupying a privileged position in systems of economic and racialized inequality mean for women?
- Does being male confer advantages independent of race or class?

- Has racialized inequality declined enough in the United States that we can dismiss race as a significant determinant of one's biography?
- When we use such phrases such as "women of color," do we inadvertently ignore diverse experiences and identities among such women?
- What happens when one occupies a subordinate position because of gender, and must simultaneously endure the social stigma of disability?

Let us begin with the situation of persons who are clearly members of the dominant group within systems of racial and economic inequality, but not in terms of the system of gender inequality. What does it mean to be white and a member of the upper class, but a woman?

PATRIARCHY IN THE LIVES OF WEALTHY WHITE WOMEN

Gendered Inequality in the Upper Class

The mass media supply much information about what it means to be a member of the upper class. But since class privilege includes the ability to purchase everything from mansions within private gated communities to public relations staff, it is difficult to know how accurate a picture is provided by the media. Television, magazine, and newspaper stories about members of "high society" at times indicate that even those with the greatest class privilege have personal and family problems. Yet the media also show heights of material affluence that presumably provide members of the upper class with much to comfort them in times of trial and tribulation and resources to address their problems. Through articles in upscale magazines such as *Town and Country* and *Vanity Fair*, and occasional television programs that allow a glimpse into the lifestyles and homes of some of the wealthy, a material side to life in the upper class is revealed that one might associate with royalty.

Yet the popular media are in the business of entertainment, not sociological analysis. A sociological analysis of those who occupy the very highest positions of power in U.S. society reveals that they are not only disproportionately from the upper class (Domhoff, 2009), but that they are also overwhelmingly heterosexual white males (Zweigenhaft and Domhoff, 2006). Moreover, when one looks closely at gendered relations within the upper class, one of the most striking facts is gendered inequality.

Upper-Class Women's Subordinate Gender Roles

Compared with women of other classes, upper-class women may seem to "have it all," but their possessions do not enable them to escape sexism and subordination by gender. Their class membership provides them with enormous security, as does their **white-skin privilege,** a term that refers to the social advantages provided simply by their race (McIntosh, 1992). (Note that white-skin privilege exists for whites regardless of their economic status). Nonetheless, the demands that upper-class men place on them to conform to particular gendered roles circumscribe upper-class women's life chances.

Nowhere is this clearer than in the data provided by Susan Ostrander (1984), a sociologist who conducted interviews with women of the upper class. Her sample may not be representative of all upper-class women, since it was drawn from one large mid-western city. It consists of women whom she identified through an upper-class acquaintance and who agreed to be interviewed. Nonetheless, her data provide unique insights into the otherwise hidden relations between men and women of privilege.

Ostrander was interested in the roles upper-class women play as wives and mothers, so she interviewed women who were either married and living with their husbands or recently widowed. Most of the women, ranging in age from the mid-thirties to the mid-eighties, were descendants of the oldest families in the city. Their husbands almost all held top positions in major corporations or in family-owned firms in business and law.

The women tended to be highly educated, often at exclusive private liberal arts colleges long patronized by members of their class. By many criteria, women of the upper class are among the most privileged women in the world, and the access to wealth such women have allows them to "have the upper hand in social transactions with other people, especially those outside their own class and racial/ethnic categories" (Kendall, 2002: 2). Yet, the women Ostrander studied are also caught up in a system of gendered inequality that dictates that they subordinate their interests and needs to those of their husbands.

To characterize husband-wife relations among those she interviewed, Ostrander presents the words of four women:

> *He expects me to make a nice home to come to, to be a cheery companion, to be ready to go on vacations when he wants to. He expects me to go along with what he wants to do.*
> *My husband has never helped around the house or done anything for the children. If I were starting life over he certainly would.*
> *He wanted to move to the country, and I didn't so we moved to the country.*
> *My husband never asks me what I think. He just tells me how it's going to be (Ostrander, 1984: 37).*

In the interviews the women said they were expected to play very traditional female roles, that is, be supportive, nurturing, and compliant to their husbands' needs. While perhaps not typical, the situation described in the following statement, from one of Ostrander's subjects, reveals how far such women might have to go to please:

> *When he comes home in the evening the house must be perfectly quiet. I've told everyone the phone must not ring after five o'clock. He wants me to be pleasant, pretty and relaxed. I can't dare cry in front of him or show any emotion. I never bring a problem to him, except during forty-five minutes set aside on Sunday mornings for that purpose. I keep a list (Ostrander, 1984: 39).*

Upper-class women are expected to run the household (which includes supervising domestic help) and in general take on all home responsibilities that would otherwise distract their husbands from full-time attention to their work. While these women are clearly capable of pursuing their own careers, most do not and many of those who do are likely to wait until their children are grown. Instead, they devote time outside the home to volunteer work, such as serving in leadership and fundraising positions on boards of local charitable and health organizations and in voluntary associations that support music and the arts (Daniels, 1988; Kendall, 2002).

Obviously, upper-class women do not need to work for pay. Not only do their husbands earn substantial amounts, but many of the women have their "own money" from family trusts and inheritances (although most of Ostrander's subjects said that they had given control over their money to their husbands). Even so, an important additional reason why the women do not pursue their own careers is that they need to be available to their husbands at short notice to organize social gatherings, entertain clients, or accompany their husbands on business travel.

The implication is, of course, that any activities these women undertake are, by definition, secondary to the activities of their partners. Indeed, when women of the upper class become too involved and successful in outside volunteer work, their husbands are likely to become jealous and resentful. The husbands see this commitment to something outside the home as a threat to their wives' role.

Ostrander concludes:

> The wives' tasks reflect not only the division of labor, or social differentiation, but also a clear subordination of the women to the men. . . . The general mode makes it difficult, if not impossible, for the women to have life agendas independent of the men (Ostrander, 1984: 49).

Ostrander points out one further irony. The women do not have to work, and they often pay other women to perform the bulk of home tasks (cooks, cleaning women, nannies). Thus the benefits they derive from class privilege over other women subvert inclinations they may have to strongly challenge the gendered inequality they themselves simultaneously experience. Due to the important role that being a member of the dominant class plays in their lives, women of the upper class may well find it difficult to share the heartfelt commitment of many other women to feminism. Class seems to "trump" gender for women of the upper class, according to sociologist G. William Domhoff. He suggests that the dominant class position occupied by such women leads them to identify their interests as being complementary with those of upper-class men, such that there is "class solidarity between men and women toward the rest of society" (Domhoff, 2002: 56). We should also note that insofar as upper-class women's gender subordination aids their husbands' ability to accumulate wealth and exercise power, in effect the system of gendered inequality helps to strengthen the system of economic inequality at its very top. Notably, not much has changed in nearly 30 years since Ostrander's study: Similar findings emerged more recently in Jessica Holden Sherwood's (2010) research, suggesting the strong institutional impact of these status intersections and inconsistencies.

WHITE WOMEN EMPLOYERS AND DOMESTIC WORKERS OF COLOR
Racial and Class Inequalities in Household Settings

White women of the upper class may tolerate gender dominance in relationships with their husbands. However, their race and class allow them to dominate certain other persons within their households: domestic workers. This capability is also there for middle-class white women who employ domestic help as they attempt to balance housework or childcare with careers.

In many cases domestic service in the United States involves a female-to-female relationship between a white, middle- to upper-class employer and a working-class woman of color, either native-born or, as is increasingly the case, an immigrant from Latin America, the Caribbean, or Asia (Chang, 2000; Hondagneu-Sotelo, 2001; Rio, 2005). Here, racial and class differences are played out through the subordination of one group of women by another, blurring the fact that both experience subordination within the system of gendered inequality.

Within most husband–wife households, such activities as cleaning, laundering, caring for children, shopping for necessities, and cooking are still primarily considered "women's work" in the sexual division of labor. But these at-home tasks are not culturally defined as "work" in the same sense as jobs and careers outside the home, nor are they well rewarded even when they are performed as a paid occupation. Women who make a living working as domestics—cleaning other people's homes, doing their laundry, watching their children, running their errands, cooking and serving their meals—often do not even receive the legal minimum hourly wage.

Women who are full-time, year-round, private-household service workers have lower median incomes than workers in any other occupational category. In 2012, the median weekly earnings of such workers were only $395 (U.S. Bureau of Labor Statistics, 2012 available at http://data.bls.gov/search/query/results?q=median+weekly+earnings+by+occupation). Moreover, the people who employ domestic workers provide them with few, if any, benefits. Employers are unlikely to offer paid sick days, paid vacation days, health or retirement benefits. Some employers do not even pay or withhold required Social Security or income taxes. A study of Latina cleaners and nannies conducted in Los Angeles found that employers were not doing so in many cases because they did not consider work performed in their homes to be "real work," especially if it was part-time (Hondagneu-Sotelo, 1997, 2001).

Women who do domestic work have few job protections, are nonunionized, and may be asked to work under arduous conditions. They are unlikely to get workers' compensation for injuries. Many women who perform such work do not know or fully understand their rights under the law. They may find themselves subjected to treatment ranging from being cheated out of legitimately earned wages to sexual harassment and assault by males in the household. Sociologist Mary Romero has referred to employers' frequent economic exploitation and mistreatment of domestic workers as a little-noticed form of "white collar crime" (Romero, 1999).

Domestic workers are often hesitant to assert themselves in response to poor treatment by the affluent women who employ them, lest they lose wages that their families desperately need. Women who are immigrants, and particularly those who are without proper immigration or residency papers, are especially vulnerable to exploitation since employers know they are highly unlikely to complain. Faced with a confusing system of bureaucratic public agencies and courts, often lacking English language proficiency and unable to afford legal help, many women fear that contact with government officials will backfire and somehow expose them to immigration or citizenship complications, or that they could even have their children taken away, be jailed, or be deported (Romero, 1992).

Women of color who do domestic work not only must contend with the system of gendered inequality that restricts job opportunities for women in general. They are victims as well of the system of racialized inequality that operates to "ghettoize" people of color disproportionately into low-wage service occupations. The system of economic inequality places those who are heavily dependent on income from domestic service near the bottom in class terms. Hence, women domestic workers of color experience the combined disadvantage of being at the bottom of intersecting systems of racialized, economic, and gendered inequality.

Women Oppressing Women

While Kathryn Stockett's (2009) best-seller, *The Help*, explored this intersection of race, class, and gender from the vantage point of fictionalized 1960s Mississippi, the truth is that these same relations can be seen in more recent empirical scholarship. Sociologist Judith Rollins conducted some unique research on the relationships between African American domestic workers and white female employers in the Boston area. Rollins used a variety of techniques to gather her data: She interviewed domestics and employers, worked alongside domestic workers in the guise of being their "cousin," drew on her own experiences as a worker in a number of settings, and interviewed personnel at agencies dealing with domestic workers (Rollins, 1985).

While Rollins discovered a variety of relationships between women employers and their domestics, she found that some overall patterns prevailed. Patterns somewhat similar to those she identified have also been documented for employer relationships with domestic workers other than African Americans, such as Latinas from Mexico, Central America, and South America (Romero, 1992; Hondagneu-Sotelo, 2001), as well as Filipinas (Parrenas, 2001). As with our earlier discussion of white women of the upper class, these relationships shed light on the significance of where one is situated within systems of gendered, racialized, and economic inequality.

In Rollins's view, the close one-to-one interaction, carried out in the physical and social isolation of a private home, can give rise to a type of psychological exploitation. Employers are less concerned with the productivity of household domestics than with their personality traits.

For example, employers expect domestics to express deference—in everything from language ("Yes, Ma'am," "Of course, Ma'am") to behavior toward the employer's property and personal space. This deference must even be paid when the employer expresses attitudes and behaviors not deserving of respect. The domestic worker's deferential behavior toward her female employer reflects workers' respective positions in the systems of economic and racialized inequality. Domestics may be of the same sex as their employers, but racialized and class differences prevent them from treating each other as equals.

The employer–domestic relationship often also entails dynamics of maternalism. The women employers tend to regard their workers as childlike, in need of mother-like protection, support, and guidance. The maternalistic treatment meted out—giving gifts, offering loans, assisting with reading bills, interceding with travel plans, offering to meet male friends—often must be accepted by domestic workers in the interests of survival. To reject such treatment would be to jeopardize one's job.

One domestic described the situation:

> *[My employer] was always offering me bags of stuff. But if it was something I didn't want, I'd thank her, walk out of there, go around that corner and the first trash can I got to, I'd throw it in. But you take it, whatever they give. . . . But it was all just more dead weight I had to get rid of. She felt like she was really being nice (Rollins, 1985: 190).*

Another woman domestic explained it this way:

> *I didn't want most of that junk. But you have to take it. It's part of the job, makes them feel like they're being so kind to you. And you have to appear grateful. That makes them feel good too (Rollins, 1985: 191).*

Giving places one in a position of superiority; having nothing to give back except expressions of gratitude relegates one to a position of inferiority. Thus the employers' expressions of maternalism become part of the psychological exploitation domestics must endure.

Rollins believes that the fact that both parties are women intensifies the psychological exploitation. The woman employer, like the domestic worker, holds subordinate status in this society on the basis of sex. Yet employing another woman gives her a position of power that housewives do not usually possess (Rollins, 1985). In this way, the employer can attempt to compensate for the inequalities in power that she experiences in her interactions with her husband.

But the implications of the dynamics between a white, middle-class employer and her domestic servant of color are much broader in Rollins's view:

> *The presence of the "inferior" domestic, an inferiority evidenced by the performance she is encouraged to execute and her acceptance of demeaning treatment, offers the employer justification for materially exploiting the domestic, ego enhancement as an individual, and a strengthening of the employer's class and racial identities. Even more important, such a presence supports the idea of unequal human worth: it suggests that there might be categories of people (the lower classes, people of color) who are inherently inferior to others (middle and upper classes, whites). And this idea provides ideological justification for a social system that institutionalizes inequality (Rollins, 1985: 203).*

Rollins's research stresses the oppressive aspects of the employer–domestic relationship. Women workers of color often actively struggle, frequently alone, at times in concert with other workers, to resist depersonalization, loss of dignity, and attacks on their self-worth as they go about their work (Dill, 1988; Romero, 1992; Hondagneu-Sotelo, 2001).

In the next section we shall examine the situation of lower-class African American men, persons who many whites apparently believe are inherently inferior to themselves and of unequal human worth.

AFRICAN AMERICAN MEN IN THE LOWER CLASS
When Race and Class Trump Male Privilege

The fact that women of all classes find themselves caught up in a system of gendered inequality does not necessarily mean that being male makes one immune to subordination in other systems of inequality. This is clearly the case with regard to African American men (Cose, 2002). Even those black men who have broken through discriminatory barriers, earning success in traditionally "white" occupations and professions, find that race and racism continue to be salient in defining opportunities and day-to-day relations with others (Feagin and Sikes, 1994; Cose, 1995).

All African Americans, regardless of gender or class, must contend with the prevailing system of racialized inequality (Bonilla-Silva, 2001). Our focus here will be on one particular subset of the African American population: African American men in the lower class who reside in this nation's racially segregated, impoverished, inner-city "ghettos." Their life situations are often so harsh, and their life chances so limited, that such men have been referred to as an "endangered species" (Gibbs, 1988).

The experiences of African American men in the lower class are underscored by the poignant story of Gregory Howard Williams, who grew up as a member of the white middle class for the first 10 years of his life (Williams, 1996). When his parents separated in the 1950s, Williams moved with his father and a brother from their home in Virginia to be near family members on his father's side in Muncie, Indiana. There Williams discovered that while the mother they left behind was white, his father was in actuality a light-skinned African American. His father had been passing for white in Virginia, but could not do so in Muncie where his African American family and ancestry were known. In Muncie, Williams himself was not considered or treated by others as white and was shunned by white adults and children alike. He resided in the racially segregated and extremely poor black community. Growing up as a black male in the lower class, confined to a ghettoized neighborhood, Williams experienced intense white racial prejudice and discrimination that made his impoverished childhood and public school experiences especially harsh and difficult. He ultimately became a college president and is thus an unusual success story. Many other African American men in the lower class experience far less positive outcomes in their personal biographies.

What is happening to African American men in the United States? The following are indicators of what many are experiencing and confronting (www.census.gov; www.sentencingproject.org; see also Cose, 2002, Butterfield, 2003):

- African American men, including those with college educations, are more than twice as likely as their white counterparts to be jobless.
- Perhaps as many as two-thirds of African American men living in high-poverty neighborhoods of U.S. cities are either underemployed or not in the workforce at all.
- African American men have been increasingly less likely to enter marital relationships: Only about a third are married.
- African American men are less likely than their white counterparts to attend college; indeed, their college attendance rates have been declining in recent years.
- More African American men are under the control of the criminal justice system than are enrolled in higher education.
- Approximately one in four African American men between ages 20 and 29 is caught up in the criminal justice system and is either in prison, on parole, or on probation.
- Twelve percent of all African American men between the ages of 20 and 34 were in jail or prison in 2002, as compared to 1.6 percent of white men in that age group.
- The probability that an African American man will be imprisoned at some time during his life is 28 percent, far higher than is the case for white men.
- While rates of illegal drug use are higher for whites, an ever-increasing percentage of arrests of African American men involve drug offenses (for example, unlawful possession and sale).
- African American men are six to ten times as likely as white men to die from homicide.

- Suicide rates for African American men peak among men in their twenties; for whites the rates do not peak until old age.
- African American men in racially segregated ghetto neighborhoods are less likely to live to age 65 than men in the extremely poor nation of Bangladesh.

Effects of Ghettoization on African American Men

Racially segregated ghettos, while harboring only a small percentage of the nation's total poverty population, constitute almost half of the high-poverty neighborhoods within U.S. cities (Jargowsky, 1998). The dense concentration of low-income people of color in these neighborhood areas renders them highly visible, at the same time as their communities face formidable problems (Wilson, 1996). Severely limited employment opportunities and low wage jobs for both sexes, but especially for men, make it impossible for many households to avoid poverty. The difficulties associated with living below the poverty line in turn undermine stable male–female partnerships and marriages and create obstacles to getting married in the first place. This then fosters female-headed households, compelling many mothers and their children to rely on a combination of meager public assistance and low-wage jobs, and negates the role that adult men could be playing as providers and role models in the household (Wilson, 1987).

Poverty also encourages criminal behavior, such as property crime and drug offenses, and in general fosters an overall social climate that can be threatening, stressful, and conducive to impulsive acts of interpersonal violence (Anderson, 1999). The high arrest and conviction rates for black males does not, however, mean their actual rates of criminal behavior are in fact high in comparison to whites of similar class backgrounds. The difference is that unlike white males, African American males are frequently subject to practices of "racial profiling" by police, who often act as if they are an occupying army when patrolling poor black neighborhoods. When members of one particular group are more likely than others to be stopped and searched, and almost automatically considered crime suspects, the probability increases that police will find some reason to make arrests. One outcome is the extraordinary rate of imprisonment of black men, way out of proportion to their presence in the U.S. population (www.sentencingproject .org; Miller, 1996).

The majority of ghetto dwellers abhor the conditions in which they find themselves trapped. Many deeply resent the popular racist stereotype that African American males who live in poor, racially segregated neighborhoods are "dumb, deprived, dangerous, deviant, and disturbed" (Gibbs, 1988: 3; Feagin, Vera, and Batur, 2001; Rome, 2002). Most ghetto dwellers are deeply concerned and unhappy with the negative features of the climate within which they reside. Coping with problems of living is a constant, unrelenting challenge. But conditions in many communities are such that a significant minority of ghettoized African American males—especially the young—are driven or drawn into behaviors harmful to themselves or others. In part, these behaviors must be understood with reference to the system of gendered inequality and ways in which black males experience it.

While undergoing change in recent decades, within this society's system of gendered inequality men have long been encouraged to see themselves as the dominant sex. Much of the male claim to dominance rests with their ability to command wages that can contribute in a meaningful way to the support of a family, to earn a "family wage." By placing substantial barriers to do so in the way of African American men, systems of racialized and economic inequality combine to symbolically emasculate them. One important barrier is employer mistreatment or outright rejection. For example, a study of black men in the Los Angeles area found that, in comparison to whites and Latinos, they are not only disadvantaged in finding employment by residency in high-poverty areas, low levels of education, and connection with the criminal justice system. Far more than others, black men "have been the victims of systematic exploitation or discrimination" by employers (Johnson, Farrell, and Stoloff, 2000: 708–709).

Many young African American males in the lower class pursue a sense of empowerment in other ways. For some boys and young men this may mean gang membership, rebellion against the authority of school and law, involvement in the local illegal drug economy, macho posturing, and out-of-wedlock fatherhood (Anderson, 1999). Being a member of the dominant gender but imprisoned by the treatment one receives due to color and class may kick off a relentless and at times fruitless search for validation of one's manhood. As the homicide and suicide statistics on young African American males indicate, that search may entail a tragically short life trajectory.

RACISM AND MIDDLE-CLASS AFRICAN AMERICANS

Economic Success in the Face of Racism

A popular stereotype holds that, aside from popular entertainers and athletes, the vast majority of African Americans are inner-city ghetto dwellers or members of the poverty population. While it is true that African Americans are disproportionately represented in lower income brackets in comparison to the proportion of the U.S. population that they comprise, there is a sizable black middle class. More than one-third of all African American families have solid middle-class incomes of $50,000 per year or more. Nearly one in four black families has an annual income of $75,000 or more (www.census.gov). The more than 2 million adults in these more affluent families tend to be married, middle-aged, employed, and well-educated, and most own their own homes. While most members of the African American middle class are city dwellers (Pattillo-McCoy, 1999), many live in suburbs or small towns. The black middle class is far better off in income terms than the millions of whites who make up the majority of America's poor. Even so, does being middle-class mean that one's racial-group membership becomes irrelevant? Do African Americans who occupy professional and executive positions in the labor force face racism?

There has been much debate among academics and public policy makers over the alleged **declining significance of race** (Wilson, 1980; Willie, 1989; Niemonen, 2002). Some have argued that most barriers to black advancement have been removed. Whites are less prejudicial in their attitudes, civil rights laws have been passed, and previously closed educational and occupational opportunities have been opened up. Indeed, the election and reelection of Barack Obama as president of the United States in 2008 and 2012 are often taken by many observers as evidence that we are now a "post-racial" society. One's color, the argument goes, is no longer the key social determinant that it once was in our society. The growth of the black middle class since the 1960s is offered as evidence that the significance of race has declined. More and more African Americans are finding a place in the mainstream of society. Some social scientists even argue that lack of skills and credentials, not racism, is the sole reason for poverty among blacks (Mead, 1992).

In contrast, other social scientists have compiled data that suggest that racism continues to play a significant and determining role in the lives of African Americans, including those who are part of the nation's middle class (Feagin and Sikes, 1994; Feagin, 2010). Critics of the "declining significance of race" thesis hold that not only does racism continue to exist, but that African Americans are denied the unearned "white-skin privilege" that whites possess (Lipsitz, 1998). One of these privileges is the ability to go about one's business secure in the knowledge that one's skin color will not meet with negative reactions or the demeaning surveillance and mistreatment that often accompanies racial profiling. Yet, when interviewed, many middle-class African Americans complain of racist treatment by service workers in restaurants and public accommodations, by police officers and strangers on the street, by people with whom they interact at work and school, and by those from whom they seek to rent and buy housing (Feagin and Sikes, 1994; Feagin, 2010).

The negative treatment experienced by African Americans affects their lifestyles and life chances. Racism's cumulative and present-day effects have not only resulted in a smaller proportion of African Americans than whites achieving middle-class status. Due to differences in household wealth and occupational attainment, those African Americans who occupy positions in the middle class are generally in a far more economically fragile and precarious situation than middle-class whites. African Americans are less likely than whites to have achieved the "American Dream" of home ownership, and on average possess far less wealth and property (Oliver and Shapiro, 1995). In fact, African Americans have been far more likely than whites to lose their homes to foreclosure after being targeted for predatory lending practices by mortgage banks since the 1990s (Beeman, Glasberg, and Casey, 2010).

Racial Segregation of the Black Middle Class

In urban metropolitan areas, housing discrimination (by mortgage lenders, insurers, real estate agencies, property sellers and renters) works to confine many middle-class African Americans to racially segregated neighborhoods. Often these are neighborhoods once occupied and abandoned over time by whites. Frequently, middle-class African Americans find themselves forced to live adjacent to or even in areas that have lost businesses and jobs, spiraled into decline, and developed high rates of poverty, along with all the social problems that often accompany it (Massey and Denton, 1993; Pattillo-McCoy, 1999.

Mary Pattillo-McCoy (1999) spent three years living in and studying "Groveland," a black middle-class neighborhood on Chicago's South Side. She observed many families with nice homes, backyards, and two-car garages. However, while possessing many of the surface privileges of a middle-class lifestyle, these families had to deal with perils that most middle-class whites are able to escape or avoid. The perils stemmed in large part from Groveland's spatial location, segregated away from stable middle-class white neighborhoods, but not from low-income and poverty-stricken black neighborhoods with drug and crime problems.

Young Groveland residents in particular were far more likely than youth in typical white middle-class communities in metropolitan Chicago to be exposed to the realities of gang life and drug abuse. Children in Groveland were, at the same time, being bombarded by a consumer culture that romanticized and encouraged emulation of criminal and other outlaw behaviors popularly associated with living in the "'hood." Parenting black children in Groveland thus carried particularly difficult challenges with which most white middle-class parents are unlikely to be burdened (Pattillo-McCoy, 1999).

Sociologist Raymond S. Franklin (1991) argues that many white people in the United States view all African Americans through the same lens that they use to look at black members of the lower class. Whites are strongly disposed to perceive African Americans collectively as less hardworking, less intelligent, more prone to violence, and more likely to prefer living off government welfare benefits than are whites themselves (Gilens, 1999; Rome, 2002). Recent survey data (see Table 8.1) confirm that whites are far more likely to apply these stereotypes to people of color than to themselves.

Franklin believes that such ideas may derive from the fact that African Americans are "over-crowded"—that is, statistically overrepresented—in the lower class. Racist stereotypes about the character and worth of lower-class blacks, in Franklin's view, cast a "shadow" over African Americans who are middle-class. In his words,

> *The shadow that is cast and generalized from the economically subordinate portion of the black population determines the attitudes and behavior of all whites toward all blacks, and, specifically, toward the more affluent and educated members of the black population who have class characteristics comparable to their white cohorts (Franklin, 1991: 122).*

In other words, middle-class blacks are frequently viewed and treated as if they carried the attributes that whites stereotypically associate with African Americans in the lower class. This

Table 8.1: Whites' Trait Ratings of Whites, African Americans, Latino/as, and Asian Americans

Trait	Percentage of White Respondents Applying Trait to:			
	Whites	African Americans	Asian Americans	Latino/as
Lazy	2.8	14.3	11.6	4.8
Hard-working	19.8	8.2	14.0	31.9
Violence-prone	6.9	23.4	16.6	5.8
Not Violence-prone	17.1	6.7	7.1	16.7
Unintelligent	2.7	5.3	8.6	4.6
Intelligent	23.7	10.8	8.8	24.9
Poor	1.5	27.4	35.4	12.7
Rich	14.1	1.7	2.3	10.8

Source: 2006 General Social Survey, (authors' calculations), National Opinion Research Center (available at www.norc.org/gss)

may help to explain why, when middle-class blacks begin moving into an all-white middle-class neighborhood, whites begin to move out (Feagin, 2001).

In short, data on the attitudes of the racially dominant white population and the personal experiences of African Americans show that race remains highly significant in the United States. Even as more African Americans have "made it" into the middle class, many whites continue to hold racist stereotypes on the basis of skin color. Despite the advances to which proponents of the "declining significance of race" thesis point, many middle-class African Americans report experiences of discrimination. The biographies of all African Americans are still conditioned today by racial inequality, regardless of their class.

DIVERSE EXPERIENCES AMONG WOMEN OF COLOR
The Importance of Recognizing Women's Diversity

The contemporary feminist movement has long had to confront tensions among its diverse supporters. In recent years, concern with racism has been prominent among these tensions. For over three decades the feminist movement has been dominated by white, middle-class women and the issues most pressing to them. Tensions have emerged because many women of color have found that the feminist movement has not adequately addressed their felt needs and concerns (hooks, 1981; Dill, 1983; Guy-Sheftall and Cole, 1995). Some scholars and activists have called for a movement that embraces "multiracial feminism," a feminism that focuses on the multiple positions in the matrix of inequality that women occupy, and particularly the central role that inequalities associated with racial ancestry and ethnic heritage play in women's lives (Zinn and Dill, 1993; Collins, 2000).

Even if observers somehow managed to ignore class and other systems of inequality, women of color, by being simultaneously subordinated within the two systems of gendered and racialized inequality, face challenges qualitatively different from those facing white women or men of color (Spelman, 1988). But it is also important to keep in mind that the phrase "women of color" encompasses in itself a diverse population of women. It includes women from different **ethnic groups,** people who possess distinguishing cultural traits and a sense of community based on their shared heritage (Schaefer, 2004).

Even commonly used ethnic group labels mask a great deal of diversity among women. Latinas, for example, include women who are U.S. citizens of Mexican descent, Puerto Ricans, and immigrants from different Latin nations in the Caribbean as well as Central and South America. Similarly, Asian Americans include women of Chinese, Japanese, Filipino, Asian Indian, Korean, Vietnamese, Cambodian, and Thai ancestry. Native American women come from many different ancestral Indian nations. The fact that women are not "all the same" should seem like an understatement, given the ease with which our discussion in this chapter has ranged from wealthy white women to women of color who are domestic workers. The tendency of the white-dominated feminist movement to emphasize the common experiences of women has opened it to the charge of **false universalism** (Asch and Fine, 1988). This term refers to the idea that all women experience life in the same ways. Yet who could experience a relationship more differently than a white woman employer and a female domestic worker of color? Indeed, are there any experiences common to all women that are not somehow tempered by the varying positions that they may hold in the systems of racialized and economic inequality? Many scholars believe the answer to be "No" (Amott and Matthaei, 1996).

To illustrate the diversity of experiences and the different challenges that women of color face, we will consider African American women and Chicanas.

Challenges Facing African American Women

The vast majority of African American women who marry or cohabit with male partners do so with African American men. Yet, as we saw earlier, African American males are now being referred to as an "endangered species." A shortage of viable African American male partners makes it more difficult for many heterosexual African American women to form stable two-parent households (Wilson, 1987). Racism, insofar as it undermines the opportunities and life chances of black men (and women) is of immediate and pressing concern. Many African American women would like to see the feminist movement throw its full weight in the fight against racism and the harm it does to communities of color. In their minds, the feminist movement needs to be much more sensitive to what it means to be both black and female.

At the same time, African American women must deal with how they are treated as women. Their history is unique in comparison to that of other women of color in the United States, for the ancestors of almost all African American women were involuntary immigrants, kidnapped and held in bondage as slaves: legally owned as property, exploited for their labor, and freely sexually assaulted by white males—a dominant group in terms of class, race, and gender (Davis, 1983). Some scholars argue that this historical legacy continues to influence the ways in which many white males perceive and treat African American women (Jewell, 1993). Still today, many feel little reason to respect women of color, subscribing as they do to long-standing racist stereotypes about their morality and sexuality (Collins, 2000; Neubeck and Cazenave, 2001; Neubeck, 2006).

African American women must also contend with a system of gendered inequality in which they are subordinate to African American males. Disempowered by racialized inequality, many African American men seek to compensate through sexist treatment of "their" women. African American women are caught in a quandary: Should they do battle with black men, whose self-esteem and self-worth is already besieged by racism? Or should they be more understanding of these men, who are oppressed by racism even as they themselves are oppressed by the men's sexism? These kinds of issues arose in the wake of the controversial 1991 hearings held to evaluate U.S. Supreme Court candidate Clarence Thomas, during which he was charged with sexual harassment by black law professor Anita Hill (Morrison, 1992). Many African American women have come to the conclusion that elimination of the sexism of which they are victims requires combating racism. This is an insight that has not been evident to or widely shared by the white-dominated feminist movement.

Experiences of Chicanas in U.S. Society

The experiences of women of color vary a great deal, both in terms of the women's treatment in their ancestral societies and their treatment in the United States (Amott and Matthaei, 1996). Let us illustrate this point by focusing upon women of Mexican descent, or Chicanas, the largest segment of the U.S. Latina population. Some of the ways in which Chicanas' experiences and identities as women of color differ from those of African American women will become apparent.

The history of Chicanas can be traced back to the forcible conquest by Spanish invaders of what was later to be named "Mexico" (Almquist, 1989). The Spanish *conquistadores* plundered the territory's indigenous Native American nations, engaged in genocidal massacres of many of their members, and captured or bartered for the Native American women. The Spaniards treated native women as male property and intermarried with them freely. Their offspring, called *mestizos/as*, became part of a three-class system of racialized inequality in this Spanish colony: Spaniards were at the top, mestizos/as in the middle, and the remaining Native Americans at the very bottom. Important roles that women had often played in the indigenous nations were lost. The goddesses they had worshiped were replaced by a religion oriented around male domination (Almquist, 1989).

For three centuries of Spanish colonial rule the submission of women was promoted by the teachings of Roman Catholicism, the religion of the Spanish invaders. Women were exhorted to emulate the ideals associated with the Virgin Mary—remain pure and celibate before marriage, bear many children and be good mothers when called upon, suffer pain and sorrow with grace and dignity, pursue lives of self-denial, sacrifice, and even martyrdom.

Complementing this principle of *Marianisma* ("Mary-ism"), the cultural norm by which women's behavior was to be judged, was the Spaniards' norm for men called *machismo*. This was a Latino version of the myth of male superiority (Williams, 1990). Men were expected to be strong, sexually virile, and dominant over women while respecting and protecting their honor. Women were expected to be virgins at marriage and sexually faithful afterward, but men's "natural virility" allowed them to routinely have affairs and mistresses. Under Roman Catholicism, women unhappy with this situation could not seek a divorce.

In the mid-nineteenth century the U.S. government precipitated a war with Mexico in order to gain control over rich farmlands and natural resources. Upon winning the war, the government annexed much of what was then Mexico and incorporated this territory's inhabitants and their culture into the United States. The Mexicans who lived there lost control over their properties. The conquering "Anglos" dominated them politically and economically, exploiting their labor when needed and treating them with racist disdain. Most Chicanos/as today can trace their ancestry to persons living in the annexed area (Acuña, 2000).

Thus, Chicanas have long suffered subordination along the lines of race, class, and gender. As persons of Spanish and Native American ancestry, they have been oppressed by their conqueror's acting upon beliefs in Anglo racial, male gender, and European-origin cultural superiority. Chicanas' labor has been and continues to be purchased cheaply (Amott and Matthaei, 1996). Historically, Chicanas have had lower formal labor-force participation than Anglo and African American women, but this has changed dramatically in recent decades. Today, over half of all Chicanas in the United States are in the labor force, principally in the Southwest, where they are over-concentrated in low-paying seasonal jobs and in blue-collar, service, and agricultural settings (Amott and Matthaei, 1996).

Chicanas on average have very limited formal educational credentials. This is due to a combination of factors: lack of respect for their cultural heritage and language in Anglo-dominated schools; high dropout rates due to family responsibilities; and, for some, disruptions in school attendance because of family involvement in migrant labor. Their lack of formal education, coupled with racist and sexist employment practices, means that Chicanas are at a serious disadvantage in the job market (Amott and Matthaei, 1996). Moreover, they often find themselves competing for work with other women of color, including Mexican and Central American women who have entered the United States illegally with the desperate hope of finding work.

The cultural traditions of Marianisma and machismo continue to linger among both sexes, but adherence to such traditions varies within the Chicano/a population. This was a key finding in interviews conducted with Chicanas by Patricia Zavella (1987). She found that the inability of men to earn wages that will allow their wives to play their traditional roles have helped alter male-female relations. Increasing numbers of Chicanas have had to go to work to assist in supporting their families. Their entry into the job market has coincided with growth in the service sector of the U.S. economy that has opened up low-wage job opportunities for these women. Many Chicanas have, in turn, placed pressures on their husbands to take on household tasks, including childcare.

Chicanas' participation in work outside the home—work that the family depends on—gives them a sense of empowerment they would not otherwise have in their marital relationships. Zavella found that while in some cases this has led to serious conflict between men and women, in many cases it has contributed to more egalitarian relationships within the home. Her research demonstrates that cultural traditions alone do not determine gendered roles; these roles are subject to influences outside the family that may provoke both men and women to negotiate, experiment, and change.

Unlike African Americans, persons of Mexican descent did not become part of the United States through forced migration and enslavement of their ancestors. Chicanos/as were absorbed through a process similar to colonial conquest. While African Americans have long been stripped of their homeland cultures by the dominant white majority, many Chicanos/as have been able to hold on to language and practices that frequently reflect their dual cultural heritage—Native American and Spanish. While African Americans live an enormous physical and psychological distance from their continent of ancestral origin, persons of Mexican descent live in North America where their ancestors lived; the proximity of Mexico helps strengthen and renew their cultural identity. Thus, although the challenges faced by Chicanas may seem, and may indeed be, very similar to those faced by African American women, the historical and cultural contexts within which Chicanas' and African American women's biographies are forged are not the same. Moreover, as people of color, both groups of women face challenges and operate in contexts that are different from those of white Anglo women.

SPECIAL CHALLENGES FACING WOMEN WITH DISABILITIES
When Gender and Disability Meet

As we noted in the previous chapter, U.S. society has constructed a system of inequality around people's ablebodiedness. Disabilities include a physical or mental condition that substantially limits one or more life activities, such as walking, hearing, speaking, seeing, learning, and working. Members of this population have long found themselves the objects of discrimination and marginalization by the ablebodied majority (Shapiro, 1993; M. Russell, 1998).

An estimated 54 million people in the United States possess a disability, defined as "a reduced ability to perform tasks one would normally do at a given stage in life." Almost two-thirds of the latter are between 15 and 64 years of age (www.census.gov; www.cdc.gov).

Because people with disabilities are overrepresented in low-income and poverty circumstances, many of them experience subordination in U.S. society's system of economic inequality as well. As we will see, women with disabilities are particularly vulnerable to being poor. In any case, poor or not, such women simultaneously experience subordination within the system of gendered inequality. In addition, many simultaneously experience disadvantage within the system of racialized inequality. Rates of disability, for example, are higher for Native American and African American women than for white women (Bradsher, 1996).

For many years social science literature concerned with the challenges confronting persons with disabilities assumed either that the gender of such persons was irrelevant or that these persons were males. The idea that women with disabilities might face special problems not faced by ablebodied women, or men with disabilities, was largely ignored (Quinn, 1994).

Even social movements relevant to people with disabilities were slow to address specific issues of concern to women in this population. Disability-related organizations that have pushed for an end to discriminatory practices and for increased access to the U.S. mainstream (e.g., access to employment and schooling) have tended to be male-dominated. Women's voices have been largely muted within such organizations. The contemporary feminist movement has primarily been concerned with fighting sexism, not ableism. This movement has only recently begun to incorporate concerns unique to women with disabilities.

The relative invisibility of women with disabilities in the United States is clearly beginning to change, and a growing body of data has underscored their plight (Jans and Stoddard, 1999; Fairchild, 2002; Welsby and Horfall, 2011). Yet most people still remain unaware of the special problems these millions of women experience. The impact on the biographies of those forced into subordinate positions on the basis of both their sex and disability is enormous (Frank, 2000).

The Oppression of Women with Disabilities

Women are somewhat more likely than men to have a disability. In addition, women are more likely than men to have the master status of "disabled" thrust upon them by ablebodied members of society. It is hard for many women with disabilities to escape this master status. Men are more likely to resist its imposition when they can, and to be successful in resisting, because men possess more options and have access to more social roles that it is assumed they can play (Gershick and Miller, 2000).

In a classic article that helped encourage sociological thinking about women with disabilities, Michelle Fine and Adrienne Asch (1985) argue that such women often suffer from **rolelessness,** that is, the absence of socially sanctioned roles to fill. This can be clearly seen in the economic arena. Women with disabilities are frequently turned away from aspiring to economically productive roles not only through rejection by employers but also through discouragement stemming from their school experiences and even their own families. Publicly funded rehabilitation and job training programs provide more services and wage-earning outcomes for men than for women (Fine and Asch, 1985; Chatterjee and Mitra, 1998; Bates-Harris, 2012).

In the U.S. system of gendered inequality men are expected to work outside the home, and the occupational reward structure is tilted in favor of "men's jobs." Men with disabilities are thus more likely than women to feel encouraged to aspire to economically productive roles and to seek work. While employment difficulties faced by men with disabilities are common, the situation for their female counterparts is worse. In contrast to the high rates at which ablebodied women have entered the labor force in recent decades, including women with children, the labor force participation of women with disabilities lags far behind. They are far more likely than men with disabilities to be unemployed, or to be working less than full time when they are able to find work. Moreover, even when women with disabilities work full-time, their pay on average is well below that of men, since they are likely to occupy poorer-paying "women's jobs."

Thus, it should not be surprising that women with disabilities earn less on average than men and, while the poverty rate for men with disabilities is high, women are far more likely than men with disabilities to be living in poverty. Impoverishment is particularly common for women without partners or others to help support their households. One study found that 73 percent of single mothers with a disability who have children younger than 6 years of age live in poverty (LaPlante, 1996). Not surprisingly, a disproportionate percentage of impoverished mothers whose families must rely on welfare have disabilities and are among those from whom recent welfare reform policies have removed the income safety net.

Fine and Asch suggest that the rolelessness handicap extends beyond economic roles to the social arena as well. Our system of gendered inequality calls for women to play loving, nurturing, reproductive roles as partners to men, but women with disabilities are widely viewed as unable to do so. They may, for example, depart from the dominant male-generated standards for physical attractiveness. In addition, disability is stereotypically equated with being incapable of handling family and household responsibilities, another unattractive trait to many men.

Here is how one never-married woman with disabilities assesses her life:

> *If you are not a cripple, you cannot possibly imagine the way the world reduces you to that condition. For a woman, especially, normality, acceptability, and marriageability depend upon looking whole. I have been in leg and arm braces since I was three. Boys never considered me fair game for dating, even though they liked me a lot to pal around with. Teachers never thought it possible that I might accomplish what others could do. Firms that I interviewed with approached me with fear and loathing. I got through because I believed in my inner wholeness, even if my outside leaves a lot to be desired. But the world around me saw a woman without the use of her limbs, without womanliness, without a man, without children. Everything else had a cameo role (Simon, 1988: 220).*

Since men can usually determine the terms on which they will interact with women, their rejection of women with disabilities in favor of ablebodied women limits the role options of the former. In comparison to ablebodied women, women with disabilities are less likely to marry and more likely to be divorced. Although far more women than men with disabilities marry, many live without a mate because of divorce, separation, abandonment, or death (Asch and Fine, 1988). Consequently, social isolation is a chronic problem for many such women.

Poor women, particularly those of color, have historically been pressured not to bear children and many have been subjected to involuntary sterilization (Shapiro, 1985). Yet women with disabilities have been treated in this way no matter what their race or class background. It has long been widely assumed that such women cannot mother successfully and thus have no business bearing children in the first place. Many people are surprised that women with disabilities possess sex drives and have "normal" interests and needs that mirror those of the ablebodied population (Lonsdale, 1990). A lack of interest in the challenges faced by women with disabilities leaves the women in a vacuum when seeking appropriate professional advice. In contrast, men with disabilities are unlikely to be discouraged from becoming fathers (it is assumed that they have ablebodied wives to take care of parenting). And what little clinical guidance exists to assist with problems of sexual functioning is principally addressed to men.

Women with disabilities are not immune from sexual abuse, assault, rape, and other forms of serious victimization (Asch and Fine, 1988). Moreover, such women may find it more difficult than women who are ablebodied to extract themselves from exploitative and abusive relationships. The fear of social isolation and their inability to earn a living wage force many women to remain in such relationships, despite the toll on their psychological or physical well-being. While data are inadequate to definitively state that women with disabilities are more likely to experience abuse than other women, evidence does show that those who are abused endure this abuse over longer time periods than women without disabilities (Nosek and Howland, 1998).

There have clearly been important improvements in opportunities available to people with disabilities in recent years, and many of those able to do so have become more active participants in mainstream society. The progress made is endangered, however. Conservative politicians, in seeking ways to cut back on the U.S. "welfare state," have attacked a wide range of "entitlements" to protection and assistance, including those that are relied upon by women with disabilities. Like others who are subordinated within the U.S. system of economic inequality, people with disabilities are being told to stop looking to government assistance and to instead take individual "personal responsibility" for solution to their plight (M. Russell, 1998). In addition, political conservatives have been attacking the Americans with Disabilities Act of 1990, which was intended to put an end to discriminatory practices. The contemporary feminist movement, which had long ignored the unique problems faced by women with disabilities, may yet prove to be an important ally in the unfinished and embattled disability rights movement.

UNRAVELING THE MATRIX OF SYSTEMS OF INEQUALITY

While often referred to as "minorities," together women and people of color make up the numerical majority of U.S. society's members. Much of our discussion in this chapter has focused on this numerical majority. But it is equally important to stress that white males do not all make their way through U.S. society enjoying positions of unchallenged privilege. Being a member of the dominant racial group and the dominant gender does not protect white males from blocked economic opportunities or poverty-level living. Moreover, not only do many white males experience economic insecurity and disadvantage; many are made to suffer because they are gay or have disabilities. Their race and gender does not necessarily protect white males from harm imposed by the positions they occupy within other parts of the matrix of systems of inequality.

We have said that all the systems of inequality within the matrix are interconnected. In many ways these systems are also mutually supportive of or dependent on one another. For example, if women of color are successful in combating racism, this can help reduce the sexism to which they are also exposed. The reduction of racism and sexism would help to undermine the system of economic inequality, and reduce the overconcentration of women of color who are living in poverty. Overcoming ableism would also improve the economic position of women of color, who are more likely than white women to have disabilities. Understanding more precisely the ways in which aspects of the matrix interconnect, and the implications for individuals' biographies, poses a provocative challenge for sociologists.

The oppressive effects of the matrix of systems of inequality rob society of important contributions from many of its members. U.S. society is thus far less enriched than it otherwise could be in such areas as healthcare, the sciences, engineering, business, literature and the arts, and law. This is a situation in which everyone—including white upper-class males—loses.

 ## CHAPTER SUMMARY

- This chapter stressed the importance of the positions each individual occupies in a matrix of systems of inequality. Each individual simultaneously occupies positions of advantage or disadvantage within systems of inequality organized around differences in class, race, gender, sexual orientation, and state of ablebodiedness.

- The positions people occupy in this matrix relative to other individuals and groups affects their life chances and hence their biographies. Changes in the nature of one or more of the systems of inequality that comprise the matrix can have important effects on people's lives.

- Women are at risk of subordination with the system of gendered inequality regardless of their class position. Occupying a dominant position within the system of economic inequality does not allow upper-class women to escape male domination.

- Women who are privileged by virtue of their class and race may dominate over other women who hold subordinate positions within systems of economic and racialialized inequality. Women may be oppressed by other women.

- Being male does not automatically mean one occupies a privileged position in society. The ability of males to dominate can be adversely affected by their positions in systems of racialized and economic inequality, as shown through the example of African American men in the lower class.

- Success in the system of economic inequality can simultaneously be offset by subordination within the system of racialized inequality, as is the case for the black middle class. Its members' economic success has not allowed them to avoid experiences of racial segregation.

- Women do not all have uniform life experiences within the system of gendered inequality. Women of color have quite different life experiences than do white women. Experiences likewise differ between different women of color, such as African American women and Chicanas.

- Men with disabilities experience advantages over women in dealing with the social stigma of disability. Women with disabilities experience subordination within two systems of inequality: gendered inequality and inequality based on state of ablebodiedness.

- The matrix of systems of inequality has oppressive effects and robs society of the possible contributions of many of its members.

THINKING CRITICALLY

1. As you have learned in this chapter, white women of the upper class are subordinate in terms of gender but dominant in terms of race and class. For black men in the lower class, the situation is reversed. What, if anything, do both groups have in common?

2. Some white males feel threatened by advances in education and employment made by women and people of color. Should white males view such gains positively? Give arguments to support your opinion.

3. In discussing some of the problems women with disabilities face, we talked in very general terms about disability itself. What difference do you think the *type* of disability makes in terms of how women are treated? Why?

4. Identify several negative stereotypes about people of color. Include some that are specific to males and others that are specific to females. How are these stereotypes similar? How are they different? How are these stereotypes fostered and maintained? What facts contradict them? What functions do such stereotypes play?

5. Discuss the advantages that white-skin privilege provides for whites. How is this privilege affected when one takes into account gender? Class? Ablebodiedness? Sexual orientation?

 KEY TERMS

white-skin privilege **197**
declining significance of race **205**
ethnic groups **208**

false universalism **208**
rolelessness **212**

DEVIANCE, CRIME, AND SOCIAL CONTROL

9

Through socialization into the commonly shared ideas and practices of a culture, members of society learn the boundaries of acceptable behavior. Sociologists refer to these boundaries as **norms.** Norms are standards that define the obligatory and expected behaviors of people in various situations. They are, in effect, rules.

As we discussed in Chapter 5, there are different types of norms. These range from *folkways* (the least formal or important norms, involving everyday conventional routines) to *mores* (more formal and important, defining behaviors that absolutely must or must not occur) to *laws* (norms so vital, often to dominant interests, that they are translated into a written legal code and enforced by the state).

Thus, norms as folkways may pertain to everyday interactions such as replying "Hi" to a friend's greeting. Norms may, as mores, pertain to behaviors about which there are strong and widely held feelings, such as childhood sex play. Or, norms may be laws, institutionalized and backed by state power, such as laws prohibiting evasion of taxes. Through the processes of socialization, discussed in Chapter 6, people become aware of an enormous number and variety of norms outlining acceptable behavior.

The term **deviance** is used by sociologists to refer to behavior that violates or departs from norms held by society's members. Persons whose deviant behavior violates prevailing norms may be seen as being anything from odd or eccentric to annoying, disruptive, or even dangerous to the functioning of society. Since social life is possible only if people generally abide by norms, members of society must develop means of **social control,** that is, means of minimizing deviant behavior (Davis and Stasz, 1990). Some types of behavior, such as destruction of property or violence, must be checked; otherwise, the cooperation among its members that any society needs to function will be jeopardized.

Social control of deviant behavior can be informal, as when a teacher chides a student for misbehavior, or formal, as when an individual is brought to trial in a judicial system. Social control generally calls for the use of **sanctions,** that is, the meting out of punishments or rewards. **Negative sanctions** serve to punish norm violators and to remind others of what could happen to them if they engage in similar behavior. Such sanctions can range from expressions of disapproval by members of one's primary group (family, friends, coworkers) to imprisonment or capital punishment by the state. The nature of the negative sanction depends upon such factors as the norm violated, the importance attached to it, the circumstances under which the violation occurred, the status of the violator within society, and the remorse he or she has shown.

Positive sanctions also serve to encourage conformity, but they do so from a different direction. By rewarding persons who abide by the rules, positive sanctions reinforce their behavior and remind others of the benefits of behaving according to expected norms. The reward one receives for returning a lost wallet to its owner communicates the virtue of honesty over theft. The ceremonies honoring police officers and firefighters who heroically risked or lost their lives in the line of duty remind everyone of the courageous work they do and encourage members of those professions to remain motivated. By seeing what is honored, we can often tell what would bring dishonor. In this case bravery is honored, and by implication expressions of cowardice in the line of duty are condemned.

In this chapter we shall explore such questions as these:

- Who or what determines that certain people are "deviants"?
- To what degree and in what ways do the ideas of dominant groups play a role in this process?
- Are people sometimes treated as deviant on the basis of attributes other than their behavior?
- Why do people engage in behavior that is considered deviant?
- How "just" is the criminal justice system in its treatment of law violators who differ by race or class?
- Are there circumstances under which deviant behavior may play important functions for society?

THE SOCIAL CONSTRUCTION OF DEVIANCE

How do observers know what deviance is? Does deviance reside in an act itself, or is it defined by society's members? Some have argued that certain acts, such as taking another person's life, are inherently deviant. Other sociologists reject this argument (Becker, 1963). In their view, determining that certain behaviors are deviant is a subjective process and one that tells us something about those making the rules (Orcutt, 1983). According to this view, deviant behavior is *socially constructed*. Let us look at what this means.

For many years sociologists focused their attention almost solely on the deviant and his or her behavior. In the last several decades, however, sociologists have explored ways in which deviance gets defined, or the **social construction** of deviance. Sociologists today readily acknowledge that deviant behavior is always defined with reference to a set of rules, or social norms. One could argue that there is no act in which human beings can engage that is inherently deviant in and of itself. Social norms must be present. When a person or an act is held to be deviant in the context of a set of norms, the social construction of deviance is taking place. Deviance, then, is relative to time, place, and circumstance. Its determination may be shaped by prevailing power relations in a society (Curra, 2010). What is considered deviant may change over time in a single culture or society, or differ between cultures or societies at a single point in time. And it may vary according to specific circumstances within a single culture at a single point in time.

For example, whether taking the life of another human being is defined as deviant depends on the normative context. Killing a bank teller in the course of a robbery would be considered deviant by most people, but not by criminals for whom killing in the course of a robbery is normative. Mass murder is obviously a crime. But seeking out and killing another person—even many persons—may at times receive recognition as a positive accomplishment; an example is the killing of enemy soldiers in a war. In contrast, some people are committed to norms, based on religious beliefs or matters of conscience, that hold any killing to be intolerable. As these examples show, judgments made in the context of social norms determine whether deviance exists (Akers, 1985).

In another example, alcoholic manufacture, sale, and consumption is illegal in Saudi Arabia (and much of the Middle East) but legal in the United States. But it was not always legal in the United States: It was illegal during the early twentieth century, during a period called Prohibition, to manufacture, distribute, or consume alcoholic beverages. The law was routinely ignored by large numbers of people, and eventually repealed, so that now it is a legal activity. Where there are few or no restrictions on who may consume alcoholic beverages in places like France or Amsterdam, there are specific circumstances in the United States that govern its legality: One must be over 21 years of age, and some states, such as Connecticut, still maintain a form of "blue laws" that forbids sale of alcohol after 9 PM and on certain holidays. There are cultural norms in the United States that define appropriate times and situations in which one may drink, such as after 4 PM ("happy hour") and at certain celebrations such as weddings and birthdays, and even situations when it is culturally acceptable for people to drink excessively, such as New Year's Eve and St. Patrick's Day. The example of the social construction of deviance concerning the production, distribution, and use of alcohol thus illustrates how deviance is relative to time, place, and circumstance.

If deviant behavior is a social construction, then, in theory, *any* act could be considered deviant by someone. The use of the term *deviant behavior* implies a social process whereby the **label** *deviance* is attached to the acts of an individual or group (Becker, 1963). From this perspective no act is deviant unless people define it as such within the context of norms, be they folkways, mores, or laws.

Does this mean that sociologists believe there is no right or wrong? No—sociologists, like most other people, have ethical and moral standards. Saying that deviant behavior is socially constructed is not the same as saying that everything is morally relative and that societal members should be permitted to act however they choose. Sociologists are merely pointing out that a society's members regularly make decisions about what they hold to be right, wrong, moral, or immoral. Indeed, people have to make such decisions to facilitate the functioning of society. For this reason virtually all societies develop some kind of rule-making processes and systems of sanctions, both formal and informal. If deviant behavior is a social construction, what is considered deviant may vary over time. For example, before 1973, abortion was against the law in many parts of the United States, and this law was widely accepted. People who did not adhere to the law, including both those performing abortions and the women having them, were subject to criminal penalties. Because their behavior violated existing norms as formalized in law, it was considered deviant. Over time, however, views toward abortion changed. More and more people came to the conclusion that women should have the right to make their own decisions about something as personal and private as childbearing. In 1973, the U.S. Supreme Court legalized abortion nationwide through its decision in the case of *Roe v. Wade*. Many people still hold steadfastly to views condemning abortion and disagree with the court's decision, but under the law abortion is no longer defined as deviant.

This example suggests another fact about deviant behavior. There may be little consensus as to whether an act is deviant, and laws may express the normative views of some people but not others. Since the U.S. Supreme Court's decision, groups disagreeing with *Roe v. Wade* have struggled to reverse it. The court has not acceded to the decision's opponents, but it has allowed individual states to restrict the ease with which abortions may be obtained. Likewise, Congress has come under pressure to deny federal funds for abortions in government healthcare programs and to prohibit foreign aid from going to family planning programs in impoverished nations that offer abortion to women as an option. This example emphasizes the social construction of deviance: The same act can be considered deviant by some groups and not others. And while the law may stipulate that something is legal the dependence upon resources such as financial aid may in fact enable the holder of the much-needed resource to set down restrictions that the law does not.

Only in small, homogeneous societies, where all members tend to share the same norms, is one likely to find considerable consensus as to what behaviors are deviant. Members of larger, more heterogeneous societies, such as the United States, are more likely to disagree about what is deviant. In U.S. society, performing or having an abortion is not the only behavior on which people disagree. Consider also using marijuana, driving above the posted speed limit, leaving home (by young people) to join religious cults, engaging in homosexual acts (by consenting adults), and fudging on tax returns. Some people would find one or more of these acts perfectly acceptable, while other people would vigorously condemn them all.

As seen with the example of legalizing abortion, defining deviant behavior may involve struggle and conflict. People may feel very strongly about whether a particular behavior is deviant, depending upon the norms by which they believe others should abide. Groups may be at such odds with one another that it is difficult or even impossible to resolve their differences. In the case of abortion, debate in the United States as to when human life begins and differing views over the right of women to control reproduction have forced opposing parties to seek relief in courts and legislatures. And even when courts or legislatures may assert a norm as a law, subcultural norms may conflict with dominant norms in a society. Such is the case with abortion: Although the law stipulates a woman has a legal right to access abortion, some religious subcultures may strongly disagree with that norm.

Of course, what is considered deviant behavior differs not only over time and from group to group within a society. The social construction of deviance means that whole societies may also differ in what is considered deviant (Edgerton, 1978). People who go abroad routinely come into contact with the different norms of other cultures. Often it is considered a sign of respect for visitors to adapt to another culture's norms.

At times the need for adaptation even arises in the midst of international conflict. Prior to the war it initiated against President Saddam Hussein's regime in Iraq in 2003, the U.S. government used its military power to wage the Persian Gulf War in response to Iraq's 1990 invasion of Kuwait. So as not to show disrespect to the gender norms in nearby Saudi Arabia, a U.S. ally against Iraq, female troops stationed at a Saudi air base shortly after the invasion were ordered to remain completely covered at all times despite the severe desert heat. They were also housed in sex-segregated quarters, told to avoid public fraternization with male colleagues, and restricted as to when and where they could drive (Moore, 1990). In the heavily patriarchal (male-dominated) Saudi culture, men commonly suppress public expressions of female sexuality and independence by demanding strict adherence to gender norms pertaining to dress and conduct. (Currently there are signs that some limited liberalization in these cultural practices may be slowly underway.)

In sum, deviance is socially constructed and involves a labeling process. Members of a group, a community, or a whole society may develop norms that make certain behaviors socially unacceptable. These norms take the form of folkways, mores, and laws. Norm violators are labeled deviant and subjected to sanctions intended to minimize such behaviors.

In large heterogeneous societies, such as the United States, people not only disagree about what behaviors are unacceptable but also possess different amounts of power to define who or what is deviant. In the next section we shall look at ways in which dominant groups may impose their norms on others.

THE ROLE OF POWER IN DEFINING DEVIANCE

Although societal members define deviant behavior, doing so is not a simple process of reaching a consensus or measuring the majority public opinion. For each behavior in question, some people's opinions count more than others' opinions. In short, not all individuals and groups possess equal power to determine whether a particular behavior will be considered deviant (see Adler and Adler, 2008). In Chapter 7 we saw that some people dominate others within systems of inequality and thus play a strong role in influencing others' life chances. One way to influence people's life chances is to exercise social control over their behaviors. Dominant groups within a society typically have the power to decide what is deviant and what is not.

Writing in his classic work on deviance, *Outsiders*, Howard S. Becker states (1963: 17–18):

> *To the extent that a group tries to impose its rules on other groups in the society, we are presented with a question: Who can, in fact, force others to accept their rules and what are the causes of their success? This is, of course, a question of political and economic power. . . . Differences in the ability to make rules and apply them to other people are essentially power differentials. . . . Those groups whose social position gives them weapons and power are best able to enforce their rules. Distinctions of age, sex, ethnicity, and class are all related to differences in power, which accounts for differences in the degree to which groups so distinguished can make rules for others.*

We will illustrate Becker's point by using the case of women and deviance.

Norms That Restrict Women

In his provocative book *Labeling Women Deviant* (1984), sociologist Edwin M. Schur suggests that in patriarchal societies many norms function to control women and keep them "in their place." Among those he identifies are *appearance norms* and *motherhood norms*. Control over behavior in such areas, Schur feels, serves "as a capsule statement of what male domination entails" (1984: 53). In the last several decades, these norms have been subject to question and change in the United States, and are held more strongly by some members of U.S. society than others. Still, the continued presence of these norms means that women who depart from them may risk being labeled deviant.

Appearance Norms

In Schur's view, **appearance norms** encourage women to be preoccupied with what are, in effect, male standards of attractiveness. Most women feel an obligation to be concerned about their appearance and are conscious of how they present themselves, not only in the eyes of men but in the eyes of other women (Halprin, 1995). In the United States, commercial advertising has long played a powerful role in stimulating and reinforcing this concern on the part of women (Crane, 2001; Currie, 1997). Whole industries—such as fashion, cosmetics and beauty aids, diet and weight control, and cosmetic surgery—thrive on it.

Yet the role models for female beauty typically presented in advertising, and in the media in general, cannot be emulated in real life by the vast majority of women. No matter how hard they try, most women cannot make themselves resemble those in the annual swimsuit issue of *Sports Illustrated:* young, usually white, long-haired, highcheek-boned, blemish-free, and slimly proportioned, with the exception of unusually large breasts (Sutton, 1992). From magazines to Hollywood films to MTV, the mass media present standards of beauty that women compare themselves to and are judged by. In Schur's view, the more a woman falls short of appearance norms, whether by choice or through an inability to conform, the more likely it is she will be labeled as deviant by many males.

Behaviors on the part of women that manifest a preoccupation with personal body shape may reflect the internalization of the appearance norms that Schur describes. Many women try to reshape themselves through cosmetic surgery; they undergo breast implants, facelifts, nose jobs, collagen injections, and liposuction. Diet regimes, health clubs, aerobics classes, and jogging are only in part motivated by health concerns. Some women will risk their health rather than fall short of appearance norms. Some types of artificial breast implants have had serious side effects, and controversy over the adequacy of manufacturers' warnings regarding the safety of breast implants has led to law suits (see Chapple, 1998). For many women, however, these activities are part of the endless pursuit of the "perfect body" (Glassner, 1988). Obviously, genetics places many limitations on the possibilities for success in this pursuit.

Motherhood Norms

Besides appearance norms, Schur suggests that, **motherhood norms** are also directly tied into the system of male dominance (see also Campbell, 1999). Pointing to lesbian couples and heterosexual women (married and single) who choose to be child-free, Schur argues that there is no scientific evidence for the existence of a universal, invariant "maternal instinct" in all females that drives them to childbirth and child rearing. In Schur's view, the belief that nature has equipped women with such an instinct is best understood as part of the patriarchal biology-is-destiny ideology (discussed in Chapter 7) that has justified the channeling of women into narrow sex-typed roles and responsibilities.

According to Schur, motherhood norms include the notion that "normal" women get married and bear children. Married women who wish to bear children but cannot are objects of sympathy, while wives who make it known that they (and their spouses) choose not to bear children may be labeled as deviant by friends, acquaintances, and even family members. *Refusal* to mother is an act that flaunts the norm. Women who make this decision may find little social support for it and may be stigmatized as immature, self-centered, and inclined to lead barren, unfulfilled lives.

Men can appeal to motherhood norms to pressure reluctant partners into bearing unwanted children or more children than women really want. Cultural norms of masculinity may prompt males who have chauvinistic attitudes toward women, or who do not succeed in the traditional role of husband and main breadwinner, to seek to establish or gain recognition of their "manhood" through fatherhood, a situation facilitated by the existence of motherhood norms.

Schur observes that another motherhood norm is the concept of not giving birth out of wedlock. This norm varies in intensity among different groups within society. Given the problems facing African American men that we discussed in Chapter 8, African American women have proportionately fewer choices of male partners of their "race" than do white women, and those who wish to become mothers are more likely to face the prospects of single motherhood. However, the norm against bearing children out of wedlock may be shifting overall, given the high rates of out-of-wedlock births in recent years, including an especially rapid rise in rates for white females. However, despite this growing shift, such births still often meet with negative evaluations, often expressed through pejorative phrases like "unwed mother" and "illegitimate child." Some politicians portray nonmarital births as a breakdown of "family values" that threatens the family as a social institution.

Schur points out that when a birth occurs out of wedlock, it is primarily the woman who is judged to have done something wrong. However, attitudes may be changing on this notion as well. There is currently much more of a focus on paternity because of political clamors over the costs of public assistance for impoverished female-headed families, the need to place more responsibility for child support on fathers from all economic levels, and technological advances that make establishing paternity easier. Still, the fathers of children born out of wedlock are not as routinely condemned as are the mothers. Until recently, many fathers simply disappeared from the picture.

The norm against giving birth out of wedlock pressures women to marry even when they do not wish to. The alternative is to take on the heavy parental responsibilities and economic challenges that often come with being a single mother. Many unmarried pregnant women choose neither marriage nor unwed motherhood; they opt for abortion instead. Obviously, for many in our society abortion itself is a violation of motherhood norms and thus subject to condemnation.

Married women who do not wish to have children and unmarried women who do not want to bear children out of wedlock face hurdles. There is no contraceptive that is 100 percent effective. Some forms of birth control can pose threats to women's health and safety. Abortion to end an unwanted pregnancy not only remains controversial, but government actions have made access to abortion increasingly difficult for women, particularly those who are poor.

Some women who become mothers unwillingly—whether within or outside marriage—may take out their frustrations on their children; some may engage in child neglect. For such women a new label denoting deviance is waiting: "unfit mother." In Schur's view, motherhood norms not only include the notion that "normal" women marry and have children within marriage but also include expectations that women will strive toward a maternal ideal of self-sacrifice, unconditional love, and nurturance.

Motherhood norms can also make it difficult for women who want to have children outside a conventional marriage. Heterosexual single women who intentionally conceive and give birth may be labeled as deviant. But attitudes toward such behavior are changing, at least with regard to single women with careers. Such change in attitudes may be signaled by the notable lack of controversy over out-of-wedlock births among female celebrities in the entertainment industry and the tolerant treatment of unwed motherhood on popular television programs. Witness the unwed pregnancies of Rachel on *Friends* and Eleanor on *The Practice*.

Lesbian women who choose to become mothers are viewed as even more deviant than single heterosexual women who do so (F. Nelson, 1999). In a 1993 court ruling in Virginia, a judge awarded custody of a lesbian's baby to its grandmother, reasoning that the lesbian's sexual orientation made her "unfit" to raise the child. Both lesbian and single heterosexual mothers challenge the notion that adequately fulfilling the motherhood role requires dependence on a male partner. The notion that two parents find it easier to rear a child than one parent certainly has merit, particularly since that arrangement may allow for the sharing of the economic burden of running a household and the everyday responsibilities of parenting. However, there is little reason to conclude that the two parents must be of a different sex, or that single women cannot do a fine job as mothers. Many millions have done so. To the degree to which such sentiments are held by other members of society, they pressure women not to choose motherhood outside marriage.

Challenges to the Label "Deviant"

In a patriarchal society, men have the power to make and enforce rules that determine what is socially constructed as "normal" behavior for women. In the United States, in part due to the existence of an active feminist movement for women's rights, that power has been challenged. Appearance and motherhood norms still exist and exert control over women who could become "deviant," but in various ways and in various places these norms have been breaking down (Edut, 1998; Crane, 1999; Feasey, 2012). The feminist movement has inspired many women to depart from gender-based norms that restrict their right to make choices and has encouraged women to capture greater control over their own life chances.

The ability of other dominant groups in U.S. society to attach the label "deviant" to the behavior of those over whom they exercise power has also been under attack. Gay males and lesbians have been fighting against heterosexual-imposed norms that define homosexuality as deviant (D'Emilio Turner, and Vaid, 2000; Smith and Windes, 2000; Berman, 2011). People of color have been challenging the norm that calls for them to be quietly passive and acquiesce to racist treatment by members of the dominant white majority (Ancheta, 1998; Pinkey, 2000). And people with disabilities have been using political activism to dismantle norms that have excluded them from sharing in activities engaged in by the ablebodied (Shapiro, 1993; Charlton, 2000; Dowrick, 2001).

These examples suggest that people may at times resist the label "deviant" that dominant groups attempt to bestow upon them. In the next section we shall look closer at people's resistance to being defined as deviant.

DEVIANCE AND RESISTANCE

Thus far in this chapter we have defined deviance as *behavior* that is in violation of social norms. Most sociologists would agree with this traditional definition. We have emphasized that dominant groups may use their power to determine what behaviors will be considered deviant. But it is also apparent that power allows dominant groups to define others as deviant in terms of their very *being*. Thus, being a woman, a person of color, a gay male or lesbian, a person with a disability, an elderly person, or a poor person often means being defined as a deviant by dominant groups, even in the absence of any actual behavior that violates behavioral norms.

Deviance as Behavior versus Deviance as Being

Groups with power tend to define themselves as normal and those they dominate as "the other." Arturo Madrid (1998: 8) describes what it is like to be defined as the other by dominant groups:

> *Being* the other *means feeling different; is awareness of being distinct; is consciousness of being dissimilar. It means being outside the game, outside the circle, outside the set. It means being on the edges, on the margins, on the periphery. Otherness means being excluded, closed out, precluded, even disdained and scorned. It produces a sense of isolation, of apartness, of disconnectedness, of alienation. . . . Being* the other *involves a contradictory phenomenon. On the one hand being the other means being invisible. . . . On the other hand, being* the other *sometimes means sticking out like a sore thumb. What is she/he doing here?*

In Chapter 5 we saw how language can socially construct a definition of who is "normal" through the use of qualifying labels that subtly identify some people as "the other." For example, when a political leader is identified as a "gay legislator," a surgeon as a "woman doctor," or an athlete as a "black golfer," it subtly suggests that the normal incumbent of these positions is heterosexual, male, or white. In contrast, when persons holding these positions conform to the assumed statuses of "normal," such qualifiers are neither necessary nor used. Similarly, using the generic term "man" or "mankind" to indicate all of humanity implicitly suggests males are the "normal" human beings, and females are the "other."

In addition to language, the very physical structuring of the everyday environment communicates who is considered a "normal" member and participant of society. When public buildings and classrooms are only accessible using stairs, bathrooms are accessible only through narrow doors that cannot accommodate wheelchairs, or important signs are posted using only printed words without also using braille, it asserts that ablebodiedness is a requirement of inclusion as a "normal" member of society. The ways in which our society is physically arranged often serve to marginalize people with disabilities as outsiders and denies them the right to fully participate in and benefit from opportunities available to the ablebodied.

Persons who by their being (as the other) or behavior are defined as deviant may be considered "outsiders," a term introduced by Howard S. Becker:

> *But the person who is thus labeled an outsider may have a different view of the matter. He may not accept the rule by which he is being judged and may not regard those who judge him as either competent or legitimately entitled to do so (Becker, 1963: 1–2).*

Becker thus suggests that outsiders may resist efforts on the part of dominant groups to bestow the label "deviant" or otherwise marginalize them in response to their behavior or on the basis of their being (see Falk, 2001). It is noteworthy, however, that in many ways it is certainly easier, should one choose to do so, to alter one's behavior to avoid a label of deviant; it is not an option when the label of deviant is applied to someone on the basis of his or her very being (setting aside, of course, the question of whether or not one *should*): Our ascribed statuses are largely unchangeable. The label of deviant in the case of ascribed statuses makes the notion of power and dominant norms in the social construction of deviance abundantly clear.

Resistance to Being Labeled Deviant for One's Behavior

One of the most familiar settings in which struggles take place over being labeled deviant on the basis of one's behavior is the courtroom. Each year police arrest literally millions of people and charge them with crimes ranging from misdemeanors to felonies. In many cases charges are dropped, but arrests for the most serious offenses result in a court appearance for the accused. There, a battle ensues between the prosecutor, whose job it is to prosecute the case, and the defense attorney, who is intent on achieving a positive outcome for his or her client. The accused does not want to suffer the consequences of being successfully prosecuted and will, through the medium of the defense attorney, resist imposition of the label "criminal." Ordinarily, the higher one's class position, the greater the level of effective resistance, as individuals in higher positions have more economic resources to bring to bear in financing a defense (Reiman, 2009).

While it is rarely pursued, despite the impression one might gain from sensational cases reported in the media, the insanity defense is another example of the struggle over labeling persons deviant whose behavior violates social norms (Robinson, 1996; Mitchell, 2003). In this instance, the accused attempts to resist the unwanted label "criminal" by demanding to be given a substitute label: "insane." The goal is to be found not guilty by reason of insanity.

Insanity is a legal term, not a medical one, and individual states differ as to the criteria they use to judge its existence. The defense may argue that the accused was not in his or her right mind when performing the act in question; the prosecution will say that the defendant knew exactly what he or she was doing and knew that it was wrong. Each side is likely to bring in professional psychiatric experts to support its case. While individual cases may receive much publicity, in reality only a tiny percentage of accused criminals attempt an insanity defense. Moreover, of these only a small proportion of the attempts to substitute the label "insane" for the label "criminal" are successful. Judges and juries seem loath to accept insanity as an excuse for serious crimes, in part because psychiatrists themselves often disagree on diagnoses.

Witness the controversy over the use of the insanity plea in the case of Andrea Yates, a woman in Texas who drowned all five of her small children in 2001. Her attorneys argued that she suffered severe psychosis of post-partum depression and was therefore insane when she killed her children. The prosecutor rejected that argument. Both sides marshaled several psychiatric professionals to argue their points of view on her insanity defense, illustrating the lack of consensus even among the professionals concerning such a diagnosis.

At times, people whose behavior violates social norms are given the label "mentally ill." Once this label is bestowed, through a court process or other routes to diagnosis by mental health professionals, people may find it difficult to ever successfully resist being treated as outsiders (Link et al., 1987). According to sociologist Erving Goffman (1963), such individuals carry a negative social **stigma,** a "damaged identity" by which they are marked by others (Phelan et al., 1997; see also Nelson, 2001 for a similar analysis of the "damaged identity" relative to other status groups, such as Roma, transsexuals, and mothers, treated as subnormal and subjected to stigmas and marginalization).

For example, persons with a history of mental illness may face rejection by others for such social roles as employee or spouse. Within U.S. society, an element of fear is commonly connected with the idea of associating with the mentally ill, and it frequently results in the avoidance and exclusion of persons so labeled. Even when a person has undergone treatment and no longer has any symptoms of being ill, the label "mentally ill" may remain. Should discrimination interfere with the ability of such a person to enter and perform important roles, the stigmatization may actually contribute to mental illness. This then leads to an "I told you so" attitude on the part of those who would not let the label go (Link et al., 1997).

A similar "looping" process occurs when people are released from prison. Often those released have trouble finding employment because they have been labeled with the stigma "criminal." Employers expect applicants to report criminal convictions, but then they frequently refuse to hire those who do. Seeing little choice if they are to survive, former inmates frequently end up again committing crimes and, if caught, are reinstitutionalized. This pattern is reflected in statistics that show very high rates of **recidivism,** that is, the return to prison of many persons who have already been there. Conviction of persons released from prison for additional criminal behavior simply serves to confirm for employers the wisdom of not hiring those labeled criminal in the first place.

Resistance to Being Labeled Deviant for One's Being

Obviously, it is one thing to resist a label like "criminal" or "mentally ill" that is imposed in response to one's behavior, but something else again to resist being labeled deviant on the basis of one's very *being.* As we mentioned earlier, certain categories of people are often defined and treated by dominant groups as "the other." The dominant group views itself as normal and the other as deviant by definition. Resistance to being labeled deviant often requires that persons who make up "the other" openly question the legitimacy of the dominant group's judgments and assertions about them.

For example, gay men and lesbians who stay "in the closet" do so largely because of the discriminatory treatment they know they otherwise will have to endure, not because they are homosexual. This discriminatory treatment follows a labeling process in which many members of the dominant group—heterosexuals—define homosexuals as unnatural creatures, freaks of nature, and perverts. Gay resistance to being considered the other, as inferiors deserving of oppression, includes questioning the accuracy and legitimacy of the dominant group's stereotypes and assertions. Gay males and lesbians are people who differ from heterosexuals only in their sexual orientation. The stigma of being homosexual is often fought by emphasizing that being different is not the same as being inferior.

Likewise, people with disabilities remain socially and economically marginalized not because of their disability but because of discriminatory and exclusionary attitudes and practices on the part of the ablebodied. People with disabilities are, by definition, considered to be deviant, or the other, by many members of the ablebodied majority. From the perspective of this dominant group, people with disabilities are less-than-whole people. They are missing important physical or mental attributes that would render them decidedly "normal" human beings. Thus, the disability rights movement has emphasized the importance of using the term *people with disabilities*, as opposed to "disabled" or "handicapped" people. Such individuals are people first, just like everyone else. What they have in common with the ablebodied is far more significant than the differences associated with a disability. Again, being different is not the same as being inferior.

In the struggle to resist and overcome the label "deviant," some groups defined as the other have been more successful than others. The civil rights movement and the feminist movement have operated for some time and can cite substantial victories. The disability rights movement is much more recent, but it has made some important strides in combating discrimination, as have groups supporting rights and protections for older persons. The gay rights movement has been somewhat less successful than the others. There is much ignorance about homosexuality and a great many stereotypes about homosexuals. Gay rights activists must also contend with groups who strongly condemn homosexuality on the basis of religious doctrines. But this movement too has had some notable breakthroughs.

In recent years, street demonstrations and court cases have focused upon *racial profiling*, the practice of targeting people for surveillance, investigation, or arrest on the basis of their race or ethnicity. This is a perfect example of resisting being labeled deviant for reasons other than behavior. It is not unusual for people of color to be stopped on the roads or on the streets and questioned, searched for contraband, or arrested by police even when they have not broken any laws. That they may fit a racist stereotype as to who is the "typical" criminal can be enough of an "offense" to be treated as if they have actually broken a law, when the only "crime" committed may be "driving while black" (Harris, 1999; Meeks, 2010; www.aclu.org/profiling).

Racial profiling practices expanded and intensified in the United States in the aftermath of the terrorist acts of September 11, 2001. Muslims and Middle Eastern people in the United States found themselves targeted as suspected terrorists by police as well as by the public. Fears of further terrorist attacks encouraged many members of U.S. society to tolerate the harassment and abuse of Muslims and violations of their civil rights as the price "we" had to pay to be secure. In the year after September 11, the Council on American-Islamic Relations reported almost 1,700 cases of discrimination, intimidation, denial of services, harassment, physical assault, and law enforcement detainment of people who "looked" Middle Eastern or who had Muslim-sounding names (Awad, 2002).

Racial profiling marginalizes people and denies them the basic right of the presumption of innocence until proven guilty. It denies them the right to equal treatment under the law that members of racially dominant groups take for granted. The possible negative consequences of challenging the police or panicked neighbors have proven frightening to people of Middle Eastern ancestry or nationality who are subject to profiling, surely prompting many to remain quiet and docile. Legal actions to combat profiling and mistreatment by U.S. law enforcement and immigration officials have been pursued by national organizations such as the American Civil Liberties Union.

Finally, impoverished people suffer more silently than most people who are subject to oppression under the "deviant" label. Despite the large size of the U.S. poverty population—nearly 43 million people in 2009 (www.census.gov)—its members are often labeled and treated as "the other" by those who are more affluent. Many view poor people as deviants whose economic circumstances alone are sufficient to call their character into question (Mead, 1992). The large numbers and the diversity of the types of individuals who live under the poverty line, as well as the changing membership composition of the poor as people move into and out of poverty, complicate efforts to organize resistance to this labeling. For many poor people, a sense of fatalism and hopelessness contributes to political stagnation; some accept the dominant view that they are at heart inferior by nature in comparison to their economic superiors. Resistance to being defined as the other and being negatively treated thus is not as visible among poor people as it is among some other marginalized groups.

CRIME AS DEVIANCE

Whereas deviance is defined as a violation of norms in general, **crime** is a particular form of deviance. It is a violation of a law. As we mentioned earlier in this chapter, laws are the most formal of norms. As such, the term *deviance* refers to violations of folkways and mores, whereas the term *crime* specifically refers to those behaviors that violate norms encoded in the penal code. Punishments of crimes are therefore commonly harsher and more formalized. But these punishments are not necessarily uniformly applied: Patterns of inequality are quite common. We will discuss this in greater detail shortly. First, let's explore the importance of class inequality for how criminal behavior gets defined.

Bias in the Treatment of Different Types of Crimes

The Federal Bureau of Investigation (FBI) reports statistics on criminal activity each year in its Uniform Crime Reports (UCR), and how the agency counts such activity is telling. The UCR measures the incidence, arrests, and trends for the violent crimes of murder and voluntary manslaughter, forcible rape, robbery and aggravated assault. (Figure 9.1 provides an indication of the magnitude of violent crime offenses in the United States.)

Figure 9.1:   Violent Crimes in the United States, 1980–2009 (in millions)

Year	Murder	Forcible Rape	Robbery	Aggravated Assault
1980	23.0	83.0	566	673
1985	19.0	87.7	498	723
1990	23.4	102.6	639	1,055
1995	21.6	97.5	581	1,099
2000	15.6	90.2	408	912
2005	16.7	94.3	417	862
2009	15.2	88.1	408	807

Source: www.census.gov

The UCR also reports on property crimes: burglary, larceny-thefts, motor vehicle theft, and arson. The crime reported on in the UCR is committed by individuals, and those arrested and convicted of these crimes are disproportionately the poor and the relatively powerless in society (Reiman and Leighton, 2009).

What is not reported or even counted in the UCR are law violations that are more commonly engaged in by professionals and by corporations, even though these crimes may in fact cause more deaths and injuries and result in greater monetary losses than those individual crimes that are counted. Crimes not reported in the FBI's Uniform Crime Report include such activities as insider trading and securities fraud; fraudulent predatory lending resulting in home foreclosures; deaths and diseases caused by employers' noncompliance with occupational health and safety regulations; medical malpractice resulting in death (including inadequate emergency medical care, lethal prescription, or surgical errors related to practicing under the influence of drugs or alcohol); excessive force by police resulting in death; toxic waste dumping; corporate malfeasance; and embezzlement. The failure of the state to report on these crimes creates the impression that crime is something done only by individuals and primarily persons who are poor or otherwise marginal to mainstream society. Nothing could be further from the truth. This becomes especially clear when one examines the case of white collar and corporate crime.

The Case of White Collar and Corporate Crime

While members of dominant groups in society are in a power position to define others as deviant, they themselves may violate norms without necessarily having their own behavior defined as deviant, or be sanctioned differently when their acts do come to light. As we mentioned above, white collar and corporate crimes committed by the more affluent members of society are not reflected in the Uniform Crime Reports.

White collar crimes are violations of the law by individuals in the course of their occupations or professions and are typically crimes that benefit them. Such crimes are often committed by people who occupy high-level positions and who thus have access to criminal opportunities that are not accessible to most workers. For example, in the normal course of doing their jobs, corporate executives are often in a position to enrich themselves at the expense of the firm, consumers, stockholders, or lower-level workers in their companies. Among corporate executives, white collar crimes sometimes take the form of embezzlement, fraud, and insider trading (illegally timing sales or purchase of company stock based on privileged information). Executive treasurers, head bookkeepers, and key accountants who keep track of and control a firm's finances may be in a position to transfer funds from their company into their own accounts and to hide these transactions for a long time. This is no less a crime than if these individuals broke into someone's home and stole money and often causes great monetary losses, but it is not reflected in the Uniform Crime Reports.

One infamous example of very costly white collar crimes involved an executive in the financial services industry, Michael Milken. In the Milken case of the late 1980s, several "arbitrageurs" engaged in insider trading that provided them with literally millions of dollars in profit while stockholders and many smaller firms suffered billions of dollars of loss. The job of an arbitrageur is to put together two or more companies in a potential merger, much like a match-maker. Mergers between major corporations commonly tend to send their stock values soaring, so that anyone holding stock in the firms before they merge stands to make a terrific profit. The law therefore forbids arbitrageurs from investing in the firms that may be merging, because their job provides them with information that could significantly affect the price of the stock and therefore places them in an unfair advantage relative to everyone else. Yet that is exactly what Michael Milken and his friends did at Drexel, Burnham Lambert, a major securities trading firm.

Milken would match firms as merger partners, inform his friends of the impending match so they could purchase the low-priced shares of stock in the merging firms (for themselves as well as for Milken) before any public announcement of the merger, and then his friends would sell the stocks for a huge profit when their value jumped after the merger (Zey, 1993). Smaller investors who were unaware of this insider trading scheme lost a great deal of money when they sold the cheap shares because they did not know the mergers were about to take place. Had they known, they could have held onto their shares longer to benefit from the price boost the mergers produced. Only Milken and his friends benefitted, amassing hundreds of millions of dollars by the time the scheme was uncovered. Milken was prosecuted and fined $200 million, but was required to serve less than two years of a 10-year sentence.

As part a series of similar revelations a decade later, in 2003 10 of the financial services industry's largest firms were forced by the federal government's Securities and Exchange Commission (SEC) to agree to pay $1.4 billion in fines and restitution for employee wrongdoing. The SEC found that members of the firms' staffs were providing investors with advice that in some cases was both misleading and fraudulent. The firms involved included such industry giants as Merrill Lynch, Credit Suisse First Boston, and Salomon Smith Barney. According to the SEC, financial analysts in these companies were recommending that investors buy certain stocks, knowing full well that these stocks were unlikely to provide good financial returns. While those who followed the analysts' recommendations to channel their money into these stocks suffered losses, the analysts (and their companies) profited handsomely from handling the investors' accounts. Under the terms of the $1.4 billion settlement, the firms neither admitted nor denied misleading investors (Gordon, 2003).

More recently, Bernie Madoff, a stockbroker, wealth manager, and investment advisor ran a Ponzi or pyramid scheme in which he convinced wealthy investors to let him invest substantial sums of money for them with promises of huge profits. He paid earlier clients with the money given to him to invest by newer clients, thereby creating the image that he was an incredibly savvy investor, which itself prompted earlier investors to give him even more money to invest. Meanwhile, he kept billions of dollars for himself by skimming from clients' investment accounts. The pyramid began to collapse in 1999 when financial analyst Harry Markopolos told the Securities and Exchange Commission that it was not legally or mathematically possible to generate the profits Madoff was claiming (Markopolos, 2011). Although Markopolos's claims were ignored for several years, Madoff's illegal scheme finally fell apart in 2008 when he could no longer financially support the pyramid and continue to pay the earliest investors their customary gains. By then, client accounts were found to be missing nearly $65 billion. Madoff was sentenced in 2009 to 150 years in prison and was forced to forfeit over $17 billion. Although he certainly forfeited an astonishing amount of personal wealth, it hardly covered the massive amount of money embezzled from some of the wealthiest investors in the United States. And it represented an amount of money that a street criminal could not possibly amass.

White collar crimes are different from corporate crimes. **Corporate crimes** are violations of the law done by officers in corporations in the course of setting policy or standard operating procedures that benefit the firm. In effect, the firm itself is the criminal. Examples of corporate crimes include activities such as fraud, toxic waste dumping, stock manipulation, failure to fix known design flaws in products that result in consumer injuries or deaths, and violations of worker health and safety requirements that cause workers to die or get severely injured or diseased on the job.

An example of corporate crime can be seen in the case of Goldman Sachs, arguably the largest multinational investment banking firm that deals in securities, investment management, and global finance; it is a central figure in marketing and dealing in U.S. Treasury funds. Goldman Sachs was a key investment bank in the 2008 economic meltdown and benefitted handsomely from the subsequent $10 billion preferred stock investment by the U.S. Treasury under the federal Troubled Asset Relief Program (TARP) to bail out major banks. The Securities and Exchange Commission charged the firm in 2010 of securities fraud because it developed a security (Abacus Mortgage) that was deliberately designed to fail in the firm's attempt to profit from the housing market debacle and the federal government's bailout programs. They then encouraged customers to invest in Abacus without disclosing that the security was designed to fail. Investors lost millions of dollars in investments in a fraudulent scheme so that the firm could profit. The company settled the case with a payment of $550 million, a mere fine for a company worth nearly $3 billion at the time (Ferguson, 2012; http://topics.nytimes.com/top/news/business/companies/goldman_sachs_group_inc/index.html).

Some of these crimes may be understood in the context of the market environment in which these firms do business (Zey, 1998). Corporations operate in a market environment that includes competition between firms, the competitive advantages of large corporations over smaller firms, government policies that may actually encourage or enable corporate violations of the law, and investors who can move their investments into and out of corporations quickly if they do not produce immediate and substantial profits every business quarter. Corporate executives are under pressures to produce significant profits to appease stockholders, to successfully compete with other firms in their market environment, and to do so while attempting to comply with the legal constraints under which they are supposed to operate. The environment of the market thus encourages corporate officers to break laws and cut corners to generate quick profits. State policies that reduce government regulation of industries may also pave the way for corporate crimes, insofar as deregulation removes the oversight needed to monitor corporate compliance with existing laws.

An example of corporate crime is provided by the fraudulent standard operating procedures that Bankers Trust Company used throughout the 1990s. The firm convinced customers to become involved in financial deals that generated huge profits for the firm but cost enormous losses for its clients by misrepresenting investment opportunities to them. It enticed customers who lost money to invest in even more complicated transactions, supposedly to help them recover their losses, resulting in even bigger losses for the client and more bank profits. A mass of documents evidenced a "culture of greed and duplicity" at the bank. Said one observer, "Fraud was so pervasive and institutional that Bankers Trust employees used the acronym 'ROF'–short for rip-off factor, to describe one method of fleecing clients" (Holland and Himmelstein, 1995:108).

Sometimes illegal activities represent a hybrid of white collar and corporate crimes, to the extent that they benefit both the individuals involved as well as the firm. The collapse of Enron in 2002, the biggest bankruptcy in U.S. history, will probably take several more years to unravel. But in the immediate aftermath of the announcement of Enron's demise, it became increasingly clear that top-level executives benefitted from highly creative and generally unacceptable accounting practices. These practices hid the true, deeply troubled financial picture of this major energy-trading Fortune 500 firm. While continuing to encourage investors (including their own employees) to buy shares of stock in Enron as a solid, very profitable investment, the top executives of the firm were quietly and energetically selling their own shares. Indeed, Enron's rank and file workers were explicitly forbidden to sell their shares, which many bought as part of their participation in the company's retirement program.

In contrast to top-level executives who personally made many millions of dollars in this scheme, other Enron workers lost their jobs and in some cases most of their life savings. Meanwhile, Enron's accounting firm, Arthur Andersen, began shredding its Enron-related documents, even after the bankruptcy became evident and after investigations into events began (Sloan, 2002). It will likely take years to sort out how much of what went wrong at Enron was explicitly criminal and how much was a systemic failure of all the usual safeguards against these abuses. But it already appears that at least some of what occurred can serve to illustrate a combination of white collar and corporate crime.

EXPLANATIONS FOR DEVIANT BEHAVIOR

Why do people engage in behavior that violates norms, including those that take the form of laws? How can observers explain deviant behavior? Sociologists and other social scientists have proposed many different types of explanations for such behavior: physiological, psychological, social-psychological, and sociological (Liska and Messner, 1998; Rubington and Weinberg, 2004). Much attention has been focused on why people engage in illegal acts, so our discussion will emphasize criminal behavior more than other forms of deviance.

Physiological explanations argue that deviant behavior is rooted in some type of physical peculiarity or malfunction. Or perhaps the tendency to engage in the behavior in question is inherited and resides in the genes. **Psychological explanations** hold that deviant behavior is an expression of psychological problems or unusual personality traits. Such problems or traits often are said to stem from one's experiences with family members and other persons in a position to influence psychological development.

Social-psychological explanations look at the influence of people's immediate social environment on their thinking and behavior. This environment encompasses not only the family, but also the people with whom one associates in the neighborhood, at school, or in the workplace. While psychological explanations might view deviant behavior as evidence of a personality deficiency, social-psychological explanations often emphasize the role played by peer-group influences. Finally, **sociological explanations** examine the ways in which a society is structured and the demands it makes upon its members. Such explanations stress that the factors contributing to deviant behavior may lie well outside the control of the individuals and groups engaging in it.

For example, certain forms of mental illness, such as schizophrenia, are thought to be linked to physiological traits. Substance abuse may in many cases be a form of psychological escapism, a way of relieving stress or combating depression. Peers not only may teach novices the skills needed to successfully commit crimes but may provide informal pressures that compel them to engage in repeated criminal acts. A society that fails to deal successfully with economic recessions and the loss of jobs will foster frustration and anger on the part of the unemployed that can be reflected in high rates of partner, spouse, and child abuse. Notice how the discussion here shifted from one type of explanation to another in commenting on the possible causes of different types of deviant behavior.

Obviously, the nature of the explanation that one finds most useful for a particular form of deviant behavior will considerably affect one's approach to solutions. If, for example, higher rates of spouse abuse are "caused" by breakdowns in the economic system such as rising unemployment, then the way to address this deviant behavior is not simply to pass stricter laws and parcel out harsher punishments but also to improve the workings of the economic system.

There is, however, a popular tendency toward **reductionism** when most people think about explanations for deviant behavior. That is, people are quick to reduce explanations for deviance to the psychological or even the physiological level. Thus, if some individuals are assaulting their spouses, there must be "something wrong with them." Since most people do not abuse their family members, the deviant behavior must stem from defects or deficiencies in the abusers. Sociologists tend to be very leery of reductionist explanations when they are offered dogmatically and without reasonable consideration of other explanatory factors, such as the impact of social-group memberships or the effects of societal-level factors. In the next sections we shall consider different types of explanations for deviant behavior in more detail, providing additional illustrations.

Physiological Explanations

Being deviant in terms of one's behavior implies being different from others in some way. Why, then, could deviants not be different from everyone else in terms of their physiological characteristics? The search for biological traits that would distinguish persons engaging in deviant behavior from everyone else has gone on for a long time and encompassed a variety of behaviors. Some scholars have explored the possibility that the propensity for criminal behavior is inherited. They have even tried to correlate it with physical features, such as racial ancestry, head shape and body build, or chromosomal differences (Fishbein, 1990). Physiological causes have been explored for other forms of deviance as well, including mental illness, alcoholism, and suicide.

A relationship does exist between physiological characteristics and deviant behavior in some areas. For example, brain damage accompanying aging or alcohol abuse can cause people to act in unusual ways, as in the case of Alzheimer's disease and alcoholic psychosis. Newborns may suffer physiological damage due to their mothers' alcohol and drug use, which can in turn affect their behavior as children or adults. There are indications that for some people heredity may play a role in acquiring an addiction to alcohol (Begleiter and Kissin, 1995). Some perpetrators of violent crimes have suffered from brain damage or tumors to which their behavior may somehow be linked. But for most types of behavior that are considered deviant, physiological explanations thus far have proved inadequate.

While we no doubt will learn more in the future about the relationship between physiological characteristics and behavior, sociologists and other social scientists tend to dislike reductionist explanations and are likely to point to what they leave unexamined. People not only have bodies; they have minds. Explanations for deviant behavior must take into account people's thought processes. People also have friends, relatives, and associates whose behavior bears upon their own. Human beings are social animals whose biographies are very much forged by the statuses they occupy within society and by the changing nature of society itself. Even if it can be scientifically proven that physiology is involved in some expressions of deviant behavior, is it not also likely that non-physiological factors have much to do with the behavior as well?

Psychological Explanations

One of the most influential psychological explanations for a wide range of deviant behavior is based upon the work of Sigmund Freud (Clinard and Meier, 1992). Freud argued that mental illness stemmed primarily from unconscious conflicts. Depending on their nature, such conflicts could lead individuals to violate social norms.

Following Freud's lead, many psychologists have searched for personality traits that distinguish the deviant from the non-deviant (Clinard and Meier, 2003). For example, while some researchers have argued that alcoholism is a disease, possibly inherited, and thus best understood in terms of a physiological explanation, others have argued that there is such a thing as an "alcoholic personality" with distinct traits. Researchers have even reached a rough consensus on what the traits of this personality are. Unfortunately, the traits in question can also be found within the nonalcoholic population.

Psychological explanations for deviant behavior often flounder in the face of the fact that there do not seem to be any psychological traits that clearly distinguish deviants from nondeviants. For example, mental illness does not seem to be any more prevalent within the population of known criminals than it is among persons not known to have committed criminal acts.

More broadly speaking, psychological explanations for deviant behavior are limited to inferences or educated guesses about what goes on in the minds of those defined as deviant. Such explanations are at times criticized as reductionist, since often too little attention is paid to the nature and relative importance of social influences on the individual who engages in deviant behavior. While it is very important that researchers continue to study the role psychological factors play in various forms of deviance, sociologists would argue that researchers should not do so at the cost of ignoring the possible role of the social environment.

Social-Psychological Explanations

Individuals are constantly aware of the people around them and the fact that these others are conscious of what the individuals are doing in their presence. Social-psychological explanations for deviant behavior are based upon people's sensitivity to their immediate social environment. Such explanations suggest that others help shape the behavior that comes to be defined as deviant (Hagan, 1994). Let us look at some examples of social-psychological explanations. Many of these explanations are influenced by symbolic interactionism, an intellectual tradition in sociology discussed in Chapter 1.

Differential Association Theory

Sociologists interested in crime and juvenile delinquency often stress the importance of the associates of persons engaging in deviant behavior. One social psychological explanation for deviant behavior, known as **differential association theory,** posits that individuals learn to engage in deviant behavior by communicating and interacting with those already disposed to do so (Sutherland and Cressey, 1974). Novices are taught the skills and techniques involved in committing crimes and are shown why such behavior is worthwhile, and they are encouraged to adopt others' rationalization for flaunting the law.

Take the example of marijuana use. In his now-classic research on how people become users of this drug, Howard S. Becker notes that deviant behavior does not necessarily require a pre-existing psychological motivation to engage in the act (1963). Rather, he argues, the reverse can be true: An individual may be urged into certain behavior and only then become motivated to do it again. People are usually encouraged to try marijuana by experienced users with whom they are associating. They may agree to do so simply out of curiosity. Someone who has never used the substance must first be taught the way to use it, the circumstances under which it is best used, and the kinds of sensations to watch for. The novice must also be taught to interpret these sensations as pleasurable.

An individual may have to try marijuana several times with experienced users before learning to enjoy its effects. After the initiation period, these associates may continue to be important in providing access to the substance and sharing in behavior that is ordinarily conducted in secrecy because of its illegality. A person who does not associate with marijuana users, or associates with people who condemn its use, is unlikely to engage in this particular deviant behavior. Becker's analysis thus underscores the important role group membership can play in encouraging deviant behavior. Explanations that focus only on the psychological characteristics of marijuana users would miss the importance of this factor.

Control Theory

A second social-psychological explanation is known as **control theory** (Costello and Vowell, 1999; Hawdon, 1999). This explanation suggests that deviance is due to the absence of social control or other external constraints on individual behavior (Hirschi, 1969). It assumes that human nature contains flaws that lead people to act in ways that are "bad" and that it is necessary to control these innate tendencies if society is to function. Those social scientists who favor control theory tend to differ on where the most important sources of control originate.

Containment Theory

In **containment theory** (Reckless, 1961), the sources of control are said to be both external *and* internal to the individual. Containment theory proceeds from this question: Why doesn't much more deviant behavior take place in society? The answer, according to containment theory, is that people encounter both external and internal controls that contain the temptation toward deviance. External controls include community standards for behavior and the institutions that function to uphold them. Internal controls exist within the individual. They result from social-ization experiences people undergo through the family, education, and religion, and they supply the individual with self-control capabilities. People who engage in deviant acts are said to do so through a lack of sufficient means of self-control or the absence of clear community standards and social pressures to conform.

Social Reinforcement

A different type of social-psychological explanation suggests that deviant behavior is the result of **social reinforcement.** In this view, humans, as a species, are psychologically motivated to seek out pleasure and avoid pain, but their behavior is directed by past experiences and specula-tions as to the likely outcomes of future behavior (Akers, 1985). If people feel that the rewards from acts of deviance outweigh the punishments (or potential punishments), they are likely to engage in such acts. From this point of view, people who commit crimes, engage in substance abuse, or take their own lives do so because this behavior has been reinforced in their minds as desirable by the calculus of punishment and rewards. The criminal or substance abuser may have found that the deviant behavior was rewarding enough to be initiated or repeated, while the suicide victim may have found that life was punishing enough to be avoided.

Labeling Theory

Finally, **labeling theory** draws attention to how people come to be defined as deviant (as in our earlier discussion of the social construction of deviance). But labeling theory also addresses the social-psychological impact of this label on individuals and its effect on their subsequent behav-ior. Sociologist Edwin Lemert (1967) made the important distinction between *primary devi-ance* and *secondary deviance*. With primary deviance, individuals violate a norm and are labeled as deviant by others, but reject this label as not fitting their self image. They by and large see themselves as conformists, and there are no significant effects on their subsequent behavior from the labeling process. With secondary deviance, individuals violate a norm and are labeled as deviant, but they accept the label and internalize it, thus altering their self-image. Having done so, such individuals assume a deviant role that includes future norm violations. They may in effect become career deviants. This social-psychological explanation points to the possibility that efforts at social control of deviant behavior can actually produce more deviance.

Shortcomings of Social-Psychological Explanations

Social-psychological explanations consider the behavior of people within their immediate social environments. Such explanations explore the nature and relative importance of social influ-ences. Yet social-psychological explanations have critical shortcomings. In the case of differen-tial association, there are many forms of deviance to which the theory does not seem to apply. In most murders, for example, a person impulsively kills a relative, friend, or acquaintance. The murderer usually has never associated with others committing similar acts and has never mur-dered before.

Similarly, although containment theory may make a lot of intuitive sense, there seem to be many instances for which it is less than useful. For instance, a highly successful, middle-aged local business owner—a family man well known and respected throughout his community for his philanthropy and acts of community service, suddenly shoots his equally accomplished and socially involved wife and then takes his own life (Brown, 1993). How does one explain such sudden, seemingly impulsive behavior on the part of someone who by all criteria should be "contained"?

Theories of deviant behavior that stress the importance of reinforcement (through rewards and punishment) lack adequate empirical support. They tend to be applied after the fact: "He must have done that because he found it rewarding." Such theories cannot be used in predicting who is likely to engage in deviant behavior, since people differ greatly in terms of what they are likely to find rewarding.

Labeling theory does not really address why the violation of norms occurred in the first place. And it poses the very difficult challenge of figuring out how and under what circumstances primary deviance becomes transformed into secondary deviance. This social psychological explanation does have the virtue of drawing attention to the possibility that some people who are labeled as deviant will be propelled into future deviant behavior. But can observers reasonably predict who such people will be?

In general, social-psychological explanations are broader and encompass more factors bearing on deviant behavior than explanations that stop short at the physiological or psychological level. In that sense, proponents of social-psychological explanations are usually able to avoid charges of reductionism. Yet some sociologists argue that social-psychological explanations do not go far enough. They suggest that features of the larger society itself may make deviant behavior "normal."

Sociological Explanations

When individuals engage in deviant behavior, they do so within the context of the particular society in which they live and the ways in which its features impact upon them. Sociological explanations focus on ways in which such factors may prompt or encourage some individuals to engage in deviant behavior (Hagan, 1994).

Opportunity Structure Theory

Perhaps the best-known sociological explanation bearing on deviant behavior is Robert Merton's **opportunity structure theory** (1957). Merton noted that U.S. society places enormous stress on the pursuit of material success. Indeed, he sees this success as a cultural goal that most people share in common. It is unusual for individuals to say that they have no interest in being better off economically or for privileged persons to express no interest in holding on to or further enhancing their high economic status.

Along with the cultural goal of material success, Merton points out, there are socially approved, legitimate means for pursuing this goal. These include working, saving, and investing. Most people have access to and make use of these means in their quest for material success. But what happens in cases in which the approved means and the cultural goal do not coincide? In Merton's view, the stage is set for individuals to engage in a *mode of adaptation* that can entail deviant behavior.

For example, people may choose the mode of adaptation Merton called *innovation*—they make money illegally. Thus, a society whose culture stresses material success, but which offers only some members the means to pursue it, is a society in which one should expect to see deviant behavior in the form of burglaries, robberies, drug trafficking, prostitution, and other types of crime.

Still other people, faced with a gap between the cultural goal of material success and access to the approved means, may reject both. Choosing the mode of adaptation Merton called *retreatism*, they may adopt an alternative lifestyle as a vagrant, pursue altered states of consciousness through substance abuse, or even commit suicide. Retreatism entails removing oneself from a reality that just does not seem workable.

In contrast to retreatism, the mode of adaptation Merton termed *rebellion* involves inventing new cultural goals and new means of achieving them. The goals are likely to be quite different from, or even radically counter to, those that dominate the existing society. Persons who dedicate their lives to revolutionary organizations or transformative social movements (see Chapter 10) are adapting through rebellion.

Finally, in Merton's scheme of things, the means-goal gap may result in the mode of adaptation he calls *ritualism*. Seeing the goal of material success as hopeless, people abandon it; nonetheless, they go through the motions of working each day, rationalizing that the means themselves are worth pursuing. Since jobs that do not pay well are often also unrewarding in other ways, this can prove to be a rather hollow rationalization.

Merton suggests that since most people are able to utilize socially approved means to pursue the cultural goal of material success, they have little reason to engage in deviant behavior. Yet for others access to these means is problematic. A flawed opportunity structure creates conditions that pressure some people into modes of adaptation that may violate social norms. Much deviant behavior, from this point of view, originates outside the individual's control. Its origins lie in the characteristic features of society itself, such as values promoted by dominant culture and their impact. To reduce such deviance, society itself must undergo fundamental change.

Merton's analysis is very compelling. It provides a larger context for understanding the role of social-psychological factors in producing deviance (see Anderson, 1998). Its critics are likely to point out, however, that it does not explain why people adopt any one particular mode of adaptation. Why, for example, in the United States, are there so many thieves and so few revolutionaries? Why do people of affluence, who have access to socially approved means for material success, commit financial crimes? And how can one explain criminal behavior on the part of the extremely well-rewarded executives of large corporations?

Merton's theory seems to contain a bias toward deviant behavior as exhibited by the excluded and downtrodden, while saying comparatively little about deviance on the part of societal elites (Coleman, 1989; Simon and Eitzen, 1990). It is also highly tailored to cultural and social conditions in the United States. Finally, the focus of the model on behaviors does not lend itself to an understanding of those labeled deviant on the basis of their being rather than their actions. Nonetheless, in pointing to the influence of a society's cultural values and structure on its members' behaviors, Merton has greatly enriched sociological thinking about the origins of deviant behavior.

Deviance and Capitalism

A different, but related, type of sociological explanation for deviant behavior involves the concept of *alienation*. This explanation has its origins in the work of Karl Marx, who we discussed in Chapter 1 as a social thinker influential in the development of the conflict perspective in sociology. Contemporary sociologists borrowing from his ideas can be termed "neo-Marxists" (McGuire and McQuarie, 1994). The focus of the **Marxist theory of deviance** is on the demands that an industrial capitalist society imposes on people (Greenberg, 1993; Taylor, 1999).

An industrial capitalist society is one in which the means of producing goods and services (factories, farms, offices, mines, railroads, communication systems) are privately owned. Ownership tends to be concentrated in the hands of a few, among members of a group called the capitalist class or *bourgeoisie*. Most people, in order to survive, must work and sell their labor power to members of the capitalist class in return for wages. Marx calls this working-class group the *proletariat*. A problem arises because the self-interests of the capitalist class and those of the working class are in fundamental opposition.

The capitalist class wants to maximize profits in order to expand its wealth and property holdings and further enrich itself. Capitalists thus try to hold wages down to the bare minimum and organize industrial production in cost-saving ways that are often physically and psychologically harmful to their workers. In contrast, the working class wants adequate wages and working conditions. But, since its members are not owners of the means of production, this class lacks the power to get its needs met. Consequently, workers experience a sense of **alienation,** or estrangement, from their labor. This is extremely damaging because, in the neo-Marxist view, labor is the principal vehicle through which the human species expresses itself and seeks fulfillment.

Suffering from low wages, sporadic bouts of unemployment, and a sense of alienation, members of the working class are driven into behaviors that are defined as deviant. Crimes of violence, property offenses, and drug crimes are symptoms of the economic oppression and alienation they experience. The structure and workings of society—in this case, its capitalist features—turn the majority of its members into victims. Acting out their alienation from a system that fails to meet their fundamental human needs, members of the working class engage in activities that are harmful to themselves and/or to others (Taylor, Walton, and Young, 1973, 1975).

Neo-Marxists find that this sociological explanation for deviant behavior fits the United States (see Quinney, 1979; Hagan, 1997). The U.S. capitalist economy is characterized by chronic unemployment, poverty-level standards of living for the jobless and low-wage families, and workplace alienation, as indicated by worker tardiness, absenteeism, turnover, and acts of sabotage (Sprouse, 1992). Neo-Marxists see economic oppression and alienation as the main reason for the high incidence of crimes of violence, property crimes, and drug offenses at the lower levels of the U.S. class structure. In the neo-Marxist interpretation, capitalists' white collar and corporate crimes, such as unethical and illegal business practices, are indications that members of the capitalist class also experience a sense of alienation from the economic system in which they participate, even as they accept the logic of capitalism. But they have the most to gain from retaining the system.

Marx argued that workers in industrial capitalist societies, when pushed to the limit, would develop a revolutionary class consciousness and join in social movements to overthrow capitalism. In its place they would construct a "socialist" society in which the workers themselves collectively owned and controlled the means of production. With worker ownership and control, goods and services would be produced to serve the needs of the masses of people, not to enrich the profit of the few. Contrary to what many Marxist analysts have predicted, socialist revolutions have not taken place in industrial capitalist societies, such as the United States.

Revolutionary movements seeking to build socialism *have* arisen in some underdeveloped, agriculturally based societies. These movements built socialist economies in such widely different settings as the People's Republic of China, Cuba, and the former Soviet Union. Yet, to varying degrees, deviant behavior has been found to exist in these and other socialist societies.

Thus, while the demands made by capitalism may well drive many people into deviant behavior, clearly the dynamics of capitalism need not always be present for such behaviors to occur. The organization and operation of socialist economic systems may also contribute to deviance, a phenomenon that relatively little sociological research has explored.

CRIME AND PUNISHMENT: DIFFERENTIAL APPLICATION OF SANCTIONS

If dominant groups in society have the power to define what is "normal" and what is not, they also have the power to identify what behaviors are deserving of negative sanctions. But not everyone who engages in the same behaviors is sanctioned, and not everyone who is sanctioned receives the same kind or degree of punishment. Those who are poor are more likely than the affluent to be detained, arrested, and held in jail before trial, convicted, imprisoned, and even executed. This does not mean that poor people are more prone to break laws. One reason for their greater rates of conviction in the criminal justice system is the greater ability of the affluent to afford private attorneys who can devote adequate time to aiding clients accused of crimes, in contrast to the poor's reliance on overburdened public defenders. Moreover, judges and many jurors are also likely to identify and sympathize with more affluent defendants during trials (Reiman, 2009).

Table 9.1:   Comparison of Sentencing by Race

	Proportion of Incarcerated(c)		Prisoners under Executed(d)	
	Total Population	(2011)	Sentence of Death(d) (2010)	(2010)
Total(a)		3,739	3,158	46
White men(b)	39.8%	12.8%	55.4%	71.7%
African American men(b)	14.3	80.8	41.7	28.3

[a] Includes American Indians, Alaska Natives, Asians, Native Hawaiians, other Pacific Islanders, and Hispanic inmates for whom no other race was identified.

[b] The reporting of race and Hispanic origin differs from that presented in other tables in this document. In this table, counts of white and black inmates include persons of Hispanic/Latino origin.

[c] Source: A. Carson and W. Sobel, 2012, "Prisoners in 2011." U.S. Department of Justice, Bureau of Justice Statistics.

[d] Source: Tracy L. Snell, 2011. "Capital Punishment, 2010: Statistical Tables." U.S. Department of Justice Bureau of Justice Statistics.

Race is also a critical factor in the differential application of sanctions. Data suggest that people of color are more likely than whites to be arrested, found guilty, sent to prison or death row, and executed (Tonry, 2012; 1995) (see Tables 9.1 and 9.2).

Overall, African American men are imprisoned more than six times more often than white men (Kerby, 2012). In recent years many people of color have been sent to prison for drug offenses. Although white high school students are four times more likely to regularly use cocaine than African American students, African Americans who are arrested on drug charges are one and one-half times more likely to be sent to prison (U.S. Department of Justice, 1996; Centers for Disease Control, 1999; see also Quigley, 2010). ../Local Settings/Temporary Internet Files/Content.Outlook/NQ6J0991/(www.hrw.org/campaigns/drugs/war/key.facts.htm)

Table 9.2: Executions and Other Dispositions of Inmates Sentenced to Death, by Race and Hispanic origin, 1977–2010

| Origin | Prisoners Executed | | | Prisoners Who Received Other Dispositions (a) | |
	Total under Sentence of Death, 1977–2010 (b)	Number	% of Total	Number	% of Total
Total	7,879	1,234	15.7%	3,487	44.3%
White (c)	3,816	700	18.3	1,710	44.8
Black (c)	3,225	424	13.1	1,497	46.4
Hispanic	715	96	13.4	231	32.3
All other races (c, d)	123	14	11.4	49	39.8

Note: In 1972, the U.S. Supreme Court invalidated capital punishment statutes in several states (*Furman v. Georgia*, 408 U.S. 238 (1972)), effecting a moratorium on executions. Executions resumed in 1977 when the Supreme Court found that revisions to several state statutes had effectively addressed the issues previously held unconstitutional (*Gregg v. Georgia*, 428 U.S. 153 (1976) and its companion cases).

[a] Includes persons removed from a sentence of death because of statutes struck down on appeal, sentences or convictions vacated, commutations, or death by other than execution.

[b] Includes 5 persons sentenced to death prior to 1977 who were still under sentence of death on December 31, 2010; 374 persons sentenced to death prior to 1977 whose death sentence was removed between 1977 and December 31, 2010; and 7,500 persons sentenced to death between 1977 and 2010.

[c] Excludes persons of Hispanic/Latino origin.

[d] Includes American Indians, Alaska Natives, Asians, Native Hawaiians, and other Pacific Islanders.

Source: Tracy L. Snell, 2011. "Capital Punishment, 2010: Statistical Tables." Bureau of Justice Statistics Bulletin, December, 2011, p. 17. Available at http://bjs.gov/index.cfm?ty=pbdetail&iid=2236

People of color are also disproportionately represented among those receiving the ultimate punishment: the death penalty (see Table 9.2). And African Americans are twice as likely as whites to be executed, particularly if the victim was white (Fox, 2010; for statistics on capital punishment, see www.ojp.usdoj.gov/bjs/cp.htm).

Moreover, the race of the crime victim appears to be an important factor as well: a U.S. General Accounting Office study found that when comparing homicides committed under similar circumstances by defendants with similar criminal histories, the death penalty was "several times more likely" to be imposed when the victim was white than when the victim was African American (www.aclu.org/death-penalty/race.html). Most chilling is the fact that DNA testing increasingly reveals that there is an apparent rush to judgment clouded by racism that all too often sends innocent men of color to death row. As of 2012, at least 141 people had been exonerated at least in part as a result of DNA testing, and the majority of these have been African American and Latino (http://www.deathpenaltyinfo.org/innocence-list-those-freed-death-row; see also Alter, 2000).

People of color are likely to be required to post bail bonds substantially higher than those required of whites in order to obtain their freedom while they await trial. This is the case even when one compares people who have committed the same crime and who have similar criminal histories. Such practices occur despite the fact that no evidence exists to support the claim that people of color are more likely to flee before being brought to trial. One study found that in the case of drug charges such as possession or sale of illegal drugs, African Americans and Latinos paid average bail bonds that were four times greater than those paid by whites charged with similar law violations (Houston and Ewing, 1991, 1992; Ayres and Waldfogel, 1994).

This discriminatory pattern of setting bail bonds reverberates throughout the trial and sentencing process. National studies have found that people accused of crimes who are held in jail prior to trial because they cannot afford to post bail tend to receive longer sentences than defendants who are able to do so. Being jailed can impede the accused's ability to adequately participate in the preparation of his or her defense. It may also create the impression that the accused is guilty (Houston and Ewing, 1991). Since people of color are more likely than whites to be unemployed or disadvantaged in the labor market, and are disproportionately found among the poor, a system based on ability to pay bail imposes a greater burden on them whether they are guilty or innocent. In large measure, this means that the right to the presumption of innocence until proven guilty—with all its symbolic and practical implications—is compromised for people of color and the poor.

Furthermore, in some states, the civil liberties and rights of convicted felons are not only limited while they are imprisoned. They may continue to be denied long after prisoners have served their sentences and paid their debt to society. Four states permanently deny convicted felons the right to vote; seven other states allow some convicted felons to vote under strict conditions. The denial of voting rights after fully serving a sentence, particularly if that denial is permanent, limits ex-felons' lawful participation as citizens of their own nation. African American men in particular suffer this fate, since they are disproportionately represented among those convicted. Nationally, one in seven African American men is barred from voting; in states that carry out such penalties after time has been served, the rate is one in four (Katz, 2000; Hull, 2006; Manza and Uggen, 2008).

Taken together, these data indicate the power of dominant groups to determine not only who and what is deviant, but to also mete out differential sanctions to people committing the same infractions. Patterns of racial inequality suggest that the criminal justice system operates as a powerful social control mechanism, one that serves to punish people of color more harshly than whites. Labels and stigmas of conviction and imprisonment can follow a person long after time has been served. This compounds pre-existing patterns of inequality, making it more difficult for individuals who have been caught up, fairly or unfairly, in the system at one point in their lives to resist the label thereafter.

Note that major corporations and top-level executives who commit crimes are in a better position than the average worker to avoid the imposition of the label of deviance on their behavior, and to thus evade punishments and stigma (Reiman, 2009). Even when those engaging in white collar or corporate crimes are caught and punished, the sanctions are typically not as harsh as those suffered by persons convicted of the types of crimes of violence and property crimes found in the Uniform Crime Reports. The sentences imposed against executives who break the law commonly involve monetary fines that, even when substantial (as in the case of Michael Milken), are far less damaging in their impact than the smaller fines levied against the poor.

Convictions for white collar and corporate crimes often carry less prison time than convictions for those in the Uniform Crime Reports (with the notable exception of Bernie Madoff's sentence of 150 years for his monumental pyramid scheme, which most notably robbed from some of the wealthiest people in the United States), and imprisonment typically takes place in minimum security prisons where amenities and treatment of prisoners are far better than in medium or maximum security prisons. White collar and corporate felons do not usually lose their right to vote permanently, nor are their crimes punished by the death penalty, even when large numbers of individuals lose their lives as a result of their offenses. Executives who break the law are free to return to the political participation in which they can influence the laws that bind them and the sanctions they receive should they violate them.

Between 1992 and 2001, federal prosecutors pursued criminal charges against 525 of 609 corporate executives identified by the Securities and Exchange Commission as having committed offenses. Of those charged, 142 were found guilty of a crime. Only 87 of those found guilty served any time in jail, and most of them served only a few months. Ironically, in many instances it is legal for those forced to make restitution for their high-level financial crimes to claim much of it as a tax write-off (Smith, 2002). This pattern continued into the next decade: By 2010, the FBI had investigated 1,510 cases of securities and commodities fraud, resulting in only 306 convictions, and 592 cases of corporate fraud that resulted in 156 convictions (www.fbi.gov). Although corporate crimes result in a significantly greater dollar value of loss compared to individual street crimes, they are far more difficult to convict and do not carry the weight of stigma and hefty sanctions attached to street crimes.

DO SOCIETIES "NEED" DEVIANT BEHAVIOR?

Virtually all societies, however they may differ from one another, contain behavior that comes to be defined as deviant. In light of this fact, some sociologists have suggested that perhaps societies *need* deviant behavior. Rather than viewing deviant behavior negatively, perhaps one should see it as functional to society. This **functionalist theory of deviance** was first put forth by the

French sociologist Émile Durkheim (1964). Durkheim's importance to the more general functionalist perspective in sociology was addressed in Chapter 1.

Durkheim pointed out that deviance is not simply found in poorly organized, unstable societies. Rather, the best of societies (using whatever criteria one wishes) contain deviant behavior. Crime of one sort or another, for example, can be found everywhere. According to Durkheim, the occurrence of crime is actually a service to society; the anger and dismay crime generates function to bring people together and strengthen their solidarity as a group. The deviance reminds people of their commonly shared morality. As a sociologist who was interested in the bases of social order, Durkheim saw deviant behavior as contributing to societal stability. Without periodic opportunities to collectively condemn unwanted behavior, it would be harder to reinforce social order. In effect, deviant behavior functions as an internal threat against which societal members must rally.

Sociologist Kai Erikson elaborated on Durkheim's thoughts in *Wayward Puritans* (1966). Erikson uses the term *boundaries* to refer to the norms that evolve in human groups:

> *Human behavior can vary over an enormous range, but each community draws a symbolic set of parentheses around a certain segment of that range and limits its own activities within that narrower zone. These parentheses, so to speak, are the community's boundaries (Erikson, 1966: 10).*

Since the boundaries, or norms, are not always apparent, undergo change, and yet still must be internalized by new group members, some way must exist to demonstrate what they are. In Erikson's view, deviant behavior serves this function:

> *The deviant is a person whose activities have moved outside the margins of the group, and when the community calls him to account for that vagrancy it is making a statement about the nature and placement of its boundaries. It is declaring how much variability and diversity can be tolerated within the group before it begins to lose its distinctive shape, its unique identity (Erikson, 1966: 11).*

Thus Erikson sees the actions of *policing agents* as important in demonstrating where a group's norms, or boundaries, lie. Policing agents take many forms and include criminal justice systems, the psychiatric profession, military institutions, and religious bodies. These agents, confronting people who wander outside society's boundaries, show everyone where the boundaries are.

Erikson points out that much of what observers call "news" in the mass media concerns deviant behavior and its consequences. Many of the programs that appear on entertainment television also focus on deviant behavior. In recent years much "reality" programming has centered on police activities, most wanted criminals, and unsolved crimes. Erikson's argument is that the mass media play an important role in reinforcing societal norms by showing people repeatedly testing them and policing agents enforcing them.

Erikson suggests that deviant behavior is so important to societal stability that society actually encourages it. The failure of prisons to rehabilitate and of mental hospitals to cure actually ensures a steady supply of deviants who will violate norms, generate activity on the part of policing agents and regularly reinvigorate the majority's sense of the boundaries of socially acceptable behavior. Indeed, the segregation of deviants into such institutions ensures their continued alienation from society. Moreover, while institutionalized, deviants have the opportunity to learn new styles and techniques of norm violation from one another, an education that may assist some in pursuing a "career" of deviant behavior (Erikson, 1966).

Erikson's ideas do not really address the sources of the behavior that violates norms, but these sources are a major concern of sociologists. Nor does his argument that deviance may be beneficial, or functional, to society address the enormous harm done by many deviant acts. But he does force observers to think about whether a minimal degree of norm violation by a society's members is unavoidable if that society is to operate successfully. Accepting Erikson's ideas might cause one to view deviant behavior as a phenomenon that makes important contributions to society.

The logic of Erikson's views regarding the important functions that deviance may play within society may be extended to the practice of labeling other societies as deviant. Demonizing other societies, a common political practice, creates an "us versus them" mentality that often defines "us" as normal and "them" as evil, less civilized, and less deserving of existence. Political and military elites in the United States and elsewhere frequently identify and portray other societies ("them") as external threats. What functions does this play for society? For one, it can encourage societal members to at least temporarily suspend norms against killing so that participation in wars becomes a civic duty around which people across society will unite. The demonization of other societies as threats may also function to distract societal members from the failure of their government to address serious social problems (e.g., unemployment, poverty). External threats can make society's rank-and-file members feel dependent upon their government for information about and protection from these threats, thus reinforcing the ability of political elites to hold on to political power even as serious domestic social problems persist.

DEVIANCE AND SOCIAL CHANGE

There is another perspective from which deviant behavior may be viewed as serving important functions. People may intentionally violate norms to draw attention to societal conditions that they consider wrong and to bring about or increase pressures for social change. History is filled with examples of people "going against the system" even when it meant making enormous sacrifices of their livelihoods or even their lives.

As participants in the U.S. civil rights movement, many social activists violated norms and risked negative sanctions as they sought to end racial segregation and other discriminatory practices (Williams, 1987). Consider the importance we now attach to the historic refusal of a Montgomery, Alabama, seamstress, Rosa Parks, to give up her seat in a segregated city bus to a white man. On the day this occurred in 1955, the norms governing appropriate behavior for African Americans in the nation's South included a detailed and intricate body of rules of interracial etiquette (see Doyle, 1971). African Americans, for example, had to enter the front of the bus to pay and then had to go back outside and enter the rear of the bus to sit in the "colored only" section. Violators of such rules, some of which were unspoken while others were written into law, invited harsh sanctions from members of the dominant white majority.

Parks' action led to her arrest, which sparked a major boycott of public transportation and local white-owned businesses in Montgomery by members of the African American community.

The boycott proved successful. The buses were desegregated. The Montgomery bus boycott demonstrated to the nation that segregation could be fought by collective grassroots action. From that point on norms governing black-white relations underwent a sustained attack, including an all-out assault on such common features of everyday life as "whites only" restrooms, schools, bus station entrances, water fountains, cemetery sections, phone booths, motels, blood banks, lunchrooms, movie theater seats, swimming pools, and beaches.

By the early 1960s African Americans and their supporters, including many whites, were flagrantly contesting the norms of racial segregation through peaceful, racially integrated marches, boycotts, and sit-ins across the South. Groups such as the National Association for the Advancement of Colored People, the Congress of Racial Equality, the Student Nonviolent Coordinating Committee, and Dr. Martin Luther King's Southern Christian Leadership Conference provided leadership, legal assistance, and other resources to help advance what had become a major social movement.

Many southern civil rights workers and other supporters of the movement were targeted for negative sanctions, such as harassment, loss of their jobs, and threats or acts of violence directed against themselves and their families. Widely condemned acts of racist terrorism occurred, including a church bombing in Birmingham, Alabama, that killed four African American children, and the murder of three young civil rights workers in Mississippi (a black state resident and two white New Yorkers). These acts were the response of whites who felt their world shattering as the civil rights movement, building on its day-by-day successes, overturned laws permitting racial segregation.

The civil rights movement helped inspire others to violate norms, question injustices, and engage in deviant behavior to challenge "business as usual." The feminist movement, the disability rights movement, and the gay rights movement are but three examples. Within the gay rights movement, an organization known as ACT UP became concerned with the slowness of AIDS research and drug trials and angered over the high costs of drugs used to delay the onset of AIDS. ACT UP achieved results through dramatic demonstrations during the 1990s that harassed and embarrassed government and pharmaceutical industry officials (Shepard and Hayduk, 2002).

But not all change requires a group protest or a broad social movement. Sometimes an individual willing to take risks for what he or she believes in can have an important impact. Even if the person is unsuccessful in bringing about change, efforts in this direction can inspire others. A good example is that of **whistleblowers** within corporate or governmental settings. These people, at great risk to their jobs and career chances, speak out to the mass media about such issues as unsafe corporate practices, unethical and illegal acts, wasteful spending, fraudulent policies, corruption, and incompetence (Glazer and Glazer, 1999; Miethe, 1999; Alford, 2002).

For example, in the early 1990s a technician at Tennessee's Oak Ridge National Laboratory, a federal nuclear facility managed by Martin Marietta Energy Systems, appeared on a CBS news program to "blow the whistle" about suspiciously high rates of cancer among the laboratory's workers. The technician himself had recently undergone treatment for colon cancer. In his view, the cancers were caused by unsafe working conditions that exposed workers to dangerous radiation. Managers at the facility retaliated by assigning the technician to "a room filled with toxic and radioactive chemicals" and ordering him "to perform useless work there"

("Whistle-Blowing," 1993). He ultimately won a legal action requiring compensation for the way he was mistreated by the laboratory's managers. Through his whistleblowing deviance, the technician was also successful in helping to draw attention to the issue of worker health and safety at nuclear facilities in the United States. The dangers of radioactive contamination and pollution for people working in or living around such facilities has since become a major public health issue.

More recently, Sherron S. Watkins, a former vice president at Enron Corporation, became a whistleblower when she told both the chief executive of Enron and the firm's auditor at the accounting firm of Arthur Andersen about serious and illegal irregularities in Enron's accounting procedures. She termed them "an elaborate accounting hoax. . . . I am incredibly nervous that we will implode in a wave of accounting scandals," she wrote to Kenneth Lay, Enron's chief executive officer (www.time.com/time/pow/article/0,8599,194927,00.html; Pellegrini, 2002). She also told Congress and helped launch an investigation into what quickly became arguably the largest and most scandalous and criminal, corporate bankruptcy in U.S. history. As thanks for her whistleblowing, Watkins was treated like an "outcast" and publicly vilified by her employers in the press.

Watkins' experience in the aftermath of her whistleblowing is not unusual. Often a battle for credibility emerges when the whistleblower's superiors attempt to cast discredit on the disclosures and tarnish the whistleblower's reputation (Alford, 2002; Hilts, 1993). The whistleblower's actions violate norms that call for organizational loyalty, communication only through proper channels, and maintenance of confidentiality of internal information. Such actions reverberate in the executive suite. What if all employees got it into their heads to act like this? Hence employers are likely to engage in social control through negative sanctions to eliminate this deviant behavior.

 ## CHAPTER SUMMARY

- Whether behavior is considered deviant depends upon the norms that people develop and use to judge others. Negative and positive sanctions are used to exercise social control over deviant behavior. Norms and social control over deviance are necessary for any society to function.

- This chapter stressed the idea that deviance is a social construction. In a heterogeneous society, what is considered deviant will differ from group to group and may change over time. Norms also differ from society to society.

- Deviance involves a labeling process. The distribution of power in society helps to determine which behaviors and whose behaviors will be labeled as deviant. The label of deviant may carry a negative social stigma, one that is difficult to shed.

- Not all labeling of people as deviant involves their behavior. People may be labeled deviant simply because they are seen to differ in their characteristics from a dominant group in some way. Dominant groups tend to view those they dominate as "the other," as people who have characteristics that render them deviant by their very being.

- Since dominant groups frequently impose the "deviant" label on people who do not want it (e.g., because it portrays them as inferior people, because it leads to unjust treatment), there is often resistance to the labeling process. The more powerful the group doing the labeling, the more difficult resistance becomes.

- Sociologists have long been interested in why deviant behavior occurs, and particularly crime. Explanations that focus principally on physiological or psychological shortcomings of those who engage in deviant behavior have been of limited value. Most people engaging in deviance are similar to those not engaging in such behavior.

- Social-psychological explanations examine the influence of one's immediate social environment on deviant behavior. Sociological explanations focus on how people's behavior is affected by group memberships and features of society over which they may have little control. Sociologists explore ways in which societal conditions (e.g., blocked economic opportunities, class inequalities) may be conducive to or encourage some types of deviance.

- Since deviant behavior exists in all societies (although societies often differ on what behavior is considered deviant), the issue arises as to whether societies "need" deviance. Some would argue that deviance is functional to society, since norm violations remind people of what the norms are, thus encouraging social stability and order.

- Societies may benefit from those groups and individuals who rise up and deviate from norms that support harmful and unjust social conditions. Harsh inequalities and abuses of power may call forth counter actions and social movements.

- From the revolutionary to the whistleblower, people at times challenge what those more powerful would prefer to be considered normal. Such forms of deviant behavior can produce social change, even while entailing significant risks for those seeking to alter the status quo.

 THINKING CRITICALLY

1. Discuss the role played by power in definitions of what behavior will be considered deviant. Are people who have power or who are otherwise privileged able to "get away with" behaviors that might be considered norm violations if engaged in by others? Why? Give examples.

2. We pointed out that what is considered deviant may differ from society to society, given that societies have different norms associated with their cultures. On the basis of other courses you have taken, experiences of your friends and family members, or observations you have made while traveling, discuss some examples of these differences and speculate about why they exist.

3. In Chapter 5 we discussed subcultures. Subcultures often have their own norms, which differ in various ways from those that prevail elsewhere in society. Are there norms that must not be violated within the college student subculture? What are they? What happens to people who violate them, and why?

4. Are there circumstances in which you have felt that you were defined and treated as deviant simply on the basis of who you are rather than because of your behavior (for example, on the basis of your sex, class, race or ethnicity, sexual orientation, or state of ablebodiedness)? How did you feel, and why? How did you respond?

KEY TERMS

norms **217**

deviance **217**

social control **217**

sanctions **217**

negative sanctions **217**

positive sanctions **218**

social construction (of deviance) **218**

label **219**

appearance norms **222**

motherhood norms **222**

stigma **227**

recidivism **227**

crime **229**

white collar crime **230**

corporate crime **232**

physiological explanations **233**

psychological explanations **233**

social-psychological explanations **233**

sociological explanations **234**

reductionism **234**

differential association theory **236**

control theory **236**

containment theory **236**

social reinforcement theory **237**

labeling theory **237**

opportunity structure theory **238**

Marxist theory of deviance **240**

alienation **240**

functionalist theory of deviance **248**

whistleblowers **247**

SOCIAL CHANGE AND SOCIAL MOVEMENTS

10

Societies and cultures rarely stand still: They are frequently involved in a process of change, slow or rapid, incremental or radical. Social scientists have always been fascinated by the rapid changes that accompanied the Industrial Revolution in the mid- to late nineteenth century. Radical changes generated by political revolutions such as those in France, Russia, China, and Cuba are also a source of great interest to social scientists. Probably of greater interest to most people living today are the changes that have occurred in their own lifetimes. Just talk with your grandparents and ask them how different the world is today than when they were your age: Ask them about such things as dating rituals, sexual mores, child–parent relations, race relations, technology, and transportation. Ask your parents about the tremendous social changes ushered in by the women's rights movement, the civil rights movement, the students' rights movement, and the antiwar movement during the 1960s and 1970s. And you yourself may already be aware of how everyday life has dramatically changed since September 11, 2001. Consider, for example, how different it is now to get on a plane, work in a skyscraper, check out a book on explosives from the library, or simply open an unsolicited piece of mail. Some of the questions these changes inspire include:

- What is social change?
- Why does it occur?
- How does it occur?
- What forces and factors affect the direction and magnitude of social change?
- Are all social changes as dramatic as revolutions?
- What are the consequences and ramifications of social change?
- Does social change provide advantages and benefits to some and not to others?
- What is the impact of social change on various groups in society and on world relations?
- Is social change inevitable, or can people affect social change?

THE MEANING OF SOCIAL CHANGE

When sociologists talk about **social change,** they are referring to significant variations or alterations in social structures and cultures over time. Social change may occur on varying levels and in varying amounts of intensity. For example, **social reforms** are adjustments in the content of cultural patterns of behavior or normative systems, adjustments that do not

251

fundamentally alter the social structure. Alterations in U.S. minimum wage laws—for example, requiring that employers increase the wages of the lowest-paid workers—do not change the structure of society: Corporations remain in control of the production of goods and services, and federal laws are still made by Congress. **Social revolutions,** on the other hand, are fundamental and radical upheavals of existing social structures. Revolutions sometimes involve bloody battles between identifiable organizations of armies, but this is not always the case. The Industrial Revolution, for example, fundamentally altered the processes of production and the power and control workers had over those processes, and therefore it changed institutions, roles, and statuses (Thompson, 1966; Gutman, 1977; see also Evans, 1999). But it did not occur on a battlefield between clearly organized armies. The battlefield was the shop floor in the factories, and the conflict was initially between individual workers and owners (although, to be sure, the struggles in the labor movement that emerged many years later were at times quite bloody).

It is also useful to consider that some social change is **manifest:** It is largely recognized and intended. In many cases a large or powerful group (not necessarily a majority) deliberately and consciously organizes a movement for change. For example, the colonists began the American Revolution to gain independence from Great Britain. The feminist movement arose when women began pressing for social, political, and economic equality. Similarly, the civil rights movement emerged out of a collective, concerted effort by many people to confront and challenge racism in the United States.

Other social change is **latent:** It is largely unrecognized and unintended. For example, the baby boom that occurred in the United States after World War II was not recognized until it was well under way. It produced a demographic "bubble" that had many consequences. Schools became overcrowded when that age cohort entered kindergarten and elementary school, and the situation prompted a national scramble to build more schools and hire more teachers. Competition for jobs intensified as baby boomers entered the labor market, and by the 1980s unemployment and underemployment had become a greater possibility for more people. Baby boomers became a political force in the late 1960s and early 1970s when they participated in several social movements. The antiwar movement hastened an end to the Vietnam War. Critical analyses of the war, the military draft, and the political process raised by the antiwar movement also prompted a lowering of the legal voting age from 21 to 18. The growing feminist movement gained women more access to higher education and better jobs. In turn, the new opportunities for women had the unintended consequence of reducing birth rates in the United States. When baby boomers retire early in this century, they will impose great demands on the Social Security system. At that time the labor force will be much smaller and perhaps be unable to support those demands without major reforms in public policy.

Explaining Social Change

How do sociologists explain social change? Is it a natural, inevitable phenomenon? How much affect can people have on it? Is a society's social change propelled by forces within that society, or do external forces contribute to changes in all societies? What are the forces of global social change? Are these forces neutral and natural, or are they social constructions in response to the interests of particular groups?

Sociologists generally agree that whether it is manifest or latent, social change is an ongoing process; it is not a singular, discrete event in a vacuum of time and place. In the discussion of the baby boom, it became apparent that an initial social change may set the stage for later changes. Beyond this fact, there is wide disagreement over how to explain social change. Several theoretical perspectives attempt to explain it as a normal, natural force that is part of a stable social system. But another perspective views conflict as the key catalyst for social change.

Cyclical Theory

Some sociologists see social change as a natural cycle in the rise and fall of social systems. This analysis is called **cyclical theory** (Sorokin, 1957; Pareto, 1963). In this view, societies are likened to an organism. Every society is presumed to pass naturally and inevitably through the same age phases as individual biological organisms (particularly the human being) pass through: infancy, childhood, adolescence, adulthood, old age, and, finally, decay and death. Oswald Spengler (1926) argued that each phase lasted a definite and predictable length of time for all societies. He suggested that all societies possess an internal biological clock determining their natural life span, which he believed to be a millennium (1,000 years).

However, some societies have lasted beyond a millennium (such as Egypt, China, and India) and others seem to perish "prematurely" (such as the Union of Soviet Socialist Republics, which lasted slightly more than half a century). Even when a society perishes, it is questionable whether it is, in fact, dying a "natural" death from old age. The division of Germany into the Federal Republic of Germany (FRG) and the German Democratic Republic (GDR) after World War II was a political act taken by the Allied countries to ensure that Germany would never again be an international threat. And the reunification of these two countries into a single Germany in 1989, effectively causing the demise of the GDR and FRG as independent nations, was also a political, not a natural, development.

Spengler's cyclical theory also leaves little room for an examination of the effect of external forces on a given society's life span. For example, it ignores the role that invasion, war, annexation, exploitation, or genocide inflicted by other societies may play in hastening a society's death. More recent cyclical analyses of social change have sought to correct this limitation by examining societies' rise-and-decline patterns as part of a global system. For example, in his book, *The Rise and Fall of the Great Powers*, Paul Kennedy (1987) argued that some societies rise economically and politically while others around them decline, in large part because the ascending societies ultimately conquer the faltering ones. This type of rise-and-decline cycle is influenced by a society's economic production, its fiscal strength, and its military strength. Rising states tend to capitalize on technological developments to enhance and increase production, which increases taxable wealth. This in turn provides the state more funds to support military expansion, which facilitates the ability of rising states to conquer declining states.

Although Kennedy's analysis does recognize external factors that may affect societies' cycle of social change, it overemphasizes military conquest as an important factor in the rise and decline of states. Take the example of Japan's successful competition in the global market of the 1980s. Japan had capitalized on technological innovations to increase production, but it did not invest the state's revenues in military expansion, nor did it militarily conquer anyone. One might also argue that although the Soviet Union did not exploit technological innovation effectively in the 1980s, it did invest a great deal of its state revenues in military expansion, and yet it still declined without being militarily conquered. Both cases call Kennedy's analysis into question.

Evolutionary Theory

Other sociologists favor an **evolutionary theory** to explain social change. They share cyclical theory's assumption that societies are like organisms, but evolutionary theory likens social change to Darwin's notion of biological evolution. Societies go through a natural series of stages based on increasing complexity, propelled toward more advanced and developed states of existence. Thus, evolutionary theory favors a notion of progress, wherein each new stage of development is more advanced than the one before. All societies are believed to progress through the same stages in the same order while evolving into ever-higher forms (Durkheim, 1964; Comte, 1966; Fei and Ranis, 1997). But whereas cyclical theory sees the death of a society as the natural end to the social life cycle, evolutionary theory makes no such presumption. Some societies might die off, but only as a result of "natural selection." Recent analyses argue that this natural selection is governed by a society's cultural inheritance of technological innovations, which permits a society to command greater control over its environment. Only those societies that invest in technological innovation will survive (see Lenski, Lenski, and Nolan, 1991; Lopreato and Crippen, 1999). That is, the "fittest" societies survive. Sociologists call this last argument **social Darwinism.**

The problem with social Darwinism is that it does not analyze the ways societies might differ in their access to information and technology or the role conquest plays in the demise of societies. Furthermore, evolutionary theory's presumption that all societies must pass through the same stages in the same order, and that each successive stage is necessarily more advanced, denies the unique histories societies may have. It assumes that all societies have access to the same resources to achieve the same levels of evolution. Its implicit use of Western nations as models of "advanced" societies denies the possibility that non-Western societies may be advanced as well. Social Darwinism does not address the possibility that societies may have "advanced" by taking advantage of resources from the "less advanced" societies. We will return to this issue shortly.

Equilibrium Theory

Other sociologists believe social change naturally occurs as societies become more and more complex. The increasing complexity demands greater and greater specialization of social structures and social roles that function together in order to keep society in balance. This analysis, called **equilibrium theory,** shares cyclical and evolutionary theories' analogy of society as a biological organism (Parsons, 1951; Ogburn, 1964; Alexander and Colomy, 1990). Societies are likened, for example, to the human body, in which the circulatory, digestive, endocrine, and musculature systems are interdependent. Each system requires the functioning of all the others in order to function adequately itself. Any disturbances or alterations in one of these bodily systems prompts adjustments in the others so that the body as a whole remains in equilibrium. Like an organism, social systems are seen to have a natural tendency toward stability. As such, when a disturbance or change occurs in one sector of a social system, the great interdependence of sectors prompts changes in all other sectors to accommodate the initial change and achieve stability in the overall system (Parsons, 1951). From the viewpoint of equilibrium theory, social change entails a series of minor adjustments, rather than fundamental alteration of the structure of society.

The problem here lies in the question of the source of disturbances or changes in particular sectors of the social system. What causes such changes to occur in the first place if all the parts are integrated and harmoniously in balance? And if stability is the normal state of existence for a social system, how do sociologists explain radical social change like revolution?

Equilibrium theory is imprecise in its notion of "social system," a central concept. It is unclear just what constitutes a social system: Is it a neighborhood, a city, a nation? If the social system were to be defined as a nation, how do observers take account of the economic interdependence today that in fact creates a world-system? If one nation changes its trade relations, for example, the change affects other nations. Economic recessions in one nation can have painful economic and political repercussions in others. Thus, one of the difficulties of equilibrium theory is that it neglects the possibility that changes may come from outside the social system.

Finally, equilibrium theory emphasizes how order and stability are maintained, but it ignores conflict. Critics question the failure of equilibrium theory to discuss the role that conflict and power differentials may play in destabilizing society (see, for example, Gouldner, 1970).

Marxist Theory

In contrast to theoretical perspectives focusing on change as gradual and natural, another one sees *conflict* as a normal, constant state of affairs that makes change a regular feature in all social structures. Sociologists refer to this view as a conflict perspective. What causes conflicts to erupt and generate social change?

Some sociologists point to **Marxist theory** to explain the conflicts as rooted in unequal power relations between those who own the means of production and those who do not, and the ongoing resolutions of those conflicts as the engine of social change. Karl Marx and Friedrich Engels (1967) referred to the ongoing process of social change as the **dialectic.** Every social structure begins as a **thesis,** or its current (temporary and momentary) state of existence. But every state of existence contains serious fundamental contradictions and crises that commonly intensify until challenges to the status quo erupt. The challenge is called the **antithesis.** The conflict that accelerates between the thesis and antithesis eventually must resolve itself into what Marx and Engels called the **synthesis.** The synthesis is a wholly new social structure carrying some elements from the thesis and some from the antithesis. This new structure eventually becomes normalized as a new thesis that carries its own contradictions and crises, prompting the dialectic process to continue.

For example, Marx and Engels argued that there are inherent contradictions and antagonisms in every social structure of production and that conflicts percolate between two classes, those who own the means of production (e.g., **capitalists**) and those who do not (e.g., **proletariat,** or workers). Sharp class antagonisms in a capitalist system arise because of contradictions between social production, in which goods and services are produced by groups of workers cooperating together, and private ownership of a firm's productive resources by the capitalists. While capitalists pay workers a wage for their labor, workers are producing far greater wealth than the value of their wages. The difference between what workers are paid and the wealth they create is profit for the capitalist. Capitalists are constantly looking for ways to increase their profit at the workers' expense. Conflict takes the form of continual organized struggle between the proletariat and the capitalists over the fruits of workers' labor. When workers' organized struggle produces a fundamental change in who owns the means of production and capture control over all the wealth these produced, it creates an antithesis to capitalism. Marx believed that the conflict between capitalism and the struggle for worker ownership would produce socialism as its synthesis. For Marx, social change is thus the outcome of an ongoing process of class struggle between these two groups. Marx saw the entire history of humanity as the history of such class struggles.

According to this analysis, order in society comes about only with conflict and change. Hence, conflict is not necessarily a negative, destructive force. Marx and Engels saw conflict as a positive, restructuring force, a prerequisite for social change and progress.

While conflict theory may respond to many of the limitations of other theories of social change, it does not explain social stability. If conflict and change are natural features of social structure, how is social stability possible? Is it not possible for social change to occur without conflict?

In sum, these theories of social change offer quite different explanations for how and why individual societies may change. Each also implies some explanation for unequal development throughout the world. Is the modern world-system, marked by unequal economic growth and development, a sum total of each nation's individual social change processes, or is each nation an element of a larger, more globally interrelated process? We now turn to this question.

MODERNIZATION, DEVELOPMENT, AND UNDERDEVELOPMENT

Evolutionary theory implies that social change entails progress and that all societies must follow the same path in their development. Poor nations are presumed to need to embrace the values and imitate the norms and experiences of industrialized Western nations in order to become modernized and civilized (Hoselitz, 1960; Rostow, 1960; Harrison, 2000). The poverty of some nations and their failure to modernize are attributed to their failure to adopt the "appropriate," "progressive" Western values and ways of doing things. **Modernization theory,** a global version of the culture-of-poverty analysis (see Chapter 5), argues that the normative and value systems of poor nations interfere with their development and modernization. Such nations are therefore "less developed" or "more primitive" than the "developed" nations.

Many industrialized nations may have exported their contemporary goods and modern technologies to poor nations. While these goods and services may help poor nations better address pressing basic needs, that they do not produce these themselves is not enough to explain why they are poor in the first place. It is important to understand clearly why a particular nation is poor, rather than dismissing it as primitive because it has different normative and value systems.

The Meaning of Development

Critics have questioned the meaning of development implied in modernization theory (Frank, 1967; Todaro, 2011). A high level of development is frequently defined as an advanced degree of urbanization and industrialization, characterized by the use of state-of-the-art technology and the generation of large amounts of wealth. This definition is simply a description of the West; it is based on the ethnocentric assumption that Western nations are the most highly evolved.

Furthermore, during the 1950s and 1960s many underdeveloped nations became more industrialized and increased their manufacturing production rates. Urbanization, including some electrification and sewer systems, increased, and commercial transportation systems emerged in some places. Yet the standard of living for most people in these nations did not improve (Seers, 1969). This contradiction between the growth of urbanization, industry, and wealth production on one hand and the stagnation of poverty on the other called into question the conventional meaning of development. It showed that development benefitted some people but not others in these nations. Moreover, such extremes of inequality could be found in the "developed" nations of the West as well. How, then, do observers measure development?

Studies frequently measure development in terms of kilowatt-hours of electricity used per capita and the amount of wealth a nation produced, or its gross national product per capita. These measures are reflections of urbanization and industrialization. The problem here is that such measures simply average out the wealth produced and the electricity consumed over the entire population, thereby skirting the important question of distribution: Does everyone in the population receive an equal amount of the wealth produced? Arriving at only one statistic for an entire population implies that distribution is equal. The use of an aggregate measure, such as gross national product per capita, provides a measure for comparing the overall wealth of nations but ignores regions of poverty, patterns of inequality, and hunger and homelessness that exist even within so-called developed countries (see Figure 10.2). Likewise, it allows observers to define countries such as Haiti or the Philippines as less developed while overlooking their regions of wealth and their elites.

Some critics suggest replacing the definition of development with a definition of **basic needs** (Streeten, 1981; Wood, 1986; Basu, 1996; Sundaram, 1996). Using this definition, observers would look at how evenly the basic goods and services needed for survival are distributed within the entire population. Basic needs are measured in terms of health (such as life expectancy at birth and infant mortality rates), education (such as literacy rates and the proportion of the population age 5 to 14 enrolled in school), food (a proportion of minimum daily requirements for human survival), water supply (the percentage of the population with access to clean water), and sanitation (the percentage of the population with access to sewers and other sanitation facilities). The basic-needs approach to development makes it clear that even nations like the United States would have difficulty being defined as fully developed.

Critics also have argued that modernization theory looks at individual nations as if they existed in a vacuum, focusing only on internal dynamics and normative and value systems as causal factors for development. This ignores international power dynamics and global historical processes. Each nation has occupied a particular structural position and played a particular role in the development of the world-system. As we discussed in Chapter 3, a world-system is an international structure organizing the production, distribution, and consumption of goods and services. In that arrangement, peripheral or global south nations are generally poor, providing primary goods for production and cheap, unskilled, exploitable labor for huge multinational corporations to manufacture goods and services that are then sold mostly to consumers in the wealthier, more powerful core or global north nations. Peripheral nations are clustered in Africa, Latin America, and Asia, while the core nations are concentrated in Western Europe and North America, as well as Japan, and Australia. Nations therefore have different sets of experiences, histories, and social and economic structures, not by choice or value system but by virtue of their historical relationships with other nations, relationships marked by differential power and privilege (Frank, 1967; Wallerstein, 1974, 1997). For example, by the late seventeenth century India's economy was more advanced than economies in Europe: It had a large, thriving manufacturing sector that produced many luxury commodities, including textiles such as silk and cotton. Yet by the end of the eighteenth century India's economy, particularly its manufacturing sector, had declined significantly because Great Britain destroyed India's textile industry by flooding India with cheaper British-made cotton in an effort to eliminate competition for its own textiles (Griffin, 1979). Therefore, India's status as an underdeveloped nation resulted not from its own "primitive" normative and value systems but, rather, from its inequitable trade relationship with a more powerful industrialized nation.

Poor or peripheral nations are thus not simply at an earlier stage of development and modernization already experienced by industrialized nations, and industrialized nations did not at one time take the same path now traveled by peripheral nations. Rather, peripheral nations are **underdeveloped nations.** That is, their historically disadvantageous relationships with more powerful industrialized or core nations, often as colonies conquered or taken over by core nations, have imposed severe limitations on development opportunities. Industrialized countries today were never *under*developed: They did not face exploitation by stronger, colonizing economies and thus severe restrictions on their access to opportunities and resources for development (Frank, 1967). Such structured national inequalities continue to deepen as the world enters the new millennium because of centuries of entrenched world-system relations that are often marked by colonialism and imperialism (Chase-Dunn, 1998; Chase-Dunn and Hall, 1997).

Dependency and Development

We may understand the historical dynamic of underdevelopment by examining three different types of relationships (often referred to as forms of dependency) between nations: trade dependency, dependent development, and debt dependency.

Trade Dependency

In his historical analysis of the world-system, Wallerstein (1980) traced the outcomes of trade-dependency relationships. **Trade dependency,** which dominated the world-system between the fifteenth and nineteenth centuries, is characterized by limited numbers of trade partners for peripheral nations. Typically, a peripheral nation would be colonized by a core nation and focus its productive activities on a limited number of commodities, usually mineral and agricultural products. Such was the case, for example, in the sixteenth and seventeenth centuries, when England had economically colonized Ireland, from whom England took wool to produce textiles. Peripheral nations sent the raw materials to the core colonizers and imported more expensive finished consumer goods from these same colonizers. Initially this arrangement may have been useful to the peripheral nation: It was able to concentrate limited economic resources on a few activities, rather than trying to produce everything it needed. The peripheral nation also had a guaranteed market for its primary commodities.

In the long run, however, this arrangement hurt the development of peripheral nations (Delacroix and Ragin, 1981). Since its economic activity was concentrated on the production of a limited number of basic goods, the peripheral nation developed a distorted economy rather than a diversified one. Its economy therefore could not absorb economic shocks from trade disruptions, extreme weather patterns, and changes in consumer demands in the core. For example, if a peripheral nation focused on sugar crops and coal, it would not able to withstand a decrease in sugar consumption in the core, destruction of the sugar crop from a season of floods, or shifts in the core from the use of coal to other energy sources. Loss of the market for its goods would seriously damage the entire economy of the peripheral nation. In a nation with a diversified economy, shocks to one industry can usually be offset by the health of other industries. Therefore, a nondiversified economy produces a structural blockage to development in the periphery.

Trade dependency creates other economic troubles. Primary commodities are cheaper than finished consumer goods. Trading relatively cheaper primary commodities for more expensive finished goods creates an imbalance of trade for the peripheral nation, because it often pays for the finished goods with the relatively low earnings generated by its exports. Throughout the world-system there has been a drain of money and resources away from the periphery to the core, which has seriously harmed the peripheral nations' ability to support their own development. The one notable exception to this trend appears to be the oil-producing nations. But these nations have operated together for many years in a cartel (the Organization of Petroleum Exporting Countries—OPEC), so together they have greater control over the supply and price of a basic commodity everyone needs for production. They also trade with many global partners rather than with a few. They therefore do not suffer the restrictions imposed by trade-partner concentration.

Finally, researchers have found that trade dependency deepened income inequalities between urban and rural areas, between elites and masses, and between men and women within peripheral nations (Bornschier and Chase-Dunn, 1985; Scott, 1995; Momsen, 2010). Local elites in the periphery often cooperated with core elites to control trade arrangements, the benefits of which were rarely redistributed equally throughout the peripheral nation. Income inequalities also were aggravated because male elites from the core typically awarded the trade routes to men in the periphery (Boserup, 1970; Papanek, 1979). Moreover, males in the periphery were often charged with the more lucrative cash-crop farming, mining, and manufacturing for trade, while women were left with the responsibility of subsistence farming to feed the local population (Deere, Humphries, and deLeal, 1982). For example, women in South Africa and Lesotho increasingly worked the farmlands by themselves, while the men in their families were drafted to work the mines (Mueller, 1977). In Latin America, corporations sought out Peruvian and Colombian men to work in the factories, while women were recruited into agriculture (Deere and deLeal, 1981).

Unequal power relationships within the periphery allow elites to own and control most of the fertile land, a situation that continues today. They decide what will be grown on it and what market the crops will go to. Wealthy landowners typically grow cash crops and luxury items for export and elite consumption (such as sugar, coffee, and cocoa) rather than food needed for landless workers' and their families' survival. As a result, most workers are poor, and many suffer chronic hunger and malnutrition, which are often misunderstood as a problem of overpopulation. Poverty and hunger in the periphery is, more accurately, a product of the lack of local control over the land by the masses. Thus, inequitable trade relations between the core and periphery reach into the everyday lives of individuals in the periphery, particularly the peasants, the rural dwellers, and women and children. Their lives are impoverished not because they have not adopted the norms and values of the West but because elites in their countries and in core nations maintain trade relationships that principally benefit themselves.

Dependent Development

By the 1930s, having successfully rebelled against colonial domination, peripheral nations such as Brazil, Mexico, and India attempted to resolve the problem of the resource drain and the unequal benefits accompanying trade dependency on the core. One strategy was to substitute locally produced goods for imported goods (**import substitution**) as well as to manufacture goods for sale abroad (**export processing**). This dual strategy is referred to as **dependent development**, because it is a strategy for development adopted by peripheral and semi-peripheral nations that requires dependency on private (usually corporate) actors from the core. Peripheral nations attempted to bring about economic development with focused and planned foreign investment in certain manufacturing sectors. This investment would enable them to employ local workers in a more diverse economy and to manufacture the consumer goods they previously imported, thereby reducing the cost of the goods. Peripheral nations encouraged corporations from the core to invest in them by promising a low-wage, exploitable labor force, inexpensive natural resources, few if any labor and environmental regulations, and large markets.

The real effects of dependent development began to solidify by the 1960s. In their cross-national statistical analysis of 103 countries between 1965 and 1977 Bornschier and Chase-Dunn (1985) found that in the short run the flow of investment capital to build new plants and the generation of new jobs in the factories did stimulate the local economy. So, too, did the increase in construction activity on peripheral nations' roads, railways, airports, sewage and electrification systems, schools, and housing required by corporations.

In the long run, however, the presence and dominance of these corporations entrenched and intensified underdevelopment. For one thing, most profits earned locally by the corporations flowed back to core nations, where the companies were headquartered. Furthermore, rather than bringing in outside money, the core-headquartered corporations often used local capital, depriving local entrepreneurs of an investment source (Muller, 1979; see also De Oliver, 1995). Bornschier and Chase-Dunn found that income inequality remained high in peripheral nations because any profits that did not drain back to the core were concentrated in the hands of the local elites.

Export-oriented factories more recently emerged in electronics, pharmaceuticals, and textiles and apparel in nations such as the Philippines, Mexico, Sri Lanka, and Hong Kong. Employers hire women rather than men because they are seen as a more docile, cheaper labor force. However, researchers have found that wages at such jobs are typically insufficient to support the women workers and their children. Women who receive wages lack benefits or protective legislation (Enloe, 1989; Ponniah and Reardon, 1999; Visvanathan et al., 2011). In fact, the economic situation for many women in peripheral countries has deteriorated to the point where they must often work a daily **triple shift** combining employment in factories with bartering and street trade and the work of managing the household (Hossfeld, 1989; Ward, 1990; Dickinson, 1997). Researchers have found that both trade dependency and dependent development have increased hunger and infant mortality rates throughout the periphery (Ward, 1984; Shen and Williamson, 2001; Visvanathan et al., 2011). World-system trade relations favoring core corporations have helped impoverish women and children in peripheral nations and altered their life courses, their family relations, their work, their economic and social status, and their very survival.

How do these core-periphery trade relationships affect individuals who live in the more privileged and powerful core nations? The relative wealth of the core does not insulate residents there from the effects of these core-periphery economic arrangements (Massey, 2002). Workers in the core lose jobs, partly because core corporations relocate factories to the periphery and partly because inexpensive goods from peripheral nations flood core markets and compete with more expensive domestic goods. As core manufacturers go out of business, unemployment rises. Competition for low-wage jobs in the core may be heightened with the influx of jobless immigrants from peripheral nations whose quest for survival leads them to the core. Workers' lives in the core are, then, affected by world-system trade relations. Many people in the core suffer from the increased unemployment; some lose their homes because they cannot maintain mortgages, and some experience poverty, hunger, and even homelessness.

Indeed, the North American Free Trade Agreement (NAFTA) was supposed to reduce the negative consequences of the unequal global trade relations between the United States, Canada, and Mexico by stimulating jobs and prosperity for everyone in North America. Yet only five years after its passage in 1996, NAFTA had succeeded in destroying hundreds of thousands of production jobs in the United States, because corporations moved these just across the border to the subcontracting production zone in Mexico where wages were much cheaper (Cypher, 2001). While NAFTA was supposed to stimulate wages in Mexico to rise to meet those paid to workers in the U.S., workers' wages in both nations have instead dropped significantly (Wallach and Sforza, 1999; Cormier and Targ, 2001). This illustrates how the core is not immune to the effects of core-periphery trade relationships.

Ironically, the very conditions producing the deterioration of the lives of women, children, and the poor in the periphery may also increase the possibilities of their resistance to these unequal relationships: People working under similar oppressive and exploitive circumstances have begun forming networks of organizations within and between regions, and that may help to pave the way to global workers' and feminist movements (Bacon, 2001; Compa, 2001; Moghadam, 1999; Visvanathan et al., 2011). For example, women in Mexico's *maquilladora* have increasingly mobilized and at times organized strikes against their employers. Given the close location of the production area to the United States, struggles for unionization are likely to draw attention and participation from U.S. organized workers who recognize the need for solidarity among all workers in North America and beyond.

Debt Dependency

Governments in peripheral countries have sought to boost development with international aid and loans from core nations and international development agencies such as the International Monetary Fund, the World Bank, and the Organization for Economic Cooperation and Development (Corm, 1982; Lichtensztejn and Quijano, 1982; Dale and Mattione, 1983). Sociologists call reliance on loans for development **debt dependency.**

Unfortunately, in the 1970s and 1980s many underdeveloped nations found that declines in the value of the goods they produced and exported eroded their incomes and their ability to pay the high interest on their bank debts (Debt Crisis Network, 1985). For example, in 1983 one of Nicaragua's main export goods was coffee, a commodity that is so hugely popular around the world that one would think it had a terrific market and would be very profitable. But its export value had so badly declined that Nicaragua had to export more than 11 tons of coffee to be able to buy a tractor that would have cost it little more than 4 tons of exported coffee in 1977. And interest rates on loans during the early 1980s for countries like Nicaragua soared to as high as 17 percent (Wood, 1986). This meant that Nicaragua had to struggle to sharply increase its export of coffee just to pay the interest on its debt. Increasingly, peripheral nations like Nicaragua were forced to take out new loans from private banks in the core nations simply to pay off their old debts. Loans that should have helped with development now only helped the profitability of private banks in the core.

Studies have shown that while loans initially stimulate development, over time they impair development (Glasberg and Ward, 1993; Sharma and Kumar, 2002). This is not surprising. Money that is borrowed at increasingly higher interest rates to pay off old debt means that more and more money will be drained from the peripheral nation. Because the vast majority of private banks providing the loans are headquartered in the core nations, the interest paid is not reinvested in the periphery. By the early 1980s, a chronic debt crisis existed throughout the peripheral world, a crisis that was particularly pronounced in Latin America and that continued into the new century. For example, by 1999 Argentina's debt rose to $140 billion, and 70 percent of its government budget had to be devoted to debt service payments (www.jubilee2000uk.org). That left precious little for the state to devote to any development projects or to social needs, prompting massive social unrest and political upheaval that continued into 2003 in response to rising hunger and malnutrition.

When peripheral nations reach the point where they are unable to continue to pay the interest on their debt, private banks refuse to provide new loans to pay off the old ones. At this point, the International Monetary Fund (IMF) steps into the breach. The IMF is an international organization of nations that is supposed to provide temporary help to poor nations trying to overcome economic obstructions to development. When these nations run the danger of bankruptcy or default of massive, crushing debt, the IMF's role is to push them to restructure their economies to focus on market-oriented policies and make it attractive once again for investments by private banks and core-based corporations. The IMF does this by imposing a standard austerity program on the ailing peripheral economy in return for the promise of economic assistance.

The requirements of the standard austerity program (SAP) typically include (1) devaluation of the recipient nation's currency, making its money worth less; (2) decreases in the amount of money the peripheral nation spends on social welfare, including subsidies for consumer goods, and the elimination of price controls; (3) increases in control of labor unions, including the suppression of labor strikes for better working conditions and higher wages; (4) increases in the amount of money the peripheral nation allocates to military spending (to help enforce the austerity program by suppressing labor strife, food riots, and insurrections and to secure the general political climate for core corporations' investments); (5) decreases in or elimination of state control of industry, including the selling of state-owned industries to wealthy groups of individuals or corporations; (6) sharp reductions of imports and increases in manufacturing for export; and (7) dramatic increases in the amount of money the peripheral nation devotes to paying off its debt (Debt Crisis Network, 1985). The IMF's rationale is that this program will force peripheral nations to keep their expenditures down while they pay off their debts and their economies get healthy once again.

While these requirements might seem to make fiscal sense, unfortunately, the track record of the IMF's austerity program is not very impressive. Several case studies have documented how the austerity program ignites political unrest sparked by the meager availability and unaffordability of basic resources (Auvinen, 1996; Walton, 2001), damages prospects for development (Weeks, 2000), and helps drain even more capital from the periphery and semiperiphery to the core (see also V. Sidel, 2000; Bienefeld, 2000). For example, in a study of Mexico's 1982 debt crisis, Glasberg (1987, 1989) found that the standard austerity program resulted in serious declines in the value of Mexico's money and sharp reductions in the state's subsidies for food. The price of frijoles (beans that are a protein staple in Mexico) increased 250 percent in less than two weeks when state subsidies were withdrawn. Workers lucky enough to still have jobs found that their wages had been frozen or reduced; since the value of their money was much lower than it had been, and prices incredibly higher, they were increasingly unable to pay for food.

IMF demands for sharp reductions in imports seriously hurt Mexico's economy, because its critical petroleum industry relied on imported machinery. The petroleum industry, which was supposed to save Mexico economically, was unable to import the spare parts it needed to keep running and be profitable. The result of the IMF's austerity program was that Mexico was unable to recover economically and, indeed, was back in a debt crisis less than two years later. The country's mixed economic outlook today is due partly to U.S. guarantees of Mexico's debt (principally to U.S. banks) and to trade and production agreements with the United States that ultimately export U.S. production jobs to Mexico. Evidence of the long-term effects of such relationships on peripheral nations in the past should alert observers to the possibility that Mexico's economic health may be an issue for some time to come.

We have already noted the alarmingly high proportion of Argentina's government budget that is earmarked for repayment of its debts. The nation's newspapers are dominated almost daily with the heartbreaking stories of children dying from malnutrition, with no relief in sight. The IMF gave the national government a reprieve in 2003 by postponing a scheduled repayment of $141 million, but it merely postponed the problem: The national economy continued its free-fall because of the crushing debt that continued to mount almost daily. Indeed, the IMF's own austerity program is part of the crisis: One of its conditions for continued support of Argentina has been an insistence that Argentina increase its profits from exports in order to pay off its debts. Argentina is the fifth largest exporter of agricultural products in the world, but more than half of its population lives below the poverty line, and the malnutrition and starvation rate among its children has skyrocketed. Food is plentiful in Argentina, but not for its residents. The need to repay its loans has come to dominate its budget as well as its policies, skewering social welfare in return (http://archives.here-now.org).

Peripheral nations' debts to private banks are thus being paid off at the expense of the poor, the workers, women, and children, the very groups that did not benefit from previous efforts to develop (Miller, 1997). The real winners in the economic restructuring imposed by the IMF are the wealthy elites in the periphery and corporations and private banks in the core.

This discussion of trade relationships, dependent development, and debt dependency shows that development is *not* simply a matter of poor nations following the steps to modernization taken by industrialized nations. Nor are peripheral nations simply in an earlier stage of development long surpassed by industrialized nations. Rather, the historical role of peripheral nations in the world-system has meant that they have had to follow a path that the industrialized nations have not. Underdevelopment is best understood within a global context of private profit generation, rather than as a problem of improper cultural norms and value systems. Underdevelopment is a *political* process and a public issue involving economic and military power differentials. It is not simply a problem of national cultural dynamics or a matter of slow, inevitable progression toward development through the adoption of more "modern" values.

Creative strategies to address the problems of underdevelopment, crushing debt burdens, and global inequality have begun to link these problems with global environmental issues. **Debt-for-nature swaps** are arrangements in which debt-ridden governments agree to purchase or set aside land to conserve as state-owned parks and to protect their natural resources in exchange for a debt cancellation. The first such swap occurred in 1987 between Bolivia and Conservation International, a private U.S. organization that had purchased Bolivia's debt from Citicorp Bank. Conservation International agreed to pay off the debt in exchange for Bolivia's promise to protect almost 4 million acres around the Beni Biosphere Reserve. Nineteen other, similar debt-for-nature swaps have been arranged since 1987. By 2000, such arrangements cancelled $1.5 billion in developing countries' debt while preserving valuable natural resources (www. napa.ufl/edu/2003news/debtnature.htm). And while most debt-for-nature swaps have involved Latin America's rain forest areas, such as those in Ecuador, the Dominican Republic, and Costa Rica, swaps have also been arranged for land in the Philippines, Nigeria, Madagascar, Zambia, and Poland (Lugar and Biden, 1998 on www.csmonitor.com). These swaps underscore the interdependence of nations in the global economy as well as in the environment, and they highlight the possibilities for change in the politics of underdevelopment.

Such arrangements must be approached with caution, however, to prevent the larger global power structures from using the desperately needed economic help as leverage to reassert corporate dominance, heighten existing gender and class inequality, and subvert popular struggles against elite advantage (C. Hamilton, 1995; Turner and Craig, 1995; DeBoeck, 2000). This is because the more advantaged participants in these arrangements can potentially insist on conditions beyond protection of the environment in exchange for debt relief.

TECHNOLOGICAL AND SOCIAL CHANGES

Many contemporary observers view technological innovation as the generator of social change. What is the role of technology in processes of social change? Where do technological developments come from? Why do some technologies develop and not others? Is technological development a neutral process, wherein "necessity becomes the parent of invention"? Who determines the meaning of necessity, and who decides what is necessary? Who benefits and who is hurt by technological development?

Energy Production

Among the more visible differences between core and peripheral countries' development is the greater availability of advanced technology in the core. Many people have been taught that the Industrial Revolution was a time marked by a sudden explosion of inventions that revolutionized production processes and everyone's lives, generally in a positive way. New technologies improved people's lives and made society more progressive. Those who argued against the increasing reliance on technology were often criticized as being old-fashioned or standing in the way of progress.

We learned that **inventions**—new practices and objects developed out of existing knowledge—"happened" because necessity dictated their development. For example, the steam engine was invented because people needed a large source of power to modernize industry. But who decides that a particular invention is needed? Who supports the development of particular inventions as solutions to problems? Why are some inventions developed, and others not (even though they may, in fact, be needed)?

For example, why is the technology for nuclear power generation and energy production based on the burning of fossil fuels so well developed, while the technology for solar energy remains relatively primitive and inefficient? The answer may have to do with who benefits and who is hurt by society's continued dependence on certain kinds of energy production. Nuclear energy and fossil fuels are nonrenewable energy sources: They are based on resources that are mined or extracted from the earth (such as coal, petroleum, and uranium). Society cannot use the resources indefinitely without depleting them and cannot turn them into usable energy without the technological help provided by energy corporations and utility firms.

Solar, wind, and geothermal energy are based on renewable resources. Consumers can indefinitely derive energy from these resources as long as the sun shines fairly regularly, the winds blow, and the earth continues to contain warmth. While these resources still require some technological aid in delivering their energy to consumers in usable forms, it is not necessary to rely on energy corporations and utilities to provide them. Once the technology is in place, the resources are self-sustaining in their delivery of energy.

It is not surprising, then, to find that energy corporations and utilities use their considerable economic power and resources to sponsor research to invent technologies that rely on nonrenewable sources of energy. These same companies purchased several patents for useful solar technologies from independent developers in the 1970s and then never used them (Reece, 1980). Now, major energy corporations like BP Amoco carefully control the development of these solar technologies to ensure that if there is to be renewable energy production at all, people will remain dependent on them (Berman and O'Connor, 1997). This is not an option readily available to nonelites, given the level of economic and power inequality between large corporations on one hand and consumer and community groups on the other. Were consumers to have access to those technologies that rely on renewable sources of energy and that therefore challenge substantially the dominance of energy corporations and utilities, they might be independent of the energy corporations and the utilities after the initial construction of facilities. Large corporate interests benefit greatly from society's dependence on them as providers of energy; everyone loses a great deal from their ability to turn that reliance into expensive (for consumers) and profitable (for them) energy production.

Technological Change and the Labor Process

Framing the analysis of technological development and social change in terms of who benefits and who is hurt also points to the rise of the factory during the late 1800s and early 1900s as a major *social* change rather than as an inevitable, neutral result of technological progress. Prior to the eighteenth century, individuals manufactured many consumer goods in their homes, using manual labor—a system often referred to as **cottage industries.** They sewed clothing, cobbled shoes, built furniture, and created pottery using their hands and simple tools. This system allowed them to determine how long they worked on any given day, which days they worked, how much they produced, what they produced, and to some extent how much money they made. While capitalists provided them with the materials for making goods on order, the workers could determine how to maximize use of the materials, and they often kept the remnants to make goods for themselves or to sell to other buyers. Thus, the cottage industry system gave workers control over the work process and some power over distribution of the profits of their labor. This changed when production shifted to factories. Why did this change occur if workers stood to lose so much?

The conventional view is that factories developed in response to the invention of the steam engine as a central source of power. The steam engine was too expensive and too large for individual cottage industries to use. It was simply cheaper, according to this view, for workers to gather together under one roof and share use of the new centralized source of power. This would seem to make sense, until one examines research on forces leading up to the development of both the factory and the steam engine.

Through his historical analysis of industry in the United States, Dan Clawson (1980) clearly establishes that there was a terrific struggle from the mid-eighteenth century to the late nineteenth century between workers in the cottage industries and capitalists wishing to exert greater control over the work process. Capitalists were dismayed by workers' retention of remnants of materials that the capitalists had paid for and by workers' sometimes erratic work hours. And they were displeased that workers could determine what the capitalists would pay for production. In order to gain greater control over the labor process, capitalists built factories and tried unsuccessfully to coerce workers into them. Workers were well aware that they stood to lose much by giving the power of managing the work process to the capitalists. Capitalists countered by using the coerced, unpaid labor of prisoners, slaves, and orphans in the factories. The use of such an inexpensive labor force began to erode the cottage industries' ability to compete with the factories' economy of scale, volume of production, and lower-priced commodities. Poverty and lack of alternatives eventually forced the cottage industry workers to join the workers already in the factories.

All this took place *before* the introduction of the steam engine. Prior to the late eighteenth and early nineteenth centuries the factory merely gathered the workers together under one roof, but the technological aspects of the production process remained essentially the same as before the development of the factory. It was *after* the factory took hold that the steam engine was introduced and became a technological justification of the factory. What workers lost in control of the work process capitalists gained. The capitalists could determine the commodities produced, the way they were produced, the hours and days worked, and the wages earned. The introduction of the steam engine, then, was stimulated by the conflict between workers and capitalists over control of the production process and the resultant profits. Use of steam power firmly tilted that struggle in favor of the capitalists, rationalizing the social change in production that had already taken place.

Currently, the rise of personal computers has ironically recreated the isolation of the cottage industry as an increasing number of workers (especially women) telecommute to work for corporate employers from home, but without the element of worker power and control over the work process previously held by workers before the Industrial Revolution. That isolation decreases the likelihood that telecommuting workers will be able to communicate and develop informal peer groups, develop a sense of common bond, and organize against management.

Technology and Reproductive Issues

While most analyses of social change brought about by technology focus on its effects on work and production, there have also been profound technologically generated changes in the area of human reproduction (Franklin and Ragone, 1998; Baker, 2000; Lay et al, 2000; Evans, 2010). Technological developments such as fetal monitors can measure the heart rate of the fetus and thus determine whether the fetus is in distress during labor. Such devices are quite useful in increasing the chances of a healthy, live birth. But critics note that they have also given more control over the birthing process to doctors and technicians. One alarming indicator of this shift is the number of caesarian births over the last decade: After slowly declining in the early 1990s, the rate of caesarian section births is once again on the rise, so that one-third of all births in the United States are now delivered through surgery (Menacker and Hamilton, 2010). The American College of Obstetrics and Gynecology noted that doctors' habits rather than medical necessity were a major factor producing the increase, an assessment that suggests the power of doctors to use technology and impose their interests over and above those of the mother and the child in the labor and birth process.

Some would argue that the increase in caesarian section deliveries represents greater knowledge about health and safety for both the mother and the baby. However, there are other, perhaps more compelling incentives for physicians' increasing reliance on fetal monitors and other technologies to justify interventions like caesarian deliveries. Because caesarian sections are surgery, they are expensive, and the surgeon can count on being paid by the mother's health insurance company. The combination of insurance coverage and the profit motive in organized medicine has prompted technological developments that invest greater control of the birth process with doctors and less with women.

Technology has also altered the process of conception and pregnancy, thereby throwing society into a storm of controversy over several ethical issues. Some technologies increase the chances for sex pre-selection in conception and may reinforce cultural patriarchal notions of males as a "preferred" sex (Stearney, 1996). Amniocentesis can identify genetic defects in a fetus, revealing conditions such as Down syndrome, Tay-Sachs disease, sickle-cell anemia, and a whole host of other genetic abnormalities. It can also identify the sex of the fetus. Critics have long argued that such information could lead to the abortion of a fetus that happens to be the "wrong" sex or have unwanted disabilities (Bouchard et al., 1995). And, since many societies value males more strongly than females, there is an increased danger of abortion of female fetuses simply because they are females (Gill, 1998; www.nytimes.com/2002).

The abortion of "defective" fetuses, or those with potential disabilities, also raises an issue: When is a defect life-threatening, and when is it simply a departure from social constructions of the "perfect" human being? While the technology of procedures like amniocentesis may be very useful in early identification of fetal genetic disorders and infections in order to promote treatment, that same technology holds great potential for abuse: It allows people to identify and destroy fetuses that fail to conform to the culturally dominant image of perfection—a human being with no genetic, physical, or mental "defects." Technological innovations in reproduction (including the human genome project that is mapping human genetic material) have also opened the door to genetic engineering (Mehlman and Botkin, 1998; Ho, 2000). While this may help doctors to correct gene mutations that produce life-threatening conditions and diseases, it also introduces the chilling potential of eradicating populations who are determined by members of the dominant groups to be undesirable on the basis of a wide variety of criteria (Roberts, 1997).

In vitro fertilization has increased the chances of becoming parents for infertile couples or those who have had difficulty establishing a pregnancy. This technology is not readily available to those who can't afford the high costs of such care (Merchant, 1996). The class inequality issues this raises are also apparent in that reproductive technology has made it possible for a couple to hire a third party to carry the fertilized egg, give birth to the child, and then turn it over to them for parenting. Observers refer to the person who carries the fertilized egg and gives birth as the **surrogate mother** (although there are some controversies concerning the very definition and identification of who is the mother, who is the surrogate, who is the biological parent, and so forth).

The technology of in vitro fertilization raises several thorny issues concerning class dynamics. Poor women could be contracted to carry and deliver babies for middle-class and wealthy couples. Poverty could create a situation in which poor women "rent out" their wombs, much like poor and working-class families during the early twentieth century rented out rooms in their homes to lodgers to help pay the rent. Such a situation has the potential for seriously exploiting the surrogate.

Surrogacy contracts also enable the brokers to control the lives of the surrogates, both economically and socially. The contract typically specifies behaviors that are strictly forbidden (such as drinking, smoking, drug use, and dieting) and those that are required (eating healthy foods, taking vitamins, getting plenty of sleep, and avoiding risky activities, which may include certain kinds of jobs). Like the workers in the factories Dan Clawson studied, surrogate mothers become workers who can be carefully controlled by those who stand to profit a great deal from that control.

Clearly, the main beneficiaries of surrogacy are the lawyers who broker such contracts. Surrogacy brokering is a highly lucrative business, aided by the development of reproductive technologies that raise ethical and social questions. Meanwhile, poor and working-class women and people of color can be hurt in these arrangements. Consider that they are paid for a full nine months of their lives (and *not* merely for eight hours per day, five days per week) and factor out what they are getting paid per hour; even at a wage of $10,000 they are poorly paid.

Moreover, surrogates' bodies undergo the physical risks of any pregnancy, and they are often emotionally battered by the process of giving birth and then having the baby taken away because of a contract. While it may be relatively easy to agree to be a surrogate in exchange for more money than many of these women can earn in a year, it is not always so easy to adhere to the contract.

Surrogacy also raises gender issues. For example, the contracts are commonly developed between the adoptive father and the surrogate mother. What is the role, then, of the adoptive mother? Which of these women is the "mother"? Which one has the right to participate in determining the fate of the child? What is the relationship between the two women, and between each of them and the adoptive father? This uncertainty of the women's respective roles gives the adoptive father greater power in the contractual arrangement.

This discussion illustrates the tremendous changes in human reproduction that have been brought about by technological developments. But it also highlights the fact that cultural change has lagged behind the technology: Although science enables these changes to occur, social and cultural processes have not yet determined whether they *should* occur or how to deal with their effects if they do. This implies that social change is not just a process made possible by technological inventions and innovations; it is also a political process.

Technological Innovation, Power, and Inequality

Technology is not a neutral force. It is driven by many factors, including profit motives and vested interests in control over such processes as work and reproduction. Technology is not necessarily the natural response to necessity; it is a social and political response to necessity as defined by those who stand to benefit most from its development and who have the power and the economic resources to support such development.

Technological developments frequently affect individuals' daily lives, enhancing some aspects and restricting others. For example, factory technology meant that workers would no longer be able to control their work or their earnings. Their life choices became more restricted as they lost control of the work process. Similarly, while reproductive technology may enhance the chances that infertile couples can have babies, it also increases the medical establishment's control over reproduction and can aggravate class, gender, and race inequalities.

Ironically, technological developments that enhance the power of the already privileged may also introduce unintended benefits to the *disadvantaged*. For example, while the rise of the factory concentrated power in the hands of capitalists, it also made the production process more efficient than it had been under the cottage industry system. More goods were available to more people at lower costs than previously was the case. The rise of the factory also stimulated the rise of the labor movement, which enabled workers to collectively resist capitalists' greater control and exploitation. Since workers were now engaged in the work process under one roof, they could more easily communicate and develop common viewpoints, common strategies for resistance, and more strength in their combined organized efforts to challenge capitalists' power.

SOCIAL MOVEMENTS

Our discussion of technology and social change so far implies a "top-down" view of social change: elites define issues and needs, direct resources to address those needs, and produce changes consistent with their interests (Figure 10.1).

But are people little more than captives of dominant groups' seemingly overwhelming power to guide and govern technological and social changes, or can they affect the direction and the content of social change? Since social change is a human, social construction, humans do have

Figure 10.1: Top-Down Social Change

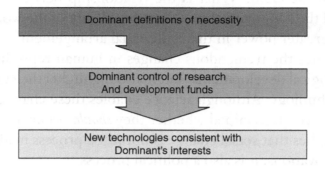

Figure 10.2: Bottom-Up Social Change

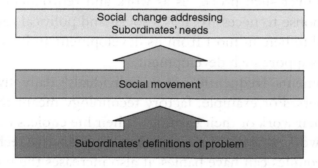

the ability to affect how societies change. Social change does not just happen like the weather; what people do alters the content of social structures and sometimes alters the very structures themselves. How do people effect social change, if so much is made to happen by and for the already privileged? Must individuals always adjust to the changes dictated by people who are powerful and advantaged, or are there options to counter those forces? Can change be stimulated from the bottom up?

The key to these questions has to do with collective, organized action. Individuals are fairly powerless by themselves to challenge the social changes introduced by the powerful and advantaged members of society. One voice alone may not be heeded or even heard. However, organized, collective efforts by many similar-minded individuals have historically posed formidable challenges to the powerful, even if they have had variable success (Figure 10.2).

For example, when factory owners introduced machinery into the stocking industry in Great Britain in the nineteenth century, workers collectively rebelled by smashing the machinery they saw as displacing their labor (Rude, 1964, 1985). While the rebellion only temporarily postponed the introduction of the new machinery, it represented collective action taken to resist the use of technology that benefited factory owners but hurt workers.

We call persistent, organized, collective efforts to resist existing structures and cultures, or to introduce changes in them, **social movements.** They often permit the less powerful members of society to effectively challenge and resist the more powerful members. As such, social movements may offer organizational opportunities for producing change from the bottom up within societies. Social movements also sometimes allow the relatively powerless to affect inter-societal relations. For example, the U.S. anti-war movement during the 1960s and early 1970s increased the pressure on the United States to redefine and end its military role in Vietnam. The impact of the anti-war movement in that instance had lasting effects on U.S. military relations: The War Powers Act restricted the ability of future presidents to militarily intrude into other countries' internal affairs. Social movements, then, can be the vehicle through which individuals working together may be able to address issues that otherwise seem too big, too daunting, and overwhelming to them.

Types of Social Movements

Social movements differ in the types of change they pursue and the amounts of change they aim for (Aberle, 1966) (see Figure 10.3).

For example, **redemptive movements** do not attempt to change society; their efforts target individuals, and their goal is for individuals to reshape the entirety of their lives around a particular set of principles. Many redemptive movements are religious movements seeking to convert individuals. Evangelists who preach on television and Jehovah's Witnesses who knock on doors to talk to people are engaged in similar attempts to convince individuals to convert from sinful pursuits to Christianity.

Alterative movements also seek changes among individuals. But while redemptive movements seek total changes in how individuals arrange their lives, alterative movements focus on limited, but specifically defined, changes. Students Against Drunk Driving (SADD), an organization of high school and college students, for example, seeks to convince other students to resist the peer pressures to drive under the influence of alcohol or other drugs. SADD has chapters throughout the country, but it does not try to change society. Rather, it focuses on trying to alter the behaviors of individual students. It also is not interested in reshaping the principles around which individual students live; its goal is to alter students' combination of driving and drinking or using drugs.

On the other hand, Mothers Against Drunk Driving (MADD) is a **reformative movement**, in that it aims to change society more than just individuals. This nationally organized group actively lobbies for strict national and state legislation criminalizing driving under the influence of alcohol. What MADD seeks is a limited, but specifically defined, change in societal rather than individual norms, and it is not seeking to do so by completely altering the entire structure of society.

Figure 10.3: Types of Social Movements

	Amount of Change Sought:	
Type of Change Sought:	Total	Limited but specific
Individuals	Redemptive	Alternative
Society	Transformative	Reformative

Source: David Aberle, 1966. The *Peyote Religion among the Navajo* (Chicago: Aldine).

Similarly, the AARP (formerly the American Association of Retired Persons) is a reformative movement comprising more than 32 million members over the age of 50. The AARP lobbies legislators for better legal protection of the rights of the elderly, and it informs the rest of society about those rights through education, advocacy, and service in the community. The AARP also engages in voter registration drives and voter education campaigns, and it presses for attention to healthcare and quality-of-life issues that concern retired persons. The AARP's goal is not to radically change the structure of society but to reform institutional politics and change societal norms toward treatment of the elderly.

The goal of **transformative movements,** like that of reformative movements, is change in society rather than in individuals. But while reformative movements work toward limited, specific changes, transformative movements seek total, structural change in society. Revolutions are good examples of transformative movements. Their goal is radical and total change of the social structure, resulting in a society that is completely different from the existing form. The Cuban revolution of the 1950s, for example, worked to overthrow the dominating capitalist social structure that produced gross inequalities of wealth, power, and privilege and to replace it with a socialist structure that favored collective production for the common good rather than for individual wealth.

While this typology is useful for differentiating many social movements, it is important to note that it is limited: Not all social movements seek change at all, but rather work to preserve the status quo. Indeed, social movements that achieve once-sought changes may shift to protect these changes from efforts to repeal them. For example, abortion rights activists who successfully fought for the right to access legal abortions in the 1960s and 1970s now struggle to protect that right against attempts to undo the Supreme Court's 1973 *Roe v. Wade* decision. Similarly, anti-war activists who helped eliminate the military draft system in the United States in the 1970s are now faced with the prospect of opposing efforts to change from an all-volunteer military to a new military draft system in support of new anti-terrorism programs. This new role as protector of the status quo makes it difficult to classify the movement within the typology.

Note, too, that this new role of the abortion rights and anti-war movements underscores that some movements may begin as one type of movement in the typology but later may morph into another type over time. For example, Mothers Against Drunk Driving initially began as an alterative movement focused on discouraging individuals from operating a motor vehicle after consuming alcohol; it has more recently become more of a reform movement as it shifted toward efforts to influence federal and state policies criminalizing drunk driving.

Within large social movements several types of movements (based on their goals and strategies) may coexist. For example, the feminist movement actually consists of several different movements (Ferree, Lorber, and Hess, 1999). The liberal feminist movement, articulated by organizations such as the National Organization for Women (NOW), is a reformative movement. Its goal is to integrate women better into existing political, social, and economic institutions, thereby increasing the equal participation of women in society. Such organizations do not question or challenge the existing social structures; they challenge the discrimination against women that occurs within those structures. Their efforts, therefore, focus on legislative lobbying, antidiscrimination suits in the courts, and public education and consciousness raising.

In contrast, the radical feminist movement defines men as the enemy and seeks to change existing institutions viewed as patriarchal. Marriage, in particular, is seen as an oppressive institution for women; radical feminists seek to redefine the structure of family to eliminate the traditional restrictive roles that inhibit women's development as independent individuals. For example, families of women living together to support one another and perhaps their children do not include men and are not based on male-dictated and gendered divisions of labor. Radical feminists, then, support one another's individual resistance to oppressive institutions. While the ultimate goal is to have so many women resist that the existing institutions change, radical feminists work primarily to convince individual women to alter the social structures of their personal living arrangements. In this sense radical feminists may be understood as involved in a form of redemptive movement.

Marxist or socialist feminists, however, see capitalism as the enemy rather than men per se. In their view, both men and women are victims of a system that exploits people for the benefit of the capitalist class. The conflict between men and women is viewed as a false wedge driven within the working class by the capitalist class to divide and conquer it and reduce the possibility that male and female workers will organize to challenge capitalism. Socialist feminists, then, do not seek greater integration of women into the political, social, and economic institutions of society, as do liberal feminists, since that would only legitimate the existing system of oppression. Similarly, they do not define men as the enemy, as do radical feminists, because that would divert energy and attention away from the real problem of capitalism as an oppressive social structure. The goal of socialist feminists is to have women and men recognize sexism as a vehicle of capitalist oppression and join forces in working toward a socialist society. The elimination of sexism requires the elimination of capitalism first. Socialist feminists, then, represent a transformative movement; they seek total change of society.

When a social movement consists of several types of movements, the diversity usually stems from disagreements among the participants on the definition of the source of a problem or on the strategy most appropriate for change. That much said, however, the question still remains of how social movements develop in the first place. Why do social movements occur, and how do grievances of individuals translate into efforts to bring about social change? The fact that societies are interdependent leads to another question: Do social movements in other societies have implications for individuals elsewhere?

Explaining Social Movements

Absolute versus Relative Deprivation

Karl Marx and Friedrich Engels (1967) argued that the working class and the capitalist class would eventually become so polarized that the workers would suffer immiseration, or **absolute deprivation:** They would be unable to purchase the simplest means of survival. According to this analysis, as the capitalists became richer because of their control over the labor force and work process, the workers would be forced to work longer hours at low wages just to support their own subsistence. When the workers became so poor that they were immiserated, Marx and Engels argued, they would collectively revolt to overthrow the social structure that caused their oppression. That is, revolutions, as organized resistance movements designed to challenge and replace existing social structures with new ones, would be provoked when the workers became intolerably impoverished.

The immiseration thesis is often used to frame popular media analyses of the civil rights movement in the United States. According to these analyses, the civil rights movement was touched off by a single act of resistance: When Rosa Parks finally could not take the intolerable conditions of racist oppression, she refused to give her seat on a Birmingham, Alabama, bus to a white man. The use of immiseration, or absolute deprivation theory in this instance points to one of the limitations of that thesis: Not all social movements are prompted by economic deprivation. Rosa Parks may have suffered from extreme or even absolute deprivation of civil rights, but the fact that she was employed suggests that she had at least a minimum, if not middle-class, ability to purchase what she needed for basic survival.

Some sociologists criticize the use of this thesis on still other grounds. James Davies (1962, 1969, 1974), for example, argued that revolutions historically did not occur when conditions reached an intolerable or absolute low. Rather, he noted, such organized rebellions occurred in response to **relative deprivation.** Davies argued that people's understanding of deprivation is *relative* to conditions around them, conditions they expect, or conditions that previously existed but no longer do. People revolted when a gap opened, over time, between the conditions that they expected and the conditions that actually existed (see also Klandermans, Roefs, and Olivier, 2001). Davies's relative-deprivation thesis can apply to economic as well as social and political conditions.

For example, people's expectations may gradually rise, but real conditions may gradually improve too, even if they don't quite reach expectations. In Davies's view, revolutions will not occur until real conditions begin to deteriorate somewhat relative to expectations. In this instance, real conditions do not need to deteriorate to the point of immiseration, as Marx and Engels believed; it is sufficient, according to Davies, that real conditions simply get slightly worse while expectations continue to slightly rise.

In a similar case of relative deprivation, expectations for improved conditions may rise sharply, and real conditions may also rise sharply but not quite enough to reach expectations. Revolutions will not occur until real conditions plateau while expectations continue to rise. In this instance, real conditions need not deteriorate at all; it is sufficient that real conditions stagnate while expectations continue to increase.

Finally, expectations for improved conditions may be on a sharp increase, and real conditions may be on an equally sharp incline of improvement. In this instance, revolutions will occur when expectations for improved conditions rise more sharply than real conditions. It is not necessary for real conditions to deteriorate or even stagnate; for revolutions to occur, it is sufficient, even in the face of vastly improved real conditions, that expectations dramatically increase relative to real conditions.

Resource Mobilization

Critics of both the absolute-deprivation and the relative-deprivation explanations argue that they imply a spontaneous combustion of social dissatisfaction. The theories presume that at a given point in time conditions will become absolutely intolerable, or the difference between expectations and real conditions will suddenly become intolerable, and a large group of people will revolt. This analysis ignores the question of resources. No matter how intolerable conditions become, people usually do not revolt unless they have access to resources to support their organized social movement activity. They need human resources to articulate their frustration and formulate a strategy for response; leadership to organize and mobilize others; tangible resources, such as financial backing, to spread the word, support endangered or jailed participants, and communicate widely with other potential supporters; and networks of other groups of people or existing organizations to support movement efforts (McCarthy and Wolfson, 1996). Thus, revolutions and other social movements are unlikely to occur in the absence of supportive resources and the ability of people to mobilize and apply them when political opportunities arise to create disruptions (Meyer and Staggenborg, 1996), regardless of how pronounced the feelings of absolute or relative deprivation might be. Sociologists refer to this explanation of social movements as **resource mobilization theory**.

In his study of the civil rights movement, Aldon Morris (1984, 1999) found, on the basis of extensive interviews with activists and participants, that resource mobilization was the best explanation for growth and success of the movement. Morris concluded that African Americans everywhere did not suddenly and simultaneously get frustrated enough to rebel. He documented how leaders in several African American organizations mobilized resources and combined their organizational efforts to become a powerful collective force in challenging segregation and other forms of racial discrimination in the United States.

As we noted, popular media accounts of the civil rights movement often ascribe its beginnings to a single incident, Rosa Parks's seemingly spontaneous refusal to give her seat on the Birmingham bus to a white person. Morris documents that Parks was, in fact, an active member, and the first secretary, of the local National Association for the Advancement of Colored People (NAACP). She had been arrested several times before that incident for the same action. Rosa Parks's famous act of rebellion was part of an organized, conscious resistance movement rather than an isolated, spontaneous reaction to racism. She herself insisted, "My resistance to being mistreated on the buses and anywhere else was just a regular thing with me and not just that day" (Morris, 1984: 51).

While many popular accounts personalized the civil rights movement in the charismatic leadership of Reverend Martin Luther King, Jr., Morris demonstrated that the movement was much greater than one person. Rev. King was simply the most visible and stirring articulator of the issues, a person able to galvanize and mobilize great numbers of individuals. But the civil rights movement was actually the result of the collective efforts of the NAACP, the Southern Christian Leadership Conference (SCLC), the Student Nonviolent Coordinating Committee (SNCC), and the Congress of Racial Equality (CORE), as well as African American churches, white religious organizations, labor unions, student organizations, and local small businesses. Their combined efforts mobilized vast resources in support of the movement. Instead of having to organize individuals in support of civil rights, the leadership was able to tap into existing organizations of people, communication networks, and monetary resources to quickly and effectively organize boycotts, marches, voter registration drives in hostile southern states, and acts of civil disobedience such as sit-ins at lunch counters. Morris's analysis of the civil rights movement illustrates how social movements can use resource mobilization to empower people who are powerless, disadvantaged, and largely disenfranchised from the mainstream. Against overwhelming odds, the civil rights movement managed to begin reforming a discriminatory social structure and alter rigidly racist cultural values that had denied African Americans basic civil rights.

However, some sociologists note that mobilizing resources may be necessary, but it is insufficient by itself to spark an effective social movement unless an opportunity exists or is created to apply those resources in a way that disrupts business as usual. This viewpoint is called **political process theory** (Joppke, 1993). Participants in the Occupy Wall Street movement, for example, created an opportunity to disrupt business as usual on Wall Street and in cities all around the country and the world by setting up tents in parks and other public spaces and refusing to leave, sometimes for months at a time. Their goal was to bring focused public attention to the stark economic inequality that exists in the United States and elsewhere, and to demand changes (Gitlin, 2012). While the resource they mobilized was large numbers of individuals who were willing to invest great amounts of time and endure great discomforts and risks, that resource would not have had any effect had they not carefully applied that resource to a strategy to disrupt business as usual.

Similarly, the Middle East's so-called Arab Spring mobilized large numbers of individuals, often using social media to do so, to stage mass demonstrations against oppressive regimes in Syria, Egypt, and elsewhere. Although mobilizing sizable populations over social media is important, it would not have the impact of toppling these regimes as it did were the protestors not able to create opportunities for mass disruption.

The ability to foment mass disruption is frequently met with strong responses by the state. Sometimes the state may respond positively to the demands and goals of the movement with changes in laws and practices. Other times, the state's response may be violent repression. Doug McAdam's (1988, 1999) study of the U.S. civil rights movement noted the role of the state as a factor in the rise and fall of social movements. For example, elimination of racist barriers to blacks' voting enhanced the likelihood of electing well-placed sympathetic elites such as John F. Kennedy and Lyndon B. Johnson. However, McAdam emphasized that federal support for the goals of the civil rights movement came only in response to insurgency and violent and nonviolent acts that subverted civil order. Similar findings on the role of the state in social movements, particularly in response to insurgent disruptions, can be seen in analyses of other movements, such as the labor movements in Brazil and South Africa (Seidman, 1993) and the antinuclear movements in the United States and Germany (Joppke, 1993; Meyer, 1993).

The civil rights movement has achieved only partial success in eliciting affirmative action, equal employment opportunity, and desegregation legislation. But it is important to realize that even that much was unlikely to have occurred in the absence of the pressure applied by the organized, collective efforts of the movement (Lawson, 1990). And although the legislation represents only official policy changes, and does not always necessarily alter actual practices, it is equally important to note that the movement has been less active in the past three decades. Indeed, there has been a conservative white political backlash against affirmative action and other policies that would challenge white racial privilege (Omi and Winant, 1986; Staples, 1995; Pincus, 2000). The movement may have to re-emerge, mobilizing resources and galvanizing the politically, socially, and economically disenfranchised to continue the progress toward racial equality begun in the decades between 1950 and late 1960s.

In fact, the civil rights movement seems to have begun reawakening and creating opportunities to mobilize resources so as to create disruption. For example, several organizations and groups, including the NAACP and the Rainbow Coalition, picketed the National Football League's 1994 Super Bowl game in Atlanta, Georgia, because the stadium unfurled the Georgia state flag at the game. The flag at the time included a replica of the Confederate flag, which many see as a strong historical symbol of racism. The state of Georgia was put under considerable pressure to change its flag before the 1996 Winter Olympics in Atlanta, under the scrutiny of the world. It wasn't until 2003 that the state capital unfurled the new state flag, without any replica of the Confederate flag. More recently, South Carolina agreed, after a long public boycott and intense public pressure, to remove the Confederate flag from atop the state house. It remains a focus of struggle, however, as the state continues to fly the flag on public common areas. Civil rights groups have also actively protested police brutality and racial profiling as well as racial bias in voting procedures in the 2000 presidential election. What is important here is that the increased willingness to articulate such concerns and to demand change indicates a renewed spirit in the civil rights movement and the potential for recapturing lost momentum. Some of that renewed activism and spirit could be seen in the increased participation by previously disenfranchised people of color in the political process in the 2008 and 2012 presidential elections.

If social movements require the mobilization of organizations and other resources and an application of these in a political process to create disruption, how do the poorest and least powerful groups in society get their needs addressed? In their comparative study, *Poor People's Movements* (1977), Frances Fox Piven and Richard Cloward argued that only insurgency and mass rebellions like strikes and riots brought concessions from elites for poor people. Forming and dealing with organizations, they argued, sapped energies, diverted attention, co-opted the poor into nonthreatening actions, and the false perception that the political system was fair and responsive to their needs. According to Piven and Cloward, insurgency emerges from the mass discontent and disruption of everyday life produced by poverty and deprivation. Thus, their analysis of poor people's movements (such as the welfare rights, the unemployed workers', the industrial workers', and the civil rights movements) implicitly used a deprivation model to explain how the poor and powerless wrested change from elites: The poor rebelled, rioted, and staged strikes in massive eruptions of insurgency sparked by discontent and deprivation.

Piven and Cloward rejected a resource mobilization explanation of poor people's movements. However, Jenkins and Perrow (1977), in their study of the migrant farmworkers' movement (1946–1972), demonstrated that resource mobilization was critical to the efforts of the United Farm Workers in the late 1960s and early 1970s to win the right to unionize and secure decent working conditions. The lack of resources was a key factor in the failure of the earlier National Farm Labor Union in the late 1940s and mid-1950s. Both organizations of migrant farmworkers had outside leadership, derived initial organizational sponsorship from outside their communities, and used insurgency tactics like strikes and boycotts. But widespread *sustained* support from a coalition of liberal organizations neutralized elite resistance to the farmworkers' insurgency in the late 1970s and led to the right to unionize for migrant farmworkers. Jenkins and Perrow concluded that discontent was not enough to ignite the insurgency and the successful challenges of the migrant farmworkers' movement; persistent organizational support from outside groups that had access to resources and devoted them to a group that had little was the critical difference between success and failure.

Resource mobilization, organization, and political opportunity appear to be critical as well to the increasing activism of the welfare rights movement. For example, the Kensington Welfare Rights Union (KWRU) organized a variation of the civil rights freedom riders in their national bus campaign in 1998 to gather testimonials from those harmfully affected by welfare reform. They presented thousands of these to the United Nations, demanding a human rights violation investigation. The KWRU remains highly visible and active: It has launched a Poor People's Economic Human Rights Campaign, participated in demonstrations at the Republican and Democratic national conventions in 2000, organized a Poor People's World Summit to End Poverty, and maintains a website (www.kwru.org) to disseminate information (Baptist, Jenkins, and Dillon, 1999; Cress and Snow, 2000).

We can also see evidence of resource mobilization and political process in the disability rights movement, which has been organized, vocal, and visible since the 1980s in the United States as well as elsewhere around the world (Neath and Schriner, 1998; Margaret Cooper, 1999; Hayashi and Okuyhira, 2001; Fleischer and Zames, 2011). "Disability" covers a wide range of conditions, including hearing and visual impairments, motor function limitations, mental disabilities, diseases such as AIDS and cancer, and physical appearances that depart from cultural definitions of "normality," such as obesity, cleft palate, dwarfism, and facial disfigurement (see Stroman, 1982). Such a diversity of conditions could have easily led to a splintering of the disability rights movement into separate powerless organizations, each attempting to apply pressure for legislative reforms addressed to its own constituency. Instead, over 80 different national disability organizations joined forces in the United States to form the Consortium for Citizens with Disabilities to press successfully for passage of the Americans with Disabilities Act of 1990. This act makes full and equal participation in U.S. society more accessible to people with disabilities. The consortium elicited the support of other organizations such as the American Federation of Labor and Congress of Industrial Organizations (AFL-CIO) and the American Civil Liberties Union (ACLU). Simple acts of discontent and insurgency would not have been enough to get results for people who are so marginalized. The mobilization of the vast resources of many organizations, both within the wide-ranging community of people with disabilities and outside it, was critical.

Students today are often stereotyped as apathetic and selfish, particularly when compared with the baby boom generation of politically active students of the 1960s and 1970s. But there is a great deal of evidence to suggest this stereotype is wrong. In the past decade alone, students have been key in mobilizing resources to affect globalization of the economy. In particular, the United Students Against Sweatshops has had an impressive impact on corporate use of sweatshops in peripheral countries to produce licensed products like sweatshirts, t-shirts, and other apparel with universities' and colleges' names and logos. It has organized on campuses around the country, staging sit-ins and demonstrations at college administrative offices, holding petition drives, and organizing boycotts. Its efforts have succeeded in forcing schools to withdraw from lucrative licensing contracts with corporations like Nike until the corporations agree to eliminate production of their goods in sweatshop conditions and submit to monitoring of conditions by the Workers Rights Consortium, a watchdog group that is independent of industry influence (Featherstone, 2000; Elkins and Hertel, 2011). This success has been repeated in scores of colleges and universities around the country, including some of the biggest National Collegiate Athletic Association (NCAA) schools. The students against sweatshops movement has also accomplished something that was far more difficult to find in the movements of the 1960s and 1970s: coalitions between students and organized labor (Cooper, 1999). Student coalitions with labor, as well as with faith communities was also apparent in the organized protests against the World Trade Organization in Seattle, Washington, and in Washington, DC, in 1999 and 2000 (Nichols, 2000).

Similarly, students forged alliances with the workers who clean campus buildings in the Justice for Janitors movement. Students demonstrated and staged sit-ins at campus administrative offices at colleges and universities all around the country in 2001 to demand living wages and health benefits for janitors who had been paid below-poverty wages. A three-week stand-off between students and administrators at Harvard University resulted in an agreement to raise wages and provide benefits to janitors there. Similar demonstrations and agreements have occurred at several other campuses, and many more are continuing the struggle (Marc Cooper, 1999; Bacon, 2000; McKean, 2001).

Clearly, students are not all apathetic, but rather many are highly active, and an important element in social movements affecting not just local, selfish concerns but global, world-system issues affecting far less privileged people around the world and at home. And that activism holds encouraging signs for further student participation in social movements: Research suggests that when students participate in one social movement activity, they tend to be more likely to influence the formation of new campus organizations devoted to activism (Van Dyke, 1998).

External Forces

Interestingly, most explanations for social movements look at the internal dynamics of individual societies. But it is important to emphasize that societies do not exist in a vacuum, that forces supportive of social movements or against them can come from outside a given society (Tilly, 1998). For example, we have just noted the effect the student movement against sweatshops in the United States has begun to have on conditions of production around the world. An organized international boycott and disinvestment campaign against corporations doing business in and with the white minority apartheid government in South Africa helped advance the defeat of that racist structure. And as noted earlier in this chapter, debt crises have prompted the imposition of IMF-sponsored austerity programs in many underdeveloped countries. In their cross-national comparative analysis of countries with debt crises, John Walton and Charles Ragin (1990) found that the likelihood of political protest was enhanced by increased external pressures for countries to adopt the austerity programs. Such external pressures also increased the intensity of the protests. Walton and Ragin found that although deprivation and hardship of living conditions certainly contributed to people's grievances, these were not strongly related to the protests.

Feminist movements focused on improving the well-being of women in individual nations are increasingly becoming more global in their perspective and their efforts. Networks of women's rights organizations throughout the world, with the help of resources like the Internet, are helping to shape a more international feminist movement, applying pressure on governments and international agencies to secure women's political and human rights, access to education and healthcare, and access to jobs. They also work to raise consciousness among women locally about their rights (Ferree and Subramaniam, 2000).

The gay rights movement has similarly organized forces across national boundaries, linking many national gay rights organizations in North America, South America, Asia, Europe, Australia, and Africa in the International Gay Association (IGA). The IGA helps movement organizations join forces, share experiences and information, and support one another's national agenda for gay male and lesbian civil rights. The gay rights movement has also organized in solidarity with other groups' movements, including those of women, labor, and people of color, drawing on shared experiences of oppression and the shared desire for change. For example, in a cross-national analysis of gay rights movements, Barry Adam noted that the Mexican Gay Pride Day activities offered support to the people of El Salvador in their struggle for self-determination and, in return, the Farabundo Marti National Liberation Front in El Salvador gave its support to the international gay rights movement (Adam, 1987: 165). Similarly, the International Lesbian and Gay Association has gained status as a consulting organization with the Economic and Social Council to address human rights violations in member nations in the European Union (Sanders, 1996). Thus, external resources may combine with internal resource mobilization to provoke and sustain social movements across national boundaries.

CHAPTER SUMMARY

- Social change is not simply a neutral, natural life force in societies. It is, rather, a political process that involves organized struggles between the powerful, advantaged segments of society, on the one hand, and the disadvantaged and disenfranchised segments, on the other. People with power and privilege are often in a better position to define the content and direction of change in a way that preserves and enhances their power and privilege.

- Development is similarly a political process, marked by unequal historical relationships among nations in a world-system. As such, countries are not on a continuum from advanced to less developed, as if all countries mature through a single series of steps to modernization. Rather, some countries are *under*developed because they have historically been thrust into a disadvantaged position by other countries that have dominated them through colonization or military intervention, or by other means exploited their resources and drained their economies.

- Technological innovation as a force of social change is also the product of power inequalities: Dominant groups are in the best position to define technological needs according to their own interests. Technological innovations tend to enhance the power and control of dominant groups over the less powerful, whether the technology pertains to the workplace or to such personal affairs as human reproduction.

  However, despite the strong sense that power inequalities direct social change in order to reinforce and reproduce those inequalities, people are not entirely powerless to affect this process.

- Social movements are the means through which the less powerful, the disadvantaged, and the disenfranchised can challenge and alter the status quo. And they may even be organized across national boundaries to produce larger, stronger movements with access to greater resources than otherwise possible.

What, then, do processes of social change mean for individuals' daily lives?

- New technologies are introduced almost every day, many of which make individuals' existence easier or more comfortable, such as air conditioners, dishwashers, refrigerators, and cars. Yet these same technologies help to deplete nonrenewable resources, including fossil fuels, and pose waste disposal and even pollution problems.

- Some technologies make work safer, such as robots that perform dangerous jobs. Those same technologies, however, may also cost workers their jobs, as machines displace human labor. Educational technologies introduce the problem of unequal access to information, as personal computers, copy machines, and cell phones become increasingly central to the education process. Those of you who are unable to afford your own personal computers or word processors know that writing papers and other assignments is more difficult and time-consuming for you than for students who have this equipment.

- Reproductive technologies are making it possible for many women to conceive and give birth who might otherwise not have had the chance. But the cost of such technologies means that the hope they offer for fertility is available only to relatively affluent women. And these technologies are also contributing to a continuing battle over women's control of the birth process. Women today may have a greater chance than their mothers had to have a baby, but they will need to be highly assertive with their doctors and midwives to have the pregnancy and birth experience they want.

- In addition to technological changes, global changes in trade and production also alter people's existence. World-system relationships that affect development in Latin America, Asia, and Africa also affect people in countries like the United States. When corporations shift production to poor countries to take advantage of inexpensive labor, consumers in the United States may be able to purchase clothing and electronics more cheaply than before. But they may also find that their jobs disappear as a result of that shift. (We will discuss this problem in greater detail in Chapter 12.)

Finally, once it becomes clear that social change is a political process rather than an inexorable neutral force, people become more empowered to participate in that process.

- Individuals have generally found it very difficult to combat oppressive forces, but organized groups of individuals have had greater success in resisting social arrangements and institutions they saw as oppressive. This means that you have the potential to participate in the process of social change, from the social organization of the classroom to the institutional arrangements of the economy and the state.

 ## THINKING CRITICALLY

1. We often feel powerless as individuals against the institutions of society. Yet sometimes individuals do alter how they are affected by institutions. Consider efforts on your own campus to change something. How did students manage to instigate change? What resources

did they marshal on behalf of the issues that concerned them? Did they, in fact, do this alone? Which theory of social movements best explains this analysis?

2. Select a recent technological innovation and discuss how it might alter society. How might it make life easier or better? What might be some of the limitations or problems generated by this technology? Now consider: Who would benefit from this technology and who would be hurt? Why? How might this technology alter your life?

3. The early 1990s saw the breakup of the Soviet Union into separate, independent countries. How has this dramatic social change in Eastern Europe affected the United States? How has it affected your daily existence? What does this suggest about the sources of social change?

4. Select a social movement (such as Occupy Wall Street, the Tea Party Movement, the nuclear freeze, gay rights, disability rights, women's rights, labor, pro-choice, antiabortion, fundamentalist movement or some other movement of your own choosing). Examine the successes and setbacks of this movement. What factors might account for its successes? What factors might account for its setbacks? Who benefits and who is hurt by the movement's successes? How? Which theory of social movements best explains this movement?

5. Compare your daily life with that of your parents or grandparents at your age (it might be useful and interesting to talk with them if possible and to talk to both males and females). How is your life different from theirs? Why? How is it similar? How might gender or class explain some of these differences and similarities? Which theory of social change or social movements might explain the differences or similarities?

 KEY TERMS

absolute deprivation 273

alterative movements 271

antithesis 255

basic needs 257

capitalists 255

cottage industries 266

cyclical theory 253

debt dependency 261

debt-for-nature swaps 264

dependent development 260

dialectic 255

equilibrium theory 254

evolutionary theory 254

export processing 260

import substitution 260

inventions 265

latent 252

manifest 252

Marxist theory 255

modernization theory 256

political process theory 276

proletariat 255

redemptive movements 271

reformative movements 271

relative deprivation 274

resource mobilization theory 275

social Darwinism 254

social movements 270

social reforms 251

social revolutions 252

surrogate mother 268

synthesis 255

thesis 255

trade dependency 258

transformative movements 272

underdeveloped nations 258

THE STATE, CAPITAL AND POWER

11

Consider the effect the institutions of the state and the economy may have on you. Perhaps you or someone you know has been called to serve in the war in Iraq. Whose interests are served when someone like you goes to war? Or perhaps someone you know needs financial assistance in order to survive day to day. Where does such assistance come from, who decides if it will be available, and how much will individuals receive? Who decides who gets to make such decisions on your behalf? Do you get to participate in deciding who will make policy affecting your life? These kinds of questions suggest that two of the most powerful institutions affecting individuals' biographies are the state and the economy.

The term **state** refers to the organization of political positions and the structure of political relations in society. The state, then, as an institution, is different from **government**, which refers to the politicians who occupy positions within the state and its agencies and bureaus. As individual politicians come and go, the government may change specific policies or views, reflecting individuals' personal styles, perspectives, party affiliations, interests, and so forth. However, the structure of political relations—electoral processes, policy-making processes, relations between the government and corporations, labor, consumers, and others—remains intact regardless of the individuals who occupy positions within the institution of the state.

The **economy** comprises the structures, relationships, and activities that produce and distribute wealth in society. Both the state and the economy are quite influential in shaping individuals' opportunities and their places in the larger society. These institutions do not operate in isolation from each other but, rather, intersect in various ways to affect peoples' lives. In the United States as well as most Western industrialized and post-industrialized nations, the economy is a capitalist one: The means of production (or **capital**) are privately owned, as are the profits these generate. But the process of production is performed by workers, who do not own the means of production, nor do they own the wealth and the profits their labor produces.

Note that this arrangement in the economy is not universal: Not every nation adopts this same approach to production and distribution of wealth. Moreover, not all states respond to the economy in the same way. Some, like the United States, claim to adopt a position in which the state maintains a "hands-off" approach to the economy: They attempt to let the marketplace control the economy and economic actors rather than allow legislation to do so. Other states may take a much more activist role in participating in the economy, regulating and controlling the markets and economic actors. The varying ways that economies may be arranged, and the ways the state may participate or not participate in these arrangements, suggests the need to explore several questions:

- What is the nature of the relationship between political and economic institutions within a capitalist society?
- Can a society in which economic ownership is concentrated in relatively few hands function democratically?
- Is the state a neutral arbiter among competing interests, legislating in the common good?
- What is the relationship between the military, the state, and private capital?
- In what ways do the needs of owners and controllers of capital clash with the fundamental needs of workers or of the poor, and with what results?

This chapter will explore how sociologists use different perspectives to examine these questions. In particular, we will focus on the corporate economy and power in this chapter; we will emphasize the role of labor in the economy and the structure of the labor market more specifically in Chapter 12, "Work and Production." In this chapter we will look at voting patterns in the United States and at the way the institutions of the state and economy affect how well voters can influence their elected leaders in government. We will also examine the relationship between workers, private corporations, and the state and consider how this relationship affects the functioning of government. In short, we will discuss various ways in which the state and the economy intersect. Finally, we will look at an example of how these relationships can affect people's daily existence by examining welfare reform of the 1990s: How has the relationship between the institutions of state and economy shaped social perceptions about poverty and the development of social policy that addresses this issue?

THE RELATIONSHIP OF STATE AND ECONOMY

The discussion of the relationship between the state and the economy begins first with an understanding that these institutions are not completely isolated from one another. The state must often enact policies concerning economic actors and relationships in order to avoid chaos and economic crises. So, for example, Congress may enact legislation to regulate wages, taxes, banking and stock market practices, and labor relations in order to prevent devastating economic depressions. These sorts of legislation are examples of how the state and economy intersect and overlap. That intersection often operates in ways that privilege one set of interests over others, creating systems of structured class inequality. Sociologists refer to the intersection of the institutions of state and economy as **political economy**.

There are three major forms of political economy: *capitalism*, *socialism*, and *communism*. **Capitalism** is a political economy characterized by an arrangement of production in which workers cooperate to produce wealth that is then privately owned by whoever hired the workers. Workers own their labor power and are paid a wage to use their labor to produce wealth; capitalists own or control the means of production, and therefore own the wealth that workers produce using these means. The state is structured on the assumption that it is generally the responsibility of individuals to provide for their own basic needs and that it is the legitimate right of employers to own the wealth produced by workers. Inequality becomes based in part on whether one is an owner of the means of production or an owner only of one's own labor power. The system of structured class inequality based on ownership of the means of production often intersects, as well, with gender and race inequalities. Clearly, this is the political economy that dominates the United States and most if not all of the wealthy, industrialized and post-industrialized countries of the world.

Compare this to the political economy of **socialism**, in which production of goods and services involves the social cooperation between workers to create wealth, as it is in capitalism. And workers are paid a wage in exchange for their labor, as they are in a capitalist economy. But where the means of production under capitalism are privately owned, under socialism these are more likely to be owned or controlled by the state. As such, the state becomes the owner and controller of the wealth produced, and then has the power to determine its distribution. Systems of structured inequality in this political economy may still be class-based, as they are under capitalism, but that inequality is more likely to be moderated by the state in its provision or subsidization of basic goods and services for all. In such a system, for example, the state often becomes a provider of healthcare, housing, food, and income support when employment is unavailable. This does not mean that class inequality is nonexistent or that it does not intersect with other systems of inequality, such as gender, religion, or ethnicity and race. But the stark gaps between wealth and poverty that are common under capitalism are less likely to be found under socialism because of the state's activist role in providing for basic needs. Cuba provides a familiar example. Variations of the socialist political economy can be found in Sweden and Norway, often referred to as "social democracies" or "mixed economies" since they contain elements of both capitalism and socialism.

In **communist** political economies workers must still cooperate to produce the goods and services needed, but ownership of the means of production are collectively owned by the workers themselves. In this case, since ownership of the means of production guarantees ownership of the wealth produced, the workers are in a position to determine its distribution. Clearly, the decision-making process of the distribution of wealth may invite the creation of structured systems of inequality, as criteria must be used to determine who gets what. Karl Marx envisioned a distribution formula whereby wealth would be distributed from each according to one's ability to produce for the group as a whole and to each according to one's need regardless of ability to produce (although he was not specific about how to evaluate either ability or need). Israeli *kibbutzim* are small-scale examples of a communist political economy where wealth distribution is in part determined by amount of time commitment to the collective: Those who have been living in the kibbutz longest receive the greatest benefits. Structured inequality in this instance becomes a function of longevity and loyalty to the collective. That does not mean that other systems of structured inequality do not matter; gender, as well as race, ethnicity, and religion are still likely to intersect with length of time one has been a member of the kibbutz in determining distribution of wealth.

Note that these political economy types are more like ideal types than actual, discretely different types. This is because most actual examples are more a hybrid of these types. The United States, for example, is often understood to be the prototypical example of the capitalist political economy, but the state here still has at various points in time taken an activist role in subsidizing basic needs or in participating in the functioning of the economy. And there are hundreds of worker-owned production facilities (like Joseph Industries, Inc., a forklift parts manufacturer in Streetsboro, Ohio, that is entirely worker-owned) and worker cooperatives (like Ithaca's Moose-wood Inn) in the United States. Similarly, the former Soviet Union has often been identified as the prime example of the communist political economy, but the workers there did not own the means of production nor did they own or control the wealth they produced. Indeed, the state owned the means of production and workers were paid wages in exchange for their labor, making the former Soviet Union's political economy more one of "state capitalism" than pure communism. The point here is that differences between political economies are more likely to be ones of degree than of actual type.

In this chapter we will focus on the capitalist political economy in order to explore how this political economy may affect individuals' lives. Other political economic structures produce their own latent institutional consequences and systems of inequality. An understanding of how a capitalist political economy may affect people's lives will help shape similar questions regarding how other political economic structures may do so for people in other nations. What, then, is the relationship between the state and the economy in a capitalist political economy?

There are two basic views of the relationship between the state and the economy, particularly in a capitalist, democratic society: pluralism and power elite theory. One sees the state and economy as separate institutions whose relationship is minor at best, and the other sees the state and economy as fused in significant ways.

PLURALISM

Some sociologists argue that the state and the economy are two entirely separate institutions. These scholars generally presume that the economy is a neutral institution governed by its own "laws" of the market, such as supply and demand, and they focus their analyses of the state on how political structures affect people's lives and how individuals may affect the political (that is, electoral) process. The economy and the state are not seen as linked in any significant way. Sociologists call this theory of the state **pluralism.** There are two strands of pluralist thought: group pluralism and elite pluralism.

Group Pluralism

According to advocates of the theory of **group pluralism**, democratic society is composed of a wide variety of groups which develop around specific needs or interests (Truman, 1951). These **interest groups** compete to get their goals met, and none of them is omnipotent or more powerful than any other. Individuals engage in political activity through these groups to affect the workings of government. People may choose to belong to one or more of these interest groups, and many people very likely belong to several such groups. Each of these groups pressure the state in order to get its needs met. In doing so, the groups compete against one another, often making conflicting demands on the state. Examples of interest groups include the National Rifle Association, the American Medical Association, the National Association of Manufacturers, the American Banking Association, the Teamsters Union, the National Organization for Women, the National Association for the Advancement of Colored People, and the American Association of Retired Persons (today simply called the AARP).

In this view, the state acts as a neutral referee, weighing and balancing competing demands, evaluating the legitimacy of each, and ultimately making policy in the common good of society. In this way, the state ensures a balance of power between many groups, thereby lending stability to society. That stability is also ensured by several other characteristics of democratic political systems. For example, a balance of power may occur between the interest groups, because none of them is strong enough to win whatever it wants each time. This leads groups to form alliances with one another on a variety of issues. These alliances are likely to shift and change as focal issues change, and this prevents permanent alliances from becoming entrenched and too powerful. Groups also realize that each has a sort of veto power over the others: If any group did attempt to thwart the interests of the others, the others would form an alliance against the transgressor. This interaction among groups is said to ensure the common good of society as a whole. Moreover, since members of society are likely to belong to several interest groups, the overlapping memberships serve to create pressures that dilute each group's powers. Interest groups must compromise with others to avoid losing members who may find the conflict between their various memberships too great.

Group pluralists further believe that society is balanced and stable because everyone agrees on the basic rules governing interest-group competition. This means that when people have an interest or a goal they want the state to address, they approach the state through democratic procedures, including elections, petitions to legislators, lawsuits filed in the courts, and so on. Adherence to these procedures ensures legislation in the common good.

Society is also stabilized by the existence of *potential* interest groups. When existing interest groups do not address the needs or interests of people, or when the state ignores people's interests, individuals may mobilize to form a new active interest group and enter into the democratic process of appealing to the state. The possibility of such a mobilization prevents existing groups from ignoring the interests of others.

Critics argue that group pluralists tend to treat all existing groups as if they had the same relative strength and power. But some groups have access to greater resources than others, some are larger in membership than others, and some represent more powerful constituencies. Moreover, some important interests have historically been weak and disregarded in the democratic process, such as those of children, the homeless, undocumented workers, people of color, and the poor. It is difficult to argue that all groups, both existing and potential, are equally powerful when some groups have consistently had great success in obtaining many of their goals while others have had little success.

Group pluralists would counter this criticism by arguing that the reason some groups seem more successful is that their interests and objectives are more consistent with the common good. However, the meaning of this term is unclear. Who defines the common good? Is it possible that what the state defines as the common good may hinder or eliminate the ability of some groups to have their objectives met? What are the social background characteristics of those who define the common good? Pluralists assume that the state is neutral and that individuals within that institution make decisions impartially. Their analysis assumes that governmental officials have no interest-group ties of their own, or that at the very least their social background characteristics are representative of the diversity of the society at large so as to present a balance of interests in which no single interest group prevails.

Critics of group pluralism also take issue with the notion of potential interest groups. How can the power of potential groups be gauged if they do not yet exist? How can the effectiveness of potential groups in altering or modifying the behavior of existing groups or elite politicians be analyzed? Existing interest groups and elected officials may, indeed, worry about challenges from ignored interests, but how much do they worry, and how much does that concern alter their pursuit of their own objectives?

Finally, critics often argued that group pluralists overemphasized groups and ignored the important role that elites play in society. It is difficult to ignore that political elites matter in democracies: Individual voters cast ballots for individual candidates. How can we explain the role of these elites in a pluralist model of the relationship between the state and the economy? Are these elected political elites separate from economic elites?

Elite Pluralism

Where group pluralists emphasize the importance of competing interest *groups*, advocates of **elite pluralism theory** emphasize the swirl of competing political *elites* in the electoral process. Politicians, as political elites, compete for people's votes in the same way that consumer products compete for their dollars. Just as competing interest groups are balanced by the need for cooperation and alliances, competing candidates are balanced by the fact that various constituents ignored today may be needed tomorrow for coalitions and support. So politicians must legislate in the common good because their own political fate is in the hands of voters. If elected officials do not pay attention to certain interests, they run the danger of being voted out of office by angry constituents. If they ignore issues of concern to people who do not regularly participate in the electoral process, politicians still run the danger of being voted out of office when those individuals become politically active (Lipset, 1960; Pinderhughes, 1987).

For example, elected officials have consistently ignored or attacked the interests and needs of the gay community. In response, gays have become increasingly active politically. They have organized and mobilized their resources in the electoral process to replace unsympathetic elected officials with more supportive candidates. In the 1970s there were fewer than five openly gay elected officials in the United States; by 2010 there were over 500 (www.victoryfund.org).

Critics of elite pluralism have argued that while this perspective presents a picture of how people might like to think the state and democracy works in the United States, it still does not explain the persistence of serious social problems such as racism, poverty, sexism, suppression of political dissent, and homelessness. If the system is balanced by the need for politicians to heed the interests of their constituents, why do so many people feel left out? Why do so few people vote? Pluralism does not adequately account for the many people who are not politically well represented or involved.

Furthermore, elite pluralists suggest that voting is the way in which people can hold elites whose decisions fundamentally affect their lives accountable. But how do they hold nonelected elites accountable? The decisions of economic elites, such as corporate chief executive officers, banking officials, and the like, affect people's livelihoods in the most basic ways, including whether someone will have a job at all, get a mortgage to buy a house, have access to credit, and so forth. Since they are not elected, how can people hold them accountable for their decisions? And, more to the point, are political elites and economic elites separate groups of elites? Or are they one and the same?

POWER ELITE THEORY

According to the pluralist model, power is diluted by the dynamics of countervailing interests and competing elites so that no one group is omnipotent. Power is dispersed across a wide array of interest groups and across a large number of political elites. On the other hand, C. Wright Mills (1957) suggested in his book, *The Power Elite*, that there is a select, or elite, group of individuals in whom power is concentrated. Their advantaged position of power ensures that their interests will prevail over all others. Pluralism focuses on the electoral and interest group processes as those relate to policy making by the state. The assumption is that the state and the economy are separate institutions. In contrast, power elite theory examines some of the ways the institutions of the state and the economy intersect or are fused. Unlike pluralists, these theorists argue that the state cannot be neutral, because of the common interests and views of the **power elite** (Mills, 1957). The power elite are those people who fill the key leadership positions of three main institutions: the state, the corporate economy, and the military. The power elite is composed of relatively few members who hold common interests and share a similar world view because they come from similar backgrounds of class, education, religion, social milieu, and so forth.

Mills argued that the members of the power elite tend to be unified by three related processes: *class identity*, *co-optation*, and the *interchangeability* of the institutional elites. **Class identity** results from the common life experiences of members of the elite, which give them a sense of being members of an exclusive group. Members of the power elite have usually attended the same few prestigious private prep schools and Ivy League colleges, hold common memberships in exclusive social clubs, live in affluent communities and enclaves, and travel in cliques. Their children tend to marry one another, thereby sealing wealth and power between families (Domhoff, 2009). In this way they are unlikely to confront views held by members of other classes that challenge those they share. They are unified in their beliefs about what is best for society and how the world works, because these beliefs are constantly reaffirmed by their class peers.

That shared arena of interaction extends into the boardroom, where these same elites are likely to sit on several corporate boards of directors together. Overlapping memberships on corporate boards not only provide a common point of view between corporations, but also reinforces elites' shared interests and adoption of a normative system shaped by corporate ideals and goals.

Co-optation involves the socialization of prospective and new members of the elite so that they come to share the world view of the power elite. That is, individuals who aspire to elite positions must be willing to adopt the prevailing world view and ideology held by the existing elite, who select new members into their circle of privilege. Only those who share that ideology will be selected. Once selected, new members of the elite become surrounded by that ideology, and they further internalize it.

Finally, the power elite are unified by their **interchangeability** across three major institutions: the state, the corporate economy, and the military. Changing from a position of power in one institution to another is not uncommon among those at the pinnacle of power. This mingling of leadership blurs any sharp distinctions in experience, perspective, ideology, or world view such leaders may have. For example, Alexander Haig, Jr., was a president of United Technologies (a major defense contractor), a former four-star general in the U.S. Army, and Secretary of State under Ronald Reagan (1981–1982). George Shultz, president of the Bechtel Corporation (another major defense contractor), was Reagan's Secretary of State (1982–1989) as well as a previous Secretary of the Treasury and Secretary of Labor (Dye, 1990: 91). More recently, President George W. Bush was an executive with Harkin Energy, an oil corporation. Vice President Richard Cheney was the Chief Executive Officer of Halliburton Oil Company from 1995 until 2000, and the Secretary of Defense from 1989 until 1993. Donald Rumsfeld, the Secretary of Defense under President George W. Bush, served as the Chief Executive Officer of G.D. Searles, a major pharmaceutical corporation. He also served as chairman of the RAND Corporation, a major military think tank. And Secretary of State Colin Powell was an Army officer, National Security Advisor from 1987 to 1989, and served as director in AOL Time Warner, as well as Gulfstream Aerospace and General Dynamics, both major Department of Defense Contractors (Dye, 2002) (Table 11.1 presents additional examples of former cabinet members and their institutional ties).

Table 11.1: Institutional Ties Of Former Cabinet Members, 1973–2013

Cabinet Members	Institutional Ties
Secretaries of State	
Henry Kissinger (1973–1977)	Project director for Rockefeller Brothers Fund and the Council on Foreign Relations
Cyrus Vance (1977–1980)	Member of the board of directors of IBM and Pan American World Airways; trustee of Yale University, the Rockefellar Foundation, and the Council on Foreign Relations; former secretary of the army under President Lyndon Johnson
Alexander M. Haig (1981–1982)	President, United Technologies Corp.; former four-star general, U.S. Army; for Supreme Allied Commander, NATO forces in Europe
George P. Shultz (1982–1989)	President, Bechtel Corp.; former director, General Motors, Borg-Warner, and Dillon, Read & Co.
James A. Baker III (1989–1992)	Houston attorney with oil industry interests
Warren Christopher (1993–1997)	Former law clerk for U.S. Supreme Court Justice William Douglas; partner, O'Melvany & Meyers; director of California Edison, First Interstate Bancorp., Lockheed, and chairman of the Board of Trustees, Carnegie Corp.

Madeleine Albright (1997–2001)	Member, Council on Foreign Relations
Secretaries of Treasury	
William E. Simon (1974–1977)	Director of Federal Energy Office; former senior partner of Salomon Brothers
Warner Michael Blumenthal (1977–1979)	President, Bendix Corporation; former vice president, Crown Cork Co.; trustee of Princeton University and the Council on Foreign Relations
G. William Miller (1979–1981)	Chairman and Chief Executive Officer, Textron Corp.; former partner, Cravath, Swaine & Moore; former director of Allied Chemical and Federated Department Stores; former Chairman of the Federal Reserve Board
Donald T. Regan (1981–1985)	Chairman of the board and Chief Executive Officer, Merrill Lynch & Co. Inc.; former vice-chairman, New York Stock Exchange; trustee, University of Pennsylvania and the Committee for Economic Development; member, policy committee of the Business Roundtable
James A. Baker III (1985–1989)	see above
Nicholas Brady (1989–1993)	Former Chairman, Dillon, Read & Co.; director of Purolator, NCR, Georgia International, ASA, and Media General
Robert E. Rubin (1995–2001)	Chairman of Goldman Sachs; trustee, Carnegie Corp.
Timothy Geithner (2009–2013)	President, Federal Reserve Bank of New York
Secretaries of Defense	
James R. Schlesinger (1973–1977)	Director, Central Intelligence Agency; former chairman of Atomic Energy Commission; research associate, RAND Corporation (a major military think tank)
Harold Brown (1977–1981)	President, California Institute of Technology; member of the board of directors, IBM and the Times-Mirror Corp.; former Secretary of the Air Force under President Lyndon B. Johnson

(Continued)

Table 11.1 *(Continued)*

Caspar W. Weinberger (1981–1989)	Vice president and director, Bechtel Corp.; member of the board of directors, Pepsico and Quaker Oats Co.; former chairman of the Federal Trade Commission
Richard B. Cheney (1989–1993)	Chief Executive Officer, Halliburton Co.
Les Aspin (1993–1994)	Former Chairman, House Armed Forces Committee
William J. Perry (1994–1997)	Former director, Electronic Defense Laboratories of GTE; former director of Stanford University Center for International Security
Willam S. Cohen (1997–2001)	Attorney
Charles Hagel (2013–)	Founder and CEO, Vanguard Cellular; Deputy Director of the 1990 G7 Summit; member, Council on Foreign Relations

Source: (of all but the Obama administration cabinet members): Pages 74–77 in Thomas R. Dye, *Who's Running America? The Bush Restoration* (7th Edition). 2002. Upper Saddle River, NJ: Prentice Hall.

More recently, the interchangeability of elites can be seen in the revolving doors between government and the likes of Goldman Sachs, arguably the largest multinational investment banking firm that deals in securities, investment management, and global finance; it is a central figure in marketing and dealing in U.S. Treasury funds. Many of its top-level personnel have served in major state positions. Robert Rubin, for example, was the U.S. Secretary of the Treasury during the Clinton administration, as was Henry Paulson during the George W. Bush Administration. Mark Patterson, Goldman Sachs lobbyist, became Treasury Secretary Timothy Geithner's chief of staff in the Obama administration. Former Goldman Sachs director Stephen Friedman became Chairman of the Federal Reserve Bank in New York in 2008. Others served in key international state positions. Mario Monti, for example, was the Prime Minister of Italy, and Mario Draghi was the Governor of the European Central Bank (Ferguson, 2012).

C. Wright Mills argued that the interchangeability of elites among the three most powerful institutions results in a fusion of views among leaders. They do not develop viewpoints and interests specific to one institution. When the power elite switch hats from one institutional realm to another, they bring with them their prejudices, their beliefs, and their interests. No seriously divisive viewpoints are expressed, then, among leaders. There is only one viewpoint, expressed by one group of people: the power elite. As such, the interests of Halliburton, the Pentagon, and the White House become fused into one set of common interests, each benefitting quite well from the war against Iraq that began in 2003. And the interests of Goldman Sachs, the White House, and the Pentagon become fused into one set of interests when the federal government bailed out banks during the severe economic recession beginning in 2008.

If one accepts that there is a power elite, what effect do its members have on the relationship between the state and the economy? According to some social scientists, their influence occurs through the actions of the **military-industrial complex.** What is the military-industrial complex? How does it affect the state and the economy?

The Military-Industrial Complex

The military-industrial complex is composed of the uniformed military, the aerospace-defense industry, the civilian national security managers, and the U.S. Congress (Pilisuk and Hayden, 1965; Hooks, 1991). Each of the components of the military-industrial complex works to advance its own interests while simultaneously promoting and reinforcing the interests of the others (Abdolali and Ward, 1998; Jones, 2001).

What does each of these components want? The uniformed military needs to maintain—and preferably expand—its capability to wage war. Its massive budgets enable it to conduct public relations campaigns portraying military goals as patriotic and justified (Herman and Chomsky, 1988; Wagner, 1989).

An even more influential component of the military-industrial complex is the corporate sector, particularly the large aerospace-defense industry. This industry supports military expenditures because it benefits from huge procurement contracts. In 2011, for example, U.S. military contracts totaled $377.6 billion, 39 percent of which went to just 10 U.S. corporations (www.govexec.com/magazine/2009/08/top-100-defense-contractors/29761../Local Settings/temp/7zO1D.tmp/www.cdi.org/issues/usmi/complex/top15fy99.html). Such sizable contracts guarantee substantial profits without the risks of the free market. After the end of the Cold War in the late 1980s, Congress reduced the growth of the military budget. However, the reductions did not return the military budget to pre-Cold War proportions. More importantly, Congress began to reverse these reductions by 1997, and by 2011 the total Department of Defense budget had grown to over $768 billion, more than any year since 1980 (www.census.gov).

The civilian national security managers support military spending because they tie American national security to access to global resources and markets and develop foreign policy with that goal in mind. These managers are influenced heavily by their backgrounds in large corporate firms. For example, Domhoff (2002:85) found that the Council on Foreign Relations (CFR) was dominated in 2000 by representatives of industrial corporations and financial institutions: 70 percent of the top 100 industrial corporations had at least one officer serving as a member of the CFR, as did 21 of the top 25 banks and 16 of the top 25 insurance companies. Not surprisingly, then, civilian national security managers' views on national security and foreign policy are consistent with those of corporate leaders.

Finally, members of Congress consistently grant the military a large proportion of the federal budget because doing so creates jobs for their voting constituents both in the military (on its hundreds of bases) and in the aerospace-defense industry (see www.census.gov). Furthermore, since members of Congress tend to be affluent, they are likely to be stockholders in major American corporations, including aerospace-defense contractors. And so are their major campaign contributors (Domhoff, 2009). The positions that representatives take, then, on defense spending may affect both their own personal wealth and their chances of getting reelected.

The primary interest unifying these components of the military-industrial complex is the protection of private profit making. For close to 50 years, U.S. military expenditures and foreign policy had been fueled by Cold War fears of communism. More recently, they have been influenced by fears that underdeveloped countries will restrict or eliminate U.S. access to crucial resources. At the same time, thousands of U.S. corporations have opened production facilities abroad, particularly in underdeveloped countries. But those countries characterized by widespread poverty and oppression are vulnerable to revolutions and popular support for socialist economic systems. These systems threaten capital-accumulation interests, because they may institute state control of production, nationalize industries, and restrict employers' exploitation of labor. Vast military expenditures have been devoted, then, to securing the political environment in which U.S. corporations operate abroad. This protection has often extended to U.S. military and paramilitary (for example, CIA) interventions in other countries, such as Chile in the 1970s, Nicaragua in the 1980s, Iraq in 1991 (and 2003), and the Balkans in the late 1990s.

Why are private capital-accumulation interests so important to the state? In 2011, the top 500 corporations identified by *Forbes Magazine* employed over 17 million workers in the United States, representing more than 12 percent of the total U.S. labor force. And they produced revenues of $10.8 trillion, the equivalent of nearly three-fourths of the entire national Gross Domestic Product (http://money.cnn.com/2011/05/04/news/companies/fortune500_top_50_walmart.fortune/index.htm; www.fortune.com/fortune/fortune500/giants.html). They also flexed their economic muscle that year by outsourcing over 2.4 million jobs over the previous decade (Jilani, 2011). These firms are clearly at the center of the nation's economic well-being. When they succeed in growing and in generating profits, the economy avoids stagnation, recession, or, worse, depression. Thus, as former Secretary of Defense and General Motors Chairman Charles E. Wilson once said, what's good for General Motors is good for the United States.

In order to grow, many major firms must expand their operations beyond the shores of the United States. When firms operate production and trade facilities in other countries, sociologists call them **multinational** (or **transnational**) **corporations.** Most of the money such corporations have invested abroad has gone to the economies of industrialized and post-industrialized countries where American corporations provide manufactured goods. The remaining investment capital has gone to Middle East countries rich in petroleum and to underdeveloped countries, where corporations can capitalize on inexpensive, nonunionized labor, lax or nonexistent environmental and labor laws, and various tax breaks. Since U.S.-based multinational corporations' earnings from their foreign operations account for 50 percent or more of their annual earnings, they want to be sure that the environment in which such earnings are produced is secure. Thus, the economic well-being of the United States depends significantly on U.S. corporations' ability to do business abroad.

Not coincidently, the ability of these firms to operate in other countries also gives them access to—and often control over—critical raw materials. These resources, needed in aerospace-defense industries, are often inaccessible or expensive to mine in the United States. Therefore, it is in both the economic and the military interests of the state to secure the safety of U.S. corporations that procure these materials in other countries and enable them to continue operations in times of political unrest.

The global expansion of U.S. capital-accumulation interests has been aided, then, by congressional willingness to provide tax dollars for military expenditures and by the foreign policy devised by civilian national security managers. These managers, typically drawn from business and finance circles, formulate foreign policy that is consistent with the need to protect corporations' foreign operations. For example, U.S. national security managers have supported economic and military aid to underdeveloped countries. Economic aid often requires the recipients to purchase goods and services from U.S. corporations. Military aid similarly requires the recipients to purchase military equipment and supplies produced by the U.S. aerospace-defense industry. This arrangement has enormous economic consequences for U.S. corporations: In 2011, U.S. arms manufacturers delivered $66.3 billion in weapons to over 170 countries the world over, more than three times as much as Russia, the second-largest arms exporter whose sales of $4.8 billion made it a distant second to the United States (Shanker, 2012). Overall, the United States alone supplied more than three-fourths of all the arms exported globally.

The Gulf Wars The power of the military-industrial complex was exercised forcefully in 1991, when the United States entered into the Gulf War against Iraq. Ostensibly, American intervention after Iraq's invasion of Kuwait was based on the need to maintain U.S. access to Kuwait's vast oil reserves. Yet U.S. national security managers had previously notified Iraq's Saddam Hussein that Iraq could settle its disputes with Kuwait in any manner that it saw fit. Why, then, did the United States, with the approval of Congress, go to war against Iraq?

In the aftermath of the war, it became clear that the big winners were the components of the military-industrial complex. One was the Raytheon Corporation, the manufacturer of the Patriot missiles, which became a military symbol of U.S. strength and resolve. The profits of Exxon and other oil corporations increased by an astonishing rate of 75 percent in just the first weeks of the war (Hayes, 1991). This is because the war created a disruption in oil production, thereby allowing U.S. oil corporations to sharply raise their prices. Other big winners included the military, which was facing vast budget cuts at the end of the Cold War against the Soviet Union. Finally, among the major winners were members of Congress whose home districts benefitted economically from the military buildup and the prospects of future orders for military hardware from several Middle East countries. Clearly, then–President George H. W. Bush benefitted from the Gulf war as well. His approval rating in the United States reached the highest point in his presidency, boosting his political capital a great deal. People in the United States and abroad perceived him as a strong, no-nonsense president and international leader. Many in the media characterized the Gulf War as an end to the "Viet Nam syndrome," wherein political leaders in the post–Vietnam era hesitated to become involved in international conflicts for fear of strong criticism and resistance in the United States. All components of the military-industrial complex, then, benefited handsomely from massive expenditures connected with the war with Iraq, even if the poor, the hungry, the homeless, the working-class unemployed, women, and schoolchildren in the United States, as well as non-elites in Iraq and Kuwait, did not.

It is not surprising, then, given these strong corporate, especially oil, interests tied to the Bush administration, to find the United States aggressively at war against Iraq in 2003. Some may argue that a war against Iraq was necessary for world security because of that country's previous use of chemical and biological weapons against the Kurds in 1991 and its supposed pursuit of nuclear weapons of mass destruction in 2002. However, no such weapons have been located, even after toppling Saddam Hussein and his administration. It is also notable that no such case about the need to protect the world against weapons of mass destruction has been made for war against North Korea, a state that has withdrawn from an international nuclear disarmament treaty and announced an expansion of its nuclear arsenal. One difference between these two countries is that Iraq controls huge oil supplies needed by the United States and the industrialized nations in which its multinational corporations have investments, and North Korea does not. Notice that Halliburton Corporation has alone been awarded the highly lucrative contract to rebuild Iraq in the aftermath of the war. And remember Halliburton's substantial connections to the George W. Bush administration: Vice President Dick Cheney was Halliburton's Chief Executive Officer before joining President Bush in the White House.

A Power Elite Analysis of the State and Economy Relationship

The discussion of the military-industrial complex illustrates the kinds of insights one can develop by using the power elite perspective. In contrast to pluralists, power elite theorists suggest that the state is not neutral or independent; it is heavily influenced by capital and corporate interests. Voting processes simply make the existing state *appear* legitimate; they channel people's energies into activities that appear to empower them but do not fundamentally challenge elites' interests. Electoral politics also distract people's attention from an understanding of the relationship between the state and the economy and therefore create the false security of believing that the state legislates for the common good.

It is noteworthy, too, that the power elite are typically white male Protestants educated at prestigious institutions. Analyzing the power elite in 2000, for example, Thomas R. Dye (2002) found that only 10 percent of the top 7,314 economic and political institutional positions in the power elite were filled by women, and people of color were almost nonexistent among the power elite, where African American representation was almost entirely restricted to high-level government positions but not chief executives in major American corporations. Dye also found that 54 percent of the corporate elite and 42 percent of the state elite were graduates of the 12 most exclusive private universities (2002:148). And more than two-thirds of the institutional elite were members of exclusive social clubs; more than one-third belonged to one or more of a few prestigious social clubs. Together, these data suggest a strong race, class, and gender bias among the power elite.

Given the combined processes of co-optation and class identity, it is not surprising to find evidence of an overwhelmingly white, male, relatively affluent network of individuals mentoring, supporting, and promoting new elites much like its existing members. Yet there is also evidence that this network is not powerful enough to be entirely closed; it is possible for someone outside the network to break into elite ranks. While there are still few women holding executive-level positions in the powerful institutions of society, it is reasonable to expect to see more women in these positions in the future. Note, however, that in spite of the limited progress of women and people of color as well as gays and lesbians in their representation among the power elite to date (with noticeable strides forward during the Obama years), there has been even less progress in terms of class: The power elite remain firmly drawn from among the most economically privileged in society (Zweigenhaft and Domhoff, 2006).

The evidence of increasing diversity in the power elite, however small thus far, points to a weakness in power elite theory: Mills mistakenly attributed a sense of omnipotence to the elite and therefore overlooked the dynamics of struggle and conflict identified in Chapter 10 that can affect the composition of the power elite. For example, the civil rights and feminist movements combined to open some opportunities for cooptation into the elite previously unavailable to anyone but white males.

Mills also assumed that the three main power elite institutions are equally significant, but he did not provide evidence supporting this equality. Nor did he provide a concrete analysis of how the main institutions of society operate together to produce an omnipotent institutional structure. Nonetheless, he opened up a lively debate with pluralist sociologists over power and its exercise at the national level.

VOTING: WHO PARTICIPATES?

Most people are not central actors in the power elite. How, then, do non-elites participate politically? Pluralists emphasize the importance of elections and voting. However, power elite theorists point out that while voters may elect some of the power elite, they do not elect all of the leaders (such as the Supreme Court), nor do they elect those who run the corporate economy and the uniformed military. Voters have no way to hold these nonelected elite leaders accountable. Pluralists assume that everyone agrees on how people are to behave politically and that the only acceptable means of affecting government is through electoral politics. But the norms of political behavior are determined by the people in power and the people who benefit most from the existing system. For example, regulations defining who may vote, based on residence qualifications, are determined by Congress, which is disproportionately populated by persons who are relatively advantaged. One must have a permanent address in order to qualify to vote. Thus, the homeless are systematically denied the right to participate in selecting the leaders whose decision making will affect their lives. Electoral politics may channel certain issues and problems into a controlled institutional arena, but what happens when elites consistently ignore some issues?

In any case, voters in the United States turn out in notoriously low numbers. As you can see in Figure 11.1, voting participation rates have steadily declined from an all-time high of around 63 percent in the 1960 national elections. By the 2008 presidential election, only 53.3 percent of the eligible voters actually participated (www.census.gov). Participation rates are even worse in state and local elections. In fact, the United States has one of the lowest voter participation rates

Figure 11.1   U.S. Voting Turnout, 1932–2012

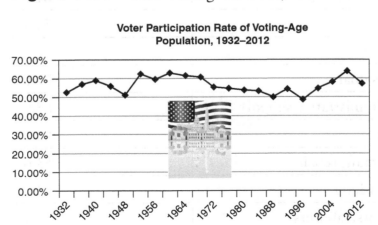

Voter Participation Rate of Voting-Age Population, 1932–2012

among industrialized capitalist democracies (only Switzerland has a lower rate) (Wattenberg, 2002). What do such poor voter turnouts in the United States mean?

Pluralists argue that the low rates indicate the population is satisfied with the existing leadership and feels no need to participate. When the electorate becomes dissatisfied, they argue, it will mobilize and vote to unseat the unsatisfactory political elites. To pluralists, then, low voter turnout rates suggest that the system is working and that voters are happy with the current state of affairs.

Table 11.2 shows the characteristics of persons who vote. Such data make it more difficult to accept the pluralist interpretation. Overwhelmingly the highest turnout rates occur within the higher-income, higher-education, and higher-status-occupation groups. And whites, as a group, tend to turn out more than people of color. One might interpret these data as evidence that people who benefit most from the status quo are more likely to participate in electoral politics than people whose interests are ignored and who are thus disadvantaged by it.

Some pluralists counter that it is good that the better-educated are the most likely to vote, since they are more likely than the poorly educated or illiterate to make intelligent choices and are not likely to be exploited by political extremists (Banfield and Wilson, 1963). Some also argue that the language skills of highly educated people and the political

Table 11.2   Characteristics Of Voters, 2010

Characteristic	Percentage Voting
Education	
Less than eighth grade	27.0%
Some high school	37.8
High school graduate	54.0
Some college	65.5
Bachelor's degree or higher	72.5
Labor Force Status	
Employed	61.5
Unemployed	52.3
Occupation [a, b]	
Managerial, professional	79.0
Technical, sales, administrative support	68.0
Service occupations	52.2
Precision product, craft, repair	53.6
Farming, forestry, fishing	54.2
Operators, fabricators, laborers	46.4

Income [c]	
Under $10,000	41.3
$10,000–$14,999	41.2
$15,000–$19,999	44.3
$20,000–$29,999	48.0
$30,000–$39,999	54.4
$40,000–$49,999	58.2
$50,000–$74,999	65.9
$75,000–$99,999	72.6
$100,000–$149,999	74.9
$150,000 +	78.1
Race	
White	61.6
African American	58.8
Latino/a	33.8
Sex	
Male	57.9
Female	61.5

[a] www.census.gov/population/socdemo/voting/cps1998

[b] These data are for 1992; the Census Bureau did not report out this characteristic for 2000

[c] Data for 2008 election; Source: http://ddoublep.wordpress.com/2012/01/18/organization-and-voting-matters/

Sources: www.census.gov

skills entailed in high-status occupations easily translate into the skills required to participate effectively in electoral politics. Others argue that political participation (particularly those activities that go beyond voting) requires a great deal of time, money, and energy—resources that the poor and working class are not likely to have in great quantities (Lipset, 1960).

Critics of pluralism point out that the electoral system is set up to *discourage* some people from participating. Registration and voting procedures raise mechanical obstacles to participation by the poor, the working class, and the poorly educated. Indeed, registration rates for African Americans and Latino/as, as well as the poor, have tended to lag behind those of whites and more affluent groups. Deliberate bureaucratic obstructions hinder efforts to register voters of color and the poor, including states' failure to deputize registrars or to set up registration posts at satellite locations and the lack of bilingual registration and election forms. Indeed, during the 2008 presidential election, when registration rates of African American and Latino/a voters showed encouraging signs of increases, some states engaged in deliberate campaigns to suppress votes in election districts with large numbers of voters of color (e.g., Florida officials admitted to having engaged in such efforts). In addition, the confusion associated with absentee ballots (for students, migrant workers, and military personnel), poorly phrased and confusing legalistic jargon on referenda, confusing appearances of ballots (such as the infamous "butterfly" ballots in Florida in the 2000 elections), hostility at registration and voting sites toward voters of color, repeated reallocations of voting districts, and endless primaries all serve to reduce participation rates among those groups (Piven and Cloward, 2000).

Taken together, these analyses of differential participation suggest that there are numerous reasons why the advantaged are more likely to vote than the disadvantaged. Yet, an examination of who does *not* vote reveals that nonparticipation cuts across all categories, including the more advantaged groups: Substantial segments of even the most advantaged groups still do not vote. And even greater numbers refrain from other forms of political participation as well. What does such nonparticipation mean?

A likely explanation for the lack of a pattern in the social background characteristics of nonvoters is that there is a great deal of disaffection and alienation among a wide variety of people within the existing political system (Boggs, 2000; Conway, 2000; Harrigan, 2000). When Marx spoke of **alienation** as an overwhelming sense of normlessness, powerlessness, and meaninglessness, he was referring to workers' estrangement from their work (Marx, 1844/1964; see also Seeman, 1959). But alienation can also affect people's political behavior. For many people, electoral politics simply does not address their interests or their needs. Why, then, should they vote? One survey suggested a reason people might not think voting makes any difference is because they do not have confidence in the leadership of elected officials: In a 2010 public opinion survey, 88 percent of the respondents agreed that "Politicians from both parties go to Washington and pursue their own party's agenda—ignoring the needs of regular citizens and the country" (Democracy Corps/Campaign for America's Future Poll, November 2010). Another survey found that 62 percent of respondents agreed that "elected officials don't care what people like me think" (Democracy Corps/Women's Voices, March 2012). Census data also indicate a similar erosion of confidence in leaders: 47 percent of respondents said they had "very little confidence" in Congress, and another 5 percent indicated that they had "none" (Gallup Poll, June 2012).

In addition, many people may feel alienated from electoral politics because voting occurs in the political process long after many important decisions have already occurred without their participation. Most people do not participate in selecting party candidates, nor do they get to determine the campaign issues. And the candidates from which they may choose on Election Day bear such strong similarities to each other as to present very little difference, either in their social background characteristics or in their ideological positions. However, this did change during the 2008 presidential election, when Barack Obama became the first African American candidate, and ultimately president of the United States. That shift did, in fact, appear to energize and galvanize large numbers of previously disenfranchised voters of color and younger voters to participate.

Political alienation is not the same thing as **apathy.** When people are apathetic, they do not care what the outcome is. When people are politically alienated, they care about the outcome but do not feel that the system is fair or just. Why are people alienated? They are alienated in part because the way the system actually works is not the way they were taught that it is *supposed* to work. Modern political history has contributed to voter alienation. The Vietnam era imbued a generation with the realization that elected officials could conduct a war against the wishes of vast segments of the population. Several government scandals—including Watergate in the Nixon era, the Iran-Contra affair of the Reagan administration, the Whitewater investigation and sexual scandals of the Clinton administration, and, more recently, questions surrounding vote counts in the Bush/Gore presidential election in 2000—indicated to voters that political elites are less trustworthy and ethical than one would like to believe. Thus, although people are taught that voting is the means by which they can hold elected officials accountable, and that voting is the exercise of power, their experiences suggest that voting is not necessarily an effective way to control political elites or to get them to address their concerns.

Critics of pluralism point out that the electoral process involves far more than simply voting. Campaign formation, candidate selection, and the party agenda are important aspects of the electoral process that occur before anyone enters the voting booth in November (Domhoff, 2009). The participants at these early stages of the electoral process are likely to be persons already advantaged by the system as well as active members of one of the two major parties. Party candidates have typically come up through the ranks of the party organization. The party is not likely to champion outsiders and challengers to the system because they have not invested loyalty, time, money, energy, and work in the party organization.

Moreover, the huge expense of running a campaign usually means that aspiring candidates will try to articulate positions that attract the support of powerful interests. It is not surprising, for example, that Bill Clinton received the enthusiastic support of the computer industry in his 1992 presidential campaign after he forcefully advocated developing an expansive "information superhighway." The computer and communications industries stood to gain huge profits from such a project. Nor was it surprising to see presidential candidate Mitt Romney in 2012 receive massive campaign support from some of the most affluent members of the corporate class: They stood to gain a great deal from Romney's insistence on protecting the huge tax advantages of the wealthiest members of society while proposing major reductions in spending on social support programs that benefit the poor and working and middle classes. Thus, political elites are most likely to listen and respond to the interests of privileged groups, particularly corporations and affluent individuals, during candidate selection and campaign planning.

Even when third party candidates emerge, expressing interests ignored by candidates representing the two major parties, voters often are discouraged from voting for them: In a two-party system where the winner takes all, voting for third party candidates may steal votes from one of the major candidates and throw the election to the more objectionable of the two. Indeed, notice the energy that the Democratic Party invested in reminding the growing number of supporters of Ralph Nader in the 2000 presidential election that a vote for Nader would take votes away from the Democratic candidate Al Gore and therefore strengthen the likelihood that Republican George W. Bush would get elected. That threat served to remind many voters to stay away from Nader and vote for Gore. It may very well have also served to discourage alienated citizens from participating altogether.

The 2000 presidential elections also may have alienated voters, especially people of color, because of the unusual circumstances in Florida. Thousands of ballots, particularly in voting districts with heavy populations of people of color, remained uncounted because the use of cardboard punch ballots produced unclear results when "chads" (the piece of cardboard that gets pushed out to select a candidate) did not fully break off. Many ballots in these districts were designed in a side-by-side butterfly fashion that seriously confused voters as to which chad corresponded with which candidate. And many people of color complained that they were harassed by police as they waited in line to vote or were told by election monitors that they were at the wrong voting district and could not vote there. Together, the irregularities in Florida caused a long delay in declaring a presidential winner there for weeks while the courts attempted to deal with the problem. Ultimately, it was the Supreme Court, not the voters, who decided the winner in Florida. In a very tight presidential race, Florida's electoral votes would determine the outcome of the national election; in essence, the Supreme Court appointed the president by declaring a winner of the state. Many voters became quite cynical in the aftermath of the 2000 elections, a cynicism that could easily translate into political alienation that appeared in lower participation rates in the 2004 election; it wasn't until the campaign of Barack Obama in 2008 that disenfranchised voters of color as well as alienated younger voters were once again energized to participate with the prospect of the first candidate of color to run in a presidential election. In that election, African American, Latino/a, and Asian voters accounted for 22 percent of those who voted, a significant increase from the 12 percent who voted in 1988. It was clear that Obama's candidacy was elemental in altering the political alienation that was previously evident among voters of color and younger voters (Chen and Reeves, 2009; Roberts and Schostak, 2012). By 2012, the changing demographics of the United States began to have a noticeable effect: Participation rates of African Americans and Latino/as held at 23 percent (Pew Research Center, 2012).

Some saw the election of Obama as a sign that the United States had become a "post-racial" society, where people's racialized identity no longer mattered and where racism was no longer an issue. However, there is compelling evidence that a deep racialized divide persists and remains highly charged. For example, a *New York Times*/CBS poll indicated that 73 percent of Tea Party members agreed that Obama "does not understand the needs and problems of people like yourself," and 75 percent agreed that he does not share the values of most Americans. Even more telling was that 52 percent agreed that "in recent years too much has been made of the problems facing black people," and 60 percent believed that "white people and black people have an equal chance of getting ahead" (*New York Times*/CBS, 2010).

Who are the Tea Party members? Twenty-eight percent of the people in the United States define themselves as Tea Party members, and 79 percent of the members were "non-Hispanic white"; 55 percent of them had annual incomes of $50,000 or more, and 65 percent had at least some college education (Saad, 2010). Far from a "post-racial" society in which racialized identity no longer matters, it appears that the election of a biracial or African American president reinforced racialized political alienation, at least among a significant portion of white, educated middle-class people (Glasberg and Shannon, 2011:107–110).

In addition to racialized politics stoking political alienation among marginalized voters, we can also see inconsistencies between the objectives of privileged voters and those of the masses in the kind of legislation that is passed, a disconnect that can make voters feel they are not heard. For example, Richard Hamilton (1972) found that during the 1950s and 1960s, most people in the working and middle classes in the United States supported the expansion of federal social welfare programs. Yet legislators consistently opposed efforts to expand such programs. Then, too, polls indicated that 63 percent of people in the United States favored the equal rights amendment (ERA) to the U.S. constitution, which would prohibit discrimination on the basis of sex. Yet the ERA was not passed because constitutional amendments require ratification by two-thirds, or 38, of the nation's state legislatures and only 35 states were willing to approve it (*Time*, 1982a, 1982b).

The class bias of elected officials also dilutes the power of voting. Members of the nation's political elite tend to come overwhelmingly from economically advantaged backgrounds (Dye, 2002; Zweigenhaft and Domhoff, 2006), partly because it is very costly to prepare for and run large campaigns. Once elected, these privileged persons are not likely to be sympathetic to the views of the disadvantaged, such as the poor, the homeless, and other groups considered marginal in U.S. society.

Our discussion of the limits of electoral politics suggests that the state and the economy are not actually separate, distinct institutions. What is the relationship between these two institutions in a capitalist system, and how does it affect individuals' daily lives?

THE STATE IN CAPITALIST SOCIETY

The discussion of the power elite and the analysis of the military-industrial complex suggest significant ways in which the state and the economy operate together in a society dominated by corporate interests. Sociologists do not necessarily agree, however, on the nature and meaning of their intersection. In *The Communist Manifesto*, Karl Marx and Friedrich Engels (1967:18) argued that "the executive of the modern state is but a committee for managing the common affairs of the whole bourgeoisie," the bourgeoisie being the capitalist business owners. Their observation has become a centerpiece of debate among various sociologists, who have engaged a spirited debate over what Marx and Engels meant: Why and how might the state manage the common affairs of capitalists? Three main theories of the state have wrestled with this question: *business dominance theory*, *capitalist state structuralist theory*, and *class dialectic theory*.

Business Dominance Theory

Business dominance theory extends the analysis of power elite theory by arguing that the state is not a neutral arbiter of the common good because the capitalists either "capture" the state or dominate it to use it as their instrument (Miliband, 1969). Capitalists may capture the state and take control of it by entering key leadership positions themselves in Congress, the White House, and the Cabinet (Useem, 1984; Dye, 2002). Or they may dominate the state by using campaign financing to gain favored access to and applying pressure on elected officials (Clawson, Neustadtl, and Weller, 1998). Capitalists may also greatly influence the state by filling positions in key advisory, regulatory, or policy committees, such as the Council on Foreign Relations, a nationally influential private organization that advises the president and Congress on foreign policy (Burris, 1992; Domhoff, 2009).

Business dominance theorists argue that the state is not free of **capitalist interests,** that is, individuals and organizations that benefit from amassing and maintaining private profits. Business dominance theorists note that the people making decisions in the name of the state are either capitalists themselves or politicians who may be beholden to them because of their massive campaign contributions. This analysis implies that it is the capitalist mentality of individuals who fill key governmental positions that determines the role of the state in capitalist society.

Capitalist State Structuralist Theory

Advocates of **capitalist state structuralist theory** agree with business dominance theorists that the state is not a neutral arbiter of the common good (Poulantzas, 1973; Jessop, 1990). But they take issue with the focus on individuals. Structuralists argue that an economy based on capitalism *forces* the state to shape its policies in ways that are consistent with capital-accumulation interests because the fate of the state rests on the economy's health. The state needs to collect taxes for social programs to discourage unrest and make its existence legitimate in the eyes of the citizenry. But it must often legislate in favor of capital-accumulation interests rather than social programs because to do otherwise would be to damage the health of the economy on which the state depends (O'Connor, 1987, 1996). The state, then, is not simply subject to the whims of individual political leaders; the needs of the corporate capitalist economy forces the state to legislate in ways that support private profit making at almost any cost or risk economic collapse. Therefore, changes in personnel in political offices do not alter the types of decisions that the state makes. State decisions will be consistent with the interests of capitalists, regardless of who is elected to fill state offices.

The influence of the economic structure on the legislative process can be seen in laws passed by the state that ostensibly control the capitalist sector but may in fact function to advance its interests. For example, a law deregulating the banking industry in 1982 prompted pronounced concentration of that industry into fewer banking institutions as larger banks could now take over smaller ones. The legislation also spawned the savings and loan (S&L) crisis of the late 1980s and the mortgage and foreclosure crisis that sparked the deep recession of 2008–2012. **Deregulation** is the process of removing or significantly relaxing government restrictions on industries. In the case of the banking industry, deregulation removed the structural and legal constraints that kept large commercial banks and smaller S&L institutions from competing against each other by limiting them to do business in different markets. Previously, S&L institutions had been legally restricted to providing low-cost home mortgages and offering low interest rates on deposits. Following deregulation, the two types of financial organizations began to compete against each other, to the decided advantage of the large commercial banks. In order to attract depositors from the commercial banks, S&L institutions offered dramatically higher interest rates on deposits but continued to collect low rates on old mortgages. That meant they were bringing in less money than they were paying out. In addition, deregulation permitted S&L institutions to engage in speculative investments that had previously been prohibited. These investments, particularly in real estate, crashed in the late 1980s, causing many S&Ls to go bankrupt. And there were now far fewer field supervisors to regularly audit the S&L institutions' books to ensure that prudent investments were being made. The lack of supervision encouraged a great deal of fraud to occur in the industry as standard operating procedure (what Calavita and Pontell, 1991, called ***collective embezzlement***).

Before long the unwise speculative investments and the shortfalls between high-interest payouts on deposits and low-interest incomes on mortgage loans caught up with the S&L

institutions, a massive national crisis erupted in the industry (Glasberg and Skidmore, 1997). Many S&L institutions failed and had to close down, leaving the government to cover their debts in the largest government bailout of private corporations and the first government bailout of an entire industry. The cost to taxpayers has proven to be immense.

More recently, deregulation of the banking industry enabled banks to engage in practices of predatory lending, in which they aggressively sought to place highly risky "balloon" mortgage instruments with people of color and poor people that ultimately resulted in millions of people losing their homes. The firestorm of foreclosures touched off deep and protracted economic recession because the severe slowdown in home construction rippled through the lumber, glass, brick, construction, plumbing, electrical, textile, durable goods, and transportation industries.

This saga of the S&L collapse and the severe mortgage and foreclosure crisis illustrates how laws passed by the state to deregulate the banking industry resulted in further concentrating the industry in fewer hands (particularly large commercial banks). This unfettered concentration of banking business advanced the interests of the largest members of the industry at the expense of working people (who relied on the S&Ls for affordable mortgages) and taxpayers (who had to pay for the bailout).

Class Dialectics and the State

Some sociologists challenge both the business dominance theorists and the capitalist state structuralists on the grounds that they tend to focus only on relations between elites in the state and in the economy and fail to examine how these relations affect and are affected by the rest of society, especially the working class. Sociologists using a **class dialectic perspective** focus on the dynamics of conflict between the working class and the capitalist class. They point to how this conflict at times results in compromises in state policy, some of which may not necessarily be in the best interests of capitalists (Levine, 1988; Quadagno and Meyer, 1989; Wysong, 1993). They ask, if the state is captured, controlled, or influenced either by members of the capitalist class itself (business dominance theory) or by the structure of the capitalist economic system that favors them (structuralist theory), how is it possible to periodically get legislation passed that favors workers or that disadvantages capitalists? For example, how is it possible to have laws guaranteeing workers the right to form unions and collectively bargain with capitalists? How is it that there have been policies increasing social welfare expenditures and expanding social welfare programs, such as the New Deal in the 1930s and the War on Poverty in the 1960s? How was any legislation regulating industries such as banks, railroads, trucks and the like, possible?

Class dialectic theorists argue that the state is the arena in which class struggles are played out. Social welfare programs (such as unemployment insurance, income support programs, food stamps, Medicare, and Medicaid), and the legal protection of workers' rights (such as the right to collective bargaining and laws protecting worker health and safety) are outcomes of prolonged struggles in that arena. According to class dialectic theorists, these outcomes actually exemplify the state's willingness to address working-class interests in order to protect capital-accumulation interests.

For example, during the late 1800s and early 1900s, workers in the United States began to press forcefully for the right to unionize. They faced serious challenges and concerted opposition by capital-accumulation interests. Capitalists fired workers who were active in organizing attempts and hired private police and paramilitary forces to beat and shoot striking workers. Sometimes, as in the cases of the Pullman railway workers' strike in 1893 and countless coal miners' strikes (particularly in the 1930s), the state sent in armed troops to quash workers' organizing efforts (Sexton, 1991). The state used various methods to undermine and discredit labor leaders. In a glaring case, Joe Hill, a leader in the International Workers of the World, was arrested for committing a murder that no one had witnessed; although no evidence ever connected Hill to the murder, he was incarcerated and eventually executed in 1915 for the crime (Foner, 1965).

At the same time, deplorable working conditions and oppressive treatment made socialism an increasingly attractive alternative for many workers. Under socialism, workers would control their working conditions. Much debate occurred within Congress and among capitalists. Capitalists abhorred collectively bargaining with workers' unions, but the threat of socialism was even more repugnant. Many understood that socialism would become much more attractive to workers who were denied the right to unionize. Collective bargaining came to be seen as the lesser of two evils. Finally, with the grudging approval of many elites in the corporate community, Congress passed the Wagner Act in 1934, guaranteeing workers the right to unionize (Weinstein, 1968; Zinn, 2010). Thus, workers' struggles with capitalists were fought out in the arena of the state, with the state acting not as an unbiased judge but as an advocate for the long-run interests of the capitalist class. The business dominance and structuralist perspectives would find it difficult to explain the state's behavior in these situations, unlike the class dialectic perspective.

THE STATE AND POLITICAL ECONOMY: NEW FEDERALISM AND WELFARE "REFORM"

We have seen that the state may be viewed as the central arena in which struggles between the interests of labor and those of capital accumulators are acted out. Organized struggles in the 1950s and 1960s succeeded in gaining many civil rights, anti-poverty, education and job training, and health programs. But since the late 1970s the state has restructured the economy more straightforwardly in favor of business interests and to the disadvantage of labor, as well as the poor, women, children, and people of color. Two key restructuring projects were the New Federalism of the 1980s and welfare reform of the 1990s.

New Federalism

What came to be called **New Federalism** was based on the conservative political philosophy that the federal government should be involved only with taxation and national defense; all else, particularly social welfare programs, should be the responsibility of state and local governments. Under New Federalism battles previously won by disadvantaged groups would have to be fought again in the future.

New Federalism began quietly in the late 1970s under President Jimmy Carter. The state responded to an ailing economy by lowering federal social welfare expenditures, reducing the burden of taxes on the wealthy in the attempt to stimulate increased saving and investment, and relaxing or eliminating federal regulation of corporations. The goal of New Federalism was to regulate the economy to the advantage of businesses, particularly large corporations. The assumption was that firms would reinvest their increased profits to improve productive capacity, thereby creating new jobs. President Ronald Reagan greatly expanded this approach, which came to be called **supply-side,** or **trickle-down, economics.** Its supporters argued that benefits to capitalists would trickle down to benefit labor; eventually everyone would benefit from New Federalism: "A rising tide raises all ships" was the supply-siders' motto.

In practice, though, some ships sank. Tax cuts instituted under President Reagan in the 1980s greatly benefited the wealthy and large corporations who did not reinvest their newfound wealth in job creation but instead invested it in stocks and other investment instruments that enriched themselves. Meanwhile, the economy continued to suffer, increasing the ranks of the poor, the hungry, and the homeless. While their needs grew, some social welfare and entitlement programs originally designed to catch economic victims in a federal safety net were slashed; others' eligibility requirements were redefined to reduce the number of people the programs served (Abramovitz, 1996).

Critics decried the New Federalism as a "mean season" attack against the welfare state and a massive attempt to dismantle it (Block et al, 1987; Piven and Cloward, 1982). The effect of the state's twist on Robin Hood could be seen on the individual level. Overall, the economic distance between the wealthy and poor in the nation widened to a gap unseen since the Great Depression in the 1930s. As Figure 11.2 shows, the average family income of the poorest 20 percent of the U.S. population declined by 10 percent between 1967 and 2000, while the average family income of the wealthiest 20 percent increased during the same period by 13.2 percent. More strikingly, the average family income of the wealthiest 5 percent increased more than 20 percent (U.S. Census Bureau, 2001). New Federalism had succeeded in redistributing income from the poorest to the wealthiest.

New Federalism particularly impoverished women. While women's share of jobs in the labor force increased during the 1980s, their share of poverty increased quite dramatically as

Figure 11.2:   The New Federalism
And Changes In Average Family Incomes,
1979–2010 (In 2011 Dollars)

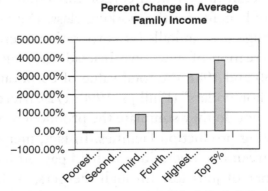

Source: Page 59 in Lawrence Mishel, Josh Bivens, Elise Gould, and Heidi Shierholz, 2012. *The State of Working America, 12th edition.* Ithaca, NY: ILR Press.

well. This was because the vast majority of new jobs created were minimum-wage, part-time service sector jobs with no health care or retirement benefits. Even if a mother of three worked full-time, year-round at the minimum wage, she would not be able to make enough on her own to rise above the federal poverty line. Working part-time guaranteed that both she and her children would be entrenched in poverty, be hungry, and possibly be homeless. If she did not have a wage-earning partner, a mother was likely to face impoverishment. Single-parent families increased from 13 percent of the total number of families in 1970 to 29.7 percent in 1992, and most of these were female-headed. While the median family income of married couples increased 9 percent between 1980 and 1993, the median income of female-headed households actually declined by 1.7 percent (U.S. Bureau of the Census, 1994). Thus, while the overall rate of poverty in the United States in 1993 was 15.1 percent, the rate of poverty among female-headed families was an astounding 35.6 percent (compared with a rate of 16.8 percent for male-headed families) (U.S. Bureau of the Census, 1994).

New Federalism also disproportionately hurt people of color. The poverty rate for whites in 1993 was 12.2 percent, but the rate for African Americans was 33.1 percent and for Latinos/as, 30.6 percent (U.S. Bureau of the Census, 1994). According to the Bureau of Labor Statistics, African Americans were more than twice as likely as whites to be unemployed in 1992, and Latinos/as were almost twice as likely. The gap between African Americans and whites in terms of wealth and median family income widened, regardless of education levels.

People with disabilities were also targeted by the New Federalism. The federal government reduced its financial responsibilities by redefining eligibility standards and reformulating the budgeting for disabilities programs. For example, greater financial responsibility for the education of children with disabilities was shifted to states and local communities, whose already-strapped budgets could not make up the shortfall of federal contributions. By 1984 the federal share of community-based services for people with disabilities had dropped to 7 percent, down from 45 percent, leaving state and local governments to make up the difference. In 1984, 70 percent of total public spending on community-based services for people with disabilities came from state-level funds. Income maintenance programs for people with disabilities declined 2 percent between 1985 and 1987 (Castellani, 1987: 43). It quickly became clear that the federal safety net had gaping holes through which the poor and people with disabilities could easily fall.

Meanwhile, the New Federalism benefited corporations quite well without producing the much-heralded expectation of benefits for the working class. Deregulation of industries, relaxation of antitrust laws, and huge tax windfalls for corporations were supposed to increase productivity and stimulate the creation of new jobs. Instead, they fueled more than a decade of merger mania. Between 1980 and 1988 the total value of corporate mergers and acquisitions "exceeded two thirds of a trillion dollars" (Phillips, 1990: 172). Mergers and acquisitions do not increase productive capacity, nor do they stimulate the production of any new jobs; they simply reshuffle who owns the existing production facilities. In fact, mergers often entail job loss, as the acquiring firm tries to streamline operations to help pay off its debt. While there is little documentation of the number of jobs lost through mergers, AFL-CIO Secretary-Treasurer Thomas Donahue testified before Congress that an estimated 80,000 union jobs were lost as a direct result of mergers and another 80,000 as an indirect result (*National Journal*, 1989). His estimate is conservative, since it does not include the number of nonunion jobs lost through mergers. Corporations were using their increased profits from New Federalism policies to buy one another out, not to create new jobs. The rising economic tide was not raising all ships. Only the largest corporations were rising; smaller businesses were capsizing. Between 1985 and 1992, there were 533,000 small-business failures, a significantly larger number than in previous years (Federal News Service, 1993).

These attempts to dismantle the welfare state continued through the 1990s under welfare reform.

Welfare Reform

The Personal Responsibility Act of 1996, more familiarly known as "welfare reform," dramatically changed how public assistance is administered and gave individual states far greater flexibility in determining how such programs would be implemented. Key provisions in the national policy included a sharp reduction in benefit amounts as well as reductions in length of time over a lifetime recipients would be permitted to collect (the Act established a national limit of five years, but 22 states have since instituted far more stringent time restrictions). Recipients must find paid employment in order to continue to be eligible for assistance (Beaulieu, 1998). These reforms were based on the stereotype of the lazy "welfare queen" who continued to live off the public dole indefinitely, refusing to work, having more children in order to increase her benefits, and acting as a financial drain on public resources (Sidel, 2000).

That stereotype, however, never matched the reality: Relatively few recipients ever actually remained very long on welfare (over 70 percent received welfare assistance for less than two years, and only 8 percent remained on welfare for over eight years); the average family size of welfare recipients, at two children, was no larger than the average middle-class family size and more than 75 percent of welfare recipients had three children or fewer; and most welfare recipients are not lazy people who refuse to work, but instead are women who have lost jobs or who work at low-wage jobs that fail to provide income above the poverty level (Seccombe, 1999; U.S. Department of Commerce, Census Bureau, 1999). These facts did not dissuade those in Congress who were intent on further dismantling social welfare programs.

When welfare reform was implemented, the number of people on public assistance or welfare dropped sharply. The assumption has been that this decline indicates the success of the program of weaning those who have grown dependent on the state by forcing them to get jobs. But the question remains: Where did these former welfare recipients go? Are they off the welfare rolls because they are now gainfully employed? Has welfare reform thus served to significantly reduce poverty? The answer to both questions apparently is "no." Many former recipients have simply run out of benefits, but have been without an opportunity to complete education or training programs to secure decent jobs. Others have jobs, but these are minimum wage or low-paying jobs that often carry few or no benefits (Casey, 1998; Abramovitz, 2000; Neubeck, 2006). The Urban Institute found, for example, that 61 percent of welfare recipients had jobs after leaving welfare, but they were earning a median wage of $6.61 per hour, and fewer than one-fourth of them had medical benefits from their jobs (Gault and Um'rani, 2000).

Evidence from individual states confirms the finding that welfare reform is not reducing poverty, even if it is reducing the number of people receiving welfare assistance. The Wisconsin Works (W-2) program reduced welfare roles by half in three years, but most participants have remained in poverty: One-fourth of those who left welfare returned for cash assistance, and half of those who found jobs are earning so little they remain below the poverty line (www.legis.state. wi.us/lab/reports/01-7full.pdf). A mother of two working full time, year round at a minimum wage job simply does not have enough income to move her family above the poverty line, and the loss of benefits such as medical care compounds the poverty. Other former recipients have simply disappeared out of the system, perhaps to the streets among the homeless.

Among the hardest hit by welfare reform has been women of color and their children. This is partly because Latinas and African American women "are more vulnerable to poverty than white women," having higher rates of both poverty and unemployment. Researchers attribute this racial disparity to educational disadvantages and both gender and racial discrimination by employers (Gault and Um'rani, 2000:2; see also Neubeck, 2006). Many states have compounded the likelihood of continued poverty among former welfare recipients, particularly among women of color and children: In their enthusiasm for welfare reform, they have failed to inform recipients and the working poor who leave welfare that they or their children are still eligible for programs like Food Stamps, Medicaid, housing assistance, and the like (Houppert, 1999).

Evidence strongly indicates, then, that welfare reform and the significant cuts in antipoverty programs under the New Federalism have served to intensify poverty, particularly among women, children, people of color, and people with disabilities (Schram and Beer, 1999). Programs such as welfare reform and the New Federalism are based on the assumption that the capitalist economy has the ability to solve social problems like poverty. However, an economy that increasingly offers minimum wage service work with no benefits as the only real option to the poor, and which does not seriously address discrimination in employment and education opportunities or the need for a living wage, is in no position to reduce structured economic inequality (Blau, 1999; Huber and Kosser, 1999; Eitzen and Baca Zinn; 2000).

Dismantling the Welfare State?

As much as the New Federalism and welfare reform have clearly contributed to a growing gap between rich and poor, between men and women, and between whites and people of color, it is important to note that these policy changes do not necessarily represent a dismantling of the welfare state. This is because these programs together constitute only one part of the welfare state, namely **social welfare,** which includes state policies and budgetary expenditures that redistribute wealth from the affluent to the poor in order to subsidize the needs of the poor and people with disabilities. There are two other components of the welfare state, however, and these remained largely untouched or even enhanced under the New Federalism. They are *gilded welfare* and *corporate welfare*.

Gilded welfare involves state policies and budgetary expenditures to redistribute wealth from the poor and working class to the middle class and the affluent. These include Social Security, Medicare, federal income tax deductions for homeownership and local property taxes, dependent children tax deductions, and home business tax deductions. While much of media and public attention has focused on social welfare expenditures, the fact is that gilded welfare spending far outweighs social welfare spending. For example, in 2011 the federal government spent over $1.3 trillion on gilded welfare programs (not including middle class and affluent tax deductions and allowances), but only $622.7 billion on antipoverty programs (www.census.gov). That means that social welfare spending represented slightly more than 16 percent of the total federal spending. Despite the media and popular perceptions that social welfare represented a drain on the federal budget, it certainly appears to be a very small slice of that pie.

Even more expensive have been the **corporate welfare** expenditures. Corporate welfare involves the state policies and expenditures that redistribute wealth to corporations and the affluent by directly or indirectly subsidizing, supporting, rescuing, or otherwise socializing the cost and risk of investment and private profit making. These include subsidies to industries such as agriculture, tax abatements, depreciation allowances for equipment, Department of Defense spending that provides guaranteed markets at noncompetitive prices, and corporate bailouts. Taken together, the corporate welfare programs represent an enormous slice of the federal budget. For example, bailout of the savings and loan industry in the late 1980s represented a massive federal commitment of taxpayers' money to subsidizing the risks of profit making in private savings and loan institutions and rescuing those that had failed as a result of investing in junk bonds and real estate speculation. The bailout itself represented a major increase in corporate welfare: Although the federal government has bailed out over 400 individual corporations since World War II (Lockheed and Chrysler among the largest), it had never before agreed to bail out an entire industry. And while previous bailouts were limited to fixed amounts over a clearly defined and relatively short time period, the savings-and-loan bailout occurred with no discussion of a limited dollar amount and no mention of a specified limited time period. This was, in fact, the first time any corporate entity was bailed out with a "blank check." And what a blank check it has been: The program has not concluded its bailouts and has thus far cost at least $250 billion. Estimates are that the total cost could reach as high as $500 billion before it is over (see Glasberg and Skidmore, 1997). Compare this expense of a single corporate welfare program to the entire budget of 1990s antipoverty expenditures, at a mere $117 billion, and it becomes clearer that the welfare state for the affluent and non-needy is, indeed, alive and well, and growing every day.

What occurred during the 1980s and 1990s was not so much a dismantling of the welfare state but more of a redistribution of resources from social welfare to gilded and corporate welfare. Indeed, when one considers the huge state expenditures devoted to corporate welfare programs, it becomes evident that, far from dismantling the welfare state, the New Federalism had resulted in an expanded welfare state, but one more devoted to corporate and gilded welfare than to social welfare. The state has never been neutral in the struggle between capital-accumulation interests and those of workers, the poor, women, people of color, people with disabilities, and children. New Federalism and the attacks on social welfare it unleashed succeeded in promoting legislation and budgeting practices that unabashedly favored capitalists and redistributed wealth from the poor and workers to the wealthy and corporations. Even conservatives like Kevin Phillips (1990, 1993) could not argue that this was in the common good.

And corporate welfare expanded once again during the recession of 2008–2012, when the federal TARP program bailed out banks' losses from predatory lending practices and subsidized banks' collective profit making with little regard for the fact that their behavior had in fact ignited that severe recession. Worse yet, the bailout occurred without the federal government insisting on the imposition of new regulations to keep track of its investment as a condition of banks receiving TARP money. Incredibly enough, banks blatantly provided huge bonuses to their executives after receiving their share of TARP money, the very same executives who oversaw the bank practices that sent the nation into an economic tailspin. Mean season, indeed. It remains to be seen if the second Obama administration can impose new controls on banks and reverse the redistribution of wealth from the poor and working and middle classes to the more affluent class that has occurred under the New Federalism.

 CHAPTER SUMMARY

- Political and economic institutions intersect in very powerful ways in the United States, a capitalist society dominated by the presence of large corporations.

- The state hardly seems to be a neutral arbiter, balancing competing demands of various interest groups and legislating in the common good. Rather, it is a very active participant in class struggles and frequently legislates in favor of capital-accumulation interests.

- At times, when groups of the disadvantaged press for change, the state finds ways to incorporate their demands as long as capitalist interests are not adversely affected. Indeed, reforms may serve to legitimate and stabilize the capitalist system.

- Even voting, which would seem to be the mechanism by which everyone, regardless of race, gender, income, occupation, or education, could participate in the political economy, does not appear to level the playing field. Participants in the political process are disproportionately likely to be individuals who are already advantaged by the existing political economy, and their participation increases the likelihood of protecting and maintaining their advantage relative to others.

- The state is not able to escape the influence of capital-accumulation interests. To undermine capital accumulation is to undermine the country's (and maybe the world's) economic health. The state is therefore constrained to make policy decisions from a very limited range of options.

- However, perceptions of what is a viable option for a given problem can be influenced by the process of class struggle. That is, conflict between the relatively advantaged and disadvantaged members of society can often redefine problems and solutions so that new ways of understanding issues can develop. For example, there is a growing welfare rights movement in the United States that has begun to mobilize and organize around the problems of welfare "reform" and its attacks against the poor (Reese and Newcombe, 1999).

- Further, there is a rising coalition of labor and faith communities struggling to get all employers to pay their workers a living wage. Allies from a variety of walks of life are forming common bonds and are encouraging harbingers of social challenge and social change in the ways the state responds to its constituents, particularly those who have received fewer advantages and resources at the state's disposal.

 THINKING CRITICALLY

1. Consider the issue of corporate welfare described in this chapter. Why is corporate welfare treated differently than social welfare for the poor, in both the press and in governmental policy? What factors and forces entered into this social construction of need?

2. Look in the newspaper for a situation that currently or potentially involves the presence of the U.S. military in a foreign country. What is at stake in that country for the United States? Whose interests are likely to be served by the military's presence, and why? Identify the components of the military-industrial complex, and analyze what each has at stake in this particular case. What effect might U.S. military involvement in this situation have on you?

3. Select an issue that is currently controversial (such as the North American Free Trade Agreement, reform of the welfare system in the United States, healthcare, abortion rights, or gun-control legislation), and sort out the various interests that are likely to be affected by that issue. Consider the different ways that such a controversy might be resolved. Whose interests are served and whose interests are hurt by each possible outcome? How are you likely to be affected by each outcome? How might you affect the outcome?

4. The Supreme Court currently includes three women, one African American, and one Latina. Does their inclusion alter the kinds of decisions made by the Court, as opposed to the decisions of an all-white, all-male Court? Why or why not? Suppose *six* of the Supreme Court members were women or people of color? Would that change the decisions made? Why or why not? What if the Chief Justice were a woman or a person of color?

5. Does the existence of the military-industrial complex, the power elite, and the dominance of the state by business mean that nonelites are powerless? Why or why not? What can you point to as evidence of nonelite power or powerlessness?

 KEY TERMS

alienation **300**	gilded welfare **310**
apathy **300**	government **283**
business dominance theory **303**	group pluralism **286**
capital **283**	interchangeability (of elites) **289**
capitalism **284**	interest groups **286**
capitalist interests **303**	military-industrial complex **293**
capitalist state structuralist theory **304**	multinational (transnational) corporations **294**
class dialectic perspective **305**	New Federalism **306**
class identity **289**	pluralism **286**
collective embezzlement **304**	political economy **284**
communist **285**	power elite **289**
co-optation **289**	social welfare **310**
corporate welfare **310**	socialism **285**
deregulation **304**	state **283**
economy **283**	supply-side (trickle-down) economics **307**
elite pluralist theory **000**	

WORK AND ECONOMY

12

When you graduate from college, do you expect your income to be better than, worse than, or the same as that of your parents when they were at that stage of their lives? What about your lifestyle? Are you likely to purchase your own home before you are 30 years old? Will you be able to afford to send your children to college? Will you be able to afford adequate healthcare? Where will you be economically in the next 20 years? The next 30? During the 1960s, a college degree was almost a guarantee of security and upward mobility. Now, that security is less certain. What has changed since then to alter the meaning of a college degree in the work world?

Since the late 1970s, people in the United States have begun to feel that they are working harder but are falling further behind in their standard of living and their economic well-being. In a survey by the Public Agenda 2000, almost half of the respondents worried that "the strong economy would turn sour in the near future" (www.publicagenda.org/issues). In that same survey, 60 percent said they did not earn enough money to live the way they wanted. By 2009, a survey conducted by Gallup/USA Today found that 83 percent of respondents were worried that the measures the government was taking to address the economic crisis "might not work and the economy will get worse" (Gallup/USA Today, 2009), results that suggest rising concern about the security of their jobs. More and more couples, particularly those with children, are finding that both partners must work full-time to be able to afford the basic necessities of their lives (Uchitelle, 1999, 2000; Tankersley, 2012). Poverty rates remain stubbornly high. But if work is the antidote to poverty, how can this be, even during robust and prosperous economic periods when presumably a rising tide raises all boats? The question of what happened to the American Dream is linked to the labor process and its place in the economy.

- What is the current structure of work and the economy in the United States?
- How has that structure changed in recent decades, and why, and what effect do the changes have on individuals?
- Who benefits and who is hurt by these changes?
- What role have labor unions played in fostering or mitigating changes in the structure of work and the economy?
- And are people helpless victims of the economy as an institution, or are there prospects for change that offer promise to workers?

315

THE MEANING OF WORK

To answer these questions requires a careful definition of the meaning of work. Generally, **work** refers to any activity "that produces something of value for other people" (U.S. Department of Health, Education, and Welfare, 1973). This activity can involve both paid and unpaid labor. That is, people need not be paid for their production of something of value in order for it to be considered work. Moreover, their efforts need not be readily visible to anyone else, publicly recognized, or performed outside the home to be considered work: As long as these activities produce something of value for someone else, they have engaged in work. So work includes paid labor (usually performed outside the home, but not necessarily) that takes place in what sociologists often refer to as the **formal labor market;** unpaid labor (both voluntary and involuntary, but excluding domestic labor), performed in the **informal labor market** (including, for example, volunteers at local soup kitchens, coaches in Little League and local soccer teams, classroom parent aids, Boy Scout and Girl Scout leaders, and bartering); and **domestic labor** (work done to maintain the home and family, usually unpaid) (Glazer, 1987: 249).

Many sociological studies have examined the relationship between work done in the formal and informal labor markets and domestic labor. Most of these studies note that it is far more common for women than for men to work in two or more of these sectors (Nelson, 1999). Men more commonly work in the formal labor market, typically outside their homes. Even when women work full-time in the formal labor market, they are still primarily responsible for the domestic labor at home. Working full-time in the formal labor market does not seem to appreciably alter the domestic division of labor. Hochschild and Machung (2012) refer to the domestic labor responsibilities facing women at the end of a full day in the formal labor market as the **second shift.** This situation may be changing somewhat in some households; but the overall pattern still indicates that when women enter the formal labor market, the total amount of time they spend each day at work (both in the formal and domestic labor spheres) increases substantially, while for male partners the total amount of time spent each day at work remains essentially the same.

Some middle-class and upper-middle-class women respond to the pressures of the second shift by transferring the domestic labor that must be done into the formal labor market. The typical arrangement is for white middle- and upper-class women to hire poor immigrants or women of color to care for their children, clean their homes, and cook their meals (Ehrenreich and Hochschild, 2004). While such arrangements do provide employment for poor women, they also highlight the assumption that such work belongs to women. Class advantage allows some women to shift the burden of gender exploitation to other, less advantaged women, whereupon they also exploit class and race inequalities (see Chapter 8).

Women are more likely than men to work in the informal labor market, engaging in the invisible unpaid labor of volunteer work and bartering (Stone and Harvey, 2001). Bartering may involve the sharing of car rides, childcare, and errand running with other women. The volunteer work done by women may be an important aspect of community as well as an aid to the careers of many women's partners (Meadows, 1996). It can involve working in local libraries, schools, and museums and developing charitable resources for the less fortunate in a community. Although women's volunteer work can build visibility, social networks, and contacts vital for their husbands' success at work, it is often devalued as unimportant in large part because it is unpaid.

In many cases, participating in the informal labor market is imperative for women living in poverty if they and their families are to survive. Many poor women must participate in all three spheres of labor every day. The following is a description of a typical day for a woman in Peru:

Soledad, age 35, with three children and a husband who works occasionally as an electrician, rises at 4 A.M. . . . She eats a stale bun with tea and packs her merchandise for the hour and a half long ride from Villa El Salvador to the centre of Lima. . . . She is one of the thousands of ambulantes or street vendors who crowd the capital's major commercial districts, hawking cigarettes, candy, magazines, lottery tickets, cheap clothing, trinkets for tourists. Before leaving around 5:30, she wakes up her teenage daughter, Manuela. She will serve breakfast for the family and make sure that her two young brothers will arrive on time at the morning shift at the local primary school. Fourteen-year-old Manuela will do some school work, but most of her morning will be spent cleaning and washing clothes at the water spigot in the shack which adjoins the house. Sometimes, she will share these tasks with her mother during the evening hours. . . . Soledad will return home sometime after noon with her morning's earnings. In her "free moments" she also knits sweaters on consignment. Since [her husband] lost his job three months ago, her work brings in the household's only regular income. Around 1:30, Soledad and Manuela will pick up the family's most important daily meal at a comedor popular. It is one of some 800 communal or "popular" kitchens which function in Lima today. The weekly fee is modest because Soledad, like the other women who organised the comedor, combine resources and take turns preparing the meals for the dozens of families served by it. Some of the women work at the comedor in the mornings. Soledad spends one afternoon a week cooking the snacks which will be distributed in the evening. But she is distracted and worried about what her younger children may be up to—no one is at home. . . . On Monday afternoons, Soledad and two of her neighbours from the local "Glass of Milk Committee" will go to the municipal depot to pick up their weekly ration of powdered milk. It will be distributed free by other members of her committee. . . . The daily struggle to ensure her family's survival adds up to an eighteen-hour work day. . . . She says, "I feel tired all the time" (North, 1988: 12).

Soledad's incredible day describes what is referred to as the **triple shift: a daily juggle of work in the formal, informal, and household labor spheres** (Hossfeld, 1989). While Soledad's story occurred more than two decades ago, little has changed in rural Peru. Moreover, although Soledad lives in a peripheral nation, many women in the United States similarly labor a triple shift, juggling paid work in the formal labor market, unpaid housework, and the informal labor of carpooling, childcare, and volunteer work connected with their children's schools and afterschool activities.

The income people get from their participation in the formal labor market affects their ability to meet such basic needs as food, clothing, shelter, education, fuel, transportation, healthcare, and income for retirement. More broadly, labor market participation affects individuals' life chances. It is important, then, to examine the formal labor market: How is it structured, and how does its structure produce differential experiences by race, class, and gender? In this chapter we will explore the formal labor market structure and how it has changed over the past several decades. We will examine how some burdens of the changes, such as unemployment, get distributed. We will also investigate the effect of these changes on wages and on the status of the middle class. And we will discuss the prospects for further change.

THE STRUCTURE OF THE FORMAL LABOR MARKET

The formal labor market in the United States is made up of different sectors: agricultural, goods producing, and service sectors. In 2012, 83.3 percent of the employed population worked in the service sector, compared with only 16.1 percent in the goods-producing sector (manufacturing, mining, and construction) and 0.6 percent in agriculture (www.bls.gov). Workers in agriculture tend to be paid minimum wage; the work is seasonal, prompting many workers to migrate from region to region to follow various growing seasons. Although some migrant farmworkers have unionized, their working conditions tend to be unstable because of the seasonal nature of their work and the uncertainty of weather conditions.

Workers in goods production (manufacturing, construction, and mining) are more likely than farmworkers to be unionized, although, like farmworkers, the majority are not. Compared with agricultural work, the work in this sector tends to be less seasonal and more secure, be better paid, and have greater benefits. However, even in this sector, job insecurity is not uncommon; factories and mines shut down production when the economy is slow or when corporations merge or shift production outside the United States. And indeed, this is precisely the sector that was hardest hit by job loss in the severe recession that began in 2008.

Only 12.5 percent of all U.S. workers were represented by unions, and workers in the service sector are the least likely to be unionized (www.bls.gov). Workers in jobs such as nurses' aides, childcare, retail, fast food, convenience stores, and janitorial services tend to be paid minimum wage (or less, if they are high school or college students), have few, if any, health and retirement benefits, and work part-time. Jobs in this sector are growing faster than those in either of the other two sectors. Research on the effects of employment sectors on earnings challenges the functionalist view that earnings of individuals simply indicate that some jobs are more important than others and that some individuals make greater investments in their training and education (Davis and Moore, 1945). It appears that the structure of labor markets can differentiate earnings according to gender and race, regardless of education level or skill (www.census.gov; England, Thompson, and Aman, 2001; Mishel et al., 2012;). And closer examination of the formal labor market helps explain why that might be the case.

THE CHANGING STRUCTURE OF PAID WORK

The structure of the formal labor market in the United States has changed over time. Look at Figure 12.1: In 1910, the formal labor market was almost evenly distributed among the agriculture, manufacturing and goods-producing (including mining and construction), and service sectors. By World War II, this distribution had shifted dramatically; employment in agriculture began to decline, while employment in manufacturing and service work continued to increase. After 1952, service employment kept on climbing as both manufacturing and agricultural jobs fell. Currently, employment in the agricultural sector is shrinking almost to extinction, as food production in the United States falls increasingly under the control of major food-processing corporations who rely primarily on heavy machinery and temporary (often undocumented) migrant farmworkers.

Figure 12.1: Distribution of Employment by Activity Sector, 1850–2012

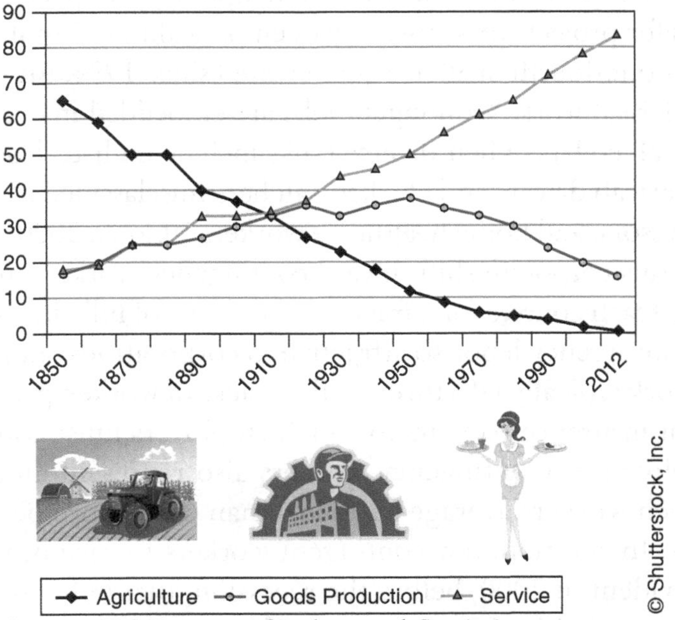

← Agriculture —○— Goods Production —▲— Service

Source: US Bureau of Labor and Statistics; US Census Bureau.

The service sector is growing by leaps and bounds: More than four-fifths of U.S. workers today are employed in this sector. And goods production activities are dramatically declining, with little more than one-fifth of the U.S. labor force engaged in manufacturing (www.bls.gov).

Strikingly, between 1970 and 1990 the greatest job growth was in involuntary part-time work (that is, jobs people accept in the absence of full-time opportunities, even when they preferred to or needed to work full-time): Such jobs increased by 121 percent, while total employment grew by only 54 percent (Folbre, 1995). By 2012 the growth in part-time work, particularly involuntary part-time work and temporary work, intensified and outpaced the growth in full-time jobs (www.bls.gov; Mishel et al., 2012). What is the significance of the dramatic increase in involuntary part-time work?

Until the late 1990s, most workers were hired by employers and placed in jobs under that employer. After that, the trend was increasingly toward temporary workers hired to perform projects and then let go when the projects were completed. This shift was signaled in 1996 when AT&T announced that it was going to lay off over 40,000 workers, with the intention of hiring many of them back as consultants and temporary workers on specific projects. These layoffs included everyone from low-level supervisors to high-level managers. AT&T insisted it was not laying off workers; it was conducting a "force management program," to reallocate its human resources by examining the skills of its workforce and deciding which people to assign to current projects. Those not invited back were simply "unassigned" (Andrews, 1996). The company proudly presented its decision as the wave of the future for all corporations: "We have to promote the whole concept of the work force being contingent. . . . [giving rise to a society that is increasingly] jobless but not workless" (Andrews, 1996: D6).

The Economic Policy Institute found that by 2012 almost one-third of the workers in the United States (around 30 million workers) were employed in temporary positions rather than secure, stable jobs (Henderson, 2012). "Temp" agencies, which hire temporary and part-time workers and lease them out to corporations for project work, themselves employ almost 3 million workers. Jobs with temp agencies account for one-fourth of all new jobs created since 1984. And these workers are not restricted to temporary clerical work: "contingent jobs are embedded in every sector of the economy, affecting workers of all collars. Their diverse ranks include high-tech software engineers and office workers; janitors, taxicab drivers and chicken catchers misclassified as independent contractors; adjunct college professors; and home healthcare workers" (Cook, 2000:15). Even colleges and universities are adopting this corporate shift toward contingency workers in their increasing reliance on adjunct faculty to teach courses for a fraction of the cost of full-time faculty (Noble, 2001).

Why is reliance on contingency labor so attractive to corporations, and what does it mean to workers? Contingency work typically falls through the cracks of worker-protection laws and is not subject to unemployment insurance benefits to which employers must contribute, making such workers more easily exploitable. Contingency workers also represent an attractive cost-saving device for employers: Such workers average $100 less than their more permanent counterparts in weekly take-home pay. In addition, few contingent workers receive healthcare or retirement benefits. It was already evident in 2000, before the recession, that only one-fifth of contingency workers have employer-provided health insurance and retirement benefits, compared to more than half of all noncontingent workers who did receive such benefits (Cook, 2000). The recession has only intensified this problem. And where goods production workers (previously the majority of the workforce) tended to be unionized, service workers in general and contingency workers in particular are not. That represents a decided political advantage to employers, whose temporary workforce is not currently organized to resist the power of their employers and whose individualized, competitive isolation reduces the opportunities for the kinds of communication networks that used to encourage worker consciousness and organized resistance to exploitation.

CAUSES OF THE STRUCTURAL TRANSFORMATION OF THE ECONOMY

What has caused this structural shift and transformation of the economy? Sociologist Beth A. Rubin (1996: 5) points to **globalization**, the "processes that create a global network of interdependent actors and activities that are unconnected to a specific place or national economy." The dramatic path-breaking developments in *technology*, particularly in microelectronics, have spurred the development of an increasingly *global economy* and the acceleration of increasing *capital mobility*. In turn, globalization has encouraged *deindustrialization* (Eitzen and Baca Zinn, 1989a: 2; Anderson and Cavanagh with Lee, 2000). Let's look at these forces one at a time.

Technology

Just as the steam engine fueled the Industrial Revolution, the computer microchip has spurred the latest structural transformation of the economy. Notably, the stimulant for both inventions was not need per se, but the need of affluent and powerful owners of the means of production to gain greater control over and profit from the production process. The microchip is capable of storing, retrieving, and manipulating mountains of data quickly and accurately and far removed from the point of production. Information can instantaneously be transmitted from one computer to another halfway around the world. Engineers and architects can anticipate and correct design problems quickly on computer screens, rather than spending months on costly experiments only to discover serious product defects. And microchips have enabled computerized robots to increase productivity in manufacturing. While these robots eliminate many tedious, boring, low-paying, and hazardous jobs, they also unfortunately displace human labor rather than create jobs (Aronowitz and DiFazio, 1994; Rifkin, 1995). Similarly, use of online and distance learning modules permanently displaces an increasing number of full-time faculty from the academic market (Noble, 2001). Thus, microchips and the technological advancements they foster have served to increase productivity, but at the cost of eliminating many higher-paying manufacturing and professional jobs.

The Global Economy

In addition to the destruction of manufacturing jobs, the microchip has also contributed to the shift toward a global economy. The speed and accuracy of information processing between computers around the world enables managers in the United States to run production processes abroad. Prior to the development of the microchip, the sheer distance separating North America from the other continents essentially protected U.S. manufacturers from international competition for the large markets within the United States. Enormous breakthroughs in transportation and communication have reduced that protection, and products from abroad now easily compete with domestic products in U.S. markets (Dolbeare, 1986).

The success of that competition can be measured by the decreasing profits of manufacturers in the United States. Many U.S. corporations have responded to the competition by stepping up the level of automated production, destroying jobs but increasing productivity. Other corporations have wrung concessions from workers, such as lower wages, moratoria on pensions, decreases in health benefits, and increases in layoffs. In addition to wringing such concessions from workers, corporations have also gained many concessions from the localities or states in which they were located. These concessions included tax benefits, eased environmental and land use restrictions, and sometimes actual cash payments or land donations. Such concessions are attractive to firms and used as incentives for firms to stay in a given location, but the costs are borne primarily by workers, whose taxes are likely to increase or whose municipal or state budgets become squeezed by the loss of corporate taxes. When these benefits are used up, corporations often move anyway, sometimes leaving the United States entirely for greener pastures in Mexico and beyond.

Capital Mobility

The globalization of the economy is related to a third force in the restructuring of the U.S. economy: capital mobility, the ability to move money and assets. Banks and manufacturers may move both financial and production resources at will anywhere they choose. They have increasingly chosen to merge their assets with other corporations and to relocate their plants abroad and invest outside the United States.

Investment Abroad

Over the past 50 years, investment abroad by U.S. corporations has grown dramatically, from $16 billion in 1950 to $4.4 trillion in 2010 (www.census.gov). Indeed, many of the largest U.S.

corporations receive a significant proportion of their revenues from their investments abroad (www.census.gov). So much of their production and revenue has shifted outside the United States that such firms are routinely referred to as multinational or transnational corporations.

Why have these corporations invested so heavily abroad? Part of the reason is that labor in other countries, particularly in the global south nations of Latin America and Asia, is nonunionized and cheaper than labor in the United States. Moreover, global south countries tend to have fewer and more lax environmental and worker health and safety regulations. Thus, production is inexpensive, if not safe and responsible. Decisions to invest abroad have the consequence of exporting U.S. production jobs.

The historic North American Free Trade Agreement (NAFTA) of 1993 was supposed to help open the political borders separating the United States, Canada, and Mexico in order to smooth the way for cheaper and easier trade between the three countries. The idea was that by eliminating trade barriers such as tariffs, and allowing corporations to engage in production and sell goods in all three countries as if they were one, the result would be prosperity, more jobs, and an improvement in environmental standards throughout North America. Five years later, evidence showed that NAFTA enhanced capital mobility for corporations but provided little else. For example, while NAFTA supporters insisted that the treaty would produce 200,000 new jobs in the United States annually, the fact is that "hundreds of thousands of U.S. jobs have been lost" (Wallach and Sforza, 1999: 7). This is because under the treaty, 40 percent of U.S. exports to Mexico are actually parts to be assembled by low-wage workers at U.S.-owned plants. The products then return to the United States as finished consumer goods, causing a huge trade deficit with Mexico for the United States. Trade deficits commonly produce layoffs because they indicate heavy importing that is not offset by sufficient exporting. So, not only are U.S. workers' jobs being exported to Mexico with the help of NAFTA, those jobs that remain here are jeopardized by trade deficits.

Moreover, not only have almost a quarter of a million workers in the United States lost their jobs as a result of NAFTA, companies that promised to create new NAFTA-stimulated jobs have not fulfilled that promise: A survey of firms that made such promises in 1993 found that almost 90 percent had failed to make good on those promises by 1999, and many had already relocated production to Mexico (Wallach and Sforza, 1999). And although one promise of NAFTA supporters was that it would stimulate increases in wages for workers in Mexico and therefore reduce the motivation for illegal immigration to the United States, workers in Mexico are no better off than U.S. workers under NAFTA: Although jobs are fleeing from the United States to Mexico, and Mexican productivity has increased by 36.4 percent, Mexican wages have declined 29 percent. Workers in Mexico's *maquiladora* production centers average such low weekly wages that nearly two-thirds of Mexican workers live below the poverty line (Wallach and Sforza, 1999: 7). So what was promised as an economic boom to everyone has provided advantages primarily to corporate elites in the United States. Notably, as low as wages are in Mexico, they are still higher than wages paid to workers in China. Multinational corporations are now relocating production from Mexico to China (Ramirez, 2003). This underscores the ease with which these firms can scour the globe seeking the cheapest wages.

Runaway Shops

U.S. corporations often decide it is profitable to relocate production and service facilities elsewhere within the United States in addition to overseas. Both forms of relocation are often referred to as **runaway shops.** The pattern has been that manufacturing corporations close plants in the North and Midwest (the "Frostbelt"), where labor unions have historically been strongest, and move production to the South and Southwest (the "Sunbelt"), where unions have been nonexistent or weak (Rifkin and Barber, 1978). By 2010, only 13.2 percent of workers in the Sunbelt were represented by unions, compared with 29 percent of workers unionized in the Frostbelt (www.census.gov). Often, such a move gives corporations the opportunity to further automate so that production can be done with less human labor.

Indeed, something of a bidding war erupted among states vying for plants to be relocated in their communities. That bidding war can be quite costly: States and cities may offer corporations gifts of land, long moratoria on taxes (many of which are lowered to attract business), infrastructural development (such as roads and schools), and lax regulations. For example, when Pennsylvania wanted to attract Norwegian global engineering and construction firm Kvaerner ASA to relocate a shipbuilding enterprise there in 1997, the state offered the company a $307 million economic incentive package. It cost the state $323,000 per job to create a mere 950 jobs, none of which paid anywhere near this figure (Barlett and Steele, 2001). Politicians have engaged in this expensive, seemingly irrational bidding war because they fear the consequences of having to explain to voters why they did not try to attract jobs to their states.

Such costs raise the issue of who the winners and losers are in the domestic relocation of productive facilities. The communities where plants shut down relied on their presence for jobs and economic security, thus runaway shops are clearly not to their advantage. But it is questionable whether the recipient communities are winners either. Some states and cities have begun to recognize that the bidding war does not work to anyone's advantage: New York City, New York State, New Jersey, and Connecticut have an agreement to stop advertisements designed to entice producers to pull up stakes and relocate. And the National Governors' Association works to explore similar ways to curb corporate relocators' power to instigate costly giveaways by states that can hardly afford them, all for the dubious distinction of creating relatively few jobs (Schwartz and Barrett, 1992).

Mergers

U.S. corporations also move investment capital into **mergers** with other corporations. That is, they invest in the purchase of other firms. The flurry of mergers or takeovers over the past two decades has been called **merger mania.** As Figure 12.2 shows, the number of mergers per year has grown from 1,719 in 1985 to 9,599 by 1999. Corporate purchases of other firms are quite expensive: The total cost of the mergers in 1999 was $3.4 trillion, up from $149.6 billion in 1985 (www.census.gov table #742). While this intense growth in mergers slowed significantly during the recession that began in 2008, by 2012 there was evidence that these were once again on the rise. Mergers are significant because these purchases take away from funds that might otherwise be invested by firms in production. In some cases, investing in a merger rather than in productive capacity can lead to corporate revenue losses that, in effect, greatly increase the price of the merger. The importance of such investment decisions can be seen in the 2000 merger between

America On-Line (AOL) and Time Warner. That merger created the largest media conglomerate in the United States, worth more than $350 billion. But less than two years later, the merged company was posting massive losses, until its value plummeted to $50 billion. Shareholders lost 45 percent of the combined value of the merged firm, and Chief Executive Officer Richard Parsons announced the company's strategy of cost control, signaling significant layoffs (*Washington Times*, 2002; Szalai, 2003).

Mergers help restructure the U.S. economy by increasing concentration in corporate America: More and more of the country's productive capacity is being owned and controlled by fewer hands. This means less competition among fewer producers and higher prices for consumer goods. Increasing concentration of productive capacity also gives corporations greater power advantages over workers and the state. They find it easier to wring concessions from workers and to elicit favorable tax policies and relaxation of state regulations. Finally, mergers tend to eliminate jobs because the acquiring firm seeks to reduce duplication and to streamline its merged operations (Russell, 1987). Merger mania, then, has been a strong factor in restructuring the U.S. economy.

Deindustrialization

As we pointed out earlier, since World War II, the economy has witnessed increasing growth in its service sector. At the same time, manufacturing activities are being shifted to the workforce in poorer countries (Collins, 1998; Mishel et al., 2012). As a result, plants in the United States are increasingly becoming empty. Either they are shutting down or the workers are simply assembling imported parts into finished goods, rather than manufacturing the parts themselves and then assembling them. Social scientists refer to this process of declining domestic manufacturing activity as **deindustrialization**.

FIGURE 12.2: Mergers and Acquisitions, 1985–2012

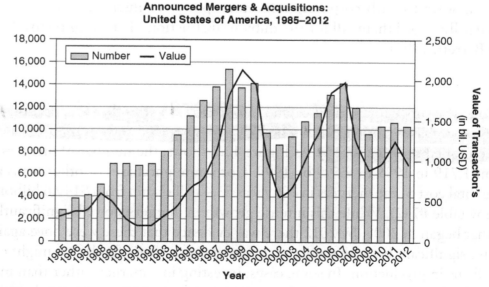

Source: Institute of Mergers, Acquisitions and Alliances (www.imaa-institute.org/statistics-mergers-acquisitions.html)

The increasing reliance on imported manufactured goods and parts has greatly affected workers in the United States. Some workers have lost their jobs (and health and retirement benefits) too close to retirement to be retrained and hired elsewhere. Other workers have relocated their families in hope of finding new jobs, only to discover that thousands of others had the same idea. What looks like a promising local job market can easily become glutted with dislocated workers in search of employment.

Some economists and politicians argue that the dislocation of workers, while admittedly uncomfortable, is temporary: As the economy undergoes its normal readjustments, new jobs will inevitably be created to replace those lost to deindustrialization. Unfortunately, research shows that although there may have been a net increase in newly created jobs, the new jobs tend to be temporary or to pay less than the old jobs that were destroyed (Heintz, Folbre, and the Center for Popular Economics, 2000; Zweig, 2000; Mishel et al., 2012). The evidence suggests that the new jobs created in the service sector have not filled the void left by deindustrialization.

In addition to permanently dislocating workers, deindustrialization can have devastating consequences on whole communities. Towns and cities that once prospered while heavily or exclusively reliant on a single company (or a single industry) find themselves facing increased poverty and loss of population when the company moves or closes (Brady and Wallace, 2001). The effects of a shutdown can reverberate throughout the community. Small businesses that once relied on the now-unemployed workers go bankrupt; industries that once supplied goods and services to the now-closed main employer lose business and thus must themselves shut down and lay off their own employees; and municipal services that once relied on income and property tax revenues must be cut back or eliminated altogether, including things like police and fire protection, sanitation removal, schools, hospitals, and so forth.

The effects of shutdowns on individuals are often devastating as well:

> *Jeff, who is 50, lost his job at Rapp Digital almost two years ago, making him one of 21,000 computer-industry professionals in New York City to have been let go since the end of 2000. . . . [H]e had three months of severance–plenty, he thought, to get him to his next position. The three months went by, then four, then five, then six. . . . "Once it hits a year, . . . there's no reason to believe it's going to be any better this time next year." [Jeff's wife finally tells him that he must find a way to contribute financially or move out]. Now, working at the Gap at $10 an hour, it takes Jeff two and a half weeks to earn what he used to make in a day at Rapp Digital. . . [A]fter "the year-and-a-half-long process of dehumanization," as Jeff calls it, he's happy to have any job. . . . Jeff's outplacement [a service provided by Rapp Digital when they laid him off] proved to be little more than a halfway house between full-time employment and full-time unemployment. . . . [S]ix months after being let go, he filed for personal bankruptcy protection. . . . "Shame is . . . about who or what you are or what you are not . . . . I felt guilty about losing my job and shame about not being able to support my family" (Mahler, 2003: 46–48, 66, 70).*

This worker's saga is not unique; it might just as easily describe the scores of similar stories that continue to emerge throughout the United States (Dandaneau, 1996; Thomas, 1997; Binkley, 2001).

Changing Corporate Organizational Structure

Why has it been possible for corporations to engage in decision making that produces deindustrialization, plant relocation, and the globalization of labor and production? The answer lies partly in the changing organizational structure of firms. Most companies were once owned and controlled by a single proprietor, who often resided in the community or close by, but firms now are owned by stockholders and controlled by managers and bankers. The change began in the late 1800s, when owners needed to raise capital to expand; they had the choice of either taking out loans and incurring debt or selling shares of ownership, or stock, in their firms. When an owner sells shares in the firm, the company structure expands to include a board of directors and potentially thousands of shareholders. Since the sales of stocks were dispersed among thousands of independent shareholders, corporate managers were able to control a corporation by owning as little as 5 percent of its stock (Berle and Means, 1932; Bell, 1973). Burnham (1941) termed this turn of events the **managerial revolution,** in which ownership and control were presumably separated, with control over corporate decision making accruing to professional managers. Critics, however, have noted that while it may be true that the sale of corporate stock separates ownership and control, shares are not as widely dispersed as previously thought: Wealthy families and banks retain the largest proprietary interests in most firms since they hold the greatest number of shares (Mintz and Schwartz, 1985; Mayer, 2001).

The stock market increasingly looms as an important factor motivating what corporations do. This is because, in addition to the interests of financial institutions as major stockholders, corporate chief executives themselves have strong vested interests in their firms' stock performance. Increasingly, chief executives' compensation is derived less from salaries (which are taxable at the highest levels as income) than from lucrative stock options. They have the option of purchasing huge blocks of stock in their firms at below-market prices, with the option of selling those shares if they wish when the asking price is highly favorable. The idea is to tie the executives' personal fortunes with those of the firm and motivate them to do whatever is in the best interest of the company on the assumption that this means making the firm more profitable.

Unfortunately, it has been quite evident that executive compensations bear little relation to profitability: Between 1978 and 2011, while the Standard and Poor's stock prices averaged an inflation-adjusted growth of 349 percent and corporate profits suffered a serious decline, chief executives posted a 759 percent increase in their compensation (Mishel et al., 2012: 289). Higher compensation, then, does not necessarily mean a more profitable or productive firm, but it does show a strong link to stock market performance. Since executives' compensation is primarily tied to the performance of their company's stock, they become motivated to make decisions that will increase the value of the stock, even if those decisions will not necessarily make the firm more profitable.

Nor do CEOs' decisions necessarily enhance workers' job security. It is widely known, for example, that mergers between large firms are likely to increase the value of a stock, even if mergers do not increase productive capacity or preserve jobs. More significantly, announcements of massive worker layoffs typically have the effect of driving up the value of shares of stock in the short run because they mean huge savings in wages for the firm; yet layoffs may harm the economy overall by stimulating recessions and decreasing the ability of consumers to afford goods. One observer went so far as to call such executives "corporate killers" suggesting that

"Wall Street loves layoffs" (Sloan, 1996: 44). No less an observer than *Business Week* wondered aloud in a 1997 cover story if "Executive pay . . . [is] out of control. . . . Don't confuse a bull market [a market in which stock prices tend to rise] with managerial genius" (Reingold, 1997: cover).

How does the separation of ownership and control, and stock prices as a force in corporate decision making, promote plant relocation and deindustrialization? Companies that are controlled by financial institutions, corporate managers, and large stockholders are not necessarily tied to the local community where the plants operate; these interests often reside elsewhere and may have little allegiance to the local community. Thus, the controlling interests of firms become an important force in the structural transformation of the economy.

In addition to undergoing a change in their ownership and control structure, corporations are no longer the individual, competitive firms they once may have been. Instead, the vast majority of the largest firms (referred to as the Fortune 500, because of their inclusion in *Fortune's* annual list of the 500 biggest corporations) are connected through interlocking boards of directors, created by economic elites who sit on multiple corporate boards. The strongest corporate interlockers are economic elites from the largest commercial banks. With large commercial banks acting as such central figures in these corporate networks, and the stock market acting as a major motivating force in chief executive and board decision making, it is not surprising to find boards of directors treating the corporation as an organization of chunks of financial assets to be bought and sold or relocated, rather than as a staple in the local community and an organization that has mutual obligations and responsibilities. Corporate boards of directors may be more concerned with keeping their firms' cash flows, stock values, and dividends high. Corporate interlocking directorates, then, may reinforce plant relocations, shutdowns, and deindustrialization as the interests of shareholders in the firm (including chief executives, financial institutions, and affluent investors) are privileged over the interests of stakeholders (including workers, consumers, and the communities in which firms do business).

THE GREAT TWENTY-FIRST-CENTURY ECONOMIC RECESSION

The global restructuring of the economy created the "perfect storm" that by 2008 triggered the deep and protracted economic recession. That recession hit not only the United States: It reverberated around the world, hitting the strongest economies in the global north as well as the more vulnerable ones in the global south. Compounding the deep effects of global economic restructuring was federal policy that removed controls that once regulated corporate behavior. More than two decades of deregulation of key industries, including financial institutions, unleashed high-risk investment behaviors, intense merger mania, and predatory lending that sent key industries like housing into turmoil. When industries central to the economy experience crises, it sends the crisis throughout the economy in spiraling ripples. This is because there are many industries that supply materials to the ailing industry, and when a central industry goes into recession, it no longer requires the volume of supplies it once did. That sends the supply industries into recession as well. In the case of the financial industry, deregulation allowed banks to engage in predatory lending and high-risk investment strategies that became economic disasters. The massive mortgage and foreclosure crisis not only caused supply industries in the housing market to go into recession; it sent the stock market tumbling to levels not seen since the Great Depression of the 1930s (Fergusen, 2012). The result was a deep and protracted recession that accelerated the structural transformation of the economy from one defined by goods production to one dominated by the service sector.

Taken together, then, technological changes, the globalization of the economy, increasing capital mobility, and deindustrialization, along with widespread industrial deregulation, have combined to generate a structural transformation of the U.S. economy that differentially affects labor and management. Exactly how has this transformation affected the daily lives of workers? We now turn to an examination of some of its effects.

ECONOMIC STRUCTURAL TRANSFORMATION AND INEQUALITY

The transformation of the economy has accentuated inequality in U.S. society. This becomes clear in an examination of these effects: (1) structural unemployment and underemployment, (2) the shift of the formal labor market from manufacturing to service work, and (3) the declining income generated by the remaining jobs in the formal labor market (Eitzen and Zinn, 1989b).

Unemployment

One indicator of the overall effect of deindustrialization and the permanent restructuring of the economy is unemployment. Between 1979 and 1983, a trend of job losses because of plant closings emerged: almost 12 million workers were permanently dislocated from their jobs. Close to 5 million of these job losses were due to plant closings; the rest were caused by the elimination of jobs or shifts, the lack of enough work to sustain the existing work force, or business failures (U.S. Department of Labor, 1985; Mishel, Bernstein and Schmitt, 1988). That trend continues: In 2012 alone, 4.5 million workers were permanently dislocated, nearly half of them because of plant closings (www.bls.gov).

These figures suggest that deindustrialization and the unemployment it generates have escalated since the 1980s. Unemployment in the United States generally deepened from the end of World War II through the early 1990s, rising from a rate in 1947 of 3.9 percent to 7.5 percent in 1992. By 2003, however, the unemployment rate hit one of its lowest points since World War II, falling to 6.0 percent of the total labor force (www.census.gov), signaling to some observers the false impression that the ravages of the economic structural transformation had come to an end.

That optimism was short-lived, as the economy took a nose-dive beginning in 2008: It became apparent that the structural transformation had generated fundamental weaknesses in the economy. Not only were massive numbers of workers losing their jobs; work was no longer the antidote to poverty it was once presumed to be. It was now quite possible for someone to be employed, even full-time, and still not make enough money to survive. We were now faced with the unthinkable reality of *underemployment* and the *working poor*.

Moreover, the patterns describing *who* the unemployed are hardly inconsequential or random. For example, in 2011, teen unemployment was 24.4 percent (Mishel et al., 2012: 337). Because teenage workers tend to be less experienced and less skilled than older workers, they are often hired for unskilled or semiskilled work. Unskilled work is frequently the first to be dislocated by automation.

FIGURE 12.3:   Unemployment Rates by Race, Gender, and Age, 2011

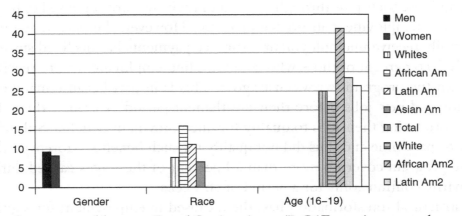

Source: www.bls.gov ../Local Settings/temp/7zO1E.tmp/www.statab.gov

*Note: The Bureau of Labor Statistics did not report out comparable data for Native Americans.

Even more telling is a breakdown of unemployment by gender and race, as shown in Figure 12.3. Women's unemployment rates were higher than the rates for men until 1995, after which their rates became the same or lower than those of men, a pattern that now continues (www.census.gov; Mishel et al., 2012: 342). And the deep and protracted recession that began in 2008 resulted in a higher unemployment rate for men relative to women. But this parity is, paradoxically, a result of continued sex discrimination. Men have had greater employment in manufacturing, precisely the sector that has suffered the most severe job losses. Women, on the other hand, have had greater employment opportunities in the service sector, which has shown pronounced increases in employment.

Racial comparisons of unemployment show a more marked pattern. Unemployment rates for African American workers have consistently remained more than twice the rates for white workers. Latino/a workers have fared only slightly better: Their rates of unemployment have consistently run more than 50 percent higher than those of white workers Mishel et al., 2012: 339). A large part of this consistent racialized difference in unemployment rates is the result of past and present-day institutional racism (see Chapter 7).

This analysis of unemployment is based on the official rates of unemployment reported by the U.S. Bureau of Labor Statistics. But these rates have come under criticism for *under*reporting the real rates of unemployment. This is because of the way the Bureau of Labor Statistics defines and counts unemployment. Persons must be considered "attached to the labor force" in order to be counted as active participants in the labor market. Anyone who has been out of the labor force and has not been actively looking for a job in the previous four weeks is not counted as unemployed. Thus, people who have become discouraged and have ceased looking for work are not included in the official statistics on the unemployed. Nor are those who work at least one day per week at a part-time job, even though they would like full-time work. And anyone who has graduated from high school or college but has not yet found a first job is not included, either. Including all the uncounted people who want to work in the formal labor market but who cannot find employment would almost double the real rate of unemployment beyond the official rate reported by the government (Mishel, Bernstein, and Schmitt, 2001).

The state determines eligibility for federal benefits for the unemployed on the basis of definitions and counts established by the Bureau of Labor Statistics. Persons who are attached to the labor force and lose their jobs through no fault of their own are supposed to be provided for under the federal unemployment insurance program. However, the percentage of the unemployed who actually receive unemployment insurance payments has declined since World War II. In 2010, only 30.6 percent of those who could not find employment were receiving benefits or payments from the program (www.census.gov). This is in part because many of the unemployed could not find new jobs before their entitlement period expired. Others did not work long enough before losing their jobs to qualify for unemployment benefits. Still others worked only seasonally or part-time and thus did not qualify for such benefits. Moreover, the payments provided by the program cover no more than 50 percent of the wages earned during employment and ordinarily continue only for a period of 26 weeks.

Economic structural transformation has, then, caused unemployment for significant numbers of U.S. workers in recent decades, a situation that has escalated and deepened in the most recent recession. Throughout this period most workers have still been employed. What has happened to them?

Underemployment and Declining Income from Existing Jobs

Beyond structural patterns of unemployment, and perhaps more significant in the new century, is the problem of underemployment, a phenomenon that is hidden by the historically low unemployment rates that especially marked the 1990s. **Underemployment** refers to the situation in which individuals are employed either at jobs that do not fully utilize their skills, that pay less than a living wage, or that do not offer opportunities for full-time employment. We have already discussed the problem of the sharp increase in involuntary part-time employment as a significant trend since the 1990s. And we have already noted the dramatic rise in contingency work as the wave of the future labor markets. Part-time and contingency work that is involuntary is an example of underemployment, which is likely to increase as a regular feature of the labor market in the coming decades.

Additionally, the growth of the service sector contributes in large measure to low wages as an element of underemployment. This is because service sector jobs are frequently minimum wage and below (www.bls.gov; see also Kim, 2000). Low wages mean that people who hold such jobs, even if they work full-time, will not rise above the poverty line. Take, for example, the case of a worker at a convenience store who works 40 hours per week for a full 52 weeks a year, at the 2011 federal minimum wage of $7.25 per hour. That person will earn $15,080 annually before taxes. Considering the fact that the poverty line for a family of three (a single adult with two dependent children under the age of 18) was $17,568 in 2010, this worker will clearly not earn enough for his or her family to rise out of poverty (www.census.gov; www.npc,umich.edu/poverty/). Once taxes are taken out of this worker's pay check, the family's situation will be much worse. This is clearly a case of underemployment: This person is working full time but is stuck in the position of being a member of the **working poor**, those people who are working full time but remain below the poverty line. By 2012 nearly 7 million U.S. workers were working two or more jobs simply to make ends meet (www.bls.gov).

Although there has been a net increase in the number of jobs created in the United States since the late 1970s, these new jobs do not compensate for the income that workers have lost as jobs have shifted from manufacturing to services. Weekly median earnings in the goods-producing sector averaged $944 in 2012; in comparison, weekly earnings in the service sector averaged $597 that same year (www.bls.gov). Thus, the greatest job growth is occurring in the sector that pays lower wages. Why is there such a gap in compensation for work in different sectors?

Part of the answer may be unionization. Workers in the service sector (with the notable exception of government workers) are unlikely to be represented by unions. Evidence shows that the collective bargaining that unions engage in typically succeeds in raising workers' wages and benefits, including health and pension coverage (www.bls.gov). Thus, it is not surprising that average annual compensation is much greater in the more unionized goods-producing sector. Jobs in the service sector are three times more likely than those in goods production to pay the minimum wage of $7.25 per hour, and many such jobs are only part-time, seasonal, or temporary work. Part-time workers typically do not receive health or pension benefits (www.census.gov; see also Mishel et al., 2012).

Another problem is that the value of the minimum wage has sharply declined since 1967. The minimum wage in 2011 could purchase little more than three-fourths of what it could purchase in 1967 (Mishel et al., 2012). This is because the minimum wage, which is established by Congress and is rarely adjusted for inflation, has not kept up with the cost of living (www.census.gov). As we noted earlier, workers who labor full-time, year-round on minimum wage cannot earn enough income to rise above the poverty line. In fact, the poverty rate for full-time, year-round workers over the age of 16 has increased since 1973, such that by 2011, 28 percent of these workers were in poverty. Full-time workers headed up 18.1 percent of all poor families in the United States that same year (Mishel et al., 2012: 432–433), and part-time workers were more than three times as likely to be poor or to head poverty-stricken families (www.bls.gov). Work, then, is not necessarily the simple antidote to poverty: Even working full-time, year-round is not a guarantee that one will not be poor, especially if one works, as do so many people in the United States, in the low-wage jobs that dominate the service sector.

Gendered and Racialized Inequality and the Labor Market

Look at the race and gender distribution of workers between and within sectors; notice the patterns of inequality that changes in the labor market have only accentuated. Since World War II, female labor-force participation rates have increased more sharply than those for males (Bianchi and Dye, 2001). But men and women do not necessarily secure employment in the same kinds of jobs, nor do they receive equal compensation for the work done (Bose and Whaley, 2001; Steinberg, 2001; Mishel et al., 2012). In 2012, women held more than 55 percent of the jobs in the service sector, where, as previously noted, wages tend to be very low. Men, in contrast, are far more likely to be employed in goods production, where wages are much better (www.bls.gov). Women were especially concentrated in clerical and service jobs, holding over 90 percent of the jobs in nursing and dental hygienics, sewing and stitching, childcare and early childhood education services, secretarial and reception work, bookkeeping, and banktelling. On the other hand, men were concentrated in higher-paying jobs, holding over 90 percent of the jobs in fields such as logging, construction work, mining, auto mechanics, plumbing and pipefitting, firefighting, engineering, and airplane piloting and navigating (www.bls.gov). These data suggest that there is a segmented labor market wherein women and men compete in different labor markets for different jobs (Rosenfeld, 1980). The significance of such a segmented labor market can be seen in comparative incomes: Female-dominated jobs pay median annual incomes ranging from $20,280 for childcare workers to $54,340 for dental hygienists, while the median annual incomes in male-dominated jobs range from $22,620 for logging equipment operators to $74,880 for airline pilots, copilots, and flight engineers (www.bls.gov).

What happens when men and women do the same job? If differences between men's and women's median annual incomes were attributable to the differential work they do, one should expect to find no gaps between incomes when men and women do the same jobs. However, the data suggest otherwise. Regardless of whether a job is performed predominantly by women or men, women tend to make less than men. In 2012, women earned 73.5 percent of the salaries paid to men in managerial jobs, 78.2 percent of that in protective services, and 73.0 percent of that in production occupations. Even in female-dominated jobs such as elementary education, women still averaged only 81.6 percent of the salaries of their male counterparts; they also averaged 86.7 percent of the salaries of male receptionists and information clerks, and 91.3 percent of male registered nurses' wages (note that there were too few men in the other female-dominated jobs to even make a comparative assessment of their wages) (www.bls.gov). Thus, even when men and women perform work in the same job category, men's income is higher. And this is the case in both female-dominated and male-dominated jobs. Why?

Examining job categories more closely reveals that they frequently contain a hierarchy of statuses, all of which are categorized as the same job. Take the occupation of baker. Female bakers are typically employed in supermarkets and similar establishments, where baking entails popping premixed dough into the oven. In contrast, men are more likely to be bakers in the traditional sense: They are more likely to be employed in bakeries, restaurants, and catering services, where baking involves measuring and mixing ingredients specified in a recipe to create fresh-baked goods, and often are rewarded for creating new items. Reskin and Roos (1990) found that exploring such gender discrepancies in the status hierarchy of job categories offered a powerful insight into wage discrepancies.

Differences in earnings also exist along racial lines. Table 12.1 shows patterns of racialized disparity in earnings. Whites typically earn considerably more than workers of color. Notably, the hours required to attain these earnings are not necessarily the same: Workers of color tend

Table 12.1: Median Weekly Earnings by Sex and Race, 2012

	Men	Women
Whites	$ 879	$710
African American	665	599
Latino/a	592	521
Asian American	1055	770

Source: www.bls.gov

*Note: No comparable date on Native Americans are available.

to work more hours than white workers, suggesting even greater wage disparities by race than comparative median weekly earnings indicate (Mishel et al., 2012: 232–233).

In addition to wage differentials based on race and gender, a **glass ceiling** faces women and people of color in promotions, particularly to managerial levels in corporations. Such workers may rise to middle-management levels but rarely are promoted to the highest executive levels (Walters, 1996; Albelda and Tilly, 1997; Maume, 1999; Russo and Hassink, 2012). According to a study by the U.S. Department of Labor (1991), the glass ceiling is lower for people of color than it is for women, but neither advance very frequently into the higher ranks of management. One reason for this ceiling is that corporate recruitment and promotion practices tend to rely on word-of-mouth referrals and networks rather than on executive-search and referral firms. Thus, an informal mentoring system in which white male executives recruit, train, and refer other white males for promotions tends to lock women and people of color out of the system.

The Department of Labor study also found that career-enhancing projects, educational opportunities, and credential-building assignments were often less accessible to women and people of color in corporations (a situation probably related to the restricted informal mentoring system). Finally, women and people of color did not always benefit from the protection of Equal Employment Opportunity Commission regulations aimed at combating discrimination. Accountability and compliance with such regulations were carefully monitored at lower levels but were highly lax for senior-level executive positions and managerial positions involving decision making. Taken together, the forces of informal mentoring, accessibility to career-building opportunities and lack of compliance with equal employment opportunity rules at higher levels in the corporation produced the glass ceiling for women and people of color. This glass ceiling helps depress their median annual-income figures relative to those for white males in the United States.

Furthermore, research has shown that job displacement caused by plant closings and industrial reorganization hits women and people of color harder than males and whites (Pastor, 2001). For example, rates of unemployment and duration of unemployment are greater for women and African Americans than for men and whites. The consequence of differential job displacement and types of employment, combined with wage discrimination based on sex and race, is that women and people of color are more likely than males and whites to be poor. In the United States in 2010, the poverty rate for women was 15.6 percent, compared with the rate of 13.0 percent for men (www.census.gov). The rate for whites was 9.9 percent, whereas the rates for African Americans (27.4 percent) and Latino/as (26.6 percent) were nearly three times that for whites (Mishel et al., 2012: 420)../Local Settings/temp/7zO1E.tmp/(www .census.gov);.

The social implications extend beyond individual workers. Families certainly are affected. Female-headed families are more than three times as likely as married-couple families to be poor: The poverty rate for female-headed families was 40.7 percent in 2010, compared with only 8.8 percent for married couple families (Mishel et al., 2012:.426). Even within these categories, there are stark racial differences, as shown in Table 12.2. Asian American families tend to have poverty rates similar to those for whites families; but African American and Latino/a families, whether married-couple or single-headed (male or female), are as much as three times more likely than white families to be poor (unfortunately, the Census Bureau did not report out comparative data for Native American families). Moreover, the workfare provisions of welfare reform that require women receiving public assistance to take any job reinforce and intensify gendered and racialized patterns of poverty. This is because the jobs available are most often menial, low-wage service sector jobs in such settings as convenience stores and other retail outlets and fast-food restaurants. This means that poor women are likely to be locked into dead-end, low-paying jobs with little chance of breaking that cycle, by order of the state. The economic structural transformation in the United States has not only accentuated racialized and gendered inequalities; it has also contributed to the disproportionate impoverishment of women and children, particularly those of color.

TABLE 12.2: Families Below the Poverty Level, 2009

Families	Poverty Rate (%)
All families	11.1%
Married-couple families	5.8
Male householder, no wife present	16.9
Female householder, no husband present	29.9
White families	9.3
Married-couple families	5.4
Male householder, no wife present	15.0
Female householder, no husband present	27.3
African American families	22.7
Married-couple families	8.6
Male householder, no wife present	25.0
Female householder, no husband present	36.7
Latino/a families	22.7
Married-couple families	16.0
Male householder, no wife present	23.0
Female householder, no husband present	38.8
Asian American and Pacific Islander families	9.4
Married-couple families	7.9
Male householder, no wife present	12.6
Female householder, no husband present	16.9

Source: www.census.gov

The Declining Middle Class

The economic structural transformation of the United States has also contributed to the erosion of the nation's middle class. For the first time in history, downward mobility has been greater than the upward mobility many have come to take for granted (Newman, 1999; Newman and Chen, 2008). Until now, members of each succeeding generation have generally been able to exceed the lifestyle their parents could afford. Now the current generation of workers is struggling just to match, let alone surpass, that lifestyle. A Gallup/USA Today poll in 2012 found that 50 percent of respondents thought it unlikely that "today's youth will have a better life than their parents" (Gallup/USA Today, 2012).

The **middle class** is loosely defined as a category of people whose income places them above the poverty line but below the wealthiest fifth of the population. It may also be conceptualized by lifestyle. Ehrenreich defined the middle class in terms of home ownership, the ability to send one's offspring to college, and "the ability to afford such amenities as a second car and family vacations" (1986: 50). Probably the most visible and telling indicator of the decline of the middle class is home ownership. While there has been no overall decline in home ownership, a breakdown by age reveals serious decreases in ownership among certain groups. For younger Americans the prospect of owning a home is becoming dimmer: between 1980 and 2012, the home-ownership rate for people younger than 35 years old fell from 51.6 to 27.8 percent, and the rate for those between the ages of 35 and 44 declined from 71.2 to 46.1 percent (www .census.gov/housing/hvs/data/histtabs.html). Clearly, home ownership, a key feature of the American Dream and middle class status, is getting more difficult for younger generations to obtain.

The ability to send their offspring to college has also begun to elude more and more members of the middle class: "For a family with 1985 earnings equal to the median national income, keeping a child in a four-year private college or university would have taken 40 percent of that income, up from 30 percent in 1970" (Phillips, 1990: 22). By the end of the 1990s, even sending a child to a state university or public college had become increasingly costly and therefore less affordable for many middle-class families, a situation that has only grown worse most recently. At the same time, government support per student for college education has stagnated (Collins and Yeskel with United for a Fair Economy, 2000). The combination of rising college tuitions and fees, rising home purchase prices, and the discrepancies of higher-paying manufacturing and lower-paying service jobs have seriously eroded the lifestyle of the middle class. Its downward mobility has been described by sociologist Katherine S. Newman (1999) as a "fall from grace" (see also Newman and Chen, 2008). Indeed, if you recall the description of Dana's family situation at the opening of this book, it is evident that at the center of much that troubled this family was its fall from grace resulting from deindustrialization and downsizing.

The structural transformation of the economy has thus made the American Dream less and less possible, for the first time in history, for many members of the middle class. Earlier manual-labor job paths to upward mobility for members of the working class and the poor either have permanently disappeared or have undergone serious income erosion. The changing structure of the economy has meant that many white-collar workers and professional and managerial workers are finding themselves unemployed for the first time. In the past, economic woes generally hit blue-collar and unskilled workers while others were largely spared. Now even persons with college degrees and good skills are joining their more traditional brethren on the unemployment, food-stamp, and soup-kitchen lines, a situation that may make middle-class victims of the structural transformation of the economy more sympathetic to the plight of the poor as they begin to share common deprivations.

PROSPECTS FOR CHANGE

Clearly, a major contributing factor to problems of deindustrialization and the structural shifts of the formal labor market is the lack of control by labor and communities over the work process. That is, the power structure of the corporation, in which decision making, which is strongly influenced by shareholders' interests and which occurs at the top of the organizational hierarchy with little or no input from workers, has greatly affected work and workers in the United States and abroad. In order to change that, any strategies for change must confront that power structure. One possible vehicle for confronting such a formidable structure in order to increase labor control is labor unions. As social movement organizations, unions historically mobilized the critical resource of workers' collective labor power to affect the power structure of work in the formal labor market to their advantage. While unions' strength has significantly declined in recent decades and their ability to mobilize collective resources has consequently been far less effective than in the decades following World War II, there is some evidence suggesting a resurgence of labor movement activity.

Unions provide definite benefits for workers. They have had a positive impact on wages, benefits, health and safety on the job, and the like. However, deindustrialization, global relocation and the twenty-first-century recession have meant a loss of jobs in goods production, the very sector where unions had made the greatest inroads in organizing workers. Labor unions have lost significant ground since 1960 in the proportion of the labor force they represent: Union membership has declined from a high of greater than 35 percent of the U.S. work force to a low of 11.3 percent in 2012 (www.bls.gov). There is evidence that this may be changing: While the proportion of workers in the total work force who are represented by unions may remain low, the numbers of new union memberships are on the rise. The reason for this seeming contradiction is that the total number of workers in the formal labor force itself is growing faster than the increase in the number of workers in unions. Therefore, the proportion of unionized workers makes it seem as if workers are continuing to disregard organized or collective bargaining as a viable strategy. The actual rise in union membership, however, suggests otherwise. Indeed, a 2012 Gallup poll on labor unions found that 52 percent of respondents approve of labor unions (Gallup, 2012). What might account for this turn of worker support for and participation in the labor movement?

Several strategies and approaches to change in unions as social movement organizations are beginning to occur. First, elections in the Teamsters Union in the early 1990s brought in a leadership devoted to reform, symbolizing the new image of greater honesty sought by unions. The Teamsters have eliminated perquisites for union executives: Gone are the union limousines, special jets, and luxury condominiums in Puerto Rico, as well as the unlimited paid vacations anywhere in the world for union executives. The image of less-privileged union executives, along with greater democratization of unions, promises to improve workers' sense of participation in union decision making and to enhance their perception that unions are functioning in their interests.

Unions are also increasingly coming to recognize the need to organize workers globally (International Labour Organization, 2013). It is no longer useful for workers in the United States to be unionized if their counterparts in other countries are not. Corporations can simply exploit the differences in pay and work conditions to undermine workers' standard of living both here and abroad. There are signs that unions are beginning to take corrective action. For example, telephone technicians in New England went on strike against Northern Telecom, a company based in Canada, and the strike lasted for months. The company was not inclined to bargain with the New England workers until the Communication and Electrical Workers of Canada supported them at the bargaining table. Within days, the New England strike was over, to the satisfaction of the workers. The lesson here: Since the division of labor has become globalized, workers must also globalize their union representation. This suggests that U.S. workers should stop seeing their counterparts in other countries as rivals and competitors.

In addition to organizing workers across national borders, much organized international activism has mobilized around the problem of sweatshops in global south countries (see Chapter 10). Pressure is mounting to force multinational corporations to comply with international standards of worker health and safety, if not living wages. Such efforts at the very least hold the potential to regularize work conditions regardless of where production takes place so as to make it less attractive to corporations to transplant jobs abroad.

Another way in which unions can make an impact is by organizing workers who have not been unionized, particularly in the non-government service sector. That sector is the least unionized of the formal-labor-market sectors. Service workers in the state sector, on the other hand, are among the most unionized of the service workers, and as a result they enjoy better wages and benefits, better working conditions, and somewhat better job security than service workers in the private sector. While union representation in manufacturing has seriously eroded, representation among government workers has remained relatively stable for nearly 30 years: By 2010, 40 percent of government workers are covered by unions, compared with 7.7 percent of private sector workers (www.census.gov). Similar progress in organizing labor can be made with service workers in the private sector. Indeed, several unions have begun energetic organizing efforts among janitors, hotel and restaurant workers, office workers, nursing home workers, and the like.

In fact, it is ironic that the very thing that undermined organized labor in the 1970s and 1980s has become important for the new century of unionization. The ability to globally relocate or automate manufacturing jobs severely damaged the effectiveness of one of the most powerful weapons labor had: the strike. But the structural transformation of the economy from goods production to services holds tremendous promise for a resurgence of the efficacy of the strike. Unlike goods-producing jobs, many service sector jobs (such as those in janitorial services, nursing home services, convenience stores, hotels and restaurants, delivery services, and so forth) are not as geographically mobile. Services are typically provided in local settings for the most part and therefore are difficult to relocate by employers seeking to avoid unionization. For workers in an organized service sector, going out on strike can be quite effective in forcing employers to negotiate living wages, decent and safe working conditions, health and retirement benefits, and perhaps even profit or power sharing. The unionized workers at the United Parcel Services demonstrated this in 1997, when they won a landmark strike against their employer (Cockburn, 1997). UPS workers, represented by the Teamsters Union, managed to gain agreements from UPS management to convert 10,000 part-time jobs to full-time jobs at twice the hourly pay rate; to increase workers' wages by 15 percent over five years for full-time workers and up to 35 percent for part-time workers; and to discontinue plans to drop out of the union's pension program (Magnusson et al., 1997: 29). No other union had succeeded in gaining such beneficial contract provisions in more than two decades. The fact that the jobs of local delivery service workers cannot be exported to another country, combined with the mobilization of workers' collective power to strike as a resource, gave these workers an advantage not experienced by labor in some time.

In addition to a renewed sense of energy in the American labor movement, there have been some promising changes in corporate worker-management relations. One such change has been **employee stock option plans**, or **ESOPs**, in which managers set up ways for workers to purchase shares of stock in their own companies. This approach provides workers with a share of the profits their labor helps create, and may motivate them to become more productive (Ford, 1988). More than 11,000 firms in the U.S. now provide ESOPs to over 9 million workers (www .nceo.org/articles/employee-stock-options-factsheet; Rosen, 1998). Such a strategy may be quite lucrative for workers, especially during periods when the stock market is highly robust. But profit sharing does not mean power sharing: Workers under ESOP plans still do not share in the decision making that affects their jobs, the work process, or the work environment (Logue, 1998). Such decisions remain in the hands of chief executive officers and boards of directors, whose decisions are likely to continue to be more strongly influenced by managerial and ownership interests, not the needs of workers. And while increased values in stocks may certainly be to the advantage of workers holding significant shares of stock in their firms, decisions that produce such increases can also mean the loss of workers' jobs (through downsizing, job export, etc.).

There are some strategies that offer promise for workers to gain more control over or voice in corporate decision making. For example, by 2012 there were approximately 11,000 majority-owned or worker-owned companies employing almost 13 million workers in the United States, almost all of which were employee or community buyouts from prior owners (as opposed to start-ups). Many of these plants or companies were about to be shut down and their operations relocated elsewhere (National Center for Employee Ownership www.nceo.org; www.nytimes .com/2011/12/15/opinion/worker-owners-of-america-unite.html?_r=0; see also Varano, 1999). The buyouts often succeeded through coalitions of community, labor, and, at times, religious organizations and municipal governments (Hodson and Sullivan, 1990: 166–167; Logue, 1998). Sometimes such buyouts are financed with workers' pensions or employee stock-option programs (Ford, 1988). When workers pool their stockholdings in the company, they may have enough capital or clout to buy out at least the plant in their community, thereby preserving jobs and the plant's productive capacity.

Once a buyout is completed, the plant may be converted to a **worker cooperative**, **which is entirely owned and operated by the workers themselves** (MacLeod, 1997; Pencavel, 2002). In the typical worker-owned cooperative, not only does the entire workforce of the company own the firm; decisions, including the selection of managers, are commonly done democratically, with each worker having one vote; and all share in the profits generated by their collective efforts (Delaney, 1996; Estey and Bowman, 2000). This ensures that ownership and operation remain locally controlled and eliminates the possibility of a runaway shop. While not all were buyouts of existing firms by workers, there are currently over 11,000 worker-owned cooperatives thriving in the United States with over $800 billion in assets and employing 13 million employee-owners (http://truth-out.org/news/item/13215-employee-owned-businesses-ignored-by-mainstream-media; http://www.nytimes.com/2011/12/15/opinion/worker-owners-of-america-unite.html).

As intriguing as worker-owned buyouts may be, however, caution must be used: As with other corporations, when financial institutions provide major loans or sit on the firm's board they may exercise considerable clout over owners' decision making. This can compromise owners' power to determine their firm's future, whether they are worker-owners or more traditional professional corporate managers.

Federal programs sometimes offer other useful strategies for communities and workers to prevent runaway shops. For example, the federal Community Reinvestment Act (CRA) offers local community organizations an opportunity to challenge banks' tendency to "disinvest" in the local community. Banks frequently take the deposits from their branches in local communities and reinvest that finance capital elsewhere, often supporting plant relocations. Bank mergers tend to reinforce patterns of disinvestment in the local community. CRA provides local community organizations an opportunity to challenge banks' practices when a bank is attempting to open intercity branches or to participate in an interstate merger between banks, because these expansions require federal approval. One factor that can affect that approval is community reinvestment. Therefore, a CRA challenge can potentially hinder banks' expansion plans and therefore can prompt negotiations between the local community and the bank, frequently resulting in greater bank commitments to invest in local and regional development (Fitzgerald and Meyer, 1986). Successful CRA challenges of banks' decisions have resulted in more than $1 trillion reinvested back into previously severely underserved low and moderate income communities since 1977 (www.enterprisefoundation.org/policy/crasummary), a shift the Federal Reserve credits with the effectiveness of the legislation (www.federalreserve.gov/boarddocs/speeches/1998). ../Local Settings/temp/7zO1E.tmp/(www.enterprisefoundation.org/policy/crasummary). These highly encouraging results, however, are just a beginning: Banks continue to deny mortgage loan applications from African Americans and Latino/as at twice the rate as applications made by whites (www.innercitypress.org/cra).

These developments suggest positive possibilities for workers to become a stronger force in the reshaping of the U.S. economy. And unions are now poised to play a more significant role in reducing gender and racial inequalities than they have in the past. If unions, as workers' own bases of power, are to grow once again, they must organize across national borders and into previously nonunionized labor sectors like the service sector and contingency work. And they must seek to include more women and people of color among their members. Unions therefore must address the issues and concerns of such workers in order to attract them as members. Through unions, women and workers of color may be able to gain a stronger voice in what happens to them in the formal labor market.

CHAPTER SUMMARY

- Several factors have worked to devalue college degrees and what they can do for people who attain them.

- The changing structure of the economy and of the formal labor market is reducing workers' control over decisions affecting their jobs and their participation in the economy. The consequences of that restructuring most negatively affect lower-level workers and the poor, women, and people of color—that is, those who have historically been disadvantaged in the formal labor market.

- The result has been increasing inequality: a widening gap between rich and poor, between men and women, between whites and people of color.

- In addition, the most recent phase of the structural transformation of the economy has hit the middle class and managerial workers, those who until recently enjoyed comparatively secure, protected positions and opportunities for upward mobility.

- Higher education (when it can be obtained) no longer guarantees upward mobility.

- The changing formal labor market suggests that the economy is hardly a neutral force devoid of politics.

- Power imbalances enable some in the economic hierarchy to make decisions that benefit themselves but adversely affect others.

- Workers can protect themselves by actively seeking a greater voice in decisions that affect the economy, their communities, and their jobs.

- Of course, work occurs not only in the formal labor market but in the informal labor market and in the unpaid domestic labor sphere as well.

- Work in these three spheres is differentially distributed along race, class, and gender lines: The poor and the working class, women, and people of color are much more likely to engage in a triple shift than the wealthy, men, and whites.

- People who are already advantaged are better able to delegate responsibility for the work done in the household and in the community to the less advantaged.

- Perhaps strategies can be formulated to more equitably distribute work in all three spheres, and devise ways to better reward both paid and unpaid labor.

THINKING CRITICALLY

1. We discussed Reskin and Roos's observation that within broad job categories there are occupational status hierarchies. Select a job category and analyze the occupational status hierarchies that it might include. Which of these occupations might pay more, and why? Who is more likely to have each of these occupations? What does this suggest about the distribution of earnings?

2. Consider the division of labor in your family. Outline the various jobs that each member does, and identify whether these are done in the formal, the informal, or the unpaid domestic labor markets. Which of these markets does each family member *primarily* work in? Is there a balance between labor markets for all members, or do some members work primarily in one market? What might explain the distribution of work in your family? For example, is gender an important factor?

3. Think of industries or corporations that left or ceased operations in your state or community. Why did they leave or close? How did these shutdowns affect your local community? Your state? Your family or the families of those you know? What could the community and/or the state do to avoid the loss of industries or to reduce the effects of their loss?

4. The North American Free Trade Agreement (NAFTA) allows free movement of goods, services, and production between the United States, Mexico, and Canada. This means that corporations in the United States may elect to produce goods in any of the three countries without incurring import tariffs (taxes) on goods produced outside the United States. Who is likely to benefit and who is likely to be hurt by NAFTA, and why? What might those who may be hurt by NAFTA do to protect themselves from possible disadvantages of the trade agreement?

 KEY TERMS

deindustrialization **324**

domestic labor **316**

employee stock option plans (ESOPs) **338**

formal labor market **316**

glass ceiling **333**

globalization **320**

informal labor market **316**

interlocking boards of directors **327**

managerial revolution **326**

mergers **323**

merger mania **323**

middle class **335**

runaway shops **323**

second shift **316**

segmented labor market **332**

triple shift **317**

underemployment **330**

work **316**

worker cooperative **338**

working poor **328**

2. Consider the division of labor in your family. Outline the various jobs that each member does, and identify whether these are done in the formal, the informal, or the underground domestic labor markets. Which of these markets does each family member work in? For which is there a balance between labor markets for all workers, or do some members work primarily in one market? What might explain the household of work in your family? For example, is gender an important factor?

3. Think of industries or communities that left for cesser operations in your current community. Why did they leave or close? How did those situations affect your local community? Your state? Your family or the families of those you know? What could a community and/or the state do to avoid the loss of industries or to reduce the loss of those jobs?

4. The North American Free Trade Agreement (NAFTA) allows the movement of goods, services, and production between the United States, Mexico, and Canada. The main three corporations in the United States may elect to produce goods in any of the three countries without incurring import tariffs (taxes) on goods produced outside the United States. Who is likely to benefit and who is likely to be hurt by NAFTA, and why? What might those who maybe hurt by NAFTA do to protect themselves from possible disadvantages of the trade agreements?

 KEY TERMS

nondash labor 324
domestic labor 315
employee-self ownership (ESOP) 318
formal labor market 316
class-caste 320
globalization 320
industrial revolution
microenterprises 325
merger 325

underground 323
informal labor 325
microloan 325
merger 316
segmented labor market 317
capitalism 317
outsourcing 318
work 316
worker cooperative 322
world trade 325

FAMILIES

13

Consider the various images of families shown on television over the last several decades, and often rebroadcast on cable stations. *In Leave It to Beaver*, the 1950s' television program, the mother is a full-time homemaker, the father works at an office in an unspecified occupation, they have two children, and they live in a comfortable suburban home. In *The Honeymooners*, a full-time homemaker is married to a bus driver, they have no children, and they live in a cramped, working-class walk-up apartment in New York City.

By the 1970s and 1980s these images began to change. *The Brady Bunch* showed a family composed of a woman and her three daughters from her previous marriage living together with her new husband and his three sons from a previous marriage. *Kate and Allie* described two single mothers and their children living together in one apartment and functioning as a family. *My Two Dads* depicted a family of two men raising a daughter. In *The Cosby Show*, mom and dad both had lucrative and satisfying professional careers; their five children lived with them in a large-city brownstone house, although at various times the children moved out or returned to their parents' home bringing with them spouses and offspring. In *Punky Brewster* the family consisted of a young foster child and the elderly man who adopted her. And *Roc* showed a working class African American family of a young, dual-occupation couple living with the husband's elderly father and unemployed brother in a single household.

During the 1990s, the images continued to change. In *Blossom*, a single father raised his children alone. In *Murphy Brown*, a single, successful professional woman decided to maintain her pregnancy and raise her child alone. In *The Golden Girls*, four middle-aged and elderly women, including one woman's mother, lived together in a Florida condominium.

By 2000, *Everybody Loves Raymond* introduced a family of three young children living with their full-time homemaker mother and full-time sports writer father. Grandparents and an uncle lived next door, but the distinctions between their households were blurred, as if there were not two separate households but one simply connected by a corridor of backyard. And by 2013 *Modern Family* and *The New Normal* depicted gay couples with adopted children, as well as interracial families, traditional nuclear families, extended families, and blended families. The New Normal, indeed.

These television families are a limited array of the various forms that the institution of the family may take. Despite the variety of forms, they are all, in some fashion, families. Your own family situation may differ significantly from the families seen on television. What, then, is a family? In this chapter we will examine the meaning of "family" by examining the following questions:

- What family forms prevail in the United States, and why?
- What factors make some forms more advantageous than others?
- Who benefits and who is hurt by different family forms?
- Does the variety of family forms, and the troubles afflicting many families, mean "the family" is breaking down as an institution?

Beyond being aware of the forms families may take, it is important to understand the dynamics among family members and the forces that might affect those dynamics. In this chapter we will explore the factors that can create problems and stress for families. We will consider how developments in other institutions affect the creation, alteration, and dissolution of family ties. For example, we will examine the roles the state and economy play in encouraging and rewarding some family forms but not others.

Let's turn first to the meaning of family.

DEFINING FAMILY

In 1949, George Murdock defined family, on the basis of an analysis of nearly 500 societies, as "a social group characterized by common residence, economic cooperation, and reproduction" (1949: 1). Murdock's definition, which he believed to be universally applicable to all societies, stated that a family consisted of "adults of both sexes, at least two of whom maintain a socially approved sexual relationship, and one or more children, own or adopted, of the sexually cohabitating adults" (1949: 1). He believed this family form was widespread because it was functional to society: It fulfilled societal needs. This definition reflects the functionalist theory of family, which emphasizes the role of the institution of family in addressing the functional imperatives of societal survival (see Chapter 3). These include reproduction to replace lost members of society, protection of societal members, transmission of cultural information to new members through socialization (see Chapter 6), and motivation of societal members to perform expected roles (Ogburn and Tibbits, 1934).

While many sociologists accept Murdock's definition, others criticize it for what it omits. For example, it does not include the realities of many family forms today: single-parent families, married couples without children, gay male and lesbian couples, multigenerational families without sexual relationships, blended families, and elderly couples with no children. It also excludes cohabitating couples, both heterosexual and same-sex.

Murdock's definition of family seems to confuse *family* (defined by a set of principles determining relatedness) with **household** (a common residential unit in which related and nonrelated individuals may live) (Andersen, 1990; Ferree, 1990). However, a family and a household are not necessarily the same thing. For example, in pre-Civil War United States, while slaves contributed to a slave owner's family as an economic unit, and were often considered part of the household, they were not accepted as legitimate family members according to the conventional definition (Jones, 1987). Consider, too, the case of children of a divorce: They may live in a separate household with only one of their parents, but they often still consider *both* parents to be their family.

Sociologists who accept Murdock's functional definition of family often recognize that there may be different types of family, based on the role it plays for the individual, and they have differentiated families on the basis of biological factors. **Families of orientation** are the families into which individuals are born or adopted, while **families of procreation** are those into which individuals marry and in which they often produce their own offspring. From your own perspective, this means that your parents and siblings are your family of orientation while your family of procreation may be you and your spouse and possibly your children. This differentiation of family by the biological role it plays for the individual assumes that most individuals will marry into a heterosexual relationship that will likely produce offspring.

But this is a very shaky assumption. Many people enter into cohabitation relationships, both heterosexual and homosexual, and a growing number of couples (both married and cohabitating) are choosing not to have children. Many gay males and lesbians increasingly refer to their relationships with their partners and their partners' relatives as **families of choice**, reflecting a family form not defined by biology (Cody and Welch, 1997; Stiers, 2000). In this form, family is defined by stable voluntary relationships based on shared economic and emotional ties in one or more households.

Sociologists have also differentiated between nuclear and extended families. **A nuclear family** is composed of two parents and their offspring living together. The classic example is the family on *Leave it to Beaver*. **An extended family** includes the nuclear family plus other members of one or both parents' families of orientation (e.g., their parents, grandparents, aunts and uncles, and siblings). TV examples are the families in *Everybody Loves Raymond*, *Roc*, *King of Queens*, and the later years of *Cosby*.

Some sociologists link these types of family to social class: The nuclear family is seen to typify the middle class, because the breadwinner earns enough to support the family without the financial help of other family members; the extended family is more commonly found among the working class and poor, since several generations or members of the same generation tend to live together out of economic necessity. Such a differentiation of family forms continues to confuse households with families. It is also historically inaccurate: Many middle-class families in the 1950s and 1960s in the United States lived in some form of extended family (particularly those including two married members, their children, and one or more grandparents) (Litwak, 1965). As will be shown later, many still do today, and their numbers are growing, owing to a struggling economy.

Research also indicates some racial and ethnic differences in the prevalence of extended families. Although most families in the United States, regardless of racial/ethnic group, are "maintained by a married couple or by a single parent with children" (Taylor, 2002: 25), African Americans are twice as likely as whites to live in extended families that "transcend and link several different households" (Farley and Allen, 1987:168; Kane, 2000; see also Gerstel, 2011). Similarly, Latino/a (Perez, 2002; Carrasquillo, 2002), Native American (Yellowbird and Snipp, 2002), and Asian American families (Nakano Glenn and Yap, 2002; Tagaki, 2002) are more likely than white families to be structured as extended families. There are clearly diverse ethnicities within each of these socially constructed racialized categories, but one thing they have in common is the likelihood that extended family structure derives, in part, from cultural histories and experiences, including racism, immigration, resettlement, internment, and exclusion in the United States. But far from being dysfunctional, these extended family forms manifest strong family-centered values and norms, egalitarian domestic divisions of labor, and adaptable family roles (Kane, 2000). Extended families may thus operate as structures that reflect resilience of the family in the face of institutional challenges (Taylor, 2002).

For example, extended families among Vietnamese Americans occur as a structure of rebuilding and reconstituting families disrupted by migration after the Vietnam War. The evacuees of the first wave of immigrants tended to be among the Vietnamese elites, who settled in the United States. Those who fled after 1975 tended to be poorer, and they fled to asylum in neighboring countries in Asia where they were placed in refugee camps and often waited as long as two years to be resettled to countries like Canada, Australia, China, and the United States. As individuals arrived from these interim arrangements, they joined the earlier arrivals, who took in both kin and nonkin in an attempt to reconstruct families within their community (Kibria, 2002).

Cultural familial norms may encourage extended families. For example, Native American, Latino/a, and Asian American cultural norms often define adult children as responsible for the care of aging parents (Phua, Kaufman, and Park, 2001). The wider community becomes part of the familial network of kin and nonkin, thereby contributing in part to the greater likelihood of extended family structures.

Extended family forms may also be a response to the economy (Aaron et al, 1999; Glick and Van Hook, 2011). While white families' household income tends to derive primarily from the incomes of one or both partners of a marriage, African American families' income is more likely to be based on the combined incomes of both partners, adult children, and extended relatives. Given the lower average annual earnings of African Americans compared with those of whites, there are clear economic pressures to pool relatively limited financial resources as a means of escaping extreme poverty.

Economic pressures are contributing to a general resurgence of extended families in the United States. Many middle-class families with aging parents are returning to a form of extended family. As reliable, adequate nursing-home care becomes increasingly expensive and inaccessible to the middle class, elderly parents are moving in with their children. Family Caregiver Alliance estimates that one-fourth of all U.S. households is caring for an elderly family member (www.caregiver.org). This is creating a **sandwich generation** of adults caring for both elders and children. In the United States, one in seven adults is caring for elderly parents and simultaneously raising children (Cravey and Mitra, 2011; De Los Santos, 2013). Notably, women are typically the caretakers, regardless of whether the elderly parent is hers or her partner's (Velkoff and Lawson, 1998; Guberman, 1999; Kunemund, 2006). In 2009, more than one-fourth of the adult U.S. population provided care for an individual who was disabled or chronically ill, including parents and partners (Family Caregiver Alliance, National Center on Caregiving, available at www.caregiver.org).

Furthermore, we are witnessing the increasing prevalence of a **boomerang generation**: As housing costs soar and shifts in the economy make decent-paying jobs scarce even for college graduates, an increasing number of middle-class offspring return home as adults to live with their parents (Veevers, Gee, and Wister, 1996; Zhu, Yang, and Liu, 2002). In 2012, 57 percent of men and 49 percent of women between the ages of 18 and 24 were living at home (Darling, 2012), and 30 percent of adults 25 to 34 were still living with their parents (Parker, 2012). So the extended family appears to be widespread among the population, reflecting a variety of social and economic circumstances.

Nearly half of all marriages end in divorce. Most divorced people remarry: Within five years after divorce, 58 percent of white women have remarried, as have 44 percent of Latinas and 32 percent of African American women (www.census.gov/statab; Bramlett and Mosher, 2001). Since many remarriages involve partners with children from previous marriages, there are an increasing number of **blended families** consisting of two new partners and their respective children. When these new marriages produce children as well, they create a family consisting of stepsiblings, half-siblings, stepparents, and parents. Joint-custody arrangements between divorced parents can mean that marriage to a new partner does not necessarily sever the relationship between a parent and his or her children. Thus, the children may live primarily with one parent but also remain part of the other parent's household. The blended family, like the new extended family, challenges the conventional definition of family since it often involves several households.

Divorce has also created a new challenge to the meaning of household and family. Some divorced couples maintain the previous household where the children live as well as their own residence; each parent cycles in and out of that household for their custodial time with the children, rather than having the children rotate between their parents' individual residences. Such an arrangement clearly requires an amicable divorce, and a fair amount of income to maintain essentially three households, which is why so few divorced couples do this. But that some do remains a challenge to the definition of family: Is this a family, even if it is split over several households? Finally, new technologies in reproduction have introduced the prospect of a variety of combinations and arrangements involving biological providers of sperm and egg, carriers of fetuses, and providers of custodial care of offspring. Such relationships became evident through painful legal dramas involving custody battles over children born as the products of "surrogate" or gestational mothers and those with whom they had contracted to carry the fetus. These relationships raise the thorny questions concerning who are the "rightful" parents and who are not. They have also gained attention when celebrities are involved, exemplified by the family created by actress Julie Cypher and rock singer Melissa Ethridge, two lesbian mothers whose two children were fathered by sperm donated by rock legend David Crosby. Cypher and Etheridge have since split, opening a discussion of how to maintain the family and whether it mattered that the parents were both lesbians.

How, then, can "family" be defined and still capture the wide diversity of forms which constitute that institution? A critical definition based on that offered by Carol D. Stack (1974: 31) can be useful because it reflects a variety of situations, including those contoured by race, class, and gender: **Family** is an organized, ongoing network of kin and nonkin who interact daily, sharing economic and household responsibilities and obligations, providing for domestic, emotional, physical, and financial needs of all members, and ensuring their survival. The family network may span several households that may be based on biology or on choice.

DIVERSITY OF FAMILY FORMS

Given that the family may be structured in different ways at different times, which forms of the family are most prevalent in the United States today, and why? As shown in Figure 13.1, the conventional understanding of the nuclear family, composed of a breadwinning father, a full-time homemaker mother, and two or more young offspring living in the same residence, describes less than 4 percent of U.S. households (www.census.gov/statab). Nearly twice as many households consist of two income-earning married adults and their children as single-earner households. Married couples with no children total almost one-third of U.S. households. Single-parent households are also common. Among these, female-headed households are more than five-and-a-half times more frequent than male-headed households (www.census.gov/statab). Unmarried cohabiting couples are also on the rise: By 2010, 8.1 million of over 117 million documented households consisted of cohabiting couples (www.census.gov). Unfortunately, the Census Bureau does not provide data for other household arrangements, such as blended families. However, despite these limitations, the data indicate that the conventional nuclear family is no longer the typical U.S. family.

Are the proportions of family types similar for white, African American, and Latino/a families in the United States? According to Figure 13.2, in 2010 white and Latino/a families were more likely to be two-parent households than were African American or Asian American families. African American families were more likely than either Latino/a, Asian American or white families to be headed by single mothers with no husband present. Wives in African American married-couple families were also more likely to work in the formal labor force than were white wives (www.census.gov).

Let's take a closer look at the diversity of family forms in the United States.

Family Forms: Cultural Choice or Institutional Response?

In a controversial speech given in 1992, Vice President Dan Quayle argued that single-parent families were largely responsible for much of what was wrong in the United States. He insisted that "appropriate" family values call for a two-parent family, in which one of the parents (presumably the mother) assumes primary responsibility for taking care of the children. He urged a return to such family values as the answer to most social problems.

FIGURE 13.1: Proportion of Family Forms in the United States, 2010

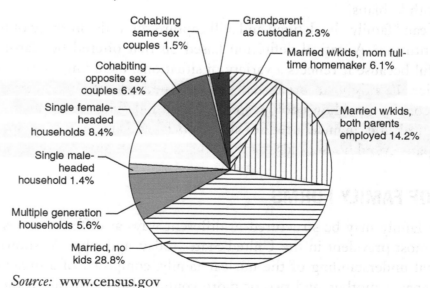

Source: www.census.gov

FIGURE 13.2:   Family Forms by Race, 2010 (as percent of population)

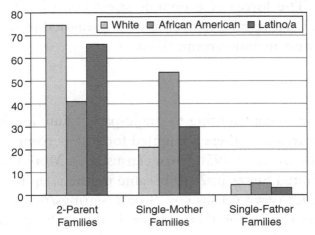

Source: www.census.gov

This attitude suggests that family forms other than the traditional nuclear family structure represent conscious choices on the part of individuals or reflect different cultural norms within the population. But what about institutional forces that might influence the form some families assume? A conflict perspective suggests that institutional forces may not only be responsible for diversity in family forms but that they may also influence the interpersonal dynamics and individual experiences within these forms (Allan and Crow, 2001).

Reasons for the Rise in Single-Parent Families

Several forces help account for the growing number of single-parent families, primary among them being divorce and unwed motherhood and the state of the economy.

Divorce

Many single-parent families are the result of divorce. While the divorce rate in the United States has declined from three out of every five marriages during the 1970s to half of all marriages, the rate is still high. What factors contribute to the high rate of divorce?../Local Settings/temp/7zO21.tmp/(www.census.gov).

Divorce has become easier to achieve since 1970 with the advent of **no-fault divorce** laws in many states. Prior to this legislation, couples were required to demonstrate that one of the partners was responsible for the destruction of the marriage, usually on the grounds of adultery or severe mistreatment. Under no-fault divorce laws, it is no longer necessary to attribute blame for misconduct in order to dissolve the marriage. One or both partners may simply apply to the courts for a divorce by citing irreconcilable differences. Such a significant change in legal requirements for divorce indicates substantial changes in society's values and cultural norms regarding marriage, the declining influence of religious institutions, and the increasing influence of the state in family affairs.

Economic conditions may also contribute to the divorce rate. Participation in the formal labor market provides some women with greater economic independence from their husbands, thereby making divorce a more viable option. A weak economy, including high rates of unemployment and inflation and a significant decline in the value of wages, may introduce serious stresses into a marriage. The forces of economic stress contributing to divorce affect some groups more than others. Divorce rates (as well as rates of marital separation and abandonment) are highest among the lowest-income groups (Kim, 2010).

Unwed Motherhood

Divorce is not the only factor contributing to single-parent families. Many such families *begin* with a single parent. Unmarried mothers accounted for 40.7 percent of all births in the United States in 2008, up from 4 percent in 1950 (www.census.gov). More than one-fifth of all never-married women in the United States in 2010 became mothers, up from slightly more than 15 percent just a decade earlier (www.census.gov../Local Settings/temp/7zO21.tmp/(www.census .gov/statabT). Part of the reason for this increase is that cultural sanctions against out-of-wedlock births are changing. Less often today do people refer to children of unwed mothers as "illegitimate." And an increasing number of affluent, over-30 single women are choosing to have babies, without plans of marriage. However, apart from this trend, teenagers constitute a significant, but declining, group among unwed mothers. Why might there be a high rate of births to single females, especially teenagers?

One factor is that girls have become capable of reproduction at increasingly younger ages, in part because of improved nutrition and health, and ironically, some believe, attributable to widespread consumption of fast food that is infused with growth hormones. An earlier onset of menstruation means that a greater percentage of females are able to become pregnant. In the late 1990s, the proportion of teenagers who were sexually active had declined from the high rates noted in 1990, but these rates still remain high. According to the Alan Guttmacher Institute, more than half have had intercourse by the time they turn 17, and 70 percent by the time they turn 19 years old (www.agi-usa.org../Local Settings/temp/7zO21.tmp/(www.agi_usa.org).). Although such teenagers may have access to contraceptives, and most do use them before their first intercourse experience, many do not use them. In 2008, 24 percent of sexually active young unmarried females did not use contraceptives during their first intercourse (www.guttmacher .org). Many pregnancies result from the female's first sexual experiences, when use of contraceptives is often neglected. In fact, the Alan Guttmacher Institute, which tracks adolescent sexual and health data, noted that sexually active teens have a 90 percent chance of becoming pregnant within a year when they do not contraceptives.

Why, then, do so many teenagers neglect using contraceptives? Part of the problem is lack of knowledge and misinformation concerning birth control and pregnancy. Sex education in the public schools takes place to some extent, but it is mired in controversy. The programs often fail to provide information about what leads to pregnancy and how to use and obtain contraceptives. Some parents fear that such information will only make teenagers *more* sexually active. But studies have found that sex education does *not* increase the rate of sexual activity among teenagers, and it may actually increase the probability that those who are sexually active will use contraceptives (Grunseit et al, 1997; Kirby and Lans, 2009).

Religious and state institutions may also discourage use of contraceptives. The Roman Catholic Church, for example, does not approve of contraceptive use by anyone. While most U.S.

married Catholics tend to ignore the church's disapproval, teenagers who are active members of the church may be discouraged from using this protection. State and federal laws restrict access to certain types of contraceptives (birth-control pills, diaphragms, and intrauterine devices) by requiring a physician's prescription. Since many teenagers are reluctant to admit sexual activity to a family doctor, or are unable to afford to see one, they may have limited access to prescribed contraceptives. Planned Parenthood and other clinics offer free exams and contraceptives, but they are not always easily accessible to teenagers (especially in rural areas). Thus, policies of such institutions as education, religion, and the state contribute to the high rates of teenage pregnancy and single parenthood.

In addition, gender socialization and cultural notions of romantic love may contribute to teenage pregnancies (Finlay, 1996). Traditional gender roles assume male aggression and sexual expertise and female docility and sexual purity. These gender roles often suggest that a "good girl" does not *plan* for a sexual encounter (Kisker, 1985). Guilt over sexual activity, coupled with the **cultural myth of romanticism,** may thus lead some females to avoid contraception. Being prepared for sexual intercourse by having contraceptives amounts to admitting that one is sexually active, but a female's sexual activity may be understood or excused if she was "swept off her feet" in the heat of a romantic moment. For teenaged males, cultural norms of masculinity and machismo are likely to discourage use of condoms (Castro-Vasquez, 2000). In this way cultural definitions of gender-specific appropriate behaviors contribute to single parenthood.

Reasons for the Rise in Other Nontraditional Family Forms

Institutional and cultural arrangements may also encourage the growth of other nontraditional family forms in the United States. For example, the lack of paid family-leave policies and government-supported childcare programs may encourage multihousehold or multigenerational extended families. Other countries, such as Sweden, use income-tax revenues to provide for parental leave from employment during the first year of a child's life, with minimal loss of income for the parents who elect to take such leave. Many governments in Europe at least partially support daycare facilities for children over the age of 1, thereby ensuring adequate institutional support for parents who must work outside the home but do not want to jeopardize the care and education of their children (Ferber, O'Farrell, and Allen, 1991; Gilbert and Van Voorhis, 2003; Tunberger and Sigle-Rushton, 2011). An economy where many hold low-wage jobs makes it necessary for both partners in a traditional nuclear family to earn income in order to survive or to achieve a standard of living above poverty. Living in an extended family where childcare help is available may be necessary. Poverty among the elderly, particularly women, may prompt the need for an extended family to provide elder care.

Increasing divorce rates have sent many women to work in order to provide for themselves and their children. But wage inequalities in the formal labor market mean that many women, especially those who are the sole providers for their families, will struggle to avoid poverty and many will not succeed. The lack of affordable dependent care for young children, persons with disabilities, and the elderly causes many families to turn to help from extended family members. For example, the U.S. Bureau of the Census found that in 2010, 42.3 percent of preschool age children whose mothers were employed in the formal labor market were cared for by relatives other than their parents; almost 30 percent of these children were cared for by their grandparents (www.census.gov). Clearly, then, varying family forms to some extent respond to such institutional forces as the dynamics of the economy and state policies in addition to diversity in cultural norms, rather than merely reflecting individual choice.

The deployment of troops to Iraq and Afghanistan beginning in 2003 has also focused attention on the issue of institutional forces prompting nontraditional family forms. When individuals who are part of two-parent families are deployed far from the family household, it at least temporarily creates single-parent families. Men with military wives who are activated for duty may be thrust for the first time into an extended experience of the double shift more commonly juggled by women. And when single parents are deployed, it forces new considerations of childcare. Grandparents may suddenly find themselves functioning as full-time primary caretakers of their grandchildren. Divorced parents may need to rearrange custody agreements. And if the unthinkable should happen and the deployed parent never returns home, these temporary arrangements may very well become permanent.

Does the diversity of family forms mean that the institution of the family in the United States is in a state of crisis? Not necessarily. The impact of powerful institutions, such as the economy and the state, make the traditional nuclear family untenable for many people. Yet other family forms and variations develop to ensure the survival and well-being of societal members. The institution of the family is not breaking down, but it is undergoing substantial change and adapting to challenges created by the manner in which other institutions like the economy and the state operate. The latent functions of these institutions are likely to prompt adaptive strategies in the institution of the family. Whether all the changes are for the good is a matter of considerable debate and a worthy subject for social science research.

POVERTY AND FAMILIES

Institutional forces not only influence family forms but also affect the experiences of families, as seen most clearly in the different patterns of poverty shown in Chapter 12 (Table 12.2). The U.S. Bureau of the Census found that in 2010, single-parent families, especially those headed by a female, were far more likely than married-couple families to be poor. And families of color were more likely than white families to be poor. Why do such patterns exist? How can these be explained in the context of the current economic climate?

The Effect of State Policies

Wage inequality makes it more difficult for single women of all racial and ethnic groups than for married couples and men to provide for their families and rise above poverty levels. For the same reason, African American and Latino/a married couples and single parents find doing so more difficult than their white counterparts. The inadequacy of the minimum wage means that even when a father works full-time, year-round, he may not earn enough to provide adequately for his family. His spouse must also participate in the formal labor market. Even when both parents work, it is not always possible for the family to remain above poverty. Unfortunately, some social welfare programs that provide assistance to the poor are specifically designed to aid *single mothers* and their children, a policy that discourages partners from remaining together during serious economic hardship.

State policy may, on the other hand, improve rather than aggravate the economic circumstances of some families. Although African American and Latino/a families are more likely than white families to be poor, not all families of color are poor. In fact, the number of African American and Latino/a middle-class families has grown since 1990 (www.census.gov). Such growth suggests that state programs aimed at providing equal educational opportunities and prohibiting discrimination in employment have had some impact.

Other research demonstrates the effect of state policies on the economic well-being of various family forms. Federal economic policies of the 1970s and 1980s that reduced support for women and children, as well as welfare reform of the 1990s that eliminated women's and children's entitlement to public assistance, exacerbated the **feminization of poverty** (Roschelle, 1999), in which an increasing proportion of the poor are female-headed families, particularly those headed by women of color. The term *feminization of poverty* has been commonly used in the mass media to describe the increased presence of women in poverty, but its usage may erroneously imply that women have either chosen to be poor (e.g., by electing to stay on welfare to remain home with their children) or somehow brought poverty on themselves (e.g., by leaving their marriages). An increasing number of observers prefer instead to refer to the **pauperization of motherhood,** a concept that more accurately points to the *institutional* forces that have impoverished women (Folbre, 1985; Amott, 1993).

The state may also contribute to the pauperization of motherhood. In the 1990s, state welfare reform programs harmed impoverished single mothers and their children, especially those of color, by imposing impossibly short time limits on eligibility for public assistance, while rewarding two-parent middle-class families with tax deductions for having dependent children and giving tax credits for childcare expenses. The state, then, can play an influential role in determining the economic viability of various family forms. Under certain state policies, family forms other than the traditional two-parent nuclear family may be economic liabilities.

The Effect of Marital Dissolution

Marital dissolution provides another glimpse into the economic effect of institutional forces on family forms. Most marriages are dissolved either by divorce or by death of one of the partners. Research shows that in both cases, women tend to suffer long-term negative economic consequences while men are less likely to (Bartfeld, 2000; Shelton and Dean, 2001; Gadalla, 2009). Poverty rates for women, for example, have a strong tendency to be higher after divorce than during marriage (www.census.gov), and female-headed households have a much greater tendency than male-headed households to be poor (see Figure 13.3). Studies have found a serious erosion in women's standard of living following divorce (Hanson, McLanahan, and Thomson, 1998; Gadalla, 2008). In contrast, marital dissolution tends to *improve* men's standard of living when they have relied on their partners for less than one-fifth of their pre-divorce household income (McManus and DiPrete, 2001), suggesting that traditional divisions of labor are economically more dangerous for women than for men. While women's ratio of income to needs drops by at least 50 percent following divorce (Burkhauser and Duncan, 1989), the ratio for men substantially increases, even after deductions for child support and alimony (Peterson, 1996).

FIGURE 13.3: Poverty and family structure: percent below poverty, 2009

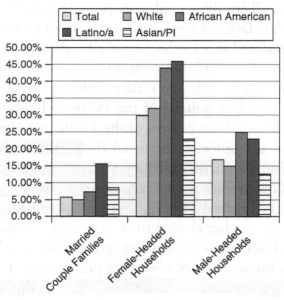

Source: www.census.gov

Why does this happen? Research suggests that institutional forces are at work here, particularly in state policies and labor-market practices (England, 2000). For example, on the assumption that women are more appropriate caregivers than men, courts tend to award women physical custody of children in a divorce, thereby reducing the economic responsibility fathers must bear. Even when courts order that fathers pay child support, few fathers comply fully, particularly after the first year. In 2009, only 36 percent of the women awarded child support payments by noncustodial fathers actually received full payment (Grall, 2011). Even when noncustodial fathers do pay the full amount of child support awarded to the custodial mothers of their children, the amounts of the payments tend to be less than the actual costs of raising children, increasing the possibility of their children living in poverty (Seltzer, 1989; Pirog-Good, 1993; Grall, 2011). In addition, sex inequalities in the formal labor market help generate greater incomes for husbands than for wives (Koretz, 2001). Together, these factors produce a situation after divorce in which "men retain a larger share of the family's income, while their economic needs decrease more than their income" (Holden and Smock, 1991).

Indeed, research indicates a trend toward greater economic interdependence in marriage, in which the incomes of both partners are crucial for the family's economic well-being. In such arrangements, divorce is likely to produce a lower standard of living for both men and women when the marriage dissolves (McManus and DiPrete, 2001). This research underscores the fact that gendered divisions of labor in marriage produce economic consequences in the aftermath of a divorce: Traditional gendered divisions of labor in which the woman is a full-time (unpaid) homemaker are likely to produce far harsher economic hardship for her than when she is employed in marriage. Men's increasing reliance on women's earnings in marriage means they will likely feel the loss of their wives' contributions in divorce.

The extent of a woman's decline in economic status after divorce seems to be related to class and race (Molina, 2000). The greatest economic decline following divorce occurs for women whose pre-divorce family incomes were highest. Research also indicates that women of color suffer significant declines in income after divorce, more so than white women (Duncan and Hoffman, 1985; Stroup and Pollock, 1999). The factors that seem to intensify the negative economic consequences of marital dissolution for women appear to be related to gender roles in traditional nuclear families and to wage inequities based on sex and race in the formal labor market (Shelton and John, 1999).

Research demonstrates that the economic effects of widowhood are often just as disadvantageous for women as divorce. Poverty rates for women tend to increase following the deaths of their husbands (Hungerford, 2001). And while higher pre-widowhood incomes may offer greater protection from post-widowhood poverty, one study found that women in higher-income groups were more likely to suffer a significant decline in their ratio of income to needs than women whose pre-widowhood incomes were lower (Holden, 1990).

The age of the wife at the onset of widowhood significantly affects her chance of poverty: Widows younger than 60 are more likely to fall into poverty (Zick and Smith, 1986; Holden, Burkhauser, and Feaster, 1988; Angel, Jimenez, and Angel, 2007; see also Gillen and Kim, 2009). This is because in many insurance policies greater benefits accrue to an older widow and because younger widows with children may face restrictions and inequalities in the formal labor market (Holden and Smock, 1991). Also, federal Social Security policy tends to penalize younger widows with no children; they are not eligible for the survivor benefits normally extended to children, and they are too young to collect Social Security benefits themselves (Holden, 1990; Holden and Smock, 1991).

Some husbands may provide their surviving wives with protection from possible poverty through their pension funds, but only if the husbands are vested (that is, they have paid into the insurance for a long enough period of time, usually five to 10 years). However, some pension funds do not extend any benefits to the surviving spouse; others may offer only a one-time lump-sum payment; and still others may deny the surviving partner any benefits until such time as the deceased would have become eligible to collect benefits as a retiree (Holden, 1990; Holden and Smock, 1991). Provisions that deny benefits altogether for widows or delay benefits for younger widows push women into poverty at the time of widowhood. In addition, while husbands may try to protect their partners from poverty in widowhood through private life insurance, research shows that they tend to seriously underinsure themselves (Auerbach and Kotlikoff, 1987). This is no surprise, particularly during serious economic downturns, like the Great Recession that began in 2008: When people have to make tough daily decisions concerning housing, food, and fuel, saving for a pension or paying for life insurance understandably falls lower on the list of priorities.

Certain state policies can aggravate the economic disadvantages women confront. For example, the state may not adequately enforce child-support payments after a divorce or facilitate the timely transfer of property following the death of a partner. Even Social Security policy continues to contribute to gendered inequality because there is still a gender gap in spousal and widow benefits that does not take into account the unpaid labor of homemakers (Meyer, 1996). And private-sector policies (such as wage inequalities, insurance policy inequalities based on age, and inadequate pension provisions) add to the institutional forces that penalize women in such circumstances.

Poverty in Nontraditional Families

For workers who have a nontraditional family form, state policies and economic forces also affect their benefits and thus their families' economic well-being. Some policies, for example, penalize families that are based on cohabitation rather than marriage. Gay male and lesbian couples, as well as cohabitating heterosexual couples, often find that employers will not cover their partners under their health insurance policies or as pension and life insurance beneficiaries. Similarly, individuals in such relationships are frequently denied the legal right to participate in decision making concerning care and continued life support of their partners in times of serious illness.

Some of this may be changing, however. Vermont now recognizes gay and lesbian civil unions as legitimate marriages, thereby extending the economic and legal benefits of marriage to such couples (Silverman, 2000). Dozens of municipalities, including Hartford, San Francisco, Seattle, and Tacoma Park, recognize relations between cohabitants as legitimate and, upon application, will certify them as licensed domestic partnerships, much like licensed marriages. A few cities, including Atlanta, extend medical insurance coverage to "domestic partners" of their employees. Moreover, a small, but growing, number of corporations recognize the legitimacy of cohabitation in their policies. Ben and Jerry's Homemade, Inc., extends the same benefits, including health and pension coverage, to cohabitants that married partners enjoy at the firm. The Lotus Development Corporation has a domestic-partners plan for gay male and lesbian couples (but not for heterosexual cohabitants) enabling them to receive family benefits. The firm's reasoning behind its homosexuals-only plan is that heterosexuals can marry to receive family benefits, whereas gays and lesbians cannot in most states. By 2003, more than 5,800 employers offered domestic partner benefits, including over 200 Fortune 500 corporations and more than 5,000 smaller private firms, nonprofit agencies, unions, colleges, and governmental employers (www .hrc.org). Such policies may help prevent poverty in nontraditional families in the event of a serious illness or retirement.

FAMILY DYNAMICS AND FAMILY ISSUES

The previous discussions use a conflict perspective to suggest how the economy and state can affect the well-being of families. Those institutions can also affect relationships between family members. For example, China maintains a state policy, instituted in 1978, mandating one-child family structures in an attempt to reduce the population growth rate. Families that restrict themselves to one child are given preferences for jobs and promotions, housing, education, and healthcare; those who do not comply are typically denied access to these rewards and resources and may also find that subsequent children are not covered at all by state-sponsored services, including health and education. Since cultural values privilege males over females, it often means that the state's policy creates an incentive for female infanticide, female-child abandonment, and abortion of female fetuses as couples strive for their one and only child to be male. Over time the one-child policy has reverberated throughout the culture as it reshapes family structures and dynamics: The concepts of siblings, cousins, nieces, nephews, aunts, and uncles evaporate because these statuses eventually lose their social meaning. It also poses challenges to families that have traditionally relied on a network of children in the extended family to care for aging parents. When two only-children marry, they alone become responsible for four aging parents because they have no other siblings to help shoulder that burden (Lev, 2000). China's one-child family policy, then, illustrates the impact that state policy can have on family structures and dynamics.

How do institutional forces affect the internal dynamics of families in the United States? How do state policies and the economy affect violence within families? How do state policies and changes in the U.S. labor market affect the domestic division of labor? And how might state policy affect reproductive and parenting rights of young women, gay males and lesbians, and people with disabilities?

Family Violence

"The family" is often idealized as providing a safe, satisfying, and secure "haven in a heartless world" (Lasch, 1977). Unfortunately, this is not always the case. All too often the family is an arena in which people experience severe violence. One common assumption is that only the mentally ill physically abuse their spouses or children and that such abuse occurs only in poor families. However, research challenges these beliefs. Approximately 4 million women are seriously assaulted by their partners each year, and nearly one in three women is assaulted by her partner at least once in the relationship (www.apa.org; www.stopfamilyviolence.org). In 2010 in the United States, nearly 6 million children were victims of abuse, most at the hands of one of their own parents; more than 1,800 children died of abuse and neglect (www.childhelp.org/pages/statistics).

Reports of elder abuse increased 150 percent over the 10-year period between 1986 and 1996, an increase that significantly exceeded the 10 percent increase in the older population. The problem has only increased since. In 90 percent of the cases where the abuser was known, perpetrators of elder abuse were family members; two-thirds of these were adult children or spouses (www.aoa.dhhs.gov/Factsheets/abuse../Local Settings/temp/7zO21.tmp/(www.aoa.dhhs.gov/Factsjeets/abuse). Almost one-third of the murders of people aged 65 and older are committed by a family member (www.apa.org), and most of the victims are women with chronic illnesses or disabilities (www.surgeongeneral.gov). Although *reported* rates of family violence are highest among low-income people, violence is, in fact, widespread and common in families of all income levels (www.ncea.aoa.gov/Library/Data/index.aspx#problem; Tower, 1996; Anderson, 2000). Mental illness has been linked to only 10 percent of acts of family violence.

If poverty and mental illness are not the principal causes of family violence, then what else might be? Gelles and Straus (1988) noted that family violence is not a new phenomenon. They suggested an interactionist perspective, focusing on the intimate interactions between the individuals involved. Violence, they argued, is related to the institution of the family itself, for it is a structure that puts individuals in close and constant contact with one another. Such a structure is likely to foster emotionally intense relationships simply because of the unrelenting proximity of family and household members who may use "biographical ammunition" against one another. Since the relationships within families are very intimate and interaction is frequent, tensions heighten as individuals know better than people outside the family which emotional buttons to push.

Constant contact may also increase the chances that some household members will become easy or convenient targets against whom other members unleash their everyday frustrations. The roles given to family members according to their age and sex also play a part in domestic violence. For example, conflicts between children and adults, or husband and wife, may reflect power differences and may be a natural outcome of family roles built around age and gender inequalities.

Using violence to resolve conflicts may also derive from social and cultural influences that encourage or reinforce violence. Many violent abusers were themselves abused or observed abuse in their families. Such experiences may lead them to see violence as an acceptable and normal way to resolve conflict. Furthermore, books, television, movies, and videos often treat the use of force as an understandable and acceptable form of behavior. Violence is a standard component of media entertainment, including sports. And the national jubilation that accompanies military victories such as the U.S. defeat of Iraq in 1991 and 2003 and the killing of Osama bin Laden in 2012 relates the use of violence to heroic acts and often directly or indirectly links this behavior to maleness. Gelles and Straus concluded that the combination of direct and indirect socialization experiences contributes to an atmosphere in which many forms of family violence are viewed as "normal" violence, because they are accepted and given legitimacy in the larger culture.

Another problem is that much family violence in the United States occurs out of public view. People in the United States value their privacy, so physical violence and abuse within the family are far less subject to public scrutiny and control than the same behaviors in many non-family settings. For example, it is not acceptable for a teacher to beat a student, an employer to beat an employee, or a religious leader to abuse followers. Thus, the use of physical violence against another person in most institutional settings outside the family is construed as assault and battery. But within the family, violence is often viewed as a way for parents to discipline their children or as an adjunct to everyday marital conflicts. The hesitation of some courts and local police to interfere in domestic disputes can leave family victims of physical violence unprotected and reinforce the legitimacy of violence as a means of coping with or resolving conflicts.

Moreover, that family violence typically occurs behind closed doors and out of public view contributes to the popular myth that it is something that happens only in poor and uneducated families. This is because wealthy families commonly live in single-family homes that are a fair distance and sometimes isolated from neighbors, making it difficult to hear or see the abuse and therefore easy to conceal. But the poor typically live in cramped apartment settings, often with thin walls between them, so that violent interactions can easily be heard in surrounding apartments and therefore more likely to be subject to involvement of police and Departments of Children and Family Services. Furthermore, the affluent are more likely to seek medical attention (if they do at all) from private physicians who, despite their legal role as mandated reporters, more likely to look the other way. The poor, on the other hand, are likely to seek medical attention at public hospitals and emergency rooms, where the role of mandated reporter is more readily invoked. Thus, family violence becomes falsely construed as a problem of the poor rather than the affluent simply because it is more readily apparent. But that does not mean it does not occur in affluent families, too.

Power Differentials in the Family

A conflict perspective offers some insight into why family violence takes on the patterns it does. Why are children, the elderly, and women most often the targets of abuse in families? The answer may lie in the question of power inequality. The structure of families carries gendered and age-based power inequalities that may contribute to family violence. In particular, children and the elderly are physically less powerful than their abusers, and typically do not have decision-making power in the family. Where children are concerned, the state enforces that power inequality in its recognition of parental rights to determine childrearing and in the relative rarity of its willingness to recognize the rights of children seeking emancipation from parental control. Further, Gelles and Straus noted that power differentials in the home were one of the most important factors affecting spouse abuse and violence (see also Whiting, Oka, and Fife, 2012; Anderson and Umberson, 2001). "The risk of intimate violence is the greatest when all decision making in a home is concentrated in the hands of one of the partners. Couples who report the most sharing of decisions report the lowest rates of violence" (Gelles and Straus, 1988: 92). Thus, gender roles that reinforce power differentials, vesting males with greater power and control in decision making, contribute to the likelihood of domestic violence.

Analyzing domestic violence in terms of internal family power structures offers new insights into gender relations. For example, observers on all sides of the controversy concerning family violence agree that while women do sometimes batter their partners, the vast majority of batterers are men. Indeed, a woman typically attacks only in self-defense, either hitting back after an attack against her, or striking first because she has been victimized before and believes she will be seriously assaulted if she does not (Kimmel, 2000). Why should this gendered pattern of violence be so? Conventional explanations suggest a biological or psychological answer, which might suggest that men are simply more innately aggressive than women. But such explanations do not address why men are more likely to vent their frustrations and anger against their female partners than against other potential targets, such as male friends and colleagues or male authority figures. Nor do they address why stress on women is not as likely to escalate into physical violence against male partners. A conflict perspective suggests the importance of issues of dominance and power differentials based on gendered social structures (Gordon, 1988; Merry, 2002; Hearn, 2012). Men more commonly attack women because women are more often socially perceived as subordinate, weaker, and less likely to strike back. In a society whose dominant culture supports the notion that men are "naturally" more powerful and dominant and in which most social institutions are dominated by men, it is likely that domestic violence by men will be accepted as unfortunate but "normal."

Sources of Stress in Families

The gendered and age-based power differentials in families provide a structural context in which expressions of frustration and stress become directed at the least powerful members of the family: women, children, and the elderly. Gelles and Straus pointed to the many sources of mounting stress confronting families in the United States that may contribute to violent behavior. The ravages of poverty and unemployment increase stress in families. *Reported* rates of violence tend to be highest among poor families (Benson et al., 2000). However, violence is not restricted to poor families alone (and note that the focus here is the reported rate, not the actual rate. The actual rate among the affluent is likely to be depressed due to the factors discussed above). Stress factors other than poverty afflict higher-income families, including performance of household responsibilities while balancing two jobs or careers, lack of adequate daycare for

children, responsibility for aging or ailing parents or dependents with disabilities, and conflicting schedules. Let's examine these stresses and their effects on the family.

Many families depend on two incomes in order to provide a middle-class standard of living. In a 2012 survey, 39 percent of the respondents felt they did not earn enough money to
live comfortably (Gallup, April 9, 2012). In another survey that same year, 35 percent of the
respondents reported that they did not have enough money for basic necessities in the past
month (www.roperweb.ropercenter.uconn.edu). Moreover, 46 percent of respondents in a 2013
poll indicated that they were not confident that they "will have enough money to live comfortably throughout their retirement years" (Helman et al, 2013:1). Such anxieties concerning the
stability and health of the economy suggest a threat of erosion of people's ability to maintain
their standard of living, and that anxiety (or, in an age of increasing layoffs, perhaps an all-too-
real situation) often drives both partners in a two-parent middle-class family to enter the paid
labor market.

Changes in the work force and the increasing frequency of dual-income couples may create another, sometimes stressful situation: women earning higher salaries than their partners.
In a society that grants the male status for being the family provider, this situation creates
status inconsistency in which one's claims to power and deference based on some statuses are
not consistent with other statuses. Status inconsistency can also occur when one's educational
attainment is much greater than one's occupational status, a source of stress for both men and
women. This stress becomes increasingly likely in an economy in which decent-paying jobs are
relatively scarce and competition for them is high. Stress can also mount when corporations
downsize and fire middle-level managers, engineers, and other professional and technical personnel, who often then must take lower-paying jobs (Hautzinger, 2003). Researchers suggest
that men's attempt to reassert dominance and privilege in the face of such stresses is related to
family violence (Anderson, 1997).

How do two-earner families cope with domestic responsibilities? When both parents work,
they frequently arrange their employment schedules so that they can take shifts caring for their
children. While such an arrangement reduces the expense of daycare, it also means that the
parents rarely see each other. This arrangement produces stress because it severely reduces the
partners' ability to interact as a couple and their ability to interact together with their children as
a family (Presser, 2000). Such stress is likely to intensify for some families in the United States:
Recent trends show an increase in part-time, low-wage employment (see Chapter 12). This suggests potential for a rise in the three-income family, in which one parent takes one job while the
other moonlights at two.

Most families know how stressful it is to balance employment with childcare. Yet the high
expense of daily childcare, and the relative scarcity of adequate care facilities, can only add to
the stress of families. Childcare difficulties become particularly acute in single-parent families,
where something of a vicious cycle occurs. Single-parent families tend to have lower incomes
relative to two-parent families, and the parent has greater difficulties securing and paying for
adequate childcare that would enable him or her to maintain a job. In 2011, the annual cost of
care for a 4-year-old in a childcare center averaged $4,100 in South Carolina to $9,600 in New
York (Child Care Aware, 2012). Childcare for younger children costs more. The Children's
Defense Fund noted that these costs in urban areas are higher than the average annual tuition

rates of public colleges in 49 states, and in some cities the cost of childcare was twice the cost of college tuition (Schulman, 2000). Low-income families typically pay between 5 and 15 percent of their incomes on childcare, while higher-income families typically spend an average of less than 5 percent of their incomes. Single-parent families spent higher proportions of their family incomes for childcare, on average, than two-earner families (www.urban.org). Of course, higher-quality childcare arrangements cost more than less-than-adequate childcare.

In the absence of good alternatives, low-income families and single-parent families have little flexibility in the care they can choose for their children. Almost 43 percent of the children whose parents work in the formal labor force are cared for by relatives, usually grandmothers (www.census.gov). This arrangement, while cheaper than daycare centers, may create family conflict, since it extends the dependence of grown children on their aging parents even as they are now raising their own children. It also imposes a burden on older caretakers, who may be less able to meet the demands of childcare.

Many families in all classes suffer the added stresses of caring for elderly relatives or family members with disabilities. Most of the elderly with disabilities were cared for by their families and friends (www.census.gov). The stress of such caregiving can be seen in a variety of ways: More than 60 percent of caregivers in the *Stress in America* survey reported having trouble sleeping through the night because of the added responsibilities of caregiving (www.apa.org/news/ press/releases/stress/2011/health-risk.aspx). Most also reported stress resulting from the limits caregiving imposed on their privacy and free personal time and from the relentless attention required by the care recipients (see also Chisholm, 1999; Singleton, 2000).

While nursing-home care may be a way to reduce some of the stresses of caregiving, it does not mean that family members are free from responsibilities. They visit relatives in nursing homes, and many often assist with chores such as laundry, shopping, financial management, management of medical appointments, and supervision of nursing-home care. And such care is expensive, although the total costs vary by state, extent of care needed, and type of room: While Medicare almost always covers short-term nursing-home care, the average annual cost of long-term nursing-home care per person in 2011 was more than $78,000 for a semi-private room, and $81,000 for Alzheimer's care (Met Life, 2011). Such costs influence families to assume greater and greater burdens of at-home care for the elderly, including the elderly with disabilities. Family Caregiver Alliance estimates that one-third to one-half of all elder caregivers are employed in the labor market. The struggle to juggle mounting family responsibilities, compounded by the demands of elder care, and work outside the home eventually forces about 5 percent to turn down a promotion and 12 percent of the caregivers to quit their jobs altogether to devote themselves full-time to providing care for elderly family members (www.caregiver .org). While this may ease the time crunch for the caregivers, it comes at a price. It means a significant loss of family income. In the absence of adequate, affordable nursing-care facilities, caring for elderly family members can easily become a major source of family stress, contributing to increasing family violence in homes at all income levels. Clearly, there are a variety of serious pressures on families in the United States. Any one of these pressures, or in combination, could raise a family's stress level so high that violence becomes increasingly possible. Violence, then, is not something that occurs only in poor families or in families where mental illness prevails.

Stress in and of itself is not a sufficient explanation for family violence. The patterns whereby men are the most likely to use violence against less powerful or weaker members of the family, particularly women, children, and the elderly, suggests the significant role of the structure of power differentials. Men don't hit women, children, and the elderly because they are simply stressed out; they hit them when they are stressed out because they can. Men don't typically hit their boss when they're stressed, or their neighbor, or the police in their neighborhood. Stress certainly may play a role in family violence, but structural power differentials identify vulnerable targets. Family violence, then, is not a personal problem of poor judgment; it is a public issue produced by structural and cultural arrangements. This analysis suggests a route to change that doesn't depend on psychological explanations. To reduce domestic violence, particularly as it victimizes women, it is crucial to address gendered power differentials.

Prospects for Change: Reducing Family Violence

Taken together, the research on family violence indicates important influences that the culture, the state, and the economy have on the production of family violence. But research also provides encouraging insights into the role these factors may play in *reducing* that violence. For one thing, where previous generations accepted family violence as a matter of course, current cultural norms in the United States no longer support such tolerance. This may be due at least in part to several decades of strong public education efforts and policy initiatives and pressures by children's and family rights advocates (Strauss, 2000). Simply put, what happens behind closed doors is not necessarily a private family matter beyond the reach or jurisdiction of the law if it involves violence.

Since limited economic means to support a family is a stress factor associated with family violence, it is not surprising to find that a healthier economic environment produces lower rates of domestic violence. The warning signal in the new century is the nation's growing gap between rich and poor. While unemployment rates in the 1990s were among the lowest in the United States since World War II, more people were working in service jobs at low wages with few if any medical or pension benefits and little job security. Since the end of the 1990s, unemployment has risen, and it sharply increased with the start of the Great Recession in 2008. The economic vise now squeezing an increasing number of families increases the likelihood of rising rates of domestic violence. Improving wages, benefits, and employment security are important measures for reducing domestic violence.

While some observers have cited the competing demands facing dual-occupation families as a stress factor that can lead to violence, other research suggests otherwise. Women may sometimes derive a greater sense of self-worth from juggling multiple roles simultaneously, while men may benefit from being less pressured about the family's financial well-being and from having more opportunities to care for and spend time with their children (Gerson, 1993). This finding calls into question analyses emphasizing psychological stress as an explanation for family violence. Indeed, female participation in the paid labor force may reduce power differentials based on income contributions within the family and therefore may reduce the potential for family violence. Providing more support for women's participation in the paid labor force could be an important way to reduce family violence. So might policies directed at addressing the challenges for both men and women to juggle work and family demands.

Other social changes have contributed to women's empowerment in the home. Women no longer need to resign themselves to abuse. Women have had an increasing number of alternatives in the last several decades, such as programs and shelters for both abuse victims and their children. While these projects still cannot support all who need them, their increased availability encourages women to realize that abuse need not be tolerated. Moreover, women's increased participation in the formal labor market provides them with an economic alternative to reliance on an abusive partner for financial support.

Despite encouraging findings that family violence may be declining, however, recent studies suggest that the incidence of intimate partner violence (Tjaden and Thoennes, 2000) and child abuse (www.calib.com/nccanch/pubs/factsheets; www.acf.dhhs.gov/programs) remain alarmingly high. That much said, greater insight into the social and economic roots of domestic violence are helping to point to more effective avenues for prevention, intervention, and treatment (Healey, Smith, and O'Sullivan, 1998). Most states now have laws mandating that teachers, health practitioners, and social workers must report cases of suspected child and partner abuse. Findings of abuse often lead to mandatory arrest of adult abusers and enrollment in a treatment program. More of these programs are needed, but their increased availability has helped many family members to address domestic violence.

Legal mandates for protection of abuse victims are far from perfect, however. A false accusation by an ignorant or vindictive teacher, for example, can tear a family apart. And given what is already known about race and class assumptions in evaluating children in the classroom, the chances that even a well-meaning teacher may define poor families and families of color as abusive are strong. Moreover, laws governing child abuse frequently tread a fine line between legal protection for abuse victims and civil liberties concerning parental rights and the right to privacy. All too often these laws still offer inadequate protection for victims of domestic violence; conversely, children in poor families and families of color may be removed from families unnecessarily (Roberts, 2001).

The same cultural and institutional factors that can greatly influence the acceptance of family violence can also serve to reduce that violence. Hence, policies that reinforce a healthy economy, that provide institutional support to balance work and family challenges, that challenge conventional and unequal gendered roles, and that provide social and economic supports to abuse victims are important in curbing and perhaps eliminating violence within families.

Reproductive and Parenting Rights and Issues

The choice to reproduce is largely understood to be a private matter, but for some families this decision is controlled or limited by the state, as our earlier discussion of China's one-child policy indicates. In such cases, the tension between the institutions of state and family affect decision-making dynamics between family members. For example, some people with disabilities must struggle against state laws or state agencies that interfere with their decision to bear and raise children. State agencies may encourage sterilization of people with severe mental or physical disabilities or refuse to extend social welfare benefits to children born of parents with disabilities (Kallianes and Rubenfeld, 1997; Brady, 2001).

Several myths prompt this social and legal resistance to reproduction and parenting by people with disabilities. These myths include the notions that disabilities are inherited or contagious, that the presence of persons with disabilities is depressing and should not be inflicted on the children, and that physical mobility is critical for adequate childrearing (Shaul, Dowling, and Laden, 1985). None of these myths are supported by evidence. The vast majority of physical disabilities are not inherited. Even those that are inherited do not necessarily cause offspring to lead less-than-full lives.

People often base assumptions about the limitations posed by disabilities and the fear of their inheritance on the false notion that people with disabilities are by definition unhealthy or sick. But most of those who have disabilities do not see themselves in that way; disability is viewed as the master status more by ablebodied observers than by persons with disabilities themselves. People with disabilities tend to focus their lives, much as everyone else does, on the demands posed by work, family, and achieving a productive and full life. Finally, many people with physical disabilities and mobility restrictions are able to raise children through creative adjustments to the challenges posed by the disabilities (Shaul, Dowling, and Laden, 1985). Institutional supports, such as access ramps to buildings and streets, wheelchair-accessible public transportation, braille notations in public areas, and so forth, can make these adjustments easier. Thus, any restrictions posed by physical disabilities for raising children appear to be based more on cultural assumptions and the failure of the state to provide institutional supports than on any intrinsic limitations posed by the disabilities themselves.

Another reproductive rights issue involves the right to end unwanted pregnancies. State-imposed restrictions on this right can affect decision-making processes between family members. For example, some states, such as Pennsylvania, have restricted access to abortions for minors. The laws in such states require parental notification when teenagers seek abortions and parental permission before they can receive abortions. These laws may pose problems for teenagers whose pregnancy is the result of incest or rape. Incest victims, for example, may face extreme danger in seeking permission for abortion from an enraged incestuous father. Thus, these laws can contribute to an increase in family violence.

On the other hand, the Food and Drug Administration's 2000 approval of RU-486 (the "morning after pill") requiring only a physician's prescription has the potential to greatly enhance women's access to greater control over their own bodies, especially in areas with few or no clinics or physicians who can perform abortions. It remains unclear if such a prescription falls under the age restrictions imposed in states with parental consent laws for abortion.

Research on childrearing shows no difference between lesbian or gay parents in comparison with heterosexual parents in parent effectiveness (Allen and Burrell, 1996; Ritenhouse, 2011). Yet gay males and lesbians often confront cultural resistance to their roles as parents (Clarke, 2001). Moreover, they frequently find that the state interferes with their rights to parent. In custody battles, the courts often resist the right of gay male and lesbian parents to retain custody of their children, regardless of their parenting abilities. Most custody decisions are made in state domestic relations courts, where the judge (rather than a jury) acts as fact finder and determines what is in "the best interest" of the child. While some state statutes require the demonstration of the existence of harm to the child in order to wrest custody from the parent, other statutes allow the judge to consider *future* potential harm to the child. In the latter situation, the bias of the judge regarding the "fitness" of gay males and lesbians to parent becomes a major influence in custody determinations (Lofstrom, 1998; Rivers, 2012). There are some indications that gay and lesbian parents are winning significant custody battles. Most states no longer routinely deny custody or visitation rights of parents simply because of their sexual orientation (www.aclu.org).

Some adoption agencies have allowed gays and lesbians to adopt openly gay adolescent children, but only when the child has expressed "a clear and definite sense of his or her sexual identity" (Raymond, 1992: 119). Such a requirement limits the possibilities of children who need caring adoptive homes, since "clear and definite" sexual identities tend to occur relatively late in adolescence (on average, age 17 for men and age 22 for women). Adoption agencies may erroneously assume that gay males and lesbians can be effective parents only of gay children, thereby focusing solely on the sexual identity of the prospective adoptive parents and ignoring the possible parenting talents they may have.

These statutes, agency practices, and legal precedents challenge conventional definitions of family and parent. But they also highlight the role of the state and of social service agencies as institutions influencing the outcome of issues such as reproduction and parenting rights. The outcomes of these critical public issues affect family forms and family dynamics as the state punishes some and rewards others on the basis of their conformity to dominant views on what comprises the "normal" family form. Indeed, the role of the state in defining the social construction of "family" was drawn very much under scrutiny in the Spring 2013 session of the Supreme Court, as justices heard arguments challenging Proposition 8 in California, asserting that the state only recognizes marriage as that between a man and a woman and effectively banning same-sex marriages, and the federal Defense of Marriage Act, defining marriage as specifically between one man and one woman. The Supreme Court's decisions on these cases will certainly affect the social constructions of marriage and family.

Contradictions between Work and Family

Conflicting demands between participation in the formal labor market and family responsibilities may produce tensions in two-parent households, particularly for women (Coltrane and Adams, 2001; Worley and Vannoy, 2001; Craig and Powell, 2012). When family responsibilities mount, adding care of the elderly, for example, to childcare and housework, it is largely women who must balance them with the demands of work in the formal labor market, turning down promotions, reducing work hours without pay, or quitting employment altogether. Since caregivers are most often women, then, the demands of caregiving mean an added hurdle for women in the workplace, damaging not only their chances for promotions and salary raises, but perhaps also their very livelihoods.

Balancing work and family care of both elders and children commonly besets women more than men, and the competing demands of these can affect her livelihood. One study describes a woman who tried working reduced hours in order to care for her small child, only to find her boss implying that she may not have her job for very long under this arrangement. She noted, "If I go back [to my job] full time pretty soon, I'll be okay. But if I keep this up much longer, I won't be. I may already be out. My boss says, 'You're walking alone right now. You're not committed here'" (Hochschild and Machung, 1989: 91). Another woman in the study, struggling with the needs of her young child (who had an ear infection) and her job, felt the pressure to reconcile the conflict by quitting her job: "I'm on the verge of quitting. . . . I'm supposed to go on a business trip tomorrow, and I have a strong urge to say, 'I'm not going.' . . . The worst thing I could possibly do [at work] is to acknowledge that my children have an impact on my life" (Hochschild and Machung, 1989: 95–96). Sometimes a woman's attempt to balance the competing demands of work and family threatens or restricts her livelihood (Budig and England, 2001; Maume, 2001), contributing to the glass ceiling limiting many women's career advancement opportunities and to women's lower wages. Such stresses are also structured into welfare reform policies that demand single mothers work but provide little help in meeting child and home responsibilities. Why do the demands of work and family collide as they do, and why do women bear the brunt of that antagonism? Although African American women and white working-class women have a long history of working outside the home for pay (Eisenstein, 1983), the world of the formal labor market was, until the end of World War II, largely defined as a male domain, and women's work was said to belong in the home. The formal labor market has been slow to recognize the permanent presence of women in the labor force, so it has failed to take steps to resolve the contradictions between their roles on the job and their roles at home. So has the state. Few state policies help reconcile those contradictions; policies like welfare reform make them worse.

The same assumptions about women's and men's "appropriate" roles in the labor market also affect the division of labor in the family. After a full day in the formal labor market women frequently come home to work full-time on domestic responsibilities, what Hochschild and Machung (2012) refer to as the *second shift*. Families use a variety of strategies to deal with these conflicting demands, but most of them disadvantage women. Some women are pressured to quit their jobs or reduce their hours in order to maintain the household, conventionally defined as women's responsibility. Others attempt to negotiate shared responsibilities within their families, with mixed and often unsatisfactory results. At the very least, such attempts frequently create tensions within the family. Men often resent being asked to assume greater domestic responsibilities.

Some progress toward redefining household responsibilities is occurring so that men share these burdens as partners with women. For example, research shows that men are beginning to spend more time engaged in parenting than previous generations (Levine, 2000), often in spite of pressures from employers not to do so. Other research demonstrates the positive benefit of this change for the social and emotional development and well-being of both daughters and sons (Warner and Steel, 1999). But there is still a long way to go before the notion of the second shift applies to men as well as women.

Of course, the gender inequalities in balancing home and work demands do not necessarily reflect all families in the United States. Research shows that these inequalities are less pronounced among African American couples than white couples. Part of the reason for this may be that African American women have historically been more likely to participate in the formal labor market than white (and, particularly, middle-class white) women. African American families may be more likely to view such participation as a matter of course and as an economic fact of life and therefore are more likely to have adjusted to sharing responsibilities more equitably (John, Shelton, and Luschen, 1995). Research also shows that egalitarian divisions of household labor found more likely in African American families is not simply a function of economic necessity. Compared with white families, African American families maintain this pattern regardless of the woman's employment status, income, and gender role values (Ross, 1987). However, despite these greater levels of egalitarianism, African American women, like their white counterparts, remain responsible for most of the traditionally female-relegated household chores like cooking, cleaning, and doing laundry (Broman, 1988).

A few changes slowly occurring in the workplace are beginning to address the tension between work and family. For example, an increasing number of firms have been instituting **flextime** to allow workers to maintain full-time job status while sharing more responsibilities at home (Glass and Estes, 1997; Blair-Loy, 2009). Some flextime programs enable workers to arrive at their jobs earlier or later than is customary, as long as a full workday is put in. Other arrangements allow employees to work 10-hour days, with three days off to care for family. These flextime arrangements are available to both men and women, facilitating greater sharing of the demands of work and family. However, evidence indicates that affluent professionals use flextime most often (Sharp, Hermsen, and Billings, 2002).

For a variety of reasons, flextime is less viable for others. Some have jobs that are not time-flexible and cannot be altered, such as teaching or shift work. Others simply don't have the power to negotiate such options with their employers. For example, according to Cynthia Fuchs Epstein (1993), many law firms provide flextime, and even emergency childcare assistance, for women attorneys but not for legal secretaries. Even unionization is not a guarantee of access to flextime. Factors such as gender of membership and leadership affect whether unions negotiate work-family benefits like flextime (Gerstel and Clawson, 2001). Thus, flextime arrangements have great potential for easing some tensions between work and family responsibilities for both men and women, but their implementation has been less than perfect and still needs much work.

Some corporations allow workers to telecommute, working from home on computers and attending meetings via Skype and other technological interfaces. However, this is an arrangement that is more common in white collar jobs and high-level positions. However, even in these settings where many sought to balance work and family by working from home the climate is increasingly chilly: At Hewlett-Packard, for example, the new CEO, herself a new mother, imposed a new policy in 2013 requiring workers to put in "face time" and work in the office rather than from home. This policy puts a huge burden on parents of young children and those caring for elder family members who must now make the unwinnable choice between earning a living or caring for family members. And that burden will most likely fall on women more than men.

Some corporations are beginning to recognize that it is in their best interest to pay attention to the difficulties of workers balancing work and family. Prompted by the United Auto Workers Union, Ford Motor Company now has an ambitious program to develop 30 Family Service and Learning Centers providing round-the-clock childcare (including care for mildly sick children and children whose parents may work the midnight shift), summer camp, tutoring, and activities for teens after school as well as retirees. Notably, these services are available to all workers, not just elite executives. And Ford is not alone: Other companies, such as IBM and JC Penney are joining their ranks in developing programs to address the needs of all workers to balance work and family (Greenhouse, 2001).

Other firms are offering **catastrophic leave policy**, which allows workers to donate unused paid time off (such as sick leave, vacation time, and personal leave time) to fellow workers facing family crises (Taylor, 2003). This policy fosters a strong sense of community among workers helping each other balance work and family demands with the support of their employer. And the employer benefits from avoiding lost productivity and perhaps lost trained and experienced personnel. However, in most cases it is fellow workers, not the employer, who are making the principal sacrifice.

FUTURE TRENDS

So far, this chapter has discussed ways that institutions such as the state and the economy are influential factors affecting the family. Not only do these institutions affect the diversity of family forms observed in the United States, they also affect the relationships between family members as well as the economic and social well-being of the family. Thus, the great diversity of families does not necessarily indicate a breakdown of traditional values and of the healthy family in the United States; rather, it indicates the broad variety of ways that people cope with pressures from the state and the economy. Since these institutions are such important influences on the family, what future policies are needed to ensure the efficacy of the family, regardless of the form it takes?

One way to answer this question is to examine the experiences of other countries. Many European countries spend freely on social welfare programs that support the family. Many European countries also provide family leave benefits through national health insurance programs, unemployment insurance, or special parental-leave programs. Employers themselves do not directly pay workers on leave; instead, the state provides parents with pay while they are on leave to care for newborn infants. State payments relieve small employers of an economic burden. Importantly, many of these programs provide leaves for fathers as well as mothers. Of course, the taxpayer ultimately pays for such programs, but the existence of these programs and the willingness of most citizens to pay for them clearly indicate that the well-being of the family is a political and social priority.

In addition, the challenge of gendering continues to define parenting as a woman's job. Congress passed the Family and Medical Leave Act in 1993, giving men in larger workplaces the legal right to take unpaid time off from work to care for a newborn. Some men decline to exercise this right because they simply cannot afford to lose the income even temporarily. But many others remain at work for fear of ridicule, of being passed over for promotion, or even of losing their job (Levine, 2000). One South Carolina state trooper reported that when he requested time off to care for his newborn daughter, his supervisor told him, "A man's job is to work, not stay home with the kids" (Ligos, 2000:G1). An Ivy League professor requesting parental leave was told he would never get tenure if he took such time off. And a human resources manager at a major corporation admits that he advises men to take vacation time and sick leave instead of parental leave to avoid the stigma on their permanent record. But in firms where senior executives have set a positive example by taking parental leave themselves, more men have been found to follow their lead and do likewise. This suggests promise for change over time. The state has put into place a legal right to parental leave (even if unpaid at present); economic institutions may play a key role in translating that right into practice by setting nurturing executive behavioral norms that challenge traditional gendered work and family roles.

European countries differ a great deal in the benefits they provide. Sweden allows for the most generous benefits: If both parents have been gainfully employed, both may share 270 days of parental leave at 90 percent of their regular salary. They are not required to use all their parental leave at once; rather, it can be spread out over the first four years of the child's life and can be used to care for a sick child. Parents are entitled by law to the same position they had prior to taking parental leave or to an equivalent position (U.S. Department of Health and Human Services, 1985; see also Ruhm, 2011). At the other end of the continuum are Greece and the Netherlands, where maternity leaves are mandated for 12 weeks (Ferber, O'Farrell, and Allen, 1991; see also Boje and Ejrnaes, 2012).

Despite their diversity, all family-leave policies in Europe are more generous than those provided in the United States, where, despite new laws, leave is still provided only on a voluntary and limited basis by many private (especially small-business) employers. Typically, such leaves are unpaid and do not necessarily ensure that parents will still have their jobs when they are ready to return to work. The lack of federal support for paid parental leave, coupled with the scarcity of affordable, adequate daycare facilities, undermines the ability of U.S. families to maintain a middle-class standard of living while caring for their children. The European approach is not perfect, however: It does not provide family-leave policies for workers to care for sick partners or elderly family members. In the face of inadequate affordable nursing-home care, and with increasing numbers of families assuming the care of sick or elderly family members themselves, such programs are clearly needed.

In the area of childcare, many European countries provide greater state subsidies for facilities than the United States does. However, like the United States, no European country fully subsidizes childcare, and none provides adequate, affordable care for *all* children from infancy on. Thus, childcare remains a source of the tension between family and work, both in Europe and in the United States. In an increasing number of families, single parents and both parents in two-parent families must earn wages in order to survive economically, and they clearly need state support to help pay for childcare. The alternative would be state income assistance that allows parents to work less, but no country places that much value on family care-taking responsibilities.

 CHAPTER SUMMARY

Individuals commonly live in structures they refer to as families. The meaning of family, however, may be very different to each person. What, then, is a family?

- A family is an organized, ongoing, and enduring network of people whose daily interactions provide for the needs and survival of members, regardless of age or gender. Family networks may be confined to a single household or stretch over several households and may be defined by biological ties as well as by ties of choice. They contain one or more adults and may or may not include children.

- Despite cultural and media depictions of the conventionality of the nuclear family (consisting of two children and two opposite-sex parents, with the female parent as full-time homemaker-mother and the male parent as sole provider), the typical U.S. family is quite different. In fact, according to U.S. Bureau of the Census figures, the most common family form in the 1990s was the dual-earner family. What are the reasons for this diversity?

- This is partly because the economy necessitates that both partners work in the paid labor force in order to maintain even a modest middle-class standard of living.

- Single-parent families (especially female-headed households) have become increasingly common, in part because of relatively high divorce rates and unwed parenthood.

- Many couples, both heterosexual and homosexual, set up households and maintain a marriage-like relationship despite the absence of state endorsement of that relationship.

- Given the disruptive dynamics of the economy, it is not unusual to find multigenerational households or families that extend over several households. Thus, the structure of institutions like the economy and the state greatly influence the structure of the family in the United States.

- These institutions also differentially reward or support various family forms. Dual-earner families often have an economic advantage over single-earner families; this, of course, depends upon the amount of income each earner gets. For example, a married male executive making over $200,000 per year can clearly support a wife and three children on the basis of that income alone, while a husband and wife working at minimum wage will barely be able to manage. Given the growth in low-wage service sector jobs and involuntary part-time work, many dual-earner families will have difficulty providing for themselves.

- Pressures from the economy can introduce stress factors that encourage such dynamics as family violence.

- State policies have different effects. Most policies tend to favor two-parent families and males. The failure of the state to adequately support daycare or elder care causes fewer stresses on two-parent families in which one parent earns enough money to support the entire family, thereby enabling the other parent to remain home and care for dependents. Health insurance and retirement benefits that are extended only to dependents or partners in state-sanctioned relationships adversely affect cohabiting couples, both homosexual and heterosexual.

- Patterns of institutional discrimination in the labor market also reward some family forms and disadvantage others. For example, income differences based on gender mean that female-headed households suffer poverty more than male-headed households or two-parent households. Income differences based on race mean that African American and Latina female-headed households are likely to be less advantaged than white female-headed households.

- Institutional influences from the economy and the state are also likely to affect the internal dynamics of various family forms. For example, when families are characterized by power inequalities, particularly those based on age and gender, family violence is most likely to occur as pressures on families increase. The stress of trying to maintain a single-parent family is increased under conditions of low pay; the stress of insufficient income is likely to be heightened when state policies do not support dependent care, healthcare, and so forth, in all family forms.

- Violence can readily occur even in dual-earner families, particularly when the wage earners work part-time and/or at minimum-wage jobs. Even in families of higher income, family violence can be precipitated by increased stress generated by the economy, such as the fear of losing one's job or the necessity of working additional hours to maintain one's position. In a society in which aggression and violence are culturally acceptable, especially for males, stress becomes manifested through violence against the least powerful family members.

- The state and the economy, then, not only contribute to the diversity of family forms but also influence the relative advantages and internal dynamics of these forms.

THINKING CRITICALLY

1. Families do not exist in a social vacuum: Social institutions can affect family forms as well as their daily experiences. What effect does the state have on family structures? How does the dominant definition of family affect families whose structures depart from that definition? What other institutions might have an affect on the structure of families? How do these institutions affect the structure of your own family?

2. An old African proverb suggests that it takes an entire village to raise a child. What does this mean? What institutions and people might be important for raising a child? Think of your community or state. What supports exist for child rearing? What is lacking? Now think of your own family. What people or institutions besides your parents participate or have participated in raising you or your siblings? What does the African proverb suggest about the definition of family?

3. Look at the wedding-announcements section of a newspaper. What sorts of information are included in these announcements? Are there race, class, and gender differences in the information or the way it is provided? What is not included in the information given? What social message might the existence of wedding-announcement sections promote? What social arrangements are *not* being promoted?

4. In 1993, advances in reproductive technology enabled several postmenopausal women in Europe to bear children. What implications does this ability have for the definition of family? How might it alter the structure and dynamics of families? What are the advantages and disadvantages of bearing children late in life? What are some social implications of this technology and the changes it might bring?

5. How would you describe the structure of your own family? What factors influence that structure? Consider who performs each of the various roles of provider and homemaker: What are the sources of family income, and who contributes the income? Who handles the household responsibilities? What factors influence who performs these roles? Have the structure and division of labor in your family always been the same as they are now? If not, what prompted the change?

 KEY TERMS

blended family   **347**

boomerang generation   **346**

catastrophic leave policy   **367**

cultural myth of romanticism   **351**

extended family   **345**

families of choice   **345**

families of orientation   **345**

families of procreation   **345**

family   **347**

feminization of poverty   **353**

flextime   **367**

household   **344**

no-fault divorce   **349**

nuclear family   **345**

pauperization of motherhood   **353**

sandwich generation   **346**

status inconsistency   **360**

EMERGING ISSUES

14

A key feature of twenty-first-century existence is **globalization, a process whereby the world-system of economic relationships becomes increasingly dominant, linking and integrating ever-larger numbers of societies into a worldwide network of economic and political relationships.** This process is neither inevitable nor equitable. It did not just happen by itself, and not everyone in the world benefits equally from it. Rather, globalization is the creation of dominant forces that have asserted their interests worldwide, regardless of the consequences for others. Globalization has been marked increasingly by sharp inequalities both between nations and within nations, between rich and poor, men and women, whites and people of color, young and old (Schaefer, 2003). Nations find their cultures and institutions, and indeed their very life chances, are influenced more and more by transnational forces and less by local interests. International trade agreements, for example, may influence internal labor relations, social expenditures, environmental conditions, and the overall economic health of individual societies. And individuals may find their statuses and life chances dramatically affected by the consequences of these international relations, resulting less from their individual or personal efforts and far more by institutional rearrangements.

Many of the issues likely to confront individuals in the new century are linked by this process of globalization. Throughout this text we have talked periodically about globalization and its effects on individuals' daily lives. For example, the global division of labor has produced a widening gap between the wealth of core, global north nations and the poverty of peripheral, global south nations (see Chapters 3 and 10). That gap is likely to widen if large, multinational corporations continue to exploit the politically and economically disadvantaged workforces of poverty-stricken peripheral nations. In the United States, continued globalization of the division of labor means more lost manufacturing jobs and pressure toward wage stagnation and decline for many U.S. workers. This change in the labor force is contributing to a widening of the gap between the nation's rich and poor. And serious economic crises in the global north reverberate around the world, affecting all nations. On the other hand, the economic pressures and dislocations resulting from globalization have also helped to energize resistance. They have, for example, reignited the labor movement and awakened an international coalition of student groups, unions, and faith communities in a challenge to organizations like the World Trade Organization. Resistance has also emerged around the world to challenging severe austerity measures that harm the most vulnerable members of society as the state tries to rein in beleaguered budgets without upsetting the advantages enjoyed by powerful economic actors.

What other effects is globalization likely to have in the future? In this chapter we will explore four emerging issues: (1) population age dynamics, (2) environmental racism, (3) the digital divide, and (4) global militarism.

In the United States, on average people are living longer, and more of them are entering their later years than ever before.

- What does this mean for society and for the quality of life that individuals can expect to have during old age?
- Will everyone face the same issues and challenges as they age, or are there differing patterns based on gender, race, and class?

The baby-boom generation promises to be the largest cohort of elderly people in the United States, and we must begin to address the implications of an aging population. But as individuals assess their own life chances in the United States, people elsewhere face shorter life spans. Peripheral nations often have much younger populations.

- How does globalization affect population age dynamics?
- Why is there a "graying of the core" at the same time as a "youth boom" in the periphery?
- What are the implications for a society in which very young people greatly outnumber the older population?
- How do these differ from the implications of a population dominated by elders?

The second issue we will explore is environmental racism. Production and consumption patterns throughout the world, but especially in the core nations, have had a negative impact on the environment globally. Pollution produced by the burning of fossil fuels and the release of a variety of chemicals into the atmosphere have contributed to erosion of the ozone layer that helps protect the earth from cancer-causing radiation. Such polluting activities are also a major culprit in climate change. Environmental issues, then, are global issues: What producers and consumers do in the core is polluting the environment for everyone. Moreover, consumption and production processes in the core raise the problem of what to do with enormous amounts of waste products.

- What is the role of racism in toxic waste siting?
- Why does this matter to everyone?
- What is the role of globalization in processes affecting racism in waste management?

Few analyses of the environment examine the roles of race and racism in decisions about where to put toxic waste. Yet there is evidence that selection of polluting and toxic waste sites may at times be racism-driven. That such practices exist, and why, is important for each of us, because they affect such fundamental matters as health and life span. They also reflect the unequal distribution of political power and access to decision making.

The third issue we will examine is the impact of the tremendous growth of the Internet on society and on the world-system. While its supporters cite the great benefits derived from this technology, a critical analysis of globalization leads to several questions:

- What is the Internet, and what can it do?
- Who controls the Internet?
- What are the social possibilities of the information superhighway, and what are the problems it may pose?

- Who has access to the Internet and who does not?
- How does the global spread of the Internet affect world-system relations?

Finally, we will explore the globalization of militarism and the rising threat of global terrorism. The Cold War ended in the early 1990s with the breakup of the Soviet Union. In the aftermath of the Cold War, industries devoted to defense contracting have had to find new markets for their goods and services. One strategy the U.S. defense industry has chosen with the apparent support of the state is to increase export of arms to other countries.

- What are the implications—for each of us, for society, and for the world—of the choices these industries make?

Further, it is hard to ignore the threat posed by global terrorism.

- How might this threat be related to the globalization of militarism?

The sociological imagination you have developed in this course invites you to examine the social context in which these issues continue to evolve. It is important to ask questions concerning the structural arrangements, institutional processes, and social relationships that help define these matters as emerging public issues. Armed with sociological concepts and a sociological imagination, you can begin to explore how your biography and others' may be affected by these issues now and in the future.

GLOBAL POPULATION: THE YOUTH EXPLOSION OF THE PERIPHERY AND THE GRAYING OF THE CORE

A good place to begin to examine this issue is by comparing a core country like the United States with a peripheral country like Sierra Leone. When you look at Figure 14.1, it becomes clear that in the United States there are more people in the older age groups than in the younger age groups. This figure is a **population pyramid**, a graph that illustrates the distribution of ages and sex to get a visual appreciation of population dynamics in a particular place. In Sierra Leone, the population pyramid looks like a cone: There are far more people in the youngest age groups than in the older groups, with roughly equal distributions of men and women in each age group. In the United States, the population pyramid looks more bloated in the middle and certainly fuller at the top than in Sierra Leone, and women more numerous in older groups. What might explain these differences?

One way to understand the different population distributions is to look at basic demographic indicators, such as *birth rate*, *death rate*, *infant mortality rate*, and *life expectancy at birth* (see Table 14.1). Birth and death rates measure the number of births and deaths each year per 1,000 in the mid-year population. The difference between these two rates provides a rough measure of the growth of population overall. The birth rate in 2010 in Sierra Leone was more than two and a half times greater than that in the United States; its death rate was twice that of the United States. This suggests that the overall population in Sierra Leone was growing at a faster rate. It also helps explain why the younger groups in Sierra Leone's population are larger than those in the United States.

Figure 14.1: Population Pyramids, U.S. and Sierra Leone, 2010

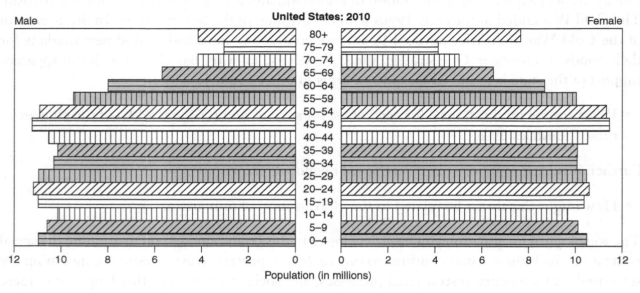

U.S. Population Pyramid for 2010

Age and sex distribution for the year 2010:

United States: 2010

Sierra Leone Population Pyramid for 2010

Age and sex distribution for the year 2010:

Sierra Leone: 2010

Source: www.nationmaster.com/country/us/Age_distribution, www.nationmaster.com/country/sl-sierra-leone/Age_distribution.

To better understand the factors affecting the population distributions in the two nations, it's useful also to look at infant mortality rates and life expectancies at birth. *Infant mortality* rates indicate the number of children who die before their first birthday per 1,000 live births in a given year. In Sierra Leone, the infant mortality rate in 2010 was 16 times greater than the rate in the United States. High infant mortality rates can reduce the impact of high birth rates. However, if the birth rate is high enough, even a high infant mortality rate will not necessarily alter the relative proportions of the age groups in a country's population. This will especially be the case if life expectancy at birth is low for that country.

Table 14.1:   Comparing population dynamics in the United States and Sierra Leone, 2010

Indicator	United States	Sierra Leone
Birth Rate	14	38.6
Death Rate	8	15.3
Adult Mortality Rate (Men)	138.6	464
Adult Mortality Rate (Women)	80	444.5
Infant Mortality Rate	7.5	119.2
Life Expectancy at Birth (Men)*	75.9	47.2
Life Expectancy at Birth (Women)*	80.7	48.4
Age Dependency Ratio	50.1	81
Total Fertility Rate	2.1	4.9
Adolescent Fertility Rate	50.1	112.1
Child Immunization Rate for DPT	94	84
Child Immunization Rate for Measles	90	80
Percentage of Population with Access to		
Improved Water Source	99	55
Improved Sanitation Facilities	100	13
Percentage of Children (aged 10–14) in Labor Force (not including child slavery or military)	0	53.7

Source: World Bank, 2012. *World Development Indicators*. Washington, DC: The World Bank.
*Source: www.odci.gov/cia

Life expectancy at birth, or the number of years someone born in a given year may be expected to live if the existing patterns of mortality that year remain the same throughout that person's life, also affects the size of the age groups: Longer life expectancies mean people will survive to join the older age groups in the population, making these older groups larger than those where life expectancies are low. In 2010, Sierra Leone's life expectancy was about 33 years shorter than that of the United States (World Bank, 2012). Taken together, these data suggest a shorter average life in Sierra Leone than in the United States, so that the older age groups in the United States are much larger than those in Sierra Leone. Coupled with the higher birth rate in Sierra Leone producing larger younger age groups, Sierra Leone's population distribution looks like an inverted version of that of the United States. What factors help to explain these stark differences?

Consider, first, our discussion in Chapter 3 of the global division of labor in the world-system. Peripheral countries are among the poorest as a result of centuries of economic exploitation and dominance by the core. As a result, famine, war, natural disaster, chronic malnutrition, and poor health are key factors that limit life chances. For example, in Sierra Leone a civil war has raged since 1991, resulting in the displacement or deaths of more than one-third of the population (www.odci.gov/cia). Much of the fighting is over control of the production and sale of diamonds, a valuable resource in the global economy (www.amnestyusa.org). The displacement of large segments of the Sierra Leone population has resulted in high rates of hunger and malnutrition and a shortage of vital resources such as healthcare. Moreover, the poverty-stricken people of peripheral countries typically have limited access to clean water and sanitation systems, making intestinal bacteria and diarrhea a common and deadly occurrence. In Sierra Leone, 55 percent of the population have access to drinkable water (what the World Bank calls "improved water sources"), compared to 99 percent of the population in the United States; 13 percent of the Sierra Leone population have access to "improved sanitation facilities," compared to 100 percent in the United States (World Bank, 2012).

Global inequality between the core and the periphery also means unequal access to medical care and drug treatment for critical diseases. In Sierra Leone, 80 percent of the children under 12 years old have access to vaccination against measles, and 84 percent have access to immunization against diphtheria, pertussis, and whooping cough (DPT); compare that to the United States, where 90 percent of the children under 12 have access to measles vaccinations, and 94 percent to DPT immunizations (World Bank, 2012). Children in Sierra Leone are thus more vulnerable to childhood diseases, since their immune systems are likely to be compromised by chronic malnutrition. As a result, any health challenges, from simple diarrhea to more serious illnesses, can frequently kill. Moreover, there is less access to medical care in peripheral nations. In Sierra Leone, there are only 0.12 physicians per 1,000 people in the population, compared to 2.4 physicians per 1,000 people in the United States. Even when people become ill with treatable diseases, in Sierra Leone they are less likely to have access to a doctor to prevent the disease from causing death.

While the spread of the Human Immunodeficiency Virus (HIV) and the number of cases of Auto Immune Deficiency Syndrome (AIDS) have slowed considerably in core nations like the United States, they are increasing in peripheral nations like Sierra Leone. This is, in part, because access to preventive education is more readily available in the core. Moreover, the very expensive drugs currently used to control AIDS symptoms are generally unavailable or unaffordable to most in the periphery. The World Bank noted that sub-Saharan Africa has the fastest growing increase in the rate of new adult HIV infections in the world; by 2012 the region held 69 percent of all AIDS cases worldwide (www.allafrica.com). In 2001, at least 44,000 of the population older than 15 in Sierra Leone were HIV-positive in 2011 (World Bank, 2003). And while infants are vulnerable to maternally transmitted HIV infection, the number of children younger than 14 years old living with HIV in 2011 was relatively low (4,300) in Sierra Leone (World Health Organization, available at www.unaids.org).

In contrast, demographers have long noted that the population of the United States is aging. The average life span has been steadily increasing since the 1950s, largely as a result of advances in nutrition, exercise, and medicine. Children born in 2010, for example, can expect to live an average of 78.3 years (../Local Settings/temp/7zO24.tmp/(www.census.gov/statabWorld Bank, 2012). In addition, the baby-boom generation (persons born between 1946 and 1964) has begun to enter middle age. While the birth rate since the 1980s has been increasing somewhat in an "echo boom" of the earlier baby boom, it is not as large an increase as that following World War II. This means that the number of people age 65 and over is larger than it has ever been.

Estimates vary about exactly how large this older group may grow to be, but there is wide consensus that the increase will be rather dramatic. In 2010, 5.54 million people in the United States were 85 years old or older (www.census.gov). Meanwhile, the growth of the younger segments of the population is slowing down. In 1960, for example, 16.5 million children were 5 years old or younger; by 2010, the number had grown to 20.2 million. But the growth in the 65-and-older age group was far more pronounced: In 1960 there were 16.7 million people in this group, roughly the same as the youngest age group; but by 2010, the number of elders had more than doubled, to 40.3 million (www.census.gov). Observers agree that this elder age group will continue to increase rapidly.

In large measure, then, the core nations' greater access to life-enhancing resources based on their privileged position in the world-system is producing an increasingly aging population, in stark contrast to the experience of peripheral nations, where limited access to vital resources stemming from their exploited and dominated position in the world-system is producing a population that is clearly younger. The globalization process is exacerbating the gaps between the core and periphery. What are the social implications of these population age dynamics?

The Youth Boom of the Periphery

When a population is dominated by younger age groups, it is likely to stimulate population growth, since a younger population is likely to be more fertile than an aging one. Indeed, in 2010 Sierra Leone's *fertility rate* (the number of children that would be born to a woman if she lived through her child-bearing years and reproduced consistently at her age-group's fertility rate) was more than two and a half times the rate in the United States. More telling is the relative *adolescent fertility rate* (the number of births to women age 15–19 years old per 1,000 women in the same age group) (see Table 14.1): Sierra Leone's adolescent fertility rate was more than twice that of the United States. This means strong pressures toward a continuing increase in population growth rates in a country that suffers limited access to vital resources supporting life chances as a result of its peripheral position in the global political economy.

In a population that has proportionately fewer adults in the age groups usually responsible for production and labor, children become an important asset. High infant mortality rates that threaten the survival of children make high fertility rates a strategy that increases the chances that at least some will survive to contribute labor and income to the family. Large cohorts of very young children coupled with smaller cohorts of working-age adults (15–64) mean that working-age people are placed under greater pressure to provide for a very large number of dependents. Sierra Leone's *age dependency ratio* (the ratio of people younger than 15 and older than 65 to the number of people aged 15–64) is nearly 50 percent higher than that of the United States. While this dependency ratio can also mean providing for those who are 65 or older, in peripheral nations like Sierra Leone people do not commonly live that long. As such, Sierra Leone's greater age dependency ratio indicates that there are too few working-age people to support a young, dependent population or to provide a labor force sufficient to meet current societal needs. And this dependency ratio is further complicated by the fact that a high rate of HIV among adults has produced a startling number of orphaned children. Since the beginning of Sierra Leone's AIDS epidemic, more than 75,000 children have lost their mother or both parents to AIDS; there are currently more than 18,000 children orphaned by the disease there (World Health Organization, available at www.unaids.org).

Because of the higher dependency ratio in Sierra Leone, there is a greater likelihood that children will be used as workers in the formal and informal labor force, and they frequently are abducted or sold into slavery (Bales, 1999). This is because the resources available are insufficient to support the sheer number of people who must be provided for. With so few adults to produce or obtain what is needed, and so many children available, children become a source of labor. Children are commonly active as slave labor in the informal labor markets of peripheral nations, engaging in street vending and bartering and even prostitution. In addition, sweatshops and mines frequently use young children as slaves because they are an easily exploitable, readily available labor force. While the true extent of child slavery is difficult to count, nations often report on the number of children officially employed. In Sierra Leone in 2010, 53.7 percent of the children aged 10–14 participated in the formal low-wage labor force (not including child slavery and military service), compared with 0 percent in the United States (see Table 14.1). This figure does not include the number of children who have been forced or sold into slavery.

Children are also more likely to be used as soldiers in countries dominated by younger age groups. There are simply not enough adults to fight the increasing incidence of civil wars and international wars often fueled by tensions arising from the unequal distribution of vital resources. The United Nations issued a report in 2001 noting the rise of child soldiers, particularly in the periphery, and Human Rights Watch (HRW) issues reports tracking child soldiers. The U.N. report estimated that more than 300,000 children under the age of 18—and sometimes as young as 7 or 8—were involved as soldiers in conflicts, and HRW identifies at least 14 countries where child soldiers prevail (www.hrw.org). Amnesty International cited Sierra Leone in particular, where an estimated 10,000 children under the age of 18 (and some as young as 5) were used as combatants by both government and opposition forces during the civil war there (www .amnestyusa.org; www.hrw.org). Participation as both a worker and a soldier means that the notion of childhood that dominates in the core, where children are seen as innocent and carefree and where they are protected from exploitation as laborers or as soldiers, is unlikely to prevail in the periphery. It is not that peripheral cultures do not value children or human life as do those in the core; it is that the effects of centuries of unequal relations in the global division of labor on population age dynamics have vastly different implications for the periphery and the core. And a large, poverty-stricken population with an enormous abundance of very young people becomes more vulnerable to exploitation and slavery of children (Bales, 1999).

The Graying of the Core

Let's look at the United States as an example of a core nation to explore the contrasting implications posed by an aging population. In this case, the growing population of elders is occurring in a nation that has benefitted from the globalization process, such that more people live longer and there are more resources to assist them. Nonetheless, elders face problems and challenges.

Within the next few decades, the age distribution in the United States will have shifted so dramatically toward the elderly that society is likely to look quite different than it does today. Imagine the impact an aging population will have on institutions such as the family, the economy, and the government. Many social institutions will have to change in order to accommodate the pressures imposed by a large elderly cohort.

An aging population in general increases pressures on the institution of the state, particularly on programs designed to address the issues and needs of the elderly. People commonly become more vulnerable to chronic illnesses as they age and thus require more medical care. Of course, aging does not necessarily entail becoming frail, feeble, or senile, but the older people get the more susceptible they become to chronic or long-term illnesses such as arthritis, heart disease, Alzheimer's disease, and various types of cancer. Some chronic conditions are exacerbated by extended exposure to environmental pollution and toxins or by other factors such as smoking, alcohol abuse, lack of exercise, or high-fat diets. The longer people live, the more these factors affect them. Chronic illnesses are typically among the most expensive to treat; thus, the more elderly there are in the population, the greater the expense of healthcare for the nation.

At present, one must be extremely poor to receive Medicaid assistance to pay for nursing-home and other long-term care (e.g., visiting nurses and caretakers). Relatively few elderly have private long-term care insurance. Many older persons and their families thus face the terrifying prospect of being bankrupted by the costs of nursing-home care. As noted in Chapter 13, the average annual cost of such care per person in 2011 was more than $78,000, and some states averaged as much as $81,000 per year (www.ltcfeds.com; The American Association of Homes and Services for the Aging www.aahsa.org). The elderly and their families pay more than 56 percent of that cost, with the remainder currently paid by Medicaid. In 2001, when the total national bill for nursing-home care was $137 billion, Medicaid and other governmental health-care programs paid out $73 billion of that amount (www.census.gov). Adding the cost of care paid by the elderly and their families to the government bill would significantly increase the tax burden on the younger working population.

The institution of the family is greatly affected by these pressures on the U.S. healthcare system. In Chapter 13 we noted that the high cost of nursing-home care was causing more families to care for their frail or disabled elderly members themselves. Indeed, many of the elderly with disabilities are cared for by their own families, either in the elders' own homes in the same community or in their children's homes. By the turn of this century, more than one-third of the elderly with disabilities are cared for by their children, compared with only 5 percent in nursing-home care (Cancian and Oliker, 2000). The remainder struggle to care for themselves or are cared for by other aging relatives and friends. The impact this has on families is important. Children of elderly parents with disabilities are often ill-equipped to care for them, since many of the children either are working couples or are unemployed or underemployed. In this way class influences the impact of aging on families.

Gender figures prominently in the effects of elder care. Studies indicate that women are care-givers far more often than men (Merrill, 1997). One study found that 72 percent of elder caregivers were women (Cancian and Oliker, 2000); more recent studies indicate this has not changed (www.caregiver.org). Such women spend an average of nearly 22 hours per week on elder care, and many spend much more, depending on the severity of the dependence (www.caregiver.org).

An aging population also places pressures on the Social Security system. Originally designed as a social contract with America's workers, the Social Security system relies on payments from current workers to pay benefits to current retirees; the assumption is that when these current workers retire and begin to collect their entitlements, enough workers will fill their vacated places in the labor market to support them throughout retirement. This assumption may be in jeopardy in the coming decades. If more elderly people in the United States are living longer after they retire, and fewer younger and middle-aged people are in the labor force to pay their entitlements, pressures on the Social Security system could mount to crisis proportions. Indeed, over the past decade many people have debated whether the system is on the verge of bankruptcy or in danger of becoming so (this debate, of course, conspicuously ignores the option of reducing spending in other areas such as defense, or raising taxes on wealthy corporations and individuals, to better meet rising Social Security needs).

Such budgetary fears raise the question of the social construction of retirement. Currently, most workers retire between 62 and 65 years of age. Most retire willingly, but for many, retirement is involuntary (Neubeck and Neubeck, 1997). Because of improvements in healthcare and health awareness, most people in the United States are still quite healthy physically and mentally when they retire, and many can expect to live 20 or more additional years. For some, this creates a role strain, for a person may want to fulfill the obligations of a productive citizen but may not have the opportunity to do so. What does retirement mean, then, when a retiree is still able and willing to be productive? And how is an aging person to live for 20 or more years on an income that is just a fraction of that on which he or she may have been relying?

Some retirees seek employment after retirement. Fast-food firms such as McDonald's have made a point of hiring retirees as counter workers. Retirees who do not necessarily need the income of a paying job but want to continue making positive contributions to their communities often perform important volunteer services. Many donate time and skills as daycare workers, hospital aides, soup-kitchen aides, cancer-care volunteers, and so forth. All these pursuits suggest that the social construction of retirement in the United States is driven by antiquated stereotypes of elderly fragility, senility, and declining productivity. Yet a shrinking labor market encourages continuation of these stereotypes, as younger workers pressure older workers to retire to make room for them.

In addition to its effects on the economy, the state, and the family, the aging of America also affects the political process. As the baby-boom generation ages and lives longer, it has a greater impact on voting and the legislative process, in part because it represents one of the largest age cohorts in the voting population. Studies show that political participation rates tend to increase with age (www.census.gov). As we saw in Chapter 11, politicians are paying increasing attention to the issues and needs of older people because there is a significant and growing number of them, and because they vote.

Of course, political clout among elders is dependent upon the development of **age consciousness,** the awareness of common interests based on age. Older people can have a tremendous political impact by organizing and mobilizing their collective effort for change. Opportunities for increasing age consciousness are growing as a result of such trends as segregated housing for the elderly in retirement communities and programs that stimulate interaction among the elderly, such as senior centers.

Their potential for organized political clout has not been lost on aging persons in the United States. They have been organizing into powerful political groups ever since the Gray Panthers was founded in the 1970s. With a current membership of over 70,000 in over 50 networked chapters, the Gray Panthers have frequently challenged ageist stereotypes and age discrimination in the workplace and elsewhere. They also seek to increase awareness among legislators of the need for policies to assist and protect the elderly (see www.graypanthers.org). Much larger groups, such as the 40 million member AARP (formerly the American Association of Retired Persons) have a greater impact on the political process. As the elderly population increases, and as elders find their voice through influential organizations, the political process will pay more and more attention to issues and interests affecting them.

The shift in the population pyramid has an interesting effect on a culture that has focused primarily on youth since the 1960s, when baby boomers became relatively affluent and the largest and most vocal segment of the population. Films, television, and advertising have strongly celebrated youth. Over the past several years, however, more commercials have been appearing for products pitched to an aging population, such as adult disposable diapers for incontinence, vitamins designed for older people, erectile dysfunction medications, electric light switches that operate at the clap of a hand, voice-activated emergency alert systems, and life insurance programs available regardless of age. Where once only young models could be seen in advertisements and fashion magazines, now increasingly older, gray-haired models peer out from the pages and the screen. Television programs and films contain older actors, who are depicted as vibrant, sexually active, and productive.

Still, the dominant culture's emphasis on the desirability of youth has hardly disappeared. As the population ages, advertisements offer anti-baldness products and hair dyes to cover the gray, facial creams to smooth out wrinkles, and senior citizen exercise videotapes promising to make their users look and feel young. While people may be living longer, advertisers emphasize that they need not look "old." The population shift to older cohorts, then, also increasingly affects the culture whose themes simultaneously celebrate and resist the aging process.

Why is this population shift of concern to you now? First, you may have parents or other relatives who are currently elderly, and thus you are learning firsthand what the population shift already means to their existence (and to that of their primary caretakers, who may very likely be you). Second, if current trends continue, everyone may eventually become part of those increasingly larger older age groups. Who will underwrite the retirement income and healthcare programs on which older people will have to rely? How will decisions made today concerning the federal budget and spending affect the reliability of programs such as Medicare, Social Security, and elder care when people are eligible for them? How will current decisions regarding a national healthcare policy affect the quality of life in retirement? How can people improve their economic well-being while they are in the labor force so as to protect their life chances when they retire? It is important not to frame questions and analyses in terms of a pitched battle between the young and the elderly; rather, these should be framed in the context of people's life-cycle relationships to such macro-level social structures as the economy, the state, and the intersection of race, class, gender, and age within institutions, all of which are affected by the relationship between the United States and others in the globalization process that is currently under way.

ENVIRONMENT: TOXIC IMPERIALISM AND ENVIRONMENTAL RACISM

No one lives in environmental isolation. What happens to the environment in one part of the world ultimately affects the environment in other parts of the world. Never was this made clearer than in 1986, when an overheated nuclear power reactor in Chernobyl in the former Soviet Union's Ukraine released more radioactivity into the atmosphere than ever before in world history, "equivalent to the fallout from several dozen Hiroshima bombs" (Hohenemser and Renn, 1988:5). Notably, the fallout did not remain over or near the Ukraine alone, although the largest impact was clearly in the former Soviet Union and Western Europe; it traveled to cover the entire Northern Hemisphere. While that event was certainly notable in its enormity, it was not simply an isolated freak accident.

Similarly, the enormous earthquake in Japan in 2011 not only left more than 16,000 people dead; it severely damaged an active nuclear reactor there, causing a meltdown. And it touched off a devastating tsunami that inundated significant proportions of the nation. But the flooding damage was not restricted to Japan: Two years later huge amounts of debris from the flood continue to wash up on shores halfway around the world. The debris carries not only contaminants from the earthquake and the tsunami; it brings invasive ocean species that pose potential serious environmental challenges to the ecosystem.

These two events make it clear that how we live in the modern world has serious consequences on the environment, consequences that will affect us all, now and in the future. Moreover, environmental catastrophes, both natural and human-made, do not remain isolated within the countries where they initially occur; their effects are felt worldwide. This also raises questions as to the relationship between environmental danger and inequality within and between societies, inequality that is in many instances increasing with globalization.

National and worldwide attention has focused on environmental concerns since the first Earth Day celebration in 1970. Increasing awareness of the effects individuals' daily actions have on the health and stability of the environment has caused many to modify their lifestyles and patterns of consumption. Political action has increasingly focused on industrial production and on ways to curb corporate contributions to environmental instability and climate change. However, the sociological imagination leads to several questions: What effect does globalization have on the environment? Does everyone suffer the consequences of environmental pollution equally? How are toxic waste sites selected and pollution cleanups assigned? Are they distributed equitably throughout the world and in this country? How do power relationships and processes affect the selection of sites for toxic waste dumps?

Toxic Imperialism

Scant attention has been paid to exploring the possible intersection of environmental issues and issues of globalization and inequality. Yet evidence suggests that this question warrants close scrutiny (Simon, 2000). For example, there are indications that international trade agreements are likely to make the environment worse, as countries seek to minimize or eliminate what they perceive to be barriers to trade and production. For example, the North American Free Trade Agreement (NAFTA) has been implicated in the environmental deterioration of the *maquiladora* factory zones lining the United States–Mexico border as a result of relaxed environmental protection standards in the United States and Mexico, selective enforcement of standards, and the improper disposal of toxic waste byproducts of production, all in the interest of enhancing trade and production (www.globalexchange.org/ftaa/topten.html). This situation is likely to spread, since the United States would like to expand NAFTA to all of Central and South America. ../Local Settings/temp/7zO24.tmp/(www.globalexchange.org/ftqaa/topten.html).

In addition, corporations and core nations like the United States have been dumping toxic wastes and polluting products in peripheral nations such as Nigeria, Guinea, and Haiti, as well as in black townships in South Africa (Marks and Brown, 1990; Clapp, 2001; Block, 2002). U.S. corporations like HoltraChem Manufacturing Co. have dumped hundreds of tons of mercury waste products in India (Judd, 2001). And tons of hazardous waste from Australia, Germany, and the United States are routinely dumped in South Pacific nations and islands (www .greenleft.org). The Earth Day/Wall Street Action Group has referred to toxic dumping in semi-peripheral and peripheral nations by major multinational corporations and core nations as **toxic imperialism** (Cohen, 1990).

Why are such nations targeted as viable sites for toxic waste dumping? Part of the answer can be understood in the context of world-system relations. Semi-peripheral and peripheral nations are far less powerful and much poorer economically than core nations like the United States. Indeed, overwhelming debt has prompted some peripheral nations such as the Philippines and Cambodia to accept toxic waste in exchange for payments as a way of raising money to reduce debt burdens (www.hrw.org).

Loopholes in U.S. federal laws regulating toxic materials, especially the Federal Insecticide, Fungicide and Rodenticide Act (FIFRA), have encouraged exports of toxic materials, even when these substances have been banned for use in the United States. Legislative efforts since 1978 to close the loopholes have failed. Federal policy initiatives and lax enforcement of regulatory laws have made it profitable for corporations to export products that are deemed a threat to U.S. residents (O'Neill, 2000). Few poor nations have regulatory policies governing toxic substances and pesticides. Governments in those that do often do not adequately enforce them. This gives the large international pesticide producers and toxic waste producers the freedom to export these substances without restriction (www.panna.org/panna/resources).

The governments of many nations do not wish to publicly acknowledge the level of environmental poisoning caused by toxic imports. Press reports of contaminated food, water, and land could severely depress tourism in poor nations. Furthermore, many of their governments are understandably reluctant to admit that their lack of legal controls or inability to enforce them has aided and abetted the endangerment of their own citizens. And finally, any admission that toxic substances are present in the land or water of other nations invites investigation by the U.S. Food and Drug Administration (FDA) of all food imports into this country, thereby potentially damaging poor nations' important source of trade income (Weir and Schapiro, 1981; see also Adeola, 2000). Taken together, these factors make it easy for corporations based in core nations to dump unsafe substances and toxic wastes in poorer areas of the world.

The corporations that are most likely to pollute the poorer nations may be based in the core, but they are acting like stateless entities: huge multinational corporations that do business all around the world, globally spreading their toxic waste, yet seem beyond control by governments. But multinational corporations do not restrict their practice of dumping of toxic wastes to poorer nations. They also pollute neighborhoods in core nations like the United States (see Simon, 2000). What is notable, however, is that they do not spread their wastes randomly. When they dump toxic waste in the United States, they tend to select neighborhoods of color and poverty, a practice called **environmental racism**.

Environmental Racism

The kinds of relationships that exist between global inequality and environmental degradation are reproduced more locally. A growing body of research has begun to focus on the issue of inequality and toxic pollution within the United States (Stretskey and Hogan, 1998; Cassidy, Judge, and Sommers, 2001; Malley, Scroggins, and Bohon, 2012). In a 1987 study of the relationship between toxic wastes and racial composition of communities, the Commission for Racial Justice (under the auspices of the United Church of Christ) noted that there were "clear patterns which show that communities with greater minority percentages of the population are more likely to be the sites of commercial hazardous waste facilities. The possibility that these patterns resulted by chance is virtually impossible" (Chavis and Lee, 1987: 23). Little had changed more than a decade later (Hind and Reese, 1998; Maher, 1998).

Commission for Racial Justice researchers found that poverty-stricken neighborhoods and communities of color continue to bear a disproportionate burden as recipients of the 6 billion tons of toxic waste and environmental pollution produced in the United States annually. As many as 50 percent of African Americans and 60 percent of Latinos live in communities in which levels of air pollutants exceed federal regulations (Hatfield, 2003). Indeed, they found that communities in which commercial waste sites existed had twice the proportion of people of color as communities that did not have any such sites. And communities that had two or more commercial toxic waste sites had more than three times the proportion of people of color than those that had no such sites. Moreover, racial composition correlated with the location of a commercial toxic waste site more strongly than any other variable, including socioeconomic variables such as average household income and average home values (Been, 1994; Pollack and Vitas, 1995;). Researchers came to similar conclusions regarding air pollution (Gelobter, 1992; Daniels and Friedman, 1999), as well as the effects of toxic waste dumping on people who consume fish caught in dump site waters (West et al., 1992).

Some researchers refer to this pattern as a problem of environmental racism (C. Lee, 1992, 1994; Pulido, 2000; Westra and Lawson, 2001), in which the invisible, unearned privileges of whiteness and affluence include the relative freedom from pollution in one's immediate neighborhood. Why have communities of color in the United States become the disproportionate recipients of toxic waste sites? Various studies have begun to unravel this issue. The sociological imagination points to at least four important factors related to inequality.

First, land values in neighborhoods of color and heavily integrated communities are often depressed. This is because properties in white communities are frequently defined by real estate agencies and mortgaging banks as more desirable investments. In fact, banks often **redline** heavily integrated communities and neighborhoods of color, a practice that defines these areas as ineligible for mortgage or repair loans, or small-business loans. One study found that in 2001 African Americans were more than twice as likely to be denied a mortgage as white applicants, regardless of income; Latinos were 1 ½ more likely than whites to be denied such loans (www .uaw.org). Redlining also frequently makes it difficult for small businesses to obtain insurance, a situation that can escalate the flight of businesses from communities in transition. Land is consequently readily available and cheap, with owners eager for a buyer (J. T. Hamilton, 1995). Furthermore, the combination of racial discrimination in housing and poverty often means that both poor and middle-class people of color have far less mobility than middle-class whites. They may not be able to sell their property or afford to move from a community where toxic waste sites are located (Boerner and Lambert, 1995; Bullard, 2002).

People of color also often have fewer political and economic resources and often are not well organized politically. When commercial toxic waste sites are targeted for their communities, they are not able to respond with as strong an organized opposition as that put forth by white middle-class communities (Bullard and Wright, 1987; Chavis and Lee, 1987). And beyond the question of organization is the lack of access to influential governmental and nongovernmental leaders and institutions. People of color and the poor are underrepresented in government and almost entirely absent on policy boards and other key advisory bodies (Pinderhughs, 1996). Therefore, their interests and concerns are far less likely to be heard. As a result, governmental agencies charged with overseeing the environment not only do not recognize the relationship between systems of racial and economic inequality and environmental issues, but they also fail to protect communities of color and poverty. Penalties for violations of environmental laws are often more lax or poorly enforced in these communities compared with those in affluent white communities (Boerner and Lambert, 1995). Mainstream nongovernmental environmental organizations are not any more likely to recognize the role of systems of inequality and to articulate the problem, as most are primarily concerned with the conservation of nature and wildlife preservation rather than with the human health risks of exposure to toxic waste (Austin and Schill, 1994).

Finally, those promoting the toxic waste facilities often promise jobs and other economic benefits for the host communities, thereby mitigating some of the opposition that might develop. Communities of color may have unemployment rates that are two to three times higher than those of white communities. Economically depressed communities are thus vulnerable to promises of much-needed jobs (J. T. Hamilton, 1995).

It should not be assumed that people of color are unconcerned about dump sites in their neighborhoods. Evidence suggests that African Americans are just as concerned about the environment as are whites (Mohai, 1990). Indeed, one recent study found that the poor and people of color are *more* concerned with environmental issues than whites and the affluent (Uyeki and Holland, 2000). Native Americans have organized an environmental action group, Citizens Against Ruining Our Environment, which helps residents on tribal lands resist toxic waste dumping in their communities (see also www.njrs.org). This task is complicated by the fact that Native lands are not subject to the same state and federal regulations as non-Native lands (Wei, 1991). And the National Association for the Advancement of Colored People increasingly links civil rights issues to the issue of environmental racism (www.naacp.org; Cole and Foster, 2001).

Despite these resistance efforts, toxic waste sitings continue to be overwhelmingly located in communities of color. Resistance is hampered by lack of information. Even when grassroots activists attempt to resist these facilities, they often find it difficult to obtain key information necessary to organize their efforts. Community groups often note that they confronted obstacles when they tried to obtain information, and many cite government agencies as those obstacles (Bullard, 1993, 2002). Chavis and Lee (1987) noted that such "institutional resistance" to providing access to information is likely to increase when agencies deal with groups that they believe are not powerful (see also Gould, 1993).

It is crucial for everyone to understand environmental racism and toxic imperialism as a public issue. Why? First, when toxic wastes and other unsafe materials are exported to underdeveloped countries, they can return to the United States in imports of such things as produce, coffee, meat, and fish. Notably, toxic pesticide dumping remains high: Between 1997 and 2000 U.S. exports of toxic pesticides increased by 15 percent over the exports between 1992 and 1996 (www.panna.org/panna/resources/panups/panup_20020111.dv.html). By 2003, almost 28 million pounds of pesticides banned in the United States were exported (www.huffingtonpst.com). Toxic wastes and carcinogenic materials such as mercury, dioxins, and lead dumped in other countries thus find their way into the food chain, and they may return to the United States and onto people's dinner plates.

The factors uncovered by studies of the relationship between inequality and environmental danger suggest that *all* communities are potentially at risk. That is, any community that is not well organized or does not have access to political and economic resources is vulnerable. Furthermore, in an economy where jobs are continuing to disappear, many communities that are stable now could change and become susceptible to the appeal of jobs and financial compensation in exchange for accepting the risks and hazards of toxic waste facilities. Similarly, a recessionary economy frequently attacks the real estate values of many communities, including previously stable middle-class white neighborhoods. Such depreciated areas become increasingly vulnerable to hazardous waste sitings. Together, these factors suggest that everyone would benefit from an understanding of how the systems of racial and economic inequality relate to toxic waste and pollution.

Finally, individuals may be relieved that such hazards and risks presently occur in someone else's community and not their own, but the fact is that everyone ends up sharing in increased healthcare costs related to illnesses from dangerous toxic waste sitings. Ultimately, tolerating toxic waste sites in anyone's community cedes power to those who produce and dump hazardous and toxic substances. As long as these polluters believe that jobs and cash can appease communities, and as long as governmental agencies feel free to keep information from those who seek to fend off unwanted risks, everyone will be less able to struggle against these forces if or when their own community is targeted.

TECHNOLOGY AND GLOBALIZATION: THE DIGITAL DIVIDE

Increasing globalization has stimulated and in turn has been encouraged by the development of new technologies. In particular, the Internet, or information superhighway, has dramatically altered the way societies produce and consume goods and services, communicate, and gain access to information and other resources. Multinational corporations that have shifted production overseas to peripheral countries use it to connect management in core headquarters with labor and materials abroad. Likewise, Internet communications enable global military operations to be directed from the United States. Drones, for example, fly guided by computerized guidance rather than by human pilots in the cockpit, able to conduct surveillance and bomb targets from afar without jeopardizing the life of the pilot. With keystrokes, entire communities, nations, and regions around the world are affected by economic, political, and military decision makers.

Those with Internet access can obtain information about jobs all around the country or the world. This greatly expands job search capabilities beyond the local newspaper listings. It is increasingly possible for some workers to telecommute to work from the comforts of home using personal computers. Such an arrangement can be invaluable to people struggling to balance family responsibilities with the need to earn income, including workers with preschool-age children or family members who require constant care, such as people with disabilities or aging parents. Telecommuting often reduces the need for costly childcare or home companion arrangements. And daily errands after work can similarly be made more convenient because in addition to telecommuting to work, it is possible to shop online and have the merchandize delivered to one's door.

The Internet also offers many educational opportunities. Anyone with access can obtain all sorts of reference materials from the comforts of home and not be restricted by the limited resources of local library facilities or by geographic isolation of living in remote rural areas. It's increasingly possible for teachers to place reference materials and reading assignments for courses online or post these materials on website blackboards, so that commuting students can access these beyond the restricted hours their libraries may be open. Journals, newspapers, and magazines can publish online instead of printing thousands of copies to distribute to libraries and book stores, thus saving trees from wanton destruction. People more and more complete whole courses and degree programs online in distance-learning arrangements, allowing full-time and shift workers, full-time parents and homemakers, as well as homebound people (such as the frail elderly or people with severe disabilities) and those who live in isolated communities to access educational opportunities they might ordinarily be denied.

The environmental and community benefits of the Internet can be significant. Online shopping and educational opportunities, as well as telecommuting, can benefit the environment as fewer cars (or even mass transit) are needed, thus reducing the pollution caused by burning fossil fuels. The Internet can also offer a virtual community for people who have difficulties connecting to others who live in their immediate geographic communities, providing valuable support networks and information. For example, gay and lesbian adolescents can find refuge in online chatrooms and information sites without risking rejection, punishment, and perhaps violence associated with coming out in their geographic communities (Egan, 2000). The Internet also allows users to "travel" around the world to talk to a diverse range of people about their perspectives and lives in places that are unfamiliar. And it is increasingly recognized as an invaluable tool for people suffering from Asperger's syndrome and other forms of autism spectrum disorders to communicate and connect to the social world that may otherwise be inaccessible to them.

On the other hand, the very nature of the Internet's promise also poses many new and interesting questions about power and inequality. For example, telecommuting to work using personal computers at home signals a return to a form of cottage industry, as more and more workers become "mobile workers" with PCs, fax machines, email, Skype, etc. While this may be cheaper and easier for both workers and employers, it also means workers become increasingly isolated from each other and therefore encounter fewer opportunities to develop a sense of community and to organize around common problems. Generally, telecommuters are not unionized; that means that they may be more easily subjected to unfair or abusive work conditions. There is emerging evidence, for example, that many telecommuting workers are enduring the same conditions long suffered by workers in sweatshops common in the garment and electronics industries, including low wages, no benefits, long hours, and oppressive supervisory control (Ross, 1999). The reliance on technology keeps workers plugged in long past the conventional workday, so that there is virtually no end to the workday (Sandberg, 2013): it creates "the new economy's round-the-clock work imperative" (Losse, 2013). Furthermore, laws designed to protect the physical environment that workers must endure are difficult to enforce; it is impossible to legislate desk heights, appropriate seating and lighting, fair lunch and coffee breaks, and other occupational health and safety factors in people's homes.

In addition to the problems facing many workers now engaged in telecommuting, increasing reliance on the Internet poses many cultural costs. Online educational opportunities and distance learning certainly offer the potential of linking isolated individuals and schools to the mainstream of society. However, the Internet also has the potential to displace human labor, since fewer instructors will be needed to teach larger numbers of students electronically. And it can mean far less human contact between students and teachers who are online, thereby removing an important piece of the educational process: the give and take of discussion and the mentoring relationship. Who, then, will write recommendation letters for faceless students who complete these courses and then try to find jobs or admission to postgraduate educational programs? Placing books, magazines, reference materials, and newspapers online also means a cultural shift in how individuals relate to printed material. It means a substantial change in the social construction of leisure, as it becomes more difficult to enjoy the simple pleasures of reading at the beach, on a subway, under a tree, sitting up in bed late at night, or even while snuggling with a young child in a comfortable chair. The popularization of e-readers allows readers to overcome many of these limitations. But as countless airline passengers have discovered, when they are required to power down all electronics on takeoff and landing: They cannot continue reading (as can those using print media) during precisely the most stressful moments of the flight that could be relieved by the distraction of reading. And e-readers make it far more difficult if not impossible to experience one of the joys of reading: passing around and sharing loved books and magazines with friends and family.

Increasing reliance on Internet publications means that the more affluent will likely have better access to vital information, thereby widening the gap between the haves and the have-nots. For example, access to job ads posted on the Internet is predicated on a working knowledge of how to use the Internet, and, more importantly, on access to a computer and the ability to pay for an Internet service provider. This is important, since more and more employers are posting job openings on the Internet instead of placing job ads in newspapers. They do this for several reasons. First, it acts as a prescreening device, in that only those with some computer skills will even know about and apply for the job; even if the job does not require these skills, people who have them are likely to have an ability to learn new skills and be able to keep up with technological changes in the workplace. Further, posting jobs on the Internet is less expensive than paying for ads in the newspapers; and once the job is filled, its listing can be instantaneously removed from the Internet, unlike newspaper ads that will run for the entire time period that has been paid for, even if the job has already been filled. What this means is that those with no computer skills or with no regular access to a computer will be left behind in a labor market that is increasingly polarized between a limited number of entry-level jobs with strong potential for upward mobility, good pay, and decent benefits at one pole and millions of dead-end, low-wage jobs with no benefits and little or no prospect for advancement at the other pole.

Because issues of power and inequality rise with Internet use, it becomes sociologically revealing to ask who controls and who uses the Internet. While many people often think of the

Internet as the new frontier where no one controls or censors the content or access, the fact is that there are several layers of people and organizations that control the Internet to some degree (Biegel, 1996; Goldsmith and Wu, 2008). First, the federal government exerts some control over the Internet, which was initially intended to connect the defense and military establishments, universities, and research institutions around the country and the globe. Other examples include recent government actions to control the display of pornography, to capture those who would prey on children, and to remove information that might be used by terrorists.

Private corporations are also among those controlling the "information superhighway." Internet service providers affect who has access to the Internet. They determine the service fees to be charged, and they can decide to deny services to some users. Communications companies, such as local television cable service providers, are increasingly expanding their services to include high-speed digital and cable connections to the Internet, for a fee. Since they are financing the infrastructure needed to provide this service, they can determine who has access by deciding which communities will receive the infrastructural investment and which ones will not. In addition to these companies, others, most notably Apple and Microsoft, develop the computers and the software necessary to connect to the Internet. These firms have a strong ability to influence, if not control, how people use the Internet (McChesney, 2013). Microsoft, for example, has been highly successful in its strategy of preloading most new personal and laptop computers with its Windows file management system, so that almost everyone now uses Windows.

In addition to their role as Internet service providers, corporate actors can shape perceptions by posting or withholding information on the thousands of websites they maintain ("dot.coms"). They are joined by thousands of government agencies, as well as faculty at colleges and universities who develop new computer programs and post massive amounts of information and data on the Internet. Together, they shape what people see and learn and what they can do on the Internet. And finally, there is the Internet Society, chartered by the federal government for the express purpose of evaluating Internet policies and acting as federal watchdog over other task forces and committees that address these policies (www.isoc.org). Together, these individuals and organizations have the very real capacity to shape, influence, and control the future direction of as well as access to what is increasingly becoming an indispensable resource.

In addition to the concern of Internet control, a related issue is who uses the Internet. How diverse is the online community? Does it reflect the diversity of the real world? What are the implications of user patterns? U.S. Census data indicate that initially there was a notable gender gap in computer use and Internet access, such that men were far more active in cyberspace than women. But that gap has quickly evaporated: In 2010, the Census Bureau noted that among adults with online access and usage, 48.4 percent were men and 51.6 percent were women (www.census.gov). Beyond gender, however, other patterns of inequality noted throughout this textbook are replicated online, a situation referred to as the **digital divide**. Those who are of the dominant statuses relative to class, race, ability, and age enjoy privileged access to the Internet (Luke, 1997).

For example, the Internet is not economically diverse: The poor have relatively little access. As recently as 2010, the poor seriously lagged behind the more affluent in their entrance into the Information Age (see Table 14.2).

Table 14.2: Household Internet usage in and outside of the home by class and race, 2010

	In the Home	**Anywhere**
Income (per year)		
<$15,000	39.6%	57.2%
15,000–24,999	52.6	66.4
25,000–34,999	63.3	76.0
35,000–49,000	77.9	87.1
50,000–74,999	87.1	93.5
75,000 –99,999	93.8	97.2
100,000–149,000	96.4	98.2
150,000 +	98.0	99.0
Race:		
African American	57.8%	72.6%
Latino/a	59.1	73.8
Native or Alaskan American	56.8	72.6
Asian American/Pacific Islander	82.8	87.5
White	74.9	82.2

Source: www.census.gov

Worse yet, when the poor do gain access, they do so with technology that is several developmental cycles or generations behind that used by the affluent, thereby being deprived of the latest tools with which to compete effectively for jobs and other opportunities, or must rely on limited Internet access in public places like libraries (Goslee, 1998; U.S. Department of Commerce and National Telecommunications and Information Administration, 2000). Notably, the technology gap between social classes is not the result of personal choices being made by individuals, but rather a function of the inequality of infrastructural development in communities. Telephone, cable, and communications companies have been much quicker to wire affluent communities, particularly in the suburbs, but have ignored poorer neighborhoods.

Why does this matter? The widening technology gap between the poor and the affluent has economic implications for communities and individuals, as well as for the larger society. When poor neighborhoods lack the infrastructure to help individuals link to the Internet, this poses obstacles to economic development in those communities. Communities with obsolete telecommunications capabilities are unattractive locations for businesses. The result is likely to be a downward cycle of limited economic opportunities and jobs for residents, many of whom already have limited means of mobility to travel to jobs that are increasingly located in communities wired for state-of-the-art technology. The deepening poverty of urban communities, for example, makes them even more unattractive for other investments, thus intensifying the cycle of poverty as jobs evaporate in poor city neighborhoods while they sprout in the suburbs. The result is a highly "fractured" labor market in many urban areas. The only work remaining for the unskilled is increasingly found in the service sector in jobs where, as seen in Chapter 12, wages are low, and benefits, job security, and opportunity for advancement are frequently limited or nonexistent. The U.S. Office of Technology Assessment cited the poor distribution of information access technologies and the supportive infrastructure as increasingly significant factors contributing to inequality in the United States because of "the concentration of poverty and the deconcentration of opportunity" (c.f. Goslee, 1998:2; Bucy, 2000).

The effect of this digital divide on individuals is not only a loss of possible employment opportunities for those who lack access to the Internet (Sangmon, 2001). Increasing reliance by the state on the Internet to connect individuals to vital services introduces further obstacles to the poor in gaining access to important resources. Since three-fourths of all interactions between individuals and the state, including the delivery of food stamps, Social Security benefits, and Medicaid information, occur online, people with little or no access to the Internet are at a serious disadvantage (Goslee, 1998).

Ironically, at precisely the time when the state is demanding that the poor be self-sufficient, technological inequality is making it far more difficult for impoverished communities and individuals to help themselves. This is because more and more of the occasions that once nurtured leadership development and citizen participation occur online. With fewer face-to-face meetings and associations that previously were significant in the development of communication, coordination, and encouragement of community action, poor communities find themselves increasingly bereft of the necessary networks to address social problems. This does not mean there are no community organizations actively pursuing strategies to help their neighborhoods address the serious social problems confronting them. But lack of access to the communications technology that can link isolated, small, and poor communities in more powerful networks makes it much more difficult to obtain the resources they need. It becomes harder for such communities to find out about funding opportunities, legislative developments that might affect them, and strategies used in other neighborhoods.

Lack of access to new technology not only impairs the ability of poor communities and individuals to help themselves; democratic processes may also be harmed (Lockard, 1997; Hurwitz, 1999; see also Sylvester and McGlynn, 2010). Increasingly, political leaders are communicating with their constituents online, and that means those with greater access to the Internet will be more likely to have access to those who make policy decisions. As we saw in Chapter 11, access to legislators is a key factor in shaping how they define problems and policy solutions to these. Political Action Committees (PACs) have been an important mechanism enabling the affluent and corporations to gain the attention of legislators and thus to increase their chances of achieving favorable treatment in legislative policies. Technological inequality reinforces PACs' privileged access to legislators, and thus effectively magnifies their political clout.

Patterns of technological access relative to racially defined status echo those relative to class: Racially dominant groups have a strong advantage. Whites and Asian Americans are more likely to have Internet access than African Americans, Latino/as, and Native Americans. Owning a computer is closely associated with household income levels. Our discussions in Chapter 7 indicated a strong intersection of class and race in the United States, such that African Americans and Latino/as are three times more likely than whites or Asian Americans to be poor, and therefore unlikely to have sufficient financial resources to support computer ownership or Internet access.

Beyond the ability to purchase computer equipment and Internet access service is the problem of a sort of high-tech "redlining" of African American and Latino/a communities. When communications companies install high-speed fiber optic cables to connect users to the Internet, they often focus their efforts on affluent communities and areas serving businesses. The result is that the infrastructure information superhighway put in place often bypasses communities of color. Technology is thus less likely to be available to support Internet access to people of color, even if they have their own home computers.

One alternative to providing individuals with access to the Internet at home is to provide it through public institutions such as schools. But funding school budgets through property tax revenues means fewer resources in poor communities, including poor communities of color, to finance either the infrastructure of high-speed fiber optic cables or the computers themselves. Without fundamental changes in how schools are financed, schools in such communities will continue to be shortchanged in their access to computers and the Internet. Public libraries are in a similar bind.

In addition to reinforcing patterns of inequality relative to class and race, increasing reliance on the Internet may deepen inequality based on ablebodiedness. People with disabilities, such as illiteracy, dyslexia, and blindness, face barriers to fully participate in the great potential future promised by the Internet (see Borchert, 1998; Vicente and Lopez, 2010). While this is not surprising, the implications are significant: If people are becoming increasingly reliant on the Internet as a critical resource, many individuals with disabilities will likely be left behind. Unless societies develop tools to connect them with the mainstream of the Internet, and make these affordable and accessible, they will have a difficult time benefitting from all that this resource has to offer, thereby increasing the gap between the ablebodied and those with disabilities.

Age inequalities are also replicated and reinforced in the virtual world of the Internet, mimicking earlier patterns of inequality witnessed in the United States in the first half of the twentieth century (Loos, 2012). Adult immigrants to the United States during this period often found that their native language and culture limited their ability to interact and participate in the social mainstream. But their children quickly learned English and the new culture through their participation in the public school system. Children often became their elders' teachers, translators, and protectors as they helped their parents navigate the complexities of institutions in their new location, producing a role reversal and a generational status inconsistency. Now, the older, less Internet-savvy generation is much like these earlier geographic adult immigrants: Today's older generation is less literate in computer and Internet language and culture. But their children, particularly affluent children, are more likely to be computer-literate and well-versed in usage and vocabulary of the Internet because of computer education and access in school. Today's children often become the Internet teachers and technological translators for their parents, producing the same generational role reversals and status inconsistencies earlier geographic immigration created between young and old.

These patterns of inequality of access to the Internet reverberate globally, thereby intensifying the global inequalities discussed in Chapters 3 and 10. Although there are certainly inequalities in access between classes in every nation, core and periphery alike, in general, members of the core nations have privileged access to the Internet while the semi-periphery and the periphery lag woefully behind. Most nations have at least some direct Internet connection, regardless of their world-system status. This is not surprising, since such connections are necessary to support multinational corporations doing business around the world. These connections link managers in the core with production facilities and workers in the semi-periphery and the periphery, and with markets everywhere. But some peripheral nations, particularly in Africa, have no Internet connection at all. Others, again primarily in Africa, have only email capabilities (www.isoc.org/images/mapv15.gif). This pattern of unequal access to global connectivity means that the periphery is being left behind in the great information revolution.

Why does this matter? If Internet connectivity is an increasingly critical resource for development, the gap between the wealth and power of the core and the poverty and relative powerlessness of the periphery is sure to widen even further, intensifying the differences in people's life chances that already exist in the world-system. The lack of connectivity discourages foreign investment, impedes economic development, and reduces the chances of global political participation.

Even in nations with Internet connection capabilities, individuals in the periphery and semi-periphery have far less access than do individuals in the core. This is because connectivity in these countries is more typically over telephone lines rather than through the high-speed fiber optical cables more common in the core. The number of telephones per 1,000 people provides a picture of the difficulty of individual access to the Internet: The fewer phones there are to be shared by more people, the less likely it is that one will be able to tie up those lines to be connected to the Internet for very long, if at all. In the core, there are significantly more phones than in the periphery and semi-periphery. In the United States, Western Europe, and Australia, for example, there are 400 to 700 phones for every 1,000 people, but in much of Latin America, Asia, and Africa, this figure drops sharply, to 1 to 99 phones per 1,000 people (see United Nations Development Programme, www.undp.org). People in the core, then, have a much better opportunity than those in the periphery or semi-periphery to gain access to information for empowerment, and perhaps enhanced life chances.

Ironically, technology itself is beginning to offer an important resource for bypassing these limitations to development in the periphery and semi-periphery. The rapidly declining cost of cellular telephones is making global interconnectivity an increasingly real opportunity for people in countries left behind in the revolution taking place on the Internet. This is because cell phones do not depend upon the expensive infrastructure required of conventional telephone lines and are not subject to the whims of private investors, despotic rulers seeking to keep populations ignorant and under control, or the ravages and disruptions of wars. Particularly in Africa, cellular phones are becoming an increasingly common possession. In Botswana, for example, more than 12 percent of the population owns a cellular phone. The result: a "quiet revolution" of potential political and economic empowerment. In Senegal in 2000, 40 years of one-party rule finally ended when voters ousted President Abdou Diouf. Cellular phones enabled poll watchers to immediately report election results to independent broadcasters, making it all but impossible for Diouf to preserve his rule by incorrectly claiming to have won (Ashurst, 2001). The use of cellular phones to provide access to the Internet is likely to increase in such countries, as wireless technology now increasingly available in the core spreads to the periphery and semi-periphery.

Cyberspace and the Promise for Social Change

Many people throughout the world have turned to the Internet as a potent social movement resource, particularly when states have sought to silence them. Women in Chiapas, Mexico, for example, have found the Internet a useful networking tool, sending news of state oppression and human rights violations there outside of the remote isolation of the area and gaining political and financial support for their cause beyond their immediate location (Glusker, 1998). In Taliban-controlled Afghanistan, women in RAWA (Revolutionary Association of Women in Afghanistan) sought and gained international support through the Internet for their struggles against the fundamentalist dictatorship that denied women education, healthcare, employment, and freedom of movement as well as speech. Their efforts succeeded in the unprecedented inclusion of at least two women in the provisional governing alliance put in place in Afghanistan after the fall of the Taliban government in 2001.

In recent years, a number of citizen groups in the United States have experimented with the use of computer networks as a tool for monitoring government agencies and organizing citizens, thereby creating virtual communities among individuals who are otherwise marginalized from power and participation (Stoecker and Stuber, 1999; Bennett, 2012). Today, using the Internet, it is possible to obtain information on a wide range of important topics and share it among literally millions of persons at a very low cost. There are also bulletin boards social media opportunities for announcing demonstrations and other actions that one can join, addresses to write letters, and lists of companies currently being boycotted for various reasons. The Internet sites are often interactive, allowing citizens to talk with each other, exchange feedback, offer pointers, and debate facts and strategies. Some provide links so that people can contact their legislators to register their point of view. In 2003, as the United States pushed for a war against Iraq, anti-war activists used the Internet and email to rally hundreds of thousands of protestors in a "virtual demonstration," clogging legislators' emails and phone systems with messages imploring them to withdraw their support of President Bush's planned attacks. Social media, such as Facebook and Twitter, offer similar outlets. Empowerment is enhanced when citizens have free or low-cost access to the Internet, databases of government information, social media, and email systems. The Internet can be enormously empowering, if one has such access and knows how to use it.

The key issue of the future in cyberspace, then, is democratizing access. One way to encourage greater access is to install more computers in public schools and libraries, senior centers, daycare centers, welfare and unemployment offices, community centers, etc. Public Internet cafes where anyone may come and use the Internet, much like a public library's noncirculating reference materials, might also help. Such cafes might also become community gathering places, encouraging greater interaction between neighbors than could otherwise be accomplished when individuals are isolated in their own homes away from other community members. Ironically, one of the more recent developments in Internet access, wireless connectivity, has opened up potential for access that is difficult to control: Wireless connections "bleed" beyond the walls they are intended to serve. Users can often find wireless "hotspots" and "pirate" access to the Internet for free. Communities may thus empower people by harnessing the technological quirk of hotspots and deliberately create these to enhance everyone's access regardless of income.

GLOBALIZATION, MILITARISM, TERRORISM, AND SOCIAL CHANGE

The power of globalization is such that even the core must deal with the ramifications of alterations in the structure of the global economy. By the 1990s, the Cold War between the East and the West had come to an end. The Berlin Wall separating East and West Germany had been torn down, and the German Democratic Republic and the Federal Republic of Germany reunited after existing separately since World War II. The Soviet Union ceased to exist following the restructuring of Soviet society, or *perestroika*, and its republics became independent nations. The end of the Cold War escalated the process of increasing globalization as former Eastern bloc nations shifted their economies to mixtures of capitalism and socialism and sought inclusion into international security and trade organizations from which they had previously been excluded. The end of the Cold War opened new markets for core capitalist nations for a whole range of products, from soda and burgers to guns and other weapons.

Furthermore, despite evidence of a rise of neo-fascist, ultra-right-wing parties and candidates in Russia and other Eastern European countries, the military threat posed by the communist bloc largely disappeared for the West. With no identifiable enemy to fill the void, the United States was left with the question of how to deal with its huge industrial apparatus developed in support of the military. One response to this challenge facing the United States military-industrial complex was to increase the sale of arms and weapons systems abroad (Bixby, 1992; www.fas.org). While this response may make economic sense to the defense-contracting corporations, it is important to ask critical questions: What are the consequences of this globalization of arms? Moreover, how does government justify continuing large-scale military expenditures and weapons production in the face of the evaporation of the communist threat? In light of the insistence of all of the components of the military-industrial complex that external threats continue to exist, who or what might those threats be? Are military responses likely to be effective against such threats? Who benefits and who is hurt by the military-industrial complex's response to these questions?

The question of what to do with massive sectors of the economy devoted to defense production is not simply a question of U.S. foreign policy and the future of its military. It is inextricably linked to the structure of the entire military-industrial complex, as well as to the health and future of the U.S. economy as a whole. While the end of the Cold War raised fitting debates about what to do with the anticipated "peace dividend" of money no longer needed for defense that could have resulted from that momentous change in global politics, and some defense spending cuts occurred, the U.S. Department of Defense has nonetheless continued to absorb significant proportions of the federal budget. The total military budget expenditure in 2010 was $768.2 billion (www.census.gov). By 2012, United States military spending accounted for 41 percent of total world military expenditures of $1.7 trillion (www.fas.org; www.globalissues .org). U.S. military expenditures have since been growing, particularly with the 2003–2012 war against Iraq and the expansion of the War on Terror into Afghanistan.

Prior to the September 11, 2001, terrorist attacks, some observers suggested alternative approaches to the continued high levels of military spending, arguing that winding down the East-West arms race in and of itself would make the world a more secure place. More attention could be focused on severe domestic problems such as hunger and homelessness, unemployment, deteriorating infrastructure, inadequate education facilities, and racial inequality. Further, with reduced military spending, research and development monies previously allocated to military projects could be turned to civilian needs. Finally, workers who would be laid off from defense contractors are highly trained and educated; such workers could be redeployed into nondefense skilled jobs where serious labor shortages exist. And some observers point out that civilian expenditures can actually produce more jobs than military spending: Where "$1 billion in military procurement generates 21,500 jobs directly and indirectly [,] the same $1 billion invested in industrial renewal, mass transit, housing, education, and health care will produce on average 33,100 jobs" (Melman, 1997; www.webcom.com/ncecd).

Even before September 11, the United States ignored these potential benefits of winding down military production and expenditures with the end of the Cold War, and instead chose a different path. President George W. Bush resurrected Ronald Reagan's hugely expensive and much criticized Star Wars defense plan, claiming it to be a desperately needed missile defense system. He did not, however, clearly identify the sources of the alleged missile threats to United States security that might necessitate such a multibillion dollar program. In the aftermath of the September 11, 2001, attacks on the World Trade Center and the Pentagon, and the spread of anthrax through the United States mail, it became apparent that the greatest threat to security was not individual nations but international terrorists. Yet the Bush administration increased conventional defense spending to a degree not seen in years. That raises the pressing and undebated question: Do expenditures on conventional military responses and missile defense systems increase U. S. security against terrorist attacks? Meanwhile, defense contractors are busy defending their own economic interests by fueling the international market for arms. What effect does this international market have on United States or world security, and on the rise of international terrorism? Let's look at these emerging global issues.

Export of Arms

In 2012, the United States was by far the leading arms-exporting nation in the world. U.S. arms manufacturers delivered $66.3 billion in weapons to over 170 countries the world over, more than three times as much as Russia, the second-largest arms exporter whose sales of $4.8 billion made it a distant second to the U.S. (Shanker, 2012). Overall, the United States alone supplied more than three-fourths of all the arms exported globally. And, most notably, the United States helped fuel global conflicts, supplying arms or military technology in more than 92 percent of the conflicts that flared up around the world, often supplying arms as well as military training to both sides at the same time. For example, both India and Pakistan received weapons from the United States, as did both Azerbaijan and Armenia. Many of the nations locked in extended and bitter disputes in the Middle East, notable among them Israel, Egypt, Oman, Saudi Arabia, Lebanon, and Kuwait, all receive arms from the United States. Conservative estimates are that in 2006 and 2007 alone, the United States sent more than $16.2 billion in arms to countries where violations of international human rights treaties are rampant, including the use of children as soldiers in combat (Gamage, 2009; www.cdi.org;../Local Settings/temp/7zO24.tmp/(www.cdi .org; www.fas.org). These exports occurred even as the elder Bush administration publicly spoke in 1992 of a "new world order" stimulated by arms restraint, and lectured other countries to join the United States in such restraint.

How is it possible to take this position and still sell others arms? One rationale for allowing such exports is the necessity to save U.S. jobs that would otherwise be lost were there to be cuts in government defense spending in the United States. Indeed, in a tight battle for his reelection in 1992, President Bush tried the unsuccessful political alchemy of turning jobs into votes by approving several new foreign arms sales, including sales to Saudi Arabia and Taiwan. Such sales have continued unabated into the new century. And although Congress has the constitutional power to veto these sales, the fact is that it has not. Why? Each senator and congressperson has constituents who desperately need jobs, and it would be political suicide to refuse arms sales that give them employment.

Who has benefitted and who has been hurt by this strategy of arms export? The main beneficiaries of arming the world have been the weapons-manufacturing corporations. The Center for Defense Information found that such corporations have reaped great profits from international arms sales (Hellman, 2000: www.cdi.org/issues/usmi/complex/top15fy99.html). In many ways, the Gulf war against Iraq in 1991 became a live commercial for arms manufacturers such as Raytheon (the manufacturer of the Patriot missile), as potential international buyers saw dramatic videos purporting to show "evidence" (later found to be far less spectacular in reality) of the efficiency and kill-power of U.S. weapons systems. More recently, widespread news reports of the successful use of drones in targeting and killing "enemy combatants" in Iraq and Afghanistan functioned as commercials for the manufacturers of unmanned systems like Northrop Grumman and General Atomics.

Not surprisingly, given the changing organization of work and production we discussed in Chapter 11, defense industry workers in many cases have lost jobs. For the arms manufacturers, increased profits from exports in a competitive world market do not offset profit slowdowns when they are unable to obtain enough lucrative contracts from the Department of Defense. For example, United Technologies Corporation, the eighth-largest arms exporter in the United States, decided to downsize in the early 1990s because of government defense spending cutbacks and laid off 14,000 workers; its Pratt & Whitney division eliminated 7,500 jobs, even as it seemed it would be the likely manufacturer of the engines for the jets sold to Saudi Arabia and Taiwan (Bixby, 1992: A7). By 1996, only about 2.3 million United States workers were employed in defense-related industries, a 36 percent decline in such jobs from the height of the Cold War in 1987 (Melman, 1997: www.webcom.com/ncecd). But by 2011, owing to the twin wars in Iraq and Afghanistan, such figures swelled: 6.1 million U.S. workers were employed in defense-related industries (3.1 million civilian and military employees by the Defense Department and an additional 3 million workers by defense contractors) (Rizzo, 2011).

While profits are made by weapons producers, increased arms exports are not making the world any safer. In fact, they are increasing the likelihood of armed conflicts and arms buildups everywhere. Arms have become a key commodity traded in the world-system. With nations becoming ever more heavily armed in regions of the world where tensions are quite high, the probability of future armed conflicts between nations increases immeasurably. And arms sales to drug dealers and traffickers has fueled violence in many countries as drug lords and powerful gangs battle over turf.

The terrorist attacks in the United States in 2001 have raised the question of the role of the international arms market in contributing to the heightened sophistication of and dangers posed by terrorists around the world. The State Department estimates that 28 terrorist organizations operate from 18 nations. While the United States does not directly sell arms to these terrorist groups, throughout the 1990s it sold weapons and provided military assistance and training to 16 of the 18 governments that host these organizations and tolerate them, such as Saudi Arabia, Algeria, Iraq, Lebanon, and Sri Lanka (www.cdi.org). What may have seemed like a good idea at one time often becomes a highly regrettable one, to say the least. For example, the United States played a significant role in arming and training the Taliban military in Afghanistan in the early 1990s, in support of its military conflict with the former Soviet Union. This was part of the approach the United States has frequently adopted in international affairs, in which "the enemy of my enemy is my friend." Once the Taliban had successfully defended Afghanistan against Soviet forces, the imported weapons and the Afghanis' training expertise remained. These became key elements in the strengthening of the international al Qaeda network, which was identified as the terrorist perpetrator of the September 11, 2001, suicide attacks against the World Trade Center, the Pentagon, and other targets. These horrific events are forcing people to come to grips with the rise of international terrorism: What is terrorism? Is this a new phenomenon? Will greater investment in conventional military responses provide adequate defense and security against such attacks if they are aimed at the United States?

Terrorism

Global economic and political inequalities, largely propped up by the huge proliferation of military might in the core and elsewhere, U.S. arms exports to other nations, and U.S. military support for "friendly" militaristic regimes throughout the world, have helped fuel international terrorism. But what exactly is terrorism? People use this word to describe a wide range of behaviors, and acts that are described as "terrorism" by some observers may be termed by others as acts of "patriotism." U.S. officials insisted that the September 11 attacks represented acts of war against the United States, requiring a military response. What is the difference between "war" and "terrorism"? It would seem important to sort out these issues, then, in order to understand the new realities of life in an era of globalization.

War is an organized, armed conflict between nations (Palen, 2001: 472). Armed conflicts that occur within nations between organized factions are termed "civil wars" to distinguish these from international armed conflicts. Wars can be officially and formally declared, or may be unofficially waged (as when the U.S. government referred to its war in Vietnam as a "conflict" rather than declare a formal "war," or as when it wages an undeclared war against Iraq in 2003). In either case, war is a fairly constant feature of world history, and certainly of the United States, which has participated in more than a dozen major wars and has sent troops around the world to participate in "peacekeeping missions" and other assorted armed conflicts nearly 200 times (Leckie, 1992).

Terrorism is the use of violence as a strategy to gain political objectives; it may be used often by individuals or groups who usually have relatively little power otherwise. When used in this way, terrorism has been called a "weapon of the weak" (Scott, 1985), and "diplomacy from below" (Kumamoto, 1991).The power of terrorism is its ability to incite tremendous fear and sense of vulnerability in people through acts of unpredictable, random violence, or by leveling violence against society's critical institutions, leaders, and symbols. Terrorism commonly interrupts business and life as usual by altering people's freedom of movement, their comfort in their surroundings, and their confidence that the full force of the state or other social institutions can protect them. As such, terrorism from below can create a legitimacy crisis for the state and destabilize or disrupt existing governments.

It is often difficult for the state to confront terrorism because the enemy is not always apparent, and thus may be unresponsive to conventional social control mechanisms (including police, military repression, and counterviolence). Terrorism has tremendous potential to undermine the invisible, unearned privileges that come with living in the core, including the ability to live without the threat of the violence that is so common elsewhere in the world, and to go to work every day, to shop, to travel, to vote, to simply open the daily mail, without fear of loss of life and limb.

While terrorism is frequently a weapon of the weak, it can also be used by governments to coerce their own resistant populations to acquiesce to their will and to eliminate challengers to state power. For example, the military in Argentina and Chile in the 1970s used kidnaping, murder, and torture to purge these countries of leftist critics, thousands of whom remain among the "disappeared." Former President of Yugoslavia Slobodan Milosevic was charged in an international tribunal with sanctioning rape, murder, and kidnaping (among other charges) as terrorist tactics in 1999 in an attempt to "ethnically cleanse" Kosovo of Albanians by scaring them into leaving Kosovo or by killing them.

Terrorism, like war, is not new or unusual, although the incidence of terrorist acts has certainly been on the rise all around the world. For example, terrorist bombings have occurred in Great Britain, Northern Ireland, the Middle East, and elsewhere fairly regularly for decades. In the United States, such bombings showed a steady increase from the early 1980s through the 1990s (Eitzen and Baca Zinn, 1997). Terrorism is also not something used only by "others," that is, people outside the United States. The Ku Klux Klan and other white supremecist groups have frequently used terrorist tactics in their disputes with the federal government's policies in support of civil rights, as have anti-abortionists, and extremists in the anti-war movement in the 1960s, to name a few. When a bomb tore through the Federal Building in Oklahoma City in 1995, killing 167 people, many people in the United States, including those in the media, immediately assumed that the culprits were probably Middle Eastern terrorists. It quickly became clear, however, that the perpetrators were U.S. citizens involved in local militia groups disgruntled with the federal government. In fact, Timothy McVeigh, the man ultimately convicted and executed for the bombing, was a veteran of the United States military. This case highlighted the fact that terrorism is a tactic used by "home-grown" groups as a strategy for achieving their political objectives, and not only by groups located elsewhere around the world. The characteristic that terrorists often have in common is the possession of far less power relative to that of the governments they seek to challenge.

What actions should be defined as terrorism is not always agreed on by everyone. Some even view "terrorism" as indistinct from "patriotism." What is the difference? Individuals involved in domestic terrorism in the United States are often part of a loose configuration of groups that refer to themselves as the "Patriot" movement. They believe that the federal government increasingly violates the basic premises of the Constitution and consider it their patriotic duty to subvert and challenge that government wherever and however possible (Berlet and Lyons, 1995; Wills, 1995). Similarly, members of the Irish Republican Army (IRA) considered themselves to be patriots defending the right of Northern Ireland to self-determination apart from the control of Great Britain; and members of the radical Islamic jihad movement believe they are being patriotic in attacking governments that violate their interpretation of Islamic law. Indeed, colonists in the American Revolution saw the Boston Tea Party as an act of patriotism. Such examples are not intended to justify the use of property destruction and violence to gain a political objective, but they do raise the critical issue of perspective and relativity: One person's terrorism is another's patriotism. While we don't hold that terrorist crimes against humanity are acceptable if they're defined as acts of "patriotism," it is useful to consider these issues in order to approach some understanding as to why terrorist acts occur.

Despite President George W. Bush's insistence that the world is clearly defined in camps of "evil doers" and "us," reality is much more complex and ambiguous. In an increasingly globalized world, it becomes necessary to understand the complexities. For example, it is useful to appreciate the relationship between the United States and other core nations on one hand and underdeveloped and oppressed populations on the other. Increased expenditures on conventional military responses to terrorism against the core that arise out of that context are unlikely to provide increased security (Luban, 2005). Viable solutions will likely emerge only when people more fully understand the global context in which terrorism occurs.

What social, political, and economic factors are likely to influence the growth of international terrorism? Some research suggests that the experience of intensifying ethnic and religious rifts, accompanied by feelings of alienation, social isolation, and threatened survival, often underscored by a sense of religious imperative, are common features shared by many international terrorist groups (Hoffman, 1995). Other researchers point to the widening global gap between wealth and poverty, the continuing dominating military role of the United States, and the global expansion of the culture-invasive Internet as critical trends to watch (Jensen, 2001).

As the United States struggles to combat terrorism, questions of who will bear the greatest burden of that effort become critical. Under a system of an all-volunteer military in the United States, structured racial and class inequality (see Chapter 7) means that people of color are disproportionately likely to be among those called to place themselves in harm's way in conventional military responses against terrorism. For example, while African Americans constitute 13.6 percent of the total U.S. population, they represent more than 17.3 percent of the active duty military. Almost 21 percent of the Army, the branch most likely to function as ground troops and therefore to be placed in greatest danger, are African Americans. They are also far less likely to be among the more elite branches of the military: 14.7 percent of the Air Force, 10.6 percent of the Marines, and 19 percent of the Navy are African American (www.defense.gov/home/features/2007/blackhistorymonth/index.html).../Local Settings/temp/7zO24.tmp/(http:/www.census.gov/prod/2001pubs/statab/sec11.pdf. This means that people of color are at a relatively higher risk than whites to be harmed by the decision to resort to conventional military responses to terrorism.

While it is true that in the military actions in both the Persian Gulf and Afghanistan ground troops played a relatively minor role and suffered few casualties, such troops remain more likely to be injured or killed than jet pilots flying at high speeds above their targets or military technicians far removed from harm's way guiding drones over dangerous enemy territory. Those on the ground are closer to the danger (including improvised explosive devices [IEDs] and the potential to become part of the "collateral damage" of erroneous bombing and other forms of "friendly fire"). In the 2003 war with Iraq, ground troops figured prominently as the troops pressed toward Baghdad in a search for both presumed "weapons of mass destruction" and personnel such as Saddam Hussein himself. Tens of thousands were potentially exposed to feared biological and chemical weapons, which fortunately were not used against U.S. troops (and may not have been in the Iraqi arsenal at the time of the U.S. attack). Similarly, tens of thousands of ground troops were jeopardized in the search of Osama bin Laden in Afghanistan.

In addition to the unequal burden of danger faced by people in the military, individual civilians face serious consequences of war and terrorism. In such instances, the consequences are not just individual: Everyone stands to lose. Xenophobic fear and anxiety fueled by a combination of international terrorism and the U.S. military-industrial complex's hunger for war produces suspicion of visitors and immigrants from abroad. Fears of terrorism have led U.S. government agencies to profile individuals in an attempt to defend the nation against future attacks, not because they have done anything wrong but because of their national origins.

Might there be other, perhaps more effective, responses to international terrorism? How helpful, for example, might the United Nations be in focusing widespread international pressure on states that support terrorists? Might the creation of an international court of justice devoted to handling terrorists be effective in convening fair trials, meting out appropriate sanctions and upholding international norms outlawing terrorist acts? Is it useful for the United States to isolate itself from the concerns of the rest of the world except when it serves its own dominant interests? And, perhaps most importantly, how do societies address the global problems that feed terrorism, such as poverty, lack of democratic governance, violations of refugees' human rights, and so forth? Would addressing these issues help reduce the fertile grounds spawning terrorism? How these questions are answered will affect everyone in this new century.

 CHAPTER SUMMARY

Globalization of economic relationships increasingly dominates social life and has a significant effect on social arrangements and individuals alike.

- The global division of labor has worsened the gap of wealth and poverty between core and peripheral nations, and that has contributed to stark population patterns.

- While core nations are increasingly dominated by older population cohorts, the periphery struggles to support an ever-younger population.

- Societies with large older cohorts must find ways to address the medical, economic, and social needs of an aging population. Those with significantly larger populations under the age of 15 face quite different challenges, including the care and feeding of more dependent members of society as well as the problem of production of necessary goods and services and the defense of the nation.

- Increasing globalization also creates a problem of what to do with the toxic waste generated by the production of the world's goods and services. The power imbalances of the world-system and the related economic disparities created by the global division of labor means that core nations have the power to discard their toxic waste in peripheral countries with very little challenge.

- Similarly, unequal power, coupled with systems of inequality around race and class in core nations like the United States, leads to environmental racism. Poor neighborhoods and communities of color are far more likely than affluent and white communities to become the unwilling recipients of much of the toxic and nuclear waste of the nation.

- Globalization is furthered by the rapid rise of the Internet. While this new technology offers tremendous promise for information and communication access for everyone, it is not quite living up to that promise.

- There is a substantial digital divide, in which access to the Internet and all that it promises remains sharply unequal. Poor people, people of color, and peripheral nations have far less access to the Internet and to the new opportunity structures for improved integration and participation in society. Some, including many nations in Africa, people with severe visual disabilities, and the very poor, are left out entirely.

- Increasing globalization of economic relations promotes not only greater opportunities for trade and wider distribution of goods and services. It also promotes increasing political tensions around the world, in part because of the widening gap between wealth and poverty among nations and the need for core nations to protect their economic interests in peripheral and semi-peripheral nations.

- While the end of the Cold War in the 1990s presumably made the world safer from the threat of nuclear war between the East and West, it actually worsened the promise of world peace. Core nations, particularly the United States, stepped up their sale of arms worldwide, and hence substantially contributed to a widening destabilization of global relations and violence around the world.

- In addition, international terrorism has spread the threat of violence from its previous concentration in peripheral and semi-peripheral areas of the globe to the core as well. Responding to terrorism that spawns from networks of groups across many nations is much more difficult than responding to violence from an easily identifiable single nation.

Our discussion concerning emerging issues suggests that using a sociological imagination helps us to begin to frame questions concerning new issues and concerns as they develop. It is not necessary to wait for someone else to do the research in order to ask questions. A well-developed sociological imagination should provide the tools to analyze aggregate statistics and averages; to figure out who benefits and who is hurt by certain relationships and processes; and to see the implications changes might have for different members of U.S. society and those in other societies around the world. Armed with a tool kit of sociological concepts such as those we have introduced in this text and applied in our analysis of emerging issues, individuals may be able to anticipate future trends. In short, people can learn to link their personal, individual biographies to the larger institutions in society and their history, and thereby better understand the societal patterns and processes that affect them. Doing so may lead individuals to see how *they* can contribute to change, and thus give them the greater freedom of being actors in their world, not just people who are acted upon.

 THINKING CRITICALLY

1. Suppose you were in charge of developing strategies to close the digital divide. What approaches would you suggest to accomplish this goal? How would you work toward greater access for the poor? For people of color? For people with disabilities? For the elderly? For peripheral and semi-peripheral countries? Who will likely benefit and who will likely be hurt by your proposals, and why? What institutions would need to be changed, and how? What institutions will likely be changed by your proposals, and why?

2. Look at the population pyramids in Figure 14.1. What are the implications of these different age and sex distributions between the United States and Sierra Leone? What might these mean for the next 50 years relative to family structures and dynamics, the economy, health, and politics?

3. Increasing longevity is causing more people to reconsider the meaning of retirement and "old age." Perhaps some people you know are currently retired. What have they done to redefine their retirements? How do their experiences compare with how their parents defined retirement? What factors may explain the differences, if any, between the people you know and their parents? Which institutions affect the retirement experiences of the people you know and their parents? How? How might these institutions need to change in the future in order to accommodate the presence of a larger elderly cohort?

4. Is an unannounced plant shutdown an act of terrorism? Is rape an act of terrorism? Is a school shooting an act of terrorism? Why or why not? What differentiates these from acts such as the attacks against the World Trade Center in 2001, if anything? How are they similar?

5. Suppose you were asked to offer a plan for toxic waste disposal that addresses the problem of environmental racism. What factors would you consider in the development of your plan? Why? Who is likely to benefit and who is likely to be hurt by your proposal? Are there things that you can do to minimize or eliminate the differential impact of your plan? What institutional changes, if any, would have to take place in order to accommodate your plan?

6. Select an emerging issue that has not been covered in this chapter (perhaps reproductive technology, privatization of public services like prisons, gays in the military, decriminalization of drugs, or any other that you may find interesting). Using your sociological imagination, explore the institutional arrangements that might contribute to the issue. Examine who benefits and who is hurt by the issue as it currently stands and try to assess why. What alternative arrangements would you suggest to deal with the issue? Are there race, class, and gender factors to be considered when examining this emerging issue? Be specific.

KEY TERMS

age consciousness **382**

digital divide **391**

environmental racism **385**

globalization **373**

perestroika **397**

population pyramid **375**

redline **386**

terrorism **400**

toxic imperialism **385**

war

REFERENCES

Aaron, Vanetta, Keith D. Parker, Suzanne Ortega, and Thomas Calhoun. 1999. "The extended family as a source of support among African Americans." *Challenge: A Journal of Research on African American Men* 10(2): 23–36.

Abbott, Franklin (ed.). 1998. *Boyhood, Growing Up Male: A Multicultural Anthology*. Madison, WI: University of Wisconsin Press.

Abdolali, Nasrin, and Daniel S. Ward. 1998. "The Senate Armed Services Committee and defense budget making: The role of deference, dollars, and ideology." *Journal of Political and Military Sociology* 26(2): 229–252.

Aberle, David. 1966. *The Peyote Religion among the Navaho*. Chicago: Aldine.

Abramovitz, Mimi. 1996. *Regulating the Lives of Women: Social Welfare Policy from Colonial Times to the Present*. Boston: South End Press.

_____. 2000. *Under Attack, Fighting Back: Women and Welfare in the United States*. New York: Monthly Review Press.

Acuña, Rodolfo. 2000. *Occupied America: A History of Chicanos*, 4th ed. Boston: Addison-Wesley.

Adam, Barry D. 1987. *The Rise of the Gay and Lesbian Movement*. Boston: Twayne.

Adeola, Francis O. 2000. "Cross-national environmental injustice and human rights issues: A review of evidence in the developing world." *American Behavioral Scientist* 43(4): 688–706.

Adler, Patricia. 1985. *Wheeling and Dealing*. New York: Columbia University Press.

_____, and Peter Adler (eds.). 1994. Constructions of Deviance: Social Power, Context, and Interaction. Belmont, CA: Wadsworth Publishing Co.

_____, and Peter Adler (eds.). 2008. *Constructions of Deviance: Social Power, Context, and Interaction*, 6th ed. Belmont, CA: Wadsworth Publishing Co.

Akers, Ronald L. 1985. *Deviant Behavior*, 3rd ed. Belmont, CA: Wadsworth.

_____. 1999. *Criminological Theories: Introduction and Evaluation*. Chicago: Fitzroy Dearborn Publishers.

Albelda, Randy, and Chris Tilly, 1997. *Glass Ceilings and Bottomless Pits: Women's Work, Women's Poverty*. Boston: South End Press.

Alexander, Jeffrey C., and Paul Colomy (eds.). 1990. *Differentiation Theory and Social Change: Comparative Historical Perspectives* New York: Columbia University Press.

Alford, C. Fred. 2002. *Whistleblowers: Broken Lives and Organizational Power*. Ithaca, NY: Cornell University Press.

Allan, Graham, and Graham Crow. 2001. *Families, Households, and Society*. New York: Palgrave.

Allen, Brandeanna D., John M. Nunley, and Alan Seals. 2011. "The effect of joint-child-custody legislation on the child-support receipt of single mothers." *Journal of Family and Economic Issues* 32(1): 124–139.

Allen, Mile, and Nancy Burrell. 1996. "Comparing the impact of homosexual and heterosexual parents on children: Meta-analysis of existing research." *Journal of Homosexuality* 32: 19–35.

Allen, Tammy D., Stacy E. McManus, and Joyce E.A. Russell. 1999. "Newcomer socialization and stress: Formal peer relationships as a source of support." *Journal of Vocational Behavior* 54(3): 453–470.

Allen-Meares, Paula. 1990. "Educating black youths: The unfulfilled promise of equality." *Social Work* 35(3): 283–286.

Almquist, Elizabeth M. 1989. "The experience of minority women in the United States." Pages 414–445 in Jo Freeman (ed.), *Women: A Feminist Perspective*, 4th ed. Mountain View, CA: MayWeld.

Alter, Jonathan. 2000. "The death penalty on trial." I (June 12):24–34.

Alwin, Duane F. 1984. "Trends in parental socialization values: Detroit, 1958–1983." *American Journal of Sociology* 90: 359–382.

Amato, Paul R., and Frieda Fowler. 2002. "Parenting practices, child adjustment and family diversity." *Journal of Marriage and the Family* 64(3): 703–716.

American Association of University Women and the Wellesley College Center for Research on Women. 1992. *How Schools Shortchange Girls*. Washington, DC: AAUW Educational Foundation.

American Psychological Association. 2009. "Who are family caregivers?" Available at www.apa.org

American Sociological Association. 1997. *Code of Ethics*. Washington, DC: Author. Available at www.asanet.org

Amott, Teresa. 1993. *Caught in the Crisis: Women and the U.S. Economy Today*. New York: Monthly Review Press.

_____, and Julie A. Matthaei. 1996. *Race, Gender, and Work: A Multicultural Economic History of Women in the United States*, rev. ed. Boston: South End Press.

Ancheta, Angelo N. 1998. *Race, Rights, and the Asian American Experience*. New Brunswick: Rutgers University Press.

Andersen, Margaret L. 1990. "Feminism and the American family ideal." *Journal of Comparative Family Studies* 22: 35–46.

_____, and Patricia Hill Collins (eds.). 2001. *Race, Class, and Gender: An Anthology*, 4th ed. Belmont, CA: Wadsworth.

Anderson, Kristin L. 2000. *"Not to People Like Us": Hidden Abuse in Upscale Marriages.*

Anderson, Elijah. 1999. *Code of the Street: Decency, Violence, and the Moral Life of the Inner City.* New York: W.W. Norton.

_____. 2003. *A Place on the Corner*, 2nd ed. Chicago: University of Chicago Press.

Anderson, Kristin L. 1997. "Gender, status, and domestic violence: An integration of feminist and family violence approaches." *Journal of Marriage and the Family* 59(3): 655–669.

_____, and Debra Umberson. 2001. "Gendering violence: Masculinity and power in men's accounts of domestic violence." *Gender & Society* 15(3): 358–380.

Anderson, Sarah, and John Cavanagh with Thea Lee. 2000. *Field Guide to the Global Economy.* New York: The New Press.

Anderson, Tammy L. 1998. "A cultural identity theory of drug abuse." *Sociology of Crime, Law, and Deviance* 1: 233–262.

Andrews, Edmund L. 1996. "Don't go away mad, just go away: AT&T's gentle but firm effort to cut 40,000 jobs." *New York Times* February 13: D1, D6.

Angel, Jacqueline L., Maren A. Jimenez, and Ronald J. Angel. 2007. "The economic consequences of widowhood for older minority women." *The Gerontologist* 47(2): 224–234.

Antill, John K., Jacqueline J. Goodnow, Russell Graeme, and Sandra Cotton. 1996. "The influence of parents and family context on children's involvement in household tasks." *Sex Roles* 34(3-4): 215–236.

Apple, Michael W. 1992. "Constructing the captive audience: Channel One and the political economy of the text." *International Studies in Sociology of Education* 2(2): 107–131.

Arnett, Jeffrey Jensen. 1995. "Adolescents' uses of media for self-socialization." *Journal of Youth and Adolescence* 24(5): 519–533.

Aronowitz, Stanley. 1998. "The new corporate university: Higher education becomes higher training." *Dollars and Sense* 216 (Mar.-Apr.): 32–35.

_____. 2000. *The Knowledge Factory: Dismantling the Corporate University and Creating True Higher Learning.* Boston: Beacon Press.

_____, and William DiFazio. 1994. *The Jobless Future: Sci-Tech and the Dogma of Work.* Minneapolis: University of Minnesota Press.

Ascenzi, Joseph, 2000. "Toxic suit cites PG&E in 4 deaths; action by 56 plaintiffs says toxic water used to fill swimming pools." August 14 www.fumento.com/buspress.html

Asch, Adrienne, and Michelle Fine. 1988. "Introduction: Beyond pedestals." Pages 1–37 in Michelle Fine and Adrienne Asch (eds.), *Women with Disabilities.* Philadelphia: Temple University Press.

Ashurst, Mark. 2001. "Now, a 'quiet revolution." *Newsweek* August 27: 32.

Associated Press. 2000. "Associated Press Poll." May 17–21.

Auerbach, A. J., and L. J. Kotlikoff. 1987. "Life insurance of the elderly: Its adequacy and determinants." Pages 229–267 in G. Burtless (ed.), *Work, Health, and Income among the Elderly*. Washington, DC: Brookings Institute.

Austin, Regina, and Michael Schill. 1994. "Black, brown, red, and poisoned." *The Humanist* July/August: 9–16.

Auvinen, Juha Y. 1996. "IMF intervention and political protest in the Third World: A conventional wisdom refined." *Third World Quarterly* 17(3): 377–400.

Awad, Nihad. 2002. "The effect of racial and religious profiling in the American Muslim community since September 11, 2001." Paper presented to the United States House of Representatives House Judiciary Committee., www.cair-net.org

Ayres, Ian and Joel Waldfogel. 1994. "A market test for racial discrimination in bail setting." *Stanford Law Review* 46: 987–1047.

Ayers, William, Jean Ann Hunt, and Therese Quinn (eds.). 1998. *Teaching For Social Justice: A Democracy and Education Reader*. New York: The New Press.

Babbie, Earl. 2010. *The Basics of Social Research*, 5th ed. Belmont, CA: Wadsworth.

_____. 2012. *The Practice of Social Research*, 13th ed. Belmont, CA: Wadsworth

Bacon, David. 2000. "No justice for janitors." *In These Times* May 15.

Bagdikian, Ben H. 2000. *The Media Monopoly*, 6th ed. Boston: Beacon Press.

Baker, Robin. 2000. *Sex in the Future: The Reproductive Revolution and How It Will Change Us*. New York: Arcade Publishers.

Bales, Kevin. 1999. *Disposable People: New Slavery in the Global Economy*. Berkeley, CA: University of California Press.

Bane, Mary Jo, and David T. Ellwood. 1991. "Is American business working for the poor?" *Harvard Business Review* (September–October): 58–66.

Banfield, Edward. 1974. *The Unheavenly City Revisited*. Boston: Little Brown.

_____, and James Q. Wilson. 1963. *City Politics*. New York: Vintage.

Baptist, Willie, Mary Bricker Jenkins, and Monica Dillon. 1999. "Taking the struggle on the road: The new Freedom Bus-Freedom from unemployment, hunger, and homelessness." *Journal of Progressive Human Services* 10(2): 7–29.

Baratz, Steven S., and Joan C. Baratz. 1970. "Early childhood intervention: The social science base of institutional racism." *Harvard Educational Review* 40: 29–50.

Barker, Martin and Julian Petley (eds.). 1997. *Ill Effects: The Media/Violence Debate*. London: Routledge.

Barlett, Donald L., and James B. Steele. 2001. "Corporate Welfare." Pages 87–97 in Amanda Konradi and Martha Schmitt (eds.), *Reading Between the Lines: Toward an Understanding of Social Problems*, 2nd ed. Mountain View, CA: Mayfield Publishing Co.

Barnett, Bernice McNair. 1993. "Invisible southern black women leaders in the civil rights movement: The triple constraints of gender, race, and class." *Gender & Society* 7(June): 162–182.

Barnett, Mark A. 1977. "The role of play and make believe in children's cognitive development: Implications for social class differences and education." *Journal of Education* 159(4)(November): 38–48.

Barnhurst, Kevin G., and Ellen Wartella. 1998. "Young citizens, American TV newscasts and the collective memory." *Critical Studies in Mass Communication* 15(3): 279–305.

Barnes, Sandra L. 2003. "The Ebonics enigma: An analysis of attitudes on an urban college campus." *Race, Ethnicity and Education* 6(3): 247–263.

Baron, Dennis. 2000. "Ebonics and the politics of English." *World Englishes* 19(1): 5–19.

Barry, David S. 1993. "Growing up violent." *Media and Values* 62(Summer): 8–11.

Bartfeld, Judi. 2000. "Child support and the postdivorce economic well-being of mothers, fathers, and children." *Demography* 37(2): 203–213.

Barthel, Diane. 1988. *Putting on Appearances: Gender and Advertising*. Philadelphia: Temple University Press.

Basu, Malika. 1996. "Humanization and development: The question of basic needs." *Social Action* 46(3): 249–261.

Bates-Harris, Cheryl. 2012. "Segregated and exploited: The failure of the disability service system to provide quality work." *Journal of Vocational Rehabilitation* 36(1): 39–64.

Battles, Kathleen, and Wendy Hilton-Morrow. 2002. "Gay characters in conventional spaces: Will and Grace and the situation comedy genre." *Critical Studies in Media Communication* 19(1): 87–105.

Beaulieu, Lionel J. 1998. "Welfare reform: An overview of key provisions." *Southern Rural Development Center Information Brief* 1(January): 1–3.

Becker, Howard S. 1963. *Outsiders: Studies in the Sociology of Deviance*. New York: Free Press.

Been, Vicki. 1994. "Locally undesirable land uses in minority neighborhoods: Disproportionate siting or market dynamics?" *The Yale Law Journal* 103: 1383–1413.

Beeman, Angie, Davita Silfen Glasberg, and Colleen Casey. 2010. "Whiteness as Property: Predatory Lending and the Reproduction of Racialized Inequality." *Critical Sociology* 37(1):27–45.

Begleiter, Henir and Benjamin Kissin (eds.). 1995. *The Genetics of Alcoholism*. New York: Oxford University Press.

Bell, Daniel. 1973. *The Coming of Post-industrial Society*. New York: Basic Books.

Bennett, Lance W. 2012. "The personalization of politics: Political identity, social media, and changing patterns of participation." *The Annals of the American Academy of Political and Social Science* 644(1): 20–39.

Benson, Michael L., Greer Litton Fox, Alred De Maris, and Judy Van Wyk. 2000. "Violence in families: The intersection of race, poverty, and community context." *Contemporary Perspectives in Family Research* 2: 91–109.

Berberick, Stephanie Nicholl. 2010. "The objectification of women in mass media: Female self-image in misogynist culture." *The New York Sociologist* 5: 1–15.

Berger, Peter L. and Thomas Luckmann. 1966. *The Social Construction of Reality*. Garden City, NY: Doubleday.

Berle, Adolph, and Gardiner C. Means. 1932. *The Modern Corporation and Private Property*. New York: Harcourt, Brace & World.

Berlet, Chip, and Matthew N. Lyons. 1995. "Militia nation." *The Progressive* 59(June): 22–25.

Berman, Daniel M., and John T. O'Connor. 1997. *Who Owns the Sun? Politics and the Struggle for a Solar Economy*. White River Junction, VT: Chelsea Green Publishing.

Berman, Steve. 2011. *Speaking Out: LGBTQ Youth Stand Up*. Bold Strokes Books.

Best, Joel. 1998. "Too much fun: Toys as social problems and the interpretation of culture." *Symbolic Interaction* 21(2): 197–212.

Bianchi, Suzanne M., and Jane Lawler Dye. 2001. "The participation of women and men in the United States labor force: Trends and future prospects." Pages 460–472 in Dana Vannoy (ed.), *Gender Mosaics*. Los Angeles: Roxbury.

Bienefeld, Manfred. 2000. "Structural adjustment: Debt collection device or development policy." *Review–Fernand Braudel Center* 23(4): 533–582.

Biegel, Stuart. 1996. "Does anyone control the Internet?" *The UCLA Online Institute for Cyberspace Law and Policy*. www.gse.ucla.edu/iclp/control.html

Billings, Dwight B., and Kathleen M. Blee. 2000. *The Road to Poverty: The Making of Wealth and Hardship in Appalachia*. New York: Cambridge University Press.

Binkley, Bonnie. 2001. "A case study of the impact of deindustrialization in Memphis, Tennessee." Paper presented at the annual meetings of the Southern Sociological Society.

Bixby, Lyn. 1992. "Peace dividend: More markets for arms makers." *Hartford (CT) Courant*, October 25:A6-A7.

Black, Amy E., and Jamie L. Allen. 2001. "Tracing the legacy of Anita Hill: The Thomas/Hill hearings and media coverage of sexual harassment." *Gender Issues* 19(1): 33–52.

Blair-Loy, Mary. 2009. "Work without end? Scheduling flexibility and work-to-family conflict among stockbrokers." *Work and Occupations* 36(4): 279–317.

Blau, Joel. 1999. *Illusions of Prosperity: America's Working Families in an Age of Economic Insecurity*. New York: Oxford University Press.

Block, Alan A. 2002. "Environmental crime and pollution: Wasteful reflections." *Social Justice* 29(1–2): 61–81.

Block, Fred, Richard A. Cloward, Barbara Ehrenreich, and Frances Fox Piven. 1987. *The Mean Season: The Attack on the Welfare State*. New York: Pantheon Books.

Blumberg, Rhoda Lois. 1991. *Civil Rights: The 1960s Freedom Struggle*, rev. ed. Boston: Twayne.

Boerner, Christopher, and Thomas Lambert. 1995. "Environmental justice." *The Public Interest* 118 (Winter): 61–81.

Boggs, Carl. 2000. *The End of Politics: Corporate Power and the Decline of the Public Sphere*. New York: Guilford Press.

Boggiano, A. K., and M. Barrett. 1991. "Strategies to motivate helpless and mastery-oriented children: The effect of gender-based expectancies." *Sex Roles* 25: 487–510.

Boje, Thomas P., and Anders Ejrnaes. 2012. "Policy and practice." *International Journal of Sociology and Social Policy* 32(9–10): 589–605.

Bonanno, Alessandro, Douglas H. Constance, and Katherine L. Lyman. 1997. "Corporate crime in the global era: The Enimont case." *Critical Sociology* 23(2): 63–88.

Bonilla-Silva, Eduardo. 2001. *White Supremacy and Racism in the Post-Civil Rights Era*. Boulder, CO: Lynne Rienner.

Borchert, Mark. 1998. "The challenge of cyberspace: Internet access and persons with disabilities." Pages 49–63 in Ebo Bohash (ed.), *Cyberghetto or Cyberutopia? Race, Class, and Gender on the Internet*. Westport, CT: Praeger.

Bornschier, Volker, and Christopher Chase-Dunn. 1985. *Transnational Corporations and Underdevelopment*. New York: Praeger.

Bose, E. Christine, and Rachel Bridges Whaley. 2001. "Sex segregation in the U.S. labor force." Pages 228–239 in Dana Vannoy (ed.), *Gender Mosaics: Social Perspectives*. Los Angeles: Roxbury.

Boserup, Esther. 1970. *Women's Role in Economic Development*. New York: St. Martin's Press.

Bouchard, Louise, Marc Renaud, Odile Kremp, and Louis Dallaire. 1995. "Selective abortion: A new moral order? Consensus and debate in the medical community." *International Journal of Health Services* 25(1): 65–84.

Bouchard, Thomas J. Jr., and Matthew McGue. 1990. "Genetic and rearing environmental influences on adult personality: An analysis of adopted twins reared apart." *Journal of Personality* 58(1): 263–292.

Bowker, Lee H. 1972. "Red and black in contemporary history texts: A content analysis." Pages 101–110 in Howard M. Bahr, Bruce A. Chadwick, and Robert C. Day (eds.), *Native Americans Today: Sociological Perspectives*. New York: Harper & Row.

Bowles, Samuel, and Herbert Gintis. 1976. *Schooling in Capitalist America: Educational Reform and the Contradictions of Economic Life*. New York: Basic Books.

Bowman, Philip, and Cleopatra Howard. 1985. "Race-related socialization, motivation, and academic achievement: A study of black youth in three-generation families." *Journal of the American Academy of Child Psychiatry* 24:134–141.

Boxer, Paul, L. Rowell Huesmann, Brad J. Bushman, Maureen O'Brien, and Dominic Moceri. 2009. "The role of violent media preference in cumulative developmental risk for violence and general aggression." *Journal of Youth and Adolescence* 38(3): 417–428.

Boyle, Sarah Patton. 1962. *The Desegregated Heart: A Virginian's Stand in Time of Transition*. New York: William Morrow.

Bradsher, Julia E. 1996. "Disability among racial and ethnic groups." Abstract 10 (July). San Francisco: Disability Statistics Center, University of California.

Brady, David, and Michael Wallace. 2001. "Deindustrialization and poverty: Manufacturing decline and AFDC recipiency in Lake County, Indiana 1964–93." *Sociological Forum* 16(2): 321–358.

Brady, Susan M. 2001. "Sterilization of girls and women with intellectual disabilities: Past and present justifications." *Violence Against Women* 7(4): 432–461.

Bramlett, Matthew D., and William D. Mosher. 2001. "First marriage dissolution, divorce, and remarriage: United State." Department of Health and Human Services Centers for Disease Control. *Advance Data* Number 323 (May 31).

Brand, Peg Zeglin (ed.). 2000. *Beauty Matters*. Bloomington: Indiana University Press.

Brault, Matthew W. 2012. "Americans with Disabilities." Current Population Reports P70-131. Washington DC: U.S. Department of Commerce, U.S. Census Bureau.

Brecher, Jeremy, Tim Costello, and Brendan Smith. 2000. *Globalization from Below: The Power of Solidarity*. Cambridge, MA: South End Press.

Brint, Steven. 1998. *Schools and Societies*. Thousand Oaks, CA: Pine Forge Press.

Broman, Clifford L. 1988. "Household work and family life satisfaction of blacks." *Journal of Marriage and the Family* 50: 743–748.

Brown, Dee Alexander. 2001. *Bury My Heart at Wounded Knee: An Indian History of the American West*. New York: Henry Holt & Company.

Brown, Tina A. 1993. "Police seek motive in murder-suicide." *Hartford Courant* (August 8): B1.

Bucy, Erik. 2000. "Social access to the Internet." *Harvard International Journal of Press/Politics* 5(1): 50–61.

Budig, Michelle J., and Paula England. 2001. "The wage penalty for motherhood." *American Sociological Review* 66(2): 204–225.

Bullard, Robert D. 1993. *Confronting Environmental Racism: Voices from the Grassroots*. Boston: South End Press.

_____. 2002. "Poverty, pollution, and environmental racism: Strategies for building health and sustainable communities." Available at www.ejrc.cau.edu

*_____, and Beverly Hendrix Wright. 1987. "Environmentalism and the politics of equity: Emergent trends in the black community." *Mid-American Review of Sociology* 12(2): 21–38.

Bureau of Labor Statistics. 2013. "Women in the labor force: A databook." Available at www.bls.gov

Burgess, Melina C.R., Steven Paul Stermer, and Stephen R. Burgess. 2007. "Sex, lies, and video games: The portrayal of male and female characters on video game covers." *Sex Roles: A Journal of Research* 57(5-6): 419–433.

Burke, Jude Miller and Mark Attridge. 2011. "Pathways to career and leadership success: Part 2—striking gender similarities among $100k professionals." *Journal of Workplace Behavioral Health* 26:207-39.

Burkhauser, R.V. and G.J. Duncan. 1989. "Economic risks of gender roles: Income loss and life events over the life course." *Social Science Quarterly* 70:3-23.

Burnham, James. 1941. *The Managerial Revolution*. New York: John Day.

Burns, Ailsa and Ross Homel. 1989. "Gender division of tasks by parents and their children." *Psychology of Women Quarterly* 13(1):113-25.

Burris, Val. 1992. "Elite policy-planning networks in the United States." *Research in Politics and Society* 4: 111–134.

Business Week. 1980. "Industry's schoolhouse clout." October 13:156-60.

Butsch, Richard. 1995. "Ralph, Fred, Archie, and Homer: Why television keeps recreating the white male working-class buffoon." Pages 403–412 in Gail Dines and Jean M. Humez (eds.), *Gender, Race, and Class in Media*. Thousand Oaks, CA: Sage Publications.

Butterfield, Fox. 2003. "Prison Rates Among Blacks Reach a Peak, Report Finds." New York Times (April 7): A11.

Calavita, Kitty, and Henry Pontell. 1991. "'Other people's money' revisited: Embezzlement in the savings and loan insurance industries." *Social Problems* 38(1): 94–112.

_____, Henry Pontell, and Robert H. Tillman, 1997. *Big Money Crime: Fraud and Politics in the Savings and Loan Crisis*. Berkeley: University of California Press.

Callan, Valerie, and Jared S. Rosenberger. 2011. "Media and public perceptions of the police: Examining the impact of race and personal experience." *Policing & Society* 21(2): 167–189.

Campbell, Anne. 1991. *The Girls in the Gang: A Report from New York City*. New York: Basil Blackwell.

Campbell, Nancy D. 1999. "Regulating 'maternal instinct': Governing mentalities of late twentieth century U.S. illicit drug policy." *Signs* 24(4): 895–923.

Cancian, Francesca M., and Stacey J. Oliker. 2000. *Caring and Gender*. Thousand Oaks, CA: Pine Forge Press.

Cannon, Carl M. 1993. "Honey, I warped the kids." *Mother Jones* 18(July–August): 16–17.

Carrasquillo, Hector. 2002. "The Puerto Rican Family." In Ronald L. Taylor (ed.), *Minority Families in the United States: A Multicultural Perspective*, 3rd ed. Upper Saddle River, NJ: Prentice Hall/Pearson.

Casey, Timothy J. 1998. "Welfare reform and its impact in the nation and in New York." New York: Federation of Protestant Welfare Agencies, Inc. www.wnylc.com/frames/menus/. . . law/resource-material/welrefor.htm

Cassell, Justine, and Henry Jenkins (eds.). 1998. *From Barbie to Mortal Kombat: Gender and Computer Games*. Cambridge, MA: MIT Press.

Cassidy, Elizabeth, Rebecca P. Judge, and Paul M. Sommers. 2000. "The distribution of environmental justice: A comment." *Social Science Quarterly* 81(3): 877–878.

Castro-Vasquez, Genaro. 2000. "Masculinity and condom use among Mexican teenagers: The Escuela Nacional Preparatoria No. 1's case." *Gender and Education* 12(4): 479–492.

Cermak, Sharon, and Victor Groza. 1998. "Sensory processing problems in post-institutionalized children: Implications for social work." *Child and Adolescent Social Work Journal* 15(1): 5–37.

Cerulo, Karen A. 2000. "Packaging violence: Media, story sequencing, and the perception of right and wrong." Pages 153–176 in Mark Gottdiener (ed.), *New Forms of Consumption: Consumers, Culture, and Commodification*. Lanham, MD: Rowman & Littlefield.

Chalabaev, Aina, Phillipe Sarrasin, Paul Fontayne, Julie Boiche, and Crentin Clement-Guillotin. 2013. "The influence of sex stereotypes and gender roles on participation and performance in sport and exercise: Review and future direction." *Psychology of Sport and Exercise* 14(2): 136–144.

Chang, Grace. 2000. *Disposable Domestics: Immigrant Women Workers in the Global Economy*. Boston: South End Press.

Chapple, Constance L. 1998. "Dow Corning and the silicone breast implant debacle: A case of corporate crime against women." Pages 179–196 in Lee H. Bowker (ed.), *Masculinities and Violence*. Thousand Oaks, CA: Sage.

Charlton, James I. 2000. *Nothing About Us Without Us: Disability Oppression and Empowerment (new edition)*. Berkeley: University of California Press.

Chase-Dunn, Christopher. 1997. *Rise and Demise: Comparing World Systems*. Boulder, CO: Westview Press.

_____. 1998. *Global Formation: Structures of the World Economy*. Lanham, MD: Rowman & Littlefield Publishers.

_____and Thomas Hall, 1997. *Rise and Demise: Comparing World-Systems*. Boulder, CO: Westview Press.

Chatterjee, Lata, and Monika Mitra. 1998. "Evolution of federal and state policies for persons with disability in the United States: Efficiency and welfare impacts." *Annals of Regional Science* 32(3): 347–365.

Chavis, Benjamin F., Jr., and Charles Lee. 1987. *Toxic Wastes and Race in the United States: A National Report on the Racial and Socio-Economic Characteristics of Communities with Hazardous Waste Sites*. New York: United Church of Christ Commission for Racial Justice.

Chen, Lanhee J. and Andrew Reeves. 2011. "Turning out the base or appealing to the periphery? An analysis of county-level candidate appearances in the 2008 presidential campaign." *American Politics Research* 39(3):534-56.

Cheney, George. 2002. *Values at Work: Employee Participation Meets Market Pressure at Mondragon*, Rev. ed. Ithaca, NY: Cornell University Press.

Child Care Aware of America. 2012. "Parents and the cost of child care." Available at www.naccrra.org

Chisolm, June F. 1999. "The sandwich generation." *Journal of Social Distress and the Homeless.* 8(3): 177–191.

Chomsky, Noam. 1997. *Media Control: The Spectacular Achievements of Propaganda*. New York: Seven Stories Press.

_____. 1999. "The current bombings: Behind the rhetoric." Znet (www.zmag.org/current_bombings.htm).

_____. 2002. *Media Control: The Spectacular Achievements of Propaganda*, 2nd ed. New York: Seven Stories Press.

Chossudovsky, Michel. 1997. "Dismantling former Yugoslavia, recolonizing Bosnia." *Capital and Class*, 62(summer): 1–12.

Citizens for Tax Justice. 2011 "The hidden entitlements." Report (www.ctj.org/html.publist.htm).

Clapp, Jennifer. 2001. *Toxic Exports: The Transfer of Hazardous Wastes from Rich to Poor Countries.* Ithaca, NY: Cornell University Press.

Clark, Charles S. 1991. "Youth gangs." *Congressional Quarterly Researcher* 1(22): 753–776.

Clark, Kenneth B., and Mamie P. Clark. 1947. "Racial identification and preferences in Negro children." Pages 169–178 in Theodore M. Newcomb and Eugene L. Hartley (eds.), *Readings in Social Psychology*. New York: Holt, Rinehart and Winston.

Clarke, Victoria. 2001. "What about the children? Arguments against lesbian and gay parenting." *Women's Studies International Forum* 24(5): 555–570.

Clawson, Dan. 1980. *Bureaucracy and the Labor Process: The Transformation of U.S. Industry, 1860–1920*. New York: Monthly Review Press.

_____. 2003. *The Next Upsurge: Labor and the New Social Movements*. Ithaca: ILR Press.

_____, Alan Nedstadtl, and Mark Weller. 1998. *Dollars and Votes: How Business Campaign Contributions Subvert Democracy*. Philadelphia: Temple University Press.

Clawson, Rosalee A. 2002. "Poor people, black faces: The portrayal of poverty in economics textbooks." *Journal of Black Studies* 32(3): 352–361.

_____, and Elizabeth R. Kegler. 2000. "The 'race-coding' of poverty in American government college textbooks." *Howard Journal of Communications* 11(3): 179–188.

Clendinen, Dudley, and Adam Nagourney. 2001. *Out for Good: The Struggle to Build a Gay Rights Movement in America*. New York: Touchstone Books.

Clinard, Marshall B., and Robert F. Meier. 1992. *Sociology of Deviant Behavior*, 8th ed. Fort Worth, TX: Harcourt Brace Jovanovich.

_____, and Robert F. Meier. 2003. *Sociology of Deviant Behavior*, 12th ed. Belmont, CA: Wadsworth Publishing Co.

CNN/ORC. 2012. "CNN/ORC Poll." May 29–31.

CNN/Time. 1998. "CNN/Time Poll." October 14–15.

Cockburn, Alexander. 1997. "The big win." *The Nation* September 8/15: 8.

Cody, Paul J., and Peter L. Welch. 1997. "Rural gay men in northern New England: Life experiences and coping styles." *Journal of Homosexuality* 33(1): 51–67.

Cohen, Mitchell. 1990. "Toxic imperialism: Exposing Pentagonorrhea." *Z Magazine*, October: 78-79.

Cole, David. 1999. *No Equal Justice: Race and Class in the American Criminal Justice System*. New York: The New Press.

Cole, Luke W., and Sheila R. Foster. 2001. *From the Ground Up: Environmental Racism and the Rise of the Environmental Justice Movement*. New York: New York University Press.

Coleman, James William. 1989. *The Criminal Elite*. New York: St. Martin's Press.

Collins, Patricia Hill. 2000. *Black Feminist Thought: Knowledge, Consciousness, and the Politics of Empowerment*, 2nd ed. New York: Routledge.

Collins, Chuck, and Felice Yeskel with United For a Fair Economy. 2000. *Economic Apartheid in America: A Primer on Economic Inequality and Insecurity*. New York: The New Press.

Collins, Susan. 1998. "Economic integration and the American worker: An overview." Pages 3–45 in Susan Collins (ed.), *Imports, Exports, and the American Worker*. Washington, DC: Brookings Institution Press.

Coltrane, Scott, and Michele Adams. 2001. "Men, women, and housework." Pages 145–154 in Dana Vannoy (ed.), *Gender Mosaics: Social Perspectives*. Los Angeles: Roxbury.

Compa, Lance. 2001. "NAFTA's labor side agreement and international labor solidarity." *Antipode* 33(3): 451–467.

Comstock, George, and Haejung Paik. 1991. *Television and the American Child*. San Diego, CA: Academic Press.

Comte, Auguste. 1966. *System of Positive Polity*, vol. 3. New York: Burt Franklin.

Conley, Dalton. 1999. *Being Black, Living in the Red*. Berkeley: University of California Press.

Connecticut Department of Education. 1999. *Connecticut Public Schools: Town and School District Profiles*. Hartford: State Department of Education.

Conway, M. Margaret. 2000. *Political Participation in the United States*. Washington, DC: CQ Press.

Cook, Christopher D. 2000. "Temps demand a new deal." *The Nation* March 27: 13–19.

Cookson, Peter W., and Caroline Hodges Persell. 1985. *Preparing for Power: America's Elite Boarding Schools*. New York: Basic Books.

Cooley, Charles Horton. 1902. *Human Nature and the Social Order*. New York: Scribner.

_____. 1929. *Social Organization*. New York: Scribner.

Cooper, Marc. 1999. "No sweat: Uniting workers and students: A new movement is born." *The Nation* June 7: 11–15.

Cooper, Margaret. 1999. "The Australian disability rights movements lives." *Disability and Society* 14(2): 217–226.

Corm, Georges. 1982. "The indebtedness of the developing countries: Origins and mechanisms." Pages 15–110 in J. C. Sanchez Arnau (ed.), *Debt and Development*. New York: Praeger.

Cormier, David, and Harry Targ. 2001. "Globalization and the North American worker." *Labor Studies Journal* 26(1): 42–59.

Cose, Ellis. 1995. *The Rage of a Privileged Class*. New York: Perennial.

_____. 2002. *The Envy of the World: On Being a Black Man in America*. New York: Washington Square Press.

Costello, Barbara J., and Paul R. Vowell. 1999. "Testing control theory and differential association: A reanalysis of the Richmond Youth Project Data." *Criminology* 37(4): 815–842.

Craig, Lyn, and Abigail Powell. 2012. "Dual-earner parents' work-family time: The effects of atypical work patterns and non-parental childcare." *Journal of Population Research* 29(3): 229–247.

Crane, Diana. 1999. "Gender and hegemony in fashion magazines: Women's interpretations of fashion photographs." *Sociological Quarterly* 40(4): 541–563.

_____. 2001. *Fashion and Its Social Agendas: Class, Gender, and Identity in Clothing*. Chicago: University of Chicago Press.

Cravey, Tiffany, and Aparna Mitra. 2011. "Demographics of the sandwich generation by race and ethnicity in the United States." *The Journal of Socio-Economics* 40(3): 306–311.

Cress, Daniel M., and David A. Snow. 2000. "The outcomes of homeless mobilization: The influence of organization, disruption, political mediation, and framing." *American Journal of Sociology* 105(4): 1063–1104.

Croissant, Jennifer L. 2001. "Can this campus be bought? Commercial influence in unfamiliar places." *Academe* September-October: 44–48.

Cruz, Barbara C. 2002. "Don Juan and rebels under palm trees: Depictions of Latin Americans in US history textbooks." *Critique of Anthropology* 22(3): 323–342.

Cubbins, Lisa A. 2001. "The legacy of patriarchy in today's Russia." Pages 174–183 in Dana Vannoy (ed.), *Gender Mosaics: Social Perspectives*. Los Angeles: Roxbury.

Cuklanz, Lisa M. 2000. *Rape on Prime Time: Television, Masculinity, and Sexual Violence*. Philadelphia: University of Pennsylvania Press.

Cummings, Scott, and Del Taebel. 1978. "The economic socialization of children." *Social Problems* 26(December): 198–210.

Cummins, Robert A., and David Dunt. 1988. "Evaluation of a de-institutionalization program in Australia: The St. Nicholas Project." *International Journal of Rehabilitation Research* 11(4): 395–396.

Cunningham, Mick. 2001. "Parental influences on the gendered division of labor." *American Sociological Review* 66(2):184–203.

Curra, John. 2010. *The Relativity of Deviance*, 2nd ed. Thousand Oaks, CA: Sage.

Currie, Dawn H. 1997. "Decoding femininity: Advertisements and their teenage readers. *Gender & Society* 11(4): 453–477.

Curtiss, Susan. 1977. *Genie: A Linguistic Study of a Modern Day "Wild Child."* New York: Academic Press.

Cutler, James Elbert. 1969. *Lynch-Law: An Investigation into the History of Lynching in the United States*. Montclair, NJ: Patterson Smith.

Cypher, James M. 2001. "NAFTA's lessons: From economic mythology to current realities." *Labor Studies Journal* 26(1): 5–21.

Cyrus, Virginia (ed.). 2000. *Experiencing Race, Class, and Gender in the United States*, 3rd ed. Mountain View, CA: Mayfield.

Dale, Richard S., and Richard P. Mattione. 1983. *Managing Global Debt*. Washington, DC: Brookings Institute.

Dandaneau, Steven P. 1996. *A Town Abandoned: Flint, Michigan Confronts Deindustrialization*. Albany, NY: State University of New York Press.

Daniels, Arlene Kaplan. 1988. *Invisible Careers: Leaders from the Volunteer World*. Chicago: University of Chicago Press.

Daniels, Glynis, and Samantha Friedman. 1999. "Spatial inequality and the distribution of industrial toxic releases: Evidence from the 1990 TRI." *Social Science Quarterly* 80(2): 244–262.

Darling, Nancy. 2012. "Are today's 20-somethings slackers?" *Psychology Today*, February 26. Available at www.psychologytoday.com

Davies, James. 1962. "Toward a theory of revolution." *American Sociological Review* 27(1): 5–19.

_____. 1969. "The J-curve of rising and declining satisfactions as a cause of some great revolutions and a contained revolution." Pages 671–709 in H. D. Graham and T. R. Gurr (eds.), *Violence in America*. New York: Signet.

_____. 1974. "The J-curve and power struggle theories of collective violence." *American Sociological Review* 39: 607–610.

Davis, Angela Y. 1983. *Women, Race and Class*. New York: Vintage.

Davis, D. M. 1990. "Portrayals of women in prime-time network television: Some demographic characteristics." *Sex Roles* 23(5–6): 325–332.

Davis, Kingsley. 1940. "Extreme social isolation of a child." *American Journal of Sociology* 45 (January): 554–564.

_____. 1948. *Human Society*. New York: Macmillan.

_____, and Wilbert Moore. 1945. "Some principles of stratification." *American Sociological Review* 10: 242–249.

Davis, Nanette J., and Clarice Stasz. 1990. *Social Control of Deviance*. New York: McGraw-Hill.

DeBoeck, Guy. 2000. "Green zones or greenbacks? The debt-nature exchange: Green neocolonialism and environmental exploitation." *Contradictions* 92: 99–110.

Debt Crisis Network. 1985. *From Debt to Development: Alternatives to the International Debt Crisis*. Washington, DC: Institute for Policy Studies.

Deegan, Mary Jo. 1998. "Harrie Martineau, patriarchal gatekeeping and sociological theory: Multiple assaults on the historical canon." Paper presented at the International Sociological Association.

Deere, C., and M. Leon deLeal. 1981. "Peasant production, proletarianization, and the sexual division of labor in the Andes." *Signs* 7(2): 338–360.

_____, J. Humphries, and M. Leon deLeal. 1982. "Class and historical analysis for the study of women and economic change." Pages 87–116 in R. Anker, M. Buvinic, and N. Youssef (eds.), *Women's Roles and Population Trends in the Third World*. London: ILO.

Dei, George J. Sefa, Josephine Mazzuca, Elizabeth McIsaac, and Jasmin Zine. 1997. *Reconstructing "Drop-Out": A Critical Ethnography of the Dynamics of Black Students' Disengagement from School*. Ontario: University of Toronto Press.

Delacroix, Jacques, and Charles C. Ragin. 1981. "Structural blockage: A cross-national study of economic dependency, state efficacy, and underdevelopment." *American Journal of Sociology* 86:1311–1347.

Delaney, John T. 1996. "Workplace cooperation: Current problems, news approaches." *Journal of Labor Research* 17(1): 45–56.

De Los Santos, Brian. 2013. "Middle-aged breadwinners become part of the 'sandwich generation'." NPR. Available at www.npr.org

D'Emilio, John, William B. Turner, and Urvashi Vaid (eds.). 2000. *Creating Change: Sexuality, Public Policy, and Civil Rights*. New York: St. Martin's Press.

Demo, David H., and Alan C. Acock. 1993. "Family diversity and the division of domestic labor: How much have things really changed?" *Family Relations* 42(3): 323–331.

Democracy Corps. 2010. Campaign for America's Future Poll. November.

_____. 2012. Women's Voices Poll. March.

Dennis, Everette E., and Edward C. Pease (eds.). 1996. *The Media in Black and White*. New Brunswick, NJ: Transaction Publishers.

Dennis, Rutledge M. 1981. "Socialization and racism: The white experience." Pages 71-85 in Benjamin P. Bowser and Raymond G. Hunt (eds.), *Impacts of Racism on White Americans*. Beverly Hills, CA: Sage.

DeOliver, Miguel. 1995. "Structural consolidation: The Colorado Delta Region, 1900–10." *Review* 18(4): 565–588.

DeParle, Jason. 1990. "War, class divisions, and burden of service." *New York Times* (November 13): A14.

Deutscher, Guy. 2010. "Does your language shape how you think?" *New York Times*, August 26. Available at www.nytimes.com

DeVaney, Ann (ed.). 1994. *Watching Channel One: The Convergence of Students, Technology, and Private Business*. Albany: State University of New York Press.

Dewan, Shaila. 2012. "More men enter fields dominated by women." *New York Times*, May 20. Available at www.nytimes.com

Dickinson, Torry D. 1997. "Selective globalization: The relocation of industrial production and the shaping of women's work." *Research in the Sociology of Work* 6: 109–129.

Dietz, Tracy L. 1998. "An examination of violence and gender role portrayals in video games: Implications for gender socialization and aggressive behavior." *Sex Roles* 38(5-6): 425–442.

Dill, Bonnie Thornton. 1983. "Race, class, and gender: Prospects for an all-inclusive sisterhood." *Feminist Studies* 9(1): 131–150.

_____. 1988. "'Making your job good itself': Domestic service and the construction of personal dignity." Pages 33–52 in Ann Bookman and Sandra Morgen (eds.), *Women and the Politics of Empowerment*. Philadelphia: Temple University Press.

Dill, Karen, and Kathryn P. Thill. 2007. "Video game characters and the socialization of gender roles: Young people's perception mirror sexist media depictions." *Sex Roles: A Journal of Research* 57(11–12): 851–864.

Dines, Gail. 1992a. "Pornography and the media: Cultural representation of violence against women." *Family Violence and Sexual Assault Bulletin* 8(3): 17–20.

_____. 1992b. "Capitalism's pitchmen: The media sells a business agenda." *Dollars and Sense* 176 (May): 18–20.

Dobash, Emerson R. et al. 2000. *Changing Violent Men*. Thousand Oaks, CA: Sage Publications.

Dolbeare, Kenneth M. 1986. *Democracy at Risk: The Politics of Economic Renewal*, rev. ed. Chatham, NJ: Chatham House.

Domhoff, G. William. 2002. *Who Rules America? Power and Politics*, 4th ed. New York: McGraw-Hill.

_____. 2009. *Who Rules America? Challenges to Corporate and Class Dominance*. New York: McGraw-Hill.

Dorwick, Peter W. and Christopher Keys. 2001. *People With Disabilities: Empowerment and Community Action*. New York: Routledge.

Dowrick, Peter W. 2001. *People with Disabilities: Empowerment and Community Action*. New York: Routledge.

Doyle, Bertram Wilbur. 1971. *The Etiquette of Race Relations in the South: A Study in Social Control*. New York: Schocken Books.

Du Bois, W.E.B. 1989/1903. *The Souls of Black Folk*. New York: Penguin.

Dudley, William (ed.). 1999. *Media Violence: Opposing Viewpoints*. San Diego, CA: Greenhaven Press.

Duncan, G.J. and S.D. Hoffman. 1985. "Economic consequences of marital instability." Pages 427-67 in M. David and T. Smeeding, eds., *Horizontal Equity, Uncertainty, and Economic Well-Being*. Chicago: University of Chicago Press.

Duneier, Mitchell. 1992. *Slim's Table: Race, Respectability, and Masculinity*. Chicago: University of Chicago Press.

Dunning, Eric. 1993. "Sport in the civilising process: Aspects of the development of modern sport." Pages 39–70 in Eric G. Dunning, Joseph A. Maguire, and Robert E. Pearton (eds.), *The Sports Process: A Comparative and Developmental Approach*. Champaign, IL: Human Kinetics Press.

Durkheim, Émile. 1964. Trans. George Simpson. *The Division of Labor in Society*. New York: Free Press.

Durning, Alan Thein. 1994. "Redesigning the forest economy." Pages 22–40 in Lester R. Brown (ed.), *State of the World, 1994*. New York: Norton.

Dye, Thomas R. 1990. *Who's Running America? The Bush Era*. Englewood Cliffs, NJ: Prentice-Hall.

_____. 2002. *Who's Running America: The Bush Reconstruction*. Englewood Cliffs, NJ: Prentice-Hall.

Edgerton, Robert B. 1978. *Deviance: A Cross-Cultural Perspective*. Menlo Park, CA: Cummings.

Edin, Kathryn, and Laura Lein. 1997. *Making Ends Meet: How Single Mothers Survive Welfare and Low-Wage Work*. New York: Russell Sage Foundation.

Edsall, Thomas B., and Mary D. Edsall. 1992. *Chain Reaction: The Impact of Race, Rights, and Taxes on American Politics*. New York: Norton.

Edwards, Richard. 1979. *Contested Terrain: The Transformation of the Workplace in the Twentieth Century*. New York: Basic Books.

Edut, Ophira (ed.). 1998. *Adios, Barbie: Young Women Write About Body Image and Identity*. Seattle, WA: Seal Press.

Egan, Jennifer. 2000. "Lonely gay teen seeking same." *New York Times Magazine* (December 10):110–117; 128–133.

Egan, Timothy. 1998. "The swoon of the swoosh." *New York Times Magazine* (September 13): 66–70.

Ehrenreich, Barbara. 1986. "Is the middle class doomed?" *New York Times Magazine* (September 7): 44 ff.

_____. 2001. *Nickel and Dimed*. New York: Owl Books.

_____, and Arlie Russell Hochschild (eds.). 2004. *Global Woman: Nannies, Maids, and Sex Workers in the New Economy*. New York: Metropolitan Books.

Eisenstein, Sarah. 1983. Give Us Bread but *Give Us Roses: Working Women's Consciousness in the United States, 1890 to the First World War*. London: Routledge & Kegan Paul.

Eitzen, D. Stanley, and Maxine Baca Zinn. 1989 "The forces reshaping America." Pages 1–18 in D. Stanley Eitzen and Maxine Baca Zinn (eds.), *The Reshaping of America: Social Consequences of the Changing Economy*. Englewood Cliffs, NJ: Prentice Hall.

Eitzen, D. Stanley and Maxine Baca Zinn. 1989b. *The Reshaping of America: Social Consequences of the Changing Economy*. Englewood Cliffs, NJ: Prentice Hall.

_____. 1997. *Social Problems*, 7th ed. Boston: Allyn and Bacon.

_____. 2000. "The missing safety net and families: A progressive critique of the new welfare legislation." *Journal of Sociology and Social Welfare* 27(1): 53–72.

Elias, Robert. 1986. *The Politics of Victimization: Victims, Victimology, and Human Rights*. New York: Oxford University Press.

Elkins, Julie, and Shareen Hertel. 2011. "Sweatshirts and sweatshops: Labor rights, student activism, and the challenges of collegiate apparel manufacturing." Pages 9–21 in William T. Armaline, Davita Silfen Glasberg, and Bandana Purkayastha (eds.), *Human Rights in Our Own Backyard: Injustice and Resistance in the United States*. Philadelphia: University of Pennsylvania Press.

England, Paula. 2000. "Marriage, the costs of children, and gender inequality." Pages 320–342 in Linda J. Waite, Christine Bachrach, Michelle Hindin, Elizabeth Thomson, and Arland Thornton (eds.), *The Ties That Bind: Perspectives on Marriage and Cohabitation*. New York: Aldine de Gruyter.

_____, Jennifer Thompson, and Carolyn Aman. 2001. "The sex gap in pay and comparable worth: An update." Pages 551–565 in Ivar Berg and Arne L. Karleberg (eds.), *Sourcebook of Labor Markets: Evolving Structures and Processes*. New York: Kluwer Academic/Plenum.

Enloe, Cynthia. 1989. *Bananas, Beaches, and Bases: Making Feminist Sense of International Politics*. Berkeley: Universityof California Press.

Entman, Robert M., and Andrew Rojecki. 2000. *The Black Image in the White Mind: Media and Race in America*. Chicago: University of Chicago Press.

Epstein, Cynthia Fuchs. 1993. *Women in Law*, 2nd ed. Urbana: University of Illinois Press.

Erikson, Erik. 1963. *Childhood and Society*. New York: Norton.

Erikson, Kai T. 1966. *Wayward Puritans*. New York: Macmillan.

Estey, Ken, and Betsy Bowman. 2000. "What is a co-op?" *GEO (Grassroots Economic Organizing) Newsletter* 43(Sept.–Oct.): 2.

Euben, J. Peter. 1997. *Corrupting Youth: Political Education, Democratic Culture, and Political Theory*. Princeton, NJ: Princeton University Press.

Evanoff, Richard. 2001. "Co-ps for older workers on the rise in Japan." *GEO (Grassroots Economic Organizing) Newsletter* 46 (March-April).

Evans, Chris. 1999. "Work and workloads during industrialization: The experience of forgemen in the British iron industry." *International Review of Social History* 44(2): 197–215.

Evans, John H. 2010. *Contested Reproduction: Genetic Technologies, Religion, and Public Debate*. Chicago: University of Chicago Press.

Fabig, Heike, and Richard Boele. 1999. "The changing nature of NGO activity in a globalising world: Pushing the corporate responsibility agenda." *IDS Bulletin* 30(3)(July): 58–67.

Fairchild, Sherry R. 2002. "Women with disabilities: The long road to equality." *Journal of Human Behavior in the Social Environment* 6(2): 13–28.

Falk, Erika. 2003. "The glass ceiling persists: The 3rd annual APPC report on women leaders in communications companies." Available at www.annenbergpublicpolicycenter.org

Falk, Gerhard. 2001. *Stigma: How We Treat Outsiders*. Amherst, NY: Prometheus Books.

Family Caregiver Alliance. 2012. "Selected caregiver statistics." Available at www.caregiver.org

Farley, Reynolds, and Walter R. Allen. 1987. *The Color Line and the Quality of Life in America*. New York: Russell Sage Foundation.

Farrell, Bill, and Larry Koch. 1995. "Criminal justice, sociology, and academia." *American Sociologist* 26(1): 52–61.

Fausto-Sterling, Anne. 2000. *Sexing the Body: Gender Politics and the Construction of Sexuality*. New York: Basic Books.

Feagin, Joe R2010. *Racist America: Roots, Currents Realities and Future Reparations*, 2nd ed. New York: Routledge.

_____ and Clairece B. Feagin. 1986. *Discrimination American Style*, 2nd ed. Malabar, FL: Krieger.

_____ and Melvin P. Sikes. 1994. *Living with Racism: The Black Middle-Class Experience*. Boston: Beacon Press.

_____, Hernan Vera, and Pinar Batur. 2001. *White Racism: The Basics*, 2nd ed. New York: Routledge.

Feasey, Rebecca. 2012. *From Happy Homemaker to Desperate Housewives: Motherhood and Popular Television*. Anthem Press.

Featherstone, Liza. 2000. "The new student movement." *The Nation* (May 15): 11–18.

Federal Bureau of Investigation. 2009. "2009 Financial Crimes Report." Available at www.fbi.gov

Federal News Service. 1993. "White House press briefing: Secretary of the Treasury Lloyd Bentsen" (March 10).

Fei, John C. H., and Gustav Ranis. 1997. *Growth and Development from an Evolutionary Perspective*. Malden, MA: Blackwell Publishers.

Fein, Melvyn L. 1990. *Role Change: A Resocialization Perspective*. New York: Praeger.

Feltey, Kathryn M. 2001. "Gender violence: Rape and sexual assault." Pages 363–373 in Dana Vannoy (ed.), *Gender Mosaics: Social Perspectives*. Los Angeles: Roxbury.

Ferber, Marianne A., Brigid O'Farrell and La Rue Allen. 1991. *Work and Family: Policies for a Changing Work Force*. Washington, DC: National Academy Press.

Ferguson, Charles H. 2012. *Predator Nation: Corporate Criminals, Political Corruption, and the Hijacking of America*. New York: Crown Business.

Ferree, Myra Marx. 1990. "Beyond separate spheres: Feminism and family research." *Journal of Marriage and the Family* 52(November): 866–884.

_____, and Elaine J. Hall. 1996. "Gender, race, and class in mainstream textbooks." *American Sociological Review* 61(6): 929–950.

_____, Judith Lorber, and Beth B. Hess (eds.). 1999. *Revisioning Gender*. Thousand Oaks, CA: Sage Publications.

_____and Mangala Subramaniam. 2000. "The international women's movement at century's end." Pages 496–506 in Dana Vannoy (ed.), *Gender Mosaics: Social Perspectives*. Los Angeles: Roxbury.

Fine, Cordelia. 2010. *Delusions of Gender: How Our Minds, Society, and Neurosexism Create Difference*. New York: Norton.

Fine, Gary Alan. 1986. "The dirty play of little boys." Pages 171–179 in Michael S. Kimmel and Michael A. Messner (eds.), *Men's Lives*. New York: Macmillan.

_____. 1987. *With the Boys: Little League Baseball and Preadolescent Culture*. Chicago: University of Chicago Fine, Michelleand Adrienne Asch. 1985. "Disabled women: Sexism without the pedestal." Pages 6–22 in Mary Jo Deegan and Nancy A. Brooks (eds.), *Women and Disability: The Double Handicap*. New Brunswick, NJ: Transaction Books.

Finlay, Andrew. 1996. "Teenage pregnancy, romantic love and social science: an uneasy relationship." Pages 79–96 in Veronica James and Jonathan Gabe (eds.), *Health and the Sociology of Emotions*. Oxford, England: Blackwell.

Finn, Patrick J. 1999. *Literacy with an Attitude: Educating Working-Class Children in Their Own Self-Interest*. Albany, NY: State University of New York Press.

Fishbein, Diane H. 1990. "Biological perspectives in criminology." *Criminology* (28): 27–72.

Fitzgerald, Joan, and Peter B. Meyer. 1986. "Recognizing constraints to local economic development." *Journal of the Community Development Society* 17(2): 115–126.

Flanagan, Cara. 1999. *Early Socialisation: Sociability and Attachment*. New York: Routledge.

Fleischer, Doris Zames, and Frieda Zames. 2001. *The Disability Rights Movement: From Charity to Confrontations*. Philadelphia: Temple University Press.

_____. 2011. *The Disability Rights Movement: From Charity to Confrontations*, 2nd ed. Philadelphia: Temple University Press.

Folbre, Nancy. 1985. "The pauperization of motherhood: Patriarchy and public policy in the U.S." *Review of Radical Political Economics* 16(4): 72–88.

_____. 1995. *The New Field Guide to the U.S. Economy*. New York: The New Press.

_____. 2012. "Homemaker dad, breadwinner mom." *New York Times*, January 16. Available at www.economix.blogs.nytimes.com

Foner, Phillip S. 1965. *The Case of Joe Hill*. New York: International Publishers.

Ford, Ramona L. 1988. *Work, Organization and Power*. Boston: Allyn and Bacon.

Foster, John. 1999. *The Vulnerable Planet*. New York: Monthly Review Press.

Fox, James Alan. 2010. "Death penalty: Still racist after all these years." Available at www.boston.com

Fox, James Alan and Marianne W. Zawitz. 2010. "Homicide trends in the United States.: Department of Justice Statistics, available at bjs.gov/content/pub/pdf/htius.pdf

Fox News/Opinion Dynamics. 2000. "Fox News/Opinion Dynamics Poll." January 12–13.

Frank, Andre Gunder. 1967. *Capitalism and Underdevelopment in Latin America: Historical Studies of Chile and Brazil*. New York: Monthly Review Press.

Frank, Gelya. 2000. *Venus on Wheels: Two Decades of Dialogue on Disability, Biography, and Being Female in America*. Berkeley, CA: University of California Press.

Franklin, Barry M. 1986. *Building the American Community: The School Curriculum and the Search for Social Control*. Philadelphia: Falmer Press.

Franklin, Raymond S. 1991. *Shadows of Race and Class*. Minneapolis: University of Minnesota Press.

Franklin, Sarah, and Helena Ragone (eds.). 1998. *Reproducing Reproduction: Kinship, Power, and Technological Innovation*. Philadelphia: University of Pennsylvania Press.

Fraser, Jill A. 2001. *White Collar Sweatshop: The Deterioration of Work and Its Rewards in Corporate America*. New York: W. W. Norton.

Free, Marvin D. 1996. *African Americans and the Criminal Justice System*. New York: Garland Pub.

Freiberg, P. 1991. "Separate classes for black males?" *APA Monitor* (May): 1, 47.

Freud, Sigmund. 1946. *Civilization and Its Discontents*. London: Hogarth Press.

Fromberg, Doris Pronin, and Doris Bergen (eds.). 1998. *Play from Birth to Twelve and Beyond: Contexts, Perspectives, and Meanings*. New York: Garland Pub.

Gadalla, Tahany M. 2008. "Gender differences in poverty rates after marital dissolution: A longitudinal study." *Journal of Divorce and Remarriage* 49(3-4): 225–238.

_____. 2009. "Impact of marital dissolution on men's and women's incomes: A longitudinal study." *Journal of Divorce and Remarriage* 50(1): 55–65.

Gallas, Karen. 1998. *"Sometimes I Can Be Anything": Power, Gender, and Identity in a Primary Classroom*. New York: Teachers College Press.

Gallup Poll. 1999. February 19–21.

Gallup Poll. 2012. June 7-10.

_____. August 9-12.

Gallup/USA Today Poll. 2009. February 20-22.

_____. 2012. December 14-17.

Gamage, Daya. 2009. "US weapons sold to human rights violators/undemocratic nations." *Asian Tribune*

Gans, Herbert. 1982. *The Urban Villagers*, rev. ed. New York: Free Press.

Garfinkel, Harold. 1956. "Conditions of successful degradation ceremonies." *American Sociological Review* 61: 420–424.

Garfinkel, Irwin, Sara S. McLanahan, Daniel R. Meyer, and Judith A. Selzer. 1998. *Fathers Under Fire: The Revolution in Child Support Enforcement*. New York: Russell Sage Foundation.

Garson, Barbara. 1994 . *All the Livelong Day: The Meaning and Demeaning of Routine Work*. New York: Penguin.

Gault, Barbara, and Annisah Um'rani. 2000. "The outcomes of welfare reform for women." *Poverty and Race* 9(4): 1–6.

Gelles, Richard J., and Murray A. Straus. 1988. *Intimate Violence*. New York: Simon & Schuster.

Gelobter, Michel. 1992. "Toward a model of environmental discrimination." Pages 64–81 in B. Bryant and P. Mohai (eds.), *Race and the Incidence of Environmental Hazards: A Time for Discourse*. Boulder, CO: Westview Press.

Gerschick, Thomas J. and Adam Stephen Miller. 2000. "Coming to terms: Masculinity and physical disability." Pages 135-37 in Tracy E. Ore (ed.), *The Social Construction of Difference and Inequality: Race, Class, Gender, and Sexuality*. Mountain View, CA: Mayfield.

Gerson, Kathleen. 1993. *No Man's Land: Men's Changing Commitments to Family and Work*. New York: Basic Books.

Gerstel, Naomi. 2011. "Rethinking families and community: The color, class, and centrality of extended kin ties." *Sociological Forum* 26(1): 1–20.

Gerstel, Naomi, and Dan Clawson. 2001. "Unions' responses to family concerns." *Social Problems* 48(2): 277–297.

Gerstle, Gary, and John Mollenkopf (eds.). 2001. *E Pluribus Unum? Contemporary and Historical Perspectives on Immigrant Political Incorporation*. New York: Russell Sage.

Gerth, Hans, and C. Wright Mills (eds.). 1968. *From Max Weber: Essays in Sociology*. New York: Oxford University Press.

Gervasi, Sean. 1996. "Why is NATO in Yugoslavia?" Paper presented at the Conference on the Enlargement of NAT in Eastern Europe and the Mediterranean. Prague, Czech Republic (January).

Gibbs, Jewel Taylor (ed.). 1988. *Young, Black and Male in America: An Endangered Species*. Dover, MA: Auburn.

Gilbert, Neil, and Rebecca A. Van Voorhis. 2003. "The paradox of family policy." *Society* 40(6): 51–56.

Gilens, Martin. 1999. *Why Americans Hate Welfare: Race, Media, and the Politics of Antipoverty Policy*. Chicago: University of Chicago Press.

Gill, Gurjeet K. 1998. "Female feticide as a contemporary cultural practice in the Punjab." *Dialectical Anthropology* 23(2): 203–213.

Gillborn, David, Nicola Rollock, Carol Vincent, and Stephen J. Ball. 2012. "'You got a pass, so what more do you want?': Race, class and gender interactions in the educational experiences of the Black middle class." *Race, Ethnicity and Education* 15(1): 121–139.

Gillen, Martie, and Hyungsoo Kim. 2009. "Older women and poverty transition: Consequences of income source changes from widowhood." *Journal of Applied Gerontology* 28(3): 320–341.

Gilligan, Carol, Nona P. Lyons, and Trudy J. Hanmer (eds.). 1990. *Making Connection: The Relational Worlds of Adolescent Girls at Emma Willard School*. Cambridge, MA: Harvard University Press.

Gilmore, Sean, and Alicia Crissman. 1997. "Video games: Analyzing gender identity and violence in this new virtual reality." *Studies in Symbolic Interaction* 21: 181–199.

Gitlin, Todd. 2012. *Occupy Nation: The Roots, the Spirit, and the Promise of Occupy Wall Street*. New York: It Books.

Glasberg, Davita Silfen. 1987. "International finance capital and the relative autonomy of the state: Mexico's foreign debt crisis." *Research in Political Economy* 10: 83–108.

_____. 1989. *The Power of Collective Purse Strings: The Effect of Bank Hegemony on Corporations and the State*. Berkeley: University of California Press.

_____and Deric Shannon. 2011. *Political Sociology: Oppression, Resistance, and the State*. Los Angeles: Sage.

_____ and Dan Skidmore. 1992. "State policy formation and unintended consequences: Bank deregulation and the savings and loan crisis." Paper presented at the annual meeting of the American Sociological Association, Pittsburgh.

_____and Dan Skidmore. 1997. *Corporate Welfare Policy and the Welfare State: Bank Deregulation and the Savings and Loan Bailout*. New York: Aldine de Gruyter.

_____ and Kathryn B. Ward. 1993. "Foreign debt and economic growth in the world system." *Social Science Quarterly* 74(4): 703–720.

Glass, Jennifer L., and Sara Beth Estes. 1997. "The family responsive workplace." *Annual Review of Sociology* 23: 289–313.

Glassner, Barry. 1988. *Bodies*. New York: Putnam.

Glazer, Morton Peretz, and Penina Migdal Glazer. 1999. "On the trail of courageous behavior." *Sociological Inquiry* 69(2): 276–295.

Glazer, Nona Y. 1987. "Servants to capital: Unpaid domestic labor and paid work." Pages 236–255 in Naomi Gerstel and Harriet Engel Gross (eds.), *Families and Work*. Philadelphia: Temple University Press.

Glick, Jennifer E., and Jennifer Van Hook. 2011. "Does a house divided stand? Kinship and the continuity of shared living arrangements." *Journal of Marriage and Family* 73(5): 1149–1164.

Glusker, Susannah. 1998. "Women networking for peace and survival in Chiapas: Militants, celebrities, academics, survivors, and the Stiletto Heel Brigade." 39(7–8): 539–557.

Goffman, Erving. 1961. *Asylums: Essays on the Social Situation of Mental Patients and Other Inmates*. Chicago: Aldine.

_____. 1963. *Stigma: Notes on the Management of Spoiled Identity*. Englewood Cliffs, NJ: Prentice-Hall.

Goidel, Kirby, Stephen Procopio, Dek Terrel, and D. Denis Wu. 2010. "Sources of economic news and economic expectations." *American Politics Research* 38(4): 759–777.

Goldsmith, Jack, and Tim Wu. 2008. *Who Controls the Internet? Illusions of a Borderless World*. New York: Oxford University Press.

Goode, Erich. 1996. "The ethics of deception in social research: A case study." *Qualitative Sociology* 19(1): 11–33.

Goodwin, M. H. 1980. "Directive-response sequences in girls' and boys' task activities." Pages 157–173 in S. McConnell-Ginet, R. Borker, and N. Furman (eds.), *Women and Language in Literature and Society*. New York: Praeger.

Gopaul-McNicol, Sharon-Ann. 1988. "Racial identification and racial preference of black pre-school children in New York and Trinidad." *Journal of Black Psychology* 14(February): 65–68.

Gordon, Linda. 1988. *Heroes of Their Own Lives*. New York: Viking Penguin.

Gordon, Mary. 2003. "Wall Street firms to pay 1.4b in SEC deal." Associated Press Online, April 29.

Goslee, Susan. 1998. "Losing ground bit by bit: Low-income communities in the information age." Washington, DC: Benton Foundation (www.benton.org/library/low-income).

Gossett, Thomas F. 1997. *Race: The History of an Idea in America*, Rev. ed. New York: Oxford University Press.

Gould, Kenneth A. 1993. "Pollution and perception: Social visibility and local environmental mobilization." *Qualitative Sociology* 16(2): 157–178.

Gould, Stephen J. 1996. *The Mismeasure of Man*, Rev. ed. New York: W. W. Norton.

Gouldner, Alvin W. 1970. *The Coming Crisis of Western Sociology*. New York: Avon.

Gow, Joe. 1996. "Reconsidering gender roles on MTV: Depictions in the most popular music videos of the early 1990s." *Communication Reports* 9(2): 151–161.

Grall, Timothy S. 2011. "Custodial mothers and fathers and their child support: 2009." *Current Population Reports* P60-240. Washington, DC: U.S. Department of Commerce, U.S. Census Bureau.

Gramsci, Antonio. 1971. *Selections from the Prison Notebooks*. New York: International Publishers.

Granovetter, Mark S. 1973. "The strength of weak ties." *American Journal of Sociology* 78(May): 1360–1380.

Grant, Carl A., and Christine F. Sleeter. 1988. "Race, class and gender and abandoned dreams." *Teachers College Record* 90(1)(Fall): 19–40.

Green, Charles, and Ian Isidore Smart. 1997. "Ebonics as cultural resistance." *Peace Review* 9(4): 521–526.

Greenberg, Bradley, and Jeffrey E. Brand. 1993. "Television news and advertising in schools: The 'Channel One' controversy." *Journal of Communication* 43(1): 143–151.

Greenberg, David F. 1988. *The Construction of Homosexuality*. Chicago: University of Chicago Press.

_____ (ed.). 1993. *Crime and Capitalism: Readings in Marxist Criminology*. Philadelphia: Temple University Press.

Greenhouse, Linda. 2003a. "Justices back affirmative action by 5 to 4." *New York Times*, June 24, p. A1.

Greenhouse, Linda. 2003b. "Justices, 6-3, legalize gay sexual conduct." *New York Times*, June 27, p. A1.

Greenhouse, Steven. 2001. "Child care, the perk of tomorrow?" *New York Times* May 13 (Week in Review).

Griffin, Keith. 1979. "Underdevelopment in history." Pages 77–90 in Charles K. Wilber (ed.), *The Political Economy of Development and Underdevelopment*, 2nd ed. New York: Random House.

Grossman, Dave, and Gloria DeGaetano. 1999. *Stop Teaching Our Kids to Kill: A Call to Action Against TV, Movie, and Video Game Violence*. New York: Crown Publishers.

Grunseit, Anne, Susan Kippax, Peter Aggleton, Mariella Baldo, and Gary Slutkin. 1997. "Sexuality education and young people's sexual behavior: A review of studies." *Journal of Adolescent Research* 12(4): 421–453.

Guberman, Nancy. 1999. "Daughters-in-law as caregivers: How and why do they come to care?" *Journal of Women and Aging* 11(1): 85–102.

Gunter, Whitney D., and Kevin Daly. 2012. "Causal or spurious: Using propensity score matching to detangle the relationship between violent video games and violent behavior." *Computers in Human Behavior* 28(4): 1348–1355.

Gutman, Herbert G. 1977. *Work, Culture, and Society in Industrializing America*. New York: Vintage.

Guy-Sheftall, Beverly, and Johnetta Betsch Cole (eds.). 1995. *Words of Fire: An Anthology of African-American Feminist Thought*. New York: New Press.

Hackett, Robert, and Megan Adam. 1999. "Is media democratization a social movement? *Peace Review* 11(1): 125–131.

Hagan, John. 1994. *Crime and Disrepute*. Thousand Oaks, CA: Pine Forge Press.

-----------. 1997. "Crime and capitalization: Toward a developmental theory of street crime in America." Pages 287–308 in Terence P. Thornberry (ed.), *Developmental Theories of Crime and Delinquency*. New Brunswick, NJ: Transaction.

Hagedorn, John M. 1998. "Gang violence in the postindustrial era." *Crime and Justice* 24: 365-419.

Hall, Kira, and Mary Bucholtz (eds.). 1995. *Gender Articulated: Language and the Socially Constructed Self*. New York: Routledge.

Hall, Stuart, and Paul du Gay (eds). 1996. *Questions of Cultural Identity*. Thousand Oaks, CA: Sage.

Haller, William J., and Vijai P. Singh. 1996. "Technology, producer services, and the new international division of labor." *Journal of Developing Societies* 12(1): 4–18.

Halprin, Sara. 1995. *Look at My Ugly Face: Myths and Musings on Beauty and Other Perilous Obsessions with Women's Appearance*. New York: Viking.

Hamilton, Cynthia. 1995. "Industrial racism, the environmental crisis, and the denial of social justice." Pages 189–196 in *Cultural Politics and Social Movements*, edited by Marcy Darnovsky, Barbara Epstein, and Richard Flacks. Philadelphia, PA: Temple University Press.

Hamilton, James T. 1995. "Testing for environmental racism: Prejudice, profits, political power?" *Journal of Policy Analysis and Management* 14(1): 107–132.

Hamilton, Richard. 1972. *Class and Politics in the United States*. New York: Wiley.

Hamper, Ben. 1991. *Rivethead: Tales from the Assembly Line*. New York: Warner Books.

Hampton, Robert L. et al (eds.). 1993. *Family Violence*. Newbury Park, CA: Sage Publications.

Hanania, Joseph. 1999. "Playing princesses, punishers and prudes." *The New York Times* March 7: 35, 38.

Handleman, David. 1990. "ACT UP in Anger." *Rolling Stone* (March 8): 80 ff.

Hanson, Thomas L., Sara S. McLanahan, and Elizabeth Thomson. 1998. "Windows on divorce: Before and after." *Social Science Research* 27(3): 329–349.

Harkness, Sara, and Charles M. Super (eds). 1996. *Parents' Cultural Belief Systems: Their Origins, Expressions, and Consequences*. New York: Guilford Press.

Harrigan, John J. 2000. *Empty Dreams, Empty Pockets: Class and Bias in American Politics*. New York: Longman.

Harris, David A. 1999. "Driving while black: Racial profiling on our nation's highways." American Civil Liberties Special Report. (www.aclu.org/profiling/report).

Harrison, Lawrence E. 2000. "Promoting progressive cultural change." Pages 296–307 in *Culture Matters: How Values Shape Human Progress*, edited by Lawrence E. Harrison and Samuel P. Huntington. New York: Basic Books.

Hartman, Andrew. 2003. "Language as oppression: The English-only movement in the United States." *Socialism and Democracy* 171: 187–208.

Harvard Law Review. 1988. "Developments in the law: Race and the criminal process." 101: 1472.

Hatfield, Heather. 2003. "Toxic communities: Environmental racism." Available at www.cbcf-health.org

Hautzinger, Sarah. 2003. "Researching men's violence: Personal reflections on ethnographic data." *Men and Masculinities* 6(1): 93–106.

Havens, Timothy. 2000. "'The biggest show in the world': Race and the global popularity of *The Cosby Show*." *Media Culture and Society* 22(4): 371–391.

Hawdon, James E. 1999. "Daily routines and crime: Using routine activities as measures of Hirschi's involvement." *Youth and Society* 30(4): 395–415.

Hawkesworth, Marian. 2001. "Disabling spatialities and the regulation of a visible secret." *Urban Studies* 38(2): 299–318.

Hayashi, Reiko, and Masako Okuhira. 2001. "The disability rights movement in Japan: Past, present, and future." *Disability and Society* 16(6): 855–869.

Hayes, Thomas C. 1991. "Earnings soar 75% at Exxon." *New York Times* (April 25): D1, D10.

Healey, Kerry, and Christine Smith with Chris O'Sullivan. 1998. "Batterer intervention: Program approaches and criminal justice strategies." U.S. Department of Justice, Office of Justice Programs, National Institute of Justice.

Hearn, Jeff. 2012. "A multifaceted power analysis of men's violence to known women: From hegemonic masculinity to the hegemony of men." *The Sociological Review* 60(4): 589–610.

Heintz, James, Nancy Folbre, and the Center for Popular Economics. 2000. *The Ultimate Field Guide to the U.S. Economy: A Compact and Irreverent Guide to Economic Life in America*. New York: The New Press. Held, David, Anthony McGrew, David Goldblatt, and Jonathan Perraton. 1999. *Global Transformations: Politics, Economics, and Culture*. Stanford, CA: Stanford University Press.

Hellman, 2000. www.cdi.org/issues/usmi/complex/top15fy99.html.

Helman, Ruth, Mathew Greenwald and Associates, Nevin Adams, Craig Copeland, and Jack VanDerhel. 2013. "The 2013 Retirement Confidence Survey: Perceived Savings Needs Outpace Reality for Many." Employee Benefit Research Institute. Available at www.ebri.org/surveys/rcs .

Hemenway, David, Tomoko Shinoda-Tagawa, and Matthew Miller. 2002. "Firearm availability and female homicide victimization rates among 25 populous high-income countries." *Journal of the American Medical Women's Association* 57(2).

Henderson, Maureen J. 2012. "Careers are dead. Welcome to your low-wage, temp work future." *Forbes*. Available at www.forbes.com

Henry, Jules. 1963. *Culture against Man*. New York: Vintage Books.

Herman, Edward S., and Noam Chomsky. 1988. *Manufacturing Consent: The Political Economy of the Mass Media*. New York: Pantheon.

Hesse-Biber, Sharlene. 1996. *Am I Thin Enough Yet? The Cult of Thinness and the Commercialization of Identity*. New York: Oxford University Press.

Hibbard, David R., and Duane Buhrmester. 1998. "The role of peers in the socialization of gender-related social interaction styles." *Sex Roles* 39(3-4): 185–202.

Hill, Nancy. 1997. "Does parenting differ based on social class? African American women's perceived socialization for achievement." *American Journal of Community Psychology* 25(5): 675–697.

Hill, Shirley. 1999. *African American Children: Socialization and Development in Families*. Thousand Oaks, CA: Sage Publications.

Hilts, Philip J. 1993. "Why whistle-blowers can seem a little crazy." *New York Times* (June 13): E6.

Hind, John A., and Michael Reese. 1998. "The distribution of environmental quality: An empirical analysis." *Social Science Quarterly* 79(4): 693–716.

Hirschi, Travis. 1969. *Causes of Delinquency*. Berkeley: University of California Press.

Ho, Mae-Wan. 2000. *Genetic Engineering: Dream or Nightmare? Turning the Tide on the Brave New World of Bad Science and Big Business*. New York: Continuum.

Hochschild, Arlie. 1997. *The Time Bind: When Work Becomes Home and Home Becomes Work*. New York: Metropolitan Books.

_____, with Anne Machung. 1997. *The Second Shift: Working Parents and the Revolution at Home*. New York: Avon Books.

_____. 2012. *The Second Shift: Working Parents and the Revolution at Home*, Rev. ed. New York: Penguin Books.

Hodson, Randy. 1991. "The active worker: Compliance and autonomy at the workplace." *Journal of Contemporary Ethnography* 20 (April): 47–78.

_____. 1995. "Worker resistance: An undeveloped concept in the sociology of work." *Economic and Industrial Democracy* 16 (1): 79–110.

_____. 2001. *Dignity at Work*. New York: Cambridge University Press.

_____, and Teresa A. Sullivan. 1990. *The Social Organization of Work*. Belmont, CA: Wadsworth.

Hoffman, Bruce. 1995. "'Holy terror': The implications of terrorism motivated by a religious imperative." *Studies in Conflict and Terrorism* 18(4): 271–284.

Hohenemser, Christopher, and Ortwin Renn. 1988. "Chernobyl's other legacy." *Environment* 30(April): 5.

Holden, Karen C. 1990. *Social Security Policy and the Income Shock of Widowhood*. Working Paper No. 3, Madison, WI: University of Wisconsin, Institute of Public Affairs.

_____, R. V. Burkhauser, and D. J. Feaster. 1988. "The timing of falls into poverty after retirement and widowhood." *Demography* 25: 405–414.

_____ and Pamela J. Smock. 1991. "The economic costs of marital dissolution: Why do women bear a disproportionate cost?" *Annual Review of Sociology* 17: 51–78.

Holland, Kelley, and Linda Himelstein. 1995. "The Bankers Trust tapes." *Business Week*, October 16: 106–111.

Holmstrom, Lynda Lytle, David A. Karp, and Paul S. Gray. 2002. "Why laundry, not Hegel? Social class, transition to college, and pathways to adulthood." *Symbolic Interaction* 25(4): 437–462.

Hondagneu-Sotelo, Pierette. 1997. "Affluent players in the informal economy: Employers of paid domestic workers." *International Journal of Sociology and Social Policy* 17 (3/4): 131–159.

_____. 2001. *Domestica: Immigrant Workers Cleaning and Caring in the Shadows of Affluence*. Berkeley, CA: University of California Press.

Hooks, bell. 1981. *Ain't I a Woman: Black Women and Feminism*. Boston: South End Press.

Hooks, Gregory. 1991. *Forging the Military-Industrial Complex: World War II's Battle of the Potomac*. Urbana and Chicago: University of Illinois Press.

Horowitz, Irving Louis (ed.). 1967. *The Rise and Fall of Project Camelot*. Cambridge, MA: M.I.T. Press.

Hoselitz, Berthold Frank. 1960. *Sociological Aspects of Economic Growth*. Glencoe, IL: Free Press.

Hossfeld, Karen. 1989. "The triple shift: Immigrant women workers and the household division of labor in Silicon Valley." Paper presented at the annual meeting of the American Sociological Association, Atlanta.

Houppert, Karen. 1999. "You're not entitled! Welfare 'reform' is leading to government lawlessness." *The Nation* October 25: 11–18.

Houston, Brant and Jack Ewing. 1991. "Justice jailed." *Hartford (CT) Courant*, June 16:A1, A10-11.

Houston, Brant and Jack Ewing. 1992. "Racial inequality still evident in setting of bail." *Hartford (CT) Courant*, May 17:A1, A6.

Howard, Judith A., and Jocelyn A. Hollander. 1997. *Gendered Situations, Gendered Selves: A Gender Lens on Social Psychology*. Thousand Oaks, CA: Sage Publication.

Huber, Melissa S., and Ellen Ernst Kosser. 1999. "Community distress predicting welfare exits: The under-examined factor for families in the United States." *Community, Work and Family* 2(2): 173–186.

Huff, C. Ronald (ed.). 1996. *Gangs in America*. Thousand Oaks, CA: Sage Publications.

Hughes, Bill. 1999. "The constitution of impairment: Modernity and the aesthetic of oppression." *Disability and Society* 14(2):155-72.

Hughes, Diane, and Lisa Chen. 1997. "When and what parents tell children about race: An examination of race-related socialization among African American families." *Applied Developmental Science* 1(4): 200–214.

Hull, Elizabeth. 2006. *The Disenfranchisement of Ex-Felons*. Philadelphia: Temple University Press.

Humphreys, Laud. 1975. *Tearoom Trade*. Chicago: Aldine.

Hungerford, Thomas L. 2001. "The economic consequences of widowhood on elderly women in the United States and Germany." *Gerontologist* 41(1): 103–110.

Hurwitz, Roger. 1999. "Who needs politics? Who needs people? The ironies of democracy in cyberspace." *Contemporary Sociology* 28(6): 655–661.

Ichilov, Orit. 2002. "Citizenship perceptions of Soviet immigrants in Israel." *International Review of Sociology* 12(1): 5–22.

International Labour Organization. 2013. "More than 52 million domestic workers worldwide." January 9. Available at www.ilo.org

Isaac, T. M. Thomas, Richard W. Franke, and Pyaralal Raghavan. 1998. *Democracy at Work in an Indian Industrial Cooperative*. Ithaca, NY: Cornell University Press.

Iyengar, Shanto. 1990. "The accessibility bias in politics: Television news and public opinion." *International Journal of Public Opinion Research* 2(1): 1–15.

Jackall, Robert. 1988. *Moral Mazes: The World of Corporate Managers*. New York: Oxford University Press.

_____ , and Henry M. Levin (eds.). 1984. *Worker Cooperatives in America*. Berkeley: University of California Press.

Jackson, Janine. 2000. "Anything but racism: Media make excuses for 'whitewashed' TV lineup." www.fair.org/extra/0001/tv-racism.html .

Jaffee, David. 2002. *Organization Theory: Tension and Change*. New York: McGraw-Hill.

Jans, Lita, and Susan Stoddard. 1999. *Chartbook on Women and Disability in the United States*. Washington, DC: U.S. Office of Education.

Jargowsky, Paul A. 1988. *Poverty and Place: Ghettos, Barrios, and the American City*. New York: Russell Sage Foundation.

Jencks, Christopher, and Meredith Phillips (eds.). 1998. *The Black-White Test Score Gap*. Washington, DC: Brookings Institute.

Jenkins, J. Craig and Charles Perrow. 1977. "Insurgency of the powerless: Farm workers movements, 1946-72." *American Sociological Review* 42(2):249-68.

Jensen, Carl J. III. 2001. "Beyond the tea leaves: Futures research and terrorism." *American Behavioral Scientist* 44(6): 914–936.

Jessop, Bob. 1990. *State Theory: Putting the Capitalist State in Its Place*. University Park: Pennsylvania State University Press.

Jewell, K. Sue. 1993. *From Mammy to Miss America and Beyond*. New York: Routledge.

Jilani, Zaid. 2011. "Profits at largest 500 corporations grew by 81 percent in 2010." *Think Progress*, May 5. Available at www.thinkprogress.org

John, Daphne, Beth Anne Shelton, and Kristen Luschen. 1995. "Race, ethnicity, gender, and perceptions of fairness." *Journal of Family Issues* 16(3): 357–379.

Johnson, Allan G. 1997. *The Forest and the Trees: Sociology as Life, Practice, and Promise*. Philadelphia: Temple University Press.

_____ . 2001. *Privilege, Power, and Difference*. Mountain View, CA: Mayfield.

Johnson, Bradley. 1989. "California moves to ban Whittle's 'Channel One.'" *Advertising Age* 60 (May 29): 1, 48.

Johnson, Dirk. 1990. "More prisons using iron hand to control inmates." *New York Times* (November 1).

Johnson, James E., James F. Christie, and Thomas D. Yawkey. 1999. *Play and Early Childhood Development*. New York: Longman.

_____ , Walter C. Farrell Jr., and Jennifer A. Stoloff. 2000. "An empirical assessment of four perspectives on the declining fortunes of the African American male." *Urban Affairs Review* 35 (May): 708–709.

Jones, Christopher M. 2001. "Roles, politics and the survival of the V-22 Osprey." *Journal of Political and Military Sociology* 29(1): 46–72.

Jones, Jacqueline. 1987. "Black women, work, and the family under slavery." Pages 84–110 in Naomi Gerstel and Harriet Engel Gross (eds.), *Families and Work*. Philadelphia: Temple University Press.

Joppke, Christian. 1993. *Mobilizing against Nuclear Energy: A Comparison of Germany and the United States*. Berkeley: University of California Press.

Judd, Neville. 2001. "USA/India: Toxic shipment under fire." Available at www.corpwatch.org

Kagan, Jerome, J. Steven Resnick, and Nancy Snidman. 1988. "Biological bases of childhood shyness." *Science* 240(April 1): 167–171.

Kallianes, Virginia, and Phyllis Rubenfeld. 1997. "Disabled women and reproductive rights." *Disability and Society* 12(2): 203–221.

Kane, Connie. 2000. "African American family dynamics as perceived by family members." *Journal of Black Studies* 30(5): 691–702.

Kane, Michael B. 1970. *Minorities in Textbooks: A Study of Their Treatment in Social Science Texts*. Chicago: Quadrangle.

Kanfer, Stefan. 1993. *The Last Empire: De Beers, Diamonds, and the World*. New York: Farrar Straus Giroux.

Kaplan, Howard B., Robert J. Johnson, and Carol A. Bailey. 1987. "Deviant peers and deviant behavior: Further elaborations of a model." *Social Psychology Quarterly* 50(4): 227–252.

Katz, Jesse. 2000. "For many felons, voting ban is forever." *Hartford Courant* (April 26): A12.

Kendall, Diana. 2002. *The Power of Good Deeds: Privileged Women and the Social Reproduction of the Upper Class*. New York: Rowman and Littlefield.

Kennedy, Paul. 1987. *The Rise and Fall of the Great Powers*. New York: Random House.

Kennedy, Randall. 1997. *Race, Crime, and the Law*. New York: Pantheon Books.

Kerbo, Harold R2011. *Social Stratification and Inequality: Class Conflict in Historical, Comparative, and Global Perspective*, 8th ed. New York: McGraw-Hill.

Kerby, Sophia. 2012. "1in 3 Black men go to prison? The 10 most disturbing facts about racial inequality in the U.S. criminal justice system." Available at www.alernet.org

Kibria, Nazli. 2002. "Vietnamese families." In Ronald L. Taylor (ed.), *Minority Families in the United States: A Multicultural Perspective*, 3rd ed. Upper Saddle River, NJ: Prentice Hall/ Pearson.

Kilbride, Howard W., David L. Johnson, and Ann Pytkowicz Streissguth. 1977. "Social class, birth order, and newborn experience." *Child Development* 48(4)(December): 1686–1688.

Kim, Jeounghee. 2010. "A diverging trend in marital dissolution by income status." *Journal of Divorce and Remarriage* 51(7): 396–412.

Kim, Marlene. 2000. "Women paid low wages: Who they are and where they work." *Monthly Labor Review* September: 26-30.

Kimmel, Michael S. 2000. *The Gendered Society*. New York: Oxford University Press.

Kindlon, Daniel J., Michael Thompson, with Teresa Barker. 2000. *Raising Cain: Protecting the Emotional Life of Boys*. New York: Ballantine Books.

Kinsey, Alfred, Wardell Pomeroy, and Clyde Martin. 1948. *Sexual Behavior in the Human Male*. Philadelphia: Saunders.

————, ————, ————, and Paul Gebhard. 1953. *Sexual Behavior in the Human Female*. Philadelphia: Saunders.

Kirby, Douglas, and B.S. Lans. 2009. "Effective curriculum-based sex and STD/HIV education programs for adolescents." *Child Development Perspectives* 3(1): 21–29.

Kirschenman, Joleen, and Kathryn M. Neckerman. 1991. "'We'd love to hire them, but': The meaning of race for employers." Pages 203–232 in Christopher Jencks and Paul E. Peterson (eds.), *The Urban Underclass*. Washington, DC: Brookings Institution.

Kisker, E. E. 1985. "Teenagers talk about sex, pregnancy, and contraception." *Family Planning Perspectives* 17(2): 83–90.

Klandermans, Bert, Marlene Roefs, and Johan Olivier. 2001. "Grievance formation in a country in transition: South Africa, 1994–1998." *Social Psychology Quarterly* 64(1): 41–54.

Kleinman, Sherryl. 2002. "Why sexist language matters." *Qualitative Sociology* 25: 299–304.

Kleinman, Sherryl, Matthew B. Ezzell and A. Corey Frost. 2009. "Reclaiming critical analysis: The social harms of 'Bitch'." *Sociological Analysis* 3: 47–68.

Knee, Jonathan A. 2003. "False alarm at the FCC: Ending TV-newspaper cross-ownership rules may have little effect." Available at www.cjr.org/year/03/3/knee

Kohn, Melvin. 1977. *Social Competence, Symptoms and Underachievement in Childhood: A Longitudinal Perspective*. Washington, DC: Winston.

Koretz, Gene. 2001. "Why married men earn more." *Business Week* (September 17).

Korgen, Kathleen Odell. 1998. *From Black to Biracial: Transforming Racial Identity Among Americans*. Westport, CT: Praeger.

Kubitschek, Warren N., and Maureen T. Hallinan. 1996. "Race, gender, and inequity in track assignments." *Research in Sociology of Education and Socialization* 11: 121–146.

Kumamoto, Robert. 1991. "Diplomacy from below: International terrorism and American foreign relations, 1945–1962." *Terrorism* 14(1): 31–48.

Kunemund, Harald. 2006. "Changing welfare states and the 'sandwich generation': Increasing burden for the next generation?" *International Journal of Aging and Later Life* 1(2): 11–29.

Kurz, Demie. 2001. "Violence against women by intimate partners." Pages 205–215 in Dana Vannoy (ed.), *Gender Mosaics: Social Perspectives*. Los Angeles: Roxbury.

Lacayo, Richard. 1990. "Why no blue blood will flow: On the front lines, a disproportionate number of troops hail from minorities and the working class." *Time* (November 26): 34.

LaDuke, Winona. 1999. *All Our Relations: Native Struggles For Land and Life*. Cambridge, MA: South End Press.

Lamb, Michael E. (ed.). 1997. *The Role of the Father in Child Development*. New York: Wiley.

LaPlante, Mitchell P. 1996. "Disability and employment." Abstract 11 (January). San Francisco: Disability Statistics Center, University of California.

Lappe, Frances Moore, and Joseph Collins. 1986. *World Hunger: Twelve Myths*. New York and San Francisco:

Lasch, Christopher. 1977. *Haven in a Heartless World: The Family Besieged*. New York: Basic Books.

Lawson, Steven F. 1990. *Running for Freedom: Civil Rights and Black Politics in America since 1941*. Philadelphia: Temple University Press.

Lay, Mary M. et al (eds.). 2000. *Body Talk: Rhetoric, Technology, Reproduction*. Madison: University of Wisconsin Press.

Leckie, Robert. 1992. *The Wars of America*. New York: Harper Collins.

Lee, Charles. 1992. "Toxic waste and race in the United States." Pages 10–27 in B. Bryant and P. Mohai (eds.), *Race and the Incidence of Environmental Hazards: A Time for Discourse*. Boulder, CO: Westview Press.

_____. 1994. "Beyond toxic wastes and race." Pages 41–52 in Robert D. Bullard (ed.), *Confronting Environmental Racism: Voices from the Grassroots*. Boston: South End Press.

Lemert, Edwin M. 1967. *Human Deviance, Social Problems, and Social Control*. Englewood Cliffs, NJ: Prentice-Hall.

Lengermann, Patricia Madoo, and Jill Niebrugge. 2000. "Contemporary feminist theory," Pages 436-486 in George Ritzer, *Sociological Theory*, 4th ed. New York: McGraw-Hill.

_____. 2007. *The Women Founders: Sociology and Social Theory, 1830–1930*. Long Grove, IL: Waveland Press.

Lenski, Gerhard. 1966. *Power and Privilege*. New York: McGraw-Hill.

_____, Jean Lenski, and Patrick Nolan. 1991. *Human Societies: An Introduction to Macro-sociology*. New York: McGraw-Hill.

Lev, Michael A. 2000. "China's One-Child Rule: The Next Generation." *Hartford Courant* (May 1): B7.

Levine, Rhonda. 1988. *Class Struggle and the New Deal: Industrial Labor, Industrial Capital and the State*. Lawrence: University Press of Kansas.

Levine, Suzanne Braun. 2000. *Father Courage: What Happens When Men Put Family First*. New York: Harcourt.

Lewis, Oscar. 1959. *Five Families: Mexican Case Studies in the Culture of Poverty*. New York: Basic Books.

Lichtensztejn, Samuel, and Jose Manuel Quijano. 1982. "The external indebtedness of the developing countries to international private banks." Pages 185–265 in J. C. Sanchez Arnau (ed.), *Debt and Development*. New York: Praeger.

Lichter, S. Robert, and Daniel R. Amundson, 1997. "Distorted reality: Hispanic characters in TV entertainment." Pages 57–72 in Clara Rodriguez (ed.), *Latin Looks*. Boulder, CO: Westview Press.

Liebow, Elliot. 1967. *Tally's Corner: A Study of Negro Streetcorner Men*. Boston: Little, Brown.

"Life sentence in dragging death." 1999. *Washington Post* (November 19): A32.

Ligos, Melinda. 2000. "The Fear of Taking Paternity Leave." *New York Times* (May 31): G1.

Lindsey, Linda L., and Sandra Christy. 1996. *Gender Roles: A Sociological Perspective*, 3rd ed. Upper Saddle River, NJ: Prentice-Hall.

Ling, Nan. 2000. "Inequality in social capital." *Contemporary Sociology* 29 (November): 785–795.

Link, Bruce G. et al. 1987. "The social rejection of former mental patients: Understanding why labels matter." *American Journal of Sociology* 92(May): 1461–1500.

Linton, Simi. 1998. *Claiming Disability: Knowledge and Identity*. New York: New York University Press.

Lipset, Seymour Martin. 1960. *Political Man: The Social Bases of Politics*. Garden City, NY: Doubleday.

_____. 1990. *Continental Divide: The Values and Institutions of the United States and Canada*. New York, London: Routledge.

Lipsitz, George. 1998. *The Possessive Investment in Whiteness: How White People Profit from Identity Politics*. Philadelphia: Temple University Press.

Liska, Allen E., and Steven F. Messner. 1998. *Perspectives on Crime and Deviance*. Upper Saddle River, NJ: Prentice Hall.

Litwak, Eugene. 1965. "Extended kin relations in an industrial democratic society." Pages 290–323 in Ethel Shanas and Gordon T. Strieb (eds.), *Social Structure and the Family: Generational Relations*. Englewood Cliffs, NJ: Prentice-Hall.

Lockard, J. 1997. "Progressive politics, electronic individualism, and the myth of virtual community." Pages 219–32 in D. Porter (ed.), *Internet Culture*. New York: Routledge.

Loewen, James W. 1995. *Lies My Teacher Told Me: Everything Your American History Textbook Got Wrong*. New York: New Press.

Lofstrom, Jan. 1998. "Introduction: Sketching the framework for a history and sociology of homosexualities in the Nordic countries." *Journal of Homosexuality* 35(3-4): 1-13.

Logue, John. 1998. "Rustbelt buyouts: Why Ohio leads in worker ownership." *Dollars and Sense* (September-October): 34-38.

Long, Patrick Du Phuoc, and Laura Ricard. 1996. *The Dream Shattered: Vietnamese Gangs in America*. Boston: Northeastern University Press.

Lonsdale, Susan. 1990. *Women and Disability*. New York: St. Martin's Press.

Lont, Cynthia M. 2001. "The influence of the media on gender images." Pages 114-122 in Dana Vannoy (ed.), *Gender Mosaics: Social Perspectives*. Los Angeles: Roxbury.

Loos, Eugene. 2012. "Senior citizens: Digital immigrants in their own country?" *Observatorio (OBS)* 6(1): 1-23.

Lopez Haney, Ian. 2006. *White By Law: The Legal Construction of Race* (revised and updated). New York: NYU Press.

Lopreato, Joseph, and Timothy Crippen. 1999. *Crisis in Sociology: The Need for Darwin*. New Brunswick, NJ: Transaction Publishers.

Losse, Kate. 2013. "Feminism's tipping point: Who wins from leaning in?" *Dissent*, March 26. Available at www.dissentmagazine.org

Lowe, Marcia D. 1994. "Reinventing transport." Pages 81–98 in Lester R. Brown (ed.), *State of the World, 1994*. New York: Norton.

Luban, David. 2005. "Eight fallacies about liberty and security." Pages 242-57 in Richard Ashby Wilson (ed.), *Human Rights in the 'War on Terror.'* New York: Cambridge University Press.

Lucas, Samuel R. 1999. *Tracking Inequality: Stratification and Mobility in American High Schools*. New York: Columbia University Teachers College Press.

Lugar, Richard, and Joseph Biden. 1998. www.csmonitor.com

Luke, Timothy W. 1997. "The politics of digital inequality: Access, capability, and distribution in cyberspace." *New Political Science* 41-42 (Fall): 121-144.

Luzer, Daniel. 2010. "Economic meltdown causes surge in grad school applications." *Washington Monthly*. Available at www.washingtonmonthly.com

MacArthur, John R. 1992. *Second Front: Censorship and Propaganda in the Gulf War*. Berkeley: University of California Press.

MacLeod, Greg. 1997. *From Mondragon to America: Experiments in Community Development*. Nova Scotia: University of College of Cape Bretton Press.

Madrid, Arturo. 1992. "Missing people and others." Pages 6–11 in Margaret L. Andersen and Patricia Hill Collins (eds.), *Race, Class, and Gender*. Belmont, CA: Wadsworth.

Magnussen, Paul, with Nicole Harris, Linda Himmelstein, Biull Vlasic, and Wendy Zellner. 1997. "A wake-up call for business." *Business Week* (September 1): 28–29.

Maher, Timothy. 1998. "Environmental oppression: Who is targeted for toxic exposure?" *Journal of Black Studies* 28(3): 357–367.

Mahler, Jonathan. 2003. "Commute to nowhere: In a new kind of recession, out-of-work executives are being forced to rethink their professional identities, their personal relationships–and their most fundamental sense of who they are." *New York Times Magazine* (April 13): 44–49+.

Majors, Richard, David Gillborn, and Tony Sewell. 2001. "The exclusion of Black children: Implications for a racialized perspective." Pages 105–109 in Richard Majors, David Gillborn, and Tony Sewell (eds.), *Educating Our Black Children*. London: RoutledgeFalmer.

Majoribanks, Kevin. 1987. "Gender/social class, family environments and adolescents' aspirations." Australian Journal of Education 31(1):43-54.

Malley, Sara, Jennifer Scroggins, and Stephanie A. Bohon. 2012. "U.S. EPA enforcement of environmental regulations in Tennessee: 2005–2008." *Society and Natural Resources* 25(1): 87–96.

Maltz, D. N., and R. A. Borker. 1983. "A cultural approach to male-female miscommunication." Pages 195–216 in J. J. Gumperz (ed.), *Language and Social Identity*. New York: Cambridge University Press.

Mann, Coramae Richey, and Marjorie S. Zatz (eds.). 2002. *Images of Color, Images of Crime*. Los Angeles, CA: Roxbury Publishing Company.

Manning, Robert D. 2000. *Credit Card Nation: The Consequences of America's Addiction to Credit*. New York: Basic Books.

Manning, Steven. 1999. "Students for sale: How corporations are buying their way into America's classrooms." *The Nation* (September 27): 11–18.

Manza, Jeff and Christopher Uggen. 2008. *Locked Out: Felon Disenfranchisement and American Democracy*. New York: Oxford University Press.

Marcus, Eric. 1999. *Is It a Choice?: Answers to 300 of the Most Frequently Asked Questions about Gay and Lesbian People*, Rev. ed. San Francisco, CA: Harper SanFrancisco.

Markopolos, Harry. 2011. *No One Would Listen: A True Financial Thriller*. New York: Wiley.

Marks, Donovan, and Nicole Brown. 1990. "The next link in the dumping chain." Pages 32–33 in Dana Alston (ed.), *We Speak for Ourselves: Social Justice, Race and Environment*. Washington, DC: Panos Institute.

Martins, Nicole, and Barbara J. Wilson. 2012. "Social aggression on television and its relationship to children's aggression in the classroom." *Human Communication Research* 38(1): 48–71.

Marx, Karl. 1844/1964. *Economic and Philosophic Manuscripts of 1844*. Trans. Martin Milligan. New York: International Publishers.

_____ and Friederich Engels. 1848/1967. *The Communist Manifesto*. Baltimore: Penguin.

Massey, Douglas S. 2002. *Beyond Smoke and Mirrors: Mexican Immigration in an Era of Economic Integration*. New York: Russell Sage Foundation.

_____, and Nancy A. Denton. 1993. *American Apartheid: Segregation and the Making of the Underclass*. Cambridge, MA: Harvard University Press.

Mater, Gene P. 1989. "Monday memo." *Broadcasting* 117(July 10): 23.

Mauer, Marc. 1999. *Race to Incarcerate*. New York: New Press.

Maume, David J., Jr. 1999. "Glass ceilings and glass escalators: Occupational segregation and race and sex differences in managerial promotions." *Work and Occupations* 26(4): 483–509.

_____. 2001. "Work-family conflict: Effects for job segregation and career perceptions." Pages 240–248 in Dana Vannoy (ed.), *Gender Mosaics: Social Perspectives*. Los Angeles: Roxbury.

Mayer, Colin. 2001. "Financial institutions and the institutional foundations of a market economy." Available at www.dse.de/ef/omstm/mayer.htm

McAdam, Doug. 1982. *Political Process and the Development of Black Insurgency, 1930–1970*. Chicago: University of Chicago Press.

_____. 1988. *Freedom Summer*. New York: Oxford University Press.

_____. 1999. *Political Process and the Development of Black Insurgency, 1930–1970*. Chicago: University of Chicago Press.

McAllister, Matthew P. 1996. *The Commercialization of American Culture: New Advertising, Control, and Democracy*. Thousand Oaks, CA: Sage

McCarthy, John D., and Mark Wolfson. 1996. "Resource mobilization by local social movement organizations: Agency, strategy, and organization in the movement against drinking and driving." *American Sociological Review* 61(6): 1070–1088.

McChesney, Robert. 1997. "The global media giants: The nine firms that dominate the world." Available at www.fair.org

_____. 1999. *Rich Media, Poor Democracy: Communication Politics in Dubious Times*. Urbana, IL: University of Illinois Press.

_____. 2004. *The Problem of the Media: U.S. Communication Politics in the Twenty-First Century*. New York: Monthly Review Press.

_____. 2008. *The Political Economy of Media: Enduring Issues, Emerging Dilemmas*. New York: Monthly Review Press.

_____. 2013. *Digital Disconnect: How Capitalism is Turning the Internet Against Democracy*. New York: The New Press.

McClellan, Jeffrey A., and Mary Jo V. Pugh (eds.). 1999. *The Role of Peer Groups in Adolescent Social Identity: Exploring the Importance of Stability and Change*. San Francisco: Jossey-Bass Publishers

McFadden, Robert D. 1991. "Degrees and stacks of résumés yield few jobs for class of '91." *New York Times* (April 22): A1, B6.

McGuire, Patrick, and Donald McQuarie (eds.). 1994. *From the Left Bank to the Mainstream: Historical Debates and Contemporary Research in Marxist Sociology*. Chicago: Nelson Hall.

McIntosh, Peggy. 1992. "White privilege and male privilege." Pages 70–81 in Margaret L. Andersen and Patricia Hill Collins (eds.), *Race, Class, and Gender*. Belmont, CA: Wadsworth.

McKean, Benjamin L. 2001. "Harvard's shame." *The Nation* (May 21).

McManus, Patricia A., and Thomas A. DiPrete. 2001. "Losers and winners: The financial consequences of separation and divorce for men." *American Sociological Review* 66(2): 246–268.

McQuiston, John T. 1990. "Dozens are injured in further outbreak of Rikers Island unrest." *New York Times* (August 22): A1.

Mead, George Herbert. 1934. *Mind, Self, and Society*. Chicago: University of Chicago Press.

Mead, Lawrence M. 1992. *The New Politics of Poverty*. New York: Basic Books.

Meadows, Lynn M. 1996. "Discovering women's work: A study of post-retirement aged women." *Marriage and Family Review* 24(1-2): 165–191.

Meeks, Kenneth. 2010. *Driving While Black: Highways, Shopping Malls, Taxi Cabs, Sidewalks: How to Fight Back if You Are a Victim of Racial Profiling*. New York: Broadway.

Mehlman, Maxwell J., and Jeffrey R. Botkin. 1998. *Access to the Genome: The Challenge to Equality*. Washington, DC: Georgetown University Press.

Melman, Seymour. 1997. "From private to state capitalism." www.webcom.com/ncecd

_____. 2001. *After Capitalism: From Managerialism to Workplace Democracy*. New York: Knopf.

Menacker, Fay, and Brady E. Hamilton. 2010. "Recent trends in Cesarean delivery in the United States." U.S. Department of Health and Human Services, Centers for Disease Control and Prevention. Available at www.cdc.gov

Merchant, Jennifer. 1996. "Biogenetics, artificial procreation, and public policy in the United States and France." *Technology in Society* 18(1): 1–15.

Merrill, Deborah M. 1997. *Caring for Elderly Parents: Juggling Work, Family, and Caregiving in Middle and Working Class Families*. Westport, CT: Auburn House.

Merry, Sally Engle. 2002. "Governmentality and gender violence in Hawai'i in historical perspective." *Social and Legal Studies* 11(1): 81–111.

Merton, Robert K. 1957. *Social Theory and Social Structure*. New York: Free Press.

_____. 1968. *Social Theory and Social Structure*, enlarged ed. New York: Free Press.

Messner, Michael A. 2001. "When bodies are weapons: Masculinity and violence in sport." Pages 94–105 in Dana Vannoy (ed.), *Gender Mosaics: Social Perspectives*. Los Angeles: Roxbury.

MetLife. 2011. "Market survey of long-term care costs." Available at www.metlife.com

Meyer, David S. 1993. "Institutionalizing dissent: The United States structure of political opportunity and the end of the nuclear freeze movement." *Sociological Forum* 8(2): 157–180.

_____, and Suzanne Staggenborg. 1996. "Movements, countermovements, and the structure of political opportunity." *American Journal of Sociology* 101(6): 1628–1660.

Meyer, Madonna Harrington. 1996. "Making claims as workers or wives: The distribution of Social Security benefits." *American Sociological Review* 61(3): 449–465.

Michels, Robert. 1962. *Political Parties: A Sociological Study of Oligarchical Tendencies of Modern Democracy*. New York: Free Press.

Miethe, Terance D. 1999. *Whistleblowing at Work: Tough Choices in Exposing Fraud, Waste, and Abuse on the Job*. Boulder, CO: Westview Press.

Milgram, Stanley. 1967. "The small-world problem." *Psychology Today* 1 (1): 60–67.

Miliband, Ralph. 1969. *The State in Capitalist Society*. New York: Basic Books.

Miller, Carol Diana. 1997. *Effects of Economic Development, Trade Dependency, and Debt on Women's Share of the Labor Force: A Cross-National Study*. PhD Dissertation (University of Arizona, Tuscon). Ann Arbor, MI: Dissertation Abstracts.

Miller, Jerome G. 1996. *Search and Destroy: African American Males in the Criminal Justice System*. New York: Cambridge University Press.

Mills, C. Wright. 1957. *The Power Elite*. New York: Oxford University Press.

_____. 1959. *The Sociological Imagination*. New York: Oxford University Press.

Min, Pyong Gap. 1996. *Caught in the Middle: Korean Merchants in America's Multiethnic Cities*. Berkeley, CA: University of California Press.

Mink, Gwendolyn. 2002. *Welfare's End*. Ithaca, NY: Cornell University Press.

Mintz, Beth and Michael Schwartz. 1985. *The Power Structure of American Business*. Chicago: University of Chicago Press.

Mishel, Lawrence, Jared Bernstein, and John Schmitt, 1997. *The State of Working America, 1996-97*. Armonk, NY: M.E. Sharpe.

Mishel, Lawrence and Jacqueline Simon. 1988. *The State of Working America*. Washington, DC: Economic Policy Institute.

_____, Jared Bernstein, and John Schmitt. 2001. *The State of Working America, 2000–2001*. Ithaca, NY: ILR Press.

_____, Josh Bivens, Elise Gould, and Heidi Shierholz. 2012. *The State of Working America*, 12th ed. Ithaca, NY: ILR Press.

Mitchell, Edward W. 2003. *Self-Made Madness: Rethinking Illness and Criminal Responsibility*. London: Ashgate Publishing, LTD.

Mittal, Anuradha, and Peter Rosset (eds.). 1999. *America Needs Human Rights*. Oakland, CA: Food First Books.

Moghadam, Valentine M. 1999. "Gender and the global economy." Pages 128–160 in Myra Marx Ferree, Judith Lorber, and Beth B. Hess (eds.), *Revisioning Gender*. Thousand Oaks, CA: Sage.

Mohai, Paul. 1990. "Black environmentalism." *Social Science Quarterly* 71(4): 744–765.

_____, and Bunyan Bryant. 1992. "Environmental racism: Reviewing the evidence." Pages 163–176 in Bunyan Bryant and Paul Mohai (eds.), *Race and the Incidence of Environmental Hazards: A Time for Discourse*. Boulder, CO: Westview Press.

Molina, Olga. 2000. "African American women's unique divorce experiences." *Journal of Divorce and Remarriage* 32(3-4): 93–99.

Momsen, Janet. 2010. *Gender and Development*. New York: Routledge.

Monaghan, Peter. 1993. "Facing jail, a sociologist raises questions about a scholar's right to protect sources." *Chronicle of Higher Education* (April 7): A10.

Montgomery, James D. 1992. "Job search and network competition: Implications of the strength-of-weak-ties hypothesis." *American Sociological Review* 57 (October): 586–596.

Monti, Daniel J. 1994. *Wannabe: Gangs in Suburbs and Schools*. Cambridge: Blackwell.

Moore, Joan, and John M. Hagedorn. 1996. "What happens to girls in the gang?" Pages 205–218 in *Gangs in America* (2nd edition), edited by Ronald C. Huff. Thousand Oaks, CA: Sage.

Moore, Molly. 1990. "Crossing the culture gulf: For female soldiers, different rules." *Washington Post* (August 23): D1–D2.

Moore, Robert. 2000. "Racism in the English language." Pages 396–407 in Tracy E. Ore (ed.), *The Social Construction of Difference and Inequality: Race, Class, Gender, and Sexuality*. Mountain View, CA: Mayfield Publishing Co.

Morgan, Leslie A. 1991. *After Marriage Ends: Economic Consequences for Midlife Women*. Newbury Park, CA: Sage Publications.

Morris, Aldon D. 1984. *The Origins of the Civil Rights Movement: Black Communities Organizing for Change*. New York: Free Press.

_____. 1999. "A retrospective on the civil rights movement: Political and intellectual landmarks." *Annual Review of Sociology* 25: 517–539.

Morris, Joan, and Michale D. Grimes. 1996. "Contradictions in the childhood socialization of sociologists from the working class." *Race, Gender and Class* 4(1): 63–82.

Morrison, Toni (ed.). 1992. *Race-ing Justice, En-gendering Power: Essays on Anita Hill, Clarence Thomas, and the Social Construction of Reality*. New York: Pantheon.

Mortimer, Jeylan T., and Roberta G. Simmons. 1978. "Adult socialization." Pages 421–454 in Ralph H. Turner, James Coleman, and Renee C. Fox (eds.), *Annual Review of Sociology*, vol. 4. Palo Alto, CA: Annual Reviews.

Morton, Emma, Carol W. Runyan, Kathryn E. Moracco, and John Butts. 1998. "Partner homicide-suicide involving female homicide victims: A population-based study in North Carolina, 1988–1992." *Violence and Victims* 13(2)(summer): 91–106.

Mueller, L. 1977. "Women and men, power and powerlessness in Lesotho." *Signs* 3(1): 154–166.

Muller, Ronald. 1979. "The multinational corporation and the underdevelopment of the third world." Pages 151–178 in Charles Wilber (ed.), *The Political Economy of Development and Underdevelopment*. New York: Random House.

Munch, Allison, J. Miller McPherson, and Lynn Smith-Lovin. 1997 : "Gender, children and social contact: The effects of childrearing for men and women." *American Sociological Review* 62: 509–520.

Murdock, George. 1949. *Social Structure*. New York: Macmillan.

Murray, Stephen O. 2000. *Homosexualities*. Chicago: University of Chicago Press.

Nakano Glenn, Evelyn, and Stacey G.H. Yap. 2002. "Chinese American families." In Ronald L. Taylor (ed.), *Minority Families in the United States: A Multicultural Perspective*, 3rd ed. Upper Saddle River, NJ: Prentice Hall/Pearson.

Nanda, Serena. 1999. *Gender Diversity: Cross Cultural Variations*. New York: Waveland Press.

National Coalition of Anti-Violence Programs. 2002. "Anti-Lesbian, Gay, Transgender and Bisexual Violence in *The National Journal*. 1989. "AFL-CIO calls for legislation to control mergers, ease impact on workers, communities." 21(February 18): 395.

NBC News/Wall Street Journal Poll. 1999. June 16–19.

Neath, Jeanne, and Kay Schriner. 1998. "Power to people with disabilities: Empowerment issues in employment programming." *Disability and Society* 13(2): 217–228.

Neilson, Joyce McCarl, Glenda Walden, and Charlotte A. Kunkel. 2000. "Gendered heteronormativity: Empirical illustrations in everyday life." *Sociological Quarterly* 41(2): 283–96.

Nelson, Fiona. 1999. "Lesbian families: Achieving motherhood." *Journal of Gay and Lesbian Social Services*. 10(1): 27–46.

Nelson, Hilde Lindemann. 2001. *Damaged Identities: Narrative Repair*. Ithaca, NY: Cornell University Press.

Nelson, Margaret K. 1999. "Between paid and unpaid work: Gender patterns in supplemental economic activities among white, rural families." *Gender & Society* 13(4):518-39.

Neubeck, Kenneth J. 2006. *When Welfare Disappears: The Case for Economic Human Rights*. New York: Routledge.

_____, and Mary Alice Neubeck. 1997. *Social Problems: A Critical Approach*, 4th ed. New York: McGraw-Hill.

_____, Mary Alice Neubeck, and Davita Silfen Glasberg. 2006. *Social Problems: A Critical Approach*, 5th ed. New York: McGraw-Hill.

_____, and Noel Cazanave. 2001. *Welfare Racism: Playing the Race Card Against America's Poor*. New York: Routledge.

Neuman, W. Lawrence. 2009. *Social Research Methods: Qualitative and Quantitative Approaches*, 7th ed. Upper Saddle River, NJ: Prentice Hall/Pearson.

New York Times/CBS Poll. 2010. April 5-12.

Newman, Katherine S. 1989. *Falling from Grace: The Experience of Downward Mobility in the American Middle Class*. New York: Vintage.

_____. 1999. *Falling from Grace: Downward Mobility in the Age of Affluence.* Berkeley: University of California Press.

_____ and Victor Tan Chen. 2008. *The Missing Class: Portraits of the Near Poor in America.* Boston: Beacon Press.

Newton, Barbara J., and Elizabeth B. Buck. 1985. "Television as significant other: Its relationship to self-descriptors in five countries." *Journal of Cross-Cultural Psychology* 16(3) (September): 289–312.

Nicholas, George P. 2001. "On representations of race and racism." *Current Anthropology* 42(1): 140–142.

Nichols, John. 2000. "Now what? Seattle is just a start." *The Progressive* (January): 16–19.

Niemonen, Jack. 2002. *Race, Class, and the State in Contemporary Sociology: The William Julius Wilson Debates.* Boulder, CO: Lynne Rienner.

Noble, David. 2001. *Digital Diploma Mills.* New York: Monthly Review.

Norberg, Katarina. 2001. "The constitutive values of Swedish schooling: A challenge to the inner life of schools." *Pedagogy, Culture, and Society* 9(3): 371–386.

North, Liisa. 1988. "The women poor of Peru." *ISIS: International Women's Journal* 17(March): 12–14.

Nosek, Margaret A., and Carol A. Howland. 1998. "Abuse and women with disabilities." *Violence Against Women Online Resources,* www.vaw.umn.edu . February.

Oakes, Jeannie. 1985. *Keeping Track: How Schools Structure Inequality.* New Haven: Yale University Press.

_____. 1990. *Multiplying Inequalities: The Effects of Race, Social Class, and Tracking on Opportunities to Learn Mathematics and Science.* Santa Monica, CA: Rand Corporation.

_____. 1995. Two Cities' Tracking and Within-School Segregation. *Teachers College Record* 96(4): 681–690.

_____, and G. Guiton. 1995. "Matchmaking: The dynamics of high school tracking decisions." *American Educational Research Journal* 32 (Spring): 3–33.

O'Connor, James. 1987. *The Meaning of Crisis: A Theoretical Introduction.* New York: Basil Blackwell.

_____. 1996. "World economy in the 1990s." *Capitalism, Nature, Socialism* 7(1): 113–124.

O'Connor, Lisa A., Jeanne Brooks-Gunn, and Julia Graber. 2000. "Black and white girls' racial preferences in media and peer choices and the role of socialization for black girls." *Journal of Family Psychology* 14(3): 510–521.

Ogburn, William F. 1964. *On Culture and Social Change: Selected Papers* (edited by Otis Dudley Duncan). Chicago: University of Chicago Press.

_____, and Clark Tibbits. 1934. "The family and its functions." Pages 661–708 in *Recent Social Trends in the United States*, edited by Research Committee on Social Trends. New York: McGraw-Hill.

Oliver, Melvin L., and Thomas M. Shapiro. 1995. *Black Wealth/White Wealth: New Perspective on Racial Inequality*. New York: Routledge.

Omi, Michael, and Howard A. Winant. 1986. *Racial Formation in the United States from the 1960s to the 1980s*. New York: Routledge, Chapman & Hall.

_____. 1994. *Racial Formation in the United States: From the 1960s to the 1990s*. New York: Routledge.

O'Neill, Kate. 2000. *Waste Trading Among Rich Nations: Building a New Theory of Environmental Regulation*. Cambridge, MA: MIT Press.

Orcutt, James D. 1983. *Analyzing Deviance*. Chicago: Dorsey Press.

Ore, Tracy E. (ed.). 2000. *The Social Construction of Difference and Inequality: Race, Class, Gender, and Sexuality*. Mountain View, CA: Mayfield.

Ostrander, Susan A. 1984. *Women of the Upper Class*. Philadelphia: Temple University Press.

Page, Reba Neukom. 1991. *Lower Track Classrooms*. New York: Teachers College Press.

Palen, J. John. 2001. *Social Problems for the Twenty-First Century*. New York: McGraw-Hill.

Papanek, H. 1979. "Development planning for women: The implications of women's work." Pages 170–201 in R. Jahan and H. Papanek (eds.), *Women and Development*. Dacca: Bangladesh Institute of Law and International Affairs.

Parenti, Michael. 1993. *Inventing Reality: The Politics of the Mass Media*. New York: St. Martin's Press.

_____. 1998. *America Besieged*. San Francisco: City Lights Books.

_____. 2010. *Democracy for the Few*. Beverly, MA: Wadsworth Publishing.

Pareto, Vilifredo. 1963. *Treatise on General Sociology*. New York: Dover.

Parker, David. 2001. "Good companions: Decorative, informative, or interrogative? The role of social theory textbooks." *Sociology* 35(1): 213–218.

Parker, Kim. 2012. "The boomerang generation." Pew Research Center. Available at www.pewsocialtrends.org

Parkin, Frank. 1971. *Class Inequality and Political Order: Social Stratification in Capitalist and Communist Societies*. New York: Praeger.

Parrenas, Rhacel Salazar (ed.). 2001. *Servants of Globalization: Women, Migration, and Domestic Work*. Stanford, CA: Stanford University Press.

Parsons, Talcott. 1951. *The Social System*. New York: Free Press.

Pastor, Manuel Jr. 2001. "Economics and ethnicity: Poverty, race, and immigration in Los Angeles County." Pages 102–138 in Marta Lopez-Garza and David R. Diaz (eds.), *Asian and*

Latino Immigrants in Restructuring Economy: The Metamorphosis of Southern California. Stanford, CA: Stanford University Press.

Pattillo-McCoy, Mary. 1999. *Black Picket Fences: Privilege and Peril among the Black Middle Class.* Chicago: University of Chicago Press.

Peet, Richard (with Elaine Hartwick). 1999. *Theories of Development.* New York: The Guilford Press.

Pehlke, Timothy Allen II, Charles B. Hennon, Elise M. Radina, and Katherine A. Kuvalanka. 2009. "Does father still know best? An inductive thematic analysis of popular TV sitcoms." *Fathering* 7(2): 114–139.

Pellegrini, Frank. 2002. "Person of the Week: 'Enron Whistleblower' Sherron Watkins." *Time* online edition (Jan. 18). Available at www.time.com

Peltz, William H. 1990. "Can girls + science - stereotypes = success?" *Science Teacher* (December): 44–49.

Pencavel, John. 2002. *Worker Participation: Lessons from the Worker Co-ops of the Pacific Northwest.* New York: Russell Sage.

Perez, Lisandro. 2002. "Cuban American families." In Ronald L. Taylor (ed.), *Minority Families in the United States: A Multicultural Perspective*, 3rd ed. Upper Saddle River, NJ: Prentice Hall/Pearson.

Peterson, Gary W., and Boyd C. Rollins. 1987. "Parent-child socialization." In Marvin B. Sussman and Suzanne K. Steinmetz (eds.), *Handbook of Marriage and the Family.* New York: Plenum Press.

Peterson, Richard R. 1996. "A re-evaluation of the economic consequences of divorce." *American Sociological Review* 61: 528–536.

Pew Research Center for the People and the Press. 2000. "Poll: Market shapes news." Reported in the *Hartford Courant* (May 1): A7.

_____. 2012. "Changing face of American helps assure Obama victory." November 7. Available at www.people-press.org

Phelan, Jo, Bruce G. Link, Robert E. Moore, and Ann Stueve. 1997. "The stigma of homelessness: The impact of the label 'homeless' on attitudes toward poor persons." *Social Psychology Quarterly* 60(4): 323–337.

Phillips, Kevin. 1990. *The Politics of Rich and Poor: Wealth and the American Electorate in the Reagan Aftermath.* New York: Random House.

_____. 1993. *Boiling Point: Republicans, Democrats, and the Decline of Middle Class Prosperity.* New York: Random House.

_____. 2002. *Wealth and Democracy: A Political History of the American Rich.* New York: Broadway Books.

Phua, Voon Chin, Gayle Kaufman, and Suk Keong Park. 2001. "Strategic adjustments of elderly Asian Americans: Living arrangements and headship." *Journal of Comparative Family Studies* 32(2): 263–281.

Pilisuk, Marc, and Thomas Hayden. 1965. "Is there a military-industrial complex which prevents peace? Consensus and countervailing power in pluralistic society." *Journal of Social Issues* 21(July): 67–117.

Pincus, Fred L. 2000. "Reverse discrimination vs. white privilege: An empirical study of alleged victims of Affirmative Action." *Race and Society* 3(1): 1–22.

Pinderhughes, Dianne M. 1987. *Race and Ethnicity in Chicago Politics: A Reexamination of Pluralist Theory*. Urbana: University of Illinois Press.

Pinderhughs, Raquel. 1996. "The impact of race on environmental quality: An empirical and theoretical discussion." *Sociological Perspectives* 39(2): 231–248.

Pinkey, Andrea Davis. 2000. *Let It Shine: Stories of Black Women Freedom Fighters*. San Diego: Gulliver Books/Harcourt.

Pirog-Good, Maureen A. 1993. "Child support guidelines and the economic well-being of children in the United States." *Family Relations* 42(4): 453–462.

Piven, Francis Fox, and Richard Cloward. 1977. *Poor People's Movements: Why They Succeed, How They Fail*. New York: Vintage.

_____.2000. *Why Americans Still Don't Vote: And Why Politicians Want It That Way*. Boston: Beacon Press.

Pollack, Philip H., and M. Elliot Vitas. 1995. "Who bears the burden of environmental pollution? Race, ethnicity, and environmental equity in Florida." *Social Science Quarterly* 76(2): 294–310.

Ponniah, Gowrie, and Geraldine Reardon. 1999. "Women's labour in Bangladesh and Sri Lanka: The trade-off with technology." *Gender, Technology, and Development* 3(1): 85–102.

Pooley, Julie Ann, Lisbeth T. Pike, Neil M. Drew, and Lauren Breen. 2002. "Inferring Australian children's sense of community: A critical exploration." *Community, Work, and Family* 5(1): 5–22.

Poulantzas, Nicos. 1973. *Political Power and Social Classes*. London: New Left Books and Sheed and Ward.

Poulton, Terry. 1997. *No Fat Chicks: How Big Business Profits By Making Women Hate Their Bodies–And How to Fight Back*. Secaucus, NJ: Carol Pub. Group.

Powell-Hopson, Darlene, and Derek Hopson. 1988. "Implications of doll color preferences among black preschool children and white preschool children." *Journal of Black Psychology* 14(February): 57–63.

Pozner, Jennifer L. 2010. *Reality Bites Back: The Troubling Truth About Guilty Pleasure TV*. Berkeley, CA: Seal Press.

Press, Eyal and Jennifer Washburn. 2000. "The kept university." *The Atlantic Monthly* (March):39-54.

Pulido, Laura. 2000. "Rethinking environmental racism: White privilege and urban development in Southern California." *Annals of the Association of American Geographers* 90(1): 12–40.

Public Law 101-335, an Act to Establish a Clear and Comprehensive Prohibition of Discrimination on the Basis of Disability. 1990. Washington, DC: U.S. Government Printing Office.

Purdie-Vaughns, Valerie, Claude M. Steele, Paul G. Davies, Ruth Ditimann, and Jennifer Randall Crosby. 2008. "Social identity contingencies: How diversity cues signal threat or safety for African Americans in mainstream institutions." *Journal of Personality and Social Psychology* 94(4): 615–630.

Quadagno, Jill S., and M. H. Meyer. 1989. "Organized labor, state structures and social policy development: A case study of old age assistance in Ohio, 1916–1940." *Social Problems* 36(2): 181–196.

Quigley, Bill. 2010. "Fourteen examples of racism in criminal justice system." Available at www.huffingtonpost.com

Quindlen, Anna. 1991. "Women warriors." *New York Times* (February 3).

Quinn, Peggy. 1994. "America's disability policy: Another double standard?" *Affilia* 9(Spring): 45–59.

Quinney, Richard. 1979. *Criminology: Analysis and Critique*, 2nd ed. Boston: Little, Brown. "Race: Can we talk?" 1991. *Ms.* (July–August): 34–39.

Ramirez, Miguel. 2003. "NAFTA hasn't lived up to its billing in Mexico." *The Hartford Courant* (September 22): A7.

Raymond, Diane. 1992. "'In the best interests of the child': Thoughts on homophobia and parenting." Pages 114–130 in Warren J. Blumenfeld (ed.), *Homophobia: How We All Pay the Price*. Boston: Beacon Press.

Reckless, Walter C. 1961. *The Crime Problem*. New York: Appleton-Century-Crofts.

Reece, Ray. 1980. "The solar blackout: What happens when Exxon and DOE go sunbathing together?" *Mother Jones* (September–October): 28–37.

Reese, Ellen R., and Carnette Newcombe. 1999. "Welfare rights organizations then and now: The divergent goals and strategies of the NWRO and ACORN." Paper presented at the annual meeting of the Society for the Study of Social Problems (August, Chicago).

Reid, Penny, and Gillian Finchilescu. 1995. "The disempowering effects of media violence against women on college women." *Psychology of Women Quarterly* 19(3): 397–411.

Reiman, Jeffrey H. 1996. *—and the Poor Get Prison: Economic Bias in American Criminal Justice*. Boston: Allyn and Bacon.

_____. 2009. *The Rich Get Richer and the Poor Get Prison: Ideology, Class, and Criminal Justice*, 9th ed. Boston: Allyn and Bacon.

_____ and Paul Leighton. 2012. *The Rich Get Richer and the Poor Get Prison: Ideology, Class, and Criminal Justice*, 10th ed. Upper Saddle River, NJ: Prentice Hall/Pearson.

Reingold, Jennifer. 1997. "Executive pay: Tying pay to performance is a great idea. But stock-option deals have compensation out of control." *Business Week* April 21: 58–66.

Renard, Marie-Christine. 1999. "The interstices of globalization: The example of fair coffee." *Sociologia Ruralis* 39(4)(October): 484–500.

Rendall, Steve, and Will Creeley. 2002. "White noise: Voices of color scarce on urban public radio." www.fair.org/extra/0209/white-noise.html

Renold, Emma. 2000. "'Coming out': Gender, (hetero)sexuality and the primary school." *Gender and Education* 12(3): 309–326.

Reskin, Barbara F. 1998. *Realities of Affirmative Action in Employment*. Washington, DC: American Sociological Association.

_____, and Patricia A. Roos. 1990. *Job Queues, Gender Queues: Explaining Women's Inroads into Male Occupations*. Philadelphia: Temple University Press.

Rhem, James. 1999. "Pygmalion in the classroom." *The National Teaching and Learning Forum*. February 8(2) www.ntlf.com/html/pi/9902/pygm 1.html

Rhym, Darren. 1998. "An analysis of George Jefferson and Heathcliff Huxtable." *Journal of African American Men* 3(3): 57–67.

Riegle-Crumb, Catherine, Barbara King, Eric Brodsky, and Chandra Muller. 2012. "The more things change, the more they stay the same? Prior achievement fails to explain gender inequality in entry into STEM college majors over time." *American Educational Research Journal* 49(6): 1048–1073.

Rifkin, Jeremy. 1995. *The End of Work: The Decline of the Global Labor Force and the Dawn of the Post-Market Era*. New York: G.P. Putnam and Sons.

Rifkin, Jeremy and Randy Barber. 1978. *The North Will Rise Again: Pensions, Politics, and Power in the 1980s*. Boston: Beacon Press.

Riggle, Ellen D. B., Alan L. Ellis, and Anne M. Crawford. 1996. "The impact of "media contact" on attitudes toward gay men." *Journal of Homosexuality* 31(3): 55–69.

Rio, Cecilia. 2005. "'On the move': African American women's paid domestic labor and the class tradition to independent commodity production." *Rethinking Marxism* 17(4): 489–510.

Rist, Ray C. 1970. "Student social class and teacher expectations." *Harvard Educational Review* 40 (August): 411–451.

_____. 1973. *The Urban School: A Factory for Failure*. Cambridge, MA: M.I.T. Press.

Ritenhouse, Damon. 2011. "What's orientation got to do with it? The best interest of the child standard and legal bias against gay and lesbian parents." *Journal of Poverty* 15(3): 309–329.

Ritzer, George. 2009. *Sociological Theory and its Classical Roots: The Basics*, 5th ed. New York: McGraw-Hill

_____. 2012. *The McDonaldization of Society (20th Anniversary Edition)*. Thousand Oaks, CA: Sage Press.

Rivers, Daniel. 2012. "'In the best interests of the child': Lesbian and gay parenting custody cases, 1967–1985." *Journal of Social History* 43(4): 917–943.

Rizzo, Jennifer. 2011. "Defense cuts: The jobs numbers game." *CNN*, September 22. Available at www.secruity.blogs.cnn.com

Roberts, Dorothy. 1997. *Killing the Black Body: Race, Reproduction, and the Meaning of Liberty*. New York: Pantheon Books.

_____. 2001. *Shattered Bonds: The Color of Child Welfare*. New York: BasicCivitas Books.

Roberts, Loma and John Schostak. 2012. "Obama and the 'Arab Spring': Desire, hope, and the manufacture of disappointment: Implications for a transformative pedagogy." *Discourse* (*Abingdon*) 33(3):377-96.

Robinson, Daniel N. 1996. *Wild Beasts and Idle Humours: The Insanity Defense from Antiquity to the Present*. Cambridge, MA: Harvard University Press.

Rodden, John. 2001. "Reeducating reunified Germany?" *Society* 38(5): 66–74.

Rodriguez, Clara E. (ed.). 1997. *Latin Looks: Images of Latinas and Latinos in the U.S. Media*. Boulder, CO: Westview Press.

Roethlisberger, Frederick J., and William J. Dickson. 1939. *Management and the Worker*. Cambridge, MA: Harvard University Press.

Rogers, Mary F. 2001. "Contemporary Feminist Theory." Pages 285–296 in George Ritzer and Barry Smart (eds.), *Handbook of Social Theory*. London: SAGE Publications.

Rollins, Judith. 1985. *Between Women: Domestics and Their Employers*. Philadelphia: Temple University Press.

Rollins, Susan, and Peter C. Rollins. 1994. *Gender in Popular Culture: Images of Men and Women in Literature, Visual Media, and Material Culture*. Cleveland, OK: Ridgemont Press.

Rome, Dennis M. 2002. "Murderers, rapists, and drug addicts." Pages 71–81 in Coramae Richey Mann and Marjorie S. Zatz (eds.), *Images of Color, Images of Crime*, 2nd ed. Los Angeles: Roxbury Publishing Company.

Romero, Mary. 1992. *Maid in America*. New York: Routledge.

_____. 1999. "Immigration, the servant problem, and the legacy of the domestic labor debate." *University of Miami Law Review* 53 (July): 1045–1064.

Root, Maria P. P. (ed.). 1996. *The Multiracial Experience: Racial Borders as the New Frontier*. Thousand Oaks, CA: Sage.

Roschelle, Anne R. 1999. "Gender, family structure, and social structure: Racial ethnic families in the United States." Pages 311–340 in Myra Marx Ferree, Judith Lorber, and Beth B. Hess (eds.), *Revisioning Gender*. Thousand Oaks, CA: Sage.

Rose, Arnold. 1967. *The Power Structure*. New York: Oxford University Press.

Rosen, Corey. 1998. "ESOPs." *Dollars and Sense* (July-August): 48.

Rosenfeld, Rachel A. 1980. "Race and sex differences in career dynamics." *American Sociological Review* 45: 583–609.

Rosenthal, Robert, and Lenore Jacobson. 1968a. *Pygmalion in the Classroom*. New York: Holt, Rinehart and Winston.

_____. 1992. *Pygmalion in the Classroom*, Expanded ed. New York: Holt, Rinehart and Winston.

Ross, Andrew. 1999. "Sweated labor in cyberspace." *New Labor Forum* 4(Spring-Summer): 47–56.

Ross, Catherine E. 1987. "The division of labor at home." *Social Forces* 65: 816–833.

Rostow, W. W. 1960. *The States of Economic Growth: A Non-Communist Manifesto*. London: Cambridge University Press.

Rothschild, Joyce, and Terance D. Miethe. 1999. "Disclosing misconduct in work organizations: An empirical analysis of the situational factors that foster whistleblowing." *Research in the Sociology of Work* 8: 211–227.

Rothschild, Joyce and J. Allen Whitt. 1986. *The Cooperative Workplace: Potentials and Dilemmas of Organizational Democracy and Participation*. New York: Cambridge University Press.

Rubin, Beth A. 1996. *Shifts in the Social Contract: Understanding Change in American Society*. Thousand Oaks, CA: Pine Forge Press.

Rubington, Earl, and Martin S. Weinberg (eds.). 2004. Deviance: The Interactional Perspective, 9th ed. Boston: Allyn and Bacon.

Rude, George F. E. 1964. *The Crowd in History: A Study of Popular Disturbances in France and England, 1730–1848*. New York: Wiley.

_____. 1985. *History from Below: Studies in Popular Protest and Popular Ideology in Honour of George Rude* (edited by Frederick Krantz). Montreal: Concordia University.

Ruhm, Christopher J. 2011. "Policies to assist parents with young children." *The Future of Children* 21(2): 37–68.

Rushton, J. Phillippe. 1997. *Race, Evolution, and Behavior*. New Brunswick, NJ: Transaction Publishers.

Russell, George. 1987. "Rebuilding to survive." *Time* (February 16): 44–45.

Russell, Katheryn K. 1998. *The Color of Crime: Racial Hoaxes, White Fear, Black Protectionism, Police Harassment, and Other Macroaggressions*. New York: New York University Press.

Russell, Marta. 1998. *Beyond Ramps: Disability at the End of the Social Contract*. New York: Common Courage Press.

Russo, Giovani, and Wolter Hassink. 2012. "Multiple glass ceilings." *Industrial Relations* 51(4): 892–915.

Ryan, Jake, and Charles Sackrey. 1984. *Strangers in Paradise: Academics from the Working Class.* Boston: South End Press.

Ryan, William. 1976. *Blaming the Victim*, Rev. ed. New York: Vintage.

Saad, Lydia. 2010. "Tea Partiers are fairly mainstream in their demographics." Gallup Poll. Available at www.gallup.com/poll/127181/tea-partiers-fairly-mainstream-deographics.aspx

Sadker, David, and Myra Sadker. 1994. *Failing at Fairness: How America's Schools Cheat Girls.* New York: Scribner.

Sandberg, Sheryl. 2013. *Lean In: Women, Work, and the Will to Lead.* New York: Knopf.

Sanders, Douglas. 1996. "Getting lesbian and gay issues on the international human rights agenda." *Human Rights Quarterly* 18(1): 67–106.

Sangmon, Kim. 2001. "The impact of differential access to the Internet on earnings: A cross-sectional analysis." Paper presented at the Southern Sociological Society annual meetings.

Sapir, Edward. 1949. *Selected Writings of Edward Sapir in Language, Culture, and Personality.* Edited by David G. Mandelbaum. Berkeley, CA: University of California Press.

Scarr, Sandra. 1982. "Development is internally guided, not determined." *Contemporary Psychology* 27: 852–853.

Schaefer, Richard T. 2004. *Racial and Ethnic Groups*, 9th ed. Upper Saddle Ridge, NJ: Pearson/Prentice Hall.

Schaefer, Robert K. 2003. *Understanding Globalization: The Social Consequences of Political, Economic, and Environmental Change (2nd ed.).* Lanham, MD: Rowman and Littlefield.

Schofield, J. W. 1981. "Complementary and conflicting identities: Images and interaction in an interracial school." Pages 53–90 in S. R. Asher and J. M. Gottman (eds.), *The Development of Children's Friendships*. New York: Cambridge University Press.

_____, and Samuel H. Beer (eds.). 1999. *Welfare Reform: A Race to the Bottom?* Baltimore: Johns Hopkins University Press.

Schulman, Karen. 2000. "The high cost of child care puts quality care out of reach for many families." Children's Defense Fund.

Schur, Edwin M. 1984. *Labeling Women Deviant: Gender, Stigma, and Social Control.* New York: Random House.

Schutt, Russell K. 2008. *Investigating the Social World: The Process and Practice of Research*, 6th ed. Thousand Oaks, CA: Pine Forge Press.

Schwartz, John and Todd Barrett. 1992. "Can you top this? The war between the states—for new business—rages on." *Newsweek*, February 17:40-41.

Schwartz-Nobel, Loretta. 2002. *Growing Up Empty: The Hunger Epidemic in America.* New York: HarperCollins.

Scott, V. Catherine. 1995. *Gender and Development: Rethinking a Modernization and Dependency Theory*. Boulder, CO: L. Rienner.

Scott, James C. 1985. *Weapons of the Weak: Everyday Forms of Peasant Resistance*. New Haven: Yale University Press.

Seccombe, Karen. 1999. *"So You Think I Drive a Cadillac?" Welfare Recipients' Perspectives on the System and its Reform*. Boston: Allyn & Bacon.

Seeman, Melvin. 1959. "On the meaning of alienation." *American Sociological Review* 24: 783–791.

Seers, Dudley. 1969. *The Meaning of Development*. Paper presented at the Eleventh World Conference of the Society for International Development, New Delhi.

Segal, Mady W., David R. Segal, Jerald G. Bachman, and Peter Freedman-Doan. 1998. "Gender and the propensity to enlist in the U.S. military." *Gender Issues* 16(3)(summer): 65–87.

Seidman, Gay. 1993. *Manufacturing Militance: Workers' Movements in Brazil and South Africa, 1970–1985*. Berkeley: University of California Press.

Seltzer, J. A. 1989. *Relationships between Fathers and Children Who Live Apart*. NSFH Working Paper No. 4, University of Wisconsin–Madison, Center for Demographic Ecology.

Sen, Amartya. 2000. *Development as Freedom*. New York: Anchor Books.

Sexton, Patricia Cayo. 1991. *The War on Labor and the Left: Understanding America's Unique Conservatism*. Boulder, CO: Westview Press.

Seybold, Peter. 1987. "Beyond the veil of neutrality." Pages 175–193 in Rhonda F. Levine and Jerry Lembcke (eds.), *Recapturing Marxism*. New York: Praeger.

Shaffer, Emily S., David M. Marx, and Radmilla Prislin. 2013. "Mind the gap: Framing of women's success and representation in STEM affect women's math performance under threat." *Sex Roles* 68(7-8): 454–463.

Shanker, Thom. 2012. "U.S. arms sales make up most of global market." *New York Times*, August 26. Available at www.nytimes.com

Shanklin, Eugenia. 2000. "Representations of race and racism in American anthropology." *Current Anthropology* 41(1): 99–103.

Shapiro, Joseph P. 1993. *No Pity: People with Disabilities Forging a New Civil Rights Movement*. New York: Times Books/Random House.

Shapiro, Thomas M. 1985. *Population Control Politics*. Philadelphia: Temple University Press.

Sharma, Sohan, and Surinder Kumar. 2002. "Debt relief: Indentured servitude for the Third World." *Race and Class* 43(4): 45–56.

Sharp, Deanna L., Joan M. Hermsen, and Jodi Billings. 2002. "Factors associated with having flextime: A focus on married workers." *Journal of Family and Economic Issues* 23(1): 51–72.

Shaul, Susan, Pamela J. Dowling, and Bernice F. Laden. 1985. "Like other women: Perspectives of mothers with physical disabilities." Pages 133–142 in Mary Jo Deegan and Nancy A. Brooks (eds.), *Women and Disability: The Double Handicap*. New Brunswick, NJ: Transaction Books.

Shaw-Taylor, Yoku, and Nijole V. Benokraitis. 1995. "The presentation of minorities in marriage and family textbooks." *Teaching Sociology* 23(2): 122–135.

Sheldon, Randall G., Sharon K. Tracy, and William B. Brown. 1997. *Youth Gangs in American Society*. Belmont, CA: Wadsworth Pub.

Shelton, Beth Anne, and Daphne John. 1999. "Who does what and how much do they do? Gender and total work time." *Sociological Focus* 32: 285–300.

_____, and Rebecca E. Dean. 2001. "Divorce trends and effects for women and men." Pages 216–226 in Dana Vannoy (ed.), *Gender Mosaics: Social Perspectives*. Los Angeles: Roxbury.

Shen, Ce, and John B. Williamson. 2001. "Accounting for cross-national differences in infant mortality decline (1965–1991) among less developed countries: Effects of women's status, economic dependency, and state strength." *Social Indicators Research* 53(3): 257–288.

Shepard, Benjamin, and Ronald Hayduk (eds.). 2002. *From ACT UP to the WTO: Urban Protest and Community Building in the Era of Globalization*. New York: Verso.

Sherwood, Jessica Holden. 2010. *Wealth, Whiteness, and the Matrix of Privilege: The View from the Country Club*. Lanham, MD: Lexington Books.

Shire, Karen A. 1999. "Socialization and work in Japan: The meaning of adulthood of men and women in a business context." International Journal of Japanese Sociology 8 (Nov.): 77–92.

Sidel, Ruth. 2000. "The enemy within: The demonization of poor women." *Journal of Sociology and Social Welfare* 27(1): 73–84.

Sidel, Victor W. 2000. "Working together for health and human rights." *Medicine, Conflict, and Survival* 16(4): 355–369.

Siegel, Jessica. 1991. "What Army ads don't say." *New York Times* (January 18): A31.

Silverman, Lewis A. 2000. "Vermont civil unions, full faith and credit, and marital status." *Kentucky Law Journal* 89(4): 1075–1107.

Simon, Barbara Levy. 1988. "Never-married old women and disability." Pages 215–225 in Michelle Fine and Adrienne Asch (eds.), *Women with Disabilities*. Philadelphia: Temple University Press.

Simon, David R. 2000. "Corporate environmental crimes and social inequality: New directions for environmental justice research." *American Behavioral Scientist* 43(4): 633–645.

_____, and D. Stanley Eitzen. 1990. *Elite Deviance*, 3rd ed. Boston: Allyn and Bacon.

Singleton, Judy. 2000. "Women caring for elderly family members: Shaping non-traditional work and family initiatives." *Journal of Comparative Family Studies* 31(3): 367–375.

Sinke, Suzanne M. 1999. "Gender in language and life: A Dutch American example." *Gender Issues* 17(1)(winter): 26–51.

Sklar, Holly, Laryssa Mykyta, and Susan Wefald. 2002. *Raise the Floor: Wages and Policies That Will Work for Us All*. Boston: South End Press.

Sloan, Allan. 2002. "Who killed Enron?" *Newsweek* January 21: 18–22.

Sloan, Lacey M., and Nora S. Gustavson (eds.). 2000. *Violence and Social Injustice Against Lesbian, Gay, and Bisexual People*. New York: Harrington Park Press.

Smedley, Audrey. 1999. *Race in North America: Origins and Evolution of a World View*, 2nd ed. Boulder, CO: Westview Press.

Smith, Christian (ed.). 1996. *Disruptive Religion: The Force of Faith in Social Movement Activism*. New York: Routledge.

Smith, Greg B. 2002. "Bad execs do little time." *New York Daily News* July 14:7.

Smith, Ralph R., and Russell R. Windes. 2000. *Progay/Antigay: The Rhetorical War Over Sexuality*. Thousand Oaks, CA: Sage Publications.

Smith, Robert C. 1995. *Racism in the Post-Civil Rights Era: Now You See It, Now You Don't*. Albany: State University of New York Press.

Smitherman, Geneva, and Sylvia Cunningham. 1997. "Moving beyond resistance: Ebonics and African American youth." *Journal of Black Psychology* 23(3): 227–232.

Sorokin, Pitirim A. 1957. *Social and Cultural Dynamics*, rev. abridged ed. Boston: Porter Sargent.

Sorrels, Bobbye D. 1983. *The Nonsexist Communicator: Solving the Problems of Gender and Awkwardness in Modern English*. Englewood Cliffs, NJ: Prentice-Hall.

Soyer, Daniel. 1999. "Garment sweatshops, then and now." *New Labor Forum* 4 (spring-summer): 35–46.

Spade, Joan Z. 2001. "Gender and education in the United States." Pages 85–93 in Dana Vannoy (ed.), *Gender Mosaics: Social Perspectives*. Los Angeles: Roxbury.

Spelman, Elizabeth. 1988. *Inessential Women*. Boston: Beacon Press.

Spengler, Oswald. 1926. *The Decline of the West*. New York: Knopf.

Spickard, Paul R. 1997. "What must I be? Asian Americans and the question of multiethnic identity." *Amerasia Journal* 23(1): 43–60.

Sprouse, Martin (ed.). 1992. *Sabotage in the American Workplace: Anecdotes of Dissatisfaction, Mischief, and Revenge*. San Francisco, CA: Pressure Drop Press.

Spyrou, Spyros. 2000. "Education, ideology, and the national self: The social practice of identity construction in the classroom." *Cyprus Review* 12(1): 61–81.

Stack, Carol D. 1974. *All Our Kin: Strategies for Survival in a Black Community*. New York: Harper & Row.

Staples, Robert. 1995. "Black deprivation-white privilege: The assault on Affirmative Action." *The Black Scholar* 25(3): 2–6.

Stauber, John C., and Sheldon Rampton. 1995. *Toxic Sludge Is Good for You: Lies, Damn Lies, and the Public Relations Industry*. Monroe, ME: Common Courage Press.

Stearney, Lynn M. 1996. "Sex control technology and reproductive 'choice': The conflation of technical and political argument in the new science of human reproduction." *Communication Theory* 6(4): 388–405.

Steelman, Lala Carr, and Brian Powell. 1985. "The social and academic consequences of birth order: Real, artifactual, or both?" *Journal of Marriage and the Family* 47(1)(February): 117–124.

Steinberg, Ronnie J. 2001. "How sex gets into your paycheck and how to get it out: The gender gap in pay and comparable worth." Pages 258–268 in Dana Vannoy (ed.), *Gender Mosaics: Social Perspectives*. Los Angeles: Roxbury.

Stern, Sol. 1998. "The vanishing teacher and other UFT fictions." www.city journal.org/html/10_2_the_vanishing_teacher.html

Stevenson, Howard C., Jr. 1995. "Relationship of adolescent perceptions of racial socialization to racial identity." *Journal of Black Psychology* 21(1): 49–70.

Stiers, Gretchen A. 2000. *From This Day Forward: Commitment, Marriage, and Family in Lesbian and Gay Relationships*. New York: St. Martin's Press.

Stockett, Kathryn. 2009. *The Help*. New York: Putnam.

Stoecker, Randy, and Angela C. S. Stuber. 1999. "Building an information superhighway of one's own: A comparison on two approaches." *Research in Politics and Society* 7: 291–309.

Stohs, Joanne Hoven. 2000. "Multicultural women's experience of household labor, conflicts, and equity." *Sex Roles* 42(5-6): 339–361.

Stolen Lives Project. 1999. *Stolen Lives: Killed by Law Enforcement*, 2nd ed. New York: October 22nd Coalition to Stop Police Brutality, Repression, and Criminalization of a Generation.

Stone, Leroy O., and Andrew S. Harvey. 2001. "Gender differences in transitions to total-work retirement." Pages 258–269 in Victor W. Marshall, Walter R. Heinz, Helga Kruger, and Anil Verma (eds.), *Restructuring Work and the Life Course*. Ontario: University of Toronto Press.

Strauss, Murray. 2000. *Beating the Devil Out of Them: Corporal Punishment in American Families and Its Effects on Children*, 2nd ed. New Brunswick, NJ: Transaction.

Streeten, Paul, with Shahid Javed Burki, Mahbub ul Haq, Norman Hicks, and Frances Stewart. 1981. *First Things First: Meeting Basic Human Needs in Developing Countries*. New York: Oxford University Press.

Stretsky, Paul, and Michael Hogan. 1998. "Environmental justice: An analysis of Superfund sites in Florida." *Social Problems* 45(2): 268–287.

Stroman, Duane F. 1982. *The Awakening Minorities: The Physically Handicapped*. Washington, DC: University Press of America.

Stroup, Atlee L., and Gene E. Pollock. 1999. "Economic consequences of marital dissolution for Hispanics." *Journal of Divorce and Remarriage* 30(1–2): 149–166.

Sundaram, I. Satya. 1996. "Basic needs approach to development." *Social Action* 46(3): 225–239.

Sullivan, Harry Stack. 1953. *The Interpersonal Theory of Modern Psychiatry*. New York: Norton.

Sutherland, Edwin H., and Donald R. Cressey. 1974. *Criminology*, 9th ed. Philadelphia: Lippincott.

Sutton, Terri. 1992. "Bustin' loose: Why big breasts are back." *Utne Reader* (May–June): 60–61.

Swan, Edward T. 1995. "Equitable access to funding." *Contemporary Education* 66(4): 202–204.

Sylvester, Dari E., and Adam J. McGlynn. 2010. "The digital divide: Political participation and place." *Social Science Computer Review* 28(1): 64–74.

Szalai, Georg. 2003. "Company sees $45 billion loss, $45 billion write-down in fourth quarter." *Hollywood Reporter* 30 (January): 1.

Takagi, Dana Y. 2002. "Japanese American Families." In Ronald L. Taylor (ed.), *Minority Families in the United States: A Multicultural Perspective*, 3rd ed. Upper Saddle River, NJ: Prentice Hall/Pearson.

Tankersley, Jim. 2012. " 'I'm working really hard, but I'm not getting ahead': The new middle class trap." *The Atlantic*. Available at www.theatlantic.com

Taylor, Ian. 1999. *Crime in Context: A Critical Criminology of Market Societies*. Boulder, CO: Westview Press.

_____, Paul Walton, and Jock Young. 1973. *The New Criminology*. New York: Harper & Row.

_____. 1975. *Critical Criminology*. London: Routledge & Kegan Paul.

Taylor, Ronald L. 2002. *Minority Families in the United States: A Multicultural Perspective*, 3rd ed. Upper Saddle River, NJ: Prentice Hall/Pearson.

Taylor, Shawn. 2003. "Time to give: Workers donating paid hours off to colleagues in need." *The Hartford Courant* March 10: E1.

Thomas, Charles B. Jr. 1997. "Segregation and social inequality in a deindustrializing community: The case of Flint." *Michigan Sociological Review* 11: 64–96.

Thomas, Evan. 2003. "Fear at the front." *Newsweek* Feb. 3: 34–40.

Thomas, W. I. 1928. *The Child in America*. New York: Knopf.

Thompson, E. P. 1966. *The Making of the English Working Class*. New York: Vintage.

Thorne, Barrie. 1989. "Girls and boys together . . . but mostly apart: Gender arrangements in elementary schools." Pages 138–153 in Michael S. Kimmel and Michael A. Messner (eds.), *Men's Lives*. New York: Macmillan.

_____. 1993. *Gender Play: Girls and Boys in School*. New Brunswick, NJ: Rutgers University Press.

Thornton, Michael C. 1998. "Indigenous resources and strategies of resistance: Informal caregiving and racial socialization in black communities." Pages 49–66 in Hamilton I. McCubbin,

Elizabeth A. Thompson, Ann I. Thompson, and Jo A. Futrell (eds.), *Resiliency in African-American Families*. Thousand Oaks, CA: Sage.

Thornton, Michael et al. 1990. "Sociodemographic and environmental influences on racial socialization by black parents." *Child Development* 61:401-9.

Tilly, Charles. 1998. "Social movements and (all sorts of) other political interactions: Local, national, and international, including identities." *Theory and Society* 27(4): 453–480.

Time. 1982a. "Countdown on the ERA: As the deadline nears, supporters mount last-gasp drives." (June 14):25.

_____. 1982b. "ERA dies: But its backers will try again." (July 5):29.

Tjaden, Patricia, and Nancy Thoennes. 2000. "Extent, nature, and consequences of intimate partner violence: Findings from the National Violence Against Women survey." U.S. Department of Justice, Office of Justice Programs, National Institutes of Justice.

Todaro, Michael P. and Stephen C. Smith 2011. *Economic Development*, 11th ed. Upper Saddle River, NJ: Prentice Hall.Tomaskovic-Devey, Donald. 1993. *Gender and Racial Inequality at Work: The Sources and Consequences of Job Segregation*. Ithaca, NY: ILR Press.

Tonry, Michael. 2012. *Punishing Race: A Continuing American Dilemma*. New York: Oxford University Press.

Tower, Cynthia Crosson. 1996. *Understanding Child Abuse and Neglect*, 3rd ed. Boston: Allyn & Bacon.

Truman, David B. 1951. *The Governmental Process*. New York: Random House.

Tuchman, Gaye, Arlene Kaplan Daniels, and James Benet (eds.). 1978. *Hearth and Home: Images of Women in the Mass Media*. New York: Oxford University Press.

Tumin, Melvin. 1953. "Some principles of stratification: A critical analysis." *American Sociological Review* 18: 387–394).

_____. 1966. "Some principles of stratification: A critical view." Pages 53–58 in Rheinhard Bendix and Seymour Martin Lipset (eds.), *Class, Status and Power*, 2nd ed. New York: Free Press.

Tunberger, Pernilla, and Wendy Sigle-Rushton. 2011. "Continuity and change in Swedish family policy reforms." *Journal of European Social Policy* 21(3): 225–237.

Turow, Joseph and Matthew Mcallister (eds.). 2009. *The Advertising and Consumer Culture Reader*. New York: Routledge.

Uchitelle, Louis. 1999. "The American middle, just getting by." *New York Times* (August 1): Section 3: 1, 13.

_____. 2000. "Working families strain to live middle-class life." *New York Times* (September 10): 1, 28.*UNAIDS. 2000. *Report on the Global HIV/AIDS Epidemic*. Geneva, Switzerland: UNAIDS.

United Nations Human Development Programme. 1998. *Human Development Report, 1998*. New York: Oxford University Press.

U.S. Congress: Senate. 1989. *Americans with Disabilities Act of 1989*. Hearings before the Committee on Labor and Human Resources and the Subcommittee on the Handicapped, 101st Congress, 1st Session. Washington, DC: U.S. Government Printing Office.

_____. 1991. "Channel one: Educational television and technology." Hearings before the Subcommittee on Education, Arts, and the Humanities of the Committee on Labor and Human Resources., 102nd Congress, 1st Session. Washington, DC: U.S. Government Printing Office.

U.S. Department of Commerce and National Telecommunications and Information Administration.. 2000. "Falling through the net: Toward digital inclusion." Washington, DC: U.S. Government Printing Office.

U.S. Department of Commerce, Bureau of the Census. 1999. *Statistical Abstract of the United States, 1999*. Washington, DC: U.S. Government Printing Office.

U.S. Department of Health, Education, and Welfare. 1973. *Work in America*. Report of a Special Task Force to the Secretary of Health, Education, and Welfare. Washington, DC: U.S. Government Printing Office.

U.S. Department of Health and Human Services. 1985. *Social Security Programs throughout the World*. Washington, DC: U.S. Government Printing Office.

U.S. Department of Labor. 1985. *Displaced Workers, 1979–83*. Washington, DC: U.S. Government Printing Office.

_____. 1991. *A Report on the Glass Ceiling Initiative*. Washington, DC: U.S. Government Printing Office.

Useem, Michael. 1984. *The Inner Circle: Large Corporations and the Rise of Business Political Activity in the U.S. and U.K.* New York: Oxford University Press.

Uyecki, Eugene S., and Lani J. Holland. 2000. "Diffusion of pro-environment attitudes?" *American Behavioral Scientist* 43(4): 646–662.

Van Dyke, Nella. 1998. "Hotbeds of activism: Locations of student protest." *Social Problems* 45(2): 205–220.

Varano, Charles S. 1999. *Forced Choices: Class, Community, and Worker Ownership*. Albany: State University of New York Press.

Veevers, Jean E., Ellen M. Gee, and Andrew V. Wister. 1996. "Homeleaving age norms: Conflict or consensus?" *International Journal of Aging and Human Development* 43(4): 277–295.

Velkoff, Victoria A., and Valerie A. Lawson. 1998. "International brief: Gender and aging: Caregiving." U.S. Department of Commerce, Economics and Statistics Administration.

Verrier, Richard. 2013. "Minorities and women see gains in TV writing." *The Hartford Courant* (March 29): D3.

Vicente, Rosalia Maria, and Ana Jesus Lopez. 2010. "A multidimensional analysis of the disability digital divide: Some evidence for Internet use." *The Information Society* 26(1): 48–64.

Vigil, James Diego. 1997. *Learning from Gangs: The Mexican American Experience*. Charleston, WV: Clearinghouse on Rural Education and Small Schools, Appalachia Educational Laboratory.

Visvanathn, Nalini, Lynn Duggan, Nan Wiegersma, and Laurie Nisonoff(eds). 2011. *The Women, Gender, and Development Reader*. London: Zed Books.

Voakes, Greg. 2012. "How do video games and modern military influence each other?" Available at www.forbes.com

Wagner, Edwin M. 1989. "Air Force first-term reenlistment: The effect of held values." *Journal of Political and Military Sociology* 17(2): 223–239.

Wallach, Lori, and Michelle Sforza. 1999. "NAFTA at 5." *The Nation* (January 25): 7.

Wallerstein, Immanuel. 1974. *The Modern World System: Capitalist Agriculture and the Origins of the European World-Economy in the Sixteenth Century*. New York: Academic Press.

_____. 1980. *The Modern World System II: Mercantilism and the Consolidation of the European World Economy, 1600–1750*. New York: Academic Press.

_____. 1997. "Long waves of capitalist development: A Marxist interpretation." *Science and Society* 61(2): 264–266.

Walsh, Mark. 1990. "N.C. board sues to block the use of 'Channel One.'" *Education Week* 9 (February 28): 1, 21.

Walters, Pamela Barnhouse. 2001. "Educational access and the state: Historical continuities and discontinuities in racial inequality in American education." *Sociology of Education* extra issue: 35–49.

Walters, Ronald. 1996. "The criticality of racism." *Black Scholar* 26(1): 2–8.

Walton, John. 2001. "Debt, protest, and the state in Latin America." Pages 299–328 in *Power and Popular Protest: Latin American Social Movements*, edited by Susan Eckstein. Berkeley, CA: University of California Press.

_____, and Charles Ragin. 1990. "The debt crisis and political protest in the Third World." *American Sociological Review* 55(6): 876–890.

Ward, Kathryn. 1990. "Introduction and overview." Pages 1–24 in Kathryn B. Ward (ed.), *Women Workers and Global Restructuring*. Ithaca, NY: ILR Press.

Warner, Rebecca L., and Brent S. Steel. 1999. "Child rearing as a mechanismfor social change: The relationship of child gender to parents' commitment to gender equality." *Gender & Society* 13: 503–517.

Washington Times. 2002. "The AOL Time Warner debacle." August 8 (editorial).

Washburn, Jennifer. 2006. *University, Inc.: The Corporate Corruption of Higher Education*. New York: Basic Books.

Watson, Bill. 1971. "Counter-planning on the shop floor." *Radical America* 5 (May–June).

Wattenberg, Martin P. 2002. *Where Have All the Voters Gone?* Cambridge, MA: Harvard University Press.

Weber, Max. 1947. *The Theory of Social and Economic Organization*. Trans. A. M. Henderson and Talcott Parsons. New York: Free Press.

Weeks, John. 2000. "Latin America and the 'high performing Asian economies': Growth and debt." *Journal of International Development* 12(5): 625–654.

Wei, Ann. 1991. "Dumping on Native Americans." *Multinational Monitor*, October: 7.

Weinstein, James. 1968. *The Corporate Ideal in the Liberal State, 1900–1918*. Boston: Beacon Press.

Weir, David and Mark Schapiro. 1981. *Circle of Poison: Pesticides and People in a Hungry World*. San Francisco: Institute for Food and Development Policy.

Weitzman, Lenore J. and Mavis Maclean (eds.). 1992. *Economic Consequences of Divorce: The International Perspective*. Oxford, England: Clarendon Press; New York: Oxford University Press.

Welsby, Janette, and Debbie Horsfall. 2011. "Everyday practices of exclusion/inclusion: Women who have an intellectual disability speaking for themselves." *Disability & Society* 26(7): 795–807.

West, Patrick C., J. Mark Fly, Francis Larkin, and Roberts Marans. 1992. "Minority anglers and toxic fish consumption: Evidence from a state-wide survey of Michigan." In B. Bryant and P. Mohai (eds.), *Race and the Incidence of Environmental Hazards: A Time for Discourse*. Boulder, CO: Westview Press.

Westra, Laura, and Bill E. Lawson (eds.). 2001. *Faces of Environmental Racism: Confronting Issues of Global Justice*. Lanham, MD: Rowman and Littlefield.

"Whistle-blowing nuclear worker gains." 1993. *New York Times* (June 10): A18.

Whiting, Jason B., Megan Oka, and Stephen T. Fife. 2012. "Appraisal distortions and intimate partner violence: Gender, power, and interaction." *Journal of Marriage and Family Therapy* 38(1): 133–149.

Whorf, Bejamin Lee. 1956. "The relation of habitual thought and behavior to language." Pages 134–159 in *Language, Thought, and Reality*." Cambridge, MA: The Technology Press of M.I.T.

Williams, Brett. 1999. "The great family fraud of postwar America." Pages 65–89 in Adolph Reed, Jr. (ed.), *Without Justice for All: The New Liberalism and Our Retreat from Racial Equality*. Boulder, CO: Westview.

Williams, Gregory Howard. 1996. *Life on the Color Line: The True Story of a White Boy Who Discovered He Was Black*. New York: Plume.

Williams, Juan. 1987. *Eyes on the Prize*. New York: Penguin.

Williams, Norma. 1990. *The Mexican American Family: Tradition and Change*. Dix Hills, NY: General Hall.

Williams, Robin M., Jr. 1965. *American Society: A Sociological Interpretation*, 2nd ed. New York: Knopf.

Willie, Charles V. 1989. *Caste and Class Controversy on Race and Poverty*, 2nd ed. New York: General Hall.

Wills, Garry. 1995. "The new revolutionaries." *The New York Review* August 10: 50–55.

Wills, John S. 1994. "Popular culture, curriculum, and historical representation: The situation of Native Americans in American history and the perpetuation of stereotypes." *Journal of Narrative and Life History* 4(4): 277–294.

Wilson, Edward O. 2000. *Sociobiology: The New Synthesis*. Cambridge, MA: Belknap Press of Harvard University Press.

Wilson, John. 1992. "Cleaning up the game: Perspectives on the evolution of professional sports." Pages 65–95 in Eric Dunning and Chris Rojek (eds.), *Sport and Leisure in the Civilizing Process: Critique and Counter Critique*. Toronto: University of Toronto Press.

Wilson, William Julius. 1980. *The Declining Significance of Race: Blacks and Changing American Institutions*, 2nd ed. Chicago: University of Chicago Press.

_____. 1987. *The Truly Disadvantaged*. Chicago: University of Chicago Press.

_____. 1996. *When Work Disappears: The World of the New Urban Poor*. New York: Knopf.

Wolff, Edward N., and Richard C. Leone. 2002. *Top Heavy: The Increasing Inequality of Wealth in America and What Can Be Done About It*, 2nd ed. New York: Free Press.

Women's International League for Peace and Freedom. 1991. "Victory or defeat for people of color?" *Questions and Answers about the Gulf War* 3(April): 1–4.

Wood, Robert E. 1986. *From Marshall Plan to Debt Crisis: Foreign Aid and Development Choices in the World Economy*. Berkeley: University of California Press.

Wooden, Wayne S. 1995. *Renegade Kids, Suburban Outlaws: From Youth Culture to Delinquency*. Belmont, CA: Wadsworth.

Woodford, Maize, California School Board, James Baldwin, Patricia J. Williams, John H. McWhorter, Herb Boyd, Jaquelyne Johnson Jackson, Mumia Abu-Jamal, Geneva Smitherman, and Earl Ofari Hutchinson. 1997. "The Black Scholar Reader's Forum: Ebonics." *Black Scholar* 27(1): 2–37.

World Bank. 2003. *World Development Indicators*. Washington, DC: World Bank.

_____. 2012. *World Development Indicators*. Washington, DC: World Bank.

Worley, Jennifer Campbell, and Dana Vannoy. 2001. "The challenge of integrating work and family life." Pages 165–173 in Dana Vannoy (ed.), *Gender Mosaics: Social Perspectives*. Los Angeles: Roxbury.

Wysong, Earl. 1993. "Conflicting agendas, interests, and actors in disease prevention policy-making: Business, labor, and the High Risk Act." *International Journal of Health Services* 23(2): 301–322.

Wrong, Dennis H. 1959. "The functional theory of stratification: Some neglected considerations." *American Sociological Review* 24 (December): 772–782.

Xiao, Hong. 2000. "Class, gender, and parental values in the 1990s." *Gender & Society* 14(6): 785–803.

Yellowbird, Michael, and C. Matthew Snipp. 2002. "American Indian families." In Ronald L. Taylor (ed.), *Minority Families in the United States: A Multicultural Perspective*, 3rd ed. Upper Saddle River, NJ: Prentice Hall/Pearson.

Zajda, Joseph. 2000. "The politics of the re-writing of history in Russia: School textbooks and curriculum material." *Education and Society* 18(3): 99–123.

Zavella, Patricia. 1987. *Women's Work and Chicano Families*. Ithaca, NY: Cornell University Press.

Zeitlin, Irving M. 2009. *Ideology and the Development of Sociological Theory*, 7th ed. Upper Saddle River, NJ: Prentice Hall/Pearson.

Zey, Mary. 1993. *Banking on Fraud: Drexel, Junk Bonds, and Buyouts*. Hawthorne, NY: Aldine de Gruyter.

_____. 1998. "Embeddedness of interorganizational corporate crime in the 1980s: Securities fraud of banks and investment banks." *Research in the Sociology of Organizations* 15: 111–159.

Zhu, Xiao Di, Yi Yang, and Xiaodong Liu. 2002. "Young American adults living in parental homes." Joint Center for Housing Studies. Cambridge, MA: Harvard University.

Zick, C. D., and K. R. Smith. 1986. "Immediate and delayed effects of widowhood on poverty: Patterns from the 1970s." *Gerontologist* 26: 669–675.

Zinn, Howard.. 2010. *A People's History of the United States*. New York: Harper Perennial Classics (Dix Rep edition).

Zinn, Maxine Baca, and Bonnie Thornton Dill (eds.). 1993. *Women of Color in United States Society*. Philadelphia: Temple University Press.

Zweigenhaft, Richard L., and G. William Domhoff. 1998. *Diversity in The Power Elite: Have Women and Minorities Reached the Top?* New Haven: Yale University Press.

_____. 2006. *Diversity in the Power Elite: How it Happened, Why it Matters*. Lanham, MD: Rowman & Littlefield.

GLOSSARY

ableism   Prejudice and discrimination against a group of people because of their physical or mental disability. (Chapter 7)

absolute deprivation   The state of being unable to purchase the things related to basic survival. (*Compare with* relative deprivation.) (Chapter 10)

achieved status   Social status acquired through a person's application of resources, talent, effort, and opportunity. (*See also* status; *compare with* ascribed status.) (Chapter 4)

affirmative action   Regulations requiring that employers not discriminate in hiring and that they take positive steps to increase the number of members of racial minority groups and women in their job applicant pools. (Chapter 7)

age consciousness   The awareness of common interests based on age. (Chapter 14)

alienation   A withdrawing or separation from something; for example, in Marxist theory, workers experience a sense of estrangement from their work. (*Compare with* apathy.) (Chapters 9 and 11)

alterative movement   A type of social movement that focuses on changing individuals' thinking and behavior in a specific, limited way; for example, Students Against Drunk Driving. (*Compare with* redemptive movement, reformative movement, and transformative movement.) (Chapter 10)

anticipatory socialization   Preparation for future roles in society; for example, parents prepare their children for the world of work they are likely to be a part of when they are adults. (Chapter 6)

antithesis   According to Marx and Engels, the contradictions and antagonisms within the structure of society that challenge that structure. (*See also* dialectic, thesis, and synthesis.) (Chapter 10)

apathy   Indifference or lack of interest or concern. (*Compare with* alienation.) (Chapter 11)

appearance norms   Standards of attractiveness, often applied to women. (Chapter 9)

ascribed status   Social status over which a person has no control, such as race, sex, and class. (*See also* status; *compare with* achieved status.) (Chapter 4)

469

basic needs   What a country's population requires for survival, including health, education, food, water, and sanitation. (Chapter 10)

bias   Unwanted influences that can produce research results that are invalid or without foundation. (Chapter 2)

birth rate   The number of births each year per 1,000 live births. (Chapters 3 and 14)

bisexual   People whose sexual preferences involve individuals of the opposite sex as well as the same sex. (Chapter 7)

blended families   Families consisting of two partners and their respective children from previous partners. When these new marriages produce children as well, they create a family consisting of stepsiblings, half-siblings, stepparents, and parents. (Chapter 13)

boomerang generation   An age cohort of offspring who return home as adults to live with their parents (Chapter 13)

bourgeousie   The ownership class or group of capitalists who are the principal private owners of the society's means of production under capitalism. (Chapter 1)

bureaucracy   An organization characterized by clear-cut division of labor, hierarchy of authority, adherence to formal rules, impartiality, and rewards based on merit. (*See also* secondary group.) (Chapter 4)

business dominance theory (also known as instrumentalism)   The view that the state is not a neutral arbiter of the common good because capitalists have captured it and use it to further their own interests. (Chapter 11)

capital   The means of production (Chapter 11)

capitalism   A political economy characterized by an arrangement of production in which workers cooperate to produce wealth that is then privately owned by whoever hired the workers. (Chapters 1, 7, and 11)

capitalist interests   Individuals and organizations that benefit from amassing and maintaining private profits. (Chapter 11)

capitalist state structuralist theory   Theoretical argument that an economy based on capitalism *forces* the state to shape its policies in ways that are consistent with capital-accumulation interests because the fate of the state rests on the economy's health. (Chapter 11)

capitalists   Those who have capital invested in business and therefore own the means of production. (*Compare with* proletariat.) (Chapter 10)

catastrophic leave policy   Allows workers to donate unused paid time off (such as sick leave, vacation time, and personal leave time) to fellow workers facing family crises (Chapter 13)

class   A segment of the population whose members are similar in their possession of and access to economic resources. (Chapter 7)

class consciousness   According to Marx, workers' understanding of what capitalism was doing to them and their realization that it would be desirable to join others in a struggle against the capitalist class. (*Compare with* false consciousness.) (Chapters 1 and 11)

class dialectic perspective   The view that the conflict between the working and capitalist classes results in compromises in state policy that are not necessarily in the best interests of the capitalists. (Chapter 11)

class identity   The sense of belonging to a particular economic class, resulting from shared life experiences, as, for example, that experienced by members of an elite. (Chapter 11)

collective embezzlement   Situation in which the lack of supervision encouraged a great deal of fraud to occur in the savings and loan industry as standard operating procedure (Chapter 11)

communism   Political economy in which workers must cooperate to produce the goods and services needed, but ownership of the means of production are collectively owned by the workers themselves. (Chapter 11)

competitive individualism   The belief that individuals are completely responsible for their own economic condition so that economic success (wealth) or failure (poverty) is the result of individual effort. (Chapter 5)

compulsory heterosexuality   The norm requiring adoption of a heterosexual public persona as a prerequisite for acceptance in mainstream society (Chapter 6)

conflict theory   The view that social divisions and struggles characterize society; also the belief that social change is a result of conflict. (*Compare with* order perspective; *see also* cyclical theory, evolutionary theory, and equilibrium theory). (Chapters 1, 3, 6, and 10; see also Marxist theory)

conflict perspective on economic inequality   A view holding that extreme economic inequality in a society is neither natural nor inevitable but gives rise to conflict within society. (Chapter 7)

containment theory   A social-psychological explanation that suggests that deviant behavior is limited in society because of internal (personal) and external (societal) controls that contain the behavior of individuals. (*See also* social-psychological explanations; *compare with* differential association theory, control theory, and social reinforcement theory.) (Chapter 9)

control group   In research, a group of subjects that does not receive the special treatment designed for an experimental group. The control group serves as a baseline of comparison for the experimental group. (*Compare with* experimental group.) (Chapter 2)

control theory   A social-psychological explanation for deviant behavior that suggests that such behavior results from the absence of social control or constraints. (*See also* social-psychological explanations; *compare with* differential association theory, containment theory, and social reinforcement theory.) (Chapter 9)

co-optation   The socialization of prospective and new members of the power elite so that they come to share the world view of that elite. (*See also* power elite.) (Chapter 11)

core concepts   Fundamental ideas that are helpful in analyzing features of a society. (Chapter 1)

core nations   In a world-system, countries in which production is based on technology that relies more on machinery than on human labor and in which human labor is relatively skilled and highly paid; they are usually relatively wealthy nations. (*See also* world-system; *compare with* peripheral nations and semiperipheral nations; *also compare with* global north nations.) (Chapter 3)

corporate crime   Violations of the law by corporations in their policies or operating procedures. (Chapter 9)

corporate culture   The relationships and structures created in societies by corporate ideologies that promote and enhance the production of private profit; corporations in the core frequently export these ideologies to peripheral countries. (Chapter 5)

corporate welfare   State policies and expenditures that redistribute wealth to corporations and the affluent by directly or indirectly subsidizing, supporting, rescuing, or otherwise socializing the cost and risk of investment and private profit making. (Chapter 11)

cottage industry   A business whose labor force consists of family members who work at home using their own equipment. (Chapter 10)

counterculture   A subculture whose members embrace values, norms, rituals, and lifestyles that directly challenge those of the dominant culture. (Chapter 5)

crime   A form of behavior considered deviant because it is in violation of the law. (Chapter 9)

cultural diffusion   The sharing and incorporation of a diversity of cultures from one society to another, or of subcultures within the dominant culture. (Chapter 5)

cultural hegemony   A situation in which the ideas and values of the dominant members of society are diffused throughout society's institutions and imposed on less powerful members. (Chapter 5)

cultural lag   The time it takes from the point at which a new subculture, technology, or idea is introduced to the point at which it is accepted or incorporated into the dominant culture. (Chapter 5)

cultural leveling   Situation in which the diverse and distinctive differences between cultures become blurred as they increasingly come to resemble each other because of the common, dominating presence of corporate culture. (Chapter 5)

cultural myth of romanticism   Ideology that explains female sexual activity as the result of being "swept off her feet" in the heat of a romantic moment. (Chapter 13)

cultural relativity   A perspective that considers other cultures and their points of view as worthy of respect and understanding. (*Compare with* multiculturalism.) (Chapter 5)

culture   The social construction of reality of society's dominant groups, often imposed as a shared way of life among members of a society; it is sometimes shared and frequently challenged by subordinate groups. (Chapter 5)

culture of poverty   The belief that poor people are poverty-stricken because of a shared lack of motivation to work hard, earn a living, or gain an education. (Chapter 5)

culture shock   A feeling of confusion, uncertainty, surprise, or anxiety experienced when people are exposed to a different culture or behavior that does not conform to the prevailing norms. (Chapter 5)

cyclical theory   The view that society is like a natural organism and that each society passes naturally and inevitably through the same life cycle phases as individual biological organisms, so that ultimately social change may be viewed as part of a natural cycle. (*Compare with* evolutionary theory, equilibrium theory, and conflict perspective.) (Chapter 10)

death rate   The number of deaths each year per 1,000 in the population. (Chapters 3 and 14)

debt dependency   A strategy of development based on reliance on aid and loans from other countries, international aid agencies, and banks. (*Compare with* dependent development and trade dependency.) (Chapter 10)

debt-for-nature swaps   Arrangements in which debt-ridden governments agree to purchase or set aside land to conserve as state-owned parks and to protect the land's natural resources in exchange for debt cancellation. (Chapter 10)

declining significance of race   The belief that because of changes in attitudes, passage and enforcement of civil rights laws, and efforts to promote educational and occupational opportunities, one's race is no longer a key social determinant in the United States. (Chapter 8)

definition of the situation   *See* Thomas theorem.

degradation ceremony   The process in which socialization agents attack and devalue an individual's existing identity in an effort to break it down and build a new one. (Chapter 6)

deindustrialization   A state of decline in a nation's manufacturing activity; for example, goods may be produced in other countries and only assembled domestically. (Chapter 12)

democracy   A government, organization, or group ruled and controlled by the people, usually the majority. (Chapter 4)

dependent development   A dual strategy combining import substitution and export processing adopted by peripheral nations in order to combat the drain on their resources and the unequal benefits of trade dependency. (*See also* import substitution and export processing; *compare with* trade dependency and debt dependency.) (Chapter 10)

dependent variable   A variable in which change is caused by an independent variable. (Chapter 2)

deregulation   The process of removing or significantly relaxing government restrictions on an industry. (Chapter 11)

deviance   Behavior or a condition of being that is in violation of or departs from social norms. (Chapter 9)

dialectic   According to Marx and Engels, the ongoing process of social change marked by conflict. (*See also* thesis, antithesis, and synthesis.) (Chapter 10)

differential association theory   A social-psychological explanation for deviant behavior that suggests that such behavior results from an individual associating with people who are already disposed toward deviant behavior. (*See also* social-psychological explanations; *compare with* containment theory, control theory, and social reinforcement theory.) (Chapter 9)

digital divide   Pattern of inequality in which those who are of the dominant statuses relative to class, race, and age enjoy privileged access to the Internet. (Chapter 14)

direct democracy   A government, organization, or group in which all members participate in decision making. (*See also* democracy; *compare with* representative democracy.) (Chapter 4)

disengagement theory   The view that it is natural for all elderly people to withdraw from the social roles they occupied when they were younger because of inevitable biological and psychological decline. (Chapter 7)

disability   Any physical or mental condition that substantially limits one or more life activities of an individual. (Chapter 7)

discrimination   *Actions* toward individuals based on prejudice. (Chapter 7)

division of labor   An arrangement of work in which tasks are broken into steps or jobs performed by different individuals or nations (Chapter 3, 12)

domestic labor   Work done to maintain the home and family, usually unpaid. (*Compare with* formal labor market and informal labor market.) (Chapter 12)

double day   A situation in which women who work full time also perform most or all of the domestic chores at home; also called double shift or second shift. (*Compare with* triple shift.) (Chapters 6, 8, 12, and 13)

double shift   *See* double day.

dual labor market   economic structure in which men and women tend to work in sex-segregated employment markets, where most women hold jobs in which the majority of their coworkers are female and men hold jobs in which the majority of their coworkers are male. (Chapter 7)

economic inequality   A system of inequality characterized by a vast difference in wealth and income possessed by families and individuals. (Chapter 7)

economy   The institution made up of structures, relationships, and activities whose manifest function is to produce and distribute goods and services throughout society. (Chapters 3 and 11)

education   The institution whose manifest function is to transmit the knowledge and skills that all young members of society need to become productive members of the economy as adults. (Chapter 3)

ego   As described by Freud, the rational self that controls the urges of the individual. (Chapter 6)

elite pluralism (elite pluralist theory)   A perspective in which competing elites coexist and compromise to achieve a balanced government for the common good. (*Compare with* interest-group pluralism.) (Chapter 11)

employee stock option plans (ESOPs)   Programs in which workers purchase shares of stock in their own companies. This approach provides workers with a share of the profits their labor helps create, and may motivate them to become more productive. (Chapter 12)

environmental racism   The dumping of toxic wastes in racial minority communities to a disproportionate degree compared to dumping in other areas. (Chapter 14)

equilibrium theory   The view that society is like a biological organism such as the human body; according to this notion all systems in the organism are interdependent, and any disturbance or alteration in one of the systems requires adjustments in the other systems in order for the organism to maintain its equilibrium. (*Compare with* cyclical theory, evolutionary theory, and conflict theory.) (Chapter 10)

ethnic group People with a shared racial, religious, or national heritage who possess the same cultural traits and sense of community. (Chapters 7 and 8)

ethnocentrism The view that one's culture is the standard against which other cultures should be evaluated. (Chapter 5)

evolutionary theory The view that society is like a biological organism that evolves to a higher life form with each change, so that social change is viewed as evolutionary. (*Compare with* cyclical theory, equilibrium theory, and conflict theory.) (Chapter 10)

experimental group In research, a group of subjects that receives special treatment designed by the researcher so that the effects of that treatment may be studied. (*Compare with* control group.) (Chapter 2)

experimental research Research conducted to determine how a particular organism or object is affected by different types of treatment selected by the researcher. (*Compare with* Weld research and historical research.) (Chapter 2)

export processing The strategy adopted by peripheral nations of manufacturing goods for sale abroad in order to combat the drain on their resources and the unequal benefits of trade dependency. (*See also* trade dependency.) (Chapter 10)

extended family A family that includes the nuclear family plus other members of one or both of the parents' families of orientation, such as grandparents or aunts and uncles. (*See also* families of orientation; *compare with* nuclear family.) (Chapter 13)

false consciousness According to Marx, the failure of workers to understand that capitalism and not themselves is to blame for their alienation and misery. (*Compare with* class consciousness.) (Chapters 1 and 11)

false universalism The belief that all persons with a given status experience life in the same ways; for example, that all women have the same life experiences regardless of their race, class, or age. (Chapter 8)

families of choice A family form not defined by biology but by choice, marked by stable relationships based on shared economic and emotional ties in one or more households, such as those found where heterosexual or homosexual couples live together but are not married. (*Compare with* families of orientation and families of procreation.) (Chapter 13)

families of orientation Families into which people are born or adopted. (*Compare with* families of procreation and families of choice.) (Chapter 13)

families of procreation Families into which people marry and produce offspring. (*Compare with* families of orientation and families of choice.) (Chapter 13)

family An organized ongoing network of kin and nonkin who interact daily, sharing economic and household responsibilities and obligations, providing for domestic needs of all members, and ensuring their survival. (Chapters 3 and 13)

feminists Persons (male or female) who believe in the political, economic, and social equality of the sexes. (Chapter 7)

feminization of poverty   A situation in which a growing percentage of the poor live in female-headed households; subtly suggests that women choose to be poor and stay on welfare or somehow bring poverty on themselves. (*Compare with* pauperization of motherhood.) (Chapter 13)

fertility rate   The number of children that would be born to a woman were she to live through her child-bearing years and reproduce consistently at her age-group's fertility rate (Chapter 14)

field research   Research conducted at the place where the subjects are located so that the researcher may gain information through first-hand observation. (*Compare with* experimental research and historical research.) (Chapter 2)

flex time   An arrangement of work hours that allows more free time for the worker so long as a full day or week of work is performed; for example, some workers work four-day weeks with ten hours of work a day so that they can have three days off to take care of their families. (Chapter 13)

folkways   The least formal or important norms, usually involving conventional routines such as how many meals a day we eat. (*See also* norms; *compare with* mores and laws.) (Chapter 5)

formal labor market   Consists of people who are paid for their work, usually performed outside the home. (*Compare with* informal labor market and domestic labor.) (Chapter 12)

functionalist perspective   Views societies as adaptive social structures that help human beings adjust to their physical, political, economic, and social environment (Chapters 1 and 3)

functional imperatives   According to functionalists, the social needs that must be met in order for a society to survive. (Chapter 3)

functionalist theory of deviance   The belief that deviant behavior is a necessary and possibly even desirable thing; for example, criminals perform a service to society in that their crimes anger and upset members of society who then come together and become more cohesive as a group. (Chapter 9)

functionalist perspective on economic inequality   The belief that economic inequality is the result of beneficial forces and that different occupational levels in society should receive markedly different rewards. (Chapter 7)

gatekeepers   Schools that open different doors of opportunity for different student populations through such policies as tracking, thus depriving students from economically disadvantaged backgrounds of knowledge and school credentials that could facilitate their future upward mobility. (*See also* tracking.) (Chapters 2)

gender   The category of masculine or feminine, determined by societal expectations for behavior and ways of relating to others based on sex. (*Compare with* sex.) (Chapter 7)

gendered inequality   A system in which males and females are perceived and treated as unequals, usually characterized by a belief in male supremacy. (Chapter 7)

generalized other   A concept developed by George Herbert Mead to refer to the attitude of the larger community assumed by an individual to be important. (*Compare with* significant other.) (Chapter 6)

genocide   The systematic extermination of a group of people by those who consider themselves racially superior. (Chapter 7)

gilded welfare   State policies and budgetary expenditures that redistribute wealth from the poor and working class to the middle class and the affluent. These include Social Security, Medicare, federal income tax deductions for home ownership and local property taxes, dependent children tax deductions, and home business tax deductions. (Chapter 11)

glass ceiling   A level in a company or bureaucracy above which women or racial minorities rarely are able to rise. (Chapter 12)

global division of labor   Situation in which the work required to produce the world's goods and services is broken into separate tasks, each performed largely by different groups of nations or groups within nations. (Chapter 3)

global north nations   Industrialized and post-industrialized nations that are and have historically been relatively powerful economically, politically, and militarily, and thus able to assert their interests over and above those of less advantaged and powerful nations (Chapter 3; *compare with* global south nations; *also compare with* core nations).

global south nations   Semi-industrialized or largely agrarian nations that are relatively less powerful economically, politically, and militarily than the global north nations. They are often impoverished after centuries of exploitation and oppression, and many of these nations have histories of colonialism and imperialism at the hands of global north nations (Chapter 3; *compare with* global north nations; *also compare with* peripheral and semiperipheral nations).

globalization   A process whereby the world-system of economic relationships becomes increasingly dominant, linking and integrating ever-larger numbers of societies into a worldwide network of economic and political relationships. (Chapters 12 and 14)

government   The politicians who occupy the structure of the state. (*See also* state.) (Chapter 11)

greenhouse effect   An increase in the earth's temperature that results when carbon dioxide is released and trapped in the atmosphere; occurs, for example, when fossil fuels are burned. (Chapter 3)

group   A collection of individuals who have regular interaction. (Chapter 4)

group pluralism   A perspective that argues that democratic society is composed of a wide variety of interest groups that compete to get their goals met, and none of them is omnipotent or more powerful than any other. Individuals engage in political activity through these groups to affect the workings of government. (Chapter 11)

heterosexism   The belief that homosexuality is unnatural and immoral. (Chapter 7)

historical research   A type of research that is concerned with establishing facts about the past. (*Compare with* experimental research and field research.) (Chapter 2)

homogenization of news   A single perspective and analysis of news stories resulting from a few large conglomerates owning several media outlets. (Chapter 6)

household   A common residential unit in which related and nonrelated individuals may live. (Chapter 13)

human agency   The ability of humans to react to and change the social conditions surrounding them. (Chapter 1)

hypothesis   A carefully formulated proposition that may be either verified or discarded on the basis of the examination of relevant data. (Chapter 2)

id   As described by Freud, a primitive, almost feral self that compels individuals to focus on their own personal pleasure. (Chapter 6)

ideological hegemony   The dominance of a set of ideas that govern actions and make other options appear not to make sense. (Chapter 7)

ideology   A systematic body of ideas (for example, doctrines or myths) held by members of a class, institution, or group. (Chapters 5 and 7)

import substitution   The strategy adopted by peripheral nations of substituting locally produced goods for imported goods in order to combat the drain on their resources and the unequal benefits of trade dependency. (*See also* trade dependency.) (Chapter 10)

imposter syndrome   The feeling of people from the lower classes who succeed in life that they have fooled others into thinking that they are deserving of recognition, respect, and acceptance. (Chapter 6)

income   Money received in the form of hourly wages or annual salaries, or government benefits, or return on investments. (Chapter 7)

independent variable   One that affects another variable. A change in the independent variable causes the other variable to change. (Chapter 2)

inequality based on ablebodiedness   A system of inequality in which members with physical or mental disabilities are thought of and treated as less worthy than others. (Chapter 7)

inequality based on sexual orientation   A system of inequality in which members with a particular sexual orientation are thought of and treated as less worthy than others. (Chapter 7)

infant mortality rate   The number of infants who die within the first year of life per 1,000 live births. (Chapter 3)

informal labor market   Consists of people who are not paid for their work; may include both voluntary and involuntary work. (*Compare with* formal labor market and domestic labor.) (Chapter 12)

informal organization   A social structure that emerges spontaneously as people interact in bureaucratic or formal organizational settings. (Chapter 4)

institutional racism   Racial prejudice or discrimination embedded in the routine functioning of societal institutions. (*Compare with* personal racism.) (Chapter 7)

institutional sexism   Prejudicial or discriminatory practices that foster advantages for males that accompany the routine operations of societal institutions. (Chapter 7)

institutions   The social structures societies possess to fulfill fundamental social needs; five institutions are found in all societies—family, religion, economy, education, and the state. (Chapter 3)

instrumentalism *See* business dominance theory.

interchangeability (of elite) The mobility of members of the power elite to progress from one institutional sphere of influence to another; for example, someone may be a leader in a corporation and then move to a position of power in the state. (*See also* power elite.) (Chapter 11)

interest-group pluralism A perspective in which a variety of competing interest groups coexist and compromise to produce a balanced government for the common good. (*Compare with* elite pluralism.) (Chapter 11)

interest groups Structures in which individuals who share common needs and interests join together to address those interests (Chapter 11)

interlocking board of directors *See* interlocking corporate directorate.

invisible privileges Advantages individuals may enjoy based on their membership in dominant groups; these advantages are unearned and taken for granted. (Chapters 7, 8)

inventions New practices and objects developed out of existing knowledge. (Chapter 10)

iron law of oligarchy The inevitable tendency for organizations to be ruled by a few people, even those organizations that purport to be democratic. (Chapter 4)

label An identifying or descriptive word or phrase, often with a negative connotation when applied to people; for example, a "label of deviance" or "labeled an outcast." (Chapter 9)

labeling theory A theory of deviance that draws attention to how people come to be labeled as deviants and the impact of this label on such individuals and their subsequent behavior. (Chapter 9)

language Patterns of written symbols, audible sounds, and gestures that convey meanings. (Chapter 5)

latent function An unintended and sometimes unrecognized result that is produced as institutions carry out their manifest functions. (*See also* institutions; *compare with* manifest function.) (Chapter 3)

latent social change Social change that is largely unrecognized and unintended; for example, the effects of the baby boom in the United States. (*Compare with* manifest social change.) (Chapter 10)

laws The most formal and important norms, which are considered so vital that they are written as legal formalizations. (*See also* norms; *compare with* folkways and mores.) (Chapter 5)

liberation theology Religious teaching that stresses nonacceptance of poverty, challenge of authority if it is oppressive or punitive, civil disobedience, and the legitimacy of nontraditional lifestyles. (Chapter 6)

life chances One's ability to experience life and all its beneficial offerings. (Chapters 1 and 3)

life expectancy The average number of years a group of people all born in the same year are expected to live. (Chapter 14)

looking-glass self People's evaluation of themselves based on how they imagine others perceive and react to them. (Chapter 6)

macro-level social structures   The large-scale social structures that organize and distribute individuals into social positions, for example, institutions, societies, and the world-system. (*See also* social structure; *compare with* mid-level social structures and micro-level social structures.) (Chapter 3)

male chauvinism   A form of sexism through which men express the belief that males are superior to females and have a right to insist on the subordination of females. (*See also* sexism.) (Chapter 7)

managerial revolution   The separation of the functions of ownership and control in corporations, with the power of corporate decision-making going to managers. (Chapter 12)

manifest function   The basic social need an institution is intended to address. (*See also* institutions; *compare with* latent function.) (Chapter 3)

manifest social change   Social change resulting from a deliberate organized effort on the part of one group; for example, the American Revolution or the women's movement. (*Compare with* latent social change.) (Chapter 10)

Marxist theory   A theoretical perspective that explains social conflicts as rooted in unequal power relations between those who own the means of production and those who do not, and the ongoing resolutions of those conflicts as the engine of social change. (Chapter 10)

Marxist theory of deviance   A sociological explanation for deviant behavior that suggests that such behavior within the lower class results from a sense of alienation, low wages, and unemployment. (*See also* sociological explanations and alienation; *compare with* opportunity structure theory.) (Chapter 9)

master status   The one status (among several that each individual has) that overrides all others, thus dictating how a person is treated. (*See also* status.) (Chapter 4)

material culture   Physical artifacts that define a society; for example, a flag, style of dress, or housing. (*Compare with* nonmaterial culture.) (Chapter 5)

McDonaldization of society   As described by Ritzer, the exportation of U.S. corporate culture around the world and the consequent homogenization of global culture. (Chapter 5)

merger   The takeover or absorption of one company by another, often accomplished by the purchase of the company that is taken over. (*See also* merger mania.) (Chapter 12)

merger mania   A situation in which many mergers or company takeovers occur. (*See also* merger.) (Chapter 12)

micro-level social structures   Social structures through which individuals relate to one another, such as an individual's status or role in society. (*See also* social structure; *compare with* mid-level social structures and macro-level social structures.) (Chapter 4)

mid-level social structures   Medium-sized social structures such as groups and organizations. (*See also* social structure; *compare with* macro-level social structures and micro-level social structures.) (Chapter 4)

middle class   Loosely defined as a category of people whose income places them above the poverty line but below the wealthiest fifth of the population. It may also be conceptualized by lifestyle, including home ownership and the ability to send one's children to college. (Chapter 12)

military-industrial complex   A group, composed of the uniformed military, the aerospace-defense industry, the civilian national security managers, and the U.S. Congress, that works to advance the interests of its members while simultaneously promoting and reinforcing the interests of the others. (Chapter 11)

minority group   An inferior status assigned by the dominant group in a society to another group of people regardless of their numbers within the society. (Chapter 7)

modernization theory   The view that poor countries can move from traditional to industrial economies by adopting the value systems of industrialized Western nations. (Chapter 10)

mores   Norms specifying behaviors that must or must not occur, and to which strong feelings may be attached, such as those relating to the selection of a marriage partner. (*See also* norms; *compare with* folkways and laws.) (Chapter 5)

motherhood norms   A standard of behavior holding that normal women want and have children; in contrast, women who do not have children or who choose not to have children are exhibiting a form of deviant behavior. (Chapter 9)

multiculturalism   A perspective that acknowledges the heterogeneity of societies, examines the contributions and the intersection of many different groups at crucial moments in history, and explores the factors that affected the experiences of each group. (*Compare with* cultural relativity.) (Chapter 5)

multinational (or transnational) corporations   Companies that operate production and trade facilities in countries other than their own. (Chapter 11)

nations   Political entities with clearly defined geographic boundaries usually recognized by neighboring nations and characterized by the viewpoint and interests of their dominant groups or societies. (Chapter 3)

nature versus nurture debate   Disagreement among social scientists concerning whether genetics (nature) or environment (nurture) exerts a stronger influence on human behavior. (Chapter 6)

negative sanctions   Social control in the form of punishment meted out to those who violate the norms of society by exhibiting deviant behavior. (*See also* sanctions; *compare with* positive sanctions.) (Chapter 9)

net worth   The value of one's assets (wealth), minus the value of one's outstanding debts. (Chapter 7)

New Federalism   A political philosophy that endorses the belief that the federal government should be involved only in taxation and national defense and that all else is the responsibility of state or local governments. (Chapter 11)

no-fault divorce   The dissolution of a marriage in which neither party must attribute blame or misconduct to the other in order to be granted the divorce. (Chapter 13)

nonmaterial culture   The body of abstractions that defines the way a society's members live; abstractions include knowledge, beliefs, values, customs, rituals, and symbols. (*Compare with* material culture.) (Chapter 5)

normative indoctrination   The teaching of norms to individuals. (*See also* norms.) (Chapter 5)

norms   Rules or standards of proper behavior that are formed by interacting individuals. (Chapters 4, 5, and 9)

nuclear family   A family consisting of two parents and their offspring. (*Compare with* extended family.) (Chapter 13)

open-ended research questions   In research, exploratory questions that leave the sociologist flexibility in deciding what should be considered relevant data. (Chapter 2)

opportunity structure theory   A sociological explanation for deviant behavior that suggests that such behavior results from a society that stresses the importance of material success but does not provide all members with the same means to achieve that success. (*See also* sociological explanations; *compare with* Marxist theory of deviance.) (Chapter 9)

participant observation   A type of field research in which the researcher plays an active role in the group to the point where he or she becomes an active participant. (*See also* field research, direct observation, and passive observation.) (Chapter 2)

passive observation   A type of field research in which the researcher observes the group and records the events for later analysis and interpretation. (*See also* field research, direct observation, and participant observation.) (Chapter 2)

patriarchy   A social system in which male dominance is considered a natural, inalienable right. (Chapters 5 and 7)

pauperization of motherhood   A situation in which a growing percentage of the poor have female-headed households; subtly suggests that women are impoverished as a result of institutional forces. (*Compare with* feminization of poverty.) (Chapter 13)

perestroika   The restructuring of the Soviet Union. (Chapter 14)

peripheral nations   In a world-system, countries in which production is based on technology that relies more on inexpensive human labor than on expensive machinery; such countries are usually economically poor. (*See also* world-system; *compare with* core nations and semiperipheral nations; *also compare with* global south nations.) (Chapter 3)

personal racism   The racial prejudice or discrimination expressed by individuals or small groups of people. (*Compare with* institutional racism.) (Chapter 7)

personal troubles   Matters involving a person's character and his or her relations with others over which the individual has control. (*Compare with* public issues.) (Chapter 1)

physiological explanations   Within the context of explaining deviant behavior, explanations that attribute such behavior to a physical peculiarity or malfunction or to heredity. (*Compare with* psychological explanations, social-psychological explanations, and sociological explanations.) (Chapter 9)

pluralism   The theory that competing interest groups or elites coexist, cooperate, and maintain a balance of power to create government in the common good. (Chapter 11)

political economy   The intersection of the institutions of state and economy (Chapter 11)

political process theory A theoretical perspective of social movements that argues that mobilizing resources may be necessary for social movements to develop, but it is insufficient by itself to spark an effective social movement unless an opportunity exists or is created to apply those resources in a way that disrupts business as usual. (Chapter 10)

political socialization The process through which people internalize a political identity that defines who they are and how they should behave in the political and economic institutions of society. (Chapter 6)

population pyramid A graph that illustrates the distribution of ages and sex to get a visual appreciation of population dynamics in a particular place. (Chapter 14)

positive sanctions Social control in the form of rewards given to those who conform to the norms and abide by the rules of society. (*See also* sanctions; *compare with* negative sanctions.) (Chapter 9)

power elite People who fill the command positions of strategically important institutions, such as the state, the corporate economy, and the military, and who come from a single group and share a single world view. (Chapter 11)

prejudice Bigoted *attitudes* against individuals based on their membership in marginalized groups. (*Compare with* discrimination) (Chapter 7)

primary group A collection of individuals who interact frequently and share important connections that bring the members together; for example, family, friends, and coworkers. (*See also* group; *compare with* secondary group.) (Chapter 4)

primary sources Sources of information used in historical research that have not been interpreted, evaluated, or analyzed by others, for example, original records, diaries, official documents, eyewitness accounts, and oral histories. (*Compare with* secondary sources.) (Chapter 2)

proletariat The working class; those who do not own the means of production and must therefore sell their labor power in order to live. (*Compare with* capitalists.) (Chapter 10)

psychological explanations Within the context of explaining deviant behavior, explanations that attribute such behavior to emotional problems or unusual personality traits that often result from experiences with family members or other people in a position to influence one's psychological development. (*Compare with* physiological explanations, social-psychological explanations, and sociological explanations.) (Chapter 9)

public issues Societal conditions that transcend the individual and lie beyond his or her personal environment and control, such as rising unemployment. (*Compare with* personal troubles.) (Chapter 1)

race A category into which people are assigned based on the social meaning and significance given to certain physical (and sometimes cultural) characteristics of members of a society's population. (Chapter 7)

racial formation According to Omi and Winant, the process in which the dominant groups establish the content and importance of racial categories. (Chapter 7)

racial inequality   A system of inequality in which members of one race are thought of and treated as less worthy than members of another, resulting in discrimination and exploitation. (Chapter 7)

random   A system of sample selection in which every individual in the total population has an equal chance of being selected. (Chapter 2)

recidivism   A tendency to relapse into a previous mode of behavior; for example, people who have gone to prison more than once are recidivists. (Chapter 9)

redemptive movement   A type of social movement directed at totally changing individuals rather than society as a whole; often a religious movement. (*Compare with* alterative movement, reformative movement, and transformative movement.) (Chapter 10)

redline   A banking practice that defines certain areas, such as those with a large minority population, as ineligible for mortgages and small business loans. (Chapter 14)

reductionism   A process that reduces complex ideas or information to simple terms; for example, people who attribute deviant behavior to physiological or psychological reasons only and do not consider larger societal influences are practicing reductionism. (Chapter 9)

reference group   A group to whom people look for approval, guidance, and role models; for example, peer groups. (Chapter 6)

reformative movement   A type of social movement that aims to make limited but specific changes in society rather than just in individuals; for example, the civil rights movement. (*Compare with* redemptive movement, alterative movement, and transformative movement.) (Chapter 10)

relative deprivation   According to Davies, the state in which people's understanding of deprivation is relative to the conditions around them, to conditions they expect, or to conditions that previously existed. (*Compare with* absolute deprivation.) (Chapter 10)

religion   A body of beliefs and practices (embraced by a social group) concerned with the supernatural and the sacred that encourages followers to conduct themselves in accordance with moral prescriptions associated with the beliefs. (Chapter 3)

representative democracy   A government, organization, or group in which people choose or elect others to make decisions for them. (*See also* democracy; *compare with* direct democracy.) (Chapter 4)

research methods   The research tools used by sociologists, such as surveys, that help to generate new knowledge. (Chapter 2)

resocialization   The process in which an individual's previous self is replaced with a new, more acceptable social identity. (Chapter 6)

resource mobilization theory   The view that social movements and revolutions will not occur unless human and supportive resources are available and deployed for use regardless of how strong the feelings of the people may be. (Chapter 10)

rituals   Regularly practiced formal ceremonies, usually marking important personal or social events. (Chapter 5)

role conflict   The distress individuals experience when the demands of two or more roles they play are at odds. (*Compare with* role strain.) (Chapter 4)

role set   The multiple roles that a given individual is expected to fulfill and the relationships of these various roles to one another. (Chapter 4)

role strain   The distress individuals experience when one of the roles they play contains contradictory demands. (*Compare with* role conflict) (Chapter 4)

rolelessness   The absence of socially sanctioned roles. (Chapter 8)

runaway shops   Work facilities that are moved to locations where labor is inexpensive and often nonunionized and taxes and laws favor business interests. (Chapter 12)

sample   A set of subjects that is representative of the total population of subjects. (Chapter 2)

sanctions   Social control in the form of punishment meted out to those who exhibit deviant behavior or rewards given to those who conform to the norms of society. (Chapters 5 and 9)

sandwich generation   Generation of adults caring for both elders and children. (Chapter 13)

Sapir-Whorf hypothesis   Notion that people's understanding of the world around them can be limited by their language: They only know the world by the very words they learn and use. (Chapter 5)

second shift   *See* double day.

secondary data analysis   The analysis of data that have already been gathered by others, often for totally different purposes. (Chapter 2)

secondary group   A collection of individuals who come together for a specific purpose such as accomplishing a task or achieving a goal; primary groups may form as a result of people's participation in secondary groups. (*See also* group; *compare with* primary group.) (Chapter 4)

secondary sources   Sources of information used in historical research that have been interpreted, evaluated, or analyzed by others, for example, publications of scholars. (*Compare with* primary sources.) (Chapter 2)

segmented labor market   A divided labor market resulting from the fact that men and women, and people in different racial categories, compete in different labor markets for different jobs. (*see also* dual labor market) (Chapter 12)

self-fulfilling prophecy   The phenomenon in which people achieve to the level expected of them rather than to the level of which they may actually be capable. (Chapter 6)

semiperipheral nations   In a world-system, countries in which production is based on a mixture of intermediate levels of machinery and human labor and in which human labor is semiskilled and paid intermediate levels of wages. (*See also* world-system; *compare with* core nations and peripheral nations; *also compare with* global south nations.) (Chapter 3)

sex   The category of male or female, determined by fundamental biological characteristics. (*Compare with* gender.) (Chapter 7)

sex inequality   A system of inequality based on the belief that biological differences between the sexes require that members of each sex play different roles in society; one sex (usually women) is thought of and treated as less worthy (Chapter 7).

sexism   The systematic subordination of people on the basis of their sex. (Chapter 7)

sexual division of labor   A division of responsibilities for women and men based on biological differences; for example, because women bear children, it is often the custom that they stay home and be caretakers. (Chapter 7)

significant other   An individual who serves as the most important person, and therefore a crucial role model, in another individual's life. (*Compare with* generalized other.) (Chapter 6)

social aggregate   A collection of individuals with no real interpersonal ties or patterned relationships, such as people who attend a concert or sporting event. (Chapter 4)

social capital   A crucial social resource that all people possess to a greater or lesser degree. (Chapter 4)

social construction (of deviance)   The social process by which people come to define others as deviant, either in their behavior or by their being. (Chapter 9)

social change   Significant variations or alterations in social structures and cultures over time. (Chapter 10)

social construction   The creation of ideas regarding people and their relationships to others by members of a social group; for example, the idea that there are biologically distinct races, some of which are inferior to others. (Chapter 7)

social control   Means of minimizing socially deviant behavior. (Chapter 9)

social Darwinism   An extension of the evolutionary perspective that holds that as societies evolve and change, only the fittest will survive and those that are less fit will die out. (*See also* evolutionary theory.) (Chapter 10)

social determinism   The view that important features of society are determinants of what happens to individuals. (Chapter 1)

social facts   Social and cultural features of a society, existing independently of the individuals who make it up, which influence people's behavior. (Chapter 1)

social movements   Large-scale, persistent efforts in which individuals working together may alter how institutions and whole societies operate. (Chapters 3 and 10)

social networks   The complex patterns of social relationships and ties to others in which individuals are caught up. (Chapter 4)

social-psychological explanations   Within the context of explaining deviant behavior, explanations that attribute such behavior to conditions in people's immediate social environment that influence their thinking and actions. (*Compare with* physiological explanations, psychological explanations, and sociological explanations.) (Chapter 9)

social reform   An adjustment in the content of cultural patterns of behavior or normative systems that does not fundamentally alter the social structure. (*Compare with* social revolution.) (Chapter 10)

social reinforcement theory   A social-psychological explanation for deviant behavior that suggests that such behavior results from the belief that the rewards of deviant behavior outweigh the punishments. (*See also* social-psychological explanations; *compare with* differential association theory, containment theory, and control theory.) (Chapter 9)

social revolution   A fundamental and radical upheaval of existing social structures. (*Compare with* social reform.) (Chapter 10)

social role   The behavior expected of individuals in the various positions or statuses they hold. (Chapter 4)

social stratification   Ways in which people occupying different social positions can be ranked from high to low. (Chapter 7)

social structure   The way in which recurring patterns of relationships within a social system are organized. (Chapters 3 and 4)

social systems   The ongoing ways that groups of people organize themselves and relate to one another in order to survive. (Chapter 3)

social welfare   State policies and expenditures that redistribute wealth from the affluent to the poor and working class to reduce poverty and economic inequality (Chapter 11)

socialism   Political economy in which production of goods and services involves the social cooperation between workers to create wealth. The means of production are likely to be owned or controlled by the state. (Chapter 11)

socialization   The ongoing process of learning the ways of a culture. (Chapter 6)

socialization agents   Elements that bring about the process of socialization; the agents can be grouped into seven categories—family; peers; school; religion; work; media; and toys, games, and recreational activities. (Chapter 6)

society   An organization of people who share a common territory, govern themselves, and cooperate to secure the survival of the group. (Chapter 3)

sociobiology   The study of the biological basis of social behavior. (*See also* nature versus nurture debate.) (Chapter 6)

sociological explanations   Within the context of explaining deviant behavior, explanations that attribute the behavior to societal factors outside the control of individuals. (*Compare with* physiological explanations, psychological explanations, and social-psychological explanations.) (Chapter 9)

sociological imagination   A way of thinking that enables individuals to understand how they are affected by broad features of the society and the times in which they live. (Chapter 1)

sociology   The study of people as participants in and creators of society. (Chapter 1)

state   The institution made up of political positions and the structure of political relations whose manifest function is to protect society's members from internal and external threats. (Chapters 3 and 11)

status   The position a person occupies in a group or organization; for example, in a family a person may have the status of son and brother. (Chapter 4)

status inconsistency   A situation in which one indication of a person's standing in society is out of sync with the others; for example, immigrant parents who must rely on their children to connect them to social institutions. (Chapter 13)

stigma   A negative mark that discredits a person's worth. (Chapters 7 and 9)

stereotype threat   The anxiety experienced by individuals in marginalized groups when placed in situations there is a potential to perform in such a way as to conform to negative expectations of stereotypes. (Chapter 6)

subculture   A group whose members participate in the larger society and its institutions but who share values, norms, a heritage, and rituals that differ from those of the dominant culture. (Chapter 5)

superego   As described by Freud, the conscience that functions as the restraining force of the id and the ego, reinforcing the limiting rules of social behavior. (Chapter 6)

supply-side economics   An economic philosophy that supports the belief that benefits to capitalists will trickle down to benefit labor and ultimately to benefit everyone; also called trickle-down economics. (Chapter 11)

surrogate mother   A woman, usually hired by a married couple, who carries a fertilized egg and gives birth to a child but then turns over the baby to the other woman who will be the child's legal mother. (Chapter 10)

survey   A type of research in which the participants fill out a questionnaire or answer questions in person or over the phone. (Chapter 2)

symbolic annihilation   "The absence of experience of a group of people in the media" (Lont, 2001:119). When individuals see few people of color, women, gays and lesbians, people with disabilities, or the poor, or hear few of their voices talking about their experiences as valid, it suggests that these people do not exist or are unimportant. (Chapters 5 and 6)

symbolic interaction   An interpersonal process that uses language, symbols, and sanctions to create, maintain, and alter culture and society. (Chapter 6)

symbolic interactionism   A sociological perspective that focuses upon such topics as the ways in which shared meanings among individuals develop or change through social interaction. (Chapter 1)

synthesis   According to Marx and Engels, the result of the conflict between the thesis and the antithesis; a whole new social structure containing elements of both the thesis and the antithesis. (*See also* dialectic, thesis, and antithesis.) (Chapter 10)

systems of inequality Sets of social relationships built around an attribute, such as wealth or sexual orientation, to which members of society accord a great deal of meaning and importance in everyday life. (Chapter 7)

terrorism The use of violence as a strategy to gain political objectives, often used by individuals or groups who usually have relatively little power otherwise. (Chapter 14)

thesis According to Marx and Engels, the current or temporary state of existence of a society. (*See also* dialectic, antithesis, and synthesis.) (Chapter 10)

Thomas theorem The view that if a situation is defined as real, the consequences of actions based on that definition are quite real, regardless of whether the definition is accurate; for example, if women are defined as inferior to men, they will be treated as inferior regardless of the reality; also called definition of the situation. (Chapter 5)

total institutions Institutions in which individuals are completely isolated from the rest of society for an extended period of time; for example, mental institutions. (Chapter 6)

toxic imperialism Toxic dumping in underdeveloped countries by major corporations and industrialized or core nations. (Chapter 14)

tracking A policy in many schools wherein students are grouped for instruction on the basis of the presumption that their past classroom performance and standardized test scores are valid indicators of their ability and potential; for example, schools may divide students into academic (college-bound) and vocational (employment-bound) tracks. (*See also* gatekeepers.) (Chapter 2)

trade dependency A relationship between nations characterized by limited numbers of core trade partners for peripheral countries. (*Compare with* dependent development and debt dependency.) (Chapter 10)

transformative movement A type of social movement that aims to make sweeping, rather than limited, changes in society; for example, revolution. (*Compare with* redemptive movement, alterative movement, and reformative movement.) (Chapter 10)

transgendered Sexual identies that transcend or cross traditional boundaries that socially construct malenesss and femaleness (Chapter 7)

transsexuals People who have surgically altered or corrected their physical sex to align with their emotional or core sex. (Chapter 7)

transvestites Individuals who dress in the culturally accepted clothing of the opposite sex (Chapter 7)

trickle-down economics *See* supply-side economics.

triple shift A situation in which women work in the formal labor market and the informal labor market in addition to working at domestic labor. (*See also* formal labor market, informal labor market, and domestic labor; *compare with* double day.) (Chapters 10 and 12)

underdeveloped nation A peripheral nation that has experienced historically disadvantageous relationships with more powerful industrialized or core nations and thus has been limited in its development opportunities. (*See also* peripheral nation and core nation; global south nation.) (Chapter 10)

underemployment   The situation in which individuals are employed either at jobs that do not fully utilize their skills, that pay less than a living wage, or that do not offer opportunities for full-time employment. (Chapter 12)

values   Assumptions and judgments made about the goods, goals, or states of existence that are deemed important, desirable, and worth striving for. (Chapter 5)

variables   Attitudes, behaviors, or conditions that can vary. (Chapter 2)

war   An organized, armed conflict between nations. (Chapter 14)

wealth   The value of the assets or property that one owns. (Chapter 7)

whistleblowers   People, usually workers, who speak out against unfair, unethical, unsafe, or illegal practices of the institution for which they work. (Chapter 9)

white collar crime   Violations of the law by individuals in the course of their occupations or professions, crimes that benefit them. (Chapter 9)

white-skin privilege   Social advantages, usually unearned, provided to members of the white majority. (Chapter 8)

work   Any activity that produces something of value for other people. (Chapter 12)

working poor   People who are working full time but remain below the poverty line. (Chapter 12)

worker cooperative   A company that is owned and operated by its workers. (Chapter 12)

world-system   An international social system of cultural, normative, economic, political, and military relations organized around the exchange of goods and services; the most complete macro-level social structure which encompasses all other levels of social structure. (*See also* social structure and macro-level social structure.) (Chapter 3)